The Disability Studies Reader

The Fourth Edition of the *Disability Studies Reader* breaks new ground by emphasizing the global, transgender, homonational, and post-human conceptions of disability. Including physical disabilities, but exploring issues around pain, mental disability, and invisible disabilities, this edition explores more varieties of bodily and mental experience. New histories of the legal, social, and cultural give a broader picture of disability than ever before.

Now available for the first time in eBook format.

Lennard J. Davis is Professor of Disability and Human Development, English, and Medical Education at the University of Illinois at Chicago. He is the author of, among other works, *Enforcing Normalcy: Disability, Deafness, and the Body; Bending Over Backwards: Disability, Dismodernism, and Other Difficult Positions; My Sense of Silence: Memoirs of a Childhood with Deafness;* and *Obsession: A History.*

The Disability Studies Reader

Fourth Edition

Lennard J. Davis

NEW YORK AND LONDON

First published 2013
by Routledge
711 Third Avenue, New York, NY 10017

Simultaneously published in the UK
by Routledge
2 Park Square, Milton Park, Abingdon, Oxon OX14 4RN

Routledge is an imprint of the Taylor & Francis Group, an informa business

Library of Congress Cataloging in Publication Data
 Davis, Lennard J., 1949–
 The disability studies reader / Lennard J. Davis.—4th ed.
 p. cm.
 ISBN 978–0–415–63052–8 (hardback)—
 ISBN 978–0–415–63051–1 (pbk.)—
 ISBN 978–0–203–07788–7 (ebook)
 1. People with disabilities. 2. Sociology of disability.
 3. Disability studies. I. Title.
 HV1568.D5696 2013
 362.4—dc23
 2012024747

ISBN: 978–0–415–63052–8 (hbk)
ISBN: 978–0–415–63051–1 (pbk)
ISBN: 978–0–203–07788–7 (ebk)

Typeset in Utopia
by Swales & Willis Ltd, Exeter, Devon

CONTENTS

In light of the Americans with Disabilities Act (ADA) and the more recent ADA Amendments Act (ADAAA), in which definitions of disability and impairment narrowed with the ADA and broadened with the ADAAA, this essay speculates on whether the broader vision of disability will survive in the court system. Considering social attitudes and connections between the private and public spheres of American culture and politics, Emens predicts that the courts will ultimately find new ways to narrow the scope of the law's protections.

PART II: THE POLITICS OF DISABILITY

An exploration of the intersections of two major critical fields—Postcolonial Studies and Disability Studies—this essay discovers new approaches to literary and cultural criticism. Realizing that postcolonialism and disability are both tied to questions of power, Barker and Murray assert that Critical Disability Studies "needs to adapt its assumptions and methodologies to include and respond to postcolonial locations of disability."

This essay presents the problem of prenatal testing in relationship to disability and, while not opposing testing, raises concerns about the discrimination inherent in such interventions.

Saxton alerts readers to the possible conflict between the goals of the abortion rights movement and that of the disability rights movement, and she proposes goals for both that might bring their aspirations in line with one another.

Bérubé considers whether prenatal testing for genetic diseases fits in with our notions of democracy. Would it be in the interests of a democratic culture to promote or restrict the rights of parents to select the child they want, particularly when it comes to disability?

This essay locates disability activism in the Mad Pride movement, which fights for the rights of psychiatric survivors and consumers of mental health services.

PART VI: DISABILITY AND CULTURE

This essay argues that disability has become a major theme in memoirs and other forms of life-writing, opening up that experience to readers and taking control of the representation.

PREFACE TO THE FOURTH EDITION

In each of the previous three editions I began the preface by taking the pulse of the field of disability studies at the current moment. In the first edition I lamented the lack of traction disability studies was having in getting attention. In the second I saw disability studies on the rise. In the third edition I wrote "disability studies is definitely part of the academic world and civil society," noting that Barack Obama had included people with disabilities in his acceptance speech. Now it the fourth edition I can say that disability is not only accepted but also has become very much a critical term in discussions of being, post-humanism, political theory, transgender theory, philosophy, and the like. In a recent talk I gave at the CUNY Graduate Center, a PhD student asked the question "Why is disability studies so hot right now?" While I didn't quite agree about the relative temperature of the subject, I do think that having the question even asked at this moment is a sign of the times. As we begin to think through the complexities of being and post-identity, disability has become an almost necessary aspect of understanding the human–animal relationship, questions of interdependency and independence as well as issues around the construction or materiality of gender, the body, and sexuality.

Perhaps an indicator of the currency of disability studies is the asymptotic shortening of the time between editions (based on Routledge's assessment of the viability of the field). Between the first and second editions, there were 10 years, between the second and third there were four, and between the third and the fourth, three years. What this diminishing interim period has allowed is that we are moving to a point where this text is becoming less of an anthology and more of a yearbook. Because of that fact, I have been able to replace some very good essays in good conscience, feeling that those authors removed may well reappear in future editions, while also having the excitement of including many new and younger scholars who are dealing with the most current issues.

This is also the first *Reader* that will be available electronically. In the previous issue I lamented the difficulty of being able to provide easier access to the work because of the cost of doing business in the electronic age. This time, Routledge was deeply committed, along with me, to making the edition available as an e-book. Obviously the advantage will be that many more people with disabilities will be able to engage with the work in this more flexible and accessible format. I am particularly pleased with this advancement because the late Paul Longmore had made a particularly strong plea for an electronic version of the *Disability Studies Reader*, and am doubly glad that the volume will be accessible in this way and that an essay of Longmore's on telethons will appear as well.

As always, I have had a tough time in selecting which works would remain and which would be newly included. With the aid of Routledge's very helpful marketing department, I have been able to see which essays are being used in courses and which are not. My decisions are not made completely on a utilitarian basis, but at least the marketing information provides a bit of perspective on these factors. I am ever mindful of providing a balance between essays of foundational and historic interest in disability studies and newer ones that provide continuing conversation with the current moment. I also want to thank the many people who responded to my call on various Internet lists for suggestions of topics and particular essays to showcase. These responses really do make a difference and help me with my very difficult task.

This edition has, based on these requests and my own viewpoint, more essays relating to the global. We have more UK based academics writing, and more on law, race, social policy, visual culture, cognitive and affective disabilities, post-humanism, and reformulations of sex and gender. There are more challenges to received wisdom, as the field evolves, and more attempts to rethink some of the founding notions of disability, while holding onto what continues to work.

I would particularly like to thank Steve Rutter, my editor at Routledge, who keeps me on track and moves me along when I falter. Leah Babb-Rosenfeld provided assistance, along with her replacement Samantha Barbero. Elizabeth Geist, my research assistant at Fordham University, where I was a distinguished visiting professor this past semester, was very helpful in providing organization and support. John Harrington, the Dean of Fordham University, and the Department of English there, gave me the time and the opportunity to be able to do much of the editorial work on this project. As always, my own departments at the University of Illinois at Chicago were very helpful, as were my colleagues in disability studies and English. I would like to thank the instructors who reviewed the third edition and provided feedback:

Sarah L Allred, Berry College
Paul Marchbanks, California Polytechnic State University
Heather Garrison, East Stroudsburg University of Pennsylvania
Adriana Estill, Carleton College
Nolana Yip, Georgetown University
Diane Shinberg, Indiana University of Pennsynvania
David G. LoConto, Jacksonville State University
Michael F. Bérubé, Pennsylvania State University
Zosha Stuckey, Syracuse University
Mary Oschwald, Portland State University
Jami Anderson, University of Michigan, Flint
Chris Gabbard, University of North Florida
Rebecca Babcock, University of Texas of the Permian Basin
Kristenne M. Robison, Westminster College
Christopher Krentz, University of Virginia
Jean Franzino, University of Virginia
Sharan E. Brown, University of Washington

To help instructors with the use of this book in courses, we have provided test questions that can be obtained by contacting Routledge at textbooksonline@taylorandfrancis.com for a copy of these test items.

CHAPTER 1

Introduction: Normality, Power, and Culture

Lennard J. Davis

We live in a world of norms. Each of us endeavors to be normal or else deliberately tries to avoid that state. We consider what the average person does, thinks, earns, or consumes. We rank our intelligence, our cholesterol level, our weight, height, sex drive, bodily dimensions along some conceptual line from subnormal to above-average. We consume a minimum daily balance of vitamins and nutrients based on what an average human should consume. Our children are ranked in school and tested to determine where they fit into a normal curve of learning, of intelligence. Doctors measure and weigh them to see if they are above or below average on the height and weight curves. There is probably no area of contemporary life in which some idea of a norm, mean, or average has not been calculated.

To understand the disabled body, one must return to the concept of the norm, the normal body. So much of writing about disability has focused on the disabled person as the object of study, just as the study of race has focused on the person of color. But as with recent scholarship on race, which has turned its attention to whiteness and inter-sectionality, I would like to focus not so much on the construction of disability as on the construction of normalcy. I do this because the "problem" is not the person with disabilities; the problem is the way that normalcy is constructed to create the "problem" of the disabled person.

A common assumption would be that some concept of the norm must have always existed. After all, people seem to have an inherent desire to compare themselves to others. But the idea of a norm is less a condition of human nature than it is a feature of a certain kind of society. Recent work on the ancient Greeks, on preindustrial Europe, and on tribal peoples, for example, shows that disability was once regarded very differently from the way it is now. As we will see, the social process of disabling arrived with industrialization and with the set of practices and discourses that are linked to late eighteenth- and nineteenth-century notions of nationality, race, gender, criminality, sexual orientation, and so on.

I begin with the rather remarkable fact that the constellation of words describing this concept "normal," "normalcy," "normality," "norm," "average," "abnormal"—all entered the European languages rather late in human history. The word "normal" as "constituting, conforming to, not deviating or different from, the common type or stand-ard, regular, usual" only enters the English language around 1840. (Previously, the word had meant "perpendicular"; the carpenter's square, called a "norm," provided the root meaning.) Likewise, the word "norm," in the modern sense, has only been in use since around 1855, and "normality" and "normalcy" appeared in 1849 and 1857 respectively. If the lexicographical information is relevant, it is possible to date the coming into consciousness in English of an idea of "the norm" over the period 1840–1860.

If we rethink our assumptions about the universality of the concept of the norm, what we might arrive at is the concept that preceded it: that of the "ideal," a word we find dating from the seventeenth century. Without making too simplistic a division in the history, one can nevertheless try to imagine a world in which the concept of normality does not exist. Rather, what we have is the ideal body, as exemplified in the tradition of nude Venuses, for example. This idea presents a mytho-poetic body that is linked to that of the gods (in traditions in which the god's body is visualized). This divine body, then, this ideal body, is not attainable by a human. The notion of an ideal implies that, in this case, the human body as visualized in art or imagination must be composed from the ideal parts of living models. These models individually can never embody the ideal since an ideal, by definition, can never be found in this world. Pliny tells us that the Greek artist Zeuxis tried to paint Aphrodite, the goddess of love, by using as his models all the beautiful women of Crotona in order to select in each her ideal feature or body part and combine these into the ideal figure of the goddess. One young woman provides a face and another her breasts. The central point here is that in a culture with an ideal form of the body, all members of the population are below the ideal. No one young lady of Crotona can be the ideal. By definition, one can never have an ideal body. And there is no social pressure, we would imagine, that populations have bodies that conform to the ideal.

If the concept of the norm or average enters European culture, or at least the European languages, only in the nineteenth century, one has to ask what is the cause of this conceptualization? One of the logical places to turn in trying to understand concepts like "norm" and "average" is that branch of knowledge known as statistics. It was the French statistician Adolphe Quetelet (1796–1847) who contributed the most to a generalized notion of the normal as an imperative. He noticed that the "law of error," used by astronomers to locate a star by plotting all the sightings and then averaging the errors, could be equally applied to the distribution of human features such as height and weight. He then took a further step of formulating the concept of "l'homme moyen" or the average man. Quetelet maintained that this abstract human was the average of all human attributes in a given country. Quetelet's average man was a combination of *l'homme moyen physique and l'homme moyen morale*, both a physically average and a morally average construct.

With such thinking, the average then becomes paradoxically a kind of ideal, a position devoutly to be wished. As Quetelet wrote, "an individual who epitomized in himself, at a given time, all the qualities of the average man, would represent at once all the greatness, beauty and goodness of that being" (cited in Porter 1986, 102). Furthermore, one must observe that Quetelet meant this hegemony of the middle to apply not only to moral qualities but to the body as well. He wrote: "deviations more or less great from the mean have constituted [for artists] ugliness in body as well as vice in morals and a state of sickness with regard to the constitution" (ibid., 103). Here Zeuxis's notion of physical beauty as an exceptional ideal becomes transformed into beauty as the average.

Quetelet foresaw a kind of utopia of the norm associated with progress, just as Marx foresaw a utopia of the norm in so far as wealth and production is concerned.

Marx actually cites Quetelet's notion of the average man in a discussion of the labor theory of value.

The concept of a norm, unlike that of an ideal, implies that the majority of the population must or should somehow be part of the norm. The norm pins down that majority of the population that falls under the arch of the standard bell-shaped curve. This curve, the graph of an exponential function, that was known variously as the astronomer's "error law," the "normal distribution," the "Gaussian density function," or simply "the bell curve," became in its own way a symbol of the tyranny of the norm. Any bell curve will always have at its extremities those characteristics that deviate from the norm. So, with the concept of the norm comes the concept of deviations or extremes. When we think of bodies, in a society where the concept of the norm is operative, then people with disabilities will be thought of as deviants. This, as we have seen, is in contrast to societies with the concept of an ideal, in which all people have a non-ideal status.[2]

In England, there was a burst of interest in statistics during the 1830s. A statistical office was set up at the Board of Trade in 1832, and the General Register Office was created in 1837 to collect vital statistics. The use of statistics began an important movement, and there is a telling connection for the purposes of this essay between the founders of statistics and their larger intentions. The rather amazing fact is that almost all the early statisticians had one thing in common: they were eugenicists. The same is true of key figures in the eugenics movement: Sir Francis Galton, Karl Pearson, and R. A. Fisher.[3] While this coincidence seems almost too striking to be true, we must remember that there is a real connection between figuring the statistical measure of humans and then hoping to improve humans so that deviations from the norm diminish. Statistics is bound up with eugenics because the central insight of statistics is the idea that a population can be normed. An important consequence of the idea of the norm is that it divides the total population into standard and nonstandard subpopulations. The next step in conceiving of the population as norm and non-norm is for the state to attempt to norm the nonstandard—the aim of eugenics. Of course such an activity is profoundly paradoxical since the inviolable rule of statistics is that all phenomena will always conform to a bell curve. So norming the non-normal is an activity as problematic as untying the Gordian knot.

MacKenzie asserts that it is not so much that Galton's statistics made possible eugenics but rather that "the needs of eugenics in large part determined the content of Galton's statistical theory" (1981, 52). In any case, a symbiotic relationship exists between statistical science and eugenic concerns. Both bring into society the concept of a norm, particularly a normal body, and thus in effect create the concept of the disabled body.

It is also worth noting the interesting triangulation of eugenicist interests. On the one hand Sir Francis Galton was cousin to Charles Darwin, whose notion of the evolutionary advantage of the fittest lays the foundation for eugenics and also for the idea of a perfectible body undergoing progressive improvement. As one scholar has put it, "Eugenics was in reality applied biology based on the central biological theory of the day, namely the Darwinian theory of evolution" (Farrall 1985, 55). Darwin's ideas serve to place disabled people along the wayside as evolutionary defectives to be surpassed by natural selection. So, eugenics became obsessed with the elimination of "defectives," a category which included the "feebleminded," the deaf, the blind, the physically defective, and so on.

In a related discourse, Galton created the modern system of fingerprinting for personal identification. Galton's interest came out of a desire to show that certain physical traits could be inherited. As he wrote:

> one of the inducements to making these inquiries into personal identification has been to discover independent features suitable for hereditary investigation. . . . it is not improbable, and worth taking pains to inquire whether each person may not carry visibly about his body undeniable evidence of his parentage and near kinships.
>
> (cited in MacKenzie 1981, 65)

Fingerprinting was seen as a physical mark of parentage, a kind of serial number written on the body. But further, one can say that the notion of fingerprinting pushes forward the idea that the human body is standardized and contains a serial number, as it were, embedded in its corporeality. Thus the body has an identity that coincides with its essence and cannot be altered by moral, artistic, or human will. This indelibility of corporeal identity only furthers the mark placed on the body by other physical qualities—intelligence, height, reaction time. By this logic, the person enters into an identical relationship with the body, the body forms the identity, and the identity is unchangeable and indelible as one's place on the normal curve. For our purposes, then, this fingerprinting of the body means that the marks of physical difference become synonymous with the identity of the person.

Finally, Galton can be linked to that other major figure connected with the discourse of disability in the nineteenth century—Alexander Graham Bell. In 1883, the same year that Galton coined the term "eugenics," Bell delivered his eugenicist speech *Memoir upon the Formation of a Deaf Variety of the Human Race*, warning of the "tendency among deaf-mutes to select deaf-mutes as their partners in marriage" (1969, 19) with the dire consequence that a race of deaf people might be created. This echoing of Dr. Frankenstein's fear that his monster might mate and produce a race of monsters emphasizes the terror with which the "normal" beholds the differently abled.[4] Noting how the various interests come together in Galton, we can see evolution, fingerprinting, and the attempt to control the reproductive rights of the deaf as all pointing to a conception of the body as perfectible but only when subject to the necessary control of the eugenicists. The identity of people becomes defined by irrepressible identificatory physical qualities that can be measured. Deviance from the norm can be identified and indeed criminalized, particularly in the sense that fingerprints came to be associated with identifying deviants who wished to hide their identities.

Galton made significant changes in statistical theory that created the concept of the norm. He took what had been called "error theory," a technique by which astronomers attempted to show that one could locate a star by taking into account the variety of sightings. The sightings, all of which could not be correct, if plotted would fall into a bell curve, with most sightings falling into the center, that is to say, the correct location of the star. The errors would fall to the sides of the bell curve. Galton's contribution to statistics was to change the name of the curve from "the law of frequency of error" or "error curve," the term used by Quetelet, to the "normal distribution" curve.

The significance of these changes relates directly to Galton's eugenicist interests. In an "error curve" the extremes of the curve are the most mistaken in accuracy. But if one is looking at human traits, then the extremes, particularly what Galton saw as positive extremes—tallness, high intelligence, ambitiousness, strength, fertility—would have to be seen as errors. Rather than "errors" Galton wanted to think of the extremes as distributions of a trait. As MacKenzie notes:

> Thus there was a gradual transition from use of the term "probable error" to the term "standard deviation" (which is free of the implication that a deviation is in any sense an error), and from the term "law of error" to the term "normal distribution."
>
> (1981, 59)

But even without the idea of error, Galton still faced the problem that in a normal distribution curve that graphed height, for example, both tallness and shortness would be seen as extremes in a continuum where average stature would be the norm. The problem for Galton was that, given his desire to perfect the human race, or at least its British segment, tallness was preferable to shortness. How could both extremes be considered equally deviant from the norm? So Galton substituted the idea of ranking for the concept of averaging. That is, he changed the way one might look at the curve from one that used the mean to one that used the median—a significant change in thinking eugenically.

If a trait, say intelligence, is considered by its average, then the majority of people would determine what intelligence should be—and intelligence would be defined by the mediocre middle. Galton, wanting to avoid the middling of desired traits, would prefer to think of intelligence in ranked order. Although high intelligence in a normal distribution would simply be an extreme, under a ranked system it would become the highest ranked trait. Galton divided his curve into quartiles, so that he was able to emphasize ranked orders of intelligence, as we would say that someone was in the first quartile in intelligence (low intelligence) or the fourth quartile (high intelligence). Galton's work led directly to current "intelligence quotient" (IQ) and scholastic achievement tests. In fact, Galton revised Gauss's bell curve to show the superiority of the desired trait (for example, high intelligence). He created what he called an "ogive," which is arranged in quartiles with an ascending curve that features the desired trait as "higher" than the undesirable deviation. As Stigler notes:

> If a hundred individuals' talents were ordered, each could be assigned the numerical value corresponding to its percentile in the curve of "deviations from an average": the middlemost (or median) talent had value 0 (representing mediocrity), an individual at the upper quartile was assigned the value 1 (representing one probable error above mediocrity), and so on.
>
> (1986, 271)

What these revisions by Galton signify is an attempt to redefine the concept of the "ideal" in relation to the general population. First, the application of the idea of a norm to the human body creates the idea of deviance or a "deviant" body. Second, the idea of a norm pushes the normal variation of the body through a stricter template guiding the way the body "should" be. Third, the revision of the "normal curve of distribution" into quartiles, ranked in order, and so on, creates a new kind of "ideal." This statistical ideal is unlike the classical notion of the ideal, which contains no imperative that everyone should strive to be perfect. The new ideal of ranked order is powered by the imperative of the norm, and then is supplemented by the notion of progress, human perfectibility, and the elimination of deviance, to create a dominating, hegemonic vision of what the human body should be.

While we tend to associate eugenics with a Nazi-like racial supremacy, it is important to realize that eugenics was not the trade of a fringe group of right-wing, fascist maniacs. Rather, it became the common belief and practice of many, if not most, European and American citizens. When Marx used Quetelet's idea of the average in his formulation of average wage and abstract labor, socialists as well as others embraced eugenic claims, seeing in the perfectibility of the human body a utopian hope for social and economic improvement. Once people allowed that there were norms and ranks in human physiology, then the idea that we might want to, for example, increase the intelligence of humans, or decrease birth defects, did not seem so farfetched. These ideas were widely influential and the influence of eugenicist ideas persisted well into the twentieth century, so that someone like Emma Goldman could write that unless birth control was encouraged, the state would "legally encourage the increase of paupers, syphilitics, epileptics, dipsomaniacs, cripples, criminals, and degenerates" (Kevles 1985, 90).

One problem for people with disabilities was that eugenicists tended to group together all allegedly "undesirable" traits. So, for example, criminals, the poor, and people with disabilities might be mentioned in the same breath. Take Karl Pearson, a leading figure in the eugenics movement, who defined the "unfit" as follows: "the habitual criminal, the professional tramp, the tuberculous, the insane, the mentally defective, the alcoholic, the diseased from birth or from excess" (cited in Kevles 1985, 33). In 1911, Pearson headed the Department of Applied Statistics, which included Galton and the Biometric Laboratories at University College in London. This department gathered eugenic information on the inheritance of physical and mental traits including "scientific, commercial, and legal ability, but also hermaphroditism, hemophilia, cleft palate, harelip, tuberculosis, diabetes, deaf-mutism, polydactyly (more than five fingers) or brachydactyly (stub fingers), insanity, and mental deficiency" (ibid., 38–9). Here again one sees a strange selection of disabilities merged with other types of human variations. All of these deviations from the norm were regarded in the long run as contributing to the disease of the nation. As one official in the Eugenics Record Office asserted:

> . . . the only way to keep a nation strong mentally and physically is to see that each new generation is derived chiefly from the fitter members of the generation before.
>
> (ibid., 39–40)

The emphasis on nation and national fitness obviously plays into the metaphor of the body. If individual citizens are not fit, if they do not fit into the nation, then the national body will not be fit. Of course, such arguments are based on a false idea of the body politic—by that notion a hunchbacked citizenry would make a hunchbacked nation. Nevertheless, the eugenic "logic" that individual variations would accumulate into a composite national identity was a powerful one. This belief combined with an industrial mentality that saw workers as interchangeable and therefore sought to create a universal worker whose physical characteristics would be uniform, as would the result of their labors—a uniform product.

One of the central foci of eugenics was what was broadly called "feeble-mindedness."[5] This term included low intelligence, mental illness, and even "pauperism," since low income was equated with "relative inefficiency" (ibid., 46).[6] Likewise, certain ethnic groups were associated with feeblemindedness and pauperism. Charles Davenport, an American eugenicist, thought that the influx of European immigrants would make the American population "darker in pigmentation, smaller in stature . . .

more given to crimes of larceny, assault, murder, rape, and sex-immorality" (cited in ibid., 48). In his research, Davenport scrutinized the records of "prisons, hospitals, almshouses, and institutions for the mentally deficient, the deaf, the blind, and the insane" (ibid., 55).

The association between what we would now call disability and criminal activity, mental incompetence, sexual license, and so on established a legacy that people with disabilities are still having trouble living down. This equation was so strong that an American journalist writing in the early twentieth century could celebrate "the inspiring, the wonderful, message of the new heredity" as opposed to the sorrow of bearing children who were "diseased or crippled or depraved" (ibid., 67). The conflation of disability with depravity expressed itself in the formulation "defective class." As the president of the University of Wisconsin declared after World War One, "we know enough about eugenics so that if the knowledge were applied, the defective classes would disappear within a generation" (ibid., 68). And it must be reiterated that the eugenics movement was not stocked with eccentrics. Averell Harriman's sister, Mary Harriman, as well as John D. Rockefeller, funded Davenport. Prime Ministers A. J. Balfour, Neville Chamberlain, and Winston Churchill, along with President Theodore Roosevelt, H. G. Wells, and John Maynard Keynes, among many others, were members of eugenicist organizations. Francis Galton was knighted in 1909 for his work, and in 1910 he received the Copley Medal, the Royal Society's highest honor. A Galton Society met regularly in the American Museum of Natural History in New York City. In 1911 the Oxford University Union moved approval of the main principles behind eugenics by a vote of almost two to one. In Kansas, the 1920 state fair held a contest for "fitter families" based on their eugenic family histories; a brochure for the contest noted about the awards, "this trophy and medal are worth more than livestock sweepstakes. . . . For health is wealth and a sound mind in a sound body is the most priceless of human possessions" (ibid., 62). County fairs like these also administered intelligence tests, medical exams, and screened for venereal disease.

In England, bills were introduced in Parliament to control mentally disabled people, and in 1933 the prestigious scientific magazine *Nature* approved the Nazis' proposal of a bill for "the avoidance of inherited diseases in posterity" by sterilizing the disabled. The magazine editorial said "the Bill, as it reads, will command the appreciative attention of all who are interested in the controlled and deliberate improvement of human stock." The list of disabilities for which sterilization would be appropriate were "congenital feeblemindedness, manic depressive insanity, schizophrenia, hereditary epilepsy, hereditary St Vitus's dance, hereditary blindness and deafness, hereditary bodily malformation and habitual alcoholism" (cited in MacKenzie 1981, 44). We have largely forgotten that what Hitler did in developing a hideous policy of eugenics was just to implement the theories of the British and American eugenicists. Hitler's statement in *Mein Kampf* that "the struggle for the daily livelihood [between species] leaves behind, in the ruck, everything that is weak or diseased or wavering" (cited in Blacker 1952, 143) is not qualitatively different from any of the many similar statements we have seen before. And even the conclusions Hitler draws are not very different from those of the likes of Galton, Bell, and others.

In this matter, the State must assert itself as the trustee of a millennial future. . . . In order to fulfill this duty in a practical manner, the State will have to avail itself of modern medical discoveries. It must proclaim as unfit for procreation all those who are afflicted with some visible hereditary disease or are the carriers of it; and practical measures must be adopted to have such people rendered sterile.

(cited in Blacker 1952, 144)

One might want to add here a set of speculations about Sigmund Freud. His work was made especially possible by the idea of the normal. In fact, it is hard to imagine the existence of psychoanalysis without the concept of normalcy. Indeed, one of the core principles behind psychoanalysis was "if the *vita sexualis* is normal, there can be no neurosis" (Freud 1977, 386). Psychoanalysis through talk therapyt bring patients back to their normal selves. Although I cannot go into a close analysis of Freud's work here, it is instructive to think of the ways in which Freud is producing a eugenics of the mind—creating the concepts of normal sexuality, normal function, and then contrasting them with the perverse, abnormal, pathological, and even criminal.

The first depiction in literature of an attempt to norm an individual member of the population occurred in the 1850s during the development of the idea of the normal body. In Flaubert's *Madame Bovary*, Charles Bovary performs a trendy operation that would correct the club foot of Hippolyte, the stable boy of the local inn. This corrective operation is seen as "new" and related to "progress" (Flaubert 1965, 125). Hippolyte is assailed with reasons why he should alter his foot. He is told, it "must considerably interfere with the proper performance of your work" (ibid., 126). And in addition to redefining him in terms of his ability to carry out work, Homais adds: "Think what would have happened if you had been called into the army, and had to fight under our national banner!" (ibid., 126). So national interests and again productivity are emphasized. But Hippolyte has been doing fine in his job as stable boy; his disability has not interfered with his performance in the community under traditional standards. In fact, Hippolyte seems to use his club foot to his advantage, as the narrator notes:

> But on the equine foot, wide indeed as a horse's hoof, with is horny skin, and large toes . . . the cripple ran about like a deer from morn till night. He was constantly to be seen on the Square, jumping round the carts, thrusting his limping foot forwards. He seemed even stronger on that leg than the other. By dint of hard service it had acquired, as it were, moral qualities of patience and energy; and when he was given some heavy work to do, he would support himself on it in preference to the sound one.
>
> (ibid., 126)

Hippolyte's disability is in fact an ability, one which he relies on, and from which he gets extra horsepower, as it were. But although Hippolyte is more than capable, the operation must be performed to bring him back to the human and away from the equine, which the first syllable of his name suggests. To have a disability is to be an animal, to be part of the Other.

A newspaper article appears after the operation's apparent initial success, praising the spirit of progress. The article envisages Hippolyte's welcome back into the human community adding: "Hasn't the time come to cry out that the blind shall see, the deaf hear, the lame walk?" (ibid., 128) The imperative is clear: science will eradicate disability. However, by a touch of Flaubertian irony, Hippolyte's leg becomes gangrenous and has to be amputated. The older doctor lectures Charles about his attempt to norm this individual.

This is what you get from listening to the fads from Paris! . . . We are practitioners; we cure peo-ple, and we wouldn't dream of operating on someone who is in perfect health. Straighten club feet! As if one could straighten club feet indeed! It is as if one wished to make a hunchback straight!

(ibid., 131)

While Flaubert's work illustrates some of the points I have been making, it is important that we do not simply think of the novel as merely an example of how an historical devel-opment lodges within a particular text. Rather, I think there is a larger claim to be made about novels and norms.

While Flaubert may parody current ideas about normalcy in medicine, there is another sense in which the novel as a form promotes and symbolically produces normative struc-tures. Indeed, the whole focus of *Madame Bovary* is on Emma's abnormality and Flau-bert's abhorrence of normal life. If we accept that novels are a social practice that arose as part of the project of middle-class hegemony,[7] then we can see that the plot and character development of novels tend to pull toward the normative. For example, most characters in nineteenth-century novels are somewhat ordinary people who are put in abnormal circumstances, as opposed to the heroic characters who represent the ideal in earlier forms such as the epic.

If disability appears in a novel, it is rarely centrally represented. It is unusual for a main character to be a person with disabilities, although minor characters, like Tiny Tim, can be deformed in ways that arouse pity. In the case of Esther Summerson, who is scarred by smallpox, her scars are made virtually to disappear through the agency of love. Dinah Craik's *Olive* is one of the few nineteenth-century novels in which the main character has a disability (a slight spinal deformity), but even with her the emphasis on the deform-ity diminishes over the course of the novel so by then end it is no longer an issue. On the other hand, as sufficient research has shown, more often than not villains tend to be physically abnormal: scarred, deformed, or mutilated.[8]

I am not saying simply that novels embody the prejudices of society toward people with disabilities. That is clearly a truism. Rather, I am asserting that the very structures on which the novel rests tend to be normative, ideologically emphasizing the universal quality of the central character whose normativity encourages us to identify with him or her.[9] Furthermore, the novel's goal is to reproduce, on some level, the semiologically normative signs surrounding the reader, that paradoxically help the reader to read those signs in the world as well as the text. This normativity in narrative will by definition create the abnormal, the Other, the disabled, the native, the colonized subject, and so on.

Even on the level of plot, one can see the implication of eugenic notions of normativ-ity. The parentage of characters in novels plays a crucial role. Rather than being self-cre-ating beings, characters in novels have deep biological debts to their forebears, even if the characters are orphans—or perhaps especially if they are orphans. The great Heli-odoric plots of romance, in which lower-class characters are found actually to be noble, take a new turn in the novel. While nobility may be less important, characters neverthe-less inherit bourgeois respectability, moral rectitude, and eventually money and position through their genetic connection. In the novelistic world of nature versus nurture, nature almost always wins out. Thus Oliver Twist will naturally bear the banner of bourgeois morality and linguistic normativity, even though he grows up in the workhouse. Oliver will always be normal, even in abnormal circumstances.[10]

A further development in the novel can be seen in Zola's works. Before Zola, for example in the work of Balzac, the author attempted to show how the inherently good character of a protagonist was affected by the material world. Thus we read of the journey of the soul, of everyman or everywoman, through a trying and corrupting world. But Zola's theory of the novel depends on the idea of inherited traits and biological determinism. As Zola wrote in *The Experimental Novel*:

> Determinism dominates everything. It is scientific investigation, it is experimental reasoning, which combats one by one the hypotheses of the idealists, and which replaces purely imaginary novels by novels of observation and experimentation.
>
> (1964, 18)

In this view, the author is a kind of scientist watching how humans, with their naturally inherited dispositions, interact with each other. As Zola wrote, his intention in the Rougon-Macquart series was to show how heredity would influence a family "making superhuman efforts but always failing because of its own nature and the influences upon it" (Zola 1993, viii). This series would be a study of the "singular effect of heredity" (ibid.). "These young girls so pure, these young men so loyal, represented to us in certain novels, do not belong to the earth. . . . We tell everything, we do not make a choice, neither do we idealize" (ibid., 127).

My point is that a disabilities-studies consciousness can alter the way we see not just novels that have main characters who are disabled but any novel. In thinking through the issue of disability, I have come to see that almost any literary work will have some reference to the abnormal, to disability, and so on. I would explain this phenomenon as a result of the hegemony of normalcy. This normalcy must constantly be enforced in public venues (like the novel), must always be creating and bolstering its image by processing, comparing, constructing, deconstructing images of normalcy and the abnormal. In fact, once one begins to notice, there really is a rare novel that does not have some characters with disabilities—characters who are lame, tubercular, dying of AIDS, chronically ill, depressed, mentally ill, and so on.

Let me take the example of some novels by Joseph Conrad. I pick Conrad not because he is especially representative, but just because I happen to be teaching a course on Conrad. Although he is not remembered in any sense as a writer on disability, Conrad is a good test case, as it turns out, because he wrote during a period when eugenics had permeated British society and when Freud had begun to write about normal and abnormal psychology. Conrad, too, was somewhat influenced by Zola, particularly in *The Secret Agent*.

The first thing I noticed about Conrad's work is that metaphors of disability abound. Each book has numerous instances of phrases like the following selections from *Lord Jim*:

> a dance of lame, blind, mute thoughts—a whirl of awful cripples.
>
> (Conrad 1986, 114)

> [he] comported himself in that clatter as though he had been stone-deaf.
>
> (ibid., 183)

there was nothing of the cripple about him.

(ibid., 234)

Her broken figure hovered in crippled little jumps . . .

(ibid., 263)

he was made blind and deaf and without pity . . .

(ibid., 300)

a blind belief in the righteousness of his will against all mankind . . .

(ibid., 317)

They were erring men whom suffering had made blind to right and wrong.

(ibid., 333)

you dismal cripples, you . . .

(ibid., 340)

unmoved like a deaf man . . .

(ibid., 319)

These references are almost like tics, appearing at regular intervals. They tend to focus on deafness, blindness, dumbness, and lameness, and they tend to use these metaphors to represent limitations on normal morals, ethics, and of course language. While it is entirely possible to maintain that these figures of speech are hardly more than mere linguistic convention, I would argue that the very regularity of these occurrences speaks to a reflexive patrolling function in which the author continuously checks and notes.

The use of phrenology, too, is linked to the patrolling of normalcy, through the construction of character. So, in *Heart of Darkness*, for example, when Marlow is about to leave for Africa a doctor measures the dimensions of his skull to enable him to discern if any quantitative changes subsequently occur as a result of the colonial encounter. So many of the characters in novels are formed from the ableist cultural repertoire of normalized head, face, and body features that characteristically signify personal qualities. Thus in *The Secret Agent*, the corpulent, lazy body of Verloc indicates his moral sleaziness, and Stevie's large ears and head shape are explicitly seen by Ossipon as characteristic of degeneracy and criminality as described in the theories of the nineteenth-century eugenic phrenologist Cesare Lombroso.

In a Zolaesque moment of insight, Ossipon sees Stevie's degeneracy as linked to his sister Winnie:

he gazed scientifically at that woman, the sister of a degenerate, a degenerate herself—of a murdering type. He gazed at her and invoked Lombroso. . . . He gazed scientifically. He gazed at her cheeks, at her nose, at her eyes, at her ears . . . Bad! . . . Fatal!

(Conrad 1968, 269)

This eugenic gaze that scrutinizes Winnie and Stevie is really only a recapitulation of the novelistic gaze that sees meaning in normative and non-normative features. In fact, every member of the Verloc family has something "wrong" with them, including Winnie's mother who has trouble walking on her edematous legs. The moral turpitude and physical grimness of London is embodied in Verloc's inner circle. Michaelis, too, is obese and "wheezed as if deadened and oppressed by the layer of fat on his chest" (ibid., 73). Karl Yundt is toothless, gouty, and walks with a cane. Ossipon is racially abnormal having "crinkly yellow hair . . . a flattened nose and prominent mouth cast in the rough mould of the Negro type . . . [and] almond-shaped eyes [that] leered languidly over high cheek-bones" (ibid., 75)—all features indicating African and Asian qualities, particularly the cunning, opiated glance. The latter links up the eugenic with the racialized and national-ized matrix of identity.

I am not claiming that this reading of Conrad is brilliant or definitive. But I do want to show that even in texts that do not appear to be about disability, the issue of normalcy is fully deployed. One can find in almost any novel, I would argue, a kind of surveying of the terrain of the body, an attention to difference—physical, mental, and national. This activity of consolidating the hegemony of normalcy is one that needs more atten-tion, in addition to the kinds of work that have been done in locating the thematics of disability in literature.

What I have tried to show here is that the very term that permeates our contempo-rary life—the normal—is a configuration that arises in a particular historical moment. It is part of a notion of progress, of industrialization, and of ideological consolidation of the power of the bourgeoisie. The implications of the hegemony of normalcy are profound and extend into the very heart of cultural production. The novel form, that proliferator of ideology, is intricately connected with concepts of the norm. From the typicality of the central character, to the normalizing devices of plot to bring deviant characters back into the norms of society, to the normalizing coda of endings, the nine-teenth- and twentieth-century novel promulgates and disburses notions of normalcy and by extension makes of physical differences ideological differences. Characters with disabilities are always marked with ideological meaning, as are moments of disease or accident that transform such characters. One of the tasks for a developing conscious-ness of disability issues is the attempt, then, to reverse the hegemony of the normal and to institute alternative ways of thinking about the abnormal.

Many of the essays in the collection do just that. As disability studies progresses along with postmodernism and posthumanism, we are seeing that normality contin-ues to hold sway insofar as the body, the medical, and the push to diagnose disabilities are concerned. But the writers in this reader are not simply trying to include disability under the rubric of normal but to question the idea of normality, and to expand the def-inition of disability into such concepts as neurodiversity, debility and capacity, chronic illness, invisible conditions, and the like. In other words while consolidating the idea of disability, these critics are at the same time disarticulating the elements of disabil-ity to ponder how part and whole fit together. It's less a question of segregating the normal from the abnormal, the old eugenic game, as it is to describe, detail, theorize, and occupy the category of disability. Along these lines, intersectionality—the subject position of holding multiple identities—makes complex the general rubric of disability itself. If anything, this collection of essays serves to render complex the simple fact of impairment while rendering simple the ideological screen of normality.

NOTES

1. This thinking obviously is still alive and well. During the U.S. Presidential election of 1994, Newt Gingrich accused President Clinton of being "the enemy of normal Americans." When asked at a later date to clarify

what he meant, he said his meaning was that "normal" meant "middle class" (*New York Times*, November 14, 1994, A17).

2. One wants to make sure that Aristotle's idea of the mean is not confused with the norm. The Aristotlean mean is a kind of fictional construct. Aristotle advocates that in choosing between personal traits, one should tend to chose between the extremes. He does not however think of the population as falling generally into that mean. The mean, for Aristotle, is more of heuristic device to assist in moral and ethical choices. In the sense of being a middle term or a middle way, it carries more of a spacial sense than does the term "average" or "norm."

3. This rather remarkable confluence between eugenics and statistics has been pointed out by Donald A. MacKenzie, but I do not believe his observations have had the impact they should.

4. See my *Enforcing Disability* Chapter 6 for more on the novel *Frankenstein* and its relation to notions of disability.

5. Many twentieth-century prejudices against the learning disabled come from this period. The founder of the intelligence test still in use, Alfred Binet, was a Galton acolyte. The American psychologist Henry H. Goddard used Binet's tests in America and turned the numbers into categories—"idiots" being those whose mental age was one or two, "imbeciles" ranged in mental age from three to seven. Goddard invented the term "moron" (which he took from the Greek for "dull" or "stupid") for those between eight and twelve. Pejorative terms like "moron" or "retarded" have by now found their way into common usage (Kevles, 78). And even the term "mongoloid idiot" to describe a person with Down's syndrome was used as recently as 1970s not as a pejorative term but in medical texts as a diagnosis. [See Michael Bérubé's fascinating article "Life As We Know It" for more on this phenomenon of labelling.]

6. If this argument sounds strangely familiar, it is being repeated and promulgated in the neo-conservative book *The Bell Curve*, which claims that poverty and intelligence are linked through inherited characteristics.

7. This assumption is based on my previous works—*Factual Fictions: Origins of the English Novel* and *Resisting Novels: Fiction and Ideology* —as well as the cumulative body of writing about the relationship between capitalism, material life, culture, and fiction. The work of Raymond Williams, Terry Eagleton, Nancy Armstrong, Mary Poovey, John Bender, Michael McKeon, and others points in similar directions.

8. The issue of people with disabilities in literature is a well-documented one and is one I want generally to avoid in this work. Excellent books abound on the subject, including Alan Gartner and Tom Joe, eds., *Images of the Disabled, Disabling Images* (New York: Praeger, 1987) and the work of Deborah Kent including "In Search of a Heroine: Images of Women with Disabilities in Fiction and Drama," in Michelle Fine and Adrienne Asch, eds., *Women with Disabilities: Essays in Psychology, Culture, and Politics* (Philadelphia: Temple University Press, 1988).

9. And if the main character has a major disability, then we are encouraged to identify with that character's ability to overcome their disability.

10. The genealogical family line is both hereditary and financial in the bourgeois novel. The role of the family is defined by Jürgen Habermas thus: "as a genealogical link it [the family] guaranteed a continuity of personnel that consisted materially in the accumulation of capital and was anchored in the absence of legal restrictions concerning the inheritance of property" (47). The fact that the biological connectedness and the financial connectedness are conflated in the novel only furthers the point that normality is an enforced condition that upholds the totality of the bourgeois system.

11. I deal with the Lacanian idea of the *corps morcelé* in Chapter 6 of *Enforcing Normalcy*. In that section I show the relation between the fragmented body and the response to disability. Here, let me just say that Stevie's turning into a fragmented body makes sense given the fear "normal" observers have that if they allow a concept of disability to associate with their bodies, they will lose control of their normalcy and their bodies will fall apart.

12. See Chapter 4 of *Enforcing Normalcy* for more on the relation of freak shows to nationalism, colonialism, and disability. See also Rosemarie Garland Thompson's *Freakery: Cultural Spectacles of the Extraordinary Body* (New York: NYU Press, 1996).

WORKS CITED

Bell, Alexander Graham. 1969. *Memoir upon the Formation of a Deaf Variety of the Human Race*. Washington, DC: Alexander Graham Bell Association for the Deaf.

Blacker, C. P. 1952. *Eugenics: Galton and After*. Cambridge, Mass.: Harvard University Press.

Conrad, Joseph. 1924. "An Outpost of Progress." In *Tales of Unrest*. Garden City, NY: Doubleday, Page & Company.

——. 1990 [1968]. *The Secret Agent*. London: Penguin.

——. 1989 [1957]. *Under Western Eyes*. London: Penguin.

——. 1924. *Youth*. Garden City: Doubleday, Page & Company.

——. 1986. *Lord Jim*. London: Penguin.

Defoe, Daniel. 1975. *Robinson C rusoe*. New York: Norton.

Farrall, Lyndsay Andrew. 1985. *The Origin and Growth of the English Eugenics Movement 1865–1925*. New York: Garland.

Flaubert, Gustave. 1965. *Madam Bovary*. Trans. Paul de Man. New York: Norton.

Freud, Sigmund. 1977. *Introductory Lectures on Psychoanalysis*. Trans.

James Strachey. New York: Norton.

Kevles, Daniel J. 1985. *In the Name of Eugenics: Genetics and the Uses of Human* Heredity. New York: Alfred A. Knopf.

MacKenzie, Donald. A. 1981. *Statistics in Britain, 1865–1930*. Edinburgh: Edinburgh University Press.

Marx, Karl. 1970. *Capital*. Vol. 1. Trans. Samuel Moore and Edward Aveling. New York: International Publishers.

Porter, Theodore M. 1986. *The Rise of Statistical Thinking 1820–1900*. Princeton: Princeton University Press.

Stallybass, Peter and Allon White. 1987. *The Politics of Transgression*. Ithaca, NY: Cornell University Press.

Stigler, Stephen M. 1986. *The History of Statistics: The Measurement of Uncertainty before 1900*. Cambridge, Mass.: Harvard University Press.

Zola, Emile. 1964. *The Experimental Novel and Other Essays*. Trans. Belle M. Sherman. New York: Haskel House.

——. 1993. *The Masterpiece*. Trans. Thomas Walton. London: Oxford University Press.

ABBREVIATIONS

DAGW   M. Grmek, *Diseases in the Ancient Greek World* (Baltimore, 1989).

FGrH   F. Jacoby, Die Fragmente der griechischen Historiker (Leiden, 1923).

GG   F. Van Straten, "Gifts for the Gods," *Faith Hope and Worship* (Leiden, 1981).

LCL   Loeb Classical Library.

PCG   R. Kassel and C. Austin, *Poetae Comici Graeci* (Berlin, 1983).

PMG   D. L. Page, *Poetae Melici Graecae* (Oxford, 1967).

SEG   *Supplementurn Epigraphicum Graecum*.

WMH   H. Lane, *When the Mind Hears* (New York, 1985).

PART I

*H*istorical Perspectives

CHAPTER 2

Disability and the Justification of Inequality in American History

Douglas C. Baynton

Since the social and political revolutions of the eighteenth century, the trend in western political thought has been to refuse to take for granted inequalities between persons or groups. Differential and unequal treatment has continued, of course, but it has been considered incumbent on modern societies to produce a rational explanation for such treatment. In recent decades, historians and other scholars in the humanities have studied intensely and often challenged the ostensibly rational explanations for inequalities based on identity—in particular, gender, race, and ethnicity. Disability, however, one of the most prevalent justifications for inequality, has rarely been the subject of historical inquiry.

Disability has functioned historically to justify inequality for disabled people themselves, but it has also done so for women and minority groups. That is, not only has it been considered justifiable to treat disabled people unequally, but the *concept* of disability has been used to justify discrimination against other groups by attributing disability to them. Disability was a significant factor in the three great citizenship debates of the nineteenth and early twentieth centuries: women's suffrage, African American freedom and civil rights, and the restriction of immigration. When categories of citizenship were questioned,

challenged, and disrupted, disability was called on to clarify and define who deserved, and who was deservedly excluded from, citizenship. Opponents of political and social equality for women cited their supposed physical, intellectual, and psychological flaws, deficits, and deviations from the male norm. These flaws—irrationality, excessive emotionality, physical weakness—are in essence mental, emotional, and physical disabilities, although they are rarely discussed or examined as such. Arguments for racial inequality and immigration restrictions invoked supposed tendencies to feeble-mindedness, mental illness, deafness, blindness, and other disabilities in particular races and ethnic groups. Furthermore, disability figured prominently not just in arguments *for* the inequality of women and minorities but also in arguments *against* those inequalities. Such arguments took the form of vigorous denials that the groups in question actually had these disabilities; they were not disabled, the argument went, and therefore were not proper subjects for discrimination. Rarely have oppressed groups denied that disability is an adequate justification for social and political inequality. Thus, while disabled people can be considered one of the minority groups historically assigned inferior status and subjected to discrimination, disability has functioned for all such groups as a sign of and justification for inferiority.

It is this use of disability as a marker of hierarchical relations that historians of disability must demonstrate in order to bring disability into the mainstream of historical study. Over a decade ago, Joan Scott made a similar argument about the difficulty of persuading historians to take gender seriously. Scott noted that despite a substantial number of works on women's history, the topic remained marginal in the discipline as a whole. A typical response to women's history was "Women had a history separate from men's, therefore let feminists do women's history, which need not concern us," or "My understanding of the French Revolution is not changed by knowing that women participated in it." Scott argued that research on the role of women in history was necessary but not sufficient to change the paradigms of the profession. To change the way in which most historians went about their work, feminists had to demonstrate not just that women participated in the making of history but that gender is "a constitutive element of social relationships" and "a primary way of signifying relationships of power."[1]

To demonstrate the ubiquity of gender in social thought, Scott focused on political history, a field in which historians were especially apt to argue that gender was unimportant, and where most historians today would imagine disability to be equally so. She chose as an example Edmund Burke's attack on the French Revolution, noting that it was "built around a contrast between ugly, murderous *sans-culottes* hags ('the furies of hell, in the abused shape of the vilest of women') and the soft femininity of Marie-Antoinette." The contrast Scott highlights calls on not only gender but also notions of beauty, disfigurement, and misshapen bodies that would be amenable to an analysis informed by disability. Even more striking, however, is that in addition to the rhetoric of gender, Burke's argument rested just as fundamentally on a rhetorical contrast between the natural constitution of the body politic and the *monstrous* deformity that the revolution had brought forth. Burke repeatedly referred to "public measures . . . deformed into monsters," "monstrous democratic assemblies," "this monster of a constitution," "unnatural and monstrous activity," and the like (as well as evoking "blind prejudice," actions taken "blindly," "blind followers," and "blind obedience" and alluding to the madness, imbecility, and idiocy of the revolutionary leaders). This rhetoric of monstrosity was by no means peculiar to the conservative cause. Tom Paine, in his response to Burke, also found the monster metaphor an apt and useful one but turned it around: "Exterminate the monster aristocracy," he wrote.[2]

The metaphor of the natural versus the monstrous was a fundamental way of constructing social reality in Burke's time. By the late nineteenth and early twentieth centuries, however, the concept of the natural was to a great extent displaced or subsumed by the concept of normality.[3] Since then, normality has been deployed in all aspects of modern life as a means of measuring, categorizing, and managing populations (and resisting such management). Normality is a complex concept, with an etiology that includes the rise of the social sciences, the science of statistics, and industrialization with its need for interchangeable parts and interchangeable workers. It has been used in a remarkable range of contexts and with a bewildering variety of connotations. The natural and the normal both are ways of establishing the universal, unquestionable good and right. Both are also ways of establishing social hierarchies that justify the denial of legitimacy and certain rights to individuals or groups. Both are constituted in large part by being set in opposition to culturally variable notions of disability—just as the natural was meaningful in relation to the monstrous and the deformed, so are the cultural meanings of the normal produced in tandem with disability.[4]

The concept of normality in its modern sense arose in the mid-nineteenth century in the context of a pervasive belief in progress. It became a culturally powerful idea with the advent of evolutionary theory. The ideal of the natural had been a static concept for what was seen as an essentially unchanging world, dominant at a time when "the book of nature" was represented as the guidebook of God. The natural was good and right because it conformed to the intent or design of Nature or the Creator of nature. Normality, in contrast, was an empirical and dynamic concept for a changing and progressing world, the premise of which was that one could discern in human behavior the direction of human evolution and progress and use that as a guide. The ascendance of normality signaled a shift in the locus of faith from a God-centered to a human-centered world, from a culture that looked within to a core and backward to lost Edenic origins toward one that looked outward to behavior and forward to a perfected future.

Just as the counterpart to the natural was the monstrous, so the opposite of the normal person was the defective. Although normality ostensibly denoted the average, the usual, and the ordinary, in actual usage it functioned as an ideal and excluded only chose defined as *below* average. "Is the child normal?" was never a question that expressed fear about whether a child had *above*-average intelligence, motor skills, or beauty. Abnormal signified the *sub*normal.[5] In the context of a pervasive belief that the tendency of the human race was to improve itself constantly, that barring something out of the ordinary humanity moved ever upward away from its animal

origins and toward greater perfection, normality was implicitly defined as that which advanced progress (or at least did not impede it). Abnormality, conversely, was that which pulled humanity back toward its past, toward its animal origins.

As an evolutionary concept, normality was intimately connected to the western notion of progress. By the mid-nineteenth century, nonwhite races were routinely connected to people with disabilities, both of whom were depicted as evolutionary laggards or throwbacks. As a consequence, the concept of disability, intertwined with the concept of race, was also caught up in ideas of evolutionary progress. Physical or mental abnormalities were commonly depicted as instances of atavism, reversions to earlier stages of evolutionary development. Down's syndrome, for example, was called Mongolism by the doctor who first identified it in 1866 because he believed the syndrome to be the result of a biological reversion by Caucasians to the Mongol racial type. Teachers of the deaf at the end of the century spoke of making deaf children more like "normal" people and less like savages by forbidding them the use of sign language, and they opposed deaf marriages with a rhetoric of evolutionary progress and decline. Recent work on late-nineteenth-century freak shows has highlighted how disability and race intersected with an ideology of evolutionary hierarchy. James W. Trent argued in a recent article that at the 1904 World's Fair, displays of "defectives" alongside displays of "primitives" signaled similar and interconnected classification schemes for both defective individuals and defective races. Both were placed in hierarchies constructed on the basis of whether they were seen as "improvable" or not—capable of being educated, cured, or civilized. Whether it was individual atavism or a group's lack of evolutionary development, the common element in all was the presence or attribution of disability.[6]

Disability arguments were prominent in justifications of slavery in the early to mid-nineteenth century and of other forms of unequal relations between white and black Americans after slavery's demise. The most common disability argument for slavery was simply that African Americans lacked sufficient intelligence to participate or compete on an equal basis in society with white Americans. This alleged deficit was sometimes attributed to physical causes, as when an article on the "diseases and physical peculiarities of the negro race" in the *New Orleans Medical and Surgical Journal* helpfully explained, "It is this defective hematosis, or atmospherization of the blood, conjoined with a deficiency of cerebral matter in the cranium, and an excess of nervous matter distributed to the organs of sensation and assimilation, that is the true cause of that debasement of mind, which has rendered the people of Africa unable to take care of themselves." Diseases of blacks were commonly attributed to "inferior organisms and constitutional weaknesses," which were claimed to be among "the most pronounced race characteristics of the American negro." While the supposedly higher intelligence of "mulattos" compared to "pure" blacks was offered as evidence for the superiority of whites, those who argued against "miscegenation" claimed to the contrary that the products of "race-mixing" were themselves less intelligent and less healthy than members of either race in "pure" form.[7] A medical doctor, John Van Evrie of New York, avowed that the "disease and disorganization" in the "abnormal," "blotched, deformed" offspring of this "monstrous" act "could no more exist beyond a given period than any other physical degeneration, no more than tumors, cancers, or other abnormal growths or physical disease can become permanent." Some claimed greater "corporeal vigor" for "mixed offspring" but a deterioration in "moral and intellectual endowments," while still others saw greater intelligence but "frailty," "less stamina," and "inherent physical weakness."[8]

A second line of disability argument was that African Americans, because of their inherent physical and mental weaknesses, were prone to become disabled under conditions of freedom and equality. A New York medical journal reported that deafness was three times more common and blindness twice as common among free blacks in the North compared to slaves in the South. John C. Calhoun, senator from South Carolina and one of the most influential spokesmen for the slave states, thought it a powerful argument in defense of slavery that the "number of deaf and dumb, blind, idiots, and insane, of the negroes in the States that have changed the ancient relation between the races" was seven times higher than in the slave states.[9]

While much has been written about the justification of slavery by religious leaders in the South, more needs to be said about similar justifications by medical doctors. Dr. Samuel Cartwright, in 1851, for example, described two types of mental illness to which African Americans were especially subject. The first, Drapetomania, a condition that caused slaves to run away—"as much a disease of the mind as any other species of mental alienation"—was common among slaves whose masters had "made themselves too familiar with them, treating them as equals." The need to submit to a master was built into the very bodies of African Americans, in whom "we see *'genu flexit'* written in the physical structure of his knees, being more flexed or bent, than any other kind of man." The second mental disease peculiar to African Americans, Dysaesthesia Aechiopis—a unique ailment differing "from every other species of mental disease, as it is accompanied with physical signs or lesions of the body"—resulted in a desire to avoid work and generally to cause mischief. It was commonly known to overseers as "rascality." Its cause, similar to that of Drapetomania, was a lack of firm governance, and it was therefore far more common among free blacks than among slaves—indeed, nearly universal among them—although it was a "common occurrence on badly-governed plantations" as well.[10]

Dr. Van Evrie also contributed to this line of thought when he wrote in the 1860s that education of African Americans came "at the expense of the body, shortening the existence" and resulted in bodies "dwarfed or destroyed" by the unnatural exertion. "An 'educated negro,' like a 'free negro,' is a social monstrosity, even more unnatural and repulsive than the latter." He argued further that, since they belonged to a race inferior by nature, *all* blacks were necessarily inferior to (nearly) *all* whites. It occasionally happened that a particular white person might not be superior to all black people because of a condition that "deforms or blights individuals; they may be idiotic, insane, or otherwise incapable." But these unnatural exceptions to the rule were "the result of human vices, crimes, or ignorance, immediate or remote." Only disability might lower a white person in the scale of life to the level of a being of a marked race.[11]

By the turn of the century, medical doctors were still arguing that African Americans were disabled by freedom and therefore in need of greater oversight. J. F. Miller, writing in the *North Carolina Medical Journal*, thought it important to inquire whether "the effect of freedom upon the mental and physical health of the negroes of the South" had been "damaging or otherwise." His conclusion was that there were "more congenital defects" and a dramatic increase in mental illness and tuberculosis, which supposedly had been rare among enslaved African Americans. Freedom, for which the African American's weak mind and constitution were ill suited, had

brought to the former slave "a beautiful harvest of mental and physical degeneration and he is now becoming a martyr to an heredity thus established."[12]

While these arguments were often contradictory, incoherent, or simply ludicrous, disability was central to all of them. If freedom for African Americans was undesirable and slavery good, then it was sufficient to note that free blacks were more likely than slaves to be disabled. The decisive argument for miscegenation being morally wrong or socially injurious was that it produced disability. The contention had to be countered, and no argument on other grounds could trump it. Samuel Forry, for example, writing in the *New York Journal of Medicine* in 1844, noted that the supposedly higher rates of insanity among free blacks compared to slaves had been "seized upon by journals devoted to the peculiar institutions of the Southern States, as a powerful argument." Forry retorted, first, that the census did not allow a reliable comparison of deafness, blindness, idiocy, and insanity in free and enslaved blacks and, second, that even were it the case that free blacks in the North suffered more disability than slaves, slavery and freedom might not be the determinants. Instead, perhaps "the whole constitution of the black is adapted to a tropical region," and their mental and physical health was therefore bound to suffer in the northern climate.[13] The argument that a people might be enslaved to protect them from disability he left unchallenged.

Race and disability intersected in the concept of the normal, as both prescription and description. American blacks, for example, were said to flourish in their "normal condition" of slavery, while the "'free' or abnormal negro" inevitably fell into illness, disability, and eventually extinction. The hierarchy of races was itself depicted as a continuum of normality. Just as medical textbook illustrations compared the normal body with the abnormal, so social science textbooks illustrated the normal race and the abnormal ones. Arnold Guyot, in his 1873 textbook *Physical Geography*, under the heading "The White Race the Normal, or Typical, Race," compared the beauty, regularity of features, and "harmony in all the proportions of the figure" of the white race with those who have "gradually deviated" from the normal ideal. Similarly, Dr. John C. Nott, writing in the *American Journal of Medical Sciences* in 1843, invited the reader to "look first upon the Caucasian female with her rose and lily skin, silky hair, Venus form, and well chiseled features—and then upon the African wench with her black and odorous skin, woolly head and animal features—and compare their intellectual and moral qualities, and their whole anatomical structure." He added for good measure that the American Indian "has many peculiarities which are just as striking." In nineteenth-century freak shows, where disability and race intersected to illustrate familiar narratives of evolutionary progress, disabled adults were displayed as less-evolved creatures from far-off jungles. P. T. Barnum promoted his American Museum exhibit "What Is It?" as the "missing link" between human and animal, a "man-monkey." At least two different men played the role: a white actor with unusually short legs of uneven length and a mentally retarded black man with microcephaly who later became known by the stage name Zip. The presence of disability in both cases, in addition to race in one of them, was in effect the costume that signified the role of "subhuman."[14]

It is not new to point out that images of American blacks have commonly shown them with exaggerated lips, amusingly long or bowed legs, grotesquely big feet, bad posture, missing teeth, crossed or bulging eyes, and otherwise deformed bodies. At least since 1792, when Benjamin Rush explained that the skin color of Africans was due to their suffering from congenital leprosy, black skin itself has been treated as anomalous, a defect and a disfigurement, something akin to an all-body birthmark and often a sign of sin or degeneracy. Advertisements for soap in the nineteenth century often played on this idea of dark skin as defect with, for example, a pink-cheeked child asking an African American child, "Why doesn't your mamma wash you with Fairy Soap?"[15] Another advertisement told a tale of children who were bathed daily, "Because their mother did believe/That white they could be made/So on them with a scrubbing brush/Unmerciful she laid." The mother's efforts were fruitless until she found the right brand of soap: "Sweet and clean her sons became/it's true, as I'm a workman/And both are now completely white, Washed by this soap of Kirkman."[16] Dreydoppel Soap told a similar story of an African American boy ("A mite of queer humanity/As dark as a cloudy night") who scrubbed himself with acids, fasted, took sulfur baths, and "sampled all the medicine that ever was made or brewed" in the attempt to cure his unfortunate skin color. "He built an air-tight sweat box with the/Hope that he would bleach/The sweat poured down in rivers/but the Black stuck like a leech." That is, until he discovered Dreydoppel soap: "One trial was all he needed/Realized was his fondest hope/His face was white as white could be/There's nothing like Dreydoppel Soap."[17]

Daryl Michael Scott has described how both conservatives and liberals have long used an extensive repertory of "damage imagery" to describe African Americans. Conservatives "operated primarily from within a biological framework and argued for the innate inferiority of people of African descent" in order to justify social and political exclusion. Liberals maintained that social conditions were responsible for black inferiority and used damage imagery to argue for inclusion and rehabilitation; but regardless of their intentions, Scott argues, liberal damage imagery "reinforced the belief system that made whites feel superior in the first place." Both the "contempt and pity" of conservatives and liberals—a phrase that equally well describes historically prevalent attitudes toward disabled people—framed Americans of African descent as defective. Scott cites the example of Charles S. Johnson, chair of the social science department and later president of Fisk University, who told students in a 1928 speech that "the sociologists classify Negroes with cripples, persons with recognized physical handicaps." Like Johnson, Scott is critical of the fact that "African Americans were often lumped with the 'defective,' 'delinquent,' and dependent classes." This is obviously a bad place to be "lumped." Scott does not ask, however, why that might be the case.[18] The attribution of disease or disability to racial minorities has a long history. Yet, while many have pointed out the injustice and perniciousness of attributing these qualities to a racial or ethnic group, little has been written about why these attributions are such powerful weapons for inequality, why they were so furiously denied and condemned by their targets, and what this tells us about our attitudes toward disability.

During the long-running debate over women's suffrage in the nineteenth and early twentieth centuries, one of the rhetorical tactics of suffrage opponents was to point to the physical, intellectual, and psychological flaws of women, their frailty, irrationality, and emotional excesses. By the late nineteenth century, these claims were sometimes expressed in terms of evolutionary progress; like racial and ethnic minorities, women were said to be less evolved than white men, their disabilities a result of lesser evolutionary development. Cynthia Eagle Russett has noted that "women and savages, together with idiots, criminals, and pathological monstrosities [those with congenital disabilities] were a constant source of anxiety to male intel-

lectuals in the late nineteenth century."[19] What all shared was an evolutionary inferiority, the result of arrested development or atavism.

Paralleling the arguments made in defense of slavery, two types of disability argument were used in opposition to women's suffrage: that women had disabilities that made them incapable of using the franchise responsibly, and that because of their frailty women would become disabled if exposed to the rigors of political participation. The American anti-suffragist Grace Goodwin, for example, pointed to the "great temperamental disabilities" with which women had to contend: "woman lacks endurance in things mental. . . . She lacks nervous stability. The suffragists who dismay England are nerve-sick women." The second line of argument, which was not incompatible with the first and often accompanied it, went beyond the claim that women's flaws made them incapable of exercising equal political and social rights with men to warn that if women were given those rights, disability would surely follow. This argument is most closely identified with Edward Clarke, author of *Sex in Education; or, A Fair Chance for Girls*. Clarke's argument chiefly concerned education for women, though it was often applied to suffrage as well. Clarke maintained that overuse of the brain among young women was in large part responsible for the "numberless pale, weak, neuralgic, dyspeptic, hysterical, menorraghic, dysmenorrhoeic girls and women" of America. The result of excessive education in this country was "bloodless female faces, that suggest consumption, scrofula, anemia, and neuralgia." An appropriate education designed for their frail constitutions would ensure "a future secure from neuralgia, uterine disease, hysteria, and other derangements of the nervous system."[20]

Similarly, Dr. William Warren Potter, addressing the Medical Society of New York in 1891, suggested that many a mother was made invalid by inappropriate education: "her reproductive organs are dwarfed, deformed, weakened, and diseased, by artificial causes imposed upon her during their development."[21] Dr. A. Lapthorn Smith asserted in *Popular Science Monthly* that educated women were increasingly "sick and suffering before marriage and are physically disabled from performing physiological functions in a normal manner." Antisuffragists likewise warned that female participation in politics invariably led to "nervous prostration" and "hysteria," while Dr. Almroth E. Wright noted the "fact that there is mixed up with the woman's movement much mental disorder." A prominent late nineteenth-century neurophysiologist, Charles L. Dana, estimated that enfranchising women would result in a 25 percent increase in insanity among them and "throw into the electorate a mass of voters of delicate nervous stability . . . which might do injury to itself without promoting the community's good." The answer for Clarke, Potter, and others of like mind was special education suited to women's special needs. As with disabled people today, women's social position was treated as a medical problem that necessitated separate and special care. Those who wrote with acknowledged authority on the "woman question" were doctors. As Clarke wrote, the answer to the "problem of woman's sphere . . . must be obtained from physiology, not from ethics or metaphysics."[22]

While historians have not overlooked the use of disability to deny women's rights, they have given their attention entirely to gender inequality and not at all to the construction and maintenance of cultural hierarchies based on disability. Lois Magner has described how women were said to bear the "onerous functions of the female," which incapacitated them for "active life" and produced a "mental disability that rendered women unfit" for political engage-ment. Nancy Woloch has noted that a "major antisuffragist point was that women were physically, mentally, and emotionally incapable of duties associated with the vote. Lacking rationality and sound judgment, they suffered from 'logical infirmity of mind.' . . . Unable to withstand the pressure of political life, they would be prone to paroxysms of hysteria." Aileen Kraditor, in her intellectual history of the women's suffrage movement, wrote that antisuffragists "described woman's physical constitution as too delicate to withstand the turbulence of political life. Her alleged weakness, nervousness, and proneness to fainting would certainly be out of place in polling booths and party conventions." On the one hand, this was of course an unfounded stereotype deserving of ridicule, as Kraditor's ironic tone suggests. On the other hand, just as it was left unchallenged at the time, historians today leave unchallenged the notion that weakness, nervousness, or proneness to fainting might legitimately disqualify one for suffrage.[23]

Disability figured not just in arguments *for* the inequality of women and minorities but also in arguments *against those* inequalities. Suffragists rarely challenged the notion that disability justified political inequality and instead disputed the claim that women suffered from these disabilities. Their arguments took three forms: one, women were not disabled and therefore deserved the vote; two, women were being erroneously and slanderously classed with disabled people, with those who were legitimately denied suffrage; and three, women were not naturally or inherently disabled but were *made* disabled by inequality—suffrage would ameliorate or cure these disabilities.

References to the intelligence and abilities of women, countering the imputations of female inferiority, pervaded suffrage rhetoric. Although more common later in the century, this form of argument was already in evidence in 1848 at the Seneca Falls Woman's Rights Convention. Delegates resolved that "the equality of human rights results necessarily from the fact of the identity of the race in capabilities and responsibilitioo," and further, that "being invested by the Creator with the same capabilities . . . it is demonstrably the right and duty of woman" to participate in public political life. Rebecca M. Sandford avowed, "Our intellect is as capable as man's to assume, and at once to hold, these rights . . . for if we did not believe it, we would not contend for them." Frederick Douglass proclaimed that "the true basis of rights was the capacity of individuals."[24] The converse of their premise that equality in capacity justified political equality, was a warrant too basic to be considered explicitly: differences in capacity, if present, would be justification for political inequality.

A second powerful and recurrent rhetorical device for suffragists was to charge that women were wrongly categorized with those legitimately excluded from political life. A popular theme in both British and American suffrage posters was to depict a thoughtful-looking woman, perhaps wearing the gown of a college graduate, surrounded by slope-browed, wild-eyed, or "degenerate" men identified implicitly or explicitly as "idiots" and "lunatics." The caption might read, "Women and her Political Peers," or, "It's time I got out of this place. Where shall I find the key?" Echoing this theme, suffrage supporter George William Curtis rhetorically asked a New York constitutional convention in 1867 why women should be classed with "idiots, lunatics, persons under guardianship and felons," and at the national Woman Suffrage Convention in 1869, Elizabeth Cady Stanton protested that women were "thrust outside the pale of political consideration with minors, paupers, lunatics, traitors, [and] idiots."[25]

These challenges directly confronted the euphemisms used by the anti-suffragists, whose attributions of mental and psychological inferiority to women were couched in less direct language. Antisuffragists were wont to counter that it was "a noble sort of disfranchisement" that women enjoyed, "something wholly different from the disfranchisement of the pauper, the criminal, the insane. . . . These are set aside as persons not human; women are absolved as constituting a higher class. There is a very real distinction between being placed among the beasts, and being placed among the 'ministering angels.'"[26] The suffragist answer to these sentimental claims made clear that the antisuffrage argument was rooted in the attribution of disability.

Suffragists did on occasion take issue with the argument that rights rested on capacity. Lucretia Mott, speaking at Seneca Falls, conceded that "woman's intellect may be feeble, because she had been so long crushed; but is that any reason why she should be deprived of her equal rights? Does one man have fewer rights than another because his intellect is inferior? If not, why should woman?" But she immediately undercut the point by avowing, "Let woman arise and demand her rights, and in a few years we shall see a different mental development." Charlotte Perkins Gilman was the most prominent of those who argued that women's capacities had been stunted over time by restricted activity, which had come to represent a genetic inheritance that could be undone only by access to an unfettered social and political life. Matilda Gage similarly suggested that "obedience to outside authority to which woman has everywhere been trained, has not only dwarfed her capacity, but made her a retarding force in civilization."[27] These arguments were an implicit acknowledgment that capacity was indeed relevant to the question of rights. They are also examples of the third variant on the suffrage disability argument, that women were disabled by exclusion from political equality. This argument answered the antisuffrage accusation that women were inherently and unchangeably disabled with the claim that, given equal rights, they would attain equality in capacity. Like the antisuffrage position, it was a powerful argument precisely because of the cultural power of disability to discredit.

Ethnicity also has been defined by disability. One of the fundamental imperatives in the initial formation of American immigration policy at the end of the nineteenth century was the exclusion of disabled people. Beyond the targeting of disabled people, the concept of disability was instrumental in crafting the image of the undesirable immigrant. The first major federal immigration law, the Act of 1882, prohibited entry to any "lunatic, idiot, or any person unable to take care of himself or herself without becoming a public charge." Those placed in the categories "lunatic" and "idiot" were automatically excluded. The "public charge" provision was intended to encompass people with disabilities more generally and was left to the examining officer's discretion. The criteria for excluding disabled people were steadily tightened as the eugenics movement and popular fears about the decline of the national stock gathered strength. The Act of 1891 replaced the phrase *"unable* to take care of himself or herself without becoming a public charge," with *"likely* to become a public charge." The 1907 law then denied entry to anyone judged "mentally or physically defective, such mental or physical defect being of a nature which *may affect* the ability of such alien to earn a living." These changes considerably lowered the threshold for exclusion and expanded the latitude of immigration officials to deny entry.[28]

The category of persons *automatically* excluded was also steadily expanded. In 1903, people with epilepsy were added and, in addition to those judged insane, "persons who have been insane within five years previous [or] who have had two or more attacks of insanity at any time previously." This was reduced to one "attack" in the 1917 law; the classification of "constitutional psychopathic inferiority" was also added, which inspection regulations described as including "various unstable individuals on the border line between sanity and insanity ... and persons with abnormal sex instincts."[29] This was the regulation under which, until recently, gays and lesbians were excluded. One of the significant factors in lifting this ban, along with other forms of discrimination against gays and lesbians, was the decision by the American Psychiatric Association in 1973 to remove homosexuality from its list of mental illnesses. That is, once gays and lesbians were declared not to be disabled, discrimination became less justifiable.

Legislation in 1907 added "imbeciles" and "feeble-minded persons" to the list, in addition to "idiots," and regulations for inspectors directed them to exclude persons with "any mental abnormality whatever ... which justifies the statement that the alien is mentally defective." These changes encompassed a much larger number of people and again granted officials considerably more discretion to judge the fitness of immigrants for American life. Fiorello H. LaGuardia, who worked his way through law school as an interpreter at Ellis Island, later wrote that "over fifty percent of the deportations for alleged mental disease were unjustified," based as they often were on "ignorance on the part of the immigrants or the doctors and the inability of the doctors to understand the particular immigrant's norm, or standard."[30]

The detection of physical disabilities was a major aspect of the immigration inspector's work. The Regulations for the medical inspection of immigrants in 1917 included a long list of diseases and disabilities that could be cause for exclusion, among them arthritis, asthma, bunions, deafness, deformities, flat feet, heart disease, hernia, hysteria, poor eyesight, poor physical development, spinal curvature, vascular disease of the heart, and varicose veins. A visiting physician in 1893, when admission standards were still relatively liberal, described the initial inspection: "If a man has a hand done up, or any physical injury in any way . . ., or if a person has but one leg or one arm, or one eye, or there is any physical or mental defect, if the person seems unsteady and in any way physically incapacitated to earn his livelihood, he is passed to one side to be examined later."[31] An immigration official later recalled a young Italian couple who would have been deported (the man had a "game leg" that required use of a crutch) had not a wealthy philanthropist visiting Ellis Island taken an interest in the couple and intervened, guaranteeing that they would not become a public charge.[32]

In short, the exclusion of disabled people was central to the laws and the work of the immigration service. As the Commissioner General of Immigration reported in 1907, "The exclusion from this country of the morally, mentally, and physically deficient is the principal object to be accomplished by the immigration laws." Once the laws and procedures limiting the entry of disabled people were firmly established and functioning well, attention turned to limiting the entry of undesirable ethnic groups. Discussion on this topic often began by pointing to the general public agreement that the laws excluding disabled people had been a positive, if insufficient, step. In 1896, for example, Francis Walker noted in the *Atlantic Monthly* that the necessity of "straining out" immigrants who were "deaf, dumb, blind, idiotic, insane, pauper, or criminal" was "now conceded by men of all shades of opinion"; indeed there was a widespread "resentment at the attempt of

such persons to impose themselves upon us." As one restrictionist wrote, the need to exclude the disabled was "self evident."[33]

For the more controversial business of defining and excluding undesirable ethnic groups, however, restrictionists found the *concept* of disability to be a powerful tool. That is, while people with disabilities constituted a distinct category of persons unwelcome in the United States, the charge that certain ethnic groups were mentally and physically deficient was instrumental in arguing for *their* exclusion. The belief that discriminating on the basis of disability was justifiable in turn helped justify the creation of immigration quotas based on ethnic origin. The 1924 Immigration Act instituted a national quota system that severely limited the numbers of immigrants from southern and eastern Europe, but long before that, disabilities stood in for nationality. Superintendents of institutions, philanthropists, immigration reformers, and politicians had been warning for decades before 1924 that immigrants were disproportionately prone to be mentally defective—up to half the immigrants from southern and eastern Europe were feebleminded, according to expert opinion.[34] Rhetoric about "the slow-witted Slav," the "neurotic condition of our Jewish immigrants," and, in general, the "degenerate and psychopathic types, which are so conspicuous and numerous among the immigrants," was pervasive in the debate over restriction.[35] The laws forbidding entry to the feebleminded were motivated in part by the desire to limit immigration from inferior nations, and conversely, it was assumed that the 1924 act would reduce the number of feebleminded immigrants. The issues of ethnicity and disability were so intertwined in the immigration debate as to be inseparable.

Arguments for immigration restriction often emphasized the inferior appearance of immigrants, and here also ethnicity and disability overlapped and intertwined. Disability scholars have emphasized the uncertain and shifting line between an impairment of appearance and one of function. Martin Pernick, for example, has described the importance of aesthetics in eugenics literature—how fitness was equated with beauty and disability with ugliness. Lennard Davis has maintained that disability presents itself "through two main modalities—function and appearance." Restrictionists often emphasized the impaired appearance of immigrants. An Ellis Island inspector claimed that "no one can stand at Ellis Island and see the physical and mental wrecks who are stopped there . . . without becoming a firm believer in restriction."[36] A proponent of restriction avowed, "To the practised eye, the physiognomy of certain groups unmistakably proclaims inferiority of type." When he observed immigrants, he saw that "in every face there was something wrong. . . . There were so many sugar-loaf heads, moon-faces, slit mouths, lantern-jaws, and goose-bill noses that one might imagine a malicious jinn had amused himself by casting human beings in a set of skew-molds discarded by the Creator." Most new immigrants were physically inadequate in some way: "South Europeans run to low stature. A gang of Italian navvies filing along the street present, by their dwarfishness, a curious contrast to other people. The Portuguese, the Greeks, and the Syrians are, from our point of view, undersized. The Hebrew immigrants are very poor in physique . . . the polar opposite of our pioneer breed."[37]

The initial screening of immigrants was mostly a matter of detecting visible abnormality. Inspectors, who prided themselves on their ability to make a "snapshot diagnosis," had only a few seconds to detect the signs of disability or disease as immigrants streamed past them in single file. Inspection regulations specified that "each individual should be seen first at rest and then in motion," in order to detect "irregularities in movement" and "abnormalities of any description." If possible, inspectors watched immigrants as they carried their luggage up stairs to see if "the exertion would reveal deformities and defective posture."[38] As one inspector wrote, "It is no more difficult to detect poorly built, defective or broken down human beings than to recognize a cheap or defective automobile. . . . The wise man who really wants to find out all he can about an automobile or an immigrant, will want to see both in action, performing as well as at rest."[39]

For most immigrants, a normal appearance meant a quick, uneventful passage through the immigration station. An abnormal appearance, however, meant a chalked letter on the back: "L for lameness, K for hernia, G for goiter, X for mental illness," and so on.[40] Once chalked, a closer inspection was required. The inspection then would be general, not confined to the abnormality that set them apart, which meant that visibly disabled people—as well as those whose ethnic appearance was abnormal to the inspectors—were more likely to be set apart for close examination and therefore were also more likely to have other problems discovered and to be excluded.

Aesthetic and eugenic considerations were at least as important as concerns about the functional limitations of disabled immigrants. For example, on June 30, 1922, Israel Raskin was refused entry to the United States as "physically defective and likely to become a public charge." The diagnosis on the medical certificate was "lack of sexual development which may affect his ability to earn a living." The United States Surgeon General explained that the diagnosis warranted exclusion because "these persons present bad economic risks . . . due to the fact that their abnormality soon becomes known to their associates who make them the butt of coarse jokes to their own despair, and to the impairment of the work in hand." Since this was "recognized pretty generally among employers, it is difficult for these unfortunates to get or retain jobs, their facial and bodily appearance, at least in adult life, furnishing a patent advertisement of their condition."[41]

Medical exclusions on the basis of "poor physique" and "lack of physical development" began to appear around the turn of the century. The immigration service defined it as covering individuals "who have frail frame, flat chest, and are generally deficient in muscular development," or those who are "undersized—markedly of short stature—dwarf."[42] In part, this diagnosis represented a judgment of employability, and in part it was a eugenic judgment. Both concerns were expressed in a letter from the Bureau of Immigration, which explained that "a certificate of this nature implies that the alien concerned is afflicted with a body but illy adapted . . . to the work necessary to earn his bread." The diagnosis further indicated that the immigrant was "undersized, poorly developed [and] physically degenerate, and as such, not only unlikely to become a desirable citizen, but also very likely to transmit his undesirable qualities to his offspring, should he unfortunately for the country in which he is domiciled, have any."[43]

As one medical officer explained it, the "immigrant of poor physique is not able to perform rough labor, and *even if he were able*, employers of labor would not hire him."[44] The belief that an immigrant with a disability was unfit to work was justification for exclusion; but the belief that an immigrant was *likely to encounter discrimination* because of a disability was equally justification for exclusion. The disability that justified exclusion in these cases was largely or entirely a matter of an abnormal appearance that might invite employment discrimination.

The laws excluding disabled immigrants could be used by inspectors to target particular ethnic groups. The Hebrew Sheltering and Immigrane Aid Society in New York expressed concern in 1909 that the "lack of physical development" diagnosis was "constantly increasing" and being applied to Jewish immigrants disproportionately. An investigation by the Jewish Immigrants' Information Bureau in 1910 discovered that an inspector in Galveston was using the diagnosis to discriminate against Jewish immigrants. Nationality and disability might be implicitly linked in anti-immigration rhetoric, as when William Green, president of the American Federation of Labor, argued that quotas were "necessary to the preservation of our national characteristics and to our physical and our mental health."[45] They also were explicitly connected, as when a New York Supreme Court justice worried that the new immigrants were "adding to that appalling number of our inhabitants who handicap us by reason of their mental and physical disabilities."[46]

Historians have scrutinized the attribution of mental and physical inferiority based on race and ethnicity, but only to condemn the slander. With their attention confined to ethnic stereotypes, they have largely ignored what the attribution of disability might also tell us about attitudes toward disabled people. Racial and ethnic prejudice is exposed while prejudice against people with disabilities is passed over as insignificant and understandable. As a prominent advocate of restriction wrote in 1930, "The necessity of the exclusion of the crippled, the blind, those who are likely to become public charges, and, of course, those with a criminal record is self evident."[47] The necessity has been treated as self-evident by historians as well, so much so that even the possibility of discrimination against people with disabilities in immigration law has gone unrecognized. In historical accounts, disability is present but rendered invisible or insignificant. While it is certain that immigration restriction rests in good part on a fear of "strangers in the land," in John Higham's phrase, American immigration restriction at the turn of the century was also clearly fueled by a fear of *defectives* in the land.

Still today, women and other groups who face discrimination on the basis of identity respond angrily to accusations that they might be characterized by physical, mental, or emotional disabilities. Rather than challenging the basic assumptions behind the hierarchy, they instead work to remove themselves from the negatively marked categories—that is, to disassociate themselves from those people who "really are" disabled—knowing that such categorization invites discrimination. For example, a recent proposal in Louisiana to permit pregnant women to use parking spaces reserved for people with mobility impairments was opposed by women's organizations. A lobbyist for the Women's Health Foundation said, "We've spent a long time trying to dispel the myth that pregnancy is a disability, for obvious reasons of discrimination." She added, "I have no problem with it being a courtesy, but not when a legislative mandate provides for pregnancy in the same way as for disabled persons."[48] To be associated with disabled people or with the accommodations accorded disabled people is stigmatizing.

Even disabled people have used this strategy to try to deflect discrimination. Rosemarie Garland Thomson notes that "disabled people also often avoid and stereotype one another in attempting to normalize their own social identities." Deaf people throughout the twentieth century have rejected the label of disability, knowing its dangers; and the tendency of those with less-stigmatized disabilities to distance themselves from those with more highly stigmatized disabilities is a common phenomenon. In 1918, the associate director of what was known as the "Cleveland Cripple Survey" reported that some of those surveyed "were amazed that they should be considered cripples, even though they were without an arm or leg, or perhaps seriously crippled as a result of infantile paralysis. They had never considered themselves handicapped in any way."[49]

This common strategy for attaining equal rights, which seeks to distance one's own group from imputations of disability and therefore tacitly accepts the idea that disability is a legitimate reason for inequality, is perhaps one of the factors responsible for making discrimination against people with disabilities so persistent and the struggle for disability rights so difficult. As Harlan Hahn has noted, "Unlike other disadvantaged groups, citizens with disabilities have not yet fully succeeded in refuting the presumption that their subordinate status can be ascribed to an innate biological inferiority."[50] If Hahn is perhaps too optimistic about the extent to which women and minority groups have managed to do away with such presumptions, nevertheless it is true that such views are no longer an accepted part of public discourse. Yet the same views regarding disability are still espoused widely and openly.

Disability is everywhere in history, once you begin looking for it, but conspicuously absent in the histories we write. When historians do take note of disability, they usually treat it merely as personal tragedy or an insult to be deplored and a label to be denied, rather than as a cultural construct to be questioned and explored. Those of us who specialize in the history of disability, like the early historians of other minority groups, have concentrated on writing histories of disabled people and the institutions and laws associated with disability. This is necessary and exciting work. It is through this work that we are building the case that disability is culturally constructed rather than natural and timeless—that disabled people have a history, and a history worth studying. Disability, however, more than an identity, is a fundamental element in cultural signification and indispensable for *any* historian seeking to make sense of the past. It may well be that all social hierarchies have drawn on culturally constructed and socially sanctioned notions of disability. If this is so, then there is much work to do. It is time to bring disability from the margins to the center of historical inquiry.

NOTES

1. Joan Scott, "Gender: A Useful Category of Historical Analysis," *American Historical Review* 91 (December 1986): 1053–75.

2. Edmund Burke, Thomas Paine, *Reflections on the Revolution in France and The Rights of Man* (Garden City, NY: Anchor Press/Doubleday, 1973); for rhetoric of monstrosity, see pp. 22, 49, 81, 159, 208, 212, 224, 229–34, 244, 321; blindness: 53, 64, 185, 224; imbecility and madness: 135, 206, 219, 233, 248, 261.

3. Ian Hacking, *The Taming of Chance* (Cambridge and New York: Cambridge University Press, 1990), 160–66. See also Georges Canguilhem, *The Normal and the Pathological* (New York: Zone Books, 1989); Douglas C. Baynton, *Forbidden Signs: American Culture and the Campaign against Sign Language* (Chicago: University of Chicago Press, 1996), chaps. 5–6.

4. Francois Ewald, "Norms Discipline, and the Law," *Representations* 30 (Spring 1990): 146, 149–50, 154; Lennard Davis, *Enforcing Normalcy: Disability, Deafness, and the Body* (London: Verso, 1995); Baynton, *Forbidden Signs,* chaps. 5 and 6.

5. Late nineteenth-century educators began using "normal child" as the counterpart to "deaf child" instead of the "hearing" and "deaf" of previous generations. "Normal" appears to refer to an average, since the "average" person is hearing. Since it does not exclude those with superior hearing, however, it does not denote the average but those *above* a certain standard.

6. Daniel J. Kevles, *In the Name of Eugenics: Genetics and the Uses of Human Heredity* (Berkeley: University of California Press, 1985), 160; Baynton, *Forbidden Signs,* chap. 2; James W. Cook, Jr., "Of Men, Missing Links, and Nondescripts: The Strange Career of P. T. Barnum's 'What Is It?' Exhibition," in Rosemarie Garland Thomson, ed., *Freakery: Cultural Spectacles of the Extraordinary Body* (New York: New York University Press, 1996); James W. Trent, Jr., "Defectives at

the World's Fair: Constructing Disability in 1904," *Remedial and Special Education* 19 (July/August 1998): 201–11.

7. Samuel A. Cartwright, "Report on the Diseases and Physical Peculiarities of the Negro Race," *New Orleans Medical and Surgical Journal* 7 (May 1851): 693; George M Fredrickson, *The Black Image in the White Mind* (New York: Harper and Row, 1971), 250–51; J. C. Nott, "The Mulatto a Hybrid," *American Journal of Medical Sciences* (July 1843), quoted in Samuel Forry, "Vital Statistics Furnished by the Sixth Census of the United States," *New York Journal of Medicine and the Collateral Sciences* 1 (September 1843): 151–53.

8. John H. Van Evrie, *White Supremacy and Negro Subordination, or Negroes a Subordinate Race* (New York: Van Evrie, Horton, & Co., 1868), 153–55; Forry, "Vital Statistics," 159; Paul B. Barringer, *The American Negro: His Past and Future* (Raleigh: Edwards & Broughton, 1900), 10.

9. Cited in Forry, "Vital Statistics," 162–63. John C. Calhoun, "Mr. Calhoun to Mr. Pakenham," in Richard K. Cralle, ed., *The Works of John C. Calhoun* (New York: D. Appleton, 1888), 5: 337.

10. Cartwright, "Report," 707–10. See also Thomas S. Szasz, "The Sane Slave: A Historical Note on the Use of Medical Diagnosis as Justificatory Rhetoric," *American Journal of Psychotherapy* 25 (1971): 228–39.

11. Van Evrie, *White Supremacy,* 121, 181, 221. Van Evrie notes in his preface that the book was completed "about the time of Mr. Lincoln's election" and was therefore originally an argument in favor of the continuation of slavery but presently constituted an argument for its restoration.

12. J. F. Miller, "The Effects of Emancipation upon the Mental and Physical Health of the Negro of the South," *North Carolina Medical Journal* 38 (Nov. 20, 1896): 285–94.

13. Samuel Forry, "On the Relative Proportion of Centenarians, of Deaf and Dumb, of Blind, and of Insane in the Races of European and African Origin," *New York Journal of Medicine and the Collateral Sciences* 2 (May 1844): 313.

14. Van Evrie, *White Supremacy* 199, chap. 15 *passim;* Arnold Guyot, *Physical Geography* (1873; reprint, New York: American Book Co., 1885), 114–18; Nott, "Mulatto a Hybrid," quoted in Forry, "Vital Statistics," 163–64; Cook, "Of Men, Missing Links, and Nondescripts," 139–57; Robert Bogdan, *Freak Show: Presenting Human Oddities for Amusement and Profit* (Chicago: University of Chicago Press, 1988), 134–42.

15. Winthrop D. Jordan. *White over Black: American Attitudes toward the Negro, 1550–1812* (Chapel

Hill: University of North Carolina Press, 1968), 518–25; Rush explained not only African skin this way but the nose, lips, and hair as well. Smithsonian Institution Archives, Collection 60—Warshaw Collection, "Soap," Box 4 Folder: Fairbanks; dated 1893 or 1898 (illegible).

16. Smithsonian Institution Archives, Collection 60—Warshaw Collection, "Afro-Americana," Box 4, Folder 7, n.d.

17. Smithsonian Institution Archives, Collection 60—Warshaw Collection, "AfroAmericana," Box 4, Folder 4, n.d., ca. 1893.

18. Daryl Michael Scott, *Contempt and Pity: Social Policy and the Image of the Damaged Black Soul, 1880–1996* (Chapel Hill: University of North Carolina Press, 1997) xi–xvii; 12, 208 n. 52.

19. Cynthia Eagle Russett, *Sexual Science: The Victorian Construction of Womanhood* (Cambridge, Mass.: Harvard University Press, 1989), 63. See also Lois N. Magner, "Darwinism and the Woman Question: The Evolving Views of Charlotte Perkins Gilman," in Joanne Karpinski, *Critical Essays on Charlotte Perkins Gilman* (New York: G. K. Hall, 1992), 119–20.

20. Grace Duffield Goodwin, *Anti-Suffrage: Ten Good Reasons* (New York: Duffield and Co., 1913), 91–92 (in Smithsonian Institution Archives, Collection 60—Warshaw Collection, "Women," Box 3). Edward Clarke, *Sex in Education; or, A Fair Chance for Girls* (1873; reprint, New York: Arno Press, 1972), 18, 22, 62.

21. William Warren Potter, "How Should Girls Be Educated? A Public Health Problem for Mothers, Educators, and Physicians," *Transactions of the Medical Society of the State of New York* (1891): 48, quoted in Martha H. Verbrugge, *Able Bodied Womanhood: Personal Health and Social Change in Nineteenth-Century Boston* (Oxford and New York: Oxford University Press, 1988), 121.

22. A. Lapthorn Smith, "Higher Education of Women and Race Suicide," *Popular Science Monthly* (March 1905), reprinted in Louise Michele Newman, ed., *Men's Ideas/Women's Realities: Popular Science, 1870–1915* (New York: Pergamon Press, 1985), 149; Almroth E. Wright quoted in Mara Mayor, "Fears and Fantasies of the Anti-Suffragists," *Connecticut Review 7* (April 1974): 67; Charles L. Dana quoted in Jane Jerome Camhi, *Women against Women: American Anti-Suffragism, 1880–1920* (New York: Carlson Publishing Co., 1994), 18; Clarke, *Sex in Education*, 12.

23. Magner, "Darwinism," 119–20; Nancy Woloch, *Women and the American Experience, vol. 1: To 1920* (New York: McGraw-Hill, Inc., 1994), 339: Aileen S. Kraditor, *The Ideas of the Woman Suf-*

frage Movement (New York: W. W. Norton & Co., 1981), 20. See also Anne Digby, "Woman's Biological Straitjacket," in Susan Mendas and Jane Randall, eds., *Sexuality and Subordination: Interdisciplinary Studies of Gender in the Nineteenth Century* (New York: Routledge, 1989), 192–220.

24. *Woman's Rights Conventions: Seneca Falls and Rochester, 1848* (New York: Arno Press, Inc., 1969), 4–6; originally published as *Proceedings of the Woman's Rights Convention, Held at Seneca Falls and Rochester, N.Y., July and August, 1848* (New York: Robert J. Johnston, 1870), 4–6.

25. Lisa Tickner, *The Spectacle of Women: Imagery of the Suffrage Campaign, 1907–14* (Chicago: University of Chicago Press, 1988), illustration IV; Alice Sheppard, *Cartooning for Suffrage* (Albuquerque: University of New Mexico Press, 1994), 30; Elizabeth Cady Stanton, Susan B. Anthony, and Matilda Joslyn Gage, eds., *History of Woman Suffrage* (1881; reprint, New York: Arno Press, 1969), 2: 288, quoted in Yvonne Pitts, "'Under This Disability of Nature': Women and Constructions of Disability in the National Suffrage Debates, 1870–1920" (paper presented to the Berkshire Conference on the History of Women, June 1999); Elizabeth Cady Stanton, "Address to the National Woman Suffrage Convention, Washington, D.C., January 19, 1869," in Mari Jo Buhle and Paul Buhle, eds., *The Concise History of Woman Suffrage* (Urbana: University of Illinois Press, 1978), 256.

26. O. B. Frothingham, "The Real Case of the 'Remonstrants' against Woman Suffrage," *The Arena 2* (July 1890): 177.

27. *Woman's Rights Conventions*, 11; on Charlotte Perkins Gilman, see Kraditor, *Ideas of the Woman Suffrage Movement*, 97–101; "Preceding Causes, written by Matilda Joslyn Gage, in 1881," in Buhle and Buhle, eds., *Concise History*, 53.

28. *United States Statutes at Large* (Washington, D.C.: Government Printing Office, 1883), 22:214. *United States Statutes at Large* (Washington, D.C.: Government Printing Office, 1891), 26:1084; *United States Statutes at Large* (Washington, D.C.: Government Printing Office, 1907), 34: 899. Emphases added.

29. *United States Statutes at Large* (Washington, D.C.: Government Printing Office, 1903), 32: 1213; United States Public Health Service, *Regulations Governing the Medical Inspection of Aliens* (Washington, D.C.: Government Printing Office, 1917), 28–29.

30. *Statutes* (1907), 34: 899; United States Public Health Service, *Regulations*, 30–31, Fiorello H. LaGuardia, *The Making of an Insurgent: An Autobiography, 1882–1919* (1948; reprint, New York: Capricorn, 1961), 65.

31. United States Public Health Service, *Regulations*, 16–19; U. O. B. Wingate, "Quarenteen Immigration at the Port of New York," *Milwaukee Medical Journal* 1 (1893): 181, quoted in Elizabeth Yew, "Medical Inspection of Immigrants at Ellis Island, 1891–1924," *Bulletin of the New York Academy of Medicine* 56 (June 1980): 494.

32. Philip Cowen, *Memories of an American Jew* (1932; reprint, New York: Arno Press, 1975) 148–49.

33. U.S. Bureau of Immigration, *Annual Report of the Commissioner of Immigration* (Washington, D.C.: Government Printing Office, 1907), 62; Francis A. Walker, "Restriction of Immigration," *Atlantic Monthly* 77 (June 1896): 822; Ellsworth Eliot, Jr., M.D., "Immigration," in Madison Grant and Charles Steward Davison, eds., *The Alien in Our Midst, or Selling our Birthright for a Mess of Industrial Pottage* (New York: Galton Publishing Co., 1930), 101.

34. See James W. Trent Jr., *Inventing the Feeble Mind: A History of Mental Retardation in the United States* (Berkeley: University of California Press, 1994), 166–69.

35. Thomas Wray Grayson, "The Effect of the Modern Immigrant on Our Industrial Centers," in *Medical Problems of Immigration* (Easton, Penn.: American Academy of Medicine, 1913), 103, 107 ff.

36. Martin Pernick, *The Black Stork: Eugenics and the Death of "Defective" Babies in American Medicine and Motion Pictures since 1915* (Oxford and New York: Oxford University Press, 1996), 60–71; Davis, *Enforcing Normalcy*, 11–12. See also Harlan Hahn, "Antidiscrimination Laws and Social Research on Disability: The Minority Group Perspective," *Behavioral Sciences and the Law* 14 (1996): 54; Alfred C. Reed, "Going through Ellis Island," *Popular Science Monthly* 82 (January 1913): 8–9.

37. Edward Alsworth Ross, *The Old World and the New: The Significance of Past and Present Immigration to the American People* (New York: Century Co., 1914), 285–90.

38. Elizabeth Yew, "Medical Inspection of Immigrants at Ellis Island, 1891–1924," *Bulletin of the New York Academy of Medicine* 56 (June 1980): 497–98; United States Public Health Service, *Regulations*, 16–19; Alan M. Kraut, *Silent Travelers: Germs, Genes, and the "Immigrant Menace"* (New

York: Basic Books, 1994), 54–57.

39. Victor Safford, *Immigration Problems: Personal Experiences of an Official* (New York: Dodd, Mead, 1925), 244–46.

40. Kraut, *Silent Travelers*, 55.

41. Letter from W. W. Husband, Commissioner General, Bureau of Immigration, to H. S. Cumming, Surgeon General, United States Public Health Service, September 27, 1922; and reply from Cumming to Husband, September 29, 1922; National Archives, RG 90, Entry 10, File 219.

42. Letter from George Stoner, Chief Medical Officer, Public Health and Marine Hospital Service, to Surgeon General of the Public Health and Marine Hospital, Nov. 29, 1912, National Archives, RG 90, Entry 10, File 219.

43. Letter from F. P. Sargent, Commissioner-General of the Bureau of Immigration, to the Commissioner of Immigration on Ellis Island, April 17, 1905, National Archives, RG 90, Entry 10, File 219.

44. Allan McLaughlin, "The Problem of Immigration, "*Popular Science Monthly* 66 (April 1905): 532 (emphasis added).

45. Letter from Leon Sanders, President of the Hebrew Sheltering and Immigrant Aid Society, to Surgeon General of the Public Health and Marine Hospital, Nov. 14, 1909, National Archives, RG 90, Entry 10, File 219. Kraut, *Silent Travelers*, 65. William Green, "Immigration Should Be Regulated," in Grant and Davison, *Alien in Our Midst, 2*.

46. Norman S. Dike, "Aliens and Crime," in Grant and Davison, *Alien in Our Midst*, 81.

47. Ellsworth Eliot, Jr., M.D., "Immigration," in Grant and Davison, *Alien in Our Midst*, 101.

48. Heather Salerno, "Mother's Little Dividend: Parking," *Washington Post* (September 16, 1997): Al.

49. Rosemarie Garland Thomson, *Extraordinary Bodies: Figuring Physical Disability in American Culture and Literature* (New York: Columbia University Press, 1997), 15. Amy Hamburger, "The Cripple and His Place in the Community," *Annals of the American Academy of Political and Social Science* 77 (1918): 39.

50. Harlan Hahn, "Antidiscrimination Laws and Social Research on Disability: The Minority Group Perspective," *Behavioral Sciences and the Law* 14 (1996): 43.

CHAPTER 3

"Heaven's Special Child": The Making of Poster Children

Paul Longmore

Tiny Tim was a little "crippled" boy whose sweetness and courage and pathetic plight melted the heart of miserly Ebenezer Scrooge. Scrooge's charity toward Tim secured his own redemption. Dickens's *A Christmas Carol* was a Yuletide staple. Between 1901 and 2009, the entertainment industry produced fifty-six live-action and fifteen animated movie and television versions. Many were available on video and were rerun on TV each December.[1] Book retailers sold illustrated volumes as a holiday gift.[2] And each December it seemed that every theater in the U.S. staged the story as a play.[3] Americans saw a lot of Tim.

But Tiny Tim was more than a character in Dickens's tale. He was a ubiquitous cultural figure. The annual return of *A Christmas Carol* did not exhaust his appearances or significance. He arrived not just seasonally but almost year-round. Or rather, not Tim himself, but the Tiny Tim image was made into a constant and powerful cultural symbol, especially on telethons. Its main purveyors were the disability charities. Within both the charity tradition and the operation of the medical model, that persona helped to shape the identities of millions of people with disabilities. Disability rights advocates challenged the ideology behind that imposed identity.

Telethons in effect reenacted a version of *A Christmas Carol*. The hosts and audiences were huge Cratchit clans, with disabled children—and adults—playing Tiny Tim. Jerry Lewis on the MDA pageant, Dennis James in the UCP spectacle, Pat Boone on the Easter Seals rite, and the other hosts, male and female, conflated the roles of the Christmas Ghosts and Bob and Mrs. Cratchit. They were moral preceptors to potential donors, instructing them in their duty to look after Tiny Tim's siblings. At the same time, the hosts and the givers were the Cratchits gathered around the sweet pathetic children. Viewers at risk of becoming Scrooges peered through their TV screens and learned that they could join the family by opening their hearts to the afflicted Tims. By looking after the "most weak," they could buy a place at the telethon hearth.

Telethon Tiny Tims were not just *Jerry's* kids. They belonged to anyone who phoned in a pledge to any of the telethons. Some Easter Seals posters declared "He's yours too." Easter Seals local hosts touted "Adopt-a-Child." As with charities for Third World children, sponsors supported a particular youngster, who would write them a personal thank-you.[4] On some Easter Seals telecasts, Pat Boone spoke for those children in song:

I am your child.
Wherever you go,
You take me too.
Whatever I'll know,
I'll learn from you.
Whatever I do,
You'll teach me to do.
I am your child . . . .
You are my hope.
You are my chance.
And I am your child.[5]

"Believe me," declared UCP's Dennis James, "we're all taking care of heaven's special child."[6]

Through much of Western history, disabled and sick children were central to the practice of charity. In early modern Britain, children's hospitals drew more support than those treating adults with venereal disease. Though the latter were desperately needed, philanthropists feared they would be seen as supporting vice and debauchery. Beneficence to children instead associated them with innocent suffering. In any era, donation typically went to institutions that promised the greatest public approbation. That was one reason children were always popular as objects of charity. Older people were much less likely to receive such relief and remained desperately in need until the establishment of state pensions in the twentieth century.[7]

The eighteenth-century English artist William Hogarth may have pioneered images of children as a charity fundraising tool. A governor of London's first foundling hospital, established in 1737, he designed both "a distinctive uniform" for the infant inmates and "an affecting coat-of-arms" for the institution. The latter displayed "a new-born child flanked by the figures of Nature and Britannia, with the plaintive motto 'Help!'" He and other artists exhibited their paintings at the hospital, inviting wealthy patrons to buy them. This advanced Hogarth's aim to make British art competitive with Continental art in the British marketplace. It also anticipated twentieth-century fundraising that linked charity with commerce and patriotism.[8]

In 1930s America, the National Society for Crippled Children and Adults and the polio crusade invented child-based methods that became standard in disability-related soliciting. As the Society (founded in 1919) launched its 1934 drive, finance chair Paul King asked *Cleveland Plain Dealer* cartoonist J. H. Donahey to design a stamp supporters could purchase for a penny and place on envelopes and letters. That first Easter Seal pictured a boy wearing leg braces and leaning on crutches, his head bent sadly. Behind him was a white cross and—reminiscent of Hogarth's coat-of-arms—the words "Help Crippled Children." The design expressed clients' alleged plea "simply for the right to live a normal life." The huge public response eventually prompted the organization to rename itself the National Easter Seal Society. In 1952, it made the lily part of its logo. The flower explicitly represented spring, while implicitly referring to the season's religious holiday and the charity's "quasi-religious tenor." The Society also held annual contests in each state to select children as the public faces of its affiliates' fundraising.[9]

Meanwhile, the polio campaign crafted its own child-centered strategy. As early as 1932, the Warm Springs Foundation enlisted illustrator Howard Chandler Christy—famous for his World War I Uncle Sam "I-Want-You" recruiting poster—to design a poster featuring a disabled child. He also drew program covers for the President's Birthday Balls. Unlike later images, these drawings did not make the children's disabilities visible.[10] But as time went on, the drive began to stress those physical differences. In 1934, exhorting his audience to support the Birthday Balls, nicknamed "Paralysis Dances," syndicated columnist and radio personality Walter Winchell invoked the image of a paralyzed child. "If you buy a ticket to dance," he said, "then some little child who can't even walk may be able to dance some day." Polio publicists blazoned the slogan "Dance so that a child may walk." They filled the nation's newspapers with studies in physical contrast, photos of nondisabled adult dancers alongside pictures of children *crippled* by polio.[11]

In 1937, strategists at the new National Foundation for Infantile Paralysis "shifted the main appeal" from paying tribute to FDR as a victor over polio to "unashamed exploitation of the pathetic appeals of crippled children." NFIP's March of Dimes hammered at the radical difference between *crippled* children and *normal* kids. Its first drive in 1938 featured nondisabled children wearing buttons that proclaimed, "I'm glad I'm well."[12] In 1946, it begat its first poster child.[13] And its ominous film "The Crippler" blended sentimentality and pity with terror, fear, and hope. "A figure leaning on a crutch—sinister in its invisibility—stalks the land like death itself. . . . 'And I'm *especially* fond of children,' the voice-over intones with fiendish glee. . . ."[14]

The strategies contrived in the 1930s persisted over the next seven decades. Disability charities drew on the cult of sentimentalism's traditional tropes as they focused public attention on the icon of the innocent helpless child.[15] The agencies also used adults to illustrate their services, but the grown-ups got nowhere near the publicity beamed at the kids. Poster children were, by design, the most visible symbols of fundraising. At the back of their stages, the UCP, MDA, and Easter Seals telethons displayed photos of children. Easter Seals' 1994 opening scrolled images from past programs; nine out of ten showed children. Later, there was a montage of forty-eight years of poster children but no retrospective of adult representatives. Besides "national" children, Easter Seals and MDA exhibited state and local poster kids. UCP

had only local poster children, but its national telecasts were filled with images of youngsters.[16] Even the Arthritis Telethon used children to elicit alms. Of the thirty-seven million Americans with connective-tissue diseases, 200,000 were kids or teens with juvenile rheumatoid arthritis. Still, the telethon showcased a disproportionate number of children.[17]

At a 1986 workshop on the how-to's of telethon success, Easter Seals officials told local chapter executives: "Children raise more money than adults." Youngsters were effective fundraising tools, they explained, because the public sympathized with images of "the most weak." They also reported that girls pulled in larger amounts than boys.[18] Of the forty-eight national poster children chosen between 1947 and 1994, two out of three were girls. For MDA, the gender pattern seemed the reverse, with boys—in particular, boys with Duchenne Muscular Dystrophy—attracting more money.

Easter Seals' strategists also said that White kids drew more donations than children of color, though more nonwhite children would appear by the later decades of the twentieth century. The ethnic ratios on all telethons reflected that strategic judgment, even though disability prevalence rates were higher in minority communities.[19] Among those forty-eight Easter Seals poster children, just one—a girl—was African-American, while another girl was born in India. The selections reflected historic patterns of discrimination in health care. During the 1930s and 1940s, African-American community leaders criticized the Warm Springs Foundation and the National Foundation for Infantile Paralysis for neglecting black polio patients and then treating them in segregated facilities. Following World War II, in response to the civil rights movement and Cold War race politics, the NFIP slowly began to fund integrated training programs and medical rehabilitation facilities. Concurrently, beginning in 1947 a few African-American children were selected as poster children for local, regional, and national campaigns.[20] Beginning in the 1990s, perhaps because of the growth of the middle class in minority communities as well as the impact of civil rights movements, more disabled people of color, adults as well as children, were featured on telethons. For example, those African American and Indian girls were Easter Seal National Child Representatives in the early 1990s, and in 1996 and 1997, MDA chose a Latino lad and an African-American youngster as National Ambassadors.[21]

Given poster children's important function, their selection became an art. Fashions changed in the charity business, noted the *Los Angeles Times* in 1986, but choosing child spokespersons remained highly competitive. It had "earmarks of a beauty pageant: stage mothers trying to boost their youngsters to fame and fortune, children trying too hard to impress, and local Easter Seals officials going to great lengths to promote their nominees." One chapter "arranged for [national communications director Sandi Gordon] Perkins to be flown in on a sponsor's corporate airplane, gave her a party featuring California wine—and followed up with an angry letter when the chapter's candidate was not selected." Local leaders promoted their favorites as embodying sentimental stereotypes. Of one finalist, a functionary wrote: "His clear, sweet, high-pitched voice . . . together with his angelic face, breaks hearts." Another declared that a girl had "a special magnetism that will draw you near and steal your heart."[22]

Each charity chose youngsters who embodied its particular message. MDA and Arthritis kids were heart-tuggingly dependent; Easter Seals and UCP children were plucky overcomers. But all poster children had this much in common: picked for "practical marketing reasons," they must be congenial and presentable. They must be attractive, telegenic. "The national child doesn't have to be gorgeous," said Easter Seals' Perkins, "as long as they look OK." Poster kids must not look too different. According to the MDA telethon's producer, Jerry Lewis "prefer[red] his poster child to be ambulatory. He says he doesn't want to bend over a wheelchair to raise a buck." But in fact, Lewis was often shown bending over his "kids" seated on wheelchairs. It was a tricky balance: <u>they had to appear helpless but they mustn't be too disabled</u>.[23]

These considerations were crucial because poster children did far more than appear on the telethons. The charities displayed Tiny Tim's siblings year-round. A blizzard of poster-kid pictures blanketed the nation. Their images looked out from drugstore and supermarket displays tied to Easter Seals and MDA promotions. Their photos were fixed on MDA and UCP "banks" beside restaurant and grocery-store cash registers. Newspapers and magazines featured stories about them. They went to charity fundraisers: "bowl-a-thons," golf tournaments, and dinners honoring local business leaders. They posed with sports heroes and Hollywood celebrities. Over the song "You've Got to Have Friends," the Easter Seals Telethon screened a photo montage of national poster children with movie and TV stars.[24]

Poster kids were "seen and listened to by millions of Americans," noted the *Los Angeles Times*. Just halfway through his "reign," the 1986 National Easter Seals Child had flown tens of thousands of miles, every*where* from Washington, DC to Las Vegas to Puerto Rico. He had addressed conventions of every*one* from realtors to truck drivers. And his image had appeared "on every*thing* from Easter Seals' seals to Crayola crayons posters to Safeway delivery trucks." His image had been reproduced "roughly 70 million times." And he still had six months to go as a poster child.[25]

Especially important, these dependent children were introduced to the executives whose corporations were the charities' most prominent supporters. A review of hundreds of hours of telethons found a few segments featuring executives visiting therapy centers that served adults and just one that showed them meeting an adult with a disability in a business setting. Telethons did not present executives or their employees encountering disabled adults in situations that portrayed them as colleagues or even *potential* co-workers. But they met lots of children.

Poster children also had their pictures taken with elected officials—state governors and legislators, members of Congress, even the President of the United States.[26] From Harry S. Truman to William Jefferson Clinton, presidents annually met the national poster children of several disability charities. A photo of MDA's 1993 national child with Clinton ran in 3,900 newspapers.[27] In 1995, First Lady Hillary Rodham Clinton appeared on the UCP Telethon with a four year-old girl, a UCP client, to urge viewers to support that charity. In 1992, Easter Seals aired a medley of photos of its national children meeting every President from George H. W. Bush all the way back to Truman while viewers heard the song "Stand By Me."[28]

"The poster child is our major ambassador to the public," explained a March of Dimes spokeswoman.[29] That icon influenced business executives' attitudes about the millions of adults they might have seen as customers, employees, or colleagues, instead of recipients of their charity. It instructed lawmakers as they formulated policies that affected disabled citizens. It defined who Americans with disabilities really were and what they really needed. Reinforcing the medical model, charity images portrayed them as dependent objects of beneficence whose most important needs were medical. In late twentieth-

century America, the Tiny Tim persona was central to framing the cultural, social, and political meaning of disability. The charities depicted the representative disabled person as a vulnerable child, one of "the most weak."

NOTES

1. The names of many of the actors who played Scrooge are included with each entry. Live-action motion pictures and television programs: A Christmas Carol (1901); A Christmas Carol (Essanay, 1908); A Christmas Carol (Edison, 1910), Mark McDermott; A Christmas Carol (1912); A Christmas Carol (dir. Leedham Bantock, Zenith Film Company, 1913), Seymour Hicks; A Christmas Carol (dir. Harold M. Shaw, Fenning London Film Company, 1914), Charles Rock; The Right to Be Happy aka A Christmas Carol (dir. Rupert Julian, Universal, 1916); Scrooge (dir. George Wynn, 1922), H. V. Esmond; Tense Moments with Great Authors: "#7 Scrooge" (dir. H. B. Parkinson, W. Courtney Rowden, 1922), H. V. Esmond; Scrooge (dir. Edwin Greenwood, 1923), Russell Thorndike; Scrooge (dir. Hugh Croise, 1928), Bransby Williams; Scrooge (dir. Henry Edwards, Julius Hagen-Twickenham, 1935), Seymour Hicks; A Christmas Carol (dir. Edwin L. Marin, MGM, 1938), Reginald Owen; A Christmas Carol (dir. George Lowther, 1943), William Podmore, this version was 60 minutes and, at the time, was the longest U.S. TV program yet broadcast; A Christmas Carol (dir. James Caddigan, 1947), John Carradine; The Philco Television Playhouse: "A Christmas Carol" (dir. Fred Coe, 1948), Dennis King; The Christmas Carol (dir. Arthur Pierson, 1949), was a U.S. TV film narrated by Vincent Price with Taylor Holmes as Scrooge; A Christmas Carol (British TV, 1950), Bransby Williams; Fireside Theatre: "A Christmas Carol" (dir. Gordon Duff, 1951), Ralph Richardson; Scrooge, aka A Christmas Carol (dir. Brian Desmond Hurst, Showcorporation/ George Minter/Renown, 1951), Alistair Sim; Kraft Television Theatre: "A Christmas Carol" (1952), Malcolm Keen; Shower of Stars: "A Christmas Carol" (dir. Ralph Levy, 1954), Fredric March; The Alcoa Hour: "The Stingiest Man in Town" (dir. Daniel Petrie, 1955), Basil Rathbone; Story of the Christmas Carol (dir. David Barnheizer, 1955), Norman Gottschalk; General Electric Theater: "The Trail to Christmas" (dir. James Stewart, 1957), a cowboy tells a boy the Dickens tale with John McIntire as Scrooge; Tales from

Dickens: A Dickens Christmas: "A Christmas Carol" (dir. Neil McGuire, 1958), TV series hosted by Fredric March with Basil Rathbone as Scrooge; Mr. Scrooge (dir. Bob Jarvis, 1964), Cyril Ritchard; Carry on Christmas (dir. Ronnie Baxter, 1969), comedy with Sid James; Scrooge (dir. Ronald Neame, Cinema Center, 1970), musical version with Albert Finney; A Christmas Carol (dir. Richard Williams, 1971), British TV movie with Alistair Sim; A Christmas Carol (dir. Moira Armstrong, BBC, 1976), Michael Hordern; Scrooge (dir. John Blanchard, Canadian TV movie, 1978); An American Christmas Carol (Scherick-Chase-Slan/Scrooge Productions/Smith-Hemion, 1979), Henry Winkler as a New England "Scrooge" during the Great Depression, who is redeemed by helping the family of a boy (Chris Crabb) who needs rehabilitation from polio; A Christmas Carol at Ford's Theatre (1979); Skinflint: A Country Christmas Carol (1979), a country music version with Hoyt Axton as Cyrus Flint; A Christmas Carol (dir. Laird Williamson, 1981), William Paterson, a US TV movie; The Guthrie Theatre Presents a Christmas Carol (The Entertainment Channel, 1982), film of stage production, narrated by John Gielgud; The Gospel According to Scrooge (dir. Mark S. Vegh, 1983); A Christmas Carol (dir. Clive Donner, CBS, 1984), George C. Scott; A Christmas Carol (1994), U.S. ballet; Ebbie (dir. George Kazcender, Victor Television Productions/Maverick Crescent Entertainment Limited, 1994), Susan Lucci as a hard-driving department store owner Elizabeth "Ebbie" Scrooge, whose widowed assistant Roberta Cratchit has a son named Timmy who needs medical treatment; Ebbie decides to provide adequate health insurance for all her employees; John Grin's Christmas (1986), features an African-American Scrooge, Robert Guillaume, and no Tiny Tim, but does feature a generous and insightful blind woman; Scrooged (dir. Richard Donner, 1988), Bill Murray as a heartless executive producing a telecast of A Christmas Carol with Buddy Hackett as Scrooge; Bah! Humbug!: The Story of Charles Dickens' "A Christmas Carol" (dir. Derek Bailey, PBS, 1994), a reading by actors James Earl Jones and Martin Sheen; Ebenezer (dir. Ken Jubenvill, 1997), a Wild West version with Jack Palance as a ruthless cattle baron; Ms Scrooge (Wilshire Court/Power Pictures, 1997), Cicely Tyson as Ebenita Scrooge who, like "Ebbie," decides to pay for medical treatment for Tim (who this time has a slow-growing congenital tumor in his leg) and health insurance for her employees; A Christmas Carol (dir. David Hugh Jones, Flying Freehold, 1999), Patrick Stewart; A Christmas Carol (dir. Catherine Morshead, 2000), British TV movie, Ross Kemp as Eddie Scrooge; A Diva's Christmas Carol (dir. Richard Shankman, 2000), a TV movie made for VH1 with Vanessa L. Williams as pop singing star Ebony Scrooge; Scrooge and Marley (dir. Fred Holmes, 2001), an evangelical Christian version with Dean Jones; A Carol Christmas (dir. Matthew Imas, Hallmark, 2003), Tori Spelling as Carol Cartman, a selfish TV talk show host; A Christmas Carol: The Musical (dir. Arthur Alan Seidelman, 2004), Kelsey Grammer; A Carol of Christmas (dir. Roland Black, 2005); Chasing Christmas (dir. Ron Oliver, 2005), a time-traveling version with Tom Arnold as a Scrooge-like single dad; The Carol Project (dir. Tim Folkmann, 2006), musical; The Nutcracker: A Christmas Story (2007), a ballet combining the E.T.A. Hoffman story with the Dickens tale. Animated productions: Mister Magoo's Christmas Carol (dir. Abe Levitow, UPA, 1962); Bah, Humduck! A Looney Tunes Christmas (dir. Charles Visser, Warner, 2006), Daffy Duck; A Christmas Carol (dir. Zoran Janjic, Australia, Air Programs International, 1969), screened on US TV 1970; The Stingiest Man in Town (dirs. Jules Bass, Arthur Rankin Jr., Rankin-Bass, 1978), Walter Matthau as the voice of Scrooge and Robert Morse as the voice of Young Scrooge; A Christmas Carol (Australia, 1982); A Christmas Carol (Burbank Productions, 1982), narrated by Michael Redgrave; Mickey's Christmas Carol (dir. Burny Mattinson, Disney, 1983), Alan Young as the voice of Scrooge McDuck; The Muppet Christmas Carol (dir. Brian Henson, 1992), Michael Caine as the voice of Scrooge; A Christmas Carol (dirs. Toshiyuki Hiruma, Takashi Masunaga, Jetlag, 1994); A Flintstones Christmas Carol (dir. Joanna Romersa, 1994); A Christmas Carol (dir. Stan Phillips, DIC Entertainment, 1997), narrated by Tim Curry; Christmas Carol: The Movie (dir. Jimmy T. Murakami, 2001), Simon Callow as the voice of Scrooge; A Sesame Street Christmas Carol (dirs. Ken Diego, Victor DiNapoli, Emily Squires, Jon Stone, 2006); Barbie in A Christmas Carol (Australia, 2008); A Christmas Carol (dir. Robert Zemeckis, Disney, 2009), Jim Carrey as the voice of Scrooge. Internet Movie Database, http://www.imdb.com (accessed 20–22 November 2009); Martin F. Norden, The Cinema of Isolation, A History of Physical Disability in the Movies (New Brunswick: Rutgers University Press, 1994), 33; Patricia King Harrison and Alan Gevinson, ed., American Film Institute Catalog 1931–1940 (Berkeley: University of California Press, 1993), 347.

2. In June 1999, Books in Print listed 66 different editions of the story, including adaptations based on Dickens's basic plot.

3. In the late 1930s, the WPA Federal Theater Project in Los Angeles and other places made a theatrical version part of every Christmas Season program. William F. McDonald, Federal Relief Administration and the Arts (Columbus: Ohio State University Press, 1969), 554. That customary programming continued decades later. A sampling of the myriad stage productions from 1998 alone included not only major theaters such as Radio City Music Hall in New York City, the San Diego Repertory Theater, and the Geary Theater in San Francisco, but also the Totempole Playhouse in Chambersberg, Pennsylvania; the Bardavon Opera House in Poughkeepsie, New York; Triangle Church in Chapel Hill, North Carolina; Hale Center Theater in Orem, Utah; the Hippodrome State Theater in Gainesville, Florida; the Alley Theater in Houston; and Scrooge: The Ballet! at the Hawaii Theater Center in Honolulu. In 1999, comedian and composer Steve Allen was reportedly writing songs for a stage musical adaptation. Reed Johnson, "Steve Allen Writes Songs for 'Christmas Carol' Musical," San Francisco Chronicle, 24 November 1999. In 2007, playwright Christopher Durang satirized the Dickens's tale. Robert Hurwitt, "'Christmas Carol' Meets 'Wonderful Life' in 'Wild Binge,'" San Francisco Chronicle, 4 December 2007, http://www.sfgate.com (accessed 4 December 2007).

4. "Adopt-a-Child" donors received a statuette of a disabled child leaning on crutches behind a small dog. Easter Seals Telethon, 1990.

5. Ibid.

6. UCP Telethon, 1993.

7. William B. Cohen, "Epilogue: The European Comparison," in Charity, Philanthropy, and Civility in American History, ed., Lawrence J. Friedman and Mark D. McGarvie (New York: Cambridge University Press, 2003), 393.

8. Linda Colley, Britons: Forging the Nation 1707–1837 (New Haven: Yale University Press, 1992), 59. The London Foundling Hospital cared for children with many kinds of disabilities, medically and vocationally rehabilitating some and providing lifelong maintenance for others. Alysa Levene, Childcare-Health and Mortality at the London Foundling Hospital 1741–1800: "Left to the Mercy of the World" (Manchester: Manchester University Press, 2007), 165–8.

9. The organization officially adopted the name National Easter Seal Society in 1979. Charles A. Riley, II, Disability and the Media: Prescriptions for Change (University Press of New England,

2005), 110–11; Easter Seals Telethon, 1991; James E. Williams, Jr., "Easter Seals transforms the telethon," Fund Raising Management 26, no. 7 (September 1995): 28–32; Charlotte Snow, "Rehab Rival: Easter Seals is a Healthcare Force to be Reckoned With," Modern Healthcare 27, no. 17 (28 April 1997), 18–19, http://www.lexisnexis.com (accessed 1 June 2007).

10. Scott M. Cutlip, The Unseen Power: Public Relations. A History (Hillsdale, NJ: Lawrence Erlbaum Associates, 1994), 558–60, 561; Riley, Disability and the Media, 111–12. Christy's illustrations for the 1936, 1937, and 1938 Birthday Balls program covers are reproduced online at http://www.disabilitymuseum.org (accessed 7 July 2007).

11. Scott M. Cutlip, Fund Raising in the United States, Its Role in America's Philanthropy (New Brunswick: Rutgers University Press, 1965), 361, 365–71.

12. Ibid., 376, 383–7, quotes from 384 and 387; Richard Carter, The Gentle Legions (Garden City, NY: Doubleday, 1961), 112; David L. Sills, The Volunteers: Means and Ends in a National Organization (1957; repr., New York: Arno Press, 1980), 126–7, 169–70.

13. David Zinman, "Many Former Poster Kids Lead Normal Lives Today," Los Angeles Times, 16 December 1984; David M. Oshinsky, Polio: An American Story (New York: Oxford University Press, 2005), 83.

14. Tony Gould, A Summer Plague: Polio and Its Survivors (New Haven: Yale University Press, 1995), xi; Oshinsky, Polio: An American Story, 68, 81–3. In 1974, MDA presented a video monologue entitled "I Hate People, Especially Children," in which an actor personified muscular dystrophy and, like "The Crippler," "ominously hovers over the figure of a healthy child." The vignette was written by Budd Schulberg and directed by Jerry Lewis. Lawrence Joseph Londino, "A Descriptive Analysis of 'The Jerry Lewis Labor Day Telethon for Muscular Dystrophy'" (PhD diss.: University of Michigan, 1975), 127–8.

15. See Chapters 7–8. Cutlip, Fund Raising in the United States, 51; Riley, Disability and the Media, 111–12; Zinman, "Many Former Poster Kids Lead Normal Lives Today"; Ellen L. Barton, "Textual Practices of Erasure: Representations of Disability and the Founding of the United Way," in Embodied Rhetorics: Disability in Language and Culture, ed. James C. Wilson and Cynthia Lewiecki-Wilson (Carbondale: Southern Illinois University Press, 2001), 178–9, 184, 187, 193.

16. See for instance Shawn Hubler, "After Initial Anguish, Family of Cerebral Palsy Poster Child

is Picture of Happiness," Los Angeles Times, 21 January 1990, South Bay edition.

17. The 1988 Arthritis Telethon paraded photos of kids with arthritis while a singer urged: "Share your love with all the children of the world." See also Herbert J. Vida, "Dana Point Boy Works Hard as Arthritis Foundation Poster Child," Los Angeles Times, 8 June 1986, Orange County edition, http://www.proquest.com (accessed 7 July 2007).

18. Disability Rag 7, no. 2 (March/April 1986): 22; Dennis Hall and Susan G. Hall, American icons: An Encyclopedia of the People, Places, and Things That Have Shaped Our Culture, vol. 1 (Westport, CT: Greenwood Publishing Group, 2006), 574.

19. For a summary of disability prevalence rates in the 1990s U.S. population among African-Americans, Asian-Americans/Pacific Islanders, Hispanic Americans, and Native Americans as compared to European Americans see Rhoda Olkin, What Psychotherapists Should Know about Disability (New York: Guilford Press, 1999), 19–20.

20. Naomi Rogers, "Race and the Politics of Polio: Warm Springs, Tuskegee, and the March of Dimes," American Journal of Public Health 97, no. 5 (May 2007), 784–95; Oshinsky, Polio: An American Story, 65–7.

21. MDA Telethon, 1996; "Benjamin Gives Hope to Others-Again," Parade (31 August 1997). In 1986, the MDA poster child for the District of Columbia was an African-American lad. Anne Simpson, "People: MDA Poster Child," Washington Post, 8 May 1986. Service organizations in the black community supplied volunteers for the disability charities that may have, over the years, won them greater attention from those agencies. "First Year of Service Noted by AKA Chapter," Los Angeles Sentinel, 23 August 1979. The Chicago UCPA's 1991 poster child was a 10-year-old Latino boy. "Mutual admiration," Chicago Sun-Times, 8 January 1991.

22. Scott Kraft, "Poster Child Quest: Cute Isn't Enough," Los Angeles Times, 7 April 1986. See also Laura Kavesh, "It Takes a Tough Kid to Be a Poster Child," Chicago Tribune, 29 March 1985, c edition. On the March of Dimes selecting poster children for both medical and cosmetic reasons see Zinman, "Many Former Poster Kids Lead Normal Lives Today."

23. Kraft, "Poster Child Quest"; David Zinman, "Critics Say Drives Foster Stereotyping of Disabled," Los Angeles Times, 16 December 1984; Kavesh, "It Takes a Tough Kid to Be a Poster Child"; Fred Rothenberg, "Waking up Telethon's Wee Hours," Toronto Globe and Mail, 3 September 1982, early edition. In a TV commercial publicizing "Aisles of Smiles," he appeared with his "friend," that year's national poster child. The boy sat on a wheelchair, not a power chair he could have operated on his own, but a manual chair pushed by his paternal benefactor Lewis. The spot created an image of helplessness and dependency. Likewise, the 1993 MDA extravaganza opened with a musical number and then showed Lewis approaching and then bending to embrace the national poster child who was sitting in a wheelchair.

24. Easter Seals Telethon, 1993; Kavesh, "It Takes a Tough Kid to Be a Poster Child."

25. Kraft, "Poster Child Quest," emphasis added. See also Kavesh, "It Takes a Tough Kid to Be a Poster Child."

26. Kavesh, "It Takes a Tough Kid to Be a Poster Child."

27. Reported on MDA Telethon, 1993.

28. Easter Seals Telethon, 1991 and 1992.

29. Zinman, "Many Former Poster Kids Lead Normal Lives Today."

CHAPTER 4

Disabling Attitudes: U.S. Disability Law and the ADA Amendments Act

Elizabeth F. Emens[1]

This is an uncertain time for disability law in the United States. To understand why this is so, we need to start with a bit of history. In 1990, Congress passed the Americans with Disabilities Act (ADA), which prohibits discrimination (including the failure to accommodate) in employment, public accommodations, and government services. For nearly two decades after that, the courts made rulings that consistently narrowed the scope of the ADA's mandate. They did this, most obviously, by narrowly interpreting the term "disability," thereby limiting who could bring a claim under the Act. Responding to this increasing restriction of the ADA, in 2008 Congress passed the ADA Amendments Act (ADAAA). This new act attempts to restore a broader vision of the original ADA by, in particular, expanding the statutory definition of disability (§ 12101). Courts so far have had limited occasions to interpret the revised language. The question now looms as to whether that broader vision will survive the courts.

Public attitudes toward disability played a role in the fate of the ADA over the nearly twenty years between its passage and the new amendments act. Often laws are passed to keep up with changing societal attitudes. Other times, such as in this case, the law is out ahead of attitudes. The gap between societal attitudes and the law's demands led to the narrowing of the statute in the courts. Although the original ADA had impressive bipartisan support, it seems likely that the politicians who voted for it came together for disparate reasons. Combine a few who understand disability as a civil rights issue, with those who see it through the lens of pity, with those economically minded folks who see it as a way to get people off of welfare and onto the tax rolls, and you get the ADA.[2]

When the ADA eventually reached the courts, it encountered prevailing societal attitudes towards disability. Judges interpreted it more narrowly than the advocates expected. Because the law was out ahead of common sense, the courts did what they often do in such moments: they narrowed the law to better fit their common sense.[3]

The question now is whether the revised ADA will encounter that same fate in the courts. More than three years have passed since the new Act went into effect, but courts have interpreted the revision as not applying retroactively to events that occurred before 2009,[4] so there is currently not much case law. My prediction is that unless attitudes change, courts will find new ways to narrow the statute to comport with judges', and society's, "common sense."

So what is that common sense about disability? It is commonly assumed that disability is unfortunate, even tragic, and at the same time very costly for employers and for society. Under this view, disability should be avoided at most costs and accommodated only at a very limited cost. There is little sense that disability can have benefits (to the person with the disability or those around her), or that accommodations benefit more than the individual who requests them. Disability is, in this view, something we should just keep hoping will eventually go away if science and medicine get good enough to cure or eliminate it.[5] In the meantime, this common sense might say, "we" (the nondisabled people, or sometimes just "people") should be good enough, moral enough, to do some things to help disabled people, but not too much, lest we drag down society or the economy.

And that is just the beginning. The previous paragraph is probably a fair characterization of attitudes to the more *popular* and relatively more visible forms of disability such as paraplegia. My use of the word "popular" here is only slightly sarcastic; it is no coincidence that a person in a wheelchair is the symbol for disabled parking, restrooms, and the like. This is so because the more popular disabilities are the ones (like paraplegia) that apparently affect only a discrete part of a person, leaving open the possibility of competence in other parts. Such a disabled person might still be "worth something," from this troubling perspective.

By contrast, mental or psychiatric disabilities are presumed to affect the whole person. Many people—disabled and nondisabled alike—seem utterly unaware that discrimination against people with psychiatric disabilities is (presumptively) illegal.[6] Imagine a lawyer who says he recently hired a new secretary with an impressive resume, even though she seemed "crazy," because the law says he cannot discrimi-

nate on the basis of psychiatric disability. A friend of the employer might well respond, "Are you crazy?"

The prevailing "common sense" is often ignorant about disability. Consider the "spread effect," whereby outsiders raise their voices at blind people or assume a wheelchair signals cognitive disability. And consider people's reluctance to believe in unseen hidden physical disabilities, in light of Elaine Scarry's insights about our frequent inability to apprehend, or even believe, another's pain (Scarry 1985, 4).[7]

A caveat is in order, as this is a fairly gloomy story about what is clearly an exciting legal development. The ADAAA intervenes in the developing doctrine on disability discrimination in important ways, and the passage of this ambitious legislation is all the more impressive in a period characterized more by retrenchment than expansion of civil rights law. My hope is that the ADAAA will expand the scope of who is protected under the law and who obtains accommodation, through the many legal and extralegal actors who implement the law on a daily basis. If the ADAAA successfully brings more people with disabilities into the workplace, then attitudes toward disability should be improved through increased contact with a wide range of people with disabilities and with reasonable accommodations.[8]

While laws affect society through many channels, however, courts play an important role in shaping the parameters of the law's implementation. My concern is that the persistence of negative and ignorant attitudes to disability will lead courts either to continue to narrow the scope of the statute, in defiance of the clear mandate of the ADAAA, or, more likely, to find new ways to limit enforcement. I hope to contribute to our understanding of those negative attitudes by identifying a number of ways that they intersect with these recent changes to the law.

From an international perspective, this is also an auspicious moment to focus on attitudes to disability, in the wake of President Obama's signing of the UN Convention on the Rights of Persons with Disabilities (CRPD). The CRPD contains an "Awareness-raising" article explicitly requiring states' parties to promote more positive attitudes toward disability (ibid., art. 8). Whether and how states implement this directive will depend in part on their appreciation of the crucial role attitudes play in the creation and implementation of disability law. At this critical juncture, this essay examines U.S. disability law to help enrich our understanding of attitudes to disability in the U.S. context and, I hope, beyond.

INTRODUCING THE ADAAA

It is the intent of Congress that the primary object of attention in cases brought under the ADA should be whether entities covered under the ADA have complied with their obligations ... [rather than] whether an individual's impairment is a disability under the ADA.
—ADA Amendments Act of 2008

The ADA Amendments Act (ADAAA) expressly aims to "carry out the ADA's objectives ... by reinstating a broad scope of protection" (ADAAA § 12101(b)(1)). In important ways, the statute has made a bold attempt to fulfill this aim; in other ways, however, the ADAAA compromises the boldest structural aspect of the statute, fundamentally altering its idea of disability and of discrimination. First, let's revisit the relevant aspects of the ADA, how the courts narrowed its protection, and how the ADAAA intends to intervene.[9]

The ADA protects against discrimination on the basis of "disability," so in order to bring a claim, the plaintiff must first qualify as having a "disability." (ADA § 12112(a)). Under the ADA, before the amendments, the definition of "disability" was as follows:

(A) a physical or mental impairment that substantially limits one or more of the major life activities of such individual;
(B) a record of such an impairment; or
(C) being regarded as having such an impairment (ibid. §12102(2)).

This language was lifted from a previous law—the Rehabilitation Act of 1973—which had not been interpreted restrictively up until 1990. The ADA's proponents therefore had little reason to think these definitional prongs would later be interpreted as narrowly as they were.

When courts began hearing ADA cases, however, they interpreted this definition of disability strictly in (at least) five ways. First, in *Toyota v. Williams* (2002), the Supreme Court expressly required the plaintiff to meet a "demanding standard" of "disability." Second, consistent with this, courts interpreted "substantially limiting" restrictively: plaintiffs had to show that they were really *really* limited in a major life activity to count as disabled. This approach led to notorious losses for plaintiffs, such as the plaintiff whose cancer was posthumously declared not limiting enough (Long 2008, 218). Third, the Supreme Court held in *Sutton v. United Air Lines, Inc.* (1999) that since "substantially limited" is in the present tense, plaintiffs who have mitigated their disabilities must be considered in their mitigated state. This excludes anyone who has successfully mitigated her disability, such as someone whose contact lenses correct her vision (as with the plaintiffs in *Sutton*) or whose psychiatric medication or prosthesis are fully effective. Fourth, courts applied a restrictive view of what counted as a "major life activity." For example, activities were typically deemed not "major" enough if they were not "of central importance to most people's daily lives" (*Toyota*). Fifth, courts interpreted the "regarded-as" prong of the definition restrictively, in a variety of ways. Most notably, they required plaintiffs to prove not only the impairment the employer regarded them as having, but also *precisely* which major life activity the employer regarded them as *substantially* limited in. For instance, to show she was regarded as disabled, a plaintiff with mild arthritis would have to persuade a court not only that her employer thought she had arthritis, but also that her employer thought her arthritis substantially limited her in some particular major life activity, such as walking. Picture plaintiffs attempting to show that their employers were—lying awake at night?—imagining exactly how their employees' impairments limited them and in what activities. An absurd demand.

The ADAAA addresses most of these problems with the courts' treatment of the definition of disability. The findings of the new law explicitly reject both the "demanding" standard and the highly restrictive interpretations of the "substantially limited" language (ADAAA § 12102(4)(E)). The statute expressly indicates that plaintiffs are to be considered without regard to the ameliorating effects of any mitigating measures (other than ordinary eye glasses or contact lenses) (ibid.). The ADAAA gives "major life activity" a clearer and broader scope, by providing an illustrative list, and by introducing "the operation of a major bodily function" (also with an illustrative list) as another form of major life activity (ibid. § 12102(2)(A)). Perhaps most strikingly, for the regarded-as prong, the statute completely removes the need to show any substantial limitation in a major life activity. Instead, the plaintiff need only show that she has been "subjected to an action prohibited under this Act because of an actual or perceived physical or mental impairment" (that is not both minor and transitory, defined in the statute as hav-

ing "an actual or expected duration of 6 months or less") (ibid. § 12102(3)(B)).

Though these changes are not comprehensive, they are ambitious. But courts may nonetheless find new ways to undermine the scope of the statute's protections, perhaps by again interpreting "substantially limits" somewhat narrowly, in the absence of a statutory definition for the term. However, this approach would directly contravene the ADAAA's express rejection of a "demanding standard" for interpreting "substantially limits." Alternatively, courts could raise the bar for proving that one has an "impairment," potentially leading to a highly medicalized inquiry. But these further attempts to classify who is in and who is out would fly in the face of the statute's explicit mandate to determine whether discrimination has occurred.

As the statutory findings indicate, "it is the intent of Congress that the primary object of attention in cases brought under the ADA should be whether entities covered under the ADA have complied with their obligations . . . .[T]he question of whether an individual's impairment is a disability under the ADA should not demand extensive analysis." The ADAAA should therefore put pressure on courts to examine other parts of the statute beyond the definition of disability: who is "otherwise qualified" to do various jobs, what is "reasonable" accommodation, and what is an "undue hardship" that exempts an employer from providing a requested accommodation. In the course of addressing these questions, those courts inclined to keep the scope of the statute limited may well interpret these provisions restrictively.

CARVING UP THE DEFINITION OF DISABILITY: ABANDONING A RADICAL SOCIAL MODEL

[A] physical or mental impairment that substantially limits major life activities only as a

result of the attitudes of others toward such impairment.

—EEOC, Regulations interpreting "regarded as" disability[10]

The ADAAA's move towards a more expansive definition of "disability" seems to reflect a *social model*—the idea that disability inheres in the interaction between impairment and the surrounding social world, rather than being an individual medical problem.[11] The more expansive definition should shift the emphasis from just how limited the individual with a disability is (a *medical model*), to what happened (discrimination?) or what should happen (accommodation?) in interaction with the disability.

In a crucial way, however, the ADAAA moves away from the social model. One of the ADA's boldest features was its equal treatment of actual disability and regarded-as disability. The ADAAA, by contrast, separates actual and regarded-as into two different groups, which are expressly entitled to different remedies.

Recall the ADA's definition of disability quoted above. All three of the prongs counted equally as having a "disability." In principle, those who fell under the statute by virtue of *actually having* an impairment that substantially limited them in a major life activity, and those who fell under it by virtue of being *regarded as* such, had the same claim to protection, including accommodation, under the ADA. (As I shall discuss in a moment, courts worked hard to say otherwise, but nothing in the statute supported their position.)

Placing actually disabled and regarded-as disabled under a single rubric affirms the social model of disability in a fairly radical way. It says explicitly that others' perceptions of an impairment can be just as meaningful and real as an otherwise-limiting impairment, and consequently just as deserving of accommodation.[12]

While the ADAAA carves up the ADA's old definition in ways that broaden the scope of the statute's protection—a much-needed development—unfortunately it also creates two distinct types of disability, each with different legal protections and remedies. The ADAAA largely leaves the definition of disability as it was, but then it adds a qualifying phrase to the third prong, so that it reads as follows: "(C) being regarded as having such an impairment *(as described in paragraph (3))*" (ibid. § 12102(1)(C)). The paragraph referenced goes on to explain, as I noted above, that the regarded-as prong now requires less than before: a plaintiff counts as regarded-as having a disability if she was subjected to an action prohibited under this statute "because of an actual or perceived physical or mental impairment whether or not the impairment limits or is perceived to limit a major life activity." So far, so good: plaintiffs no longer have to jump through hoops to prove they are regarded-as having a disability.

The problem in the ADAAA comes with the later introduction of an exception to the contexts in which plaintiffs are entitled to accommodations:

(h) REASONABLE ACCOMMODATIONS AND MODIFICATIONS.—A covered entity . . . need not provide a reasonable accommodation or a reasonable modification to policies, practices, or procedures to an individual who meets the definition of disability in section 3(1) solely under subparagraph (C) of such section.

In other words, plaintiffs who are only regarded-as disabled have no right to accommodation.

Why should an employer accommodate someone who is only regarded-as disabled? Some people may find this idea absurd—as did some courts. However, if one accepts a social model of disability, then an employer's regarding the employee as "substantially limited" in a major life activity could warrant accommodation. For example, someone might have a limiting impairment but not count as *substantially limited enough* to qualify for ADA protection. In such a case, the fact that the employer regards the person as *substantially limited enough* would reasonably entitle the person to whatever accommodations might help him do his job better. Such cases should, however, become less frequent under the ADAAA, because it broadens protection for the "actually disabled" prong.

Or, one can imagine a plaintiff who is both actually disabled, and also regarded-as disabled, and who would prefer to make a claim under the regarded-as prong. As various scholars have pointed out, the ADA puts plaintiffs in a bind: they must prove both that they are substantially limited enough to count as disabled and that they are nonetheless capable enough to be "otherwise qualified" to perform the essential functions of the job, with or without reasonable accommodation.

To count as actually disabled under the ADA, plaintiffs had to prove to the court *just how limited they really are*. Some plaintiffs would surely find this requirement unappealing: what does it mean to perform one's limitations in court? We might think here, by analogy, of the critic Stephen Greenblatt's story about refusing a fellow airplane passenger's request to mouth the words "I want to die"; Greenblatt felt it was too dangerous to form those words, even as a brief favor to a stranger, because he was so keenly aware of the ways our performances become us.[13] It is easy to see how a plaintiff might prefer to prove that someone else thought he was substantially limited, yet refused to accommodate his (perceived) limitation, instead of going to great lengths to prove just how limited he really is. Hopefully, the expanded protection of the actual-disability prong will also

lessen this problem, although it will not eliminate it.

Third, sometimes other people's attitudes make a condition disabling. Facial scarring or a missing front tooth might provoke adverse reactions from others. Although neither condition creates any actual functional limitations, others' reactions could make working or interacting with some others difficult. An accommodation in this case could involve less interaction with customers, or a non-commission-based sales job instead of one based on sales commission. Of course, care should be taken to avoid segregating or stigmatizing the affected individual.

But all of these scenarios are irrelevant under the ADAAA, because regarded-as plaintiffs no longer have any statutory right to accommodation. They are in their own category, distinct from the *real* disabled, and with a limited set of rights and remedies. Indeed, the interpretive regulations recently issued by the EEOC explicitly distinguish between "actual disability" and "regarded-as disability," although they accompany these terms with a disclaimer that these terms are for "ease of reference only."[14] The statute itself does not employ these terms, and both types still fall equally under the definition of "disability." But the difference in remedies suggests to me a difference in the underlying categories. Even if there are few practical consequences, at a structural level, distinguishing between the two categories is a jarring step back from the more radical social model.

DISTINGUISHING ACCOMMODATION FROM ANTIDISCRIMINATION

[T]he normal definition of discrimination— differential treatment of similarly situated groups.

—Justice Kennedy, Olmstead v.
Zimring (1999)

The ADA defines "discriminate" to "include . . . not making reasonable accommodations to the known physical or mental limitations of an otherwise qualified individual with a disability" (ADAAA, § 12112(b)). A failure to accommodate *is* discrimination under the ADA. And yet, this remains a contested issue.

Is the ADA doing something really different from the rest (or the heart) of antidiscrimination law, or is it doing something fundamentally similar? Much scholarly energy has been spent debating this question (Jolls, 2001; Stein, 2004; Wax, 2003; Karlan & Rutherglen, 1996). In my view, a final resolution to this debate is unlikely, because ultimately it seems that both sides have some merit. On the one hand, core U.S. antidiscrimination statutes covering classifications like race and sex—such as Title VII of the Civil Rights Act of 1964—involve costs to the employer and changes to policies and practices that operate like accommodation. For instance, prohibiting discrimination in hiring may hurt the employer's bottom line, if customers prefer their pizza delivery people to be white or their flight attendants to be men. Putting in women's restrooms in a formerly all-male workplace may cost money. Similar to the ADA, then, Title VII requires employers to absorb costs and make structural changes. On the other hand, the ADA obliges employers to respond to individual requests by employees to change their practices, requiring a different kind of interaction between employer and employee.

With its two different meanings of "discriminate"—one for actually disabled plaintiffs and another for regarded-as disabled plaintiffs—the ADAAA has further complicated the relationship between discrimination and the failure to accommodate.

Justice Kennedy makes clear his view that the ADA is doing something different than previous antidiscrimination legislation, in his concurring opinions in two crucial cases, *Olmstead v. Zimring* (1999) and *Bd. of Trustees of the Univ. of Alabama v. Garrett* (2000), handed down one year apart. The epigraph above from *Olmstead*—"the normal definition of discrimination [is] differential treatment of similarly situated groups"—captures his basic view of discrimination. By this definition, it does not include the failure to accommodate, something he makes clear in these decisions, as he contrasts that with some of the newfangled concepts in this arena. In *Garrett*, Kennedy grapples with the changing times. Here is what he tells us about evolving concepts of "prejudice":

> Prejudice, we are beginning to understand, rises not from malice or hostile animus alone. It may result as well from insensitivity caused by simple want of careful, rational reflection or from some instinctive mechanism to guard against people who appear to be different in some respects from ourselves. Quite apart from any historical documentation, knowledge of our own human instincts teaches that persons who find it difficult to perform routine functions by reason of some mental or physical impairment might at first seem unsettling to us, unless we are guided by the better angels of our nature. There can be little doubt, then, that persons with mental or physical impairments are confronted with prejudice which can stem from indifference or insecurity as well as from malicious ill will.
>
> (ibid., 375)

In short, traditional prejudice arises from malice or hostile animus, as opposed to other more natural emotions and behaviors—"instinctive mechanisms"—that may lead us to behave in ways that "the better angels of our nature" would discourage. *"Our"* nature, Kennedy tells us, is to be "unsettled" by people with disabilities.

But law can help: "One of the undoubted achievements of statutes designed to assist those with impairments is that citizens have an incentive, flowing from a legal duty, to develop a better understanding, a more decent perspective, for accepting persons with impairments or disabilities into the larger society" (ibid.). The ADA is a good thing, Kennedy says, because it will get *us* "citizens" to accept *those* "persons with impairments or disabilities" into our society.

This is apparently a reason to praise the ADA—as "a milestone on the path to a more decent, tolerant, progressive society"—but it is not sufficient to make the law enforceable (ibid.). The forms of prejudice that involve "the failure to act or the omission to remedy" just are not enough to enforce the law against the states:

> It is a question of quite a different order, however, to say that the States in their official capacities, the States as governmental entities, must be held in violation of the Constitution on the assumption that they embody the misconceived or malicious perceptions of some of their citizens. It is a most serious charge to say a State has engaged in a pattern or practice designed to deny its citizens the equal protection of the laws, particularly where the accusation is based not on hostility but instead on the failure to act or the omission to remedy . . . (ibid.)

Thus, Kennedy concludes, "[t]he failure of a State to revise policies now seen as incorrect under a new understanding of proper policy does not always constitute the purposeful and intentional action required to make out a violation of the Equal Protection Clause" (ibid.).

In this opinion, Kennedy makes clear his view that our learning process about "prejudice" is as much a hierarchy of types of prejudice as it is a progression over time to greater understanding. With disability, we are not really talking about discrimination. No, he seems to be saying, discrimination is the stuff of racism. With disability, we are talking about the need for charity, perhaps, or some other (Christian?) virtue typified

by our "better angels" and contrary to our "human instincts." With disability, we are not talking about the kind of bad actions for which we (should) reserve the word "discrimination."

And now that hierarchy of types of prejudice is reproduced *within* disability law, with the ADAAA's statutory distinction between the actually-disabled people who have one definition of discrimination—which includes the failure to accommodate—and the regarded-as disabled people who have another definition of discrimination—which does not include the failure to accommodate. In this way, the ADAAA has conceded something to the accommodation-is-different camp. Although the statute still formally includes actually disabled and regarded-as disabled within the definition of disability, the legal entitlements for each group are now substantially different.

Some scholars offer a more optimistic account of the ADAAA's reconstruction of the regarded-as prong. For instance, one might read the regarded-as prong as "signal[ing] long-awaited parity between the ADA and other civil rights laws . . . [b]y defining 'disability' to include just about everyone on the continuum of impairments" (Barry 2010, 278). Indeed, the regulations present the regarded-as prong as the first port of call for plaintiffs who do not challenge a failure to accommodate.[15] This new statutory structure plainly incentivizes plaintiffs and their lawyers to bring suit under the regarded-as prong whenever possible. But will it also make lawyers less likely to take cases involving the more difficult, and now severable, accommodation claims?

Presumably at least some plaintiffs' lawyers will attempt to cast what would have previously been accommodation claims as antidiscrimination claims. This raises an interesting conceptual and practical question: What will happen when courts confront claims of discrimination that lie on the border of "accommodation"? For instance, is the failure to allow someone with mild depression to arrive and leave early one day a week to attend therapy a failure to accommodate or simple discrimination? What if the employer sometimes allows others to leave early for their children's sporting events? This is a classic selective-sympathy problem. Or consider the problem of structural changes to the workplace: Is the failure to construct accessible restrooms for the first disabled employees—or, in the example mentioned earlier, women's rooms for the first female employees—simple discrimination or does it fall in the special category of failure to accommodate? These are just a few examples of the kinds of dilemmas that straddle the line between antidiscrimination and accommodation. I admit I am not optimistic that many courts will give a broad reading to discrimination that is statutorily distinguished from "mere" failure to accommodate.[16] On the contrary, this bifurcation of types of discrimination seems to dovetail with Justice Kennedy's troubling view that while disability inspires some less-than-ideal attitudes and actions from "us," these new forms of discrimination against disabled people are not severe enough to require legal action.

MOVING THE LINE: TURNING BIDISABILITY INTO DISABILITY

Could we ask, about a concept . . . not so much 'What does it really mean?' or 'Who owns it and are they good or bad?', but 'What does it do?'—what does it make happen?—what . . . does it make easier or harder for people of various kinds to accomplish and think?
—Eve Kosofsky Sedgwick[17]

In principle, under the ADAAA, the category of disability has expanded to include those who were previously "not disabled enough" according to the ADA. The EEOC calls this the "group whose 'coverage has been clarified' under the ADAAA."[18] This category could also be called *bidisability* (or "bi-ability," as Ruth Colker would have it (1996)). It lies in between disabled and nondisabled, and overlaps with both.

There is no one right way to handle questions of line drawing and differential treatment across the spectrum of disability. Sometimes it seems sensible to draw finely honed distinctions between gradations of disability for legal purposes, while in other contexts it may be best to provide common treatment for various degrees of disability.

Many of those who were bidisabled under the ADA will presumably be absorbed within the ADAAA's broader disability definition. Bidisability does not (yet) appear to have any sort of cultural identity—unlike bisexual or biracial identity—but it is worth considering what functions this category nonetheless might have served. I think that under the ADA before the recent amendments, the not-disabled-enough group may have been providing a kind of *buffer zone* between nondisabled and disabled.

This buffer zone was comforting to some because it seemed to draw a line in the sand between people who are disabled and people who are not. Disability is a threatening category because, unlike a subordinated race or sex, anyone can fall into the category of disabled at any time. As various scholars have written, the permeability of a subordinated group does not necessarily lead to empathy from outsiders; on the contrary, the possibility of falling into a subordinated group can lead outsiders to fear group members and to distance themselves from the category (Yoshino, 2000; Emens, 2004). This is the idea behind, for example, homophobia: fear of the other in oneself makes one phobic of the other. Writing about disability, Harlan Hahn has famously called this the "existential anxiety" inspired by disabled others (Hahn 1988, 27–29).

In-between categories can sometimes provoke this kind of anxiety to an even greater degree, because it is harder to distance oneself from categories that share traits with both ends of a particular identity spectrum. Kenji Yoshino has, for instance, argued in this vein that bisexuality threatens both gays and straights, because both groups are more comfortable thinking their positions are fixed and opposite (Yoshino 2000). The existence of bisexuality makes it much harder for people to prove that they are simply straight or gay, because the fact of desire in one direction does not disprove desire in the other direction (ibid.).

Under this logic, one might think that the old ADA's highlighting of what I am calling the bidisabled would increase existential anxiety about disability. But rather than label them as "bidisabled," the ADA classified them as "not disabled." Anyone who was not "severely restricted" by her or his impairment was therefore "not disabled," and the case dismissed. It happened so frequently under the ADA that I sometimes thought, half seriously, that courts hoped their performative powers matched those of the evangelical preacher's "You can walk!"—curing the sick by declaring them healed. The net result was to create a large buffer zone of legally-designated "nondisabled" people who occupy the space between the small group of "actually" disabled people, and "us."

The ADAAA tries to eliminate, or at least shrink and shift, that buffer zone. It aims to bring us closer to a world in which "[t]here is no 'us' and 'them'" (Feldblum 2008, 228). If the ADAAA succeeds in folding many of the bidisabled into the legal category of disability, then we might also see heightened existential anxiety and associated empathy failures. The question will be how to turn the attitudinal consequences of an expanded definition of "disability" in a more favorable direction—from heightened anxiety to a better appreciation of disability law as a social insurance policy for everyone.

CODIFYING ASYMMETRY

There is a tradition [of saying] ... in the acknowledgements sections of academic books ... that others, while they might have contributed to the successful aspects of the project, are not to be held accountable for a book's "main defects[.]" From where I sit ... this strikes me as a tradition worth inverting. If there is anything disabled, queer, or crip about this book, it has come from my collaborative work with those named above, and many others. I take responsibility, however, for the moments when crip energies and ideas are contained or diluted in what follows, and I know that others will continue to push the work of this book, and the movements that made it possible, beyond those moments of containment.

—Robert McRuer (2006, p. xv)

Title VII of the Civil Rights Act of 1964, is largely a "symmetrical" statute, in that it protects everyone on the basis of some axis of identity (such as race or sex). By contrast, the ADA is an "asymmetrical" statute—it protects one group along a particular axis and not others. The ADAAA further entrenches this asymmetry, by explicitly prohibiting so-called reverse discrimination claims: "(g) CLAIMS OF NO DISABILITY.—Nothing in this Act shall provide the basis for a claim by an individual without a disability that the individual was subject to discrimination because of the individual's lack of disability" (ADAAA § 12201(g)).

Why is this possible for the ADA, when it is not for Title VII? An asymmetrical approach is based on an antisubordination model: it targets interventions to the groups that have historically been subject to systematic subordination. By contrast, an antidifferentiation approach looks skeptically upon any use of the protected classification, even if that aim is to rectify that history of discrimination. For example, a university admissions policy based on an antisubordination model might include affirmative action measures for groups who historically lacked access to educational opportunities based on race or sex. One based on antidifferentiation would, by contrast, be more likely to bill itself as "colorblind" or "sexblind." Many scholars (and more than one Supreme Court justice) have argued that an antisubordination model for antidiscrimination efforts would be more sensible for race and sex. So how do we have an explicit antisubordination model for disability and not for race and sex?

Most obviously, there is no constitutional impediment to an asymmetrical statute in the disability context. For better and worse, disability does not have the constitutional problem presented by race and sex, both of which are subject to rigorous constitutional scrutiny (so-called heightened scrutiny), which the Court has applied (nearly) symmetrically to more and less powerful groups in the context of, most notably, race. But *why* would this explicit anti-reverse-discrimination provision in the ADAAA not raise hackles or even get any publicity? Why is no one worried about, for example, the non-deaf person denied a job at a Deaf institution?

I think the answer lies in the highly negative social status of disability, in at least three ways. First, nondisabled is not yet an identity category. What is the opposite of "disabled"? Justice Kennedy calls it "us," or "citizens." Men and whites, although they have historically been the norm, or the comparator against which others were marked as "different," today can claim a sex and a race, respectively. By contrast, I doubt many nondisabled people think of themselves as "nondisabled" (Bérubé

2002). So long as no one is rushing to claim "nondisabled" as a primary identity, denying claims on the basis of this identity does not appear to violate any aspect of someone's being.

Second, disability is still so widely regarded as an inferior status that giving something to this group that no one else gets can go largely unchallenged. A nondisabled person who tried to claim the benefits of a statute designed for people with disabilities would likely face some stigma or opprobrium. True, some people complain that parents seek diagnoses to get goodies for their children in the educational context (Kelman & Lester 1997), but even if this is true for parents, persistent stigma probably hinders similar efforts by adults on their own behalf.

Third, and relatedly, disability is so deeply associated with inferiority that the specter of an insurrection—in which the subordinate group takes over and starts running the farm—is beyond most people's wildest imaginings.[19]

The easy prohibition on reverse discrimination claims in the ADAAA highlights other manifestations of these resolutely negative attitudes to disability. For instance, corporate and academic "diversity" initiatives regularly seek applicants on the basis of race or sex; rarely do they include "disability" as a sought-after category. Some recent work makes the so-called business case for hiring disabled workers and advertising to people with disabilities (Riley II 2006), and some scholars have described potential third-party benefits to the workplace and to society of accommodations requested by individual disabled people (Stein 2003; Emens 2008). But however obvious they may be to disability "insiders," the broader benefits of disability and accommodation are still typically overlooked, including by courts.

People who run diversity initiatives are (anecdotally) uncomfortable and awkward when asked why they have omitted disability. There is sometimes a general reluctance to focus affirmative action efforts on anything other than race—a concern that bringing in other groups waters down the attention that needs to be bestowed on race. But even where diversity initiatives go further than race, they usually skip disability.

Lennard Davis has recently argued that the era of the normal is over, and diversity is the new normal, *except for disability*. As a culture, he says, we celebrate diversity, until it comes to impairment. There, we still cling to a medical model; we equate difference with inferiority. (Davis 2011). I am skeptical that our cultural affinity for normality is ending—few people, I imagine, would consider it a compliment to be called "weird." But I agree with Davis that a thin conception of diversity circulates in the contemporary United States as part of an affirmative vision of identity and humanity, and I agree that that affirmative vision largely excludes disability.

A diversity rationale for integration affirms difference. In contrast to our standard antisubordination story of integration, which focuses on the harms to certain groups of historical exclusion and denigration, a diversity story focuses on the future gains to society of the rich cultural contributions of those with varied identities. Although a lively debate surrounds the diversity rationale, my aim here is not to argue for (or against) a diversity agenda. Instead, I'd like to examine what disability's relative absence from that agenda means for contemporary U.S. conceptions of disability.

At a talk I gave recently, a student raised an example that helps to illustrate disability's position in relation to diversity thinking.[20] The student had apparently not thought much about disability in the past, but our discussion that day made her think about the cultural houses at her undergraduate college. These residential sites were organized around people's interests in different topics, such as the environment or music. The African-American House was somewhat controversial, but it was framed around a focus on African-American history, which opened it up to people who were not themselves African-American, although most residents were. The student posited the possibility of a "Disability House," and immediately concluded that such a house would be even more controversial than the African-American House, though she was not entirely sure why.

I think the reaction the student anticipated to a Disability House—and the absence of Disability Houses on college campuses—reflects the same attitudes that lead to the neglect of disability in diversity initiatives, and to the ADAAA's easy inclusion of a ban on reverse discrimination suits. Disability is rarely understood as a positive state or identity with social or cultural benefits to its bearers or those around them. This negative perception ignores the idea of crip culture and the recent explosion of disability-related arts. The era of widespread institutionalization of people with physical as well as mental disabilities is far too recent to conceive of a house for people with disabilities as anything other than the product of exclusion or even warehousing.[21] (And as another student rightly pointed out, "disability houses" inadvertently materialize all the time, on campuses and elsewhere, when only one building or part of an institution is accessible.) But a Disability House sounds disturbing not only for its historical associations. Rather, the Disability House is inconceivable because mainstream culture is ill-equipped to see disability (as opposed to African-American history) as an issue that people with disabilities—much less people without disabilities—could affirmatively seek out and celebrate.

U.S. law on integration in the context

of "special education" and of community-based living for people with mental disabilities reflects and reinforces this negative conception of disability. Statutes and cases in these areas explicitly measure success by the extent to which people with disabilities are interacting with people without disabilities: the more contact, the better.[22] There are some important historical reasons for this focus, but the legal language makes the troubling assumption that interacting with nondisabled people is an unqualified good. Imagine a similar discussion about racial integration, in which one environment was repeatedly and explicitly deemed superior because of how much contact it offered with white people. (Of course, past racial integration efforts and decisions have effectively implied exactly that.)

Once one considers the possibility that people, disabled or nondisabled, could be drawn to disability—for community, culture, or concepts—the biases at the heart of the integration discussion are thrown into sharp relief. These discussions, in the disability context, are not framed *even superficially* in reciprocal terms. There is no consideration of what nondisabled and disabled offer each other, as equals. Rather, benefits are almost always seen as traveling one way—from nondisabled to disabled. In this light, why would voluntary efforts to diversify an institution incorporate disability? Why would an institution choose to seek out people who would bring costs and no benefits? And how could a university have a Disability House that students—disabled and even nondisabled—would choose to join? They wouldn't. According to this narrative, no one would seek to affiliate with this group, so eliminating the possibility of lawsuits brought by non-disabled people alleging discrimination for *not* being disabled raises no hackles, and passes into law unnoticed.

CONCLUSION

every built thing has its unmeant purpose . . .
Every built thing with its unmeant
meaning unmet purpose
every unbuilt thing
  —Adrienne Rich, "Powers of Recuperation"

When I heard Adrienne Rich read these lines in October of 2007, I was finishing an article on the unintended benefits of workplace accommodations under the ADA. "Unmeant purpose" resonated deeply with my sense of benefits developed for one use and exapted to another (Emens 2008). The built world was my frequent focus in that article, in fact and metaphor.

These lines now reach further. The "unmet purpose" of the ADA has been my subject here; indeed, it is the subject of the ADAAA. Metaphors of the built environment circulate always in discussions of the ADA, both challenging and constraining our thinking about disability. And in this Essay the broader benefits at issue extend beyond the workplace and beyond accommodations. Our inquiry now reaches towards the benefits of disability per se, for diversity efforts or antidiscrimination concepts, through the possibility of shifting attitudes. What lies ahead, in law and theory, is only every unbuilt thing.

NOTES

1. The essay included here is a condensed version of an earlier article. *See* Elizabeth F. Emens, *Disabling Attitudes*, 60 Amer. J. of Comparative L. 205 (2012). As part of the condensing, I have omitted the acknowledgements and much of the citation material; interested readers might consult the earlier article. For excellent editorial assistance with the preparation of this version of the article, I thank Laura Mergenthal and Anna Louie Sussman. For useful conversations and comments on earlier drafts, I thank Rachel Adams, Samuel Bagenstos, Kevin Barry, Noa Ben-Asher, Daniela Caruso, Chai Feldblum,

Katherine Franke, Michael Kavey, Sarah Lawsky, Laura Mergenthal, Michael Rembis, Charles Sabel, Michael Stein, Kimberly Walters, and participants in the Evolutions in Anti-Discrimination Law in Europe and North America at Harvard Law School, the Columbia Law Women's Association Workshop, and my Disability Law class in the Spring of 2011.

2. For more sustained treatment of the ADA's passage, see, for example, Joseph Shapiro, No Pity 118–19 (1993); Samuel R. Bagenstos, *The Americans with Disabilities Act as Welfare Reform*, 44 Wm. & Mary L. Rev. 921 (2003); Samuel Bagenstos, Law & the Contradictions of the Disability Rights Movement (2009).

3. The language in the original statute arguably opened itself up to that narrowing, which the drafters of the ADA did not recognize because the same definition in an earlier statute had not been interpreted narrowly—or received much scrutiny—from courts. *See* Feldblum 2000 at 91–92, 113.

4. *See, e.g.*, Lytes v. DC Water and Sewer Authority, 572 F.3d 936 (D.C. Cir. 2009). *Cf.* Jenkins v. National Bd. of Med. Examiners, 2009 WL 331638 (6th Cir. Feb. 11, 2009) (applying the ADAAA to a case filed before the ADAAA went into effect because the relief sought was injunctive).

5. *Cf.* Mary Johnson, Make Them Go Away: Clint Eastwood, Christopher Reeve & the Case Against Disability Rights (2003).

6. I say presumptively because there are defenses, such as someone's inability to perform the essential functions of her job, or her posing a direct threat to others in the workplace—the same defenses available for other disabilities.

7. For a critique of some ways of reading Scarry, see Tobin Siebers, Disability, Pain, and the Politics of Minority Identity (unpublished manuscript, on file with author, October 2011) ("Pain does not spring from and differentiate the individual. It does not belong to one person alone. It is a social invention, external to people, that marks them as individual. The dominant social representation of pain in the West is the individual alone in pain . . . . What would it mean to conceive of pain not as an individual or personal emotion—as a feeling owned by one person—but as a socially mediated identity, as a product of social forces operating external to individuals?").

8. There is an extensive literature on the so-called contact hypothesis, the idea that working side by side in cooperative ventures can reduce animus and stereotyping. For a discussion in the disability context, see, for example, Samuel R. Bagenstos, *"Rational Discrimination," Accommodation, and the Politics of (Disability) Civil Rights*, 89 Va. L. Rev. 825, 843–44 & n.55 (2003).

9. For more comprehensive treatments, see, for example, Kevin Barry, *Toward Universalism: What the ADA Amendments Act Can and Can't Do for Disability Rights*, 31 Berkeley J. Emp. & Lab. L. 203 (2010); Alex B. Long, *Introducing the New and Improved Americans with Disabilities Act: Assessing the ADA Amendments Act of 2008*, 103 Nw. U. L. Rev. Colloquy 217 (2008).

10. 29 CFR § 1630.2(l)(2).

11. For useful critical perspectives on the social model, see, for example, Tom Shakespeare, *Disability Rights and Wrongs* 29, 29–53 (2006); Vlad Perju, *Impairment, Discrimination, and the Legal Construction of Disability in the European Union and the United States*, 44 Cornell Int'l L.J. 279 (2011).

12. Protecting perceived-as discrimination is not unique, however; the UK's Equality Act of 2010 is an example of a jurisdiction that offers protection to those perceived to have a protected trait.

13. The other passenger was going to visit an ailing relative, and so wanted to make sure that he knew what it would look like for a person to mouth those words. *See* Stephen Greenblatt, Epilogue, Renaissance Self-Fashioning 255–56 (1983) ("I felt superstitiously that if I mimed the man's terrible sentence, it would have the force, as it were, of a legal sentence . . . . I was aware, in a manner more forceful than anything my academic research had brought home to me, of the extent to which my identity and the words I utter coincide, the extent to which I want to form my own sentences or to choose for myself those moments in which I will recite someone else's.").

14. *See* 76 Fed. Reg. 16980 (Mar. 25, 2011).

15. 76 Fed. Reg. 16978.

16. One approach courts may take to reading "discriminate" narrowly is to insist that plaintiffs identify "comparators" in order to prove that that the employer "discriminated" (in the statute's newly narrower meaning of that term) rather than failed to accommodate. For the definitive treatment of the comparator methodology, and a discussion of its problems, see Suzanne B. Goldberg, *Discrimination by Comparison*, 120 Yale L.J. 728 (2011).

17. *See* Clare Hemmings, *Bisexual Theoretical Perspectives: Emergent and Contingent Relationships, in* Bi Academic Intervention, The Bisexual Imaginary: Representation, Identity & Desire 1, 16 (1997) (quoting Eve Kosofsky Sedgwick, 'Bi', Queer Studies list, QSTUDY-L@UBVM.cc.buffalo.edu, Aug. 17, 1994: 15:49:34–0400) (emphases removed).

18. 76 Fed. Reg. 16987 n.3.
19. A counter example would be Rosemarie Garland-Thomson's reading of Kazuo Ishiguro's *Never Let Me Go*, and particularly the film adaptation, as dramatizing an anxiety about a world upside down in which people with disabilities use nondisabled people for their own grotesque purposes. Rosemarie Garland-Thomson, "Habitable Worlds: Eugenic Spaces and Democratic Spaces," The Ethics of Disability Studies Lecture Series, Columbia University (Feb 25, 2011).
20. Discussion with the Columbia Law Women's Association of Elizabeth F. Emens, *Intimate Discrimination: The State's Role in the Accidents of Love*, 122 Harv. L. Rev. 1307 (2009), (Mar. 23, 2011).
21. One might say that the problem with Disability House is that disabilities are so diverse; they are indeed diverse, but a Blind House seems just as likely to raise these concerns.
22. *See, e.g.*, Individuals with Disabilities Education Act (IDEA), 84 Stat. 175, as amended, 20 U.S.C. § 1412(a)(5) (requiring that participating states establish "procedures to assure that[,] . . . [t]o the maximum extent appropriate, children with disabilities . . . are educated with children who are not disabled"); Disability Advocates, Inc. v. Paterson, 653 F.Supp.2d 184, 208 (E.D.N.Y. 2009) (saying repeatedly, in a judgment that adult homes run by the state of New York violate the integration mandate of Title II of the ADA and *Olmstead*, that these "Adult Homes limit the development of relationships with people who do not have disabilities").

WORKS CITED

Anderson, Jill. "Just Semantics: The Lost Readings of the Americans with Disabilities Act." *Yale Law Journal* 117 (2008): 992.

Americans with Disabilities Act of 1990, Pub. L. No. 101–336, 104 Stat. 327 (1990).

Americans with Disabilities Amendments Act of 2008, Pub. L. No. 110–325, 122 Stat. 3553 (2008) (codified at 42 U.S.C. § 12101 *et seq.*).

Barry, Kevin. "Toward Universalism: What the ADA Amendments Act Can and Can't Do for Disability Rights." *Berkeley Journal of Employment and Labor Law* 31 (2010): 278.

Bérubé, Michael. "Afterword: If I Should Live So Long," in *Disability Studies: Enabling the Humanities*, edited by Sharon L. Snyder et al., 337. New York: Modern Language Association of America, 2002.

Bd. of Trustees of the Univ. of Alabama v. Garrett, 531 U.S. 356, 375 (2000) (Kennedy, J., concurring).

Colker, Ruth. *Hybrid*. New York: New York University Press, 1996.

Convention on the Rights of Persons with Disabilities, G.A. Res. 61/106, art. 8 (2007).

Davis, Lennard. "The End of Normal: Multiculturalism, Disability & Diversity." The Ethics of Disability Studies Speaker Series, put on by the Columbia University Department of English & Comparative Literature, the Center for the Critical Analysis of Social Difference, the Graduate School of Arts & Sciences, and the Center for American Studies (Apr. 1, 2011).

Emens, Elizabeth F. "Integrating Accommodation." *University of Pennsylvania Law Review* 156 (2008): 839–922.

Emens, Elizabeth F. "Monogamy's Law: Compulsory Monogamy and Polyamorous Existence." *New York University Review of Law and Social Change* 29 (2004): 277.

Feldblum, Chai R., Kevin Barry, and Emily A. Benfer. "The ADA Amendments Act of 2008." *Texas Journal on Civil Liberties and Civil Rights* 13 (2008): 187–240.

Feldblum, Chai R., "Definition of Disability Under Federal Anti-Discrimination Law: What Happened? Why? And What Can We Do About It?" *Berkeley Journal of Employment and Labor Law* 21 (2000): 91–165.

Goffman, Erving. *Stigma*. New York: Simon & Schuster, 1963.

Hahn, Harlan. "The Politics of Physical Differences: Disability and Discrimination," *Journal of Social Issues* 44(1) (1988): 39–47.

Jolls, Christine. "Antidiscrimination and Accommodation." *Harvard Law Review* 115 (2001): 642.

Karlan, Pamela S. and George Rutherglen. "Disabilities, Discrimination, and Reasonable Accommodation." *Duke Law Journal* 46 (1996): 1.

Kelman, Mark and Gillian Lester. *Jumping the Queue*. Cambridge: Harvard University Press, 1997.

Long, Alex B., "Introducing the New and Improved Americans with Disabilities Act: Assessing the ADA Amendments Act of 2008," *Northwestern University Law Review Colloquy* 103 (2008): 217.

McRuer, Robert. *Crip Theory: Cultural Signs of Queerness and Disability*. New York: New York University Press, 2006.

Olmstead v. Zimring, 527 U.S. 581, 614 (1999) (Kennedy, J., concurring).

Adrienne Rich, *Powers of Recuperation*, 8 A Public Space (2007), *available at* http://www.apublicspace.org/poetry/powers_of_recuperation.html.

Riley, Charles A. *Disability and Business: Best Practices and Strategies for Inclusion*. Hanover: University Press of New England, 2006.

Scarry, Elaine. *The Body in Pain*. Oxford: Oxford University Press, 1985.

Stein, Michael Ashley. "The Law and Economics of Disability Accommodations." *Duke Law Journal* 53 (2003): 79.

Stein, Michael Ashley. "Same Struggle, Difference Difference: ADA Accommodations as Anti-discrimination." *University of Pennsylvania Law Review* 153 (2004): 570.

Sutton v. United Air Lines, Inc., 527 U.S. 471 (1999).

Toyota Motor Mfg., Ky. v. Williams, 534 U.S. 184 (2002).

U.S. National Archives and Records Administration. *Code of Federal Regulations.* Title 29. Regulations Relating to Labor, 2011.

Wax, Amy L. "Disability, Reciprocity, and 'Real Efficiency': A Unified Approach." *William and Mary Law Review* 44 (2003): 1421.

Yoshino, Kenji. "The Epistemic Contract of Bisexual Erasure." *Stanford Law Review* 52 (2000): 353.

PART II

The Politics of Disability

CHAPTER 5

Disabling Postcolonialism: Global Disability Cultures and Democratic Criticism

Clare Barker and Stuart Murray

As scholars working in both Disability Studies and Postcolonial Studies, we are mindful of a number of concerns that arise when we seek to bring together these two fields. The first is our desire to explore the intersections of our interests, and not to have to hold them at a distance from one another because of the arbitrary lines that divide disciplinary areas. Secondly, we are conscious of the fact that, put simply, there has been little sustained analysis of the representation of disability in postcolonial literatures and cultures, nor of the methodological or theoretical bases that the approaches might share.[1] From an initial standpoint, then, there are some basic and foundational reasons to want to establish a dialogue between the two fields. The placement of disability as the active verb in our title, "Disabling Postcolonialism," reflects our feeling that Disability Studies has the potential to make a more urgent intervention into contemporary Postcolonial Studies than vice versa. As we will go on to delineate, Disability Studies has already begun to look toward the important work of globalizing its outlook and methodologies, whereas disability is still almost completely absent from postcolonial theory and criticism, marking a significant exclusion in the field. Even so, as a whole, contemporary Disability Studies

is not especially perceptive in its articulation of global dynamics and there is much work to be done, in both disciplines, to raise awareness and refine research methods. While, in the broadest terms, postcolonial criticism tends to treat disability as prosthetic metaphor, Disability Studies problematically transports theories and methodologies developed within the western academy to other global locations, paying only nominal attention to local formations and understandings of disability. It is these limitations that we want to address here: our central aim is to foster productive exchanges and cross-fertilizations between the two research fields, addressing silences that have existed for too long.

It is clear to us that there are significant questions at stake when considering the multiple forces that come together when we talk of disabling postcolonialism. The temptation to conceive of and express colonial processes and their consequences—postcolonial resistance, anticolonial nationalism, the development of independent states—using metaphors of disability is all too obvious. The idea that both disability and postcolonialism are, at heart, connected to questions of power is, of course, not misplaced. But it is an error to subscribe to a reading of such notions that thinks predominantly of the power *relations* involved here in terms of easy models of health, illness, absence, loss, pathology, charity or victimhood, to name just the most recognizable of such categories. These assumptions and tropes frequently haunt the discussion of disability in postcolonial contexts, but we want to argue that, in fact, the details within representations and narratives of postcolonial disability can also be understood to reorient, in a fundamental fashion, our understanding of such disability. We contend that it is in disability's material locations, in all their cultural diversity, that we find potential new forms through which to express disability experiences.

In this article we outline, through a critical investigation of the relevant arguments in each subject area, what we see as the most significant theoretical contributions to the disabling of postcolonialism to date. In addition, we seek to push the integration of the two fields further by articulating exactly *how* we think Critical Disability Studies needs to adapt its assumptions and methodologies to include and respond to postcolonial locations of disability. Here, we identify a number of key terms and approaches—situated analysis, cultural difference, environments of disability, and representational practices—which we believe have the capacity to undo the over-rigid models and vocabularies through which Disability Studies can sometimes function. In turn, we feel that an appreciation of disability, elaborated through these processes, gives greater detail to the understanding of the ways in which postcolonial cultural representations work. At the heart of our enquiry, as the second half of our title implies, is our sense that the integration of these twin viewpoints can be aligned with what Edward Said describes as *democratic* criticism. Our own interpretation of this term refers to a critical method that is sensitive to the particularities of disability as it is experienced in postcolonial societies, and

seeks to further freedom through asserting and questioning knowledge in the process of establishing research methods. We remain convinced that the best end product of such work can make a material difference to people's lives, and this conviction is the base for our thinking throughout what follows.

EDWARD SAID AND PARTICIPATORY CITIZENSHIP

In terms of potential models that might aid us in establishing the terms of a productive association between postcolonial and disability scholarship, we want to initiate the discussion of such a link through a consideration of the writings of Edward Said. With its focus on the power differential between communities in postcolonial contexts, Said's foundational work offers itself as an instructive guide for all manner of academic fields involved in similar endeavours. Within Disability Studies, both Tom Shakespeare and Rod Michalko have used Said's writings (on identity and exile respectively) to think through particular aspects of disability representations and experiences, and his early and mid-career work more generally displays the kinds of critique of power and representational systems that illuminate similar processes within disability scholarship. When, in a 1985 interview entitled "In the Shadow of the West," Said noted that the "violence" of the "*act* of representing (and hence reducing) others, almost always involves violence of some sort to the *subject* of the representation," or when he asked "what can we do outside of this system [of representation] that enables us to treat it as a productive, rather than a natural process?" (2005: 40, 44), his observations chime with the seminal work of those, such as David Mitchell, Sharon Snyder, Rosemarie Garland-Thomson, and Lennard Davis, who have, since the mid-1990s, sought to unpack the ways in which stories and images of people with disabilities have nearly always been reductive.

The classic Saidian process of critique, then, is easily aligned, at an appropriate level of abstraction, with the kinds of work disability scholarship has come to practise. In addition, we feel that his late work on humanism, especially in his 2004 text *Humanism and Democratic Criticism* (his last completed book, written as Said himself experienced a significant and disabling illness), contains perspectives highly relevant to a discussion of disability. As a postcolonial scholar choosing to stress the values of humanism, a mode of thinking deeply embedded within a European tradition, Said sought to outline a working critique that appears counterintuitive but has, in fact, radical applications in terms of global relations. Equally, we would claim that his articulation of an idea of the "human," a topic on which it is wise to be cautious given the history of humanism with regard to disability, offers a provocative but potentially progressive approach to the workings of disability in culture. In particular, Said's stress on what he calls "participatory citizenship" provides an inclusive framework within which questions pertinent to both postcolonial and disabled identities can be explored.

For Said, giving detail on this, there is

no contradiction at all between the practice of humanism and the practice of participatory citizenship. Humanism is not about withdrawal and exclusion. Quite the reverse; its purpose is to make things more available to critical scrutiny as the product of human labor, human energies for emancipation and enlightenment, and, just as importantly, human misreadings of and misinterpretations of the collective past and present.

(2004: 22)

He goes on:

In my understanding of its relevance today, humanism is not a way of consolidating and affirming what "we" have always known and felt, but rather a means of questioning, upsetting, and reformulating so much of what is presented to us as commodified, packaged, uncontroversial, and uncritically codified certainties.

(28)

Despite the problematic associations between humanism and disability, then, it is impossible not to see the potential of what Said says here for a progressive method of critique. The processes of "questioning, upsetting, and reformulating" and the attention given to "misreadings of and misinterpretations of the collective past and present" mirror the variety of disability movements and their attempts to demand a sense of "participatory citizenship" when validating disabled experiences. In addition, the example of the radical postcolonial scholar championing what many would represent as a conservative set of ideas asserts what we recognize as the against-the-grain logic of much of the best disability writing.

So it is both the detail and the shape of Said's thinking that offer a productive guide for thinking through the connections between postcolonial and disability scholarship. Bill Ashcroft and Pal Ahluwalia, discussing Said's late style, note that his writing on humanism constitutes a desire "almost single-handedly to re-orient the understanding of the term away from its deeply Eurocentric and elitist grounding to a worldly and multi-faceted consideration of human activity" (2000: 145), and we respond to this both as postcolonial scholars recognizing the challenge to Eurocentric thinking, and as disability scholars alive to the notion of "multi-faceted human activity." Above all, we find in the possibilities of a "participatory citizenship" ideas of democracy, agency and method; Said's thinking parallels the debates around activist rights discourses *and* the issues of theorizing disability that are so apparent in contemporary writing in Disability Studies. If the Viconian humanism that underpins Said's own conception of the term can, in his words, tell us that "we can really know only what we make or, to put it differently, we can know things according to the way they were made" (2004: 11), then maybe his own example of intellectual scrutiny and expression can also help us to think about what makes "us," in terms of a complex, inclusive humanity.

But, useful as they are, guiding frames still need specifics, and for all that the force of Said's thinking might inspire ideas about the connections between disability and the postcolonial, it is clear that his valorization of humanism will not work across the huge variety of global contexts in which disability is a social and cultural experience. These problems highlight once again the limits of grand theorizing that have bedevilled Postcolonial Studies since the 1980s and doubtless will shadow the attempted development of Disability Studies as the subject seeks to expand beyond its traditional Euro-American base. Mark Sherry has warned of the dangers of abusing the "rhetorical connections" that exist between disability and postcolonialism. "Neither disability nor postcolonialism," Sherry writes, "should be understood as simply a metaphor for the other experience; nor should they be rhetorically employed as a symbol of the oppression involved in a completely different experience" (2007: 21). Following on from this, those practitioners of disability scholarship who have sought to place disability within a global or postcolonial context, or have used the languages of identity politics in a manner common to much postcolonial writing, have often struggled with their accounts of the differing kinds of "experiences" that Sherry highlights here.

The majority of disability scholarship has emerged from traditions that emphasize local aspects of social application. In Europe and the U.K. especially, such work has stressed the processes of law and governance, with a resulting focus on such issues as community-based social services. In the U.S., where a discourse- and humanities-based model has played a greater part in the development of Disability Studies, it has nevertheless been the case that American examples have predominated. In both instances, there has been an understanding that such models may well have application in non-Euro-American contexts (claims for the social model, for example, assert that it can adapt to the local variants of other cultures), but there has been a singular lack of specificity as to the detail of such applications, especially as they might take into account the nature of cultures shaped by colonization and its consequences. It is this question of applicability that concerns us here. In aiming to develop strategies for postcolonial disability analysis, we aspire toward future scholarship in which the nuanced methods we find in much Euro-American-focused disability criticism are replicated in work on global disability.

QUESTIONING THE GLOBAL

Disability scholarship that has considered the value of a revisionist global dimension has often asserted the potential of such work in terms of enquiries and questions. "What do we talk about when we talk about global bodies?" asks Robert McRuer in the Epilogue to *Crip Theory: Cultural Signs of Queerness and Disability* (2006). His answer, in part, is to recognize that such talk involves movement beyond Euro-American subjects and methods, that the process of globalizing disability might mark a move toward the "extension or completion" of the project that seeks the widest possible integration of disabled lives and experiences into majority cultures (201). At the same time, however, McRuer notes that this kind of thinking creates an idea of global bodies that "also comes with its dangers," observing that "[w]hen a field covers a larger terrain and purports to be about everything ... there is always the danger that trumping, transcending, and even colonizing will displace the more urgent work—especially urgent in these times—of coalition" (201–202), a point equally true of Postcolonial Studies of course. Overall, McRuer's ruminations on what the global nature of Disability Studies might be open up a number of highly suggestive avenues—a further complication of cosmopolitanism and global neoliberal institutions, an idea of "disposable domesticity" (203)—that invite future work. His intervention in *Crip Theory*, though, is still best seen in terms of such an *invitation*, an acknowledgement that more needs to be done.

The same could be said of the cultural model of disability more generally, particularly as it is expressed in the formative work of Sharon Snyder and David Mitchell. In their *Cultural Locations of Disability* (2006), the very idea of "location" is one with obvious appeal to a postcolonial scholarship aiming to highlight specific located examples of disability in cultural contexts, whether that is within colonial processes of classification or post-independence renegotiations of citizenship. When Snyder and Mitchell claim that "[t]he definition of disability must incorporate both the outer and inner reaches of culture and experience as a combination of profoundly social and biological forces," we see—in the space given here to "culture and experience"—the promise of a productive model allowing for the cultural difference of postcolonial disability to find its expression (7). Yet, for all of the attractiveness of the shape of the thinking here, the work that might go on in any global cultural location of disability remains something gestured towards, and "cultural locations" appears more as a phrase than an actual paradigm.

The conclusion to *Cultural Locations of Disability* moves towards thinking through the issues of the location of Disability Studies as a *subject* (its final mini-chapters are on the institutionalization of Disability Studies and the development of research practices, 194–203) and, while we find such a focus useful, it does not embrace the full potential that the term "cultural locations" might suggest.

Indeed, there is a real sense that the practice of globalizing disability, the implementation of the suggestion as it were, actually works to foreground the limits of current formations of the cultural model. In reality, we find that asking the question of how disability is figured in the global, postcolonial history of the modern points to the closed parameters of what we think we know, rather than opening the door to further scholarship; again, it is still all to be done, with the precise locations of cultures of disability still to be found.

Other practitioners of disability scholarship have entered the debate surrounding culture and representation in ways, and with methodologies supplied by cognate disciplines, that should make their use in any account of postcolonial disability relatively transparent. This is especially the case with Ato Quayson, a noted postcolonial scholar (on both the specific literatures of West Africa and postcolonial culture and criticism more widely)[2] before his research turned toward disability representation in *Aesthetic Nervousness: Disability and the Crisis of Representation* (2007). With its focus on work by Wole Soyinka and J. M. Coetzee, among others, *Aesthetic Nervousness* presents what might seem like a clear entry into a discussion of specific postcolonial disability narratives. To an extent, this is the case: Quayson notes, for example, that Soyinka's "writing focuses ... on a set of ritual dispositions drawn from a traditional Yoruba and African cultural sensibility" and that "each of his plays may be read as partial allegories of the Nigerian and African postcolonial condition" (29). Yet our reading of Quayson's study overall is that it does not seek to make links between disability and postcoloniality at the level of cultural production. As is in fact obvious from his title, Quayson's focus is on questions of aesthetics and form, and subsequently on issues of ethics, and not on the determining question of how postcolonial cultures per se represent disability. For all that it does, *Aesthetic Nervousness* does not offer us a model of how we might conceive the particular interplay of postcolonial cultural history and the depiction of disability, whether individually experienced or socially constructed.

Despite his postcolonial credentials, then, Quayson does not focus on the questions of cultural and personal identity and representation that appear for many as the central axes of any initial account of postcolonial disability. At the other end of the spectrum is Tobin Siebers, whose commitment to identity politics is iterated throughout his disability work. "Identity politics," he writes in the introduction to *Disability Theory* (2008), "remains in my view the most practical course of action by which to address social injustices against minority peoples and to apply the new ideas, narratives, and experiences discovered by them to the future of progressive, democratic society" (15). This is language that has clear connections to the activist roots of much disability scholarship; it is also a statement with a clear relevance to postcolonial contexts in which "injustices" are countered in the name of "progressive" and "democratic" social and cultural formations. For Siebers, the category of the "minority"—whether "minority peoples," "minority identity" or "minority studies"—is essential to the optimism about what he terms, in *Disability Theory*, the "future of identity politics" (70–95). Yet, in his discussions of minorities, Siebers gives virtually

no thought to the processes of globalization or transnationalism and the production of minority identity politics that occur as a consequence of either past empires or the global hegemonic power of current neoliberal formations, especially those of the U.S. When he notes that "[d]isability studies has much to offer future discussions of minority identity and its politics" (95), the statement comes in the final paragraph of his chapter on the topic, and it is apparent that, as with Mitchell and Snyder, Siebers' work—though obviously sympathetic to non-American accounts of disability—has no real sense of what such instances might entail. Most contemporary disability scholarship is, it appears, all in favour of a situated theory and method that can articulate the nature of global postcolonial disability, and is very much aware of the need for such work to complicate current models of how disability is experienced and represented, but it has no real idea of what these processes might actually look like.

We feel it is time to move beyond the gesturing toward a future in which non-Euro-American disability stories, of all kinds, *might* be understood. We believe that detailed and situated analysis is the way to correct the conditional frame of such gestures, and furthermore, to return to McRuer's question, that such a critical approach will enable us to think through what is involved in a concentration on "global bodies." In so doing, we would like this article to build on what we see as the one recent intervention in disability scholarship that does engage with the specifics of globalized disability, namely Michael Davidson's notion of "the work of disability in an age of globalization" (168) in *Concerto for the Left Hand: Disability and the Defamiliar Body* (2008). Like other scholars, Davidson asks the pertinent questions—"[w]hat might a critical disability studies perspective bring to the globalization debate?"—but he also offers a working through of some potential answers. Noting that disability "unsettles a global panacea for health and human welfare," he asserts that it also "defamiliarizes the seemingly inexorable pattern of capital movement, information exchange, and market integration by which globalization is known" (171, 169). Following this, Davidson's concentration on poverty and the distribution of wealth, and his assertion of the need "to reevaluate some of the keywords of disability studies . . . from a comparative cultural perspective" (172), gives detail (in his accounts of "development" themes in recent film, or narratives of international organ sales and transplants, for example) to the shape of disability theorizing in global contexts.

SITUATING DISABILITY CULTURES

Our own analysis aims to supplement Davidson's globalized perspectives with specific references to postcolonial contexts, theory and critical practices. To an extent this continues the work begun by Pushpa Naidu Parekh and the contributors to her special issue of *Wagadu* on "Intersecting Gender and Disability Perspectives in Rethinking Postcolonial Identities" (2007), but we see our scholarship as bringing an added focus on critical methodology and the specifics of literary and cultural analyses informed by both Postcolonial Studies and Disability Studies. The main intervention we intend to make is formulated as a call to move away from the "modelling" established as the dominant mode of disability theorizing at present toward more nuanced understandings of disability in relation to cultural difference and situated experience. We believe that for Disability Studies to move forward, it is imperative to interrogate the universal approach to disability naturalized within the social model of disability in particular, and in doing so to enact what might be termed a "decolo-

nization" of Disability Studies in the vein advocated by Linda Tuhiwai Smith in her important book *Decolonizing Methodologies: Research and Indigenous Peoples* (1999).[3]

Arif Dirlik's controversial 2002 critique of postcolonial criticism up to that date demonstrated how, "focused on past legacies," the field was in his opinion "largely oblivious to its own conditions of existence and its relationship to contemporary configurations of power." Postcolonialism, he went on, "ignores the ways in which its interpretation of the past may serve to promote or, at the least, play into the hands of a globalized capitalism" (440). It is important to recognize that the social model of disability is similarly laden with priorities, value judgements and historical perspectives that are by no means neutral or transparent; Disability Studies' own "past legacies"—its "interpretation of the past" within a political framework of western minority rights activism—can equally be accused of a lack of self-reflexivity regarding its often relatively privileged "conditions of existence" within systems of "globalized capitalism." The kind of transnational "disability-and-development" projects (Nepveux and Smith Beitiks 2010) that act in the name of progressive disability politics to change attitudes and conditions in the global South without the necessary awareness of local ideologies and infrastructures to resist their own neocolonizing effects, are an offshoot of this embedded political stance on disability—a version of Gayatri Spivak's well-known paradigm of "white men saving brown women from brown men" (1999: 287).

Instead of imposing a hegemonic model of disability, then, and assuming that disability will function in comparable ways across disparate cultural texts and contexts, contemporary materialist postcolonial criticism gives us the tools to take particular, situated experiences as the starting point for disability analysis, enabling acts of criticism *emerging from and informed by* (rather than applied to) "cultural locatedness" in the first instance. In endorsing this method we echo the anthropologists Benedicte Ingstad and Susan Reynolds Whyte who, in *Disability in Local and Global Worlds* (2007), seek to orientate disability research "in the direction of greater differentiation and specificity" (5) instead of the pursuit of overarching disability models. "We are interested in people's own experiences of what is disabling in their world rather than in some universal definition" (11), they write—a sentiment that resonates with the increasing emphasis on lived experience in the humanities-based scholarship of Siebers and Snyder and Mitchell.

A vital step toward such analysis is the recognition that key Disability Studies concepts, including minority identity, normalcy, and the relationship between impairment and disability, are contingent on cultural difference and may be challenged by situated critical reading practices. In a variety of postcolonial contexts, culturally specific beliefs about embodiment, ontology, communal identity and belonging continue to shape disability experiences. For example, many indigenous communities do not identify with individualist models of impairment; in some American Indian cultures, for instance, "[t]he determination of 'normalcy' in health or wellness is dependent on whether or not the individual is in balance with all her relations" (Lovern 2008), including a balance with the natural world. For Māori in Aotearoa/New Zealand, the individuality of impairment is similarly downplayed; "health is viewed as an interrelated phenomenon rather than an intrapersonal one," meaning that "Māori are more likely to link good or bad health with interpersonal and inter-generational concerns" (Durie 1998: 71, 2). The presence of indigenous or local "cultural models"

of health and disability demonstrates that drawing generalized conclusions about the ways in which postcolonial cultures experience disability cannot account for either the ontological or the material conditions which are formative in constructing disabled lives.

As an agent of biopolitical control, normalcy in particular might not function in the same ways in different cultural contexts. Whereas in the global North, disability theorizing works from the assumption that disability is a minority subject position, and may focus on what Fiona Kumari Campbell calls "debates about the purview of citizenship" for disabled people "in advanced capitalist liberal nation-states," the case is very different in some postcolonial nation-states where there are instead "disputes regarding the best way to discern the field of not-disability (i.e. the healthy comparator)" (2009: 34). In contexts of chronic poverty or indigenous dispossession, ill health and disability may be widespread enough to shift the thresholds of health and disability, and in communities experiencing mass disablement (due to war, disaster, or industrial accident) people with disabilities often constitute a numerical majority. "Normal" lived experience in postcolonial and developing contexts might *be disabled* experience, drastically altering the categorical and exclusionary implications of "normalcy" and "non-normativity."

The acclaimed Bengali writer and activist Mahasweta Devi dramatizes these points in a powerful short story, "Shishu" ["Children"] (1993), which details an encounter between an idealistic relief officer, Singh, and an adivasi (tribal) community suffering from the compound crises of poverty, political repression, drought and famine. The narrative climaxes with Singh's realization that although "[h]e didn't have the stature of a healthy Russian, Canadian, or American" and he "did not eat food that supplied enough calories for a human body," when placed in context of the adivasis' government-sanctioned disablement, his own body—"the ill-nourished and ridiculous body of an *ordinary* Indian" (our emphasis)—represents "the worst possible crime in the history of civilization." By comparison, his "normalcy" (250) appears as obscene privilege. As Singh's "shadow" (250) is cast suggestively over the disabled and infantilized bodies of the adivasis, the narrative displays how, in a deeply stratified postcolonial society where power is exercised differentially, the "normate" (Garland-Thomson 1997: 8) is shadowy, unstable and ultimately elusive. Who sets the standards of embodied normalcy here? The middle-class relief officer who rations food parcels? The government, whose land repossessions, taxes and wars have disenfranchised and starved its resistant indigenous citizens? Or the World Health Organization, directly invoked by Singh (250), whose recommendations for calorie consumption render disabled a large proportion of India's population? By complicating normalcy to the point of diffusion, "Shishu" represents an instructive parable for disability analysis informed by postcolonial perspectives. While acknowledging global codes of health and normalcy as a spectral presence in the adivasis' lives, Devi *relativizes* such universalizing standards, foregrounding the local inflections that disable specific bodies in a historicized context of struggle.

ENVIRONMENT, TRAUMA, DISABLEMENT

Given that the history of colonialism (and its post/neocolonial aftermath) is indeed a history of mass disablement, and that the *acquisition* of disability may be tied into wider patterns of dispossession—the loss of family, home, land, community, employment—there is a pressing need, as we see it, to resist the too-easy censure of narratives that construct disability as loss.

We would caution especially against the blanket rejection and/or critique of medical discourse and medicalized terminology, which may be strategically important when campaigning for resources and raising awareness of (neo)colonial abuses. What individuals in such circumstances experience as loss should not be rendered an invalid response by arguments that fail to recognize the wider contexts and material environments in which disablement occurs.

Any engagement with the environments in which disability is created, especially by war or disaster, and the subsequent involvement of medical practice and discourse, invokes the category of trauma. The relationship between disability and trauma is one that is often cited explicitly in postcolonial literary and cultural narratives but has not yet undergone any sustained critical analysis. In fact, James Berger describes a "discursive abyss" (2004: 563) between disability scholarship and that on trauma, going so far as to say that "disability studies exhibits a significant degree of *denial* with regard to trauma and loss" (572). This is perhaps understandable, given the commitment of Disability Studies to changing perceptions of disability as tragedy or misfortune, but the confluence of disability and trauma in many postcolonial contexts raises a number of vital questions that Disability Studies should posit and attempt to answer. Do we conceptualize trauma as a disability? Or, given that the ways in which individuals acquire disabilities are often compounded by sociopolitical and cultural factors, can disability be considered just one component of the wider category of "trauma"? How do our assumptions about this relationship affect the ways in which disability is treated, administered, represented, and discussed? There are no simple answers to these questions but we would argue that the content of postcolonial narratives suggests that disability criticism should address this absence in pursuit of a more robust and inclusive theorization of how "loss" may be constituted within disability experiences.

This notion of compound trauma raises the question of whether the term *disability* is adequate in encapsulating the complex manifestations of disabled difference in specific traumatic settings. Anthony Carrigan's work (2010) draws attention to the particular forms of stigmatization and exclusion suffered by *hibakusha* ("explosion-affected people") in post-Hiroshima/ Nagasaki Japan. Caught between a general fear of radiation sickness and responses generated from the cultural memory of the bombings, the experiences of *hibakusha* are continually conditioned by their implication within the ongoing resonance of a collective trauma. As they negotiate minority subject positions, *hibakusha* potentially undergo all the forms of oppression, discrimination, coalition and activism that we recognize as aspects of disability politics, and yet *disability* as we know it does not wholly account for the range of often fraught interactions between impaired individuals and a society coming to terms with a violent and traumatic history. Once more, the specific cultural and historical meanings of disability experience in postcolonial environments challenge the foundational assumptions, and the suitability of the analytical tools, we would apply to global disability.

As this example makes clear, the production of disability in postcolonial locations involves complicated relationships between cultural and environmental factors. McRuer's (2010) timely commentary on the 2010 Haitian earthquake highlights how the disabilities caused by a seemingly "natural" disaster are necessarily entangled with economic relations and cultural discourses that form the legacy of colonialism in the state. Just as we believe that *culture* cannot be used as a universal

descriptor for a particular mode of disability theorizing, postcolonial disability experiences may similarly trouble "environment" as it is applied, in the social model, as a generic disabling force. The assumption that, as Siebers puts it, "[t]here is a one-to-one correspondence between the dimensions of the built environment and its preferred social body—the body invited inside as opposed to those bodies not issued an invitation" (2008: 85), becomes irrelevant in the context of Haiti. Events there remind us of the sometimes problematic over-emphasis within Disability Studies on the constructedness of environments according to able-bodied norms. Indeed, it could be that the competing claims for territory and resources, alternative conceptions of space and place, or the regularity of destruction in some postcolonial contexts, require that we rethink what is meant by disabling environments. Furthermore, the belief that such environments can be transformed through minority activism, the removal of barriers, and universal design, is symptomatic of a deterministic notion of environmental accessibility which does not account for environments in which exclusion and inaccessibility are by no means unique to people with disabilities.

With this destabilization of human–environment relations in mind, engagements with postcolonial environmental writing can help develop an understanding of disabling postcolonial environments. Rob Nixon points out how "[n]on-Western environmental movements are typically alert to the interdependence of human survival and environmental change" (2005: 243), and postcolonial ecocriticism has recently begun to direct much-needed attention toward the ways in which "environment" functions as "an integrated network of human and non-human agents acting historically" (Mukherjee 2010: 5) rather than simply existing as a stable, transformable, backdrop to human action in the postcolony. In fact, many of the central issues within postcolonial ecocriticism—the "corporatizing of biodiversity," "indigenous land rights, community displacement, ... toxicity, ... urban or poor rural experience," "biodegradation, ... and 'engineered environments'," "nuclear testing and nuclear pollution" (Nixon 2005: 243–45) to name just a few—have direct and obvious links to health and disability issues, whether as causal factors of disablement or as contexts that exacerbate the oppression of people with disabilities. Despite postcolonial ecocriticism's interest in the contingency and fragility of human–environmental interactions, however, it has so far failed to factor the presence of different human bodies, abilities and needs into its "network of human and non-human agents" in any notable way.

Indra Sinha's Booker Prize-shortlisted novel *Animal's People* (2007) showcases how a combination of disability and ecocritical perspectives can illuminate the complex interrelations inherent to disabling postcolonial environments. A fictionalization of the Bhopal industrial disaster of 1984, when toxic gas killed thousands of people as well as generating chronic illnesses, disabilities, and reproductive disorders in the years that followed, *Animal's People* broaches the relationship between environment, disability and the human in its protagonist's opening statement: "I used to be human once" (1). In the novel, "Animal," who has a twisted spine and moves on all fours, politicizes his socially inscribed dehumanization and is perceived as "especially abled" (23) due to his unique perspectives and skilled negotiation of his environment. Yet rather than focusing on the presence of disability, Pablo Mukherjee's analysis of the novel stresses the related concern that to Union Carbide— the multinational corporation implicated in Bhopal—the Indian "victims of gas were expendable because their poverty would

have doomed them to an early death anyway" (2010: 155).[4] Here, in a process Said would recognize only too well, the chain of events by which high-risk environments, poverty, and disability mutually produce and reinforce one another exemplifies the relationships of power that systematically devalue human lives. As a consequence, Sinha's novel, like Bhopal itself, invites a consideration of disability within the wider discourses of human rights where they intersect with sudden and violent environmental change.

CONCLUSION: REPRESENTATION, PARTICIPATION AND DEMOCRACY

Sinha's deliberately provocative construction of his protagonist using animalistic analogies points to another challenge generated by postcolonial disability writing: the need to diversify the terms of our formal analysis. The exposure, problematization, dismantling and deconstruction of oppressive representational practices—and metaphor in particular—remains an incredibly powerful tool within humanities-based disability research, but in thinking about metaphor, we agree with Amy Vidali's suggestions that criticism should "[refrain] from policing metaphor" and instead "[invite] creative and historic reinterpretations" (2010: 34) of figurative language. This process surely has to include the varying cultural inflections that attach meaning and resonance to impairment.

While disability is frequently used, problematically, as a metaphor for the "damaged" or abject postcolonial body politic, there are many semantic permutations to disability representation. Disability metaphors may be meaningful not just as "crutch[es]" (Mitchell and Snyder 2000: 49) in the telling of some "other" tale of postcolonial experience, but as part of foundational cultural and historical *disability* narratives; the depiction of scars in narrative accounts of slavery is just one conspicuous example of this. The situated reading practices we are proposing aim to highlight how particular disability experiences can shape cultural histories and are written into artistic and representational practices. Centrally, this involves consideration of what analogies might signify to the (disabled/postcolonial) community they represent and how they function within a particular literary form and cultural logic, rather than the wholesale dismissal of metaphor as damaging, ableist or stigmatizing. Ralph Savarese's (2010) identification of "postcolonial neurology" is provocative evidence of how creative cross-fertilizations between disability and postcolonial metaphors can service the most radical disability agendas. The idea of the "postcolonial brain," with its challenge to the assumptions that come with the terms *postcolonialism* or *neurology*, is, we feel, exactly the kind of productive criticism that can come when postcolonial and disability thinking are allowed to meet with an openness toward their possible interactions.

It is this sense of the radical and possible that draws us to Edward Said and ideas of democracy and "participatory citizenship." For Said, near the end of his own life and still pursuing the need for a radical engagement with culture, participation meant both the production of criticism and the possibility of democratic agency. "Critique," he wrote, "is always restlessly self-clarifying in search of freedom, enlightenment and more agency, and certainly not their opposites." Working within such terms, he observed, "means situating critique . . . as a form of democratic freedom and as a continuous practice of questioning and accumulating knowledge" (2004: 73, 74). Such statements, we feel, help us to understand that the knowledge we seek to bring to bear on thinking about postcolonial disability requires the scrutiny of such "continuous questioning" if it is to be of benefit. And they also remind us that, in the widest possible sense, "participation" allows for the formation of a full and inclusive idea of citizenship, one radical and yet everyday in its appreciation of the real value of disabled lives.

NOTES

1. For the most developed discussion of these intersections, see Barker 2011.
2. See, for example, Quayson 1997 and 2000.
3. For Smith, "research" is directly associated with "the worst excesses of colonialism" (1). Her notion of "decolonizing" research involves prioritizing the worldviews of research subjects and ensuring that the products of research—whether material, financial, social or epistemological—are communicated to, and used to benefit, the communities they represent.
4. In contrast, Michael Davidson's reading of Bhopal puts disability at the heart of the disaster when he wryly uses Union Carbide's motto, "Today, something we do will touch your life," as the epigraph to his chapter on disability and globalization (2008: 168).

WORKS CITED

Ashcroft, Bill and Pal Ahluwalia. *Edward Said*. London and New York: Routledge, 2000.

Barker, Clare. *Postcolonial Fiction and Disability: Exceptional Children, Metaphor and Materiality.* Basingstoke: Palgrave Macmillan, 2011.

Berger, James. "Trauma Without Disability, Disability Without Trauma: A Disciplinary Divide." *Journal of Advanced Composition* 24.3 (2004): 563–82.

Campbell, Fiona Kumari. *Contours of Ableism: The Production of Disability and Abledness.* Basingstoke: Palgrave Macmillan, 2009.

Carrigan, Anthony. "Postcolonial Disaster, Pacific Nuclearization, and Disabling Environments." *Journal of Literary & Cultural Disability Studies* 4.3 (2010): 255–72.

Davidson, Michael. *Concerto for the Left Hand: Disability and the Defamiliar Body.* Ann Arbor: U of Michigan P, 2008.

Devi, Mahasweta. "Shishu". Trans. Pinaki Bhattacharya. *Women Writing in India: 600 B.C. to the Present. Vol. 2: The Twentieth Century.* Ed. Susie Tharu and K. Lalita. New York: The Feminist Press, 1993. 236–51.

Dirlik, Arif. "Rethinking Colonialism: Globalization, Postcolonialism, and the Nation." *Interventions* 4.3 (2002): 428–48.

Durie, Mason. *Whaiora: Māori Health Development.* 1994. 2nd edn. Auckland: Oxford UP, 1998.

Garland-Thomson, Rosemarie. *Extraordinary Bodies: Figuring Physical Disability in American Culture and Literature.* New York: Columbia UP, 1997.

Lovern, Lavonna. "Native American Worldview and the Discourse on Disability." *Essays in Philosophy* 9.1 (2008): <http://commons.pacificu.edu/eip/vol9/iss1/14>.

McRuer, Robert. *Crip Theory: Cultural Signs of Queerness and Disability.* New York and London: New York UP, 2006.

——. "Reflections on Disability in Haiti." *Journal of Literary & Cultural Disability Studies* 4.3 (2010): 327–32.

Michalko, Rod. *The Two-In-One: Walking with Smokie, Walking with Blindness.* Philadelphia: Temple UP, 1999.

Mitchell, David T. and Sharon L. Snyder. *Narrative Prosthesis: Disability and the Dependencies of Discourse.* Ann Arbor: U of Michigan P, 2000.

Mukherjee, Upamanyu Pablo. *Postcolonial Environments: Nature, Culture and the Contemporary Indian Novel in English.* Basingstoke: Palgrave Macmillan, 2010.

Nepveux, Denise and Emily Smith Beitiks. "Producing African Disability Through African Film: *Emmanuel's Gift* and *Moja Moja*." *Journal of Literary & Cultural Disability Studies* 4.3 (2010): 237–54.

Nixon, Rob. "Environmentalism and Postcolonialism." *Postcolonial Studies and Beyond.* Ed. Ania Loomba, Suvir Kaul, Matti Bunzl, Antoinette Burton, and Jed Esty. Durham and London: Duke UP, 2005. 233–51.

Parekh, Pushpa Naidu (ed.). "Intersecting Gender and Disability Perspectives in Rethinking Postcolonial Identities." *Wagadu* 4 (2007).

Quayson, Ato. *Strategic Transformations in Nigerian Writing: Orality and History in the Works of Rev Samuel Johnson, Amos Tutuola, Wole Soyinka and Ben Okri.* Oxford/Bloomington: James Currey/Indiana UP, 1997.

——. *Postcolonialism: Theory, Practice or Process?* Cambridge: Polity, 2000.

——. *Aesthetic Nervousness: Disability and the Crisis of Representation.* New York: Columbia UP, 2007.

Said, Edward. *Humanism and Democratic Criticism.* London: Palgrave Macmillan, 2004.

——. "In the Shadow of the West." *Power, Politics and Culture: Interviews with Edward Said.* Ed. Gauri Viswanathan. London: Bloomsbury, 2005. 39–52.

Savarese, Ralph. "Toward a Postcolonial Neurology: Autism, Tito Mukhopadhyay, and a New Geopoetics of the Body." *Journal of Literary & Cultural Disability Studies* 4.3 (2010): 273–89.

Shakespeare, Tom. "Disability, Identity, Difference." *Exploring the Divide: Illness and Disability.* Ed. Colin Barnes and Geof Mercer. Leeds: Disability Press, 1996. 94–113.

Sherry, Mark. "(Post)colonizing Disability." *Wagadu* 4 (2007): 21–36.

Siebers, Tobin. *Disability Theory.* Ann Arbor: U of Michigan P, 2008.

Sinha, Indra. *Animal's People.* London: Simon & Schuster, 2007.

Smith, Linda Tuhiwai. *Decolonizing Methodologies: Research and Indigenous Peoples.* London and New York: Zed Books, 1999.

Snyder, Sharon L. and David T. Mitchell. *Cultural Locations of Disability.* Chicago and London: U of Chicago P, 2006.

Spivak, Gayatri Chakravorty. *A Critique of Postcolonial Reason: Toward a History of the Vanishing Present.* Cambridge, MA: Harvard UP, 1999.

Vidali, Amy. "Seeing What We Know: Disability and Theories of Metaphor." *Journal of Literary & Cultural Disability Studies* 4.1 (2010): 33–54.

Whyte, Susan Reynolds and Benedicte Ingstad. "Introduction: Disability Connections." *Disability in Local and Global Worlds.* Ed. Benedicte Ingstad and Susan Reynolds Whyte. Berkeley, CA: U of California P, 2007. 1–29.

CHAPTER 6

Abortion and Disability: Who Should and Should Not Inhabit the World?

Ruth Hubbard

Political agitation and education during the past few decades have made most people aware of what constitutes discrimination against blacks and other racial and ethnic minorities and against women. And legal and social measures have been enacted to begin to counter such discrimination. Where people with disabilities are concerned, our level of awareness is low, and the measures that exist are enforced haphazardly. Yet people with disabilities and disability-rights advocates have stressed again and again that it is often far easier to cope with the physical aspects of a disability than with the discrimination and oppression they encounter because of it (Asch, 1988; Asch and Fine, 1988). People shun persons who have disabilities and isolate them so they will not have to see them. They fear them as though the disability were contagious. And it is, in the sense that it forces us to face our own vulnerability.

Most of us would be horrified if a scientist offered to develop a test to diagnose skin color prenatally so as to enable racially mixed people (which means essentially everyone who is considered black and many of those considered white in the Americas) to have light-skinned children. And if the scientist explained that because it is difficult to grow up black in America, he or she wanted to spare people suffering because

of the color of their skin, we would counter that it is irresponsible to use scientific means to reinforce racial prejudices. Yet we see nothing wrong, and indeed hail as progress, tests that enable us to try to avoid having children who have disabilities or are said to have a tendency to acquire a specific disease or disability later in life.

The scientists and physicians who develop and implement these tests believe they are reducing human suffering. This justification seems more appropriate for speed limits, seat-belt laws, and laws to further occupational safety and health than for tests to avoid the existence of certain kinds of people. When it comes to women or to racial or ethnic groups, we insist that it is discriminatory to judge individuals on the basis of their group affiliation. But we lump people with disabilities as though all disabilities were the same and always devastating and as though all people who have one were alike.

Health and physical prowess are poor criteria of human worth. Many of us know people with a disease or disability whom we value highly and so-called healthy people whom we could readily do without. It is fortunate for human variety and variability that most of us are not called on to make such judgments, much less to implement them.

It is not new for people to view disability as a form of pollution, evidence of sin. Disability has been considered divine punishment or, alternatively, the result of witches' spells. In our scientific and medical era we look to heredity for explanations unless there is an obvious external cause, such as an accident or infectious disease. Nowadays, even if an infection can explain the disability, scientists have begun to suggest that our genes might have made us unusually susceptible to it.

In a sense, hereditary disabilities are contagious because they can be passed from one generation to the next. For this reason, well before there was a science of genetics, scientists proposed eugenic measures to stem the perpetuation of "defects."

THE RISE OF EUGENICS IN BRITAIN AND THE UNITED STATES

Eugenics met its apotheosis under the Nazis, which is why many Germans oppose genetic testing and gene therapy and their use is being hotly debated in the parliament. Germans tend to understand better than people in other countries what can happen when the concern that people with disabilities will become social and economic burdens or that they will lead to a deterioration of the race begins to dictate so-called preventive health policies. They are aware that scientists and physicians were the ones who developed the Nazi policies of "selection and eradication" (*Auslese und Ausmerze*) and who oversaw their execution. What happened under the Nazis has been largely misrepresented and misinterpreted in this country, as well as among Nazi apologists in Germany. To make what happened clearer, I shall briefly review the scientific underpinnings of the Nazi extermination program, which are obscured when these practices are treated as though they were incomprehensible aberrations without historical roots or meaning—a holocaust.

German eugenics, the attempt to improve the German race, or *Volk*, by ridding it of inferior and foreign elements, was based on arguments and policies developed largely in Great Britain and the United States during the latter part of the nineteenth and the beginning of the twentieth centuries. (In what follows I shall not translate the german word *Volk* because it has no English equivalent. The closest is "people," singular, used as a collective noun, as in "the German people *is* patriotic." But "people," singular, does not convey the collectivity of *Volk* because to us "people" means individuals. Therefore, we would ordinarily phrase my example, "the German people *are* patriotic.")

The term *eugenics* is derived from the Greek word for "well born." It was coined in 1883 by Francis Galton, cousin of Charles Darwin, as "a brief word to express the science of improving the stock, which is by no means confined to questions of judicious mating, but which, especially in the case of man [*sic*], takes cognizance of all the influences that tend in however remote a degree to give the more suitable races or strains of blood a better chance of prevailing speedily over the less suitable than they otherwise would have had" (pp. 24–25). Galton later helped found the English Eugenics Education Society and eventually became its honorary president.

British eugenics counted among its supporters many distinguished biologists and social scientists. Even as late as 1941, while the Nazis were implementing their eugenic extermination program, the distinguished biologist Julian Huxley (1941)—brother of Aldous—opened a semipopular article entitled "The Vital Importance of Eugenics" with the words: "Eugenics is running the usual course of many new ideas. It has ceased to be regarded as a fad, is now receiving serious study, and in the near future, will be regarded as an urgent practical problem." In the article, he argues that it is crucial for society "to ensure that mental defectives [*sic*] shall not have children" and defines as mentally defective "someone with such a feeble mind that he cannot support himself or look after himself unaided." (Notice the mix of eugenics and economics.) He says that he refuses to enter into the argument over whether such "racial degeneration" should be forestalled by "prohibition of marriage" or "segregation in institutions" combined with "sterilization for those who are at large." He states as fact that most "mental defects" are hereditary and suggests that it would therefore be better if one could "discover how to diagnose the carriers of the defect" who are "apparently normal." "If these could but be detected, and then discouraged *or prevented* from reproducing, mental defects could very speedily be reduced to negligible proportions among our population" (my emphasis). It is shocking that at a time when the Nazi program of eugenic sterilization and euthanasia was in full force across the Channel, Huxley expressed regret that it was "at the moment very difficult to envisage methods for putting even a limited constructive program [of eugenics] into effect" and complained that "that is due as much to difficulties in our present socioeconomic organization as to our ignorance of human heredity, and most of all to the absence of a eugenic sense in the public at large."

The American eugenics movement built on Galton and attained its greatest influence between 1905 and 1935. An underlying concern of the eugenicists is expressed in a statement by Lewis Terman (1924), one of the chief engineers of I.Q. testing: "The fecundity of the family stocks from which our most gifted children come appears to be definitely on the wane. . . . It has been figured that if the present differential birth rate continues 1,000 Harvard graduates will, at the end of 200 years, have but 56 descendants, while in the same period, 1,000

S. Italians will have multiplied to 100,000." To cope with this dire eventuality, eugenics programs had two prongs: "positive eugenics"—encouraging the "fit" (read "well-to-do") to have lots of children—and "negative eugenics"—preventing the "unfit" (defined to include people suffering from so-called insanity, epilepsy, alcoholism, pauperism, criminality, sexual perversion, drug abuse, and especially feeble-mindedness) from having any.

Many distinguished American geneticists supported eugenics, but none was more active in promoting it than Charles Davenport, who, after holding faculty appointments at Harvard and the University of Chicago, in 1904 became director of the "station for the experimental study of evolution," which he persuaded the Carnegie Institution of Washington to set up in Cold Spring Harbor on Long Island. His goal was to collect large amounts of data on human inheritance and store them in a central office. In 1910, he managed to persuade the heiress to the Harriman railroad fortune to fund the Eugenics Record Office at Cold Spring Harbor, for which he got additional money from John D. Rockefeller, Jr. He appointed Harry W. Laughlin, a Princeton Ph.D., as superintendent and recruited a staff of young graduates from Radcliffe, Vassar, Cornell, Harvard, and other elite institutions as fieldworkers to accumulate interview data about a large number of so-called mental and social defectives. The office and its staff became major resources for promoting the two legislative programs that formed the backbone of U.S. eugenics: involuntary-sterilization laws and the Immigration Restriction Act of 1924.

The first sterilization law was enacted in Indiana in 1907, and by 1931 some thirty states had compulsory-sterilization laws on their books. Aimed in general at the insane and "feeble-minded" (broadly interpreted to include many recent immigrants and other people who did badly on

I.Q. tests because they were functionally illiterate or barely spoke English), these laws often extended to so-called sexual perverts, drug fiends, drunkards, epileptics, and "other diseased and degenerate persons" (Ludmerer, 1972). Although most of these laws were not enforced, by January 1935 some twenty thousand people in the United States had been forcibly sterilized, nearly half of them in California. Indeed, the California law was not repealed until 1980 and eugenic-sterilization laws are still on the books in about twenty states.

The eugenic intent of the Immigration Restriction Act of 1924 was equally explicit. It was designed to decrease the proportion of poor immigrants from southern and eastern Europe so as to give predominance to Americans of British and north European descent. This goal was accomplished by restricting the number of immigrants allowed into the United States from any one country in each calendar year to at most 2 percent of U.S. residents who had been born in that country as listed in the Census of 1890 (so, thirty-four years earlier). The date 1890 was chosen because it established as a baseline the ethnic composition of the U.S. population prior to the major immigrations from eastern and southern Europe, which began in the 1890s. Laughlin of the Eugenics Record Office was one of the most important lobbyists and witnesses at the Congressional hearings that preceded passage of the Immigration Restriction Act and was appointed "expert eugenical agent" of the House Committee on Immigration and Naturalization (Kevles, 1985).

RACIAL HYGIENE IN GERMANY

What was called eugenics in the United States and Britain came to be known as racial hygiene in Germany. It was the response to several related and widely held beliefs: (1) that humane care for people with disabilities would enfeeble the "race" because they would survive to pass their disabilities on to their children; (2) that not just mental and physical diseases and so-called defects, but also poverty, criminality, alcoholism, prostitution, and other social problems were based in biology and inherited; and (3) that genetically inferior people were reproducing faster than superior people and would eventually displace them. Although these beliefs were not based in fact, they fueled racist thinking and social programs in Britain and the United States as well as in Germany.

German racial hygiene was founded in 1895, some dozen years after Galton's eugenics, by a physician, Alfred Plötz, and was based on much the same analysis of social problems as the British and American eugenics movements were. In 1924, Plötz started the *Archive of Race- and Socio-biology (Archiv für Rassen- und Gesellschaftsbiologie)* and the next year helped found the Society for Racial Hygiene (Gesellschaft für Rassenhygiene). German racial hygiene initially did not concern itself with preventing the admixture of "inferior" races, such as Jews or gypsies, in contrast to the British and American movements where miscegenation with blacks, Asians, Native Americans, and immigrants of almost any sort was one of the major concerns. The recommended means for preventing racial degeneration in Germany, as elsewhere, was sterilization. Around 1930 even some German socialists and communists supported the eugenic sterilization of inmates of psychiatric institutions, although the main impetus came from the Nazis. The active melding of anti-Semitism and racial hygiene in Germany began during World War I and accelerated during the 1920s, partly in response to economic pressures and a scarcity of available positions, which resulted in severe competition for jobs and incomes among scientists and physicians, many of whom were Jews.

Racial hygiene was established as an academic discipline in 1923, when Fritz Lenz, a physician and geneticist, was appointed to the newly created Chair of Racial Hygiene at the University of Munich, a position he kept until 1933, when he moved to the Chair of Racial Hygiene at the University of Berlin. Lenz, Eugen Fischer, and Erwin Baer coauthored the most important textbook on genetics and racial hygiene in German. Published in 1921, it was hailed in a review in the *American Journal of Heredity* in 1928 as "the standard textbook of human genetics" in the world (quoted in Proctor, 1988, p. 58). In 1931, it was translated into English, and the translation was favorably reviewed in Britain and the United States despite its blatant racism, or perhaps because of it. By 1933, eugenics and racial hygiene were being taught in most medical schools in Germany.

Therefore the academic infrastructure was in place when the Nazis came to power and began to build a society that gave biologists, anthropologists, and physicians the opportunity to put their racist and eugenic theories into practice. Looking back on this period, Eugen Fischer, who directed the Kaiser Wilhelm Institute for Anthropology, Human Genetics, and Eugenics in Berlin from 1927 to 1942, wrote in a newspaper article in 1943: "It is special and rare good luck when research of an intrinsically theoretical nature falls into a time when the general world view appreciates and welcomes it and, what is more, when its practical results are immediately accepted as the basis for governmental procedures" (quoted in Müller-Hill, 1984, p. 64; my translation). It is not true, as has sometimes been claimed, that German scientists were perverted by Nazi racism. Robert Proctor (1988) points out that "it was largely medical scientists who *invented* racial hygiene in the first place" (p. 38; original emphasis).

A eugenic-sterilization law, drafted along the lines of a "Model Sterilization Law" published by Laughlin (the superintendent of Davenport's Eugenics Record Office at Cold Spring Harbor), was being considered in 1932 by the Weimar government. On July 14, 1933, barely six months after Hitler took over, the Nazi government passed its eugenic-sterilization law. This law established genetic health courts (*Erbgesundheitsgerichte*), presided over by a lawyer and two physicians, one of whom was to be an expert on "hereditary pathology" (*Erbpathologie*), whose rulings could be appealed to similarly constituted supreme genetic health courts. However, during the entire Nazi period only about 3 percent of lower-court decisions were reversed. The genetic health courts could order the sterilization of people on grounds that they had a "genetically determined" disease, such as "inborn feeble-mindedness, schizophrenia, manic-depressive insanity, hereditary epilepsy, Huntington's disease, hereditary blindness, hereditary deafness, severe physical malformations, and severe alcoholism" (Müller-Hill, 1984, p. 32; my translation). The law was probably written by Dr. Ernst Rüdin, professor of psychiatry and director of the Kaiser Wilhelm Institute for Genealogy and Demography of the German Research Institute for Psychiatry in Munich. The official commentary and interpretation of the law was published under his name and those of an official of the Ministry of the Interior, also a medical doctor, and of a representative of the Health Ministry in the Department of the Interior who was a doctor of laws. All practicing physicians were sent copies of the law and commentaries describing the acceptable procedures for sterilization and castration.

The intent of the law was eugenic, not punitive. Physicians were expected to report patients and their close relatives to the nearest local health court and were fined if they failed to report someone with a so-called hereditary disease. Although some physicians raised the objection that this requirement invaded the doctor-patient relationship, the health authorities argued that this obligation to notify then was no different from requirements that physicians report the incidence of specific infectious diseases or births and deaths. The eugenic measures were to be regarded as health measures pure and simple. And this is the crucial point: the people who designed these policies and the later policies of euthanasia and mass extermination as well as those who oversaw their execution looked on them as sanitary measures, required in this case to cure not individual patients but the collective—the *Volk*—of threats to its health (Lifton, 1987; Proctor, 1988).

As early as 1934, Professor Otmar von Verschuer, then dean of the University of Frankfurt and director of its Institute for Genetics and Racial Hygiene and later the successor of Fischer as director of the Kaiser Wilhelm Institute for Anthropology, Human Genetics, and Eugenics in Berlin, urged that patients should not be looked on, and treated, as individuals. Rather the patient is but "one part of a much larger whole or unity: of his family, his race, his *Volk*" (quoted in Proctor, 1988, p. 105). Minister of the Interior Wilhelm Frisch estimated that at least half a million Germans had genetic diseases, but some experts thought that the true figure was more like one in five, which would be equivalent to thirteen million. In any event, by 1939 some three to four hundred thousand people had been sterilized, with a mortality of about 0.5 percent (Proctor, 1988, pp. 108–109). After that there were few individual sterilizations. Later, large numbers of people were sterilized in the concentration camps, but that was done without benefit of health courts, as part of the program of human experimentation.

The eugenic-sterilization law of 1933 did not provide for sterilization on racial grounds. Nonetheless, in 1937 about five hundred racially mixed children were sterilized; the children had been fathered by black French colonial troops brought to Europe from Africa after World War I to occupy the Rhineland (the so-called Rheinlandbastarde).

The first racist eugenic measures were passed in 1935. They were the Nürnberg antimiscegenation, or blood-protection laws, which forbade intermarriage or sexual relations between Jews and non-Jews and forbade Jews from employing non-Jews in their homes. The Nürnberg laws also included a "Law for the Protection of the Genetic Health of the German People," which required premarital medical examinations to detect "racial damage" and required people who were judged "damaged" to marry only others like themselves, provided they first submitted to sterilization. The Nürnberg laws were considered health laws, and physicians were enlisted to enforce them. So-called positive eugenics was practiced by encouraging "genetically healthy" German women to have as many children as possible. They were persuaded to do so by means of propaganda, economic incentives, breeding camps, and strict enforcement of the law forbidding abortion except for eugenic reasons (Koonz, 1987).

The next stage in the campaign of "selection and eradication" was opened at the Nazi party congress in 1935, where plans were made for the "destruction of lives not worth living." The phrase was borrowed from the title of a book published much earlier, in 1920, by Alfred Hoche, professor of psychiatry and director of the Psychiatric Clinic at Freiburg, and Rudolf Binding, professor of jurisprudence at the University of Leipzig. In their book, entitled *The Release for Destruction of Lives Not Worth Living (Die Freigabe zur Vernichtung lebensunwerten Lebens)*, these professors argued for killing "worthless" people, whom they defined as those who are "mentally completely dead" and those who constitute "a foreign body in human society" (quoted in Chorover, 1979, p. 97). At the time the program was initiated, the arguments focused on the money wasted in keeping institutionalized (hence "worthless") people alive, for in the early stages the rationale of the euthanasia campaign was economic as much as eugenic. Therefore the extermination campaign was directed primarily at inmates of state psychiatric hospitals and children living in state institutions for the mentally and physically disabled. Jews were specifically excluded because they were not considered worthy of euthanasia. (Here, too, the Nazis were not alone. In 1942, as the last inmates of German mental hospitals were being finished off, Dr. Foster Kennedy, an American psychiatrist writing in the official publication of the American Psychiatric Association, advocated killing mentally retarded children of five and older (Proctor, 1988). The arguments were phrased in humane terms like these: "Parents who have seen the difficult life of a crippled or feebleminded child must be convinced that though they have the moral obligation to care for the unfortunate creatures, the wider public should not be obliged . . . to assume the enormous costs that long-term institutionalization might entail" (quoted in Proctor, 1988, p. 183). This argument calls to mind the statement by Bentley Glass (1971) about parents not having "a right to burden society with a malformed or a mentally incompetent child."

In Germany, the propaganda was subtle and widespread. For example, Proctor (1988, p. 184) cites practice problems in a high school mathematics text published for the school year 1935–36, in which students were asked to calculate the costs to the Reich of maintaining mentally ill people in various kinds of institutions for different lengths of time and to compare the costs of constructing insane asylums and housing units. How is that for relevance?

Although the euthanasia program was planned in the mid-1930s, it was not implemented until 1939, when wartime dislocation and secrecy made it relatively easy to institute such extreme measures. Two weeks before the invasion of Poland an advisory committee commissioned by Hitler issued a secret report recommending that children born with Down syndrome, microcephaly, and various deformities be registered with the Ministry of the Interior. Euthanasia, like sterilization, was to proceed with the trappings of selection. Therefore physicians were asked to fill out questionnaires about all children in their care up to age three who had any of these kinds of disabilities. The completed questionnaires were sent to three-man committees of medical experts charged with marking each form "plus" or "minus." Although none of these "experts" ever saw the children, those whose forms were marked "plus" were transferred to one of a number of institutions where they were killed. Some of the oldest and most respected hospitals in Germany served as such extermination centers. By 1941 the program was expanded to include older children with disabilities and by 1943, to include healthy Jewish children. Also in 1939, evaluation forms were sent to psychiatric institutions for adults for selection and so-called euthanasia.

By September 1941 over seventy thousand inmates had been killed at some of the most distinguished psychiatric hospitals in Germany, which had been equipped for this purpose with gas chambers, disguised as showers, and with crematoria (Lifton, 1986; Proctor, 1988). (When the mass extermination of Jews and other "undesirables" began shortly thereafter, these gas chambers were shipped east and installed at Auschwitz and other extermination camps.) Most patients were gassed or killed by injection with legal drugs, but a few physicians were reluctant to intervene so actively and let children die of slow starvation and the infectious diseases to which they became susceptible, referring to this as death from "natural" causes. Relatives were notified that their family member had died suddenly of one of a number of infectious diseases and that the body had been cremated for reasons of public health. Nevertheless, rumors began to circulate, and by 1941 hospital killings virtually ceased because of protests, especially from the Church.

There is a direct link between this campaign of "selection and eradication" and the subsequent genocide of Jews, gypsies, communists, homosexuals, and other "undesirables." Early on these people were described as "diseased" and their presence, as an infection or a cancer in the body of the *Volk*. Proctor (1988, p. 194) calls this rationalization "the medicalization of antisemitism." The point is that the Nazi leaders shouted anti-Semitic and racist propaganda from their platforms, but when it came to devising the measures for ridding the Thousand Year Reich of Jews, gypsies, and the other undesirables, the task was shouldered by the scientists and physicians who had earlier devised the sterilization and euthanasia programs for the mentally or physically disabled. Therefore, nothing came easier than a medical metaphor: Jews as cancer, Jews as disease. And so the Nazi extermination program was viewed by its perpetrators as a gigantic program in sanitation and public health. It started with quarantining the offending organisms in ghettoes and concentration camps and ended with the extermination of those who did not succumb to the "natural" consequences of the quarantine, such as the various epidemics and hunger.

Yet a measure of selection was practiced throughout the eradication process: It was still *Auslese* as well as *Ausmerze*. At every step choices were made of who could still be used and who had become "worthless." We have read the books and seen the films that show selections being made as the cattle cars emptied the victims into the concentration camps: to work or to die? That is where Joseph Mengele, an M.D./Ph.D., selected the twins and other unfortunates to use as subjects for his scientific experiments at Auschwitz, performed in collaboration with Professor von Verschuer, at that time director of the Kaiser Wilhelm Institute for Anthropology, Human Genetics, and Eugenics in Berlin. And von Verschuer was not the only distinguished scientist who gratefully accepted the human tissues and body fluids provided by Mengele. After the war it became fashionable to characterize the experiments as "bad science," but as Beno Müller-Hill (1984) emphasizes, nothing about them would be considered "bad" were they done with mice. What was "bad" was not their scientific content but the fact that they were being done with "disenfranchised human beings" (p. 97).

PRENATAL TESTING: WHO SHOULD INHABIT THE WORLD?

I want to come back to the present, but I needed to go over this history in order to put my misgivings and those of some of the Germans who are opposing genetic testing into the proper perspective. I can phrase the problem best by rephrasing a question Hannah Arendt asks in the epilogue of her commentary on the trial of Adolf Eichmann. Who has the "right to determine who should and who should not inhabit the world?" (1977). That's what it comes down to.

So let me be clear: I am not suggesting that prenatal diagnosis followed by abortion is similar to euthanasia. Fetuses are not people. And a woman must have the right to terminate her pregnancy, whatever her reasons. I am also not drawing an analogy between what the Nazis did and what we and others in many of the industrialized countries are doing now. Because the circumstances are different, different things are being done and for different reasons. But a similar eugenic ideology underlies what happened then and the techniques now being developed. So it is important that we understand how what happened then came about—and not in some faraway culture that is altogether different from ours but in the heart of Europe, in a country that has produced artists, writers, composers, philosophers, jurists, scientists, and physicians the equal of any in the Western world. Given that record, we cannot afford to be complacent.

Scientists and physicians in this and other countries are once more engaged in developing the means to decide what lives are worth living and who should and should not inhabit the world. Except that now they provide only the tools, while pregnant women themselves have to make the decisions, euphemistically called choices. No one is forced to do anything. A pregnant woman must merely "choose" whether to terminate a wanted pregnancy because she has been informed that her future child will have a disability (although, as I have said before, usually no one can tell her how severe the disability will be). If she "chooses" not to take the tests or not to terminate a pregnancy despite a positive result, she accepts responsibility for whatever the disability will mean to that child and to her and the rest of her family. In that case, her child, her family, and the rest of society can reproach her for having so-to-speak "caused" that human being's physical pain as well as the social pain he or she experiences because our society does not look kindly on people with disabilities.

There is something terribly wrong with this situation, and although it differs in many ways from what went wrong in Germany, at base are similar principles of selection and eradication. Lest this analogy seem too abstract, let me give a few examples of how the principle of selection and eradication now works in practice.

Think of people who have Huntington's disease; as you may remember they were on the list of people to be sterilized in Germany. Huntington's disease is a degenerative disease of the nervous system and is unusual among hereditary diseases in that it is inherited as what geneticists call a dominant trait. In other words, even people in whom only one of the pair of genes that is involved with regulating the relevant metabolic processes is affected manifest the disease. Most other gene-mediated diseases, such as Tay-Sachs disease or sickle-cell anemia, are so-called recessives: Only people in whom both members of the relevant pair of genes are affected manifest the disease. In the case of recessive diseases, people with only one affected gene are called carriers: They do not have the disease and usually do not even know that they carry a gene for it. To inherit a recessive disease such as sickle-cell anemia, a child must get an affected gene from each of its parents; to inherit a dominant disease, such as Huntington's disease, it is enough is she or he gets an affected gene from either parent.

The symptoms of Huntington's disease usually do not appear until people are in their thirties, forties, or fifties—in other words, after most people who want to have children have already had one or more. Woody Guthrie had Huntington's disease, but he did not become ill until after he had lived a varied and productive life, produced a large legacy of songs, and fathered his children. At present, there is no cure for Huntington's disease, although scientists have been working to find one. However, a test has been developed that makes it possible to establish with fair reliability whether a person or fetus carries the gene for Huntington's disease, provided a sufficient number of people in that family is willing to be tested.

The existence of this test puts people with a family history of Huntington's disease in an outrageous position: Although they themselves are healthy and do not know whether they will get the disease, they must decide whether to be tested, whether to persuade as many of their relatives as possible to do the same, and whether to test their future child prenatally so they can terminate the pregnancy if the test reveals that the fetus has the gene for Huntington's disease. If it does and they decide on abortion, they are as much as saying that a life lived in the knowledge that one will eventually die of Huntington's disease is not worth living. What does that say about their own life and the lives of their family members who now know that they have the gene for Huntington's disease? If the fetus has the gene and they do not abort, they are knowingly wishing a cruel, degenerative disease on their future child. And if they refuse the test, they can be accused of sticking their heads in the sand. This is an obscene "choice" for anyone to have to make!

Some other inherited diseases also do not become evident until later in life, such as retinitis pigmentosa, a degenerative eye disease. People with this disease are born with normal vision, but their eyesight deteriorates, although usually not until midlife, and they may eventually lose their sight. (People with this disease presumably also were slated for sterilization by the Nazis because it is a form of "hereditary blindness.") There are different patterns of inheritance of retinitis pigmentosa, and prenatal diagnosis is becoming available for one of these patterns and being sought for others. What are prospective parents to do when confronted with the "choice" of aborting a pregnancy because their future child may become blind at some time during its life?

Another, rather different, problem arises with regard to the so-called neural-tube defects (NTDs), a group of developmental disorders which, in fact, are not inherited. They include anencephaly (failure to develop a brain) and spina bifida (failure of the spinal column, and sometimes also the overlying tissues, to close properly) Babies with anencephaly die before birth or shortly thereafter. The severity of the health problems of children who have spina bifida depends on where along the spinal column the defect is located and can vary from life-threatening to relatively mild. The incidence of NTDs varies geographically and tends to be higher in industrialized than in nonindustrialized areas. Women who carry a fetus with a neural-tube defect have a grater than usual concentration of a specific substance, called alpha-fetoprotein, in their blood. A blood test has been developed to detect NTDs prenatally, and California now requires that all pregnant women in the state be offered this test. The women are first counseled about NTDs and about the test and then have to sign a consent or refusal form. If they refuse, that is the end of it. If they consent, they can later refuse to abort the fetus even if the test is positive. This procedure sounds relatively unproblematical, although the requirement to sign a refusal form is coercive. (You cannot walk away; you must say no.) The trouble is that although the test detects virtually all fetuses who have NTDs, it yields a large number of false positive results that suggest that the fetus has a NTD although it does not.

Let us look at some numbers. In California there are about two hundred thousand births a year and the incidence of NTDs is about one per thousand. So, about 200 pregnant women a year carry fetuses with NTDs and 199,800 do not. However, about 5 percent of women test positive on a first test. In other words, if all pregnant women agreed to be tested, 10,000 women would have a positive test, 9,800 of which would be false positives. Those 10,000 women would then have to undergo the stress of worrying as well as further tests in order to determine who among them is in fact carrying a fetus with a NTD. And no test will tell the 200 women whose fetus, in fact, has a NTD how severe their child's health problem will be. All this testing with uncertain results must be offered at this time, when health dollars in California, as elsewhere, have been cut to the bone, and increasing numbers of pregnant women are coming to term with little or no prenatal services of any sort.

The reason I have spelled this problem out in such detail is to make it clear that in many of these situations parents have only the most tenuous basis for making their decisions. Because of the fear of raising a child with a serious disability, many women "choose" to abort a wanted pregnancy if they are told that there is any likelihood whatever that their future child may have a health problem. At times like that we seem to forget that we live in a society in which every day people of all ages are disabled by accidents—at work, on the street, or at home—many of which could be prevented if the necessary money were spent, the necessary precautions taken. What is more, because of the deteriorating economic conditions of poor people and especially women, increasing numbers of babies are born with disabilities that could easily be prevented and are prevented in most other industrialized nations. I question our excessive preoccupation with inherited diseases while callousness and economic mismanagement disable and kill increasing numbers of children and adults.

To say again, I am not arguing against a woman's right to abortion. Women must have that right because it involves a decision about our bodies and about the way we will spend the rest of our lives. But for scientists to argue that they are developing these tests out of concern for the "quality of life" of future children is like the arguments about "lives not worth living." No one can make that kind of decision about someone else. No one these days openly suggests that certain kinds of people be killed; they just should not be born. Yet that involves a process of selection and a decision about what kinds of people should and should not inhabit the world.

German women, who know the history of Nazi eugenics and how genetic counseling centers functioned during the Nazi period, have organized against the new genetic and reproductive technologies (Duelli Klein, Corea, and Hubbard, 1985). They are suspicious of prenatal testing and counseling centers because some of the scientists and physicians working in them are the same people who designed and implemented the eugenics program during the Nazi period. Others are former co-workers or students of these Nazi professors.

Our history is different, but not different enough. Eugenic thinking is part of our heritage and so are eugenic sterilizations. Here they were not carried over to mass exterminations because we live in a democracy with constitutional safeguards. But, as I mentioned before, even in recent times black, Hispanic, and Native-American women have been sterilized against their wills (Rodriguez-Trias, 1982). We do not exalt the body of the people, as a collective, over that of individuals, but we come dangerously close to doing so when we question the "right" of parents to bear a child who has a disability or when we draw unfavorable comparisons between the costs of care for children with disabilities and the costs of prenatal diagnosis and abortion. We come mighty close when we once again let scientists and physicians make judgments about who should and who should not inhabit the world and applaud them when they develop the technologies that let us implement such judgments. Is it in our interest to have to decide not just whether we want to bear a child but what kind of children to bear? If we try to do that we become entirely dependent on the decisions scientists and physicians make about what technologies to develop and what disabilities to "target." Those decisions are usually made on grounds of professional interest, technical feasibility, and economic and eugenic considerations, not out of a regard for the needs of women and children.

PROBLEMS WITH SELECTIVE ABORTION

I want to be explicit about how I think a woman's right to abortion fits into this analysis and about some of the connections I see between what the Nazis did and what is happening now. I repeat: A woman must have the right to abort a fetus, whatever her reasons, precisely because it is a decision about her body and about how she will live her life. But decisions about what kind of baby to bear inevitably are bedeviled by overt and unspoken judgments about which lives are "worth living."

Nazi eugenic practices were fairly coercive. The state decided who should not inhabit the world, and lawyers, physicians, and scientists provided the justifications and means to implement these decisions. In today's liberal democracies the situation is different. Eugenic principles are part of our largely unexamined and unspoken preconceptions about who should and who should not inhabit the world, and scientists and physicians provide the ways to put them into practice. Women are expected to implement the society's eugenic prejudices by "choosing" to have the appropriate tests and "electing" not to initiate or to terminate pregnancies if it looks as though the outcome will offend. And to a considerable extent not initiating or terminating these pregnancies may indeed be what women want to do. But one reason we want to is that society promises much grief to parents of children it deems unfit to inhabit the world. People with disabilities, like the rest of us, need opportunities to act in the world, and sometimes that means that they need special provisions and consideration.

So once more, yes, a woman must have the right to terminate a pregnancy, whatever her reasons, but she must also feel empowered not to terminate it, confident that the society will do what it can to enable here and her child to live fulfilling lives. To the extent that prenatal interventions implement social prejudices against people with disabilities they do not expand our reproductive rights. They constrict them.

Focusing the discussion on individualistic questions, such as every woman's right to bear healthy children (which in some people's minds quickly translates into her duty not to "burden society" with unhealthy ones) or the responsibility of scientists and physicians to develop techniques to make that possible, obscures crucial questions such as: How many women have economic access to these kinds of choices? How many have the educational and cultural background to evaluate the information they can get from physicians critically enough to make an informed choice? It also obscures questions about a humane society's responsibilities to satisfy the requirements of people with special needs and to offer them the opportunity to participate as full-fledged members in the culture.

Our present situation connects with the Nazi past in that once again scientists and physicians are making the decisions about what lives to "target" as not worth living by deciding which tests to develop. Yet if people are to have real choices, the decisions that determine the context within which we must choose must not be made in our absence—by professionals, research review panels, or funding organizations. And the situation is not improved by inserting a new group of professionals—bioethicists—between the technical professionals and the public. This public—the women and men who must live in the world that the scientific/medical/industrial complex constructs—must be able to take part in the process by which such decisions are made. Until mechanisms exist that give people a decisive voice in setting the relevant scientific and technical agendas and until scientists and physicians are made accountable to the people whose lives they change, technical innovations do not constitute new choices. They merely replace previous social constraints with new ones.

WORKS CITED

Arendt, Hannah. 1977. *Eichmann in Jerusalem: A Report on the Banality of Evil.* New York: Penguin.

Asch, Adrienne. 1988. "Reproductive Technology and Disability." In Sherrill Cohen and Nadine Taub, eds., *Reproductive Laws for the 1990s.* Clifton, N.J.: Humana Press.

Asch, Adrienne, and Michelle Fine. 1988. "Introduction: Beyond Pedestals." In Michelle Fine and Adrienne Asch, eds., *Women with Disabilities.* Philadelphia: Temple University Press.

Chrorover, Stephan L. 1979. *From Genesis to Genocide.* Cambridge, Mass.: MIT Press.

Duelli Klein, Renate, Gena Corea, and Ruth Hubbard. 1985. "German Women say No to Gene and Reproductive Technology: Reflections on a Conference in Bonn, West Germany, April 19–21, 1985." *Feminist Forum: Women's Studies International Forum* 9(3): I–IV.

Galton, Francis. 1883. *Inquiries into Human Faculty.* London: Macmillan.

Glass, Bentley. 1971. "Science: Endless Horizons or Golden Age?" *Science* 171: 23–29.

Kevles, Daniel J. 1985. *In the Name of Eugenics: Genetics and the Uses of Human Heredity.* New York: Knopf.

Koonz, Claudia. 1987. *Mothers in the Fatherland: Women, the Family and Nazi Politics.* New York: St. Martin's Press.

Lifton, Robert J. 1986. *The Nazi Doctors.* New York: Basic Books.

Ludmerer, Kenneth M. 1972. *Genetics and American Society.* Baltimore: Johns Hopkins University Press.

Müller-Hill, Benno. 1984. *Tödliche Wissenshaft.* Reinbek, West Germany: Rowohlt. (Translation 1988. *Murderous Science.* Oxford: Oxford University Press.)

Proctor, Robert N. 1988. *Racial Hygiene: Medicine and the Nazis.* Cambridge, Mass.: Harvard University Press.

Rodriguez-Trias, Helen. 1982. *In Labor: Women and Power in the Birthplace.* New York: Norton.

Terman, Lewis M. 1924. "The Conservation of Talent." *School and Society* 19(483): 359–364.

CHAPTER 7

Disability Rights and Selective Abortion

Marsha Saxton

Disability rights activists are now articulating a critical view of the widespread practice of prenatal diagnosis with the intent to abort if the pregnancy might result in a child with a disability. Underlying this critique are historical factors behind a growing activism in the United States, Germany, Great Britain, and many other countries, an activism that confronts the social stigmatization of people with disabilities.

For disabled persons, women's consciousness-raising groups in the 1960s and 1970s offered a model for connecting with others in an "invisible" oppressed social group and confirming the experience of pervasive social oppression. ("That happened to you, too?") Participants in such groups began to challenge a basic tenet of disability oppression: that disability *causes* the low socioeconomic status of disabled persons. Collective consciousness-raising has made it clear that stigma is the cause.

Effective medical and rehabilitation resources since the 1950s have also contributed to activism. Antibiotics and improved surgical techniques have helped to alleviate previously fatal conditions. Consequently, disabled people are living longer and healthier lives, and the population of people with severely disabling conditions has increased. Motorized wheelchairs, lift-equipped wheelchair vans, mobile respirators, and computer and communication technologies have increased the mobility and access to education and employment for people previously ostracized because of their disabilities.

Effective community organizing by blind, deaf, and mobility-impaired citizen groups and disabled student groups flourished in the late 1960s and resulted in new legislation. In 1973 the Rehabilitation Act Amendments (Section 504) prohibited discrimination in federally funded programs. The Americans with Disabilities Act of 1990 (ADA) provides substantial civil rights protection and has helped bring about a profound change in the collective self-image of an estimated 45 million Americans. Today, many disabled people view themselves as part of a distinct minority and reject the pervasive stereotypes of disabled people as defective, burdensome, and unattractive.

It is ironic that just when disabled citizens have achieved so much, the new reproductive and genetic technologies are promising to eliminate births of disabled children—children with Down's syndrome, spina bifida, muscular dystrophy, sickle cell anemia, and hundreds of other conditions. The American public has apparently accepted these screening technologies based on the "commonsense" assumptions that prenatal screening and selective abortion can potentially reduce the incidence of disease and disability and thus improve the quality of life. A deeper look into the medical system's views of disability and the broader social factors contributing to disability discrimination challenges these assumptions.

REPRODUCTIVE RIGHTS IN A DISABILITY CONTEXT

There is a key difference between the goals of the reproductive rights movement and the disability rights movement regarding reproductive freedom: the reproductive rights movement emphasizes the right to have an abortion; the disability rights movement, the right *not to have to have* an abortion. Disability rights advocates believe that disabled women have the right to bear children and be mothers, and that all women have the right to resist pressure to abort when the fetus is identified as potentially having a disability.

Women with disabilities raised these issues at a conference on new reproductive technologies (NRTs) in Vancouver in 1994.[1] For many of the conference participants, we were an unsettling group: women in wheelchairs; blind women with guide dogs; deaf women who required a sign-language interpreter; women with scarring from burns or facial anomalies; women with missing limbs, crutches, or canes. I noticed there what we often experience from people who first encounter us: averted eyes or stolen glances, pinched smiles, awkward or overeager helpfulness—in other words, discomfort accompanied by the struggle to pretend there was none.

It was clear to me that this situation was constraining communication, and I decided to do something about it. I approached several of the nondisabled women, asking them how they felt about meeting such a diverse group of disabled women. Many of the women were honest when invited to be:

"I'm nervous. Am I going to say something offensive?" "I feel pretty awkward. Some of these women's bodies are so different!" One woman, herself disabled, said that she'd had a nightmare image of a disabled woman's very different body. One woman confessed: "I feel terrible for some of these unfortunate disabled women, but I know I'm not supposed to feel pity. That's awful of me, right?"

This awkwardness reveals how isolated the broader society and even progressive feminists are from people with disabilities. The dangerous void of information about disability is the *context* in which the public's attitudes about prenatal diagnosis and selective abortion are formed. In the United States this information void has yielded a number of unexamined assumptions, including the belief that the quality and enjoyment of life for disabled people is necessarily inferior, that raising a child with a disability is a wholly undesirable experience, that selective abortion will save mothers from the burdens of raising disabled children, and that ultimately we as a society have the means and the right to decide who is better off not being born.

What the women with disabilities were trying to do at the Vancouver conference, and what I wish to do in this essay, is explain how selective abortion or *eugenic abortion*, as some disability activists have called it, not only oppresses people with disabilities but also hurts all women.

EUGENICS AND THE BIRTH CONTROL MOVEMENT

The eugenic interest that stimulates reliance on prenatal screening and selective abortion today has had a central place in reproductive politics for more than half a century. In the nineteenth century, eugenicists believed that most traits, including such human "failings" as pauperism, alcoholism, and thievery, as well as such desired traits as intelligence, musical ability, and "good character," were hereditary. They sought to perfect the human race through controlled procreation, encouraging those from "healthy stock" to mate and discouraging reproduction of those eugenicists defined as socially "unfit," that is, with undesirable traits. Through a series of laws and court decisions American eugenicists mandated a program of social engineering. The most famous of these was the 1927 U.S. Supreme Court ruling in *Buck v. Bell*.[2]

Leaders in the early birth control movement in the United States, including Margaret Sanger, generally embraced a eugenic view, encouraging white Anglo-Saxon women to reproduce while discouraging reproduction among nonwhite, immigrant, and disabled people. Proponents of eugenics portrayed disabled women in particular as unfit for procreation and as incompetent mothers. In the 1920s Margaret Sanger's group, the American Birth Control League, allied itself with the director of the American Eugenics Society, Guy Irving Burch. The resulting coalition supported the forced sterilization of people with epilepsy, as well as those diagnosed as mentally retarded and mentally ill. By 1937, in the midst of the Great Depression, twenty-eight states had adopted eugenics sterilization laws aimed primarily at women for whom "procreation was deemed inadvisable." These laws sanctioned the sterilizations of over 200,000 women between the 1930s and the 1970s.[3]

While today's feminists are not responsible for the eugenic biases of their foremothers, some of these prejudices have persisted or gone unchallenged in the reproductive rights movement today.[4] Consequently, many women with disabilities feel alienated from this movement. On the other hand, some pro-choice feminists have felt so deeply alienated from the disability community that they have been willing to claim, "The right wing wants to force us to have defective babies."[5] Clearly, there is work to be done.

DISABILITY-POSITIVE IDENTITY VERSUS SELECTIVE ABORTION

It is clear that some medical professionals and public health officials are promoting prenatal diagnosis and abortion with the intention of eliminating categories of disabled people, people with Down's syndrome and my own disability, spina bifida, for example. For this reason and others, many disability activists and feminists regard selective abortion as "the new eugenics." These people resist the use of prenatal diagnosis and selective abortion.

The resistance to selective abortion in the disability activist community is ultimately related to how we define ourselves. As feminists have transformed women's sense of self, the disability community has reframed the experience of having a disability. In part, through developing a sense of community, we've come to realize that the stereotyped notions of the "tragedy" and "suffering" of "the disabled" result from the *isolation* of disabled people in society. Disabled people with no connections to others with disabilities in their communities are, indeed, afflicted with the social role assignment of a tragic, burdensome existence. It is true, most disabled people I know have told me with certainty, that the disability, the pain, the need for compensatory devices and assistance can produce considerable inconvenience. But the inconvenience becomes minimal once the disabled person makes the transition to a typical everyday life. It is discriminatory attitudes and thoughtless behaviors, and the ensuing ostracism and lack of accommodation, that make life difficult. That oppression is what's most disabling about disability.

Many disabled people have a growing but still precarious sense of pride in an identity as "people with disabilities." With decades of hard work, disability activists have fought institutionalization and challenged discrimination in employment, education, transportation, and housing. We have fought for rehabilitation and Independent Living programs, and we have proved that disabled people can participate in and contribute to society.

As a political movement, the disability rights community has conducted protests and effective civil disobedience to publicize our demand for full citizenship. Many of our tactics were inspired by the women's movement and the black civil rights movement in the 1960s. In the United States we fought for and won one of the most far-reaching pieces of civil rights legislation ever, the Americans with Disabilities Act. This piece of legislation is the envy of the international community of disability activists, most of whom live in countries where disabled people are viewed with pity and charity, and accorded low social and legal status. Disability activists have fought for mentor programs led by adults with disabilities. We see disabled children as "the youth" of the movement, the ones who offer hope that life will continue to improve for people with disabilities for generations to come.

In part because of our hopes for disabled children, the "Baby Doe" cases of the 1980s caught the attention of the growing disability rights movement. These cases revealed that "selective nontreatment" of disabled infants (leaving disabled infants to starve because the parents or doctors choose not to intervene with even routine treatments such as antibiotics) was not a thing of the past. In this same period, we also took note of the growing number of "wrongful birth" suits—medical malpractice suits brought against physicians, purportedly on behalf of disabled children, by parents who feel that the child's condition should have been identified prenatally.[6] These lawsuits claim that disabled babies, once born, are too great a burden, and that the doctors who failed to eliminate the "damaged" fetuses should be financially punished.

But many parents of disabled children have spoken up to validate the joys and satisfactions of raising a disabled child. The many books and articles by these parents confirm the view that discriminatory attitudes make raising a disabled child much more difficult than the actual logistics of care.[7] Having developed a disability-centered perspective on these cases, disabled adults have joined with many parents of disabled children in challenging the notion that raising a child with a disability is necessarily undesirable.

The attitudes that disabled people are frightening or inhuman result from lack of meaningful interaction with disabled people. Segregation in this case, as in all cases, allows stereotypes to abound. But beyond advocating contact with disabled people, disability rights proponents claim that it is crucial to challenge limiting definitions of "acceptably human." Many parents of children with Down's syndrome say that their children bring them joy. But among people with little exposure to disabled people, it is common to think that this is a romanticization or rationalization of someone stuck with the burden of a damaged child.

Many who resist selective abortion insist that there is something deeply valuable and profoundly human (though difficult to articulate in the sound bites of contemporary thought) in meeting and loving a child or adult with a severe disability. Thus, contributions of human beings cannot be judged by how we fit into the mold of normalcy, productivity, or cost-benefit. People who are different from us (whether in color, ability, age, or ethnic origin) have much to share about what it means to be human. We must not deny ourselves the opportunity for connection to basic humanness by dismissing the existence of people labeled "severely disabled."

MIXED FEELINGS: DISABLED PEOPLE RESPOND TO SELECTIVE ABORTION

The disability *activist* community has begun to challenge selective abortion. But among disabled people as a whole, there is no agreement about these issues. After all, the "disability community" is as diverse as any other broad constituency, like "the working class" or "women." Aspects of this issue can be perplexing to people with disabilities because of the nature of the prejudice we experience. For example, the culture typically invalidates our bodies, denying our sexuality and our potential as parents. These cultural impulses are complexly intertwined with the issue of prenatal testing. Since the early 1990s, disability rights activists have been exploring and debating our views on selective abortion in the disability community's literature.[8] In addition, just like the general population's attitudes about *abortion*, views held by people with disabilities about *selective abortion* relate to personal experience (in this case, personal history with disability) and to class, ethnic, and religious backgrounds.

People with different kinds of disabilities may have complex feelings about prenatal screening tests. While some disabled people regard the tests as a kind of genocide, others choose to use screening tests during their own pregnancies to avoid the birth of a disabled child. But disabled people may also use the tests differently from women who share the larger culture's anti-disability bias.

Many people with dwarfism, for example, are incensed by the idea that a woman or couple would choose to abort simply because the fetus would become a dwarf. When someone who carries the dwarfism trait mates with another with the same trait, there is a likelihood of each partner contributing one dominant dwarfism gene to the fetus. This results in a condition called "double dominance" for the offspring, which, in this "extra dose of the gene" form, is invariably accompanied by severe medical complications and early death. So prospective parents who are carriers of the dwarfism gene, or are themselves dwarfs, who would readily welcome a dwarf child, might still elect to use the screening test to avoid the birth of a fetus identified with "double dominance."

Deafness provides an entirely different example. There is as yet no prenatal test for deafness, but if, goes the ethical conundrum, a hearing couple could eliminate the fetus that would become a deaf child, why shouldn't deaf people, proud of their own distinct sign-language culture, elect for a deaf child and abort a fetus (that would become a hearing person) on a similar basis?

Those who challenge selective or eugenic abortion claim that people with disabilities are the ones who have the information about what having a disability is like. The medical system, unable to cure or fix us, exaggerates the suffering and burden of disability. The media, especially the movies, distort our lives by using disability as a metaphor for evil, impotence, eternal dependence, or tragedy—or coversely as a metaphor for courage, inspiration, or sainthood. Disabled people alone can speak to the women facing these tests. Only we can speak about our real lives, our ordinary lives, and the lives of disabled children.

"DID YOU GET YOUR AMNIO YET?": THE PRESSURE TO TEST AND ABORT

How do women decide about tests, and how do attitudes about disability affect women's choices? The reproductive technology market has, since the mid-1970s, gradually changed the experience of pregnancy. Some prenatal care facilities now present

ith their ultrasound photo in a
le frame. Women are increas-
red to use prenatal testing un-
l imperative claiming that this
ponsible thing to do." Strangers
the supermarket, even characters in TV
sit-coms, readily ask a woman with a pregnant belly, "Did you get your amnio yet?"
While the ostensible justification is "reas-
surance that the baby is fine," the underlying communication is clear: screening
out disabled fetuses is the right thing, "the
healthy thing," to do. As feminist biologist
Ruth Hubbard put it, "Women are expected
to implement the society's eugenic prejudices by 'choosing' to have the appropriate tests and 'electing' not to initiate or to
terminate pregnancies if it looks as though
the outcome will offend."[9]

Often prospective parents have never
considered the issue of disability until it
is raised in relation to prenatal testing.
What comes to the minds of parents at the
mention of the term *birth defects?* Usually
prospective parents summon up the most
stereotyped visions of disabled people derived from telethons and checkout-coun-
ter charity displays. This is not to say that
all women who elect selective abortion do
so based on simple, mindless stereotypes. I
have met women who have aborted on the
basis of test results. Their stories and their
difficult decisions were very moving. They
made the decisions they felt were the only
ones possible for them, given information
they had been provided by doctors, counselors, and society.

Indeed, some doctors and counselors
do make a good-faith effort to explore with
prospective parents the point at which selective abortion may seem clearly "justifiable," with respect to the severity of the
condition or the emotional or financial
costs involved. These efforts are fraught
with enormous social and ethical difficulty.
Often, however, unacknowledged stereotypes prevail, as does a commitment to a

libertarian view ("Let people do whatever
they want!"). Together, these strains frequently push prospective parents to succumb to the medical control of birth, while
passively colluding with pervasive disability discrimination.

Among the most common justifications
of selective abortion is that it "ends suffering." Women as cultural nurturers and
medical providers as official guardians of
well-being are both vulnerable to this message. Health care providers are trying, despite the profit-based health care system,
to improve life for people they serve. But
the medical system takes a very narrow
view of disease and "the alleviation of suffering." What is too often missed in medical
training and treatment are the *social factors*
that contribute to suffering. Physicians, by
the very nature of their work, often have
a distorted picture of the lives of disabled
people. They encounter disabled persons
having health problems, complicated by
the stresses of a marginalized life, perhaps
exacerbated by poverty and race or gender
discrimination, but because of their training, the doctors tend to project the individual's overall struggle onto the disability as
the "cause" of distress. Most doctors have
few opportunities to see ordinary disabled
individuals living in their communities
among friends and family.

Conditions receiving priority attention
for prenatal screening include Down's syndrome, spina bifida, cystic fibrosis, and fragile X, all of which are associated with mildly
to moderately disabling clinical outcomes.
Individuals with these conditions can live
good lives. There are severe cases, but the
medical system tends to underestimate
the functional abilities and overestimate
the "burden" and suffering of people with
these conditions. Moreover, among the priority conditions for prenatal screening are
diseases that occur very infrequently. Tay-
Sachs disease, for example, a debilitating,
fatal disease that affects primarily Jews of

eastern European descent, is often cited as a condition that justifies prenatal screening. But as a rare disease, it's a poor basis for a treatment mandate.

Those who advocate selective abortion to alleviate the suffering of children may often raise that cornerstone of contemporary political rhetoric, *cost-benefit*. Of course, cost-benefit analysis is not woman-centered, yet women can be directly pressured or subtly intimidated by both arguments. It may be difficult for some to resist the argument that it is their duty to "save scarce health care dollars," by eliminating the expense of disabled children. But those who resist these arguments believe the value of a child's life cannot be measured in dollars. It is notable that families with disabled children who are familiar with the actual impact of the disabilities tend not to seek the tests for subsequent children.[10] The bottom line is that the cost-benefit argument disintegrates when the outlay of funds required to provide services for disabled persons is measured against the enormous resources expended to test for a few rare genetic disorders. In addition, it is important to recognize that promotion and funding of prenatal tests distract attention and resources from addressing possible environmental causes of disability and disease.

DISABLED PEOPLE AND THE FETUS

I mentioned to a friend, an experienced disability activist, that I planned to call a conference for disabled people and genetics professionals to discuss these controversial issues. She said, "I think the conference is important, but I have to tell you, I have trouble being in the same room with professionals who are trying to eliminate my people." I was struck by her identification with fetuses as "our people."

Are those in the disability rights movement who question or resist selective abortion trying to save the "endangered species" of disabled fetuses? When this metaphor first surfaced, I was shocked to think of disabled people as the target of intentional elimination, shocked to realize that I identified with the fetus as one of my "species" that I must try to protect.

When we refer to the fetus as a *disabled* (rather than defective) fetus, we *personify* the fetus via a term of pride in the disability community. The fetus is named as a member of our community. The connection disabled people feel with the "disabled fetus" may seem to be in conflict with the pro-choice stance that the fetus is only a part of the woman's body, with no independent human status.[11]

Many of us with disabilities might have been prenatally screened and aborted if tests had been available to our mothers. I've actually heard people say, "Too bad that baby with [x disease] didn't 'get caught' in prenatal screening." (This is the sentiment of "wrongful birth" suits.) It is important to make the distinction between a pregnant woman who chooses to terminate the pregnancy because she *doesn't want to be pregnant* as opposed to a pregnant woman who *wanted to be pregnant* but rejects a particular fetus, a particular potential child. Fetuses that are wanted are called "babies." Prenatal screening results can turn a "wanted baby" into an "unwanted fetus."

It is difficult to contemplate one's own hypothetical nonexistence. But I know several disabled teenagers, born in an era when they could have been "screened out," for whom this is not at all an abstraction. In biology class their teachers, believing themselves to be liberal, raised abortion issues. These teachers, however, were less than sensitive to the disabled students when they talked about "eliminating the burden of the disabled" through technological innovation.

In the context of screening tests, those of us with screenable conditions represent living adult fetuses that didn't get aborted. We are the constituency of the potentially aborted. Our resistance to the systematic abortion of "our young" is a challenge to the "nonhumanness," the nonstatus of the fetus. This issue of the humanness of the fetus is a tricky one for those of us who identify both as pro-choice feminists and as disability rights activists. Our dual perspective offers important insights for those who are debating the ethics of the new reproductive technologies.

DISENTANGLING PATRIARCHAL CONTROL AND EUGENICS FROM REPRODUCTIVE FREEDOM

The issue of selective abortion is not just about the rights or considerations of disabled people. Women's rights and the rights of all human beings are implicated here.

When disability rights activists challenge the practice of selective abortion, as we did in Vancouver, many feminists react with alarm. They feel "uncomfortable" with language that accords human status to the fetus. One woman said: "You can't talk about the fetus as an entity being supported by advocates. It's too 'right to life.'" Disabled women activists do not want to be associated with the violent anti-choice movement. In the disability community we make a clear distinction between our views and those of anti-abortion groups. There may have been efforts to court disabled people to support anti-abortion ideology, but anti-abortion groups have never taken up the issues of expanding resources for disabled people or parents of disabled children, never lobbied for disability legislation. They have shown no interest in disabled people after they are born.[12]

But a crucial issue compels some of us to risk making people uncomfortable by discussing the fetus: we must clarify the connection between control of "defective fetuses" and the control of women as vessels or producers of quality-controllable products. This continuum between control of women's bodies and control of the *products of women's bodies* must be examined and discussed if we are going to make headway in challenging the ways that new reproductive technologies can increasingly take control of reproduction away from women and place it within the commercial medical system.

A consideration of selective abortion as a control mechanism must include a view of the procedure as a wedge into the "quality control" of all humans. If a condition (like Down's syndrome) is unacceptable, how long will it be before experts use selective abortion to manipulate—eliminate or enhance—other (presumed genetic) socially charged characteristics: sexual orientation, race, attractiveness, height, intelligence? Pre-implantation diagnosis, now used with in vitro fertilization, offers the prospect of "admission standards" for all fetuses.

Some of the pro-screening arguments masquerade today as "feminist" when they are not. Selective abortion is promoted in many doctors' offices as a "reproductive option" and "personal choice." But as anthropologist Rayna Rapp notes, "Private choices always have public consequences."[13] When a woman's individual decision is the result of social pressure, it can have repercussions for all others in the society.

How is it possible to defend selective abortion on the basis of "a woman's right to choose" when this "choice" is so constrained by oppressive values and attitudes? Consider the use of selective abortion for sex selection. The feminist community generally regards the abortion of fetuses on the basis of gender—widely practiced in some countries to eliminate female fetuses—as furthering the devaluation of women. Yet women have been pressed to "choose" to perpetuate their own devaluation.[14] For those with "disability-positive" attitudes, the analogy with sex selection is obvious. Oppressive assumptions, not inherent characteristics, have devalued who this fetus will grow into.

Fetal anomaly has sometimes been used as a *justification* for legal abortion. This justification reinforces the idea that women are horribly oppressed by disabled children. When disability is sanctioned as a justification for legal abortion, then abortion for sex selection may be more easily sanctioned as well. If "choice" is made to mean choosing the "perfect child," or the child of the "right gender," then pregnancy is turned into a process and children are turned into products that are perfectible through technology. Those of us who believe that pregnancy and children must not be commodified believe that real "choice" must include the birth of a child with a disability.

To blame a woman's oppression on the characteristics of the fetus is to obscure and distract us from the core of the "choice" position: women's control over our own bodies and reproductive capacities. It also obscures the different access to "choice" of different groups of women. At conferences I've been asked, "Would I want to force a poor black woman to bear a disabled child?" That question reinforces what feminists of color have been saying, that the framework of "choice" trivializes the issues for nonprivileged women. It reveals distortions in the public's perception of users of prenatal screening; in fact, it is the middle and upper class who most often can purchase these "reproductive choices." It's not poor women, or families with problematic genetic traits, who are creating the market for tests. Women with aspirations for the "perfect baby" are establishing new "standards of care." Responding to the lure of consumerism, they are helping create a lucrative market that exploits the culture's fear of disability and makes huge profits for the biotech industry.

Some proponents argue that prenatal tests are feminist tools because they save women from the excessive burdens associated with raising disabled children.[15] This is like calling the washer-dryer a feminist tool; technological innovation may "save time," even allow women to work outside the home, but it has not changed who does the housework. Women still do the vast majority of child care, and child care is not valued as real work. Rather, raising children is regarded as women's "duty" and is not valued as "worth" paying mothers for (or worth paying teachers or day-care workers well). Selective abortion will not challenge the sexism of the family structure in which women provide most of the care for children, for elderly parents, and for those disabled in accidents or from nongenetic diseases. We are being sold an illusion that the "burden" and problems of motherhood are being alleviated by medical science. But using selective abortion to eliminate the "burden" of disabled children is like taking aspirin for an ulcer. It provides temporary relief that both masks and exacerbates the underlying problems.

The job of helping disabled people must not be confused with the traditional devaluing of women in the caregiver role. Indeed, women can be overwhelmed and oppressed by their work of caring for disabled family members. But this is *not caused by the disabilities per se*. It is caused by lack of community services and inaccessibility, and greatly exacerbated by the sexism that isolates and overworks women caregivers. Almost any kind of work with people, if sufficiently shared and validated, can be meaningful, important, joyful, and productive.

I believe that at this point in history the decision to abort a fetus with a disability even because it "just seems too difficult" must be respected. A woman who makes this decision is best suited to assess her own resources. But it is important for her to realize this "choice" is actually made under duress. Our society profoundly limits the "choice" to love and care for a baby with a disability. This failure of society should not be projected onto the disabled fetus or child. No child is "defective." A child's disability doesn't ruin a woman's dream of motherhood. Our society's inability to appreciate and support people is what threatens our dreams.

In our struggle to lead our individual lives, we all fall short of adhering to our own highest values. We forget to recycle. We ride in cars that pollute the planet. We buy sneakers from "developing countries" that exploit workers and perpetuate the distortions in world economic power. Every day we have to make judgment calls as we assess our ability to live well and right, and it is always difficult, especially in relation to raising our own children—perhaps in this era more so than ever—to include a vision of social change in our personal decisions.

Women sometimes conclude, "I'm not saintly or brave enough to raise a disabled child." This objectifies and distorts the experience of mothers of disabled children. They're not saints; they're ordinary women, as are the women who care for spouses or their own parents who become disabled. It doesn't take a "special woman" to mother a disabled child. It takes a caring parent to raise any child. If her child became disabled, any mother would do the best job she could caring for that child. It is everyday life that trains people to do the right thing, sometimes to be leaders.

DISABLED WOMEN HAVE A LEGITIMATE VOICE IN THE ABORTION DEBATE!

Unfortunately, I've heard some ethicists and pro-choice advocates say that disabled people should not be allowed a voice in the selective abortion debate because "they make women feel guilty." The prob-

lem with this perspective is evident when one considers that there is no meaningful distinction between "disabled people" and "women." Fifty percent of adults with disabilities are women, and up to 20 percent of the female population have disabilities. The many prospective mothers who have disabilities or who are carriers of genetic traits for disabling conditions may have particular interests either in challenging or in utilizing reproductive technologies, *and* these women have key perspectives to contribute.

Why should hearing the perspectives of disabled people "make women feel guilty"? The unhappy truth is that so many decisions that women make about procreation are fraught with guilt and anxiety because sexism makes women feel guilty about their decisions. One might ask whether white people feel guilty when people of color challenge them about racism. And if so, doesn't that ultimately benefit everyone?

Do I think a woman who has utilized selective abortion intended to oppress *me* or wishes I were not born? Of course not. No more than any woman who has had an abortion means to eliminate the human race. Surely one must never condemn a woman for making the best choice she can with the information and resources available to her in the crisis of decision. In resisting prenatal testing, we do not aim to blame any individual woman or compromise her individual control over her own life or body. We *do* mean to offer information to empower her and to raise her awareness of the stakes involved for her as a woman and member of the community of all women.

A PROPOSAL FOR THE REPRODUCTIVE RIGHTS MOVEMENT

The feminist community is making some headway in demanding that women's perspectives be included in formulating policies and practices for new reproductive technologies, but the disability-centered aspects of prenatal diagnosis remain marginalized. Because the technologies have emerged in a society with entrenched attitudes about disability and illness, the tests have become embedded in medical "standards of care." They have also become an integral part of the biotech industry, a new "bright hope" of capitalist health care and the national economy. The challenge is great, the odds discouraging.

Our tasks are to gain clarity about prenatal diagnosis, challenge eugenic uses of reproductive technologies, and support the rights of all women to maintain control over reproduction. Here are some suggestions for action:

- We must actively pursue close connections between reproductive rights groups and disabled women's groups with the long-range goal of uniting our communities, as we intend to do with all other marginalized groups.
- We must make the issue of selective abortion a high priority in our movements' agendas, pushing women's groups and disability and parent groups to take a stand in the debate on selective abortion, instead of evading the issue.
- We must recognize disability as a feminist issue. All females (including teenagers and girls) will benefit from information and discussion about disability *before* they consider pregnancy, so they can avoid poorly informed decisions.
- Inclusion of people with disabilities must be part of the planning and outreach of reproductive rights organizations. Inclusion involves not only use of appropriate language and terminology for disability issues but also *involvement of disabled people* as resources. Women's organizations must learn about and comply with the Americans with Disabilities Act (or

related laws in other countries). If we are going to promote far-reaching radical feminist programs for justice and equality, we must surely comply with minimal standards set by the U.S. Congress.
- We must support family initiatives—such as parental leave for mothers and fathers, flex- and part-time work, child care resources, programs for low-income families, and comprehensive health care programs—that help *all* parents and thus make parenting children with disabilities more feasible.
- We must convince legislatures, the courts, and our communities that fetal anomaly must never be used again as a justification or a defense for safe and legal abortion. This is a disservice to the disability community and an insupportable argument for abortion rights.
- We must make the case that "wrongful life" suits should be eliminated. "Wrongful birth" suits (that seek damages for the cost of caring for a disabled child) should be carefully controlled only to protect against medical malpractice, not to punish medical practitioners for not complying with eugenic policy.
- We must break the *taboo* in the feminist movement against discussing the fetus. Getting "uncomfortable" will move us toward clarity, deepening the discussion about women's control of our bodies and reproduction.
- In response to the imperative from medical providers to utilize reproductive technologies, we can create programs to train "NRT peer counselors" to help women to learn more about new reproductive technologies, become truly informed consumers, and avoid being pressured to undergo unwanted tests. *People with disabilities must be included as NRT peer counselors.*
- We can help ourselves and each other gain clarity regarding the decision to abort a fetus with a disability. To begin

with, we can encourage women to examine their motivations for having children, ideally before becoming pregnant. We can ask ourselves and each other: What needs are we trying to satisfy in becoming a mother? How will the characteristics of the potential child figure into these motivations? What opportunities might there be for welcoming a child who does not meet our ideals of motherhood? What are the benefits of taking on the expectations and prejudices of family and friends? Have we met and interacted meaningfully with children and adults with disabilities? Do we have sufficient knowledge about disability, and sufficient awareness of our own feelings about disabled people, for our choices to be based on real information, not stereotypes?

Taking these steps and responding to these questions will be a start toward increasing our clarity about selective abortion.

CARING ABOUT OURSELVES AND EACH OTHER

Here are some things I have learned while working to educate others on this issue. I try to be patient with potential allies, to take time to explain my feelings. I try to take nothing for granted, try not to get defensive when people show their confusion or disagreement. I must remember that these issues are hard to understand; they run contrary to common and pervasive assumptions about people and life. I have to remember that it took me a long time to begin to understand disability stereotyping myself. At the same time, I have very high expectations for people. I believe it is possible to be pushy but patient and loving at the same time.

To feminist organizations attempting to include disabled women in discussions of abortion and other feminist issues: for-

give us for our occasional impatience. To disabled people: forgive potential allies for their ignorance and awkwardness. At meetings we disabled people hope to be heard, but we also perceive the "discomfort" that nondisabled people reveal, based on lack of real information about who we are. *There is no way around this awkward phase*. Better to reveal ignorance than to pretend and thereby preclude getting to know each other as people. Ask questions; make mistakes!

I sometimes remember that not only have I taken on this cutting-edge work for future generations, but I'm doing this *for myself now*. The message at the heart of widespread selective abortion on the basis of prenatal diagnosis is the greatest insult: some of us are "too flawed" in our very DNA to exist; we are unworthy of being born. This message is painful to confront. It seems tempting to take on easier battles, or even just to give in. But fighting for this issue, our right and worthiness to be born, is the fundamental challenge to disability oppression; it underpins our most basic claim to justice and equality—we are indeed worthy of being born, worth the help and expense, and we know it! The great opportunity with this issue is to think and act and take leadership in the place where feminism, disability rights, and human liberation meet.

NOTES

1. *New reproductive technologies* is the term often used to describe procreative medical technologies, including such prenatal diagnostic tests as ultrasound, alpha fetal protein (AFP) blood screening, amniocentesis, chorionic villi screening (CVS, a sampling of a segment of the amniotic sac), and the whole host of other screening tests for fetal anomalies. NRTs also include in vitro fertilization and related fertility-enhancing technologies. The conference, "New Reproductive Technologies: The Contradictions of Choice; the Common Ground between Disability Rights and Feminist Analysis," held in Vancouver, No-

vember 1994, was sponsored by the DisAbled Women's Network (DAWN), and the National Action Council on the Status of Women (NAC).

2. David J. Kevles, *In the Name of Eugenics* (New York: Knopf, 1985).

3. Not long after eugenics became a respectable science in the United States, Nazi leaders modeled state policies on their brutal reading of U.S. laws and practices. After their rise to power in 1933 the Nazis began their "therapeutic elimination" of people with mental disabilities, and they killed 120,000 people with disabilities during the Holocaust. See Robert J. Lifton, *The Nazi Doctors: Medical Killing and the Psychology of Genocide* (New York: Basic Books, 1986).

4. Marlene Fried, ed., *From Abortion to Reproductive Freedom: Transforming a Movement* (Boston: South End Press, 1990), 159.

5. Michelle Fine and Adrienne Asch, "The Question of Disability: No Easy Answers for the Women's Movement," *Reproductive Rights Newsletter* 4, no. 3 (Fall 1982). See also Rita Arditti, Renate Duelli Klein, and Shelley Minden, *Test-Tube Women: What Future for Motherhood?* (London: Routledge and Kegan Paul, 1984); Adrienne Asch, "The Human Genome and Disability Rights," *Disability Rag and Resource*, February 1004, 12 13; Adrienne Asch and Michelle Fine, "Shared Dreams: A Left Perspective on Disability Rights and Reproductive Rights," in *From Abortion to Reproductive Freedom*, ed. Fried; Lisa Blumberg, "The Politics of Prenatal Testing and Selective Abortion," in *Women with Disabilities: Reproduction and Motherhood*, special issue of *Sexuality and Disability Journal* 12, no. 2 (Summer 1994); Michelle Fine and Adrienne Asch, *Women with Disabilities: Essays in Psychology, Culture, and Politics* (Philadelphia: Temple University Press, 1988); Laura Hershey, "Choosing Disability," *Ms.*, July/August 1994; Ruth Hubbard and Elijah Wald, *Exploding the Gene Myth: How Genetic Information Is Produced and Manipulated by Scientists, Physicians, Employers, Insurance Companies, Educators and Law Enforcers* (Boston: Beacon Press, 1993); Marsha Saxton, "The Politics of Genetics," *Women's Review of Books* 9, no. 10–11 (July 1994); Marsha Saxton, "Prenatal Screening and Discriminatory Attitudes about Disability, in *Embryos, Ethics and Women's Rights: Exploring the New Reproductive Technologies*, ed. Elaine Hoffman Baruch, Amadeo F. D'Adamo, and Joni Seager (New York: Haworth Press, 1988); Marsha Saxton and Florence Howe, eds., *With Wings: An Anthology by and about Women with Disabilities* (New York: Feminist Press, 1987).

6. Adrienne Asch, "Reproductive Technology and Disability," in *Reproductive Laws for the 1990s: A Briefing Handbook*, ed. Nadine Taub and Sherrill Cohen (New Brunswick, N.J.: Rutgers University Press, 1989).

7. Helen Featherstone, *A Difference in the Family: Life with a Disabled Child* (New York: Basic Books, 1980).

8. To my knowledge, Anne Finger was the first disability activist to raise this issue in the U.S. women's literature. In her book *Past Due: Disability, Pregnancy, and Birth* (Seattle: Seal Press, 1990), which includes references to her earlier writings, Finger describes a small conference where feminists and disability activists discussed this topic. German and British disability activists and feminists pioneered this issue.

9. Ruth Hubbard, *The Politics of Women's Biology* (New Brunswick, N.J.: Rutgers University Press, 1990), 197.

10. Dorothy Wertz, "Attitudes toward Abortion among Parents of Children with Cystic Fibrosis," *American Journal of Public Health* 81, no. 8 (1991).

11. This view must be reevaluated in the era of in vitro fertilization (IVF), where the embryo or a genetically prescreened embryo (following "pre-implantation diagnosis") can be fertilized outside the woman's body and frozen or can be implanted in another woman. Such a fetus has come to have legal status apart from the mother's body: for example, in divorce cases where the fate of these fetuses is decided by the courts.

12. Many "pro-life" groups support abortion for "defective fetuses." Most state laws, even conservative ones, allow later-stage abortions when the fetus is "defective."

13. Rayna Rapp, "Accounting for Amniocentesis," in *Knowledge, Power, and Practice: The Anthropology of Medicine in Everyday Life*, ed. Shirley Lindenbaum and Margaret Lock (Berkeley: University of California Press, 1993).

14. Suneri Thobani, "From Reproduction to Mal[e] Production: Women and Sex Selection Technology," in *Misconceptions: The Social Construction of Choice and the New Reproductive Technologies*, vol. I, ed. Gwynne Basen, Margaret Eichler, and Abby Lippman (Quebec: Voyager Publishing, 1994).

15. Dorothy C. Wertz and John C. Fletcher, "A Critique of Some Feminist Challenges to Prenatal Diagnosis," *Journal of Women's Health 2* (1993).

CHAPTER 8

Disability, Democracy, and the New Genetics

Michael Bérubé

In this essay I will try to suggest ways of thinking about biotechnology, bioethics, and disability that are compatible with democratic values. I will start with the uncontroversial proposition that we have entered an era in which our capacity for manipulating genetic material will determine what it means to be human—and in which our deliberations about what it means to be human will guide our capacity for manipulating genetic material. In saying this, I am presuming not only that political deliberations can determine the scope and direction of scientific research—that much seems obvious—but also that democratic values should prevail with regard both to the procedures and the substance of such deliberations. Affirming at the outset one's commitment to deliberative democracy in such matters does not foreordain their outcome: it remains to be determined, for instance, whether it is consonant with democracy to prohibit or permit prospective parents to engage in genetic selection for Huntington's disease or for myopia, or to prohibit or permit potential genetic therapies for Alzheimer's or multiple sclerosis. Deliberative democrats can plausibly come to different conclusions on these questions, based on opposing yet reasonable assessments of how to understand and adjudicate competing claims with regard

to individual liberties (positive and negative), ideas of distributive justice, legitimate scientific objectives, moral injunctions to prevent suffering, and beliefs about human dignity and nascent human life. However, deliberative democrats must nevertheless agree to insist at the outset that democracy is the primary value to be upheld in the deliberations—that although participants in the debate may rely on and express strongly held religious beliefs, religious beliefs in and of themselves cannot and must not determine the course or the scope of the debate.

This might sound uncontroversial, but in practice and in theory, it has important consequences that many of my fellow citizens (and many of my fellow humans) will not be willing to accept. In the course of this essay, for example, I will rehearse my position on prenatal screening for fetuses with disabilities, a position I set forth in chapter two of *Life As We Know It*, and I want to acknowledge immediately that there are many people of sound mind and good will who disagree with that position. Some of them, as I have learned over the past few years, dispute not only my calculations of the relative social goods and harms of prenatal testing, but also, and more stringently, my primary assumption that public access to and public uses of prenatal testing should be thought of in terms consonant with democratic values. As one of my interlocutors once put it, in the course of a discussion at Syracuse University's Center for Human Policy, it may be that democracy is not the highest value in such affairs. To people who start from the premise that there are divine laws the meanings of which are not subject to human deliberation, and which therefore must be imposed on humanity by the representatives of the deity, nothing I say in this essay will have sufficient persuasive force. And this is but one example of a pervasive philosophical problem that some have called, for better or worse, "postmodern": when the claims of two systems of belief—democracy and theocracy, perhaps—are opposed, there may not be any way to reconcile them under the heading of a third, more universal term. We may instead be faced with a fundamental incommensurability between discourses of justification, such that we may not even have the language in which to agree to disagree. Understanding this problem, then, and admitting that I will have no common ground with some participants in debates over genomics even as I appeal to the practice of deliberative democracy, I will begin my discussion of biotechnology and disability by talking about a Hollywood movie. But not just any Hollywood movie: the film in question, *Gattaca*, might well be the new *locus classicus* for discussions of genetic screening and enhancement, and one of its plots offers a vivid illustration of what Michael Sandel would argue some years later in *The Case Against Perfection*: namely, that a designer baby might spend its life laboring under the burdens imposed by his or her design, and that our sense of human freedom (for such children, and for their designing parents) would thereby be paradoxically diminished rather than enhanced by our increasing mastery over the genome.

Gattaca depicts a dystopian world, set in the "not-too-distant future," of widespread *in vitro* fertilization and pre-implantation screening, in which school placements, job interviews, and indeed life prospects consist of blood tests and urine samples. Children conceived the "old-fashioned" way—for example, by means of sex in the back seat of a car, as is the case for our protagonist and narrator, Vincent Freeman—are called "in-valids," "de-generates," "faith births," or "God children"; they are increasingly rare, and they make up the lower echelons of society, assigned to various forms of menial labor. Vincent, played by Ethan Hawke, is excluded from school as a child because the school cannot afford the insurance costs he entails, and consigned to a life of janitorial work even though he dreams of space flight, hoping against hope to work someday at the giant aerospace corporation, Gattaca. Throughout his childhood, he had been fascinated with space and space travel; we see him, as a scrawny, bespectacled teen, reading a book titled *Careers in Space*—and we witness his father, venting his frustration and anger by telling his son, "For God's sake, Vincent, don't you understand. The only way you'll see the inside of a space ship is if you're cleaning it." The moment Vincent is born, his initial genetic analysis, drawn from a blood sample and read instantaneously by an attending nurse, reveals the following: he will have a 60 percent probability of a neurological condition, a 42 percent probability of manic depression, an 89 percent probability of attention deficit disorder, a 99 percent probability of heart disease, and a life expectancy of 30.2 years. No, this is not a plausible representation of what genes can tell us. But my argument does not depend on this scene; what matters for my purposes is that Vincent's devastated parents, Marie and Antonio, decide to have a second child *in vitro*; "like most other parents of their day, they were determined that their next child would be brought into the world in what has become the natural way." The genetic technician/counselor informs Marie and Antonio that four eggs have been fertilized—two boys, two girls—and that they have been fully screened for "critical predispositions to any of the major inheritable diseases." Marie and Antonio indicate that they would like to have another boy, a brother for Vincent to play with. The geneticist nods. "You have specified," he goes on,

> hazel eyes, dark hair, fair skin. I've taken the liberty of eradicating any potentially prejudicial conditions—premature baldness, myopia, alcoholism and addictive susceptibility, propensity for violence and obesity—
>
> MARIE: We didn't want—I mean, diseases, yes, but—
>
> ANTONIO: Right, we were just wondering if it's good to leave just a few things to chance.
>
> GENETICIST: You want to give your child the best possible start. Believe me, we have enough imperfection built in already. Your child doesn't need any additional burdens. And keep in mind, this child is still you—simply the best of you. You could conceive naturally a thousand times and never get such a result.

The geneticist smiles indulgently when he refers to the parents' preference for "fair skin," because, as it happens, he himself is black (he is played by Blair Underwood). By this we are led to understand that in *this* brave new world, genetic discrimination is common but racial discrimination is a thing of the past. The point is reinforced a few minutes later, when Vincent recounts his experience as a young man seeking employment: "Of course," he tells us, "it's illegal to discriminate—genoism, it's called—but no one takes the law seriously. If you refuse to disclose, they can always take a sample from a door handle, or a handshake, even the saliva on your application form. If in doubt, a legal

drug test can just as easily become an illegal peek at your future in the company." And we see a human-resources manager wordlessly challenging Vincent to provide a urine sample. The manager, like the genetic counselor, is black.

I find this aspect of the movie's premise fascinating for two reasons—not only because the film so clearly (if counterintuitively and counterfactually) disarticulates racism from genoism, but also because it establishes *Gattaca* as a film about civil rights and employment discrimination. Disability in science fiction is not often discussed in such mundane terms, but perhaps it should be. Readers of Philip K. Dick will remember that one of the things that got lost in translation between the 1969 novel *Do Androids Dream of Electric Sheep?* and the 1982 film *Blade Runner* is the category of human "specials," people neurologically damaged by the nuclear fallout of World War Terminus and derisively referred to as "chickenheads" or, in severe cases, "antheads."[1] The Voigt-Kampff empathy test, central to both the novel and the film, is a device bounty hunters ("blade runners") employ to distinguish humans from androids trying to pass as human; it was originally devised, as Dick's novel explains, to identify "specials" so that they could be sterilized and consigned to the lower echelons of society. *Blade Runner* drops Dick's treatment of the relation between disability and employment by taking the novel's despised and lonely "chickenhead," J. R. Isidore, a driver for an artificial animal repair shop, and rewriting him as J. F. Sebastian, a lonely high-ranking engineer for the Tyrell Corporation (though the film does give Sebastian another disability, "Methuselah syndrome," a premature-aging disorder that effectively links him to the Nexus-6 androids who have lifespans of only four years). *Gattaca*, by contrast, builds its plot around the relation between employment and disability; its central drama focuses entirely on whether Vincent will be discovered and thrown out of work and into jail. That drama of detection and evasion, in turn, transforms the relation between race and disability into one of mutual implication: once it becomes inescapably clear that he will be unable to pursue a career in space exploration because of his genetic makeup, Vincent decides to become a "borrowed ladder," using the bodily fluids and effluvia of Jerome Morrow in order to obtain the clearance necessary for employment at Gattaca. Jerome (played by Jude Law) is a former world-class athlete who was struck by a car (we learn later that he tried to kill himself after failing to win an Olympic gold medal); paraplegic and visually marked by the most common sign for physical disability, his wheelchair, he literally sells his genetic identity to Vincent as he descends into bitterness and alcoholism, finally committing suicide in the film's final sequence. In other words, *Gattaca* is not only a science-fictional exploration of employment discrimination; it is also a member of one of the oldest genres in African American fiction, the passing narrative.

Scholars in disability studies have tended to see Jerome's character as a regrettable and gratuitous reinforcement of stereotypes of disability. Anne Finger's 1998 review has largely set the terms of the debate: arguing that the film is ultimately "scared of the radicalness of its critique," Finger suggests that Jerome's suicide is meant to reassure the contemporary able-bodied audience who largely identify with Vincent and hope that they, too, would have the determination to fight genetic determinism and succeed. "In its futuristic world," Finger notes,

> virtually everyone watching the film would be classified as a 'de-generate,' an 'in-valid.' Rather than leave the audience members in the uncomfortable position of thinking of themselves as disabled, the film had to create

a 'really disabled' person, someone who fits our social stereotype of what a crip is. In the end, despite its possibilities, *Gattaca* doesn't really challenge the terms of the debate. It tells us that with hard work and 'spirit' we can overcome, but it still leaves intact a division between 'us' and 'them,' those whose bodies succeed and those whose bodies fail. (Finger)

Likewise, Kathleen Ellis argues that "moves such as *Gattaca* contribute to the discrimination" against people with disabilities insofar as Jerome is presented as a weak, contemptible character, wallowing in vodka and self-pity (Ellis). What these critiques overlook, however, is that Jerome is not bitter and suicidal because he is disabled; he tried to commit suicide before he was disabled, solely because he had to settle for a silver medal, and he is bitter because his attempt failed: "Jerome Morrow," he tells Vincent, "was never meant to be one step down on the podium." Jerome's story is not that of *Million Dollar Baby*, in which an athlete decides that a physically disabled life is not worth living; it is an illustration of Sandel's argument against genetic enhancement—or, as Vincent's voiceover puts it, a warning about "the burden of perfection."

That said, it is notable that there are no accommodations for Jerome in this society: it is otherwise impressively high-tech, featuring twelve-fingered pianists and space travel to the moons of Saturn, but it does not appear to have a single elevator, ramp, or kneeling bus. Perhaps Jerome has reason to be bitter. He does not own a power chair (apparently such things no longer exist), and his apartment has no elevator—just a spiral staircase, an echo of the double helix, by which Jerome has to drag himself upstairs at a critical moment in the narrative. Notably, there are no wheelchair users at Gattaca Corporation, even though physical disability is clearly no impediment to becoming a first-rate computer programmer or aeronautical engineer. One is left to infer that disability discrimination in this society is severe indeed, though the film leaves this point implicit, just as it does not call attention to its representation of race. Of course, it's possible to say that the film is simply bizarrely optimistic that a society so obsessed with genetics will be a society without racism; it certainly appears to be a society composed entirely of able-bodied heterosexuals, so it is not clear why one form of pervasive bigotry has been overcome while other forms seem to rule the world. But let me turn from the implicit aspects of the film to the film's explicit presentation of what counts as uncontroversial genetic screening in this society: the elimination of all major inheritable diseases, as well as "potentially prejudicial conditions" such as premature baldness, myopia, alcoholism and addictive susceptibility, propensity for violence, and obesity. When Victor's mother demurs, saying "we didn't want—I mean, diseases, yes," surely the phrase she's thinking of and not uttering is something like "a designer baby." Which is, of course, precisely what she gets—still you, just the best of you. And the reason she goes along with it is that her child doesn't need any additional burdens—especially barriers to meaningful education and employment.

The *Gattaca* scenario presents a challenge especially to liberals who (like me) have thus far combined political support for reproductive rights, a defense of technologies of prenatal screening, a critique of cost-benefit analyses of human worth, a stringent skepticism about the workings of the United States' deeply inegalitarian insurance and health care system, and, last but not least, a defense of a aggressive social welfare state that provides need-based benefits to children and adults with disabilities. Granted, abortion is not an issue in *Gattaca,* precisely because IVF and genetic screening seem to have taken it off the table (though one does not know if there are abortion providers who cater to prospective parents who conceive accidentally in the back seats of cars). But the film does raise the question of what happens to the embryos Marie and Antonio do not select, and more importantly, it raises the question of what conditions we should screen for, and what we should do if and when we detect them. The larger question at stake, of course, is the question of who should inhabit the world, and on what terms. My own position on what is now called the ethics of "selective abortion" with regard to fetuses with disabilities is substantially identical to that of the 1999 Hastings Center Report on the Disability Rights Critique of Prenatal Genetic Testing (Parens and Asch 2000), which defended reproductive rights and prospective parents' access to prenatal screening while critiquing the idea that the detection of genetic anomaly is a self-evident justification for terminating a pregnancy.[2] Though I do not consider disability sufficient grounds for abortion, I believe that the fetus does not have a moral status equivalent to that of a child unless and until it is viable outside the womb, and I support the right of prospective parents to terminate pregnancies even for reasons that I would regard as trivial or wrongheaded.

Rayna Rapp's *Testing Women, Testing the Fetus* is replete with accounts of such parents, including the one who told Rapp that "having a 'tard, that's a bummer for life" (91) or the one who insisted that if the baby "can't grow up to have a shot at becoming the president, we don't want him" (92)—in regard to a fetus with Klinefelter's syndrome, on the basis of whose diagnosis the parents terminated the pregnancy. I remain unpersuaded that there are transcendent moral virtues to be advanced by compelling such parents to bear children with disabilities, even though the disabilities in question are relatively benign; indeed, I shudder to think how such parents will treat their disabled children if they compelled to bear them against their will. Nor do I see why it is virtuous to compel parents to bear children with far more severe conditions that involve profound physical and emotional suffering for all concerned, such as Lesch-Nyhan syndrome or Tay-Sachs disease; I submit that in a democratic society it is better to allow prospective parents to make such decisions for themselves. For that reason I have insisted (and continue to insist) that it is more consistent with the principles of democracy for people like me to *persuade* prospective parents and genetics counselors not to think of amniocentesis as part of a search-and-destroy mission, and to persuade them that many people with disabilities, even those disabilities detectable *in utero* (like Down syndrome), are capable of living lives that not only bring joy and wonder to those around them but are fulfilling and fascinating to the people living them as well. But I will not argue that some forms of childbirth should be made mandatory, nor will I demand that prospective parents be barred from obtaining genetic information about the fetus if they so desire such information.

As Rapp writes, "at the intersection of the disability rights movement and the feminist movement for reproductive rights lies a thorny problem: How is it possible to contest the eugenic and stigmatizing definition of disabilities which seems to underlie prenatal diagnosis, while still upholding the rights of individual women to determine what kind of medical care, and what sorts of pregnancy decisions, are in their own best interests?" (51) Rapp eventually crafts two moral imperatives—as well as the meta-imperative to see these two as complementary rather than contradictory: "The first is the need to champion the reproductive rights of women to carry or refuse to carry to term a pregnancy that would result in a baby with a serious disability. The second is the need to support adequate, nonstigmatizing, integrative services for all the children, including disabled children, that women bear" (7–8). The difficulty of balancing these needs is exemplified by the excruciating tensions in Ruth Hubbard's essay, "Abortion and Disability: Who Should and Should Not Inhabit the World?", which insists—four times, for good measure (three times emphatically in the course of its seven final paragraphs)—that "a woman must have the right to abort a fetus, whatever her reasons" while arguing that some of those reasons are (a) continuous with the logic of Nazi eugenics and (b) influenced by forces that appear to undermine Hubbard's faith that a woman's reasons can be her own. "Women are expected to implement the society's eugenic prejudices by 'choosing' to have the appropriate tests and 'electing' not to initiate or to terminate pregnancies if it looks as though the outcome will offend," Hubbard writes, pointedly questioning the choices she does not endorse by employing scare quotes to suggest that they are not "choices" at all. "And to a considerable extent not initiating or terminating these pregnancies may indeed be what women want to do. But one reason we want to is that society promises much grief to parents of children it deems unfit to inhabit the world" (78). What's striking about Hubbard's argument is not only that it discounts the decisions of prospective parents whose justifications for abortion she (and I) might find trivial or wrongheaded, suggesting that such decisions are imposed by "society" and on a continuum with Nazism, but also, and more remarkably, that it manages to criticize women *who choose not to become pregnant in the first place*—who do not "initiate" pregnancies—in an essay ostensibly devoted (as its title indicates) to abortion and disability. But surely a democratic society can find some way of honoring and respecting the decisions of women who do not want to pass a genetic disability on to their children. And one does not (by which, of course, I mean I do not) want to see disability rights advocates elide the difference between abortion and contraception, so that they wind up taking the position Hubbard suggests here—that the decision not to initiate a pregnancy, for reasons related to disability, is as censurable as the decision to terminate one.

For the moment, our society seems to have achieved a shaky but substantial consensus that it is morally acceptable to screen fetuses for profoundly debilitating conditions such as Tay-Sachs disease, which involves severe and ceaseless suffering over a nasty, brutish, and short life span, but morally unacceptable to terminate a pregnancy solely with regard to gender.[3] Everything else—Down syndrome, Huntington's disease, multiple sclerosis, leukemia—falls at various points in the capacious area between, and thus far the people of the United States have apparently decided to leave decisions concerning such conditions up to the people who will be most affected by them. But the *Gattaca* scenario compels us to ask which "potentially prejudicial conditions" we would allow prospective parents to eliminate if the technology were available. That is to say, even in the not-too-distant-future, we might feel a profound moral repugnance at the idea of terminating a pregnancy simply on the basis of the finding that the fetus has a genetic propensity for obesity, myopia, or premature baldness. But if we could select against these features at fertilization, would we do so, and what moral grounds would we offer for refusing to do so and preventing others, by law, from doing so?

In recent years I have taught *Gattaca* alongside Sandel's *The Case Against Perfection* and Jonathan Glover's *Choosing Children: Genes, Disability, and Design*, noting that Glover, in the course of an argument for genetic enhancement in "a regulated market, on a European model," where "which choices, if any, should be excluded would be part of democratic debate" (77), sees no problem with eliminating many "potentially prejudicial conditions": "Eliminating a genetic disposition to shyness or laziness might help someone flourish, as might making them more cheerful or boosting their ability to sing or to learn languages" (75–76). In Glover's ideal regulated-market democracy, apparently, a social consensus has been achieved that it is acceptable to tinker with character traits like shyness or cheerfulness, just as it goes without saying in the world of *Gattaca* that we should screen for premature baldness—despite the fact that the genetic counselor himself is bald (and, in my humble opinion, rather attractively so). My students have overwhelmingly found Glover's position repugnant, arguing that such traits as laziness and shyness do not rise to the level of diseases one would want to delete from the random reconfigurations of our genetic possibilities. (Some argue, however, along Sandel's lines, that it is acceptable to intervene pharmaceutically to bring someone to a baseline of health, as when one is prescribed medication for severe and debilitating shyness, anxiety, or depression.) Interestingly, however, many of my students report that they would welcome a genetic test that would screen for "propensity to violence," considering this a trait well worth deleting whenever possible. Upon noting that in class after class, my female students were nearly unanimous on this point, I began to reflect on the question of gendered violence (which, I realized, had been implicit in the discussions all along), and to suggest to students that this is one of the questions posed to us by Margaret Atwood's *Oryx and Crake*: though Crake's attempt to redesign the human species from scratch is monstrous—he is, after all, Victor Frankenstein as sophisticated genetic engineer—there is surely something to be said for a world in which there is "no more prostitution, no sexual abuse of children, no haggling over the price, no pimps, no sex slaves. No more rape" (165).

My own answer to the question of how we might determine how and why to screen for genetic traits, tentative though it be, runs as follows. In a world that possesses the kind of genetic knowledge we envision in *Gattaca*, bioethicists, philosophers, Presidential commissions, and humanists like me would have made the argument that while it is acceptable to screen for major inheritable diseases, screening out the "potentially prejudicial conditions" enumerated above—even the propensity for violence—would be highly controversial and far from routine. Our society would have had, and would still be engaged in, a wide-ranging debate about what kinds of disabilities do involve profound suffering or significantly diminished life chances for those who have them, and (by contrast) what varieties of human embodiment may be undesirable or inconvenient but, on the whole, do not constitute conditions so prejudicial as to jeopardize significantly the life chances of those who have them. Such a debate would acknowledge, moreover, that many disabilities are not detectable genetically, and that no amount and no degree of prenatal screening or *in vitro* engineering will produce a world free of people with cerebral palsy, autism, or pneumonia, not to mention people who are hit by cars.[4] Some of the debate's participants would have learned not to think of disability as synonymous with disease, and would continually try to persuade other participants that not all disabilities have disease etiologies and not all disabilities need to be considered in terms of cure or elimination (though in many cases, amelioration might be perfectly acceptable).[5] And finally, such a debate would focus not only on potentially prejudicial conditions but on actually existing prejudices, extending the protection of the social welfare state to stigmatized populations while working also to de-stigmatize previously stigmatized identities (as had been done, evidently, with regard to people of African descent in the world of *Gattaca*). The debate would produce a boundary of the unacceptable, just as we now have agreement on the desirability of forbidding human cloning to produce children and a looser agreement on the permissability but undesirability of selective abortion for gender. And in democratic fashion, the debate would seek to honor liberal freedoms and ideas of individual autonomy in decision-making while insisting nonetheless, as both Mill and Rawls would tell us, that democracy does not have to honor all the preferences and desires of every person participant therein.

It pains me deeply to admit it, but in such a society, the vast majority of people with Down syndrome would be those among the "faith births," those conceived without the benefits of IVF and genetic screening. There would still be a good number of Deaf people in this society, despite screening and despite the widespread availability of cochlear implants, partly because our social debate would have concluded that Deafness is far less damaging to one's life prospects and one's ability to participate fully in the social and political life of the polity than is Down syndrome, and partly because some of our fellow humans (Deaf and hearing) would have determined that Deaf culture is valuable, distinctive, and worth preserving in its own right, and that it has no linguistic or cultural counterpart among people with Down syndrome. I say this not because I desire to see a world absent of people with Down syndrome; I cannot even imagine what it would be like to desire such a thing. But I can imagine that if we had the power to screen for major disabilities, inheritable diseases, and potentially prejudicial conditions, many (but by no means all) of my fellow humans would see the elimination of Down syndrome as a social good; fewer would see the eradication of Deafness as a good; and fewer still would see the eradication of myopia or baldness in those terms. Such would be, on my best guess, the results of a democratic deliberation about disability and genomics.[6]

Yet one of the factors that makes this discussion so difficult is the fact that, as I mentioned at the beginning of this essay, some of us do not agree that societies should decide such matters by democratic deliberation. The debate over genetic screening, other words, necessarily includes the voices of those who do not believe that it should be taking place, or who believe that it should take place but that it should not be morally binding or dispositive when it comes into conflict with moral absolutes. Those moral absolutes concern the destruction of "nascent human life," whether by means of abortion, by means of the discarding of embryos not selected for implantation (three out of four of Marie and Antonio's options), or by means of the use of embryos for stem-cell research. For example, in a discussion of *Life As We Know It* for the Christian book review *Books and Culture*, Jean Bethke Elshtain responded to my defense of abortion rights and prenatal testing by accusing me of "subtly but inexorably blowing out the moral lights among us, as Lincoln said of Douglas's defense of popular sovereignty in the matter of slavery" (18). I find this remark at once exceptionally offensive and insufficiently morally serious, partly because it rests on Elshtain's remarkably unelaborated claim that "the fetus, of course, is human all along—what else can it be?" For Elshtain, apparently, there can be no debate about the morality of prenatal screening and selective abortion, because there can be no debate about the moral status of the fetus: there is one correct position, that the fetus is fully human (even as a zygote and

embryo, for that is what "all along" must mean) and deserves all the protections associated with ideas of inviolable human dignity, and those who disagree are simply blowing out the moral lights among us.[7]

When that hard-line position on nascent human life becomes part of a broader democratic deliberation, it produces distinctive distortions that can skew debate decisively. Take for instance the deliberation conducted by President George W. Bush's Council on Bioethics, published under the title *Human Cloning and Human Dignity: An Ethical Inquiry*. That Council unanimously endorsed a ban on "reproductive cloning," which the Council called "cloning-to-produce-children," and, by a complicated ten-to-seven margin, a four-year moratorium on "therapeutic cloning," which the Council called "cloning-for-biomedical-research." As Council chairman Leon Kass argued in *The Public Interest*, the Council construed the debate over cloning-for-biomedical-research as a clash between competing moral imperatives:

> On the one hand, we acknowledge that the research offers the prospect, though speculative at the moment, of gaining valuable knowledge and treatments for many diseases. On the other hand, this practice would require the exploitation and destruction of nascent human life created solely for the purpose of research.
>
> (40)

This seems to me a reasonable statement of the conflict, even though the second sentence is almost a word-for-word repetition of Charles Krauthammer's partisan account of the debate in his personal statement in the report's Appendix. Yet within only a few sentences, Kass reframes it in a way that can only be called tendentious:

> Each side recognized that we must face up to the moral burden of either approving or disapproving this research, namely, on the one

hand, that some who might be healed more rapidly might not be; and on the other hand, that we will become a society that creates and uses some human lives in the service of others.

(10)

Note what has happened between these two passages: both hands have changed substantially. On the one hand, at first we had speculative research that offers the prospect of treating many diseases; but now, blocking that research means only that "some who might be healed more rapidly might not be," and not that "some who might be healed *will never be.*" On the other hand, at first we were faced with the admittedly dicey prospect of "the exploitation and destruction of *nascent* human life"; but now if we permit cloning-for-biomedical-research "we will become a society that creates and uses some human lives in the service of others," and there is no longer anything "nascent" about the embryo.

The reason the President's Council did not advocate an outright ban on cloning-for-biomedical-research is that it could not get a majority of its members, even among those who oppose abortion as a matter of principle, to agree that such cloning constituted an exploitation and destruction of human life in the sense that five-day-old embryos bear the same moral weight as do five-month-old fetuses or five-year-old children or fifty-five-year-old adults. Social conservative James Q. Wilson, for instance, held to a position that would permit "biomedical research on cloned embryos provided the blastocyst is no more than fourteen days old and would not allow implantation in a uterus, human or animal" (297). The Council settled therefore for a moratorium that, as the report's executive summary puts it,

> provides time for further democratic deliberation about cloning-for-biomedical research, a subject about which the nation is divided

and where there remains great uncertainty. A national discourse on this subject has not yet taken place in full, and a moratorium, by making it impossible for either side to cling to the status-quo, would force both to make their full case before the public. By banning all cloning for a time, it allows us to seek moral consensus on whether or not we should cross a major moral boundary (creating nascent cloned human life solely for research) and prevents our crossing it without deliberate decision. It would afford time for scientific evidence, now sorely lacking, to be gathered—from animal models and other avenues of human research—that might give us a better sense of whether cloning-for-biomedical-research would work as promised, and whether other morally nonproblematic approaches might be available.

(xxxvi)

In one respect the statement is question-begging, insofar as it presumes the very point that needs to be argued—namely, that cloning for biomedical research involves crossing a major moral boundary. This claim is precisely what many proponents of stem-cell research wish to contest. But the ancillary claim that biomedical research itself might benefit from this moratorium is simply disingenuous, as Council member Elizabeth Blackburn pointed out in her personal statement in the Appendix to the report: "It may sound tempting," Blackburn wrote, "to impose a moratorium to get more information, since, despite very promising results, it is true, at this early stage of the research, that we still know only a little. But that information can *only* be gained by performing the same research that the moratorium proposes to halt" (246). Nor is it clear—and this is the distorting effect I mentioned above—that the appeal to "further democratic deliberation" is not a stalling tactic: since the nation remains divided between people who believe that stem-cell research is legitimate and people who believe it is immoral, there is no "moral consensus" to be had, and therefore no need for a waiting period during which such a consensus can be allowed to form.

Perhaps, then, the Council's appeal to democratic deliberation might be understood cynically as a temporizing move that will allow pro-life proponents to marshal their arguments and their social forces. Should that happen, and should we find ourselves living in a society whose democratic deliberations wind up by banning stem-cell research, then we will have become a society in which the value placed on the moral status of the human embryo trumps all other considerations, including the moral injunction to alleviate plausibly remediable suffering. It is altogether possible to achieve such a society by democratic means, and I want to argue strenuously against it, for it would install essentially theocratic views about human life at the center of moral debate.

Having made clear my antipathy to theocratic conceptions of human life, I should immediately make it clear that I am by no means sanguine or unworried about the life prospects for people with disabilities in a society in which it is widely assumed that identifiable disabilities should either be cured or prevented. For the *Gattaca* scenario is just another vision of the world of eugenics, and the world of eugenics is already too much with us. On this count, contemporary professions of good faith among geneticists are no guarantee that they've learned the lessons of history. As Dorothy Roberts argues in *Killing the Black Body*, the discourse of eugenics is not really "history" at all, and certainly not ancient history. And yet the new eugenics is not precisely the same as the old. Our era differs from the era of the Kansas State Fair in critically important ways: one might call these "public" and "private" eugenics, or one might call them macro and micro eugenics, as Barbara Katz Rothman has done in

Genetic Maps and Human Imaginations, or one might say (as I will proceed to) that the old eugenics saw the human population as an aggregate of various ethnic and racial traits some of which were not beneficial to the enlightened propagation of the species, whereas the new eugenics sees individuals as aggregates of biochemical traits some of which are not beneficial to the families or populations in which they occur. I believe that this molecular view of the human is inadequate and incomplete, partly because genetics is an inexact science, a science of probabilities in which we cannot be sure how a biochemical predisposition may express itself, and partly because we have limited but conscious, self-reflexive control over how we express some of the traits with which we are born. (This too is one of the lessons of *Gattaca*, unfortunately summed up by the movie's tag line, "there is no gene for the human spirit": much depends on what one does with the genetic hand one is dealt.) It is one thing, in other words, to promote genetic research on the grounds that it will eradicate Tay-Sachs or Huntington's or Alzheimer's; I would regard each of these as a universal, species-wide good comparable to the universal species-wide good of eradicating smallpox or tuberculosis or HIV. But it would be foolish and destructive, I think, to think of individuals as agglomerations of traits like "propensity to become impatient," "sense of how to arrange a room" or "ability to memorize geographical maps"—or shyness, or laziness, or plumb-cussedness—and to try to order an individual's genetic makeup accordingly.[8]

And yet this is what the libertarian position on genetic engineering would invite us to do. For bioethicists such as Julian Savulescu and Nicholas Agar, the *Gattaca* scenario represents not a dystopia but a utopia, in which prospective parents have the opportunity and the obligation to avail themselves of the technology that will allow them to design the "best" possible child—still you, just the best of you. For advocates of what Sandel calls forms of "liberal eugenics," the evil of eugenics as practiced in the first decades of the twentieth century was not that it was eugenics, but that the policies of involuntary sterilization and institutionalization represented forms of coercion visited on individuals by the state. "Private" eugenics, from this standpoint, is not an evil at all; it consists simply of individuals, in various familial arrangements, making rational decisions about what is best for them and their children. In democratic deliberation over genetics and disability, therefore, I will want to argue against both the theocratic and the libertarian positions, the former because I believe it has an inadequate account of the social basis of moral debate and the latter because I believe it has an inadequate account of the social good. Additionally (and, I think, tellingly), in some circumstances the libertarian position can rely on beliefs about eugenics that are not merely untroubled by history but also hostile to disability. It is as if individual choices about genetic enhancement are just fine, but decisions to screen *for* disability, rather than against, require state regulation. Or, perhaps, it is as if some libertarians tend to imagine that everyone who is allowed to design a child will share a moral consensus that disability is to be avoided or eliminated—that it is, as Jonathan Glover writes, to be "contrasted with human flourishing" (88), if not indeed inimical to human flourishing.

I draw from these debates two political paradoxes. The first is this: many of the people who supported the passage of the Americans with Disabilities Act of 1990 were, like White House counsel C. Boyden Gray, diehard antistatist conservatives, deeply opposed to gender-equity initiatives and race-based affirmative action and civil rights laws generally. The reason that the ADA enjoyed such bipartisan support,

however, was that its conservative and libertarian advocates championed it as a law that would free people with disabilities from dependence on the state. For them, the purpose of this public law was to return individuals with disabilities to the realm of the private. The second paradox is this: for people involved with disability, even for those of us who support reproductive rights, there is no realm of the private. Disability is always and everywhere a public issue, a matter for public policy, even or especially for political thinkers who otherwise have no conception of the public good. I want to suggest, then, that one way to think about disability, democracy, and genetics is to imagine that the public is not public enough and the private is not private enough. Those of us who support reproductive rights *and* a woman's right to prenatal testing *and* stem-cell research *and* the egalitarian provisions of the welfare state need to make the argument that intimate decisions about childbearing and care for people with disabilities should be protected from state coercion yet supported by the state's apparatus of social welfare; at the same time we need to make the argument that the state's apparatus of social welfare should seek to enhance the independence of people with disabilities from the state, but in order to do so must recognize the very real dependencies associated with some disabilities, and must expand and enhance the roles of state-funded dependency workers. These are matters to be determined by democratic deliberation, a deliberation that must include the voices of people with disabilities, their advocates, their family members, surrogates, and guardians. On one side of this deliberation, people like me will engage with moral absolutists for whom one value, one religious interpretation of human life, will always supersede all others; on the other side, we will engage with moral absolutists for whom one value, the value of individual freedom from state regulation, will supersede all others—except when some individual decisions about disability impose social costs on other individuals. This dual engagement, I submit, is central to the challenge of thinking democratically about disability in the age of genomics.

NOTES

1. Critics seem not to have noticed that disability is pervasive in the work of Philip K. Dick. *Martian Time-Slip* features a largely nonverbal character with autism (understood in 1964, both by Dick and the DSM-III, as a form of "childhood schizophrenia") who subtly controls the plot and warps the narrative; he, like many of Dick's "precogs," can see the future only because they are anomalies akin to mutants. And in Total Recall, the film version of "We Can Remember It for You Wholesale," the mutants on Mars are the result of genetic anomalies induced by exposure to radiation; they are the turbinium miners who were not given adequate protection from cosmic rays by their employers. If *Gattaca* is a film about disability-related discrimination, *Total Recall* is a film about employment-related disability. The "mutants" may have exotically anomalous bodies and minds (and at least one of them possesses psychic powers), but they are basically Martian versions of coal miners with black lung disease.

2. Apparently the feeling is mutual, insofar as the Hastings Center report cites *Life As We Know It* approvingly at crucial moments in its argument.

3. This is not to say that a child with Tay-Sachs falls under the infamous Nazi category of "life unworthy of life." I do not believe that any human being has the capacity or the right to so designate another human being. (For a compelling account of what it is like to care for a young child with Tay-Sachs, see Emily Rapp, "Notes From a Dragon Mom.") It is simply to acknowledge that the Chevra Dor Yesurim Program ("Organization for the Generations") was, as Rapp notes, "originally developed by an Orthodox rabbi living in Brooklyn who had lost three children to Tay-Sachs disease" (157). Rapp writes, "modern biomedical genetic technology here undergirds and enhances a traditional patriarchal practice" (157)—namely, arranged marriage. Insofar as no American conservative (or liberal) spokesperson has denounced any Orthodox Jewish organization for screening for Tay-Sachs, I submit that we have achieved some consensus on the acceptability of doing so.

4. This was my argument in "We Still Don't Know What 'Normal' Really Is," and here I fondly hope that the argument has won broad popular agreement—not an unreasonable hope, I submit, insofar as the proposition that many disabilities are undetectable has the virtue of being true.

5. For two regrettable examples of how disability is elided with and collapsed into disease, see Glover's analogy between disability and cancer (35) and Dan Hurley's repeated references to Down syndrome as a "disease" in his *New York Times Magazine* essay, "A Drug for Down Syndrome." My critique of Glover on this count can be found in "Humans, Disabilities, and the Humanities?"

6. At present, as Amy Julia Becker points out, "only 2 percent of all women seek a definitive diagnosis of Down syndrome or other chromosomal abnormalities through amniocentesis or chorionic villa sampling during pregnancy. But of the women who receive that definitive diagnosis, the vast majority (90 percent) choose to terminate their pregnancies." The fear, which I believe to be well-founded (and which I share), is that more prospective parents will screen for Down syndrome if they can do so in the first trimester of pregnancy and without the risk of miscarriage associated with amniocentesis. See, e.g., Pollack (both essays).

7. I call Elshtain's remark "offensive" not simply because I disagree with it, but because I believe it falls short of the standard of intellectual honesty one should expect in serious debate. First, Elshtain ignores passages in which I explicitly say things like "a fetal diagnosis of Down syndrome should not be understood, either by medical personnel or by parents, as a finding to which abortion is the most logical response" (79). Second, Elshtain argues that I caricature the pro-life position:

Bèrubè's [sic] cardboard cutout pro-life politician denies rights to living persons. One wonders who does this. Who are these people? He calls the implications of holding that humans have a right to life "only until they're born" staggering, and this would be true if anybody held to that view. But I can't think of a single pro-lifer who does, certainly not to judge from the literature I received from a number of pro-life groups.

(18)

I submit that Elshtain is too intelligent to intend

this as a serious argument. Surely she is aware of pro-life politicians who support the death penalty. Take the example of the Texas pro-life politician who not only executed dozens of living persons in his home state but publicly mocked one such person's pleas for clemency. Is he the only pro-life politician who believes that the state can take the life of a person? And whatever became of him, anyway?

Last, and far more seriously, Elshtain illegitimately interpolates her own words into a passage she cites, severely misconstruing the passage in the process:

If you had told me in August 1991—or, for that matter, after an amniocentesis in April 1991—that I'd have to feed my infant by dipping a small plastic tube in K-Y jelly and slipping it into his nose and down his pharynx into his teeny tummy, I'd have told you that I wasn't capable of caring for such a child. [In other words, had they had amniocentesis, they would likely have opted for abortion.] But by mid-October, I felt as if I had grown new limbs and new areas of the brain to direct them.

(89; Elshtain's addition in brackets)

There are three things wrong with this interpolation. First, most children with Down syndrome do not require such care as this; therefore, amniocentesis would not have "told" us that we would need to feed Jamie with a gavage tube. Second, the bracketed sentence allows Elshtain to ignore my discussion of prenatal-care counseling and the provision of prospective parents with information about disabilities on pages 67-88 of my book. The reason that's important, in turn, is that my discussion of prenatal testing is targeted in part at genetics counselors, whom I am trying to persuade not to think of the detection of trisomy-21 as a search-and-destroy operation. Third, I am also trying here to persuade prospective parents not to decide in advance that they cannot care for a child with disabilities. Before Jamie was born, I did not know how to feed an infant with a gavage tube, and I would have been terrified at the thought; after he was born, I learned how to do it, just as I learned to care for my first child without knowing how beforehand. Elshtain's "in other words" gets this important point exactly wrong.

8. I choose the traits "propensity to become impatient," "sense of how to arrange a room, and "ability to memorize geographical maps" because these traits happen to describe my own family. The first pertains to me, the second to my partner Janet, and the third to both our children—the one with Down syndrome and the one without.

WORKS CITED

Atwood, Margaret. *Oryx and Crake*. New York: Anchor, 2003.

Becker, Amy Julia. "Has Down Syndrome Hurt Us?" *New York Times* blog, "Motherlode: Adventures in Parenting." Published under the byline of Lisa Belkin. 3 Oct. 2011. http://parenting.blogs.nytimes.com/2011/10/03/has-down-syndrome-hurt-us/

Bérubé, Michael. *Life As We Know It: A Father, a Family, and an Exceptional Child*. New York: Pantheon, 1996.

——. "We Still Don't Know What 'Normal' Is." *The Globe and Mail* 3 Mar. 2007: F8.

——. "Humans, Disabilities, and the Humanities." *On the Human: A Project of the National Humanities Center*. 17 Jan. 2011. http://onthehuman.org/2011/01/humans-disabilities-humanities/.

Ellis, Kathleen. "Reinforcing the Stigma: The Representation of Disability in Gattaca." *Australian Screen Education* 32 (2003): 111-14.

Elshtain, Jean Bethke. "Idiots, Imbeciles, Cretins." Books and Culture: A Christian Review 4.1 (January/February 1998): 18.

Finger, Anne. "Invalids, De-generates, High-Tech Zombies and Old-Fashioned Hollywood Cripples." *Electric Edge: Web Edition of The Ragged Edge*, Jan/Feb 1998. http://www. ragged-edge-mag.com/jan98/movie01.htm.

Gattaca. Dir. Andrew Niccol. Perf. Ethan Hawke, Uma Thurman, Jude Law. Columbia/Tristar, 1997.

Glover, Jonathan. *Choosing Children: Genes, Disability, and Design*. Oxford: Oxford U P, 2006.

Hubbard, Ruth. "Abortion and Disability: Who Should and Should Not Inhabit the World?" *Disability Studies Reader* (this volume). 4th ed. Routledge, 2013.

Hurley, Dan. "A Father's Search for a Drug for Down Syndrome." *New York Times Magazine* 31 Jul. 2011. http://www.nytimes.com/2011/07/31/magazine/a-fathers-search-for-a-drug-for-down-syndrome.html?_r=1.

Kass, Leon. "The Public's Stake." Introduction to "Biotechnology: A House Divided." Symposium with Diana Schaub, Charles Murray, William A. Galston, and J. Bottum. *The Public Interest* 150 (Winter 2003): 38-62.

Parens, Erik, and Adrienne Asch, eds. *Prenatal Testing and Disability Rights*. Hastings Center Studies in Ethics. Washington, DC: Georgetown U P, 2000.

Pollack, Andrew. "A Less Risky Down Syndrome Test is Developed." *New York Times* 17 Oct. 2011. http://www.nytimes.com/2011/10/18/business/sequenom-test-for-down-syndrome-raises-hopes-and-questions.html?pagewanted=all

——. "The Quandary Posed by a New Down Syndrome Test." *New York Times* blog, "Prescriptions: The Business of Health Care." 18 Oct. 2011. http://prescriptions.blogs. nytimes.com/2011/10/18/the-quandary-posed-by-a-new-down-syndrome-test/

The President's Council on Bioethics. *Human Cloning and Human Dignity: An Ethical Inquiry.* Washington, DC: The White House, 2002. http://bioethics. georgetown.edu/pcbe/reports/cloningreport/pcbe_cloning_report.pdf

Rapp, Emily. "Notes from a Dragon Mom." *New York Times* 16 Oct. 2011: SR12. http://www. nytimes.com/2011/10/16/opinion/sunday/notes-from-a-dragon-mom.html

Rapp, Rayna. *Testing Women, Testing the Fetus: The Social Impact of Amniocentesis in America.* New York: Routledge, 1999.

Roberts, Dorothy. *Killing the Black Body: Race, Reproduction, and the Meaning of Liberty.* New York: Pantheon, 1997.

Rothman, Barbara Katz. *Genetic Maps and Human Imaginations: The Limits of Science in Understanding Who We Are.* New York: W. W. Norton, 1998.

Sandel, Michael. *The Case Against Perfection: Ethics in the Age of Genetic Engineering.* Cambridge: Harvard U P, 2007.

CHAPTER 9

A Mad Fight: Psychiatry and Disability Activism

Bradley Lewis

In the late summer of 2003, six people gathered at a small building in Pasadena, California and starved themselves for twenty-two days. The small group of hunger strikers were later joined by over a dozen "solidarity strikers" around the world. Their strike was about "human rights in mental health" and, in particular, it sought to protest the "international domination" of biological approaches to psychiatry and the ever-increasing and widespread use of prescription drugs to treat "mental and emotional crises" (Mindfreedom, July 28, 2003).

The hunger strike caught the attention of the *LA Times, The Washington Post* and, most important for those involved, the attention of the American Psychiatric Association (APA). One of the central aims of the strike was to challenge the main institutions in psychiatry—namely the American Psychiatric Association, the National Alliance of the Mentally Ill (NAMI) and the U.S. Surgeon General—and to rouse them into providing "evidence that clearly establishes the validity of 'schizophrenia,' 'depression' or other 'major mental illnesses' as biologically-based brain diseases" (Mindfreedom, July 28, 2003). The fasters demanded evidence that mental and emotional distress results from "chemical imbalances" in the brain; a view that underpins the biopsychiatric medical model and which currently

dominates mental health treatment in the West.

In demanding this evidence, the strikers were taking a risk. Using a hunger strike to challenge psychiatry and its scientific findings (which are now almost ubiquitously accepted throughout the medical world and wider culture), the protestors faced the possibility of being labeled "mad"—after all, isn't psychiatry a science? Shouldn't scientific questions be decided in laboratories and in peer-reviewed articles filled with graphs and statistical analysis? What sense does it make to hold a hunger strike to challenge contemporary scientific beliefs?

The hunger strikers took the risk because, indeed, they are mad. They are all members of a psychiatry disability activist group known among their friends and allies as "Mad Pride." This activist group is an international coalition devoted to resisting and critiquing clinician-centered psychiatric systems, finding alternative and peer-run approaches to mental health recovery, and helping those who wish to do so minimize their involvement with current psychiatric institutions. They affectionately call themselves "Mad Pride" because they believe mainstream psychiatry over exaggerates psychic pathology and over enforces psychic conformity in the guise of diagnostic labeling and treatment—which all too often comes in the form of forced or manipulated hospitalizations, restraints, seclusions, and medications. Like the celebratory and reappropriative uses of the terms "Crip," "Queer," and "Black Pride," the term "Mad Pride" overturns traditional distinctions and hierarchies. It signifies a reversal of standard pathological connotations of "madness." Rather than pathologizing mental difference, Mad Pride signifies a stance of respect, appreciation, and affirmation.

In this chapter, I discuss the relation of Mad Pride to disability studies, review the history the movement, and work through its contemporary struggles with psychiatry. Throughout the discussion, I highlight the importance of Mad Pride's efforts to go beyond "politics-as-usual." Mad Pride, like other forms of "biocultural" activisms (such as Women's Health Movement and AIDS Coalition to Unleash Power), is located at the interface of bioscience and politics. As such, Mad Pride continuously struggles with epistemological issues along with more typical political issues. In short, the people in Mad Pride struggle over *both* truth and values.

This commingling of politics, power, and truth is familiar ground for disability studies. Similar to Mad Pride, disability studies unpacks and undermines stereotyped representations of disability in science and popular culture to understand and intervene in how "representation attaches meanings to bodies" (Garland-Thomson 1997, 5). Michael Oliver gives a good sense of these stereotyped disability representations by dividing them into key themes of "individualism," "medicalization," and "normality" (Oliver 1990, 56, 58). *Individualism* refers to the perspective that disability is a "personal tragedy." This frame undergirds a "hegemony of disability" which views disability as "pathological and problem-oriented" (Oliver 1996, 129).

It leads to a ubiquitous *medicalization* that legitimizes the medical infrastructure for acquiring knowledge about the disabled individual. The logic of this medical infrastructure rests on notions of *normality* and the dichotomy between normal and pathological. The able-bodied and the disabled, the valued and the devalued, become co-constituted cultural divisions which structure medical and cultural preoccupations (Davis 1995). One side of the binary defines the other and both operate together as "opposing twin figures that legitimate a system of social, economic, and political empowerment justified by physiological differences" (Garland-Thomson 1997, 8).

Together, these stereotyped disability representations direct the health care industry toward a near exclusive focus on individual biomedical cures. Rather than adjust social environments to meet differing bodily needs, medical interventions seek to cure the individual "abnormal" body. Disability activists resist these individualizing and medicalizing approaches by reframing disability as a social restriction and oppression rather than simply a medical problem. Emphasizing a social model rather than a medical model they call attention to the fact that much of the suffering of different bodies comes from social exclusion, isolation, and lack of opportunity, along with the often pernicious side effects of a medical industry bent on aggressive intervention to achieve "normal" bodies.[1]

The task of undermining stereotyped representations of individualism, medicalization, and normality are also central to the Mad Pride movement. Individualistic approaches to mental difference and distress blame and punish the victim for structural problems that are often better understood as located in families, communities, and society. Medicalization, or psychiatrization, legitimizes the medical community's expert authority over the domain of mental difference. And the binary between normal and abnormal shores up this psychiatrization by providing tremendous social and psychological pressure to stay on the side of normality, or sanity. Disability studies scholars refer to social stigma and oppression against the physically different as "ableism"; those in Mad Pride refer to social stigma and oppression against mental difference as "mentalism" or "sanism" (Chamberlin 1977, 219; Perlin 2000, 21).

Despite these similarities, disability activists and Mad Pride members have had difficulty forming a sustained coalition. Part of this difficulty involves the simple fact that two groups are composed of different subcultures—with different histories, different cultural artifacts, and different networks of association. But, beyond this, there are other, deeper reasons. Some disability advocates continue to harbor sanist style associations toward mental difference and do not wish to be associated or "tarnished" by Mad Pride. Likewise, many in Mad Pride (like many in the Deaf community) express discomfort with the "disability" label. They do not see their mental difference as a disability, but rather as a valued capacity. In addition, many in Mad Pride feel that disability struggles are separate from their concerns because physical disability does not involve the same level of state coercion. People with physical differences are often inappropriately confined (through limited choices and multiple manipulations), but Mad Pride activists must deal with an additional layer of state sponsored coercion in the forms of involuntary commitment and forced medication laws.[2]

Like many in both movements, however, I believe it is wise to foreground the similarities between disability activism and Mad Pride. Clearly, all of the new social movements, in one way or another, have to struggle with both truth and values—largely because biomedical science has been used to justify such a broad range of subordination practices. But, more than most, Mad Pride and disability activism face a combined political and epistemological struggle. The very heart of these activisms begins with expressly biomedical assignments of impairment. This comes not in the form of a general pronouncement of inferiority, but in a direct and specific diagnosis and treatment process. Because of this, Mad Pride and disability activist efforts to reduce individualization, medicalization, and ableism require a dual struggle that goes beyond politics-as-usual. The challenge of this dual epistemological and political struggle requires all the allies you can get. When disability activist and Mad Pride work together, they can form a formidable coalition.

THE BIRTH OF MAD PRIDE MOVEMENT

Mad Pride activists have had extensive experience going beyond politics-as-usual. Their lesson of dual engagement goes back to the nineteenth century efforts of Mrs. Elizabeth Ware Packard, an early precursor to today's Mad Pride movement. In 1886, Packard, a former mental hospital patient and founder of the Anti-Insane Asylum Society, began publishing a series of books and pamphlets critical of psychiatry. Packard's writings challenged the subordination of women to their husbands and the remarkable complicity of the political and psychiatric establishment to this subordination (Packard 1868, 1874). As Gerald Grob explains, "When Packard refused to play the role of obedient [minister's] wife and expressed religious ideas bordering on mysticism, her husband had her committed in 1860 to the Illinois State Hospital for the Insane" (Grob 1994, 84). Packard remained incarcerated for three years and only won her freedom by going to court to challenge her confinement. The trial received national publicity and eventually led to Packard being declared sane by the court and released from the asylum. She spent the next twenty years campaigning for personal liberty laws that would protect individuals from wrongful commitment and retention in the asylums.

Even in this early precursor to today's movement, the issues of epistemological struggle and political struggle are inseparably intertwined. Packard challenged pathologizing diagnostic practices that would treat people as insane "simply for the expression of opinions, no matter how absurd these opinions may appear for others" (quoted in Geller and Harris 1994, 66). And she challenged the political abuses that occurred once the insanity diagnosis had been made. Lunatic asylums, she argued, too often left people at the complete mercy of hospital despotism where they were treated worse than convicts or criminals. Packard's dual stress on both the "facts" of insanity and the inhumane treatment of those considered to be insane reverberate into today's resistance to psychiatry.

The more proximate antecedents to today's Mad Pride movement began in the 1970's. Mad Pride activists, during these years, gained momentum from the black civil rights movement, the women's movement, and from the early stages of lesbian and gay movement and the disability movement. Like Elizabeth Packard almost a century before, the key experience that motivated Mad Pride activists was their negative treatment within the psychiatric system. Early founders of the movement shared common experiences of being treated with disrespect, disregard, and discrimination at the hands of psychiatry. Many also suffered from unjustified confinement, verbal and physical abuse, and exclusion from treatment planning.

The testimony of Leonard Roy Frank, cofounder of the Network Against Psychiatric Assault (1972), provides a helpful glimpse into the experiences of many. After graduating from Wharton, Frank moved to San Francisco to sell commercial real estate. He was in his own words "an extraordinarily conventional person" (Farber 1993, 191). Gradually, during his late twenties, he started discovering a new world within himself and began going through an "obvious clash between . . . my emerging self and that of my old self" (191). He later thought of this as a "spiritual transformation." But, at the time, he responded by doing serious reading and reflection on his emerging insights. He ended up rethinking everything in his life: "what was happening to me was that I was busy being born" (191).

A key text for Frank during his transformation was Mohandas Gandhi's autobiography. Frank took seriously Gandhi's message that one's inner life and outer life should interact and complement each other. Reading Gandhi opened his eyes to the violence of political injustice and to the power of non-violent resistance. It also raised his awareness that animals had feelings and could suffer. The more Frank thought about Gandhi's writings on meat-eating, the more he concluded it was inescapably cruel to both animals and to humans: "We can't avoid harming ourselves when we harm other beings, whether human or animal. Meat-eating was an excellent example of how this principle played out in real life . . . Because it was inherently cruel to animals and morally wrong, it affected the wrong doers by causing them to become sick and cutting short their lives" (206). This combination of insights made it difficult for Frank to continue his previous lifestyle and his work selling commercial real estate; he soon lost his job, grew a beard, became vegetarian, and devoted himself to full time spiritual exploration.

Frank was exhilarated by the process, but his parents were deeply concerned. Seeing Frank's transition through the stereotyped frames of individualization, psychiatrization, and sanism, they thought he was having a "breakdown." They tried to persuade him to see a psychiatrist, but Frank resisted. They responded by arranging an involuntary commitment. The hospital records show that Frank's psychiatrists document symptoms of "not working, withdrawal, growing a beard, becoming a vegetarian, bizarre behavior, negativism, strong beliefs, piercing eyes, and religious preoccupations" (193). The psychiatrists diagnosed him as "paranoid schizophrenia," and they started a sustained course of court authorized insulin-electroshock treatments that lasted nine months and included fifty insulin comas and thirty-five electroshocks.

When the psychiatrists were not giving him shock treatments, their "therapeutic" interactions with Frank revolved around his behavior: particularly his refusal to shave or eat meat. There was never any discussion of his emerging beliefs or his spirituality. Instead, Frank's psychiatrists focused on changing overt signs of "abnormality." They even went so far as to shave his beard while he was unconscious from an insulin treatment. Frank eventually came to realize that his hospital resistance was futile, and, with the ever increasing numbers of shock treatments, he also came to fear he was in a "life or death" situation: "These so-called [shock] treatments literally wiped out all my memory for the [previous] two-year period . . . I realized that my high-school and college were all but gone; educationally, I was at about the eighth-grade level" (196).

Rather than risk more "treatments," Frank surrendered. He played the psychiatrists' game and did what they wanted: "I shaved voluntarily, ate some non vegetarian foods like clam chowder and eggs, was somewhat sociable, and smiled 'appropriately' at my jailers" (196). After his release, it took six years to recover from his treatment. But, throughout it all, he never gave up on his beliefs, and he never saw another psychiatrist for treatment. He went on to become a major figure in early Mad Pride activism,

During the early 1970s, people like Frank began to recognize they were not alone and started organizing local consciousness-raising groups. In the United States this includes such organization as the Insane Liberation Front in Portland Oregon (1970), the Mental Patient's Liberation Project in New York City (1971), and the Mental Patients' Liberation Front in Boston (1971). These groups built support programs, advocated for hospitalized patients, lobbied for changes in the laws, and educated the public through guest lectures and newsletters. In addition, they began the process of developing alternative, creative, and artistic ways of dealing with emotional suffering and psychological difference outside the medical models of psychiatry. The publication of Mad Pride activist Judi Chamberlin's book *On Our Own* (1977) in the mainstream press was a milestone in the development of peer run alternatives (Van Tosh and del Vecchio 2000, 9). Chamberlin used the book to expose her own abuse at the hands of psychiatry and to give a detailed account of burgeoning consumer run alternatives. The eloquence, optimism, and timing of the book was a critical catalyst for many in the movement. As ex-patient Mary O'Hagan puts it: "When my mood swings died away I was angry and amazed at how the mental health system could be so ineffective. There had to be a better way. I searched the library not quite knowing what I was looking for. And there it was, a book called *On Our Own* by Judi Chamberlin. It was all about ex-patients who set up their own alternatives to the mental health system and it set me on my journey in to the psychiatric survivor movement" (quoted in Chamberlin, 1977, back cover).

The newly formed local Mad Pride groups also organized an annual Conference on Human Rights and Psychiatric Oppression to help connect local members with the wider movement. At these meetings, activists from across the country gathered to socialize, strategize, and share experiences. They gained solidarity and increasing momentum from the experience of being with like minded activists. Between meetings local groups communicated through a newspaper forum. The San Francisco local newsletter, *Madness Network News*, evolved into a newspaper format which covered ex-patient activities across North America and around the world. This publication became the major voice of the movement, with each issue containing a rich selection of personal memoirs, creative writing, cartoons, humor, art, political commentary, and factual reporting—all from the ex-patient point of view (Hirsch 1974; Chamberlin 1990, 327).

This early period of the Mad Pride movement was also the most radical in its epistemological critique. Early leaders of the movement drew philosophical support from high-profile critical writers that, as a group, came to be known as "anti-psychiatry." Writers such as Erving Goffman (1961), R. D. Laing (1967), Thomas Scheff (1966), and Thomas Szasz (1961) may have differed widely in their philosophies, but collectively their main tenets were clear. Mental illness is not an objective medical reality but rather either a negative label or a strategy for coping in a mad world. As Laing put it, "the apparent irrationality of the single 'psychotic' individual" may often be understood "within the context of the family." And, in turn, the irrationality of the family can be understood if it is placed "within the context of yet larger organizations and institutions" (Laing 1968, 15). Put in context in this way, madness has a legitimacy of its own which is erased by medical-model approaches that can only pathologize it. For many anti-psychiatry writers, mental suffering can be the beginning of a healing process and should not be suppressed through aggressive behavioral or biological interventions.

The most epistemologically radical of the anti-psychiatry writers, Thomas Szasz, had the most influence on U.S. activists. Szasz, a dissident psychiatrist, was shunned within his own field, but his prolific writings (over twenty-five books) and forceful prose gave him tremendous influence outside psychiatry (Leifer 1997). Throughout his work, Szasz's argument was always two-fold: (1) mental illness is a myth and (2) there should be complete separation between psychiatry and the state. As Szasz put it in a summary statement, "Involuntary mental hospitalization is imprisonment under the guise of treatment; it is a covert form of social control that subverts the rule of law. No one ought to be deprived of liberty except for a criminal offense, after a trial by jury guided by legal rules of evidence. No one ought to be detained against their will in a building called 'hospital,' or any other medical institution, on the basis of expert opinion" (Szasz 1998).

Consistent with others in the Mad Pride movement, Szasz combined his epistemology and his politics. Szasz's insistence on the autonomy of mental health clients rested directly on his epistemology, which he based on a strong positivist philosophy of science that emphasized a sharp demarcation between observation and conjecture. For Szasz, *physical illness* was real because it was based on actual observation, but *mental illness* was at best a metaphor. A broken leg is real because you can see the x-ray, but a "broken brain" is a myth because there is no x-ray that will show it. For Szasz, to see mental illness as "real" rather than as a metaphor was to make a serious category mistake. "Mental illness" is not objectively observable; it is a myth.

MAD PRIDE TODAY

During the last thirty years of their struggle, Mad Pride has increasingly infiltrated the mental health system rather than simply criticizing it from outside. Despite the fact that institutional psychiatry continues to ignore and denigrate their efforts, important government agencies involved in mental health policy have begun to pay attention. Mad Pride activists have been particularly successful in increasing consumer participation in treatment planning and facility governance. In addition, they have gained increasing respect for the work developing peer run treatment alternatives.

The most important agency to pay attention to Mad Pride perspectives has been the national Center for Mental Health Services (CMHS). This little known public agency is "charged with leading the national system that delivers mental health services" (Center for Mental Health Services 2002). Following on the success of Chamberlin's *On Our Own*, the agency worked with a local California peer group to publish *Reaching Across: Mental Health Clients Helping Each Other*, a "how to" manual for peer run services (Zinnman, Harp, and Budd 1987). For too long, CMHS explains, "decisions about mental health policies and services were made without any input from people who have mental illnesses or their families. As a result, some policies and programs failed to meet the needs of the people they were intended to serve" (Center for Mental Health Services 2004) CMHS worked to change this by sponsoring peer-run research, training, and technical assistance centers, and producing federally mandated documents encouraging states to include consumer-operated alternatives to traditional treatment programs. Since 1985, CMHS has also sponsored an annual, national level, Alternatives Conference that brings together consumers and ex-patients to network and to share the results of their scholarship and program development.

These political successes have gradually necessitated a change in Mad Pride's epistemological critique. Szasz's strong epistemological critique of psychiatry was useful in the early days of the movement, but it became less so as Mad Pride shifted into its more contemporary formations. The early anti-psychiatry literature set up an either/or relation between consumers and providers. People had to either be with psychiatry or against it. Szasz's rigid positivist epistemology left little room for contradiction and coalition politics. As sociologist and Mad Pride activist Linda Morrison points out, with increasing infiltration of the mental health system, many members no longer took a hard-line approach to psychiatry. These members identified themselves more as "consumers" than "survivors" or "ex-patients." Consumers, by definition, were critical of aspects of psychiatry but were willing to legitimize and participate in other aspects (Morrison 2005). Mad Pride needed to embrace these contradictions and adopt coalition politics to avoid losing these members.

Contemporary Mad Pride members have made just this kind of epistemological shift. Though activists still reference Szasz favorably, they now draw more on his political values (of autonomy and separation of psychiatry and state) than on his epistemology. Mad Pride members mark this shifting epistemology by referring to themselves as "consumer/survivor/ex-patient" groups. This hyphenated designation, usually shortened to "c/s/x" or "consumer/survivors," highlights that today's Mad Pride is a coalition of critical activists—some of whom have a more radical epistemological critique than others (Morrison 2005).

This shift has set the stage for additional coalitional possibilities between Mad Pride and critical psychiatrists. Increasingly, critical psychiatrists are moving beyond the narrow approaches of their training and drawing from interdisciplinary theory in science studies, disability studies, and the humanities. Like Mad Pride, they are developing alternative perspectives on psychiatry that emphasizes the importance of social models and of democratic research and treatment. In Britain, an influential Critical Psychiatry Network (www.critpsynet.freeuk.com/critpsynet.htm) has recently formed, bringing together a coalition of critical providers and consumer/survivors (Double 2002).[3]

Contemporary Mad Pride's political success at getting a seat at the table of mental health policy has also necessitated a change in the more radical infrastructure of the movement. The Conference on Human Rights and Psychiatric Oppression no longer meets and has now been replaced by the Alternatives Conference sponsored by CMHS. The different name of the conference is consistent with a shift in emphasis from psychiatric oppression to peer-run support and service involvement. The change is subtle as both oppression and support remain paramount for Mad Pride, but the change does mark a shift of the emphasis within the movement.

In addition, the newspaper *Madness Network News* is no longer being published. Today's Mad Pride connects its members largely through the activities of the Support Coalitions International (SCI) which brings together one hundred international local groups. Under the leadership of David Oaks, SCI has become "the epicenter of the Mad Movement" ("Windows into madness," 2002). It runs a Web site (www.mindfreedom.com), an e-mail list, a magazine (*Mindfreedom Journal*), and an online "Mad Market" (where interested parties can find "a little library of dangerous books"). Much of the success of the center comes from Oaks' capacity to build a coalition of consumers, survivors, and ex-patients. Like Packard, Frank, and Chamberlin before him, Oaks' motivation for mental health activism comes from his experiences of psychiatric abuse: including forced hospitalization and forced treatment. Like so many others, he has taken those experiences and turned them into political action.

RECENT STRUGGLES WITH PSYCHIATRY

Despite the successes Mad Pride has had within the mental health system, their epistemological and political struggle with psychiatry continues. These struggles are often complicated, and they require impressive political savvy. In this section, I work through some examples of these struggles to give a sense of the political terrain and the critical importance of today's consumer/survivor activism. The 2003 hunger strike is a good example of Mad Pride's contemporary epistemological battles. To understand the context of the strike, it is important to note that during the same time Mad Pride has complicated its epistemology, psychiatry has gone in the exact opposite direction. The last thirty years have seen a "scientific revolution" in psychiatry that primarily values quantitative, positivistic protocols for research (Lewis, 2006). The emphasis on "objective" data has created a preference for neuroscience and genetics at the expense of an array of cultural and humanistic styles of inquiry. This new scientific psychiatry, working in tandem with pharmaceutical funding, has gone on to create today's dominant clinical model of psychiatry, "biopsychiatry"— whose emphasis is almost exclusively biomedical style diagnoses and pharmacological treatments.

The blockbuster medication, Prozac, gives a window into biopsychiatry's dominance. Between 1987 and 2002 (the year Prozac came off patent), over 27 million new prescriptions for the drug were written. Combined with the multiple "me too" drugs it inspired—the class of antidepressants known as "selective serotonin inhibitors" (SSRI)—that total reached 67.5 million in the United States alone (Aldred 2004). That means almost one in every four people in the United States were started on a Prozac-type drug between 1987 and 2002. These same one in four people were dealing with sufficient emotional issues that someone thought they needed help.

For some of these people, the SSRIs may have been the best choice. But was it the best choice for 67.5 million people? Psychiatry's professional literature, its patient hand-outs, and the popular press all tell us "yes." They tout "scientific progress in the treatment of depression" as the main reason for the SSRIs extensive use (Gardner 2003; Lewis 2006; Metzl 2003). But, if we scratch the surface, we find that the SSRIs are highly controversial, and researchers have not been able to agree on even simple questions like: Do the drugs work? Or, are they safe? The *Handbook of Psychiatric Drug Therapy*, typical of most clinical reviews, claims with great authority that the SSRIs are highly effective and that they have a mild side effect profile (Arana and Rosenbaum 2000, 57, 76). But critical analysts conclude just the opposite: that the SSRIs are not much better than sugar pills and that they have major side effects—including sexual dysfunction, suicidality, and even violence (Breggin 1994, 65; Fisher and Fisher 1996; Glenmullen 2000; Healy 2004; Kirsch and Sapirstein 1998). Going further, scientific opinion is also at odds regarding the question of explanation. Some argue that the SSRIs have effects because they treat biological disease. But others argue these drugs are simply stimulants like cocaine and amphetamines. These researchers conclude that SSRIs are mood brighteners and psychic energizers because they work on the same neurotrans-

mitters as other stimulants (Breggin 1994; Glenmullen 2000).

When we take these controversies surrounding the Prozac-type drugs into account, it seems highly questionable that the SSRIs were the best choice for 67.5 million people. For most of these people, alternatives like psychotherapy, peer-support, and personal and political activism would have likely been better options than taking drugs that are expensive, are possibly no better than placebo, have multiple side effects, and may be little more than a dressed up version of speed. But, because of the hype of biopsychiatry, these controversies are not well known and alternatives are not given a chance. The SSRIs are seen as quick and easy solutions backed by advances in psychiatric science and individual medical recommendations. For most people thrown in that situation, they are seen as the only viable option.

Mad Pride's hunger strike was directed squarely at this so-called "biological revolution" in psychiatry. The fasters, organized by David Oaks and Support Coalition International, demanded evidence that emotional and mental distress can be deemed "biologically-based" brain diseases, and also evidence that psychopharmaceutical treatments can correct those "chemical imbalances" attributed to a psychiatric diagnoses (MindFreedom, July 28, 2003).

The strikers were not trying to show that the biopsychiatric model of mental illness is myth, and they were not touting another model of mental distress as better or more accurate. The protestors stated from the outset that they were aware that psychopharmaceuticals work for some people, and that they were not judging individuals who choose to employ biopsychiatric approaches in an effort to seek relief. For Oaks and his fellow protestors, there are "many ways to help people experiencing severe mental and emotional crises . . .

We respect the right of people to choose the option of prescribed psychiatric drugs. Many of us have made this personal choice. . . . However, choice in the mental health field is severely limited. One approach dominates, and that is a belief in chemical imbalances, genetic determinism and psychiatric drugs as the treatment of choice. Far too often this limited choice has been exceedingly harmful to both the body and the spirit" (MindFreedom, July 28, 2003). In demanding evidence, the strikers hoped to show that the "chemical imbalance" theory of mental distress is not watertight, and to therefore challenge the overinvestment in this "biopsychiatric approach" by the mental health institutions.

In the early days of the strike, the APA brushed off the strikers demands for evidence and told them to consult introductory textbooks on psychiatry. The strikers responded by persisting in their demands and by sending a letter to the APA written by a panel of fourteen critical scholars. The letter showed that within the very textbooks that the APA had recommended there were numerous statements that invalidated the notion that mental illnesses have specific biological bases (MindFreedom, August 22, 2003). Using psychiatry's own knowledge against itself, the hunger strikers prompted the APA to respond more fully, and a follow up communiqué from APA finally conceded that "brain science has not advanced to the point where scientists or clinicians can point to readily discernible pathological lesions or genetic abnormalities that in and of themselves serve as a reliable or predictive biomarkers of a given mental disorder" (APA 2003). This reluctant admission from the APA marked an important epistemological victory for Mad Pride. In an interview, Oaks said: "They acknowledged that they didn't have the biological evidence [of mental illness], so that's on the record" (Davis 2003). The hunger strike vividly demonstrated how problematic it is to accept without question the "truths" of biopsychiatry.[4]

Despite this small success, Mad Pride's epistemological struggle continues to be a tough one. They are battling against a veritable superpower whose main ally is the hugely profitable and very influential pharmaceutical industry. As David Davis reports in his *LA Times* article on the hunger strike, Mad Pride is up against both an American Psychiatric Association, whose conventions bustle with "brightly colored" booths of the drug companies, and a booming pharmaceutical industry whose "sales of psychotherapeutics reached $21 billion in 2002, almost double the $11 billion in sales in 1998" (Davis 2003).[5]

Because of the influence and clout of biopsychiatry, Mad Pride knows all too well that skirmishes over epistemology are only part of the struggle. While it is vital to strike at the heart of mainstream psychiatry's "knowledge" and "truths," it is just as vital to realize that the epistemology game is hard to win. Science studies scholar Bruno Latour explains that dissenters of science can only go so far by using scientific literature against itself. For alternative perspectives to successfully join in the process of science (and truth) in the making, they must build their own "counter-laboratories," which of course requires tremendous resources (Latour 1987, 79). Mad Pride clearly does not have the resources to compete laboratory for laboratory with the institutions of psychiatry and their pharmaceutical supporters. Thus, while Mad Pride continues to play the game of epistemology, and continues to have some successes destabilizing psychiatry's biomedical model, it also struggles with psychiatry on the more typically political and economic terrain.

This was particularly evident in 2002 when President George W. Bush's administration initiated what David Oaks dubbed "the Bush triple play," which prompted

Mad Pride to mobilize swiftly and energetically to fight on the political front (Oaks 2002–2003). The triple play included:

1. The planned appointment of a controversial conservative psychiatrist, Dr. Sally Satel, to the important National Advisory Council for Mental Health.
2. The announcement of budget cuts to key government sponsored consumer/survivor technical support centers.
3. The creation of a New Freedom Commission to study U.S. mental health services.

All aspects of this triple play posed direct threats to Mad Pride and to the consumer/survivor movement, and they threatened the freedoms and rights of those suffering mental and emotional crises.

The first part of the triple play began with a White House leak, with word coming out that Dr. Sally Satel was being selected by the Bush administration for a position on the advisory council for the CMHS (the very organization which has been most receptive to consumer/survivor initiatives). Dr. Satel—a fellow at the American Enterprise Institute (a conservative political think tank)—is the author of the controversial book *P. C., M.D.: How Political Correctness is Corrupting Medicine*. She is not only a vociferous advocate of the biopsychiatric model of mental illness, she is also an outspoken critic of the consumer survivor movement, and an insistent lobbyist for involuntary commitment and treatment laws. In *P.C., M.D.*, under a chapter titled "Inmates Take Over the Asylum," Satel names the leaders of the Mad Pride movement and attacks their hard fought efforts to increase peer run services and reduce involuntary treatments. She denigrates mental health administrators who have taken Mad Pride seriously: "Tragically, they [mental health administrators] seem to be willing to sacrifice the needs of those with the most severe illnesses to political correctness and to the expediency of placating the vocal and annoying consumer/survivor lobby" (76). And she even goes so far as to describe the Alternatives Conference as the "guinea pig rebellion" (50).

For Mad Pride, Satel's appointment and her public vilification of consumer-run organizations signaled an overall Bush administration strategy to aggressively push a controversial biopsychiatry paradigm, to abandon consumer run self-help and peer support programs, and to increase forced psychiatric medication.

These concerns were reinforced by the second part of the Bush triple play. Soon after the leak about Dr. Satel, the Bush administration announced budget cuts for CMHS sponsored consumer/survivor technical assistance centers. Although the cuts totaled only $2 million out of the total CMHS budget, they were targeted directly at consumer/survivors. Three out of five of these centers were consumer run, which represented a clear about face for CMHS. Joseph Rogers, director of one of the programs to be cut, the National Mental Health Consumer Self-Help Clearinghouse, commented that "We had no warning. The cuts just came out of the blue, and we've had no explanation since that makes any sense" (Mulligan 2002).

The third part of the Bush triple play was the creation of a New Freedom Commission on mental health. Bush hailed the commission as a major step toward improving mental health services, and he charged it with the ambitious goals of reviewing the quality of mental health services, identifying innovative programs, and formulating federal, state, and local level policy options. The administration stipulated that the commission be composed of fifteen members and that these members be selected from a range of stakeholder groups: including providers, payers, administrators, consumers, and family members (Bush 2002).

Although all of this sounded laudable enough, but true to Mad Pride concerns, when the New Freedom Commission's fifteen members were made public, only one person self-identified as having personally experienced the mental health system or as involved in the consumer/survivor movement. The New Freedom Commission's choice of members appeared not to be about true stakeholder inclusion, but only a crude form of tokenism.

For many consumer/survivors, the Bush triple play was not only an outrage, it was a serious danger. These three deft moves threatened to undo all the gains consumer/survivors had made over the past thirty years. Oaks put it this way: "Mental health consumers and psychiatric survivors have experienced fierce repression. But to have a well-funded think tank unite with a Presidential administration to openly attack our movement in such a way is unprecedented. As the enormity of the attacks set in, several activists said they were numb with disbelief" (Oaks 2002–2003).

Mad Pride activists could have reasonably given up at this juncture. Instead, they held a strategy meeting with colleagues from the international movement, and they decided to directly oppose each part of the Bush triple play. Opposition to Dr. Satel's appointment and the cuts to CHMS programs took the form of a blitz of emails to consumer/survivor list-servs, active lobbying of mental health administrators, and a barrage of critical faxes to Secretary Tommy Thompson of the U.S. Dept. of Health & Human Services. And, rather than being dismayed by the non-democratic message of the New Freedom Commission's selection process, consumer/survivors took full advantage of the Commission's plan to hold public hearings on psychiatric services. Four days before the first scheduled hearing, consumer/survivors gathered for an emergency meeting with a network of physical disability activists. Judi Chamberlin, who has been a long-time advocate of disability and Mad Pride coalitions, explained the rationale for involving the larger disability movement, "When a wolf wants to target a whole flock, it looks for the most vulnerable lamb. The Bush administration is targeting psychiatric survivors today, but the whole disability movement is the target tomorrow" (Oaks 2002–2003).

The meeting turned out to be a major inspiration for consumer/survivors. The first speaker that night was Justin Dart, who many call the "Martin Luther King" of the disability movement. Dart, struggling with the last stages of terminal illness (he died just eight days later), gave a rousing speech which set the tone for the meeting. Dart proposed that,

> . . . we in the disability communities must unite with all who love justice to lead a revolution of empowerment. A revolution, to create a culture that will empower every single individual including all people with psychiatric disabilities, to live his or her God given potential for self determination, productivity and quality of life.
>
> Empowerment means choices—individual choices about where we live, how we live, where we work, choices about health care. We have a right to complete quality health care of our own choosing.
>
> NO FORCED TREATMENT EVER.
> We choose our own doctors and medication. We choose the places of care. No denial of treatment ever.
> NO FORCED TREATMENT EVER.
>
> (Oaks 2002)

The combined presence of Dart and several other disability representatives created the strategic capacity to get the word out and rally support and resistance far beyond the usual consumer/survivor community. It also further advanced a cross-disability activist connection between the disability movement and consumer/survivors.

On the day of the New Freedom Commission's first public meeting, consumer/

survivor activists and their disability activist comrades made their presence known. Not only did they hand out their own press release and talk individually to members of the Bush Commission, they also made public announcements. Judi Chamberlin's testimony was typical. Announcing that she was a "psychiatric survivor" and "an advocate" on consumer/survivor issues for more than thirty years," she pointed out:

> A basic premise of the disability rights movement is simply this: Nothing About Us Without Us. The makeup of the Commission violates this basic principle. Just as women would not accept the legitimacy of a commission of "expert" men to define women's needs, or ethnic and racial minorities would not accept a panel of "expert" white people to define their needs, we similarly see the Commission as basically irrelevant to our struggle to define our own needs.
>
> (Chamberlin 2002)

Chamberlin argued that the New Freedom Commission lacked the "expertise on the consumer/survivor experience" as well as the "expertise of disability rights activists, those knowledgeable about the legal and civil rights of people diagnosed with mental illness, and experts in community integration." And she went on to detail how that expertise could be provided.

Unlike the results of the hunger strike, however, the results of Mad Pride's efforts to resist the Bush triple play can only be described as mixed. With regard to part one of the triple play, Mad Pride was unable to stop Sally Satel's appointment to the advisory board. Once on the board, she predictably advocated for more forced treatment and for discontinuation of consumer-run programs. But part two of the triple play, the planned budget cuts to peer support programs, never materialized. The three technical centers sponsored by CMHS continued to be funded.

The New Freedom Commission results were also contradictory. On the one hand, the commission was quite responsive to Mad Pride concerns. It agreed with Mad Pride that the mental health system is fundamentally broken, that it needs extensive overhaul (not just piecemeal reform), that mental health services must be consumer and family centered, that modern psychiatry over emphasizes reductionist biomedical approaches, and that consumers must be protected from unjust incarceration and the use of seclusion and restraints. Together these recommendations signified an impressive success for Mad Pride's (and their disability allies) efforts to reach the commission and have their voices included in the report.

But, on the other hand, all was not rosy with the commission's report. In addition to the above recommendations, the New Freedom Commission also recommended nationwide mental health screenings in schools, primary care offices, prisons, and the welfare system. The ominous dimension of this plan was pointed out the *British Medical Journal* (*BMJ*) in an exposé titled "Bush plans to screen whole US population for mental illness." The *BMJ* explained that the New Freedom Commission recommendation for nationwide screening was linked to their recommendation for "evidence-based" treatment protocols. In psychiatry, these protocols are code words for the Texas Medication Algorithm Project (TMAP). TMAP was started in 1995 as an alliance between the pharmaceutical industry, the University of Texas, and the mental health system to set up expert guidelines for psychiatric practices. But a whistle blower at TMAP, Allen Jones, revealed that key officials received money and perks from the drug companies to unnecessarily promote expensive on-patent drugs. As Jones explained, "the same political/pharmaceutical alliance" behind TMAP are also behind the New Freedom Commission.

This alliance is "poised to consolidate the TMAP effort into a comprehensive national policy" of over-treating mental illness with expensive medications (Lenzer 2004). When you add to this state of affairs the recent National Institute of Health conclusion that half of all Americans will meet the criteria for a *DSM-IV* disorder some time in their life, the profiteering possibilities of the New Freedom Commission's political/pharmaceutical alliance is easy to imagine (Kessler 2005).

Of course, none of this screening will go forward without resistance. In quick response to the *BMJ* exposé, Mindfreedom sent out a news release "What You Gonna Do When They Screen For You" and set up a section of its Web site titled "President Bush and the Shrinking of the USA" (see http://www.mindfreedom.org/mindfreedom/bush_psychiatry.shtml). This news board gives access to breaking stories and commentary, plus it provides answers to frequently asked questions concerning the controversy. In addition, the Mad Pride advocacy group, Alliance for Human Research Protection (AHRP), has begun to monitor closely the outcomes of the New Freedom Commission (see http://www.ahrp.org/about/about.php). At the time of this writing, AHRP reports that lawsuits are already being filed in Indiana to resist the effects of "TeenScreen Depression"—a program funded partly with new federal grants initiated by the New Freedom Commission.[6]

CONCLUSION

These recent conflicts with psychiatry provide an important window into Mad Pride's ongoing epistemological and political struggles. Against tremendous odds, the movement has worked impressively to expose psychiatry as a limited field of inquiry, to open up its clinical services to more peer-run alternatives, and to reduce coercive connections between psychiatry and the state. Their fight to reduce individualization, psychiatrization, and sanist approaches to psychic life is arduous, and at times a little "mad." But the stakes are high and the struggle must continue. With the increasing coalition with the broader disability movement and the emergence of a critical psychiatry network, the fight is becoming more and more mainstream. Soon the battle will be one about which we all know and in which we can all participate. Active biocultural citizenship regarding mental difference and distress requires nothing less.

As the editors of *Adbusters* sum up in their issue on Mad Pride, in a culture of hardening isolation, status, materialism, and environmental degradation, "Mad Pride can be a broad embrace. It is a signal that we will allow ourselves our deep sorrow, our manic hope, or fierce anxiety, our imperfect rage. These will be our feedback into the system. We reserve the right to seek relief from both our most troubling symptoms and from society's most punitive norms. The sickness runs deep; without madness, there is no hope of cure" ("Deep sadness, manic hope," 2002).

NOTES

1. Public health scholar Barbara Starfield estimates that the combined effect of medical adverse effects in the United States are as follows:

   - 12,000 deaths/year from unnecessary surgery
   - 7,000 deaths/year from medication errors in hospitals
   - 20,000 deaths/year from other errors in hospitals
   - 80,000 deaths/year from nosocomial infections in hospitals
   - 106,000 deaths/year from nonerror, adverse effects of medications

   That comes to a total to 225,000 deaths per year from iatrogenic causes—which constitutes the third leading cause of death in the United States.

Just after heart disease and cancer (Starfield 2000, 484).

2. For an extended discussion of confinement and disability see the "Confinement" entry in the *Encyclopedia of Disability Studies* (Lewis 2005).

3. The Critical Psychiatry Network organizes its members less under the banner of "anti-psychiatry" and more under the banner of "post-psychiatry" (Thomas and Bracken 2004). The epistemological underpinning of post-psychiatry avoids the either/or problems of anti-psychiatry. Relying on the philosophy of Michel Foucault, a post-psychiatric perspective blurs the binary between truth and myth as all forms of human knowledge making are understood to be both material and semantic (Bracken and Thomas 2001; Foucault 1965 and 2003; Lewis 2006). This shift moves the legitimacy question of psychiatric knowledge from "truth" to "consequences." The issue is not whether psychiatric knowledge magically mirrors the world, but who is allowed to participate in making the knowledge? What kinds of consequences (and for whom) will follow from the knowledge?

4. For an extended analysis of the exchange between Mad Pride and the APA see critical psychiatrists Duncan Double's review: "Biomedical Bias of the American Psychiatric Association" (Double 2004).

5. See former editor-in-chief of the *New England Journal of Medicine* Marcia Angell's book, *The Truth about Drug Companies: How They Deceive Us and What to do About It* (2004), for an extended discussion of the influence of the pharmaceuticals on medical research and practice. Also see Pulitzer Prize finalist Robert Whitaker's book, *Mad in America: Bad Science, Bad Medicine, and the Enduring Mistreatment of the Mentally Ill* (2002) for an historical perspective specific to psychiatry.

6. Theresa and Michael Rhoades, who filed the first suit, claim that TeenScreen sent their daughter home from school telling her she had been diagnosed with obsessive compulsive disorder and social anxiety disorder. The Rhoades "claim that the survey was erroneous, improper, and done with reckless disregard for their daughter's welfare and that they did not give the school permission to give the test" (Pringle 2005). High profile attorney John Whitehead calls the situation an "Orwellian Nightmare" and has agreed to take on the Rhoades case. However, "because of the financial backing of pharmaceutical companies and the Bush administration's support through the New Freedom Commission," even Whitehead is concerned and considers his opposition to be formidable foes (Alliance for Human Research Protection 2005).

REFERENCES

Aldred, G. (2004) "An Analysis of the Use of Prozac, Paxil, and Zoloft in USA 1988–2002." Retrieved on June 2, 2005 from the Alliance for Research Protection, http://www.ahrp.org/risks/usSSRIuse0604.pdf.

Alliance for Human Research Protection (2005). "The Rutherford Institute takes on TeenScreen case in Indiana." Retrieved on July 25 from http://www.ahrp.org/infomail/05/06/13.php.

American Psychiatric Association (2003). *Statement on diagnosis and treatment of mental disorders.* Release no. 03-39, September 25, 2003. Retrieved on July 15, 2005 from http://www.psych.org/news_room/press_releases/mentaldisorders0339.pdf.

Angell, M. (2004). *The truth about drug companies: How they deceive us and what to do about it.* New York: Random House.

Arana, G., and Rosenbaum, J. (2000). *Handbook of psychiatric drug therapy,* 4th ed. Philadelphia: Lippincott Williams and Wilkins.

Braken, P., and Thomas, P. (2001). "Postpsychiatry: a new direction for mental health." *British Medical Journal* 322:724–727.

Breggin, P. (1994). *Talking back to Prozac: What doctors aren't telling you about today's most controversial drugs.* New York: St. Martins Press.

Bush, G. W. (2002). "President's New Freedom Commission on Mental Health: Executive Order." The White House. President George W. Bush On line. Released on April, 29, 2002. Retrieved on June 17, 2005 from http://www.whitehouse.gov/news/releases/2002/04/20020429-2.html.

Center for Mental Health Services (2002). "About CMHS." Retrieved on July 20, 2005 from http://www.mentalhealth.samhsa.gov/cmhs/about.asp.

Center for Mental Health Services (2004). "Consumer affairs program." Retrieved on July 20, 2005 from http://www.mentalhealth.samhsa.gov/consumersurvivor/about.asp.

Chamberlin, J. (1977). *On our own: Patient-controlled alternatives to the mental health system.* Lawrence, MA: National Empowerment Center, Inc.

Chamberlin, J. (1990). "The ex-patients' movement: Where we've been and where we are going." *Journal of Mind and Behavior* 11 (3&4): 323–336.

Chamberlin, J. (2002). "Testimony of Judi Chamberlin." American Association of People with Disabilities On line. Retrieved on June 17, 2005 from http://www.aapd-dc.org/News/disability/testjudichamberlin.html.

Davis, D. (2003). "David Oaks and others in the 'Mad Pride' movement believe drugs are being overused in treating mental illness, and they want the abuse stopped." *L.A. Times Magazine*, Sunday, October 23, 2003 .Retrieved on July 20, 2005 from http://www.latimes.com.

Davis, L. (1995). *Enforcing normalcy: Disability, deafness, and the body*. London: Verso.

"Deep sadness, manic hope: A movement for liberty, and the pursuit of madness." (2002). *Adbusters* (10) 3.

Double, D. (2002). "The limits of psychiatry." *British Medical Journal* 324: 900-904.

Double, D. (2004). "Biomedical bias of the American Psychiatric Association." Critical Psychiatry Web site. Retrieved on June 22, 2005 from http://www.critpsynet.freeuk.com/biomedicalbias.htm.

Farber, S. (1993). "From victim to revolutionary: An interview with Lennard Frank." In *Madness, heresy, and the rumor of angels: The revolt against the mental health system*. Chicago: Open Court.

Fisher, R., and Fisher, S., (1996). "Antidepressants for children: Is scientific support necessary?" *Journal of Nervous and Mental Disease* 184: 99–102.

Foucault, M. (1965). *Madness and civilization: A history of insanity in the age of reason*. New York: Vintage Books.

Foucault, M. (2003). *Abnormal: Lectures at the College of France 1974–1975*. New York: Picador.

Gardner, P. (2003). "Distorted packaging: Marketing depression as illness, drugs as cures." *Journal of Medical Humanities* 24 (1/2): 105–130.

Garland-Thomson, R. (1997). *Extraordinary bodies: figuring physical disability in American culture and literature*. New York: Columbia University Press.

Geller, J., and Harris, M. (1994). *Women of asylum: Voices from behind the walls 1840–1945*. New York: Doubleday.

Glenmullen, J. (2000). *Prozac backlash: Overcoming the dangers of Prozac, Zoloft, Paxil, and other antidepressants with save, effective alternatives*. New York: Touchstone.

Goffman, E. (1961). *Asylums: Essays on the social situation of mental patients and other inmates*. New York: Doubleday.

Grob, G. (1994). *The mad among us: A history of the care of America's mentally ill*. Cambridge, MA: Harvard University Press.

Healy, D. (2004). *Let them eat Prozac: The unhealthy relationship between the pharmaceutical industry and depression*. New York: New York University Press.

Hirsch, S. (Ed.) (1974) *Madness Network News Reader*. San Francisco: Glide Publications.

Hogan, M. (2003) "Cover letter: Presidents New Freedom Commission on Mental Health." Retrieved on June 17, 2005 from http://www.mentalhealthcommission.gov/reports/Final Report/CoverLetter.htm.

Kessler, R. et al. (2005). "Lifetime prevalence and age-of-onset distributions of *DSM-IV* disorders in the national comorbidity survey replication." *Archives of General Psychiatry* Vol. 62. Retrieved on July 25, 2005 from http://www.archgenpsychiatry.com.

Kirsch, I., and Sapirstein, G. (1998). "Listening to Prozac but hearing placebo: A meta-analysis of antidepressant medications." *Prevention and treatment*. Retrieved on July 25, 2005 from http://journals.apa.org/prevention/volume1.

Laing, R. (1967). *The politics of experience*. New York: Ballantine.

Laing, R.D. (1968) "The obvious." In D. Cooper (Ed.). *The dialectics of liberation*. Harmondsworth: Penguin.

Latour, B. (1987). *Science in action*. Cambridge, MA: Harvard University Press.

Leifer, R. (1997). "The psychiatric repression of Dr. Thomas Szasz: Its social and political significance." *Review of Existential Psychology and Psychiatry* XXIII (1, 2 & 3): 85 –107.

Lenzer, J. (2004) "Bush plans to screen whole US population for mental illness." *British Medical Journal*. 328. June 19, 2004. Retrieved on August 10, 2004 from http://www.bmj.com.

Lewis, B. (2005). "Confinement." In G. Albrect (Ed.). *The encyclopedia of disability*. Thousand Oaks, CA: Sage Publications.

Lewis, B. (2006). *Moving beyond Prozac, DSM, and the new psychiatry: The birth of postpsychiatry*. Ann Arbor: University of Michigan Press.

Metzl, J. (2003). Selling sanity through gender: The psychodynamics of psychotropic advertising. *Journal of Medical Humanities* 24 (1/2): 79–105.

MindFreedom (July 28, 2003). "Original statement by the Fast for Freedom in Mental Health to the American Psychiatric Association, National Alliance for the Mentally Ill, and the US Office of the Surgeon General." Retrieved on July 10, 2005 from http://www.mindfreedom.org/mindfreedom/hungerstrike1.shtml#original.

Morrison, L. (2005). *Talking back to psychiatry: The consumer/surivor/ex-patient movement*. New York. Routledge.

Mulligan, K. (2002). CMHS budget cuts harm consumer involvement. *Psychiatric News* 37(6): 17.

Oaks, D. (2002). "From patients to passion: A call for nonviolent revolution in the mental health system. Plenary Address Alternatives 2002 Convention. Retrieved on March 3, 2003 from http://www.mindfreedom.org/mindfreedom/conference.shtml.

Oaks, D. (2002–2003). "President Bush's position on people with psychiatric labels." *Mindfreedom Journal* (Winter): 4–6.

Oliver, M. (1990). *The politics of disablement: A sociological approach.* New York: St. Martin's Press.

Oliver, M. (1996). *Understanding disability: From theory to practice.* London: Macmillan.

Packard, E. (1868). *The prisoner's hidden life, or insane asylums unveiled: As demonstrated by the report of the investigating committee of the legislature of Illinois.* Chicago: Published by the Author, A.B. Case.

Packard, E. (1874). *Modern persecutions, or married woman's liabilities.* Hartford, CT: Case, Lockwood and Brainard.

Perlin, M. (2000). *The hidden prejudice: Mental disability on trial.* Washington, DC: American Psychological Association.

President's New Freedom Commission (2003). "Executive Summary." Retrieved on June 17, 2005 from http://www.mentalhealthcommission.gov/reports/FinalReport/FullReport.htm.

Pringle, E. (2005). TeenScreen: The lawsuits begin. *CounterPunch.* June 13, 2005. Retrieved July 25, 2005 from http://www.counterpunch.org/pringle06132005.html.

Richman, S. (2004) "Bush's brave new world." *Washington Times.* October 17, 2004. Retrieved on July 25, 2005 from http://www.washingtontimes.com/commentary/20041016-115126-9840r.htm.

Satel, S. (2000). *P.C., M.D.: How political correctness is corrupting medicine.* New York: Basic Books.

Scheff, T. (1966). *Being mentally ill.* Chicago: Aldine.

Starfield, B. 2000. Is US health really the best in the world? *Journal of the American Medical Association* 284 (4): 483–485.

Support Coalition News (May 15, 2002). "Stop the appointment of extremist psychiatrist Sally Satel!" Retrieved on June 15, 2005 from http://www.mindfreedom.org/mindfreedom/satel_f.shtml.

Szasz, T. (1961). *The myth of mental illness: Foundations of a theory of personal conduct.* New York: Hoeber-Harper.

Szasz, T. (1998). "Thomas Szasz's summary statement and manifesto." Retrieved on July 20, 2005 from http://www.szasz.com/manifesto.html.

Thomas, P., and Bracken, P. (2004). Critical psychiatry in practice. *Advances in Psychiatric Treatment* 10: 361–370.

Van Tosh, L., and del Vecchio, P. (2000). *Consumer-operated and self-help programs: A technical report.* Rockville, MD: U.S. Center for Mental Health Services.

Whitaker, R. (2002). *Mad in America: Bad science, bad medicine, and the enduring mistreatment of the mentally ill.* Cambridge, MA: Perseus Publishing.

"Windows into madness" (2002) *Adhusters* (10) 3.

Zinnman, S., Howie the Harp, and Budd, S. (Eds.) (1987). *Reaching across: Mental health clients helping each other.* Sacramento, CA: California Network of Mental Health Clients.

CHAPTER 10

"The Institution Yet to Come": Analyzing Incarceration Through a Disability Lens

Liat Ben-Moshe

Grandmother lost her mother in the early 1900s to what was considered progressive policy. To protect society from the insane, feebleminded and physically defective, states invested enormous public capital in institutions, often scattered in remote areas. Into this state-created disability gulag people disappeared, one by one. Today, more than 1.7 million mothers and fathers, daughters and sons, are lost in America's disability gulag. Today's gulag characterizes isolation and control as care and protection, and the disappearances are often called voluntary placements. However, you don't vanish because that's what you want or need. You vanish because that's what the state offers. You make your choice from an array of one.

(McBryde Johnson 2003)

"THE INSTITUTION YET TO COME"

Institutional life, whether in a prison, hospital, mental institution, nursing home, group home, or segregated "school," has been the reality, not the exception, for disabled people throughout North American history (and globally). In this paper I suggest analyzing the reality of incarceration through the prism of disability, by showcasing the connections between institutions and prisons and the populations that inhabit them, including disabled prisoners and those institutionalized. I will also highlight those who resist incarceration by calling for the abolition of repressive institutions such as institutions for those with labels of psychiatric and intellectual disabilities and prisons.

Harriet McBryde Johnson (2003) describes in the opening paragraph her experiences and fear of the "disability gulag," the warehouse for disabled people that is often called "the institution." As she describes in her narrative, many people with significant disabilities fear that one day they will be sent there and lose their independence, if they are not living there already. In *Crip Theory: Cultural Signs of Queerness and Disability*, Robert McRuer (2006) discusses what he calls "the disability yet to come," describing both the fear that non-disabled people have of becoming disabled and the notion that if anyone lives long enough, they will eventually become disabled in some way. Intersecting Johnson with McRuer, we can conceptualize "the institution yet to come" as a looming presence in the lives of all people with disabilities, even those who don't reside in them (for the time being). The ghost of forced confinement haunts us all, but does so much more materially and immediately for marginalized populations, especially poor people, people of color, disabled people and any amalgamation of these groups (Chapman, Ben-Moshe and Carey forthcoming).

This call for connecting analysis of incarceration with disability, is also a call to pay attention to the lives of mostly poor people of color who are incarcerated worldwide in nursing homes, institutions for those with labels of mental illness and/or intellectual/developmental disabilities and prisons, and bring their perspective to bear on what Chris Bell (2006) characterized as "white Disability Studies." I want to add that the field of Disability Studies had historically not only privileged the experiences of white bodies, but in fact focused on bodies in general, at times to its detriment. Feminist and critical analysis of disability brought to the forefront a new conceptualization of disability, not just as a socially excluded category, but as an embodied identity (Thomson 1997; Wendell 1996). This focus on embodiment challenges the medical model of disability which conceives of disability as a lack and deficiency inherent in non normative bodies. It also challenges the social model of disability which encourages us to focus solely on processes of disablement as a critical framework that will end the oppression of people with disabilities (Morris 2001; Tremain 2002).

Not discounting such achievements, the (often unintended) consequence of such an enterprise is the privileging of analysis on the body and visible disabilities in the field of Disability Studies. Such focus obscures the myriad disabilities and impairments that could and should be analyzed under the purview of Disability Studies. I am not trying to suggest that the experiences and analysis of various impairments and forms of oppression should be conflated into one meta-field, called Disability Studies or anything else. I am also not suggesting that being psychiatrized, or being labeled intellectually disabled or having a physical or sensory disability are all the same. What I am trying to push for

is the understanding that the logic of compulsory ablebodiedness (McRuer 2002), handicapism (Bogdan and Biklen 1977), ableism, normalcy (Davis 1995) and disablement (Oliver 1990), are not just similar but related to forces of sanism or mentalism (Chamberlin 1977; Perlin 2000). I thus argue that Disability Studies could benefit immensely by actively taking up the theorizations and lived experiences in the field of Developmental Disability and Mad Studies. What such expansive formulations achieve is an understanding of incarceration in its broadest way in relation to hospitalization, institutionalization and imprisonment and a fuller understanding of the forces that construct medicalization and criminalization. Such analysis is especially pressing because of the immense growth of the prison machine in the US.

SOME BACKGROUND ON IMPRISONMENT AND (DE)INSTITUTIONALIZATION

For the first time in US history, in 2008, more than one in 100 American adults is behind bars. In 2009 the adult incarcerated population in prisons and jails in the US had reached 2,284,900 (BJS 2010). Another whopping 5,018,900 people are under "community corrections" which include parole and probation (BJS 2010). Race, gender and disability play a significant role in incarceration rates. By 2006, one in fifteen black men over the age of eighteen and one in nine black men age twenty to thirty-four were incarcerated. The overall incarceration rate for women increased 832% from 1997 to 2007 (Human Rights Index 2009/10). The imprisonment rate for African-American women was almost double that of Hispanic women and three times the rate of white women. If these seem like mere numbers consider the reality that today more African-Americans find themselves in penal institutions than in institutions of higher learning (Thompson 2010).

Although several attempts have been made to estimate the number of prisoners who have psychiatric diagnosis, it is impossible to quantify their number with any degree of precision, even if taking the label of "mental illness" as a viable construct. The American Psychiatric Association reports in 2000 that up to 5% of prisoners are actively psychotic and that as many as one in five prisoners were "seriously mentally ill" (APA 2000). Other attempts to estimate the prevalence appear to have used a substantially more expansive definition of mental illness. Bureau of Justice Statistics reports that in 2005 more than half of all prison and jail inmates were reported as having a mental health problem. They also report that women inmates had higher rates of "mental health problems" than men (Human Rights Watch 2006). Researchers also found that the prevalence of "mental health problems" varied by racial or ethnic group. White inmates appear to have higher rates of reported "mental health problems" than African-Americans or Hispanics (Thompson and Thompson 2008). Yet African-Americans, and especially African-American men, seem to be labeled "seriously mentally ill" more often than their white counterparts.[1]

Analyzing imprisonment from a disability studies lens also necessitates a closer look at the social and economic conditions of disablement and incarceration rather than looking at disability as a cause for criminal acts. Prisoners are not randomly selected and do not represent all statuses of society. The majority of prisoners are poor, and are people of color. Poverty is known to cause a variety of impairments and disabling conditions. In addition, the prison environment itself is disabling—from hard labor in toxic conditions and materials; to closed wards with poor air quality; circulation of drugs and unsanitary needles; and

lack of medical equipment and medication (Russell and Stewart 2001). It is also crucial to take an expansive view of what constitutes as "disability" in such environments. For instance, the high prevalence of HIV/AIDS amongst prisoners and the various impairments that come with aging in a disabling environment such as a prison, as a result of prolonged sentencing policies, should be of concern to Disability Studies scholars and those studying the effects of incarceration. Disability in this framework is not a natural biological entity, but related to economic and social conditions which lead to an increased chance of both disablement and imprisonment.

Similarly, conditions of confinement may cause further mental deterioration in prisoners entering the system with diagnoses of "mental retardation" or intellectual disabilities. Most court cases show that the right to (re)habilitation is often not fulfilled in jails, prisons and institutions, and that this further distresses those incarcerated and worsens their mental and physical health overall. Those incarcerated (in institutions or prisons) with labels of intellectual and developmental disabilities may in fact lose crucial life skills that they had before they were imprisoned such as "loss of the ability to communicate, perform daily self-care, remain physically safe, and to maintain even rudimentary emotional stability" (American Association of Mental Retardation et al. amicus brief in *Goodman v. Georgia 2005*). Prisoners who are identified as mentally ill or exhibit "disruptive behaviors" are often sanctioned to "administrative segregation" in separate units, which are often isolation units. These segregated forms of incarceration, such as supermax or SHU (security housing units), are likely to cause or exacerbate mental and physical ill-health of those incarcerated.

In contrast to the constant expansion of prisons, deinstitutionalization and closure of large state institutions for people with labels of mental health and "mental retardation" have been a major policy trend in most US states in the past few decades. Deinstitutionalization of people who were labeled as mentally ill began in 1950s onwards. The deinstitutionalization of people labeled as intellectually and developmentally disabled gained prominence in the seventies, although this of course varied by state. The population of people with intellectual disabilities living in large public institutions (serving over 16 people) peaked at 194,650 in 1967. In 2009, the number had declined to 33,732 (Braddock et al. 2011). The shift from large facility-centered to community residential services can be viewed from the fact that in 1977, an estimated 83.7% of the people with developmental disability labels who were receiving residential services lived in residences of 16 or more people. By 2009, an estimated 86.4% lived in community settings of 15 or fewer people, and 73.1% lived in residential settings with 6 or fewer people (Lakin et al. 2010). The trend in deinstitutionalization of people with intellectual disabilities resulted in closures of large state institutions across most of the US. By 2010, 11 states had closed all of their state-operated institutions for people with intellectual/developmental disabilities (Braddock et al. 2011). In contrast, seven states had not closed any public institutions (Lakin et al. 2010).

An accompanying shift occurred in the field of mental health with the establishment of community mental health centers in the 1960s and the closure of large state mental hospitals in most major cities. In 1955, the state mental health population was 559,000, nearly as large on a per capita basis as the prison population today. By 2000, it had fallen to below 100,000 (Gottschalk 2010; Harcourt 2011). In the public's eye, the first half of the twentieth century is conceived as an era of relative stability in terms of incarceration, with a later explosion in the form of the growth of prisons and jails, a phenomenon which is referred to as "mass incarceration" (Gottschalk 2010) or "hyper incarceration" (Wacquant 2010). However, as Harcourt (2006) suggests, if mental hospitalization and institutionalization were also covered in such analyses, the "rise in incarceration" would have reached its peak in 1955, when mental hospitals reached their highest capacity. Put differently, the incarceration rates in prisons and jails barely scrape the levels of incarceration during the early part of the twentieth century (controlling for population growth).

What needs to be empirically assessed, then, is not "the rise in incarceration" but the systemic and lingering effects of the continuity of confinement in modern times. What such arguments highlight is the need to reconceptualize institutionalization and imprisonment as not merely analogues but as in fact interconnected, in their logic, historical enactment and social effects. The theoretical and policy implications of such interconnectedness will also necessitate bringing in disability (psychiatric, developmental, physical etc.) as a focus in studies on incarceration, as well as working out questions of criminality and danger in studies of institutionalization and disablement.

CONNECTIONS BETWEEN PRISON AND INSTITUTIONS

First, we need to examine some of the ways in which prisons and institutions for those with intellectual and psychiatric disabilities are connected and interrelated. As Goffman described in *Asylums* (1961), the incarcerated populations in institutions and prisons are subjected to stripping of their identities and to processes of dehumanization. Also, especially for people with intellectual and psychiatric disabilities, their citizenship and personhood is questioned. This can be done in the form of taking away or denying voting rights or performing medical experimentation and, for women, denying reproductive rights, including forced sterilization (Waldman and Levi 2011).

On a theoretical level, the imperative to understand incarceration through both the prism of the prison but also that of the institution, as this paper suggests, is crucial to unveiling the underlying relations that legitimate confinement in a variety of settings. Such analysis also underscores the relation between penal and medical notions of danger, as they relate to both criminalization and medicalization. Historically, the connection between imprisonment and definitions of "abnormality" seems to have arisen out of the modernity project, as a result of a new configuration of notions of danger. From the nineteenth century, the webs of the medical and the judicial start to intertwine with the rise of a hybrid discourse, according to Foucault (2003). Its hybridity lies not just in the sense of amalgamation of several discourses (legal, medical) but also in the creation of a new power/knowledge structure in which "doctors laying claim to judicial power and judges laying claim to medical power" (2003: 39) lay down an intertwined system of surveillance, which includes psychiatric progress reports of the incarcerated, examination in court of the accused, and surveillance of "at risk" groups. According to Foucault (2003), this medico-judicial discourse does not originate from medicine or law or in between, but from another external discourse—that of abnormality. The power of normalization is cloaked by medical notions of illness and legal notions of recidivism. The history of treatment and categorization of those labeled as feebleminded, and later "mentally retarded," is also paved on cobblestones of notions of social danger, as prominent eugenicists tried to "scientifically" establish that those whom they char-

acterized as feebleminded had a tendency to commit violent crimes. In the late nineteenth century, as the eugenics movement gained momentum, it was declared that all feebleminded people were potential criminals (Rafter 1997; Trent 1995).

Another pervasive connection between institutionalization and imprisonment, both historically and at present, is offered through the framework of political economy. Many (including scholars and policy makers) believe that disabled people are a strain on the economy, especially under neoliberal ideology. But political economists of disability argue that disability supports a whole industry of professionals that keeps the economy afloat, such as service providers, case managers, medical professionals, health care specialists etc. (Charlton 1998; Oliver 1990). Elsewhere (Ben-Moshe 2012) I suggest that the forces of incarceration of disabled people should be understood under the growth of both the prison industry and the institution-industrial complex, in the form of a growing private industry of nursing homes, boarding homes, for-profit psychiatric hospitals and group homes. As an example, figures show that there is no correlation between the increase of the non-governmental institutional-industrial complex and percentage of those "needing" these services. Between 1977 and 2009, the total number of residential settings in which people with developmental disability labels received residential services grew from 11,008 to an estimated 173,042 (1,500% increase), while total service recipients increased from about 247,780 to an estimated 439,515 individuals (an increase of only 77.4%) (Lakin et al. 2010).

In a similar vein, for those drawing on the conceptualization of the prison-industrial complex, the increase in the number of prisons and cells is not seen as related to similar increases in crime, but as driven by capitalist and racist impetuses (Christie 2000; Goldberg and Evans 1997;

Gilmore 2006). According to Parenti (1999), the criminal (in)justice system generally, and the privatization of prisons specifically, exist to "manage and contain the new surplus populations created by neo-liberal economic policies," and the global flow of capital. Under this new configuration, men of color in particular have turned into commodities in high demand for the growing prison industry. The prison comprises a solution to one of the deepest inherent contradictions of capitalism itself: how to maintain a proletariat class (in this case mostly poor people of color), while controlling them from rising up against their conditions of being. The prison solves this dilemma almost seamlessly. Some perceive the carceral system as a failing system, in that is actually creates criminality rather than reduces it. The prison thus becomes a hub and training school for criminal behavior (Morris 1995). Foucault (1995) aids us in the realization that the prison has not failed, but indeed, has succeeded. Its success lies in the making of docile bodies and an underclass to imprison. This political economic analysis of imprisonment and institutionalization should therefore be of great interest to critical scholars and activists who are interested in understanding the phenomenon of "mass incarceration" from an intersectional lens.

FROM ANALOGIES TO INTERSECTIONS

While such comparisons help crystallize the coalition building potential between those placed in institutions and in prisons, they also obscure the important ways in which one identity or form of oppression is used to discredit the other. In an essay in *Justice Matters*, Bird (2006) posits the important connections she finds between the two populations but cautions: "In 1995 I began sharing my story publicly of how being paralyzed in a drunk driving crash has changed

my life. I'll never forget the first time that someone said to me "... but you got a life sentence sitting in that wheelchair and all he got was a year in a restitution center!?" (Bird 2006). Such comparisons seem to create an equation of disability with punishment, which is not a new phenomenon. One of the earliest sources of stigmatization of disability can be found in religious or magical thinking that assumed that disability is a result of punishment from the gods or a result of witchcraft.

In addition, if one listens to the narratives of disabled people who were segregated in institutions, another obvious connection emerges in which many describe their time there as a form of incarceration. Self advocates (activists with intellectual disability labels) compare institutions to living in prisons, and characterize their existence their as incarceration or being jailed while committing no apparent crime (Hayden, Lakin and Taylor 1995/6, Hayden 1997). Such statements, combined with McBride Johnson's epigraph and Bird's narrative above, help crystallize the vital connections between prisoners and people with disabilities, but may also pit one group against the other and ignore both the differences and intersections between the two populations.

I argue that today one cannot analyze the forces of incarceration without having a disability lens. For instance, a disproportionate number of persons incarcerated in US prisons and jails are disabled. As suggested above, prisoners with disabilities are a population that is hard to count (and account for) but is definitely at the intersection of the disability and imprisonment juggernaut. There is much at stake in counting the percentage of disabled prisoners. In terms of policy and legislation, if one can prove sufficiently that there is a large percentage of prisoners with a specific disability, then it would require a specific solution such as requesting more hospital units to be built in specific prisons or prescribing more medications on a particular unit. For activists, using statistics that demonstrate the high prevalence of disabled prisoners could go in several directions. If one is an activist in NAMI (National Alliance of Mental Illness), for instance, then these statistics are used to show that deinstitutionalization failed and that prisons and jails had become a dumping ground for those labeled as mentally ill with the lack of other alternatives. Such campaigns, which have been ongoing since the early 1990s, call in essence for the (re)hospitalization of those with psychiatric diagnosis (see Torrey 1996 for example). However, such critiques from activists and scholars about inappropriately placing disabled people in nursing homes or prisons reproduce the sentiment that there are those who are somehow *appropriately* placed in nursing homes and prisons. In other words, it reinscribes the notion that there are those who really need to be segregated in carceral edifices, while those who are young and disabled do not.

However, others might use these statistics to showcase the cruelty of the criminal "justice" system and call for the just treatment of all prisoners (such as abolishing the use of isolation units for everyone). The downturn of such arguments, much like those in the calls to abolish the death penalty for those who are labeled as intellectually disabled, is that they can turn into arguments which reproduce ableist rhetoric and may seem to call for the release of some prisoners (i.e. those most disabled) but not others. A similar tactic is used by those who find conditions of disabled prisoners and those institutionalized so deplorable that they call for the creation of more hospital beds in prisons, reform and overhaul of psychiatric hospitals and institutions for those labeled as intellectually disabled and the creation of more accessible prisons. Others call not for reforming these edifices, but for abolishing them altogether.

ABOLITION AS A FORM OF RESISTANCE TO INCARCERATION

In addition to the connections between the forces of incarceration and decarceration in prisons and institutions, I would like to end with an analysis of the connections between the movements that resist these forces. Instead of incarcerating people and segregating them, movements such as factions in anti-psychiatry, deinstitutionalization and prison abolition, propose radical new ways of treatment, care and governance that do not require the segregation of people from their peers.

Deinstitutionalization could be characterized not only as a process or an exodus of oppressed people outside the walls of institutions. In the eyes of those who pushed for institutional closure and community living, deinstitutionalization is perceived as a philosophy (Ben-Moshe 2011). The resistance to institutionalization and psychiatric hospitals arose from a broader social critique of medicalization and medical authority (Conrad and Schneider 1992; Zola 1991) and a new understanding of human value, especially in regards to people with disabilities, as seen in the principles of normalization (Wolfensberger 1972), the anti-psychiatry and ex-patients movement (Chamberlin 1977; Szasz 1961) and the People First movement (Williams and Shoultz 1982). Although these ideological shifts did not solely bring about deinstitutionalization nationwide, I believe that any significant decrease in institutionalized populations would have been impossible without them. Furthermore, deinstitutionalization is not just something that happened, but something for which many were relentlessly advocating. As such, deinstitutionalization can be construed as an active form of activism and as a social movement.

There are many ways in which one can fight for social justice or social change. In the struggle to eliminate institutional settings for those labeled as developmentally or psychiatrically disabled, and replacing them with community living and community-based services, there were myriad possibilities through which the struggle could have taken place. But what is illuminating in these cases is that some took the view that the *only* route for successful social change was to abolish these institutions and close them down, while others advocated for improving or reforming them. This tension between reform and abolition is a key characteristic of the prison abolitionist stance. However, there is no agreement as to how to resolve it, as the movement ranges from calls for focusing on the present circumstances of prisoners and advocating for gradual changes, to those who contend that any type of reform would lead to the growth of the prison-industrial complex and should be avoided by activists. Some (such as Knopp et al. 1976) suggest conceptualizing the long term goal of prison abolition as a chain for shorter campaigns around specific issues—like jail diversion, restitution programs, or the move of those released to community placements. Such strategic use of abolition and reform can also be applied to the context of abolishing psychiatric confinement and forced medical treatments, as suggested by anti-psychiatry activist Bonnie Burstow. In her keynote speech in the 2009 PsychOut conference, Burstow suggests that the short term goals of anti-psychiatry activists, such as reform efforts, should be kept as such, as concrete and direct partial abolitions (or reforms) on the road to long term change of abolishing psychiatry.

This contention between abolition and reform is not only a scholarly debate but one with pragmatic implications. For instance, Angela Y. Davis (2003), as a practicing abolitionist, suggests to question what kinds of reforms are sought and whether they will strengthen the system in the long run. For instance, fighting for health care for prisoners is something activists should support, as integral to abolitionist and decarcerating strategies. However, some health care initiatives are opposed by abolitionists, such as attempts to open prison hospitals or separate clinical wards, as these would only expand the scope of incarceration in the long haul. Many prison abolition and anti-psychiatry activists are insistent that the trend to develop mental health services within the prison only serves to criminalize (mostly women) with psychiatric and cognitive disabilities further, as quality health services of this nature are sparse outside the walls of the prison, while funds go to operate them within an already oppressive system.

Abolition can become a useful strategy for resistance to all forms of incarceration, as it does not acknowledge the structure as it is but envisions and creates a new worldview in which oppressive structures do not exist. It thus goes beyond protesting the current circumstances, to creating new conditions of possibility by collectively contesting the status quo. Norwegian sociologist Thomas Mathiesen conceptualizes abolition as an alternative in the making: "The alternative lies in the "unfinished," in the sketch, in what is not yet fully existing" (Mathiesen 1974: 1). According to Mathiesen, abolition takes place when one breaks with the established order and simultaneously breaks new ground. Abolition is triggered by making people aware of the necessary dilemma they are faced with- continuing with the existing order with some changes (i.e. reform) or transitioning to something unknown. The question becomes not "what is the best alternative" in its final formulation, but how this new order shall begin from the old.

The most powerful relevance of the prison abolitionist and anti-institutional stance is to analyze imprisonment and institutional segregation as a core structure that shapes social relations in society, not just for those affected directly but for everyone. It is not merely about closure of prisons or institutions, but it is a revolutionary framework, which transforms the way we analyze and understand forces that shape our histories and everyday lives: notions like "crime" or "innocence" (what gets to be defined as crime, and who gets to be defined as criminal); "disability" (as an identity not just a medical diagnosis) and rehabilitation (a benign process or a force of assimilation and normalization); ideas of punishment (justice vs. revenge or retribution); notions of community (as in "living in the community" or "community re-entry"); or "institution" (who defines what gets to be called an institution); notions of freedom and equality (can we feel free and safe without locking others away?) and on the other hand concepts of danger and protection (who do we protect by segregating people behind bars in psychiatric hospitals and prisons? Is it for "their own good?").

As Angela Y. Davis (2003) suggests, there is no one single alternative to imprisonment, but a vision of a more just society—revamping of the education system, comprehensive health care for all, demilitarization, and a justice system based on reparation and reconciliation. One of the main problems with prisons and institutions is that they become a catch all for "problematic populations" that are deemed socially undesirable or dangerous. The alternative to incarceration therefore cannot be a catch all solution, but an individual one, in relation to the harm done and the community in which one is involved. Prison abolition and deinstitutionalization, therefore, is not about helping prisoners or people with disabilities, but is about societal change that will improve the lives of all, inside and outside prisons and institutions.

According to liberal discourses that call for social change, change entails incorporating excluded groups into current structures—such as education systems, the government, corporations and politics. But these frameworks only change the hierarchy of the structures in which marginalized populations are placed, and not the structures themselves. Under a more abolitionary mindset it is clear that forms of oppression are not always characterized by exclusion, but by pervasive inclusion that sometimes does more damage. The goal of a non-carceral society is not to replace one form of control, such as a hospital, institution and prison, with another, such as psychopharmaceuticals, nursing homes and group homes in the community. The aspiration is to fundamentally change the way we react to each other, the way we respond to difference or harm, the way normalcy is defined and the ways resources are distributed and accessed. It is no wonder then that the abolitionary approach to institutionalization and imprisonment, as an epistemic change that breaks down the segregationist model altogether, did not occur overall. Or at least not yet . . .

CONCLUSION

This article suggests the pressing need to expand notions of what comes to be classified as "incarceration," as including institutionalization in a wide variety of enclosed settings, including prisons, jails, detention centers, institutions for the intellectually disabled, treatment centers, and psychiatric hospitals. Such formulations conceptualize incarceration as a continuum and a multifaceted phenomenon, not one that occurs in one locale or in one historical period, in contrast to current interpretations of "the rise in incarceration" or the success (or failure) of deinstitutionalization. Closure of large institutions has not led to freedom for disabled people, nor has it resulted in the radical acceptance of the fact of difference amongst us. My main argument here is that the (his)story of disability is the (his)story of incarceration and there is a need to connect them in terms of their history, as medico-judicial hybrids; their present, in the disproportionate number of disabled prisoners and those still institutionalized; and the future, in terms of movements that seek to abolish the segregationist model that underpins systems of incarceration. It is only through such coalitions that we can truly analyze, and perhaps circumvent, "the institution yet to come."

ACKNOWLEDGMENTS

Parts of this chapter appeared in *Critical Sociology* 37 (7) (2012) as "Disabling Incarceration: Connecting Disability to Divergent Confinements in the USA." I want to thank Dr. Michael Rembis for providing me with some of the data on disabled prisoners. I want to also acknowledge NIDRR Advanced Training in Translational and Tranformational Research to Improve Outcomes for People with Disabilities, Grant No. H133P110004 and University Center for Excellence in Developmental Disabilities, Grant No. 90-DD-0655/01 for funding my postdoctoral position at the University of Illinois-Chicago that enabled me to write this chapter.

NOTE

1. Jonathan Metzl's *The Protest Psychosis: How schizophrenia became a black disease* (Beacon Press, 2010) can provide a possible explanation of this phenomenon

BIBLIOGRAPHY

American Psychiatric Association (2000) *Psychiatric Services in Jails and Prisons* (2nd ed.). Washington D.C., American Psychiatric Association: xix.

Bell, C. (2006) Introducing white disability studies: A modest proposal. In Davis, L. J. (ed.) *The Disability Studies Reader* (2nd ed.). New York: Routledge.

Ben-Moshe, L. (2011) *Genealogies of Resistance to Incarceration: Abolition politics in anti-prison and deinstitutionalization activism in the U.S.* Unpublished dissertation. Syracuse, N.Y.: Syracuse University.

Ben-Moshe, L. (2012) Disabling Incarceration: Connecting disability to divergent confinements in the USA. *Critical Sociology* 37 (7).

Bird, A. (2006) *Disability and the Dehumanization of Prisoners.* Retrieved August 2000 from http://www.safetyandjustice.org/story/842

Bogdan, R. and Biklen, D. (1977). Handicapism. *Social Policy*, 7 (5) March/April: 14–19.

Braddock, D., Hemp, R., Rizzolo, M. C., Haffer, L., Tanis, E. S. and Wu, J. (2011) *The State of the States in Developmental Disabilities 2011.* Boulder: University of Colorado, Department of Psychiatry and Coleman Institute for Cognitive Disabilities.

Brief of the American Association on Mental Retardation et al. in Support of Petitioners, *Goodman v. Georgia*, No. 02–10168, 11th Circuit (July 29, 2005).

Bureau of Justice Statistics (BJS) (2010) *Correctional Populations in the United States 2009.* Washington D.C.: U.S. Department of Justice.

Chamberlin, J. (1977) *On Our Own: Patient-controlled alternatives to the mental health system.* National Empowerment Center.

Chapman, C., Ben-Moshe, L. and Carey, A. C. (forthcoming) Reconsidering confinement: Interlocking locations and logics of confinement. In Ben-Moshe, L. , Carey, A. and Chapman, C. (eds.) *Disability Incarcerated: Imprisonment and dis/ability in North America.*

Charlton, J. I. (1998) *Nothing About Us Without Us: Disability oppression and empowerment.* Berkeley: University of California Press.

Christie, N. (2000). *Crime Control as Industry: Towards gulags, Western style* (3rd ed.). London; New York: Routledge.

Conrad, P., and Schneider, J. W. (1992) *Deviance and Medicalization: From badness to sickness, with a new afterword by the authors* (Expanded ed.). Philadelphia: Temple University Press.

Davis, A. Y. (2003) *Are Prisons Obsolete?* New York: Seven Stories Press.

Davis, L. J. (1995) *Enforcing Normalcy: Disability, deafness, and the body.* New York: Verso.

Erickson, P. E., and Erickson, S. K. (2008) *Crime, Punishment, and Mental Illness: Law and the behavioral sciences in conflict.* New Brunswick, N.J.: Rutgers University Press

Foucault, M. (1995) *Discipline and Punish: The birth of the prison* (2nd Vintage Books ed.). New York: Vintage Books.

Foucault, M. (2003) *Abnormal: Lectures at the Colláege de France, 1974–1975.* New York: Picador.

Gilmore, R. W. (2006). *Golden Gulag: Prisons, surplus, crisis, and opposition in globalizing California.* Berkeley: University of California Press.

Goffman, E. (1961) *Asylums: Essays on the social situation of mental patients and other inmates* (1st ed.). Garden City, N.Y.: Anchor Books.

Goldberg, E. and Evans, L. (1997) *The Prison Industrial Complex and the Global Economy.* Pamphlet. Published by Prison Activist Resource Center.

Gottschalk, M. (2010) Cell blocks and red ink: Mass incarceration, the great recession and penal reform. *Daedalus* 139 (3): 62–73.

Harcourt, B. (2006) From the asylum to the prison: Rethinking the incarceration revolution. *Texas Law Review* 84: 1751–1786.

Harcourt, B. (2011) Reducing mass incarceration: Lessons from the deinstitutionalization of mental hospitals in the 1960s. U of Chicago Law and Economics, Olin Working Paper No. 542; U of Chicago, Public Law Working Paper No. 335. Available at SSRN: http://ssrn.com/abstract=1748796

Haydan, M. F. (1997) *Living in the Freedom World.* Minneapolis: University of Minnesota, Research and Training Center on Community Living, Institute on Community Integration.

Hayden, M. F., Lakin, K. C. and Taylor, S. J. (eds.)(1995/1996) *IMPACT: Feature Issue on Institution Closures* 9 (1): 8–9. Publication of the Institute on Community Integration, University of Minnesota.

Human Rights Index: US Prisons (2009–2010) *International Accents*, Vol. 26 (Winter). The University of Iowa Center for Human Rights. Retrieved February 12, 2012 from http://accents.international.uiowa.edu/worldviews/human-rights-index-us-prisons-winter-2009-2010-26/

Human Rights Watch, U.S. (September 5, 2006) Number of Mentally Ill in Prisons Quadrupled: Prisons Ill Equipped to Cope. Retrieved February 12, 2012 from http://www.hrw.org/print/news/2006/09/05/us-number-mentally-ill-prisons-quadrupled

Knopp, F. H. and Prison Research Education Action Project (1976) *Instead of Prisons: A handbook for abolitionists.* Syracuse, N.Y.: Prison Research Education Action project.

Lakin, K.C., Larson, S.A., Salmi, P., and Webster, A. (2010) *Residential Services for Persons with Developmental Disabilities: Statues and trends through 2009.* Minneapolis: University of Minnesota, Research and Training Center on Community Living, Institute on Community Integration.

Mathiesen, T. (1974) *The Politics of Abolition.* New York: Halsted Press.

McBryde Johnson, H. (2003) The disability gulag. *New York Times,* November 23.

McRuer, R. (2002) Compulsory able-bodiedness and queer/disabled existence. In Snyder, S. Brueggemann, B. and Garland-Thomson, R. (eds.). *Disability Studies: Enabling the humanities.* New York: MLA Press.

McRuer, R. (2006) *Crip Theory: Cultural signs of queerness and disability.* New York: New York University Press.

Morris, J. (2001) Impairment and disability: Constructing an ethics of care that promotes human rights. *Hypatia.* 16 (4): 1–16.

Morris, R. (1995) *Penal Abolition, the Practical Choice: A practical manual on penal abolition.* Toronto: Canadian Scholars' Press.

Oliver, M. (1990) *The Politics of Disablement: A sociological approach.* New York: St. Martin's Press.

Parenti, C. (1999) *Lockdown America: Police and prisons in the age of crisis.* New York: Verso.

Perlin, M. (2000) *The Hidden Prejudice: Mental disability on trial.* Washington, D.C.: American Psychological Association.

Rafter, N. (2004) The criminalization of mental retardation. In Noll, S. and Trent, J. (eds.) *Mental Retardation in America: A historical reader.* New York: New York University Press.

Russell, M. and Stewart, J. (2001) Disability, prison and historical segregation. *Monthly Review,* July–August issue.

Szasz, T. S. (1961) *The Myth of Mental Illness;*

Foundations of a theory of personal conduct. New York: Hoeber-Harper.

Thompson, H. A. (2010) Why mass incarceration matters: Rethinking crisis, decline, and transformation in postwar American history. *Journal of American History* 97: 3.

Thomson, R. G. (1997) *Extraordinary Bodies: Figuring physical disability in American culture and literature.* New York: Columbia University Press.

Torrey, E. F. (1996) *Out of the Shadows: Confronting America's mental illness crisis.* Hoboken, N.J.: John Wiley & Sons.

Tremain, S. (2002) On the subject of impairment. In Corker and Shakespeare (eds.) *Disability/Postmodernity: Embodying disability theory.* London: Continuum.

Trent, J. W. (1995) *Inventing the Feeble Mind: A history of mental retardation in the United States.* Berkeley: University of California Press.

Wacquant, L. (2010) Class, race and hyperincarceration in revanchist America. *Daedalus* 139 (3): 74–90.

Waldman, A. and Levi, R. (2011) *Inside This Place, Not of It: Narratives from women's prisons.* San Francisco: McSweeney Press.

Wendell, S. (1996) *The Rejected Body: Feminist philosophical reflections on disability.* New York: Routledge.

Williams, P. and Shoultz, B. (1982) *We Can Speak for Ourselves.* London: Souvenir Press.

Wolfensberger, W. (1972) *The Principle of Normalization in Human Services.* Toronto: National Institute on Mental Retardation.

Zola, I. K. (1991) The medicalization of aging and disability. *Advances in Medical Sociology* 2: 299–315.

PART III

*S*tigma and Illness

CHAPTER 11

Stigma: An Enigma Demystified

Lerita Coleman Brown

Nature caused us all to be born equal; if fate is pleased to disturb this plan of the general law, it is our responsibility to correct its caprice, and to repair by our attention the usurpations of the stronger.

—Maurice Blanchot

What is stigma and why does stigma remain? Because stigmas mirror culture and society, they are in constant flux, and therefore the answers to these two questions continue to elude social scientists. Viewing stigma from multiple perspectives exposes its intricate nature and helps us to disentangle its web of complexities and paradoxes. Stigma represents a view of life; a set of personal and social constructs; a set of social relations and social relationships; a form of social reality. Stigma has been a difficult concept to conceptualize because it reflects a property, a process, a form of social categorization, and an affective state.

Two primary questions, then, that we as social scientists have addressed are how and why during certain historical periods, in specific cultures or within particular social groups, some human differences are valued and desired, and other human differences are devalued, feared, or stigmatized. In attempting to answer these questions, I propose another view of stigma, one that takes into account

its behavioral, cognitive, and affective components and reveals that stigma is a response to the dilemma of difference.

THE DILEMMA

No two human beings are exactly alike: there are countless ways to differ. Shape, size, skin color, gender, age, cultural background, personality, and years of formal education are just a few of the infinite number of ways in which people can vary. Perceptually, and in actuality, there is greater variation on some of these dimensions than on others. Age and gender, for example, are dimensions with limited and quantifiable ranges; yet they interact exponentially with other physical or social characteristics that have larger continua (e.g., body shape, income, cultural background) to create a vast number of human differences. Goffman states, though, that "stigma is equivalent to an undesired differentness" (see Stafford & Scott, 1986). The infinite variety of human attributes suggests that what is undesired or stigmatized is heavily dependent on the social context and to some extent arbitrarily defined. The large number of stigmatizable attributes and several taxonomies of stigmas in the literature offer further evidence of how arbitrary the selection of undesired differences may be (see Ainlay & Crosby, 1986; Becker & Arnold, 1986; Solomon, 1986; Stafford & Scott, 1986).

What is most poignant about Goffman's description of stigma is that it suggests that all human differences are potentially stigmatizable. As we move out of one social context where a difference is desired into another context where the difference is undesired, we begin to feel the effects of stigma. This conceptualization of stigma also indicates that those possessing power, the dominant group, can determine which human differences are desired and undesired. In part, stigmas reflect the value judgments of a dominant group.

Many people, however, especially those who have some role in determining the desired and undesired differences of the zeitgeist, often think of stigma only as a property of individuals. They operate under the illusion that stigma exists only for certain segments of the population. But the truth is that any "nonstigmatized" person can easily become "stigmatized." "Nearly everyone at some point in life will experience stigma either temporarily or permanently. . . . Why do we persist in this denial?" (Zola, 1979, p. 454). Given that human differences serve as the basis for stigmas, being or feeling stigmatized is virtually an inescapable fate. Because stigmas differ depending upon the culture and the historical period, it becomes evident that it is mere chance whether a person is born into a nonstigmatized or severely stigmatized group.

Because stigmatization often occurs within the confines of a psychologically constructed or actual social relationship, the experience itself reflects relative comparisons, the contrasting of desired and undesired differences. Assuming that flawless people do not exist, relative comparisons give rise to a feeling of superiority in some contexts (where one possesses a desired trait that another person is lacking) but perhaps a feeling of inferiority in other contexts (where one lacks a desired trait that another person possesses). It is also important to note that it is only when we make comparisons that we can feel different. Stigmatization or feeling stigmatized is a consequence of social comparison. For this reason, stigma represents a continuum of undesired differences that depend upon many factors (e.g., geographical location, culture, life cycle stage) (see Becker & Arnold, 1986).

Although some stigmatized conditions appear escapable or may be temporary, some undesired traits have graver social consequences than others. Being a medical resident, being a new professor, being 7 feet tall, having cancer, being black, or being physically disfigured or mentally retarded can all lead to feelings of stigmatization (feeling discredited or devalued in a particular role), but obviously these are not equally stigmatizing conditions. The degree of stigmatization might depend on how undesired the difference is in a particular social group.

Physical abnormalities, for example, may be the most severely stigmatized differences because they are physically salient, represent some deficiency or distortion in the bodily form, and in most cases are unalterable. Other physically salient differences, such as skin color or nationality, are considered very stigmatizing because they also are permanent conditions and cannot be changed. Yet the stigmatization that one feels as a result of being black or Jewish or Japanese depends on the social context, specifically social contexts in which one's skin color or nationality is not a desired one. A white American could feel temporarily stigmatized when visiting Japan due to a difference in height. A black student could feel stigmatized in a predominantly white university because the majority of the students are white and white skin is a desired trait. But a black student in a predominantly black university is not likely to feel the effects of stigma. Thus, the sense of being stigmatized or having a stigma is inextricably tied to social context. Of equal importance are the norms in that context that determine which are desirable and undesirable attributes. Moving from one social or cultural context to another can change both the definitions and the consequences of stigma.

Stigma often results in a special kind of downward mobility. Part of the power of stigmatization lies in the realization that people who are stigmatized or acquire a stigma lose their place in the social hierarchy. Consequently, most people want to ensure that they are counted in the non-stigmatized "majority." This, of course, leads to more stigmatization.

Stigma, then, is also a term that connotes a relationship. It seems that this relationship is vital to understanding the stigmatizing process. Stigma allows some individuals to feel superior to others. Superiority and inferiority, however, are two sides of the same coin. In order for one person to feel superior, there must be another person who is perceived to be or who actually feels inferior. Stigmatized people are needed in order for the many nonstigmatized people to feel good about themselves.

On the other hand, there are many stigmatized people who feel inferior and concede that other persons are superior because they possess certain attributes. In order for the process to occur (for one person to stigmatize another and have the stigmatized person feel the effects of stigma), there must be some agreement that the differentness is inherently undesirable. Moreover, even among stigmatized people, relative comparisons are made, and people are reassured by the fact that there is someone else who is worse off. The dilemma of difference, therefore, affects both stigmatized and nonstigmatized people.

Some might contend that this is the very old scapegoat argument, and there is some truth to that contention. But the issues here are more finely intertwined. If stigma is a social construct, constructed by cultures, by social groups, and by individuals to designate some human differences as discrediting, then the stigmatization process is indeed a powerful and pernicious social tool. The inferiority/superiority issue is a most interesting way of understanding how and why people continue to stigmatize.

Some stigmas are more physically salient than others, and some people are more capable of concealing their stigmas or escaping from the negative social consequences of being stigmatized. The ideal prototype (e.g., young, white, tall, married, male, with a recent record in sports) that Stafford cites may actually possess traits that would be the source of much scorn and derision in another social context. Yet, by insulating himself in his own community, a man like the one described in the example can ensure that his "differentness" will receive approbation rather than rejection, and he will not be subject to constant and severe stigmatization. This is a common response to stigma among people with some social influence (e.g., artists, academics, millionaires). Often, attributes or behaviors that might otherwise be considered "abnormal" or stigmatized are labeled as "eccentric" among persons of power or influence. The fact that what is perceived as the "ideal" person varies from one social context to another, however, is tied to Martin's notion that people learn ways to stigmatize in each new situation.

In contrast, some categories of stigmatized people (e.g., the physically disabled, members of ethnic groups, poor people) cannot alter their stigmas nor easily disguise them. People, then, feel permanently stigmatized in contexts where their differentness is undesired and in social environments that they cannot easily escape. Hence, power, social influence, and social control play a major role in the stigmatization process.

In summary, stigma stems from differences. By focusing on differences we actively create stigmas because any attribute or difference is potentially stigmatizable. Often we attend to a single different attribute rather than to the large number of similar attributes that any two individuals share. Why people focus on differences and denigrate people on the basis of them is important to understanding how some stigmas originate and persist. By reexamining the historical origins of stigma and the way children develop the propensity to stigmatize, we can see how some differences evolve into stigmas and how the process is linked to the behavioral (social control), affective (fear, dislike), and cognitive (perception of differences, social categorization) components of stigma.

THE ORIGINS OF STIGMA

The phrase *to stigmatize* originally referred to the branding or marking of certain people (e.g., criminals, prostitutes) in order to make them appear different and separate from others (Goffman, 1963). The act of marking people in this way resulted in exile or avoidance. In most cultures, physical marking or branding has declined, but a more cognitive manifestation of stigmatization—social marking—has increased and has become the basis for most stigmas (Jones *et al.*, 1984). Goffman points out, though, that stigma has retained much of its original connotation. People use differences to exile or avoid others. In addition, what is most intriguing about the ontogenesis of the stigma concept is the broadening of its predominant affective responses such as dislike and disgust to include the emotional reaction of fear. Presently, *fear* may be instrumental in the perpetuation of stigma and in maintaining its original social functions. Yet as the developmental literature reveals, fear is not a natural but an acquired response to differences of stigmas.

Sigelman and Singleton (1986) offer a number of insightful observations about how children learn to stigmatize. Children develop a natural wariness of strangers as their ability to differentiate familiar from novel objects increases (Sroufe, 1977). Developmental psychologists note that stranger anxiety is a universal phenomenon in infants and appears around the age of seven months. This reaction to differences (e.g., women versus men, children versus adults, blacks versus whites) is an interesting one and, as Sigelman and Singleton point out, may serve as a prototype for stigmatizing. Many children respond in a positive (friendly) or negative (fearful, apprehensive) manner to strangers. Strangers often arouse the interest (Brooks & Lewis, 1976) of children but elicit negative reactions if they intrude on their personal space (Sroufe, 1977). Stranger anxiety tends to fade with age, but when coupled with self-referencing it may create the conditions for a child to learn how to respond to human differences or how to stigmatize.

Self-referencing, or the use of another's interpretation of a situation to form one's own understanding of it, commonly occurs in young children. Infants often look toward caregivers when encountering something different, such as a novel object, person, or event (Feinman, 1982). The response to novel stimuli in an ambiguous situation may depend on the emotional displays of the caregiver; young children have been known to respond positively to situations if their mothers respond reassuringly (Feinman, 1982). Self-referencing is instrumental to understanding the development of stigmatization because it may be through this process that caregivers shape young children's responses to people, especially those who possess physically salient differences (Klinnert, Campos, Sorce, Emde, & Svejda, 1983). We may continue to learn about how to stigmatize from other important figures (e.g., mentors, role models) as we progress through the life cycle. Powerful authority figures may serve as the source of self-referencing behavior in new social contexts (Martin, 1986).

Sigelman and Singleton (1986) also point out that preschoolers notice differences and tend to establish preferences but do not necessarily stigmatize. Even on meeting other children with physical disabilities, children do not automatically eschew them but may respond to actual physical and behavioral similarities and differences. There is evidence, moreover, indicating that young children are curious about human differences and often stare at novel stimuli (Brooks & Lewis, 1976). Children frequently inquire of their parents or of stigmatized persons about their distinctive physical attributes. In many cases, the affective response of young children is interest rather than fear.

Barbarin offers a poignant example of the difference between interest and fear in his vignette about Myra, a child with cancer. She talks about young children who are honest and direct about her illness, an attitude that does not cause her consternation. What does disturb her, though, are parents who will not permit her to baby-sit with their children for *fear* that she might give them cancer. Thus, interest and curiosity about stigma or human differences may be natural for children, but they must *learn* fear and avoidance as well as which categories or attributes to dislike, *fear*, or stigmatize. Children may learn to stigmatize without ever grasping "why" they do so (Martin, 1986), just as adults have beliefs about members of stigmatized groups without ever having met any individuals from the group (Crocker & Lutsky, 1986). The predisposition to stigmatize is passed from one generation to the next through social learning (Martin, 1986) or socialization (Crocker & Lutsky, 1986; Stafford & Scott, 1986).

Sigelman and Singleton agree with Martin that social norms subtly impinge upon the information-processing capacities of young children so that negative responses to stigma later become automatic. At some point, the development of social cognition must intersect with the affective responses that parents or adults display toward stigmatized people. Certain negative emotions become attached to social categories (e.g., *all* ex-mental patients are dangerous, *all* blacks are angry or harmful). Although the attitudes (cognitions) about stigma assessed in paper-and-pencil tasks may change in the direction of what is socially acceptable, the affect and behavior of elementary- and secondary-school children as well as adults reflect the early negative affective associations with stigma. The norms about stigma, though, are ambiguous and confusing. They teach young children to avoid or dislike stigmatized people, even though similar behavior in adults is considered socially unacceptable.

STIGMA AS A FORM OF COGNITIVE PROCESSING

The perceptual processing of human differences appears to be universal. Ainlay and Crosby suggest that differences arouse us; they can please or distress us. From a phenomenological perspective, we carry around "recipes" and "typifications" as structures for categorizing and ordering stimuli. Similarly, social psychologists speak of our need to categorize social stimuli in such terms as *schemas* and *stereotypes* (Crocker & Lutsky, 1986). These approaches to the perception of human differences indirectly posit that stigmatizing is a natural response, a way to maintain order in a potentially chaotic world of social stimuli. People want to believe that the world is ordered.

Although various approaches to social categorization may explain how people stereotype on the basis of a specific attribute (e.g., skin color, religious beliefs, deafness), they do not explain the next step—the negative imputations. Traditional approaches to sociocognitive processing also do not offer ideas about how people can perceptually move beyond the stereotype, the typification, or stigma to perceive an individual. Studies of stereotyping and stigma regularly reveal that beliefs about the inferiority of a person predominate in the thoughts of the perceiver (Crocker & Lutsky, 1986).

Stigma appears to be a special and insidious kind of social categorization or, as Martin explains, a process of generalizing from a single experience. People are treated categorically rather than individually, and in the process are devalued (Ainlay & Crosby, 1986; Barbarin; Crocker & Lutsky, 1986; Stafford & Scott, 1986). In addition, as Crocker and Lutsky point out, coding people in terms of categories (e.g., "X is a redhead") instead of specific attributes ("X has red hair") allows people to feel that stigmatized persons are fundamentally different and establishes greater psychological and social distance.

A discussion of the perceptual basis of stigma inevitably leads back to the notion of master status (Goffman, 1963). Perceptually, stigma becomes the master status, the attribute that colors the perception of the entire person. All other aspects of the person are ignored except those that fit the stereotype associated with the stigma (Kanter, 1979). Stigma as a form of negative stereotyping has a way of neutralizing positive qualities and undermining the identity of stigmatized individuals (Barbarin). This kind of social categorization has also been described by one sociologist as a "discordance with personal attributes" (Davis, 1964). Thus, many stigmatized people are not expected to be intelligent, attractive, or upper class.

Another important issue in the perception of human differences or social cognition is the relative comparisons that are made between and within stigmatized and nonstigmatized groups. Several authors discuss the need for people to accentuate between-group differences and minimize within-group differences as a requisite for group identity (Ainlay & Crosby, 1986; Crocker & Lutsky, 1986; Sigelman & Singleton, 1986). Yet these authors do not explore in depth the reasons for denigrating the attributes of the out-group members and elevating the attributes of one's own group, unless there is some feeling that the out-group could threaten the balance of power. Crocker and Lutsky note, however, that stereotyping is frequently tied to the need for self-enhancement. People with low self-esteem are more likely to identify and maintain negative stereotypes about members of stigmatized groups; such people are more negative in general. This line of reasoning takes us back to viewing stigma as a means of maintaining the status quo through social control. Could it be that stigma as a perceptual tool helps to reinforce the differentiation of the population that in earlier times was deliberately designated by marking? One explanation offered by many theorists is that stereotypes about stigmatized groups help to maintain the exploitation of such groups and preserve the existing societal structure.

Are there special arrangements or special circumstance, Ainlay and Crosby ask, that allow people to notice differences but not denigrate those who have them? On occasion, nonstigmatized people are able to "break through" and to see a stigmatized person as a real, whole person with a variety of attributes, some similar traits and some different from their own (Davis, 1964). Just how frequently and in what ways does this happen?

Ainlay and Crosby suggest that we begin to note differences within a type when we *need* to do so. The example they give about telephones is a good one. We learn differences among types of telephones, appliances, schools, or even groups of people when we need to. Hence stereotyping or stigmatizing is not necessarily automatic; when we want to perceive differences we perceive them, just as we perceive similarities when we *want* to. In some historical instances, society appears to have recognized full human potential when it was required, while ignoring certain devalued traits. When women were needed to occupy traditionally male occupations in the United States during World War II, gender differences were ignored as they have been ignored in other societies when women were needed for combat. Similarly, the U.S. armed forces became racially integrated when there was a need for more soldiers to fight in World War II (Terry, 1984).

Thus, schemas or stereotypes about stigmatized individuals can be modified but only under specific conditions. When stigmatized people have essential information or possess needed expertise, we discover that some of their attributes are not so different, or that they are more similar to us than different. "Cooperative interdependence" stemming from shared goals may change the nature of perceptions and the nature of relationships (Crocker & Lutsky, 1986). Future research on stigma and on social perception might continue to investigate the conditions under which people are less likely to stereotype and more likely to respond to individuals rather than categories (cf., Locksley, Borgida, Brekke, & Hepburn, 1980; Locksley, Hepburn & Ortiz, 1982).

THE MEANING OF STIGMA FOR SOCIAL RELATIONS

I have intimated that "stigmatized" and "nonstigmatized" people are tied together in a perpetual inferior/superior relationship. This relationship is key to understanding the meaning of stigma. To conceptualize stigma as a social relationship raises some vital questions about stigma. These questions include (a) when

and under what conditions does an attribute become a stigmatized one? (b) can a person experience stigmatization without knowing that a trait is devalued in a specific social context? (c) does a person feel stigmatized even though in a particular social context the attribute is not stigmatized or the stigma is not physically or behaviorally apparent? (d) can a person refuse to be stigmatized or destigmatize an attribute by ignoring the prevailing norms that define it as a stigma?

These questions lead to another one: Would stigma persist if stigmatized people did not feel stigmatized or inferior? Certainly, a national pride did not lessen the persecution of the Jews, nor does it provide freedom for blacks in South Africa. These two examples illustrate how pervasive and powerful the social control aspects of stigma are, empowering the stigmatizer and stripping the stigmatized of power. Yet a personal awakening, a discover that the responsibility for being stigmatized does not lie with oneself, is important. Understanding that the rationale for discrimination and segregation based on stigma lies in the mind of the stigmatizer has led people like Mahatma Gandhi and civil rights activist Rosa Parks to rise above the feeling of stigmatization, to ignore the norms, and to disobey the exiting laws based on stigma. There have been women, elderly adults, gays, disabled people, and many others who at some point realized that their fundamental similarities outweighed and outnumbered their differences. It becomes clear that, in most oppressive situations the primary problem lies with the stigmatizer and not with the stigmatized (Sartre, 1948; Schur, 1980, 1983). Many stigmatized people also begin to understand that the stigmatizer, having established a position of false superiority and consequently the need to maintain it, is enslaved to the concept that stigmatized people are fundamentally inferior. In fact, some stigmatized individuals question the norms about stigma and attempt to change the social environments for their peers.

In contrast, there are some stigmatized persons who accept their devalued status as legitimate. Attempting to "pass" and derogating others like themselves are two ways in which stigmatized people effectively accept the society's negative perceptions of their stigma (Goffman, cited in Gibbons, 1986). It is clear, especially from accounts of those who move from a nonstigmatized to a stigmatized role, that stigmatization is difficult to resist if everyone begins to reinforce the inferior status with their behavior. Two of the most common ways in which nonstigmatized people convey a sense of fundamental inferiority to stigmatized people are social rejection or social isolation and lowered expectations.

There are many ways in which people communicate social rejection such as speech, eye contact, and interpersonal distance. The stigmatized role, as conceptualized by the symbolic interactionism approach, is similar to any other role (e.g., professor, doctor) in which we behave according to the role expectations of others and change our identity to be congruent with them. Thus, in the case of stigma, role expectations are often the same as the stereotypes. Some stigmatized people become dependent, passive, helpless, and childlike because that is what is expected of them.

Social rejection or avoidance affects not only the stigmatized individual but everyone who is socially involved, such as family, friends, and relatives (Barbarin, 1986). This permanent form of social quarantine forces people to limit their relationships to other stigmatized people and to those for whom the social bond outweighs the stigma, such as family members. In this way, avoidance or social rejection also acts as a form of social control or containment (Edgerton, 1967; Goffman, 1963; Schur, 1983; Scott, 1969). Social rejection is perhaps most difficult for younger children who are banned from most social activities of their peers.

Social exile conveys another message about expectations. Many stigmatized people are not encouraged to develop or grow, to have aspirations or to be successful. Barbarin reports that children with cancer lose friendships and receive special, lenient treatment from teachers. They are not expected to achieve in the same manner as other children. Parents, too, sometimes allow stigmatized children to behave in ways that "normal" children in the same family are not permitted to do. Social exclusion as well as overprotection can lead to decreased performance. Lowered expectations also lead to decreased self-esteem.

The negative identity that ensues becomes a pervasive personality trait and inhibits the stigmatized person from developing other parts of the self. Another detrimental aspect of stigmatization is the practice of treating people, such as the ex-con and ex-mental patient who are attempting to reintegrate themselves into society, as if they still had the stigma. Even the terms we use to describer such persons suggest that role expectations remain the same despite the stigmatized person's efforts to relinquish them. It seems that the paradoxical societal norms that establish a subordinate and dependent position for stigmatized people while ostracizing them for it may stem from the need of nonstigmatized people to maintain a sense of superiority. Their position is supported and reinforced by their perceptions that stigmatized people are fundamentally inferior, passive, helpless, and childlike.

The most pernicious consequence of bearing a stigma is that stigmatized people may develop the same perceptual problems that nonstigmatized people have. They begin to see themselves and their lives through the stigma, or as Sartre (1948) writes about the Jews, they "allow themselves to be poisoned by the stereotype and live in fear that they will correspond to it" (p. 95). As Gibbons observes, stigmatized individuals sometimes blame their difficulties on the stigmatized trait, rather than confronting the root of their personal difficulties. Thus, normal issues that one encounters in life often act as a barrier to growth for stigmatized people because of the attributional process involved.

The need to maintain one's identity manifests itself in a number of ways, such as the mischievous behavior of the adolescent boy with cancer cited in Barbarin's chapter. "Attaining normalcy within the limits of stigma" (Tracy & Gussow, 1978) seems to be another way of describing the need to establish or recapture one's identity (Weiner, 1975).

Stigma uniquely alters perceptions in other ways, especially with respect to the notion of "normality," and raises other questions about the dilemma of difference. Most people do not want to be perceived as different or "abnormal." Becker and Arnold and Gibbons discuss normalization as attempts to be "not different" and to appear "normal." Such strategies include "passing" or disguising the stigma and acting "normal" by "covering up"—keeping up with the pace of nonstigmatized individuals (Davis, 1964; Gibbons, 1986; Goffman, 1963; Weiner, 1975). For stigmatized people, the idea of normality takes on an exaggerated importance. Normality becomes the supreme goal for many stigmatized individuals until they realize that there is no precise definition of normality except what they would be without their stigma. Given the dilemma of difference that stigma reflects, it is not clear whether anyone can ever feel "normal."

Out of this state of social isolation and lowered expectations, though, can arise some positive consequences. Although the process can be fraught with pain and difficulty, stigmatized people who manage to reject the perceptions of themselves as inferior often come away with greater inner strength (Jones *et al.*, 1984). They learn to depend on their own resources and, like the earlier examples of Mahatma Gandhi and Rosa Parks, they begin to question the bases for defining normality. Many stigmatized people regain their identity through redefining normality and realizing that it is acceptable to be who they are (Ablon, 1981; Barbarin; Becker, 1980; Becker & Arnold, 1986).

FEAR AND STIGMA

Fear is important to a discussion of how and why stigma persists. In many cultures that do not use the term *stigma*, there is some emotional reaction beyond interest or curiosity to differences such as children who are born with birthmarks, epilepsy, or a caul. Certain physical characteristics or illnesses elicit fear because the etiology of the attribute or disease is unknown, unpredictable, and unexpected (Sontag, 1979). People even have fears about the sexuality of certain stigmatized groups such as persons who are mentally retarded, feeling that if they are allowed to reproduce they will have retarded offspring (Gibbons, 1986). It seems that what gives stigma its intensity and reality is fear.

The nature of the fear appears to vary with the type of stigma. For most stigmas stemming from physical or mental problems, including cancer, people experience fear of contagion even though they know that the stigma cannot be developed through contact (see Barbarin, 1986). This fear usually stems from not knowing about the etiology of a condition, its predictability, and its course.

The stigmatization of certain racial, ethnic, and gender categories may also be based on fear. This fear, though, cannot stem from contagion because attributes (of skin color, ethnic background, and gender) cannot possibly be transmitted to nonstigmatized people. One explanation for the fear is that people want to avoid "courtesy stigmas" or stigmatization by association (Goffman, 1963). Another explanation underlying this type of fear may be the notion of scarce resources. This is the perception that if certain groups of people are allowed to have a share in all resources, there will not be enough: not enough jobs, not enough land, not enough water, or not enough food. Similar explanations from the deviance literature suggest that people who stigmatize feel threatened and collectively feel that their position of social, economic, and political dominance will be dismantled by members of stigmatized groups (Schur, 1980, 1983). A related explanation is provided by Hughes, who states, "that it may be that those whose positions are insecure and whose hopes for the higher goals are already fading express more violent hostility to new people" (1945, p. 356). This attitude may account for the increased aggression toward members of stigmatized groups during dire economic periods.

Fear affects not only nonstigmatized but stigmatized individuals as well. Many stigmatized people (e.g., ex-cons, mentally retarded adults) who are attempting to "pass" live in fear that their stigmatized attribute will be discovered (Gibbons, 1986). These fears are grounded in a realistic assessment of the negative social consequences of stigmatization and reflect the long-term social and psychological damage to individuals resulting from stigma.

At some level, therefore, most people are concerned with stigma because they are fearful of its unpredictable and uncontrollable nature. Stigmatization appears uncontrollable because human differences serve as the basis for stigmas. Therefore, *any* attribute can become a stigma. No one really ever knows when or if he or she will acquire a stigma or when societal norms might change to stigmatize a trait he or she already possesses. To deny this truth by attempting to isolate stigmatized people or escape from stigma is a manifestation of the underlying fear.

The unpredictability of stigma is similar to the unpredictability of death. Both Gibbons and Barbarin note that the development of a stigmatized condition in a loved one or in oneself represents a major breach of trust—a destruction of the belief that life is predictable. In a sense, stigma represents a kind of death—a social death. Nonstigmatized people, through avoidance and social rejection, often treat stigmatized people as if they were invisible, nonexistent, or dead. Many stigmas, in particular childhood cancer, remove the usual disguises of mortality. Such stigmas can act as a symbolic reminder of everyone's inevitable death (see Barbarin's discussion of Ernest Becker's (1973) *The Denial of Death*). These same fears can be applied to the acquisition of other stigmas (e.g., mental illness, physical disabilities) and help to intensify and perpetuate the negative responses to most stigmatized categories. Thus, irrational fears may help stigmatization to be self-perpetuating with little encouragement needed in the form of forced segregation from the political and social structure.

The ultimate answers about why stigma persists may lie in an examination of why people fear differences, fear the future, fear the unknown, and therefore stigmatize that which is different and unknown. An equally important issue to investigate is how stigmatization may be linked to the fear of being different.

CONCLUSION

Stigma is clearly a very complex multidisciplinary issue, with each additional perspective containing another piece of this enigma. A multidisciplinary approach allowed us as social scientists to perceive stigma as a whole; to see from within it rather than to look down upon it. Our joint perspectives have also demonstrated that there are many shared ideas across disciplines, and in many cases only the terminology is different.

Three important aspects of stigma emerge from this multidisciplinary examination and may forecast its future. They are fear, stigma's primary affective component; stereotyping, its primary cognitive component; and social control, its primary behavioral component. The study of the relationship of stigma to fear, stereotyping, and social control may elucidate our understanding of the paradoxes that a multidisciplinary perspective reveals. It may also bring us closer to understanding what stigma really is—not primarily a property of individuals as many have conceptualized it to be but a humanly constructed perception, constantly in flux and legitimizing our negative responses to human differences (Ainlay & Crosby, 1986). To further clarify the definition of stigma, one must differentiate between an "undesired differentness" that is likely to lead to feelings of stigmatization and actual forms of stigmatization. *It appears that stigmatization occurs only when the social control component is imposed, or when the undesired differentness leads to some restriction in physical and social mobility and access to opportunities that allow an individual to develop his or her potential. This definition combines the original meaning of stigma with more contemporary connotations and uses.*

In another vein, stigma is a statement about personal and social responsibility. People irrationally feel that, by separating themselves from stigmatized individuals, they may reduce their own risk of acquiring the stigma (Barbarin, 1986). By isolating individuals, people feel they can also isolate the problem. If stigma is ignored, the responsibility for its existence and perpetuation can be shifted elsewhere. Making stigmatized people feel responsible for their own stigma allows nonstigmatized people to relinquish the onus for creating or perpetuating the conditions that surround it.

Changing political and economic climates are also important to the stigmatization and destigmatization process. What is economically feasible or politically enhancing for a group in power will partially determine what attributes are stigmatized, or at least how they are stigmatized. As many sociologists have suggested, some people are stigmatized for violating norms, whereas others are stigmatized for being of little economic or political value (Birenbaum & Sagarin, 1976, cited in Stafford & Scott, 1986). We should admit that stigma persists as a social problem because it continues to have some of its original social utility as a means of controlling certain segments of the population and ensuring that power is not easily exchanged. Stigma helps to maintain the existing social hierarchy.

One might then ask if there will ever be societies or historical periods without stigma. Some authors hold a positive vision of the future. Gibbons, for example, suggests that as traditionally stigmatized groups become more integrated into the general population, stigmatizing attributes will lose some of their influence. But historical analysis would suggest that new stigmas will replace old ones. Educational programs are probably of only limited help, as learning to stigmatize is a part of early social learning experiences (Martin, 1986; Sigelman & Singleton, 1986). The social learning of stigma is indeed very different from learning about the concept abstractly in a classroom. School experiences sometimes merely reinforce what children learn about stigmatization from parents and significant others.

From a sociological perspective, the economic, psychological and social benefits of stigma sustain it. Stigmas will disappear when we no longer need to legitimize social exclusion and segregation (Zola, 1979). From the perspective of cognitive psychology, when people find it necessary or beneficial to perceive the fundamental similarities they share with stigmatized people rather than the differences, we will see the beginnings of a real elimination of stigma. This process may have already occurred during some particular historical period or within particular societies. It is certainly an important area for historians, anthropologists, and psychologists to explore.

Although it would seem that the core of the problem lies with the nonstigmatized individuals, stigmatized people also play an important role in the destigmatization process. Stigma contests, or the struggles to determine which attributes are devalued and to what extent they are devalued, involve stigmatized and nonstigmatized individuals alike (Schur, 1980). Stigmatized people, too, have choices as to whether to accept their stigmatized condition and the negative social consequences or continue to fight for more integration into nonstigmatized communities. Their cognitive and affective attitudes toward themselves as individuals and as a group are no small element in shaping societal responses to them. As long as they continue to focus on the negative, affective components of stigma, such as low self-esteem, it is not likely that their devalued status will change. Self-help groups may play an important role in countering this tendency.

There is volition or personal choice. Each stigmatized or nonstigmatized individual can choose to feel superior or inferior, and each individual can make choices about social control and about fear. Sartre (1948) views this as the choice between authenticity or authentic freedom, and inauthenticity or fear of being oneself. Each individual can choose to ignore social norms regarding stigma. Personal beliefs about a situation or circumstance often differ from norms, but people usually follow the social norms anyway, fearing to step beyond conformity to exercise their own personal

beliefs about stigma (see Ainlay & Crosby, 1986 and Stafford & Scott, 1986, discussions of personal versus socially shared forms of stigma). Changing human behavior is not as simple as encouraging people to exercise their personal beliefs. As social scientists, we know a number of issues may be involved in the way personal volition interacts with social norms and personal values.

The multidisciplinary approach could be used in a variety of creative ways to study stigma and other social problems. Different models of how stigma has evolved and is perpetuated could be subject to test by a number of social scientists. They could combine their efforts to examine whether stigma evolves in a similar manner in different cultures, or among children of different cultural and social backgrounds, or during different historical periods. The study of stigma encompasses as many factors and dimensions as are represented in a multidisciplinary approach. All of the elements are interactive and in constant flux. The effective, cognitive, and behavioral dimensions are subject to the current cultural, historical, political, and economic climates, which are in turn linked to the norms and laws. We know that the responses of stigmatized and nonstigmatized individuals may at times appear to be separate, but that they are also interconnected and may produce other responses when considered together. This graphic portrayal of the issues vital to the study of stigma is neither exhaustive nor definitive. It does suggest, however, that a multidimensional model of stigma is needed to understand how these factors, dimensions, and responses co-vary.

We need more cross-disciplinary research from researchers who do not commonly study stigma. For example, a joint project among historians, psychologists, economists, and political scientists might examine the relationship between economic climate, perceptions of scarcity, and stigmatization. Other joint ventures by anthropologists and economists could design research on how much income is lost over a lifetime by members of a stigmatized category (e.g., blind, deaf, overweight), and how this loss adversely affects the GNP and the overall economy. Another example would be work by political scientists and historians or anthropologists to understand the links between the stigmatization of specific attributes and the maintenance of social control and power by certain political groups. Psychologists might team up with novelists or anthropologists to use case studies to understand individual differences or to examine how some stigmatized persons overcome their discredited status. Other studies of the positive consequences of stigma might include a joint investigation by anthropologists and psychologists of cultures that successfully integrate stigmatized individuals into nonstigmatized communities and utilize whatever resources or talents a stigmatized person has to offer (as the shaman is used in many societies) (Halifax, 1979, 1982).

The study of stigma by developmental and social psychologists, sociologists, anthropologists, economists, and historians may also offer new insights into the evolution of sex roles and sex role identity across the life cycle and during changing economic climates. Indeed, linguists, psychologists, and sociologists may be able to chronicle the changes in identity and self-concept of stigmatized and nonstigmatized alike, by studying the way people describe themselves and the language they use in their interactions with stigmatized and nonstigmatized others (Coleman, 1985; Edelsky & Rosengrant, 1981).

The real challenge for social scientists will be to better understand the need to stigmatize; the need for people to reject rather than accept others; the need for people to denigrate rather than uplift others. We need to know more about the relationship between stigma and perceived threat, and how stigma may represent "the kinds of deviance that it seeks out" (Schur, 1980, p. 22). Finally, social scientists need to concentrate on designing an optimal system in which every member of society is permitted to develop one's talents and experience one's full potential regardless of any particular attribute. If such a society were to come about, then perhaps some positive consequences would arise from the dilemma of difference.

REFERENCES

Ablon, J. 1981. "Stigmatized health conditions." *Social Science and Medicine*, 15: 5–9.

Ainlay, S. and F. Crosby. 1986. "Stigma, justice and the dilemma of difference." In S. Ainlay, G. Becker, and L. M. Coleman, eds., *The Dilemma of Difference: A Multicultural View of Stigma*, 17–38. New York: Plenum.

Barbarin, O. 1986. "Family experience of stigma in childhood cancer." In S. Ainlay, G. Becker, and L. M. Coleman, eds., *The Dilemma of Difference: A Multicultural View of Stigma*. New York: Plenum, 163–184.

Becker, G. 1980. *Growing Old in Silence*. Berkeley: University of California Press.

Becker, G. and R. Arnold. 1986. "Stigma as social and cultural construct." In S. Ainlay, G. Becker, and L. M. Coleman, eds., *The Dilemma of Difference: A Multicultural View of Stigma*. New York: Plenum, 39–58.

Brooks, J. and Lewis, M. 1976. "Infants' responses to strangers: Midget, adult, and child." *Child Development* 47: 323–332.

Coleman, L. 1985. "Language and the evolution of identity and self-concept." In F. Kessel, ed., *The development of language and language researchers: Essays in honor of Roger Brown*. Hillsdale, N.J.: Erlbaum.

Crocker, J. and N. Lutsky. 1986. "Stigma and the dynamics of social cognition." In S. Ainlay, G. Becker, and L. M. Coleman, eds., *The Dilemma of Difference: A Multicultural View of Stigma* New York. Plenum, 95–122.

Davis, F. 1964. "Deviance disavowal: The management of strained interaction by the visibly handicapped." In H. Becker, ed., *The Other Side.* New York: Free Press, 119–138.

Edelsky, C. and Rosengrant, T. 1981. "Interactions with handicapped children: Who's handicapped?" *Sociolinguistic Working Paper 92*. Austin, TX: Southwest Educational Development Laboratory.

Edgerton, R. G. 1967. *The Cloak of Competence: Stigma in the Lives of the Mentally Retarded*. Berkeley: University of California Press.

Feinman, S. 1982. "Social referencing in infancy." *Merrill-Palmer Quarterly* 28: 445–70.

Gibbons, F. X. 1986. "Stigma and Interpersonal Relations." In S. C. Ainsley, G. Becker, and L. M. Coleman, eds., *The Dilemma of Difference: A Multidisciplinary View of Stigma*. New York: Plenum. 95–122.

Goffman, E. 1963. *Stigma: Notes on the Management of Spoiled Identity*. Englewood Cliffs, N.J.: Prentice Hall.

Hallifax, J. 1979. *Shamanic Voices: A Survey of Visionary Narratives*. New York: Dutton.

——. 1982. *Shaman: The Wounded Healer*. London: Thames and Hudson.

Jones. E. E., A. Farina, A. H. Hastof, H. Markus, D. T. Miller, and R. A. Scott, 1984. *Social Stigma: The Psychology of Marked Relationships*. New York: Freeman.

Kanter, R. M. 1979. *Men and Women of the Corporation*. New York: Basic Books.

Klinnert, M. D., J. J. Campos, J. F. Sorce, R. Emde and M. Svejda. 1983. "Emotions as behavior regulators: Social referencing in infancy." In R. Plutchik and H. Kellerman, eds. *Emotion Theory, Research, and Experience. Vol. II. Emotions in Early Development*. New York: Academic Press, 57–88.

Locksley, A., E. Borgida, N. Brekke, and C. Hepburn. 1980. "Sexual stereotypes and social judgment." *Journal of Personality and Social Psychology*, 39: 821–31.

Locksley, A., C. Hepburn, and V. Ortiz. 1982. "Social stereotypes and judgments of individuals: An instance of the base-rate fallacy." *Journal of Experimental Social Psychology*. 18: 23–42.

Martin, L. G. 1986. "Stigma: A social learning perspective." In S. Ainlay, G. Becker, and L. M. Coleman, eds., *The Dilemma of Difference: A Multicultural View of Stigma*. New York. Plenum, 1–16.

Sartre, J. 1948. *Anti-Semite and Jew*. New York: Schocken Books.

Schur, E. 1980. *The Politics Of Deviance: A Sociological Introduction*. Englewood Cliffs, N.J.: Prentice Hall.

——. 1983. *Labeling Women Deviant: Gender, Stigma, and Social Control*. Philadelphia: Temple University Press.

Scott, R., 1969. *The Making of Blind Men*. New York: Russel Sage Foundation.

Sigelman, C. and L. C. Singleton. 1986. "Stigmatization in childhood: A survey of developmental trends and issues." In S. Ainlay, G. Becker, and L. M. Coleman, eds., *The Dilemma of Difference: A Multicultural View of Stigma*. New York: Plenum. 185–210.

Solomon, Howard M. 1986. "Stigma and Western culture: A historical approach." In S. Ainlay, G. Becker, and L. M. Coleman, eds., *The Dilemma of Difference: A Multicultural View of Stigma*. New York: Plenum, 59–76.

Sontag, S. 1979. *Illness as Metaphor*. New York: Random House.

Sroufe, L. A. 1977. "Wariness of strangers and the study of infant development." *Child Development*, 48: 731–46.

Stafford, M and R. Scott. 1986. "Stigma, deviance and social control: Some conceptual issues." In S. Ainlay, G. Becker, and L. M. Coleman, eds., *The Dilemma of Difference: A Multicultural View of Stigma*. New York. Plenum, 77–94.

Terry, W. 1984. *Bloods: An Oral History of the Vietnam War by Black Veterans*. New York: Random House.

Tracy, G. S., and Gussow, Z. 1978. "Self-help health groups: A grass-roots response to a need for services." *Journal of Applied Behavioral Science* 12(3): 381–396.

Weiner, C. L., 1975. "The burden of rheumatoid arthritis: Tolerating the uncertainty." *Social Science and Medicine* 99: 97–104.

Zola, I. Z. 1979. "Helping one another: A speculative history of the self-help movement. *Archive of Physical Medicine and Rehabilitation* 60: 452.

CHAPTER 12

Unhealthy Disabled: Treating Chronic Illnesses as Disabilities

Susan Wendell

The relationship between disability and illness is a problematic one. Many people are disabled by chronic and/or life-threatening illnesses, and many people with disabilities not caused by illness have chronic health problems as consequences of their disabilities; but modern movements for the rights of people with disabilities have fought the identification of disability with illness, and for good reasons. This identification contributes to the medicalization of disability, in which disability is regarded as an individual misfortune, and people with disabilities are assumed to suffer primarily from physical and/or mental abnormalities that medicine can and should treat, cure, or at least prevent (Oliver 1990; Morris 1991). Moreover, Ron Amundson argues that, since illness is perceived as "globally incapacitating," identifying disability with illness fosters the myth that people with disabilities are globally incapacitated, which in turn contributes to the social devaluation of disabled people (Amundson 1992, 113–14). Perhaps most importantly, in the recent past, many healthy people with disabilities were forced to live in long-term care institutions under medical supervision simply because they needed services to perform tasks of daily living. In those institutions, medical personnel controlled every aspect of their lives, and little or

no provision was made for them to work, to receive education, or to participate in life outside the institutions. At least in Canada, not everyone who could live outside an institution has achieved that goal, and institutionalization (especially when support networks break down) remains a threat to some people with disabilities who have achieved independent living (for example, see Snow 1992). All these reasons motivate disabled activists and other people with disabilities to distinguish themselves from those who are ill.

For example, in her recent book *Exile and Pride: Disability, Queerness and Liberation* (1999), Eli Clare describes her resistance to the medical model of disability in terms that emphasize her distance from sick people:

> To frame disability in terms of a cure is to accept the medical model of disability, to think of disabled people as sick, diseased, ill people. . . . My CP simply is not a *medical* condition. I need no specific medical care, medication, or treatment for my CP; the adaptive equipment I use can be found in a computer catalog, not a hospital. Of course, disability comes in many varieties. Some disabled people, depending on their disabilities, may indeed have pressing medical needs for a specific period of time or on an ongoing basis. But having particular medical needs

differs from labeling a person with multiple sclerosis as sick, or thinking of quadriplegia as a disease. The disability rights movement, like other social change movements, names systems of oppression as the problem, not individual bodies. In short it is ableism that needs the cure, not our bodies.

(Clare 1999, 105–6)

Although she acknowledges that some people with disabilities have medical needs, including someone with multiple sclerosis (MS, which qualifies as a chronic illness), Clare criticizes the medical model for thinking of disabled people as "sick, diseased, ill people" and says that their bodies do not need cure. Yet some people with disabilities *are* sick, diseased, and ill. Social constructionist analyses of disability, in which oppressive institutions and policies, prejudiced attitudes, discrimination, cultural misrepresentation, and other social injustices are seen as the primary causes of disability, can reduce attention to those disabled people whose bodies are highly medicalized because of their suffering, their deteriorating health, or the threat of death. Moreover, some unhealthy disabled people, as well as some healthy people with disabilities, experience physical or psychological burdens that no amount of social justice can eliminate. Therefore, some very much want to have their bodies cured, not as a substitute for curing ableism, but in addition to it. There is a danger that acknowledging these facts might provide support for those who prefer the individualized, medicalized picture of disability. Thus, in promoting the liberatory vision of social constructionism, it is safer and more comfortable for disability activism to focus on people who are healthy disabled.

Despite the problematic relationship between disability and illness, many people who are disabled by chronic illnesses are involved in disability politics and contribute to social constructionist analyses,

and disability groups have increasingly welcomed into their activities people with HIV/AIDS, fibromyalgia, myalgic encephalomyelitis/chronic fatigue immune dysfunction syndrome (ME/CFIDS), and other chronic illnesses. However, there are important differences between healthy disabled and unhealthy disabled people that are likely to affect such issues as treatment of impairment in disability politics and feminism, accommodation of disability in activism and employment, identification of persons as disabled, disability pride, and prevention and so-called "cure" of disabilities. Here I hope to introduce and perhaps clarify some of those differences, and to open a conversation about the relationships between illness and disability and between unhealthy and healthy people with disabilities.

The issues I will be raising are particularly important to women because women are more likely than men to be disabled by chronic illnesses (Morris 1994; Trypuc 1994), and women (including women with other disabilities) suffer more ill health than men (Carroll and Niven 1993). Women live longer than men, but much of that extra living is done with a disabling chronic illness (Carroll and Niven 1993; *Report on the Health of Canadians* 1996). Accommodating chronic illnesses in disability politics and feminism is essential to many disabled women's participation in them. Thus, as we shall see, it is women with disabilities who have been most outspoken about some of these issues.

WHO IS WHO?

When I speak of people who are "healthy disabled," I mean people whose physical conditions and functional limitations are relatively stable and predictable for the foreseeable future. They may be people who were born with disabilities or people who were disabled by accidents or illnesses later in life, but they regard themselves as healthy, not sick, they do not expect to die any sooner than any other healthy person their age, and they do not need or seek much more medical attention than other healthy people (I will not try to give a definition of health, which is too big a topic to discuss here, but I am assuming that healthy people's functional limitations and bodily suffering are fairly stable and do not motivate them to seek medical treatment or cures).

Notice that "healthy disabled" is a category with fluctuating and sometimes uncertain membership. Many people who seem to have stable disabilities now will encounter illness and changing disability later in life (for example, post-polio syndrome has destabilized the health and abilities of some people who had recovered from polio, with residual disability, decades ago), and some people who seem to have stable disabilities also have chronic or recurrent health problems, either as consequences of their disabilities or independently of them. Thus, many of the problems I describe here as problems of unhealthy disabled people have been or will be problems of people who are now healthy disabled.

Defining what I mean by chronic illness would help to clarify the distinction between healthy and unhealthy people with disabilities, but it is not easy to pin down chronic illnesses with a definition.[1] Usually, they are understood to be illnesses that do not go away by themselves within six months, that cannot reliably be cured, and that will not kill the patient any time soon. I think that any practical concept of chronic illness has to be patient-centered or illness-centered, rather than based on diagnosis or disease classification, because many diseases cannot reliably be categorized into chronic and non-chronic. Nevertheless, a brief discussion of the variety of ways that diseases can cause chronic illness may be helpful.

Some diseases, such as lupus or diabetes, are known to be *typically* chronic. Physicians do not expect to cure them, and, once diagnosed, patients more or less expect to have to live with them (depending on how informed they are and how inclined they are to believe in miraculous cures or rapid progress in scientific medicine). A few patients with these diseases do recover their health instead of remaining chronically ill, but most do not. On the other hand, patients do not expect to die soon from these diseases. Nevertheless, many of the recognized chronic diseases, such as lupus, sometimes occur in acute forms that kill the patient quickly, and many of them, such as diabetes, are expected to kill the patient eventually, either by wearing down the patient's health or by creating severe, life-threatening episodes of illness.

Other diseases, such as infectious mononucleosis or Lyme disease, are usually acute but can last for years in some patients, making them chronically ill by any patient-centered definition. People who are chronically ill with these diseases are likely to have trouble getting recognition of their illnesses—if not by the medical profession, then by friends, relatives, acquaintances, employers, insurers, and others who believe that they should have recovered from their diseases long ago. Still other diseases are acute or chronic, depending on the treatment available to patients. HIV infection most often becomes the acute and deadly disease AIDS in poor countries, but in wealthy countries, where expensive treatment can slow its progress, it can frequently be a chronic disease.

Some diseases, such as MS and rheumatoid arthritis, can behave like recurring acute illnesses, with periods of extreme debility and periods of normal (or nearly normal) health, or they can have virtually constant symptoms (such as fatigue or pain) and/or be characterized by recurring acute episodes that leave behind permanent losses of function (such as paralysis caused by MS). Mental illnesses are sometimes acute, sometime recurring, and sometimes chronically debilitating. For example, schizophrenia and depression go in and out of remission for many people. Whether the mental illnesses are diseases is still controversial (see Agich 1997, 229–37), but clearly any adequate concept of illness includes them because of the involuntary suffering and loss of function they cause. I consider illnesses that go into remission chronic when they require prolonged medical treatment or surveillance, or when patients must fear recurrences because there is no reasonable expectation of cure.

The questions "Is my illness temporary?" and "How long will it last?" are often unanswered or answered uncertainly by medicine. This creates difficulties of identity both for the person who is ill (am I disabled or just sick for a while?) and for other people. Christine Overall describes an experience of being ill for more than a year with a painful, debilitating condition initially diagnosed as rheumatoid arthritis and then re-diagnosed as viral arthritis. She says that during the time she was ill, she identified with people with disabilities, was constructed as a person with disabilities, and inhabited the world of people with disabilities. However, she also experienced a strong pressure to *"pass* for normal" (Overall 1998, 155). People minimized her illness, ignored it, denied it, and urged her to get over it. Overall attributes some of this reaction to ageism, speculating that disability is "easier to recognize and tolerate . . . in older people than in younger ones" (1998, 162).

My own analysis is that young and middle-aged people with chronic illnesses inhabit a category not easily understood or accepted. We are considered too young to be ill for the rest of our lives, yet we are not expecting cure or recovery.[2] We cannot be granted the time-out that is normally granted to the acutely ill (or we were given it at first and have now used it up, overused it), yet we seem to refuse to return to pre-illness life. We are not old enough to have finished making our contributions of productivity and/or caregiving; old people with chronic illnesses may be seen to be entitled to rest until they die. And we are not expected to die any time soon, so we are going to hang around being sick for a long while. Cheri Register calls us "the interminably ill" (Register 1987, ix).

Moreover, those of us with chronic illnesses do not fit most people's picture of disability. The paradigmatic person with a disability is healthy disabled and permanently and predictably impaired. Both attitudes toward people with disabilities and programs designed to remove obstacles to their full participation are based on that paradigm. Many of us with chronic illnesses are not obviously disabled; to be recognized as disabled, we have to remind people frequently of our needs and limitations. That in itself can be a source of alienation from other people with disabilities, because it requires repeatedly calling attention to our impairments.

IMPAIRMENT

Many of the issues I raise in this article would be classified as issues of *impairment* in the literature of disability activism and disability studies. Disability activists and scholars usually distinguish impairment from disability, treating impairment as the medically defined condition of a person's body/mind, and disability as the socially constructed disadvantage based upon impairment. This distinction follows the United Nations' definition of impairment as "any loss or abnormality of psychological, physiological, or anatomical structure or function" (U.N. 1983, I.c., 6–7). The U.N.'s attempt to give an objective, universal definition of impairment, which

I have criticized elsewhere (Wendell 1996), connects impairment to the medical institutions that measure structure and function and set the standards of "normality." I believe this connection has contributed to neglect of the realities of impairment in disability activism and disability studies, because it makes attention to impairment seem irrelevant to or in conflict with the social constructionist analyses of disability they employ.

Illness is equated with impairment, even by disability activists and scholars, in ways that disability is not; hence there is anxiety to assure nondisabled people that disability is not illness. Another consequence is the pressure to be (or to pass as) healthy disabled both within disability activism and outside it. Because disability activists have worked hard to resist medicalization and promote the social model of disability, activists sometimes feel pressured to downplay the realities of fluctuating impairment or ill health. Cheryl Marie Wade (1994, 35) has criticized the new image of "the able-disabled" and the reluctance among disability activists to admit to weakness and vulnerability. She found that her identity as an activist made it difficult to acknowledge her physical limitations until her body broke down, endangering both her health and her self-esteem. Outside disability activism, there is pressure to conform to an inspiring version of the paradigm of disability. Those people with disabilities who can best approximate the activities and appearance of nondisabled people (that is, those who can make others forget they are disabled) will be allowed to participate most fully in the activities of their society.

British feminist disability activist Liz Crow has written a powerful critique of "our silence about impairment" within disability movements. She says:

> Our insistence that disadvantage and exclusion are the result of discrimination and prejudice, and our criticisms of the medical model of disability, have made us wary of acknowledging our experiences of impairment. Impairment is safer not mentioned at all This silence prevents us from dealing effectively with the difficult aspects of impairment. Many of us remain frustrated and disheartened by pain, fatigue, depression and chronic illness, including the way they prevent us from realizing our potential or railing fully against disability (our experience of exclusion and discrimination); many of us fear for our futures with progressive or additional impairments; we mourn past activities that are no longer possible for us; we are afraid we may die early or that suicide may seem our only option; we desperately seek some effective medical intervention; we feel ambivalent about the possibilities of our children having impairments; and we are motivated to work for the prevention of impairments. Yet our silence about impairment has made many of these things taboo and created a whole new series of constraints on our self expression.

> (Crow 1996, 209–10)

Crow emphasizes the need to focus on both disability *and* impairment, and she acknowledges that "impairment *in itself* can be a negative, painful experience" (Crow 1996, 219). She urges people with disabilities to adopt a new approach to impairment that includes not only the medically-based descriptions of our bodies/minds but also our experiences of our bodies/minds over time and in variable circumstances, the effects they have on our activities, the feelings they produce, and any concerns about them that impaired individuals might have.

It seems possible to pay more attention to impairment while supporting a social constructionist analysis of disability, especially if we focus our attention on the phenomenology of impairment, rather than accepting a medical approach to it. Knowing more about how people experience, live with, and think about their own impairments could contribute to an appreciation of disability as a valuable difference from the medical norms of body and mind. Moreover, recognition of impairment is crucial to the inclusion of people with chronic illnesses in disability politics. Chronic illness frequently involves pain, fatigue, dizziness, nausea, weakness, depression, and/or other impairments that are hard to ignore. Everything one does, including politics, must be done within the limitations they present. The need to accommodate them is just as great, if more problematic (see below), as the need to accommodate blindness or hemiplegia, but they cannot be accommodated if they are not acknowledged and discussed openly.

Liz Crow points out that ignoring impairment can reduce the relevance of the social model of disability to certain groups, such as women, among whom (in England) arthritis is the most common cause of impairment, manifested in pain (1996, 221). I would add that pain and/or fatigue are major sources of impairment in many chronic illnesses that are more common in women than in men, including rheumatoid arthritis, fibromyalgia, lupus, ME/CFIDS, migraine headache, MS, and depression. This is not to say that men do not suffer from impairments of chronic illness, but that attempting to ignore impairment in disability politics may alienate or marginalize more women than men. Jenny Morris reports that restoring the experience of impairment to disability politics was regarded as a women's issue in the series of meetings of disabled women that led to the book, *Encounters with Strangers: Feminism and Disability*, in which Crow's critique of the social model was published (Morris 1996, 13).

When feminist politics ignores their experience of impairment, there are different but equally disturbing sources of disabled women's alienation from feminism or their marginalization within it. Feminist organizations have become more aware of the need to make their activities accessible to women who use wheelchairs, women who need written material in alternative formats, and women who need Sign Language translation, but much feminist practice still assumes a consistently energetic, high-functioning body and mind, and certainly not a body and mind that are impaired by illness. (I will discuss accommodating chronic illnesses in political practice in the next section.) Moreover, in their writing and organizing, most feminists still assume that feminists are giving, and not receiving, care, and that all significant contributions to feminist movements happen in meetings, at public events, and in demonstrations on the streets. The accepted image of a good feminist still includes handling paid work and family responsibilities and having plenty of energy left over for political activity in the evenings or on weekends. In these circumstances, women with chronic illnesses are likely to find it difficult to participate in feminist movements or to identify themselves as feminists.

Not only unhealthy people with disabilities but many healthy disabled people would benefit from more recognition of impairment in both disability and feminist politics. Some disabilities that are not illnesses and do not cause illnesses do involve impairments similar to those caused by chronic illnesses. It has been difficult, for example, for people with some brain injuries to have their impairments understood and accommodated, because they are more like impairments of chronic illnesses—transitory and unpredictable—than those of paradigmatic, stable disabilities. They may include both fatigue and intermittent cognitive impairments that are exacerbated by fatigue, such as difficulty concentrating and recalling words.

Fatigue is one of the most common and misunderstood impairments of chronic illness. The fatigue of illness is different in three critical respects from the ordinary fatigue experienced by healthy people: it is more debilitating, it lasts longer, and it is less predictable. Every activity, including thinking, watching, listening, speaking, and eating, requires energy. It is possible to be too fatigued to do any of these. Anyone who has had severe influenza may recall being too fatigued to have a conversation, to follow a simple story, or to make a decision. That experience of fatigue is closer to the fatigue of MS, rheumatoid arthritis, fibromyalgia, depression, or ME/CFIDS than the fatigue of a healthy person at the end of a hard day. A good night's sleep rarely cures the profound fatigue of illness; it may last for days or weeks with no apparent improvement, or it may fluctuate, allowing some activity punctuated by periods of total exhaustion. And unlike the fatigue of influenza, which will gradually improve as one's body recovers from infection, the fatigue of chronic illness is unpredictable. It may appear first thing in the morning on the tenth day of a restful vacation or in the middle of an energetic day's work. Reasonable precautions may help to prevent it, but it resists control.

Fatigue may be a primary symptom of a chronic illness, or it may be caused by other symptoms, such as pain, anorexia, or depressed mood. Thus, fluctuating and severely limited energy is a common impairment of people with chronic illnesses. Of course, not everyone with a chronic illness experiences this impairment, but it is an important example, not only because many of us have impaired energy, but because it is one of the most challenging impairments to accommodate.

ACCOMMODATING CHRONIC ILLNESSES

Fluctuating abilities and limitations can make people with chronic illnesses seem like unreliable activists, given the ways that political activity in both disability and feminist movements are structured. On a bad day of physical or mental illness, we may be unable to attend a meeting or workshop, to write a letter, to answer the phone, or to respond to e-mail. We may need notice in advance of work to be done, in order to work only on good days or more slowly on days when we are very ill. We may need to work in teams, so that someone else can take over when we cannot work at all. We may need to send a written speech to a meeting to be read by someone else because we are too sick to attend and read it in person. We need others to understand that our not showing up does not mean that we are not committed to the group, event, or cause.

Commitment to a cause is usually equated to energy expended, even to pushing one's body and mind excessively, if not cruelly. But pushing our bodies and minds excessively means something different to people with chronic illnesses: it means danger, risk of relapse, hospitalization, long-lasting or permanent damage to our capacities to function (as for some people with MS). And sometimes it is simply impossible; people get too tired to sit up, to think, to speak, to listen, and there are no reserves of energy to call upon. Yet in political activity, all-day meetings and evening events after a full day's work are assumed to be appropriate. Stamina is required for commitment to a cause.

I feel uneasy describing these conflicts between the demands of activism and the realities of chronic illness, because I do not want to supply good reasons for regarding those of us who are perpetually ill as social burdens rather than social contributors. This is probably the same uneasiness that healthy disabled people feel about focusing attention on their impairments. I can only hope, as Liz Crow does (Crow 1996, 222–25), that probing these threatening topics will lead eventually to facing and solving some problems. If there is to be more than token participation by unhealthy disabled people over the long term, there will have to be changes in the structure, culture, and traditions of political activism. People will have to think differently about energy and commitment, pace and cooperation.

Implementing the accommodations of pace and scheduling needed by people with chronic illnesses may inconvenience a lot of other people in a group (although, given the general silence about limitations of energy, perhaps many more people will be relieved). Moreover, everyone knows that the people who commit the most time and energy to a group will usually acquire the most power to influence the group's activities. In order for people with impaired energy to participate as equals, the relationships between time, energy, and power will have to be discussed openly and negotiated.

None of this will be easy. Conflicts and suspicions are inevitable. Management of energy is an issue, and at times a challenge, for every adult, whether nondisabled, healthy disabled, or unhealthy disabled. And it is sometimes hard to tell the difference between someone's mismanaging her/his own energy and other people's failure to accommodate her/his impaired energy. Even those of us who have lived a long time with chronic fatigue cannot always tell whether we are not trying hard enough or experiencing a physical/mental limitation, whether we need inspiration, self-discipline, or a nap. In political activism, where external pressures such as publication deadlines or responding to governmental announcements can virtually dictate the pace of the group, someone's claim to need rest may seem like shirking responsibility, especially to people who resent contributing more time or energy than others. Thus, pace and flexibility about time are bound to be controversial in any group that tries to negotiate them. Yet the only alternative is to take them for granted

and make it difficult or impossible for people with impaired energy to participate.

Pace and flexibility about time are also issues of employment access for people with chronic illnesses, and here too conflict may arise—in this case, between the goals of healthy disabled people and the needs of unhealthy disabled people. We have learned that, even with strong legislation such as the Americans with Disabilities Act, it is hard to achieve accommodation of permanent, predictable disabilities in workplaces. Many employers (and non-disabled workers) resist the most straightforward requirements of wheelchair accessibility or Deaf translation. Understandably, disability activists want to stress the message "Remove the barriers that have been erected arbitrarily against our participation, and we will perform as well as anyone else." Insisting on accommodations of pace and time threaten this message, because working according to the employer's schedule and at the pace he/she requires are usually considered to be aspects of job performance, even in jobs where they are not critical to the adequate completion of tasks.

Iris Marion Young has pointed out that, from the perspective of most employers, "the norm of the 'hale and hearty' worker" makes a necessary contribution to workplace discipline. "The 'normal' worker is supposed to be energetic, have high concentration abilities, be alert to adapt to changing conditions, and be able to withstand physical, mental or interactive stress in good humor. Workers who fail to measure up to one or more of these standards are 'normally' considered lazy, slackers, uncooperative or otherwise inadequate. All workers must worry about *failing* in the eyes of their employers ..." (Young 2000, 172). Because many workers fail, either temporarily or permanently, to live up to this "norm," requiring accommodation of a wide range of disabilities would call the "norm" into question and challenge employers' power to set the standards of workplace performance. Employers would prefer to define disability narrowly and regard the vast majority of workers who do not meet their standards as unsuitable for their jobs.

Moreover, if people with chronic illnesses demand accommodations of pace and time, they may encounter resistance from other workers because of the "politics of resentment," described here by Young:

> Most workers feel put-upon and frustrated by their working conditions and the demands of their employers on their time and energy. They have to stand up all day, or have few bathroom breaks, or work overtime or at night, and their employer refuses to accommodate to their aching backs, their family pressures, their sleeplessness or difficulty in concentrating. Many workers, that is, find the demands placed on them next to overwhelming at times, and they feel barely able to cope. Rarely do they get a sympathetic ear to voice their frustrations, however, and the only agents they are allowed to blame for their difficulties are themselves. It is little wonder that they may resent people that the law requires employers to accommodate in order to enable them better to fit the work situation.
>
> . . . Disability is a matter of degree, and it is arbitrary where the line is drawn between not disabled enough to warrant accommodation, and disabled enough. A politics of resentment motivates some people to draw that line as far down the extreme end of the continuum as possible so that almost everyone will be legally expected to conform to the *normal* workplace demands.
>
> (Young 2000, 171)

On the basis of Young's analysis, I think we should expect strong resistance from both employers and workers to accommodating chronic illnesses in the workplace. This resistance may strain the resources and the solidarity of disability rights movements.

Yet access to work for unhealthy disabled people will require taking what Young calls "the next step toward equal opportunity for people with disabilities," that is, challenging the prerogative of employers to define the content, qualifications, and performance criteria of work (Young 2000, 173). There are some reasons for optimism: we have a lot of potential allies to whom pace and flexibility about time make the difference between working and not working, including many nondisabled women caring for children and disabled older family members; and, as Young points out, there are many other workers, who do not identify themselves as disabled, who would benefit from "more humane and individualized workplace accommodation" (2000, 173).

WHO BELONGS?

Controversy about the appropriateness of accommodations of pace and time often leads to doubts about the legitimacy of the disability for which accommodation is requested. Suspicion surrounds people with chronic illnesses—suspicion about how ill/disabled we really are, how or why we became ill, whether we are doing everything possible to get well, and how mismanaging our lives, minds, or souls may be contributing to our continuing illness (Wendell 1996). Suspicion comes from medical professionals, friends, relatives, coworkers, and, understandably, from other people with disabilities.

In her study of a group of people with disabilities in Britain, Jill C. Humphrey found that there was a conspicuous silence about impairment and an associated suspicion as to whether some people belonged in the group—in other words, whether they were really disabled. In her interviews with them, group members raised this suspicion about people whose impairments were not readily apparent. Humphrey comments:

"the propensity to treat only tangible impairments as evidence of a *bona fide* disability identity clearly marginalizes those with non-apparent impairments . . . whilst the reluctance or refusal to differentiate between impairments by identifying them bolsters up the claim by people with apparent impairments that they represent all disabled people" (Humphrey 2000, 67). Of course, suspicions about whether people with non-apparent impairments are really disabled are common, being the flip side of the ability to pass as nondisabled.

The ability to pass is a frequent, though not a universal, difference between unhealthy and healthy people with disabilities. Its advantages include avoiding the prejudices and daily acts of discrimination and patronizing behavior that people with obvious disabilities are subjected to at school, at work, and in other public places. Passing is sometimes voluntary, but it can also be involuntary, in that some of us will be perceived as nondisabled unless we draw attention to our disability, and sometimes even after we draw attention to it. The ability to pass makes a person *not* the paradigmatic person with a disability. Whether it makes her/him more or less acceptable to nondisabled people is unclear; someone who can pass but chooses not to may be seen as soliciting sympathy and special treatment. In either case, our ability to pass means that having our disabilities recognized as genuine is a major issue for many unhealthy disabled people. So much depends on that recognition—accommodation of our impairments, inclusion in disability politics, and, of course, our moral reputations. Because of what Young calls "the politics of resentment" (Young 2000, 171), people wonder whether someone whose disability is not obvious is faking or exaggerating it; the trustworthiness of people who claim to be disabled but do not look disabled is always in question.

Even when our disabilities are considered genuine, there is often suspicion about our role in causing them. Blame and responsibility for our disabilities are more persistent issues for unhealthy than for healthy people with disabilities. Although people disabled by accidents that they themselves caused (for example, by driving drunk) or risked unreasonably (by not wearing a helmet on a motorcycle, for example) may be blamed at first for their disabilities, that blame does not usually follow them for long, perhaps because their disabilities are relatively stable, and thus holding them responsible seems more and more pointless as time goes on. In contrast, people with chronic illnesses are likely to be blamed or held responsible not only during the process of seeking a diagnosis, but also during every relapse or deterioration of their condition, which they are expected (by doctors, loved ones, employers, and the general public) to control (Register 1987; Charmaz 1991). Fluctuations in our illnesses and abilities—which *can* be affected by our emotions, changes in our lives, and stress, but which may occur independently of them—contribute to the perception that we are responsible for our disabilities. In addition, an abundance of popular theories claim or imply that anyone can control her/his health with the right diet, exercise, attitudes, relationships, or religious beliefs; it follows from most of them that those who are unhealthy are doing something wrong, and that, if they have been told how to take better care of themselves, they are acting irresponsibly (see Wendell 1999).

PRIDE, PREVENTION, AND "CURE"

Health is regarded as a virtue or a blessing, depending on how well a person or group of people understands that it cannot be controlled, but it is almost always regarded as a good. Among people who have the political savvy not to give thanks publicly for being nondisabled, giving thanks for being healthy is acceptable, even commendable. Healthy people with disabilities express gratitude for being healthy, people with progressive chronic illnesses express gratitude for not having gotten sicker than they have, and people with recurring or fluctuating chronic illnesses express gratitude for coming out of a relapse (as I know I do).

Of course, many people, especially nondisabled people who have little knowledge of the lives of people with disabilities, fear other kinds of disability as much as, or more than, illness, and regard physical and mental "normality" as blessings, if not virtues. Because fear of disability contributes to the social stigma of being disabled, it is one of the goals of disability politics to replace fear with the understanding that disability can be a valuable difference and that people with disabilities can be proud of their differences from nondisabled people. The question is, does this goal make sense in relation to disabling chronic illnesses? At first glance, it seems to, because chronic illness is a kind of disability, but compare "Thank God I'm not disabled" with "Thank God I'm healthy," and you see the difficulty of applying disability pride to a chronic illness.

Is illness *by definition* an evil, or have we made less progress in recognizing chronic illnesses as potentially valuable differences than we have in relation to other disabilities? (There is a third possibility: Perhaps acute illness is by definition an evil, chronic illness is not, and people confuse them. Yet if that were the case, the news that you are not going to recover from an illness and will have to live with it would be good news; but, unless you were expecting death, it is not good news. Illness, chronic or acute, is widely regarded as an evil.) Certainly it is difficult to say that one is glad to have been ill and be believed, despite the fact that many people who are or have been ill testify

that it has changed them for the better. Of everything I said in my book about disability, *The Rejected Body* (1996), readers have most often questioned or been shocked by my statements that, although I would joyfully accept a cure if it were offered me, I do not need a cure and I do not regret having become ill (Wendell 1996, 83–84, 175). I suppose many people suspect I am making the best of a miserable fate, but then they probably think something very similar about other expressions of disability pride.

I do not think that those of us who appreciate having become ill are making a mistake or deceiving ourselves. Illness is not by definition an evil, but people fear and try to avoid illness because of the suffering it causes. Some of that suffering is social and could be eliminated by social justice for people with disabilities, but some of it is not. Solidarity between people with chronic illnesses and people with other disabilities depends on acknowledging the existence of the suffering that justice cannot eliminate (and therefore on our willingness to talk about impairment). It also depends on acknowledging that illness is not *only* suffering. Like living with cerebral palsy or blindness, living with pain, fatigue, nausea, unpredictable abilities, and/or the imminent threat of death creates different *ways of being* that give valuable perspectives on life and the world. Thus, although most of us want to avoid suffering if possible, suffering is part of some valuable ways of being. If we could live the ways of being without the suffering, some of us would choose to live them. Some of us would choose to live them even if they were inseparable from the suffering. And some of us are glad to have been forced to live them, would choose to be rid of the suffering even if it meant losing the ways of being, but would hope to hold on to what we have learned from them. There are, I think, many versions of disability pride.

Disability pride has come into conflict

with medical efforts to prevent disability, especially by selective abortion of potentially disabled fetuses, and with medical efforts to "cure" certain disabilities, especially deafness in children. Moreover, disability movements have criticized spending enormous amounts of public and donated money searching for "cures" while neglecting to provide the most basic services and opportunities that would improve the lives of people with disabilities. Prevention and cure both focus public attention on the medical model, which can lead us to ignore the social conditions that are causing or increasing disability among people who have impairments. Moreover, given the history of eugenics, there is reason to be skeptical about whether prevention and cure are intended primarily to prevent suffering or to eliminate "abnormalities" and "abnormal" people.

However, it is striking that everyone, including disability scholars and activists, tends to assume that prevention is desirable when the cause of disability is war, famine, poor medical care, accident, or illness, and that cure is desirable when the cause is illness. Perhaps, in these instances, it seems heartless to insist on preserving difference instead of preventing or ending suffering. Whatever our reasons, we sometimes insist on people's rights to have impairments and sometimes assume that they would not want them, depending on the causes and circumstances of disability. I think that when we explore these different responses further, we will discover different beliefs about how much suffering is an acceptable price to pay for a difference we value, and even different beliefs about the value of suffering itself. The perspectives of people with chronic illnesses will be essential to such an exploration, because it may be as difficult for healthy disabled people to see the value of illness as for nondisabled people to see the value of disability. Only some people know what is at stake when we contemplate preventing and curing illnesses: not only the relief of suffering, but also, as with other disabilities, ways of being human.

NOTES

Many thanks to Anita Silvers and three anonymous referees for their helpful comments on an earlier version of this paper.

1. In this article, I am using "sickness" and "illness" synonymously to mean suffering, limitation, and/or loss of function experienced by a person and attributed by her/him (or others) to a loss of health and not to a physical or mental condition present from birth or acquired by an injury to a specific part of the body. I am using "disease" to refer to some medically recognized diagnostic categories of physical or mental "abnormality." Not all sicknesses and illnesses are diseases recognized by medicine, and not all medically recognized diseases cause a person to feel sick or ill. My definitions are based on ordinary use of the words; unfortunately, ordinary use does not make precise distinctions, so there are afflictions that do not fit the definitions neatly (such as chronic inflammation of an injured limb). There is a considerable philosophical literature debating the definitions of "disease," "sickness," "illness," and related concepts. For a recent overview and samples of those debates, see Humber and Almeder (1997).

2. I have lived with ME/CFIDS since 1985. During the first two years of illness, I was severely impaired by fatigue, muscle pain, muscle weakness, dizziness, nausea, headaches, depression, and problems with short-term memory (especially verbal recall). All these impairments are still with me, but now they are intermittent and less severe than they were. I am able to work three-quarter-time as a professor by living a quiet, careful life. An account of my personal experience of being disabled by chronic illness can be found in *The Rejected Body: Feminist Philosophical Reflections on Disability* (1996).

REFERENCES

Agich, George J. 1997. Toward a pragmatic theory of disease. In *What is disease?* ed. James M. Humber and Robert F. Almeder. Totowa, N.J.: Humana Press.

Amundson, Ron. 1992. Disability, handicap, and the environment. *Journal of Social Philosophy* 23 (1): 105–18.

Carroll, Douglas, and Catherine A. Niven. 1993. Gender, health and stress. In *The health psychology of women,* ed. Catherine A. Niven and Douglas Carroll. Chur, Switzerland: Harwood Academic Publishers.

Charmaz, Kathy. 1991. *Good days, bad days: The self in chronic illness.* New Brunswick, N.J.: Rutgers University Press.

Clare, Eli. 1999. *Exile and pride: Disability, queerness and liberation.* Cambridge, Mass.: South End Press.

Crow, Liz. 1996. Including all of our lives: Renewing the social model of disability. In *Encounters with strangers: Feminism and disability,* ed. Jenny Morris. London: The Women's Press Ltd.

Humber, James M., and Robert F. Almeder, eds. 1997. *What is disease?* Totowa, N.J.: Humana Press.

Humphrey, Jill C. 2000. Researching disability politics, or, some problems with the social model in practice. *Disability and Society* 15 (1): 63–85.

Morris, Jenny. 1991. *Pride against prejudice: Transforming attitudes to disability.* Philadelphia: New Society Publishers.

——. 1994. Gender and disability. In *On equal terms: Working with disabled people,* ed. Sally French. Oxford: Butterworth-Heinemann Ltd.

Morris, Jenny, ed. 1996. *Encounters with strangers: Feminism and disability.* London: The Women's Press Ltd.

Oliver, Michael. 1990. *The politics of disablement.* London: Macmillan.

Overall, Christine. 1998. *A feminist I: Reflections from academia.* Peterborough, Ont.: Broadview Press.

Register, Cheri. 1987. *Living with chronic illness: Days of patience and passion.* New York: Bantam.

Report on the health of Canadians. 1996. Ottawa: Minister of Supply and Services Canada.

Snow, Judith A. 1992. Living at home. In *Imprinting our image: An international anthology by women with disabilities,* ed. Diane Driedger and Susan Gray. Charlottetown, P.E.I.: Gynergy Books.

Trypuc, Joann M. 1994. Gender based mortality and morbidity patterns and health risks. In *Women, medicine and health,* ed. B. Singh Bolaria and Rosemary Bolaria. Halifax, N.S.: Fernwood.

U.N. Decade of Disabled Persons 1983–1992. 1983. *World programme of action concerning disabled persons.* New York: United Nations.

Wade, Cheryl Marie. 1994. Identity. *The Disability Rag and ReSource* (September/ October): 32–36.

Wendell, Susan. 1996. *The rejected body: Feminist philosophical reflections on disability.* New York: Routledge.

——. 1999. Old women out of control: Some thoughts on aging, ethics and psychosomatic medicine. In *Mother time: Women, aging and ethics,* ed. Margaret Walker. Lanham, Md.: Rowman and Littlefield.

Young, Iris Marion. 2000. Disability and the definition of work. In *Americans with disabilities: Exploring implications of the law for individuals and institutions,* ed. Leslie Francis and Anita Silvers. New York: Routledge.

PART IV

*T*heorizing Disability

CHAPTER 13

The Cost of Getting Better: Ability and Debility

Jasbir K. Puar

There are many things lost in the naming of a death as a "gay youth suicide." In what follows, I offer a preliminary analysis of the prolific media attention to gay youth suicides that began in the United States in the fall of 2010. I am interested in how this attention recalls affective attachments to neoliberalism that index a privileged geopolitics of finance capitalism. I have been struck by how the discourses surrounding gay youth suicide partake in a spurious binarization of what I foreground as an interdependent relationship between bodily capacity and bodily debility. These discourses reproduce neoliberalism's heightened demands for bodily capacity, even as this same neoliberalism marks out populations for what Lauren Berlant has described as "slow death"—the debilitating ongoingness of structural inequality and suffering.[1] In the United States, where personal debt incurred through medical expenses is the number one reason for filing for bankruptcy, the centrality of what is termed the medical-industrial complex to the profitability of slow death cannot be overstated.[2] My intervention here is an attempt to go beyond a critique of the queer neoliberalism embedded in the tendentious mythologizing that "it gets better" by confronting not only the debilitating aspects of neoliberalism but, more trench-antly, the economics of debility. If the knitting together of finance capitalism and the medical-industrial complex means that debility pays, and pays well, then the question becomes, how can an affective politics move beyond the conventional narratives of resistance to neoliberalism?

THE COST OF GETTING BETTER

To begin, I pose two queries: one, what is contained in the category of sexuality? Two, what kinds of normative temporal assumptions are produced through the "event" of suicide? As a faculty member of Rutgers University in New Jersey, where a student, Tyler Clementi, committed suicide after videos of him having sex with a man were circulated by his roommate and another student, I want to provide better context for the local circumstances of his death. All three students (Clementi, Dharun Ravi, and Molly Wei) were living on Busch campus in Piscataway, New Jersey, already codified as the campus for science/premed "geeks" (some might say sissies). Busch is also racially demarcated as the "Asian" campus, an identity rarely disaggregated from geek at US colleges. Clementi's suicide has predictably occasioned a vicious anti-Asian backlash replete with overdetermined notions of "Asian homophobia" and predictable calls to "go back to where you came from," as seen in numerous online articles. Commenting on the biases of the criminal justice system against people of nonnormative race, ethnicity, and citizenship, a press release from a Rutgers organization called Queering the Air notes that Garden State Equality (a New Jersey LGBT advocacy group) and Campus Pride (a national group for LGBT students) have demanded the most severe consequences for Ravi and Wei, prosecution for hate crimes, maximum jail time, expulsion without disciplinary hearing, and that "18,000 people endorse an online group seeking even more serious charges—manslaughter."[3]

It seems imperative that the implications of two "model minority" students from a wealthy New Jersey suburb who targeted an effete, young, queer white man be considered beyond convenient narratives of the so-called inherent homophobia within racialized immigrant communities. Is it possible to see all three students involved as more alike—all geeks, in fact—than different? Instead of rehashing that old "gay-bashers are closet cases" canard, perhaps there is a reason to destabilize the alignments of "alikeness" and "difference" away from a singular, predictable axis through "sexuality." A letter recently circulated by Queering the Air claims that Clementi's death is the second suicide by an LGBTQ student since March and that four of the last seven suicides at Rutgers were related to sexuality.[4] What, then, is meant here by "related to sexuality"? I am prompted by Amit Rai's reformulation of sexuality as "ecologies of sensation"—as affect instead of identity—that transcends the designations of straight and gay and can further help disaggregate these binary positions from their racialized histories.[5]

Missing from the debate about Clementi's suicide is a discussion about the proclivities of young people to see the "choice" of Internet surveillance as a mandatory regulatory part not only of their subject formations but of their bodily habits and affective tendencies. For these youth, so-called cyberstalking is an integral part of what it means to become a neoliberal (sexual) subject. Think of the ubiquity of sexting, applications like Grindr, Manhunt, DIY porn, and cellphone mass circulation of images—technologies that create simultaneous sensations of exposure (the whole world is watching) and alienation (no one understands). These cyborgian practices constitute new relations between public and private that we have yet to really acknowledge, much less comprehend. "Invasion of privacy" remains uncharted territory for jurisprudence in relation to the Internet. But more significantly, to reiterate Rai, the use of these technologies impels new affective tendencies of bodies, new forms of attention, distraction, practice, and repetition. The presumed differences between "gay" and "straight" could be thought more generously through the quotidian and banal activities of sexual self-elaboration through Internet technologies—emergent habituations, corporeal comportment, and an array of diverse switchpoints of bodily capacity.

If signification and representation (what things mean) are no longer the only primary realm of the political, then bodily processes (how things feel) must be irreducibly central to any notion of the political. Clementi's participation in the testimonial spaces of the chat room to detail his roommate's invasion of his "privacy" and Clementi's use of Facebook for the explanatory "suicide note" reflect precisely the shared continuities with his perpetrators through ecologies of sensation. Accusations of "homophobia," "gay bullying," and even "cyberbullying" fail to do justice to the complex uptake of digital technologies in this story.

The apparently sudden spate of queer

suicides is also obviously at odds with the claims of purported progress by the gay and lesbian rights movement. As noted by Tavia Nyong'o, Dan Savage's sanctimonious statement "It gets better" is a mandate to fold oneself into urban, neoliberal gay enclaves: a call to upward mobility that discordantly echoes the now-discredited "pull yourself up by the bootstraps" immigrant motto.[6] (The symbolism of Clementi's transit from central New Jersey to the George Washington Bridge that connects northern New Jersey to upper Manhattan is painfully apparent.) Part of the outrage generated by these deaths is based precisely in a belief that things are indeed supposed to be better, especially for a particular class of white gay men. As I argue in my op-ed in the *Guardian*, this amounts to a reinstatement of white racial privilege that was lost with being gay.[7] Savage has also mastered, if we follow Sarah Lochlain Jain on the "politics of sympathy," the technique of converting Clementi's injury into cultural capital, not only through affectations of blame, guilt, and suffering but also through those of triumph, transgression, and success.[8]

AFFECTIVE POLITICS: STATES OF CAPACITY AND DEBILITY

The subject of redress and grievance thus functions here as a recapacitation of a debilitated body. To make my second and related point, then, I want to shift the registers of this conversation about "queer suicide" from pathologization versus normativization of sexual identity to questions of bodily capacity, debility, disability, precarity, and populations. This is not to dismiss these queer suicides but to ask what kinds of "slow deaths" have been ongoing that a suicide might represent an escape from. It is also to "slow" the act of suicide down—to offer a concomitant yet different temporality of relating to living and dying. Berlant moves us away from trauma or catastrophe, proposing that "slow death occupies the temporalities of the endemic" (756). Slow death occurs not within the timescale of the suicide or the epidemic but within "a zone of temporality . . . of ongoingness, getting by, and living on, where the structural inequalities are dispersed, the pacing of their experience intermittent, often in phenomena not prone to capture by a consciousness organized by archives of memorable impact" (759). In this nonlinear temporality, for it starts and stops, redoubles and leaps ahead, Berlant is not "defining a group of individuals merely afflicted with the same ailment, [rather] slow death describes populations marked out for wearing out" (760–61n20). That is, slow death is not about an orientation toward the death drive, nor is it morbid; rather, it is about the maintenance of living, the "ordinary work of living on" (761).

In the context of slow death, I ponder three things. First, what does it mean to proclaim "it gets better," or "you get stronger"? Second, why is suicide constituted as the ultimate loss of life? Third, how can we connect these suicides to the theorization of debility and capacity? David Mitchell's moving invocation of disability "not as exception, but the basis upon which a decent and just social order is founded," hinges on a society that acknowledges, accepts, and even anticipates disability.[9] This anticipatory disability is the dominant temporal frame of both disability rights activism (you are able-bodied only until you are disabled) as well as disability studies. As the queer disability theorist Robert McRuer writes, "It's clear that we are haunted by the disability to come."[10] Disability is posited as the most common identity category because we will all belong to it someday, as McRuer's comment implies. Yet, as David Mitchell and Sharon Snyder argue, disability is "reified as the true site of insufficiency."[11] But Berlant's formulation of slow death implies that we might not (only) be haunted by the disability to come but also disavow the debility already here.

Berlant argues that "health itself can then be seen as a side effect of successful normativity" (765). Therefore, to honor the complexity of these suicides, they must be placed within the broader context of neoliberal demands for bodily capacity as well as the profitability of debility, both functioning as central routes through which finance capital seeks to sustain itself. In my current book project, "Affective Politics: States of Capacity and Debility," I examine these heightened demands for bodily capacity and exceptionalized debility. Capacity and debility are seeming opposites generated by increasingly demanding neoliberal formulations of health, agency, and choice—what I call a "liberal eugenics of lifestyle programming"—that produce, along with biotechnologies and bioinformatics, population aggregates. Those "folded" into life are seen as more capacious or on the side of capacity, while those targeted for premature or slow death are figured as debility. Such an analysis reposes the questions: which bodies are made to pay for "progress"? Which debilitated bodies can be reinvigorated for neoliberalism, and which cannot? In this regard, Savage's project refigures queers, along with other bodies heretofore construed as excessive/erroneous, as being on the side of capacity, ensuring that queerness operates as a machine of regenerative productivity. Even though post-structuralist queer theory critically deploys registers of negativity (and increasingly negative affect) in reading practices primarily deconstructive in their orientation, such a figuration of queer theory has emerged from a homeostatic framework: queer theory is already also a machine of capacity in and after the cybernetic turn. Bioinformatics frames—in which bodies figure not as identities or subjects but as data—entail that there is no such thing as nonproductive excess but only emergent forms of new information.[12] This revaluing of excess/debility is potent because, simply put, debility—slow death—is profitable for capitalism. In neoliberal, biomedical, and biotechnological terms, the body is always debilitated in relation to its ever-expanding potentiality.

What I am proposing, then, is also an intervention into the binaried production of disabled versus nondisabled bodies that drives both disability studies and disability rights activism. Even as the demands of ableism weigh heavy and have been challenged by disability scholars and activists, attachments to the difference of disabled bodies may reify an exceptionalism that only certain privileged disabled bodies can occupy. While the disability rights movement largely understands disability as a form of nonnormativity that deserves to be depathologized, disability justice activists seek to move beyond access issues foregrounded by the Americans with Disabilities Act as well as global human rights frames that standardize definitions of disability and the terms of their legal redress across national locations. They instead avow that in working-poor and working-class communities of color, disabilities and debilities are actually "the norm." Thus a political agenda that disavows pathology is less relevant than a critique of the reembedded forms of liberal eugenics propagated by what they call the medical-industrial complex and its attendant forms of administrative surveillance. Such work suggests that an increasingly demanding ableism (and I would add, an increasingly demanding disable-ism—normative forms of disability as exceptionalism) is producing nonnormativity not only through the sexual and racial pathologization of certain "unproductive bodies" but more expansively through the ability or inability of all bodies to register through affective capacity.

What disability justice activists imply is

that slow death is constitutive to debility, and disability must be rethought in terms of precarious populations.

The distinctions of normative and non-normative, disabled and nondisabled do not hold up as easily. Instead there are variegated aggregates of capacity and debility. If debility is understood by disability justice activists to be endemic to disenfranchised communities, it is doubly so because the forms of financialization that accompany neoliberal economics and the privatization of services also produce debt as debility. This relationship between debt and debility can be described as a kind of "financial expropriation": "the profit made by financial institutions out of the personal income of workers is a form of financial expropriation, seen as additional profit generated in the realm of circulation."[13] Given the relationship of bankruptcy to medical care expenses in the United States, debt becomes another register to measure the capacity for recovery, not only physical but also financial. Debility is profitable to capitalism, but so is the demand to "recover" from or overcome it.

FROM EPISTEMOLOGICAL CORRECTIVE TO ONTOLOGICAL IRREDUCIBILITY

I am proposing, then, a methodology that inhabits the intersections of disability studies, the affective turn, and theories of posthumanism—all fields of inquiry that put duress on the privileging of (able-bodied) subject formation as a primary site of bodily interpellation. The affective turn, as I interpret it, signals intellectual contestation over sites of struggle, whose targets are now the following: social constructionism (reinvigorated interrogation of biological matter that challenges both biological determinism and also performativity), epistemology (ontology and ontogenesis), psychoanalysis (trauma rethought as the intensification of the body's relation to

itself), humanism (the capacities of non-human animals as well as inorganic matter, matters), and agency (the centrality of cognition and perception as challenged by theories of sensation). The modulation and surveillance of affect operates as a form of sociality that regulates good and bad subjects, possible and impossible bodily capacities. Here affect entails not only a dissolution of the subject but, more significantly, a dissolution of the stable contours of the organic body, as forces of energy are transmitted, shared, circulated. The body, as Brian Massumi argues, "passes from one state of capacitation to a diminished or augmented state of capacitation," always bound up in the lived past of the body but always in passage to a changed future.[14]

This understanding of capacity and debility entails theorizing not only specific disciplinary sites but also broader techniques of social control, marking a shift in terms from regulating normativity (the internalization of self/other subject formation) to what Michel Foucault calls regularizing bodies or what has been designated "the age of biological control."[15] In the oscillation between disciplinary societies and control societies, following Foucault's "security regimes" and Gilles Deleuze's "control society," the tensions have been mapped out thusly: as a shift from normal/abnormal to variegation, modulation, and tweaking; from discrete sites of punishment (the prison, the mental hospital, the school) to preemptive regimes of securitization; from inclusion/exclusion to the question of differential inclusion; from self/other, subject/object construction to micro-states of subindividual differentiation; from difference between to difference within; from the policing of profile to patrolling of affect; from will to capacity; from agency to affect; from subject to body.[16] And finally, and I believe most importantly, there is a shift underway, from Althusserian interpellation to an array of diverse switchpoints of the activation of the body.

What does it mean to rethink disability in terms of control societies? The particular binary categorization of dis/abled subjectivity is one that has many parallels to other kinds of binary categorizations propagated—in fact, demanded—by neoliberal constructions of failed and capacitated bodies. Therefore we cannot see this binary production as specific only to the distinction of disabled versus nondisabled subjects; all bodies are being evaluated in relation to their success or failure in terms of health, wealth, progressive productivity, upward mobility, enhanced capacity. And there is no such thing as an "adequately abled" body anymore. However, it is precisely because there are gradations of capacity and debility in control societies—rather than the self/other production of being/not being—that the distinction between disabled and nondisabled becomes fuzzier.

As an example, Nikolas Rose maintains that depression will become the number one disability in the USA and the UK within the next ten years. This expansion of depressed peoples will not occur simply through a widespread increase of depression but through the gradation of populations. In other words, it will occur not through the hailing and interpellation of depressed subjects—and a distinction between who is depressed and who is not—but through the evaluation and accommodation of degrees: to what degree is one depressed?[17] One is already instructed by television advertisements for psychotropic drugs such as "Abilify," claiming that "two out of three people on anti-depressants still have symptoms" and offering a top-off medication to add to a daily med regime. Through this form of medical administration, bodies are (1) drawn into a modulation of subindividual capacities (this would be the diverse switchpoints); (2) surveilled not on identity positions alone but through affective tendencies, informational body-as-data, and statistical probabilities—through populations, risk, and prognosis; (3) further stratified across registers of the medical-industrial complex: medical debt, health insurance, state benefits, among other feedback loops into the profitability of debility.

How the disaggregation of depressed subjects into various states, intensities, and tendencies will change the dimensionality of disability remains an open prospect, but at the very least it forces recognition of the insufficiency of disability as a category. The disability at stake is an affective tendency of sorts as well as a mental state, and as such challenges the basis on which disability rights frames have routed their representational (visibility) politics. A field that has been dominated by the visibility of physical disabilities is acknowledging the scope and range of cognitive and mental disabilities. This recognition, in turn, has challenged the status of rational, agential, survivor-oriented politics based on the privileging of the linguistic capacity to make rights claims. Why? Because the inability to "communicate" functions as the single determinant of mental or cognitive impairment (thereby regulating the human/animal distinction), thus destabilizing the centrality of the human capacity for thought and cognition.

In an effort to open up capacity as a source of generative affective politics rather than only a closure around neoliberal demands, I briefly return to Gayatri Spivak's "Can the Subaltern Speak?," perhaps unfashionably so.[18] In the context of disability studies, this question becomes not only a mandate for epistemological correctives but a query about ontological and bodily capacity, as granting "voice" to the subaltern comes into tension with the need, in the case of the human/animal distinction, to destabilize the privileging of communication/representation/language altogether. The ability to understand language is also where human/nonhuman animal distinctions, as well as human/technology distinctions, have long been drawn, and here disability studies, posthumanism, and animal studies may perhaps articulate a common interest in a nonanthropomorphic, interspecies vision of affective politics. Posthumanism questions the boundaries between human and nonhuman, matter and discourse, technology and body, and interrogates the practices through which these boundaries are constituted, stabilized, and destabilized. (The burgeoning field of animal studies is thus also a part of the endeavor to situate human capacities within a range of capacities of species as opposed to reifying their singularity.) If, according to posthumanist thinkers such as Manual De Landa and Karen Barad, language has been granted too much power, a nonanthropomorphic conception of the human is necessary to resituate language as one of many captures of the intensities of bodily capacities, an event of bodily assemblages rather than a performative act of signification.[19]

Our current politics are continually reproducing the exceptionalism of human bodies and the aggrieved agential subject, politics typically enacted through "wounded attachments."[20] Without minimizing the tragedy of Clementi's and other recent deaths, dialogue about ecologies of sensation and slow death might open us up to a range of connections. For instance, how do queer girls commit suicide? What of the slow deaths of teenage girls through anorexia, bulimia, and numerous sexual assaults they endure as punishment for the transgressing of proper femininity and alas, even for conforming to it? What is the political and cultural fallout of recentering the white gay male as ur-queer subject? How would our political landscape transform if it actively decentered the sustained reproduction and proliferation of the grieving subject, opening instead toward an affective politics, attentive to ecologies of sensation and switchpoints of bodily capacities, to habituations and unhabituations, to tendencies, multiple temporalities, and becomings?

NOTES

Thanks to Elena Glasberg, Dana Luciano, and Jordana Rosenberg for close readings, and to Tavia Nyong'o, Eng-Beng Lim, Ashley Dawson, and Richard Kim for feedback on an earlier version of this article, "Ecologies of Sex, Sensation, and Slow Death" published in Social Text on November 27, 2010.

1. Lauren Berlant, "Slow Death (Sovereignty, Obesity, Lateral Agency)," *Critical Inquiry* 33 (2007): 754–80. Hereafter cited in the text.

2. See David Himmelstein et al., "Medical Bankruptcy in the United States, 2007: Results of a National Study," *American Journal of Medicine* 122 (2009): 741–46.

3. "Justice Not Vengeance in Clementi Suicide," Queering the Air, October 19, 2010 (URL no longer working).

4. Queering the Air, e-mail message to author, October 1, 2010.

5. Amit Rai, *Untimely Bollywood: Globalization and India's New Media Assemblage* (Durham, NC: Duke University Press, 2009).

6. Tavia Nyong'o, "School Daze," September 30, 2010, bullybloggers.wordpress.com/2010/09/30/school-daze/.

7. "In the Wake of It Gets Better," *Guardian*, November 16, 2010, www.guardian.co.uk/commentisfree/cifamerica/2010/nov/16/wake-it-gets-better-campaign?showallcomments=true#comment-fold.

8. Sarah Lochlann Jain, *Injury: The Politics of Product Design and Safety Law in the United States* (Princeton: Princeton University Press, 2006), 24.

9. David Mitchell, Keynote Plenary (Annual Meeting, Society for Disability Studies, Temple University, June 2010).

10. Robert McRuer, *Crip Theory* (New York: New York University Press, 2007), 207.

11. David Mitchell and Sharon Snyder, *Cultural Locations of Disability* (Chicago: University of Chicago Press, 2006), 17.

12. See, e.g., Eugene Thacker, *The Global Genome* (Cambridge: MIT Press, 2006); Kaushik Sunder Rajan, *Biocapital: The Constitution of Postgenomic Life* (Durham, NC: Duke University Press, 2006).

13. Sam Ashman, "Editorial Introduction to the Symposium on the Global Financial Crisis," *Historical Materialism* 17 (2009): 107.

14. Brian Massumi, "Of Microperception and Micropolitics: An Interview with Brian Massumi," *Inflections* 3 (2008): 2.

15. Michel Foucault, *Society Must Be Defended: Lectures at the Collège de France, 1975–76*, ed. Mauro Bertani and Alessandro Fontana, trans. David Macey (New York: Picador, 2003); and Ian Wilmut, Keith Campbell, and Colin Tudge, *The Second Creation: Dolly and the Age of Biological Control* (Cambridge, MA: Harvard University Press, 2001).

16. Michel Foucault, *Security, Territory, Population: Lectures at the Collège de France, 1977–78*, ed. Michel Senellart, trans. Graham Burchell (New York: Picador, 2009); Gilles Deleuze, "Postscript on Control Societies," in *Negotiations* (New York: Columbia University Press, 1997).

17. Nikolas Rose, "Biopolitics in an Age of Biological Control" (lecture, New York University, New York, October 15, 2009).

18. Gayatri Chakravorty Spivak, Can the Subaltern Speak?," in *Marxism and the Interpretation of Culture*, ed. Cary Nelson and Larry Grossberg (Basingstoke: Macmillan Education, 1988), 271–313.

19. Manuel DeLanda, *A New Philosophy of Society: Assemblage Theory and Social Complexity* (London and New York: Continuum, 2006); Karen Barad, "Posthumanist Performativity: Toward an Understanding of How Matter Comes to Matter," *Signs: Journal of Women in Culture and Society* 28 (2003): 801–31.

20. See Wendy Brown, "Wounded Attachments," *Political Theory* 21 (1993): 390–410.

CHAPTER 14

Enabling Disability: Rewriting Kinship, Reimagining Citizenship

Faye Ginsburg and Rayna Rapp

In trying to portray my son in the literary model known as a novel, I have passed through . . . stages. In the case of a person like him with a mental disability, it isn't the individual himself but rather his family that has to pass from the "shock phase" to the "acceptance phase." In a sense, my work on this theme has mirrored that process. I have had to learn through concrete experience to answer such questions as how a handicapped person and his family can survive the shock, denial, and confusion phases and learn to live with each of those particular kinds of pain. I then had to find out how we could move beyond this to a more positive adjustment, before finally reaching our own "acceptance phase"—*in effect coming to accept ourselves as handicapped, as the family of a handicapped person.* And it was only then that I felt the development of my work itself was at last complete.

(Oe 1995: 46, emphasis added)

In 1963, when the Japanese novelist Kenzaburo Oe's son Hikari was born with a dangerous brain tumor, Oe and his wife chose to have it removed, a process that, along with a range of other kinds of supports, enabled the infant Hikari to survive, but with a profound disability. Since then, the family has had to re-create itself and its narrative. In his book, *A Healing Family*, Oe describes his family's capacity to embrace Hikari.

Healing is used here in two senses that draw our interest as researchers. The word's immediate referent would seem to be the capacity of parents and siblings to help heal the wound of difference for the affected boy. But Oe also emphasizes the work the family has undertaken to heal the wound of difference dealt to its own kinship narrative and practice. Oe, who won the Nobel Prize in literature in 1994, has written several other books chronicling the transformations in their familial universe inaugurated by the birth of Hikari. His works have helped his family and, at a remove, his readers, to imagine an unanticipated cultural future that could give meaning and possibility to the reshaped habitus of daily life with a disabled family member.[1] Oe's compassionate and frank story of how his family came to embrace "being handicapped" is representative of a kind of shift in consciousness—disability consciousness—suggestive of a more expansive sense of kinship across embodied difference that, we argue, is essential to the growing public presence of disability in contemporary postindustrial democracies.

The proliferation of publicly circulating representations of disability as a form of diversity we all eventually share—through our own bodies or attachments to others—offers potential sites of identification and even kinship that extend beyond the biological family. In the United States in particular, such public representations of the connections (and disconnections) of disabled people and their families across embodied difference have helped to introduce a sense of public intimacy that, we argue, is crucial to redeeming the ADA promissory note of a polity "beyond ramps" (Russell 1998). The simultaneous emergence of the U.S. disability rights movement along with the escalation of reproductive and neonatal technologies has intensified cultural awareness of a range of broader issues. These increasingly both shape and destabilize contemporary kinship practices as well as debates among disability rights activists, feminists, bioethicists, and health service providers.

Such concerns engage questions about medical ethics and the complexities of reproductive choice; concrete dilemmas about how to organize the practical logistics of care for disabled children; political and distributive queries about what citizens are owed; and conceptual questions about how disability is figured discursively. While such issues are often made the subject of public policy debate, they come already anchored in the daily and intimate practices of embracing or rejecting kinship with disabled fetuses, newborns, and young children. We suggest, then, that disability criticism should encompass not only the public arenas of law, medicine, and education, or the phenomenology of embodiment. It also needs to engage the intimate arena of kinship as a site where contemporary social dramas around changing understandings and practices of reproduction and disability are often first played out. Although the term *kinship* is conventionally associated with the private or domestic sphere, we stress the cultural work performed by the circulation of kinship narratives through various public media as an essential element in the refiguring of the body politic as envisioned by advocates of both disability and reproductive rights.

The efforts of families to "rewrite" kinship are crucial to creating a new cultural terrain in which disability is not just begrudgingly accommodated under the mandates of expanded post-1970s civil rights legislation, but is positively incorporated into the social body. Likewise, rejection of the disabled from the familial and social body continues to occur, occasionally played out in the public media as scandals of exclusion[2] and in more intimate arenas as the conventional limits of kinship are sustained rather than transcended.

When we began to explore the world of disability—both as parents of disabled children and as anthropologists interested in reproduction, kinship, and social activism—we were struck by narratives like Oe's and their proliferation in a world in which constructions of the body and identity are increasingly mediated by biomedical technologies.[3] We were particularly interested in contradictions between, on the one hand, burgeoning genetic knowledge and the neoeugenic practices it has fostered; and, on the other, the expansion of more inclusive democratic discourses—in particular, that of disability rights. To explore this tension, in this essay we foreground the domains of kinship and reproduction as key social sites at which many disabilities are initially assigned cultural meaning in the United States. We focus in particular on contemporary dilemmas surrounding pregnancy and the care of newborns and children with disabilities, which in turn underscore questions concerning the social location of caretaking and its political economy.

We locate our work at this nexus not only because reproductive choices—and the role played in them by the possibility of disability—are increasingly implicated in the new genetic knowledge, but also because the parent–child relationship is a nexus at which dramatic alternatives are articulated: dependency versus autonomy; intimacy versus authority; the acceptance of caretaking versus its rejection; normative cultural scripts versus alternative, more inclusive "rewritings." Clearly, the "passions and interests" (cf. Hirschman 1977) at work here can divide the points of view of children and parents. These potential divisions can be particularly acute in the case of children with disabilities, whose bodily and sensory (and, eventually, social and political) experiences may be profoundly different from those of their parents. Recent debates about cochlear implants for deaf children or facial surgery for children with Down syndrome highlight divisions over the value of mainstreaming technologies. Such issues divide families who differ over what constitutes "the best interests of their children." Although conflicts between the perspectives of parents and children are typically associated with the separation and self-definition that intensify at adolescence, we focus here on dilemmas that emerge much earlier—indeed, from the embryonic stage or before.

REWRITING KINSHIP

The birth of a child who is, in one sense, profoundly different from other family members can pose an immediate crisis to the nuclear and extended family. In addition to providing medical support for the affected child, families face the task of incorporating unexpected differences into a comprehensible narrative of kinship (Landsman 1999, 2000; Layne 1996). The birth of anomalous children is an occasion for meaning-making, whether through the acceptance of "God's special angels" or the infanticide of offspring deemed unacceptable. And in millennial America, new technologies have made the domain of kinship and reproduction—the locus classicus of anthropology—particularly charged with cultural contradictions surrounding questions of bodily difference.

A wide variety of contemporary cultural productions testify to this intensification. It is our argument that such public storytelling—whether in family narratives, memoirs, television talk shows and sitcoms, movies, or, most recently, through Web sites and Internet discussion groups—is crucial to expanding what we call the social fund of knowledge about disability. In opening up the experiential epistemology of disability, as shaped by and shaping the intimate world of nonnormative family life, such forms of public culture widen the space of possibility in which relationships can be imagined and resources claimed. We underscore the significance of this burgeoning public circulation of intimate disability stories, expanding the arguments of others regarding the place of intimacy in constituting subjectivities of all sorts. As Lauren Berlant writes in her introduction to the special issue of *Critical Inquiry* on intimacy,

> Rethinking intimacy calls out not only for redescription but for transformative analyses of the rhetorical and material conditions that enable hegemonic fantasies to thrive in the minds and on the bodies of subjects while, at the same time, attachments are developing that might redirect the different routes taken by history and biography. To rethink intimacy is to appraise how we have been and how we live and how we might imagine lives that make more sense than the ones so many are living. (Berlant 1998: 286)

In the expanded domain of "public intimacy" linked to disability, different forms of embodiment are represented within the context of domestic routines and subjectivity. If this is true of information-sharing magazines such as *Exceptional Parent* and the slick and upbeat activist publication and Web site *WeMedia*, it is no less characteristic of academic writings by scholars who may themselves be disabled (Asch 1989; Charlton 1998; Fries 1997; Handler 1998; Hockenberry 1995; Kuusisto 1998; Linton 1998; Mairs 1996), or caring for disabled family members (Beck 1999; Bérubé 1996; Featherstone 1980; Finger 1990; Jablow 1982; Kittay 1999; Seligman and Darling 1989). We suggest that such representations—what we call disability narratives—are foundational to the integration of disability into everyday life in the United States, a process that is in turn essential to the more capacious notions of citizenship championed by the disability rights movement. As authored by disabled people and/or their family members, these narratives offer revised, phenomenologically based understandings that at times also anchor substantial analyses of the social, cultural, and political construction of disability. The dissemination of such intimate insights among a broader public has helped to mobilize an extraordinary and rapid transformation since the 1970s in the way such notions as rights, entitlement, and citizenship are conceived—a transformation that is shaping public policy in areas such as health care, education, transportation, and access to built, aural, and visual environments.

Of course, not all disability narratives are so inclusive. A very different discourse about disability has emerged around the proliferation of reproductive technologies, in particular prenatal testing for detectable fetal anomalies. Certain assumptions are foundational to these processes. While U.S. genetic counselors are trained to express neutrality about the choices a pregnant woman and her partner may make around amniocentesis testing, the very existence of such a technology and the offer of such tests under the terms of consumer choice are premised on the desire for normalcy and fear of unknown abnormalities (Parens and Asch 2000). As anthropologists, our task is to understand how these neoeugenic technologies come to make cultural sense despite the emergence of more inclusive discourses of disability in other cultural domains. Prenatal screening, for example, is attractive to cost-accounting health care bureaucracies in which market forces increasingly stratify the "choices" made available to different constituencies as medical care becomes subject to the spreading hegemony of neo-liberal practices and ideologies. The attractiveness of prenatal screening to cost-conscious health bureaucracies is a case in point: with the administration of medical care increasingly under the sway of hegemonic neoliberalism, market forces come to dictate what choices are available to different constituencies.

In the United States, and increasingly throughout the postindustrial world, the anxieties that accompany pregnancy are, we argue, exacerbated by the individualized and privatized nature of medical decision-making. When it comes to information about the forms of medical and community support that might be available to the family of a child with a stigmatized difference, the access of prospective parents is limited. They are often unaware of the social fund of knowledge that would help them make a more knowledgeable choice (Ginsburg and Rapp 1999). This de facto segregation is apparent in narratives elicited by researchers from pregnant women and their supporters about their attitudes and aspirations regarding prenatal testing (Browner 1996; Kolker and Burke 1993; Press and Browner 1995; Rapp 1999; Rothman 1986). Unlike the stories discussed earlier, few encounters with prenatal testing are rendered as public narrations. While the social science literature suggests that awaiting the results of an amniocentesis is quite stressful, the stress turns out to be ephemeral for those who receive normal diagnoses of their fetuses.

They retrospectively experience the test as a nonevent; amniocentesis is quickly subsumed within the schedule of now-routine health procedures whose presumed outcome is a "normal" baby. By contrast, most of those whose diagnosis is positive choose to end the pregnancy. Such events generally pass unmarked, as is the case with most abortions in the West (for the counterexample of Japan, see Hardacre 1997). Writing about abortion, especially under circumstances such as these, when the pregnancy was initially desired, is fraught with personal and political risk. Those few pregnant women who have breached the veil of privacy surrounding prenatal testing and abortion tend to circulate their stories only in specialized medical contexts (Green 1992; Brewster 1984; but cf. Rapp 1999). In describing their decision-making processes, they tend to emphasize the limits of caretaking within an available family structure and concern for a child's potential suffering.

> Some people say that abortion is hate. I say my abortion was an act of love. I've got three kids. I was forty-three when we accidentally got pregnant again. We decided that there was enough love in our family to handle it, even though finances would be tight. But we also decided to have the test. A kid with a serious problem was more than we could handle. And when we got the bad news, I knew immediately what I had to do. At forty-three, you think about your own death. It would have been tough now, but think what would have happened to my other kids, especially my daughter. Oh, the boys, Tommy and Alex, would have done okay. But Laura would have been the one who got stuck. It's always the girls. It would have been me, and then, after I'm gone, it would have been the big sister that took care of that child. Saving Laura from that burden was an act of love. (Rapp 1999: 247)

Such stories provide an illuminating, if stark, comparison to the more established and more acceptable genre of disability narratives. The themes shaping these different genres of narratives about disability reveal the crucial role that kinship plays in social exclusion, on the one hand, and as a site for the transformative cultural work that can help resituate disability in contemporary American social life, on the other. Clearly, disability stories are complex and variable. The parenting literature, for example, is fraught with the tensions between efforts to normalize the experience of disability and the need for advocacy and special resources to accommodate those who cannot enter mainstream American society through the same pathways or trajectories as most others.

These tensions are themselves a reflection of the way that consumer capitalism is shaping the experience of reproduction in the United States. Perhaps the starkest examples are provided by the contemporary trend of increasingly aggressive medical intervention, with the new reproductive technology of prenatal testing conjuring up a familiar specter from dystopian science fiction: that of designer babies for the market (McGee 1997). At the same time, large numbers of compromised babies are able to survive thanks to advances in medicine and in therapeutic regimens such as occupational therapy and infant stimulation programs (Landsman 1999, 2000). These diverging sociomedical practices, which are increasingly part of normal obstetric and neonatal medicine, embody a doubled telos of modernity and technology. The practices of genetic testing, and other genetic research, seem to promise perfectibility for those who choose and can afford cutting-edge interventions (although what "perfectibility" might mean in practice is highly contested, as we discuss below). Concomitantly, other new technologies, medical and otherwise, offer another promise of expansive democratic inclusion and improved quality of life for those marked by difference from a hegemonic norm of embodiment (Blair 2000).

Suppressed in these narratives of modernity, which stress individual choice and achievement, is the crucial place of kinship and gender in structuring these possibilities. Specifically, this double telos places pregnant women under the very American pressure of "choice." Many women, and especially women with first pregnancies, imagine themselves entering the workplace of contemporary mothering in one of two ways. Most plan to control the balance between participation in wage labor and the domestic economy. They use prenatal testing hoping never to face a pregnancy whose outcome would demand more caretaking than they feel they could provide; selective abortion haunts this dilemma. This model of rationality fits easily with the one that has emerged with genetic counseling, which assumes the power of individuals, no matter how constrained, to make rational choices that will "improve the quality" of their lives. A minority of women approach these tests differently, without intent to abort. They view the test as a technology for appropriate preparation should they need to provide specialized support for the birth of a child with a serious disability. In both cases, the assumption endures that infant and child care are primarily the responsibility of the individual mother, with support from other kin and recourse to the marketplace, if finances permit.

The caretaking of a disabled infant requires different and expanded resources than can be provided by most kin groups without additional forms of support. The complexities of mobilizing the necessary medical, therapeutic, and social support reveal the limits of kinship within a gendered nuclear family structure. It is through this revelation, we suggest, that some begin to reimagine the boundaries and capacities of kinship and to recognize the necessity of broader support for caretaking. On occasion, they are motivated to rewrite kinship in ways that circulate within larger discursive fields of representation and activism.

THE LIMITS OF KINSHIP

Despite a quarter century of activism, policy innovation, and the substantial provision of public services, in the United States, the securing of care for disabled members rests with the family. A vast gap remains between the rhetoric of public inclusion that mandates everything from universal design to inclusive classrooms and the battles that still have to be fought on a daily basis to ensure their availability—battles which not everyone can or will fight. As the mother and the aunt of a child with significant disabilities point out in the article "Uncommon Children":

> Laws attempt to provide parity in society for disabled individuals, but do they go far enough? Underfunded and understaffed public schools may be hard-pressed to meet sophisticated or extensive needs. Parents of "special ed" children become angry at the lack of responsiveness while parents of typical children grow resentful of monies seemingly diverted from regular ed. The very people who need to work together to meet these complex challenges are often pitted against each other.
>
> We expect parents of children with disabilities to "rise to the occasion," but some don't or can't. As a nation we were recently horrified by the Kelsos, who left their profoundly disabled ten-year-old at a Delaware hospital with a note saying they could no longer care for him. Certainly, they did the wrong thing. But their desperate act should not be dismissed lightly as simply aberrant. (O'Connell and Foster 2000: 18)

When we step back from this impassioned description of a grim social landscape, we recognize this narrative as grounded in a potentially productive tension between a capacious view of liberal democracy, in which law and social services are expanding to accommodate the needs of people with disabilities, and the reality of the daily tasks of caretaking, which remain in the household, dependent on family—and overwhelmingly female—labor. At the same time, biomedical technology holds out utopian promises that elide the dilemmas of caretaking while raising others about perfectibility, exemplified in a variety of sometimes controversial supports to people with disabilities, from cochlear implants for the hearing-impaired to computer resources for "fast-forwarding" learning-disabled students. Technology has also delivered a rapidly expanding panoply of reproductive choices. Reliable and inexpensive birth control, infertility treatments, and safe and legal abortion have greatly enhanced women's ability to control the circumstances of mothering. The prenatal diagnosis of disabling conditions in fetuses is surely part of this technological modernity. The common choice to abort based on such diagnoses suggests the limits of the expansion described above and the implicit recognition that much of the labor of caretaking, especially in infancy and childhood, still falls on mothers.[4] In a sense, technologies such as amniocentesis are allowing pregnant women and their partners to construct the limits of kinship on their own terms, however constrained. Realistically, many fear that the social support that they would need for a disabled child might be difficult to obtain. This was true in many of the narratives of working-class women who chose amniocentesis, who had vivid images of what a chronically ill child might do to their lives. One woman explained her decision to have prenatal testing this way:

> With my other two, Lionel worked nights, I'm on days, we managed with a little help from my mother. When Eliza was three, my mother passed on, then my sister, she helped me out as much as she could. With this one, we're planning to ask for help from a neighbor who takes in a few kids. I couldn't keep a baby with health problems. Who would baby-sit? (Rapp 1999: 145)

Such stories poignantly illustrate how close to the edge many parents feel when they imagine the juggling of work and family obligations should disability enter an already tight domestic economy. Such stories can also mask deep-seated prejudices against the imagined "courtesy stigma" incurred by those close to people with "spoiled identities" (Goffman 1963). Yet it is important to highlight the material pressures under which many families with two working parents find themselves and that serve as the matrix in which the decision to use prenatal testing is made.

As we noted above, some have argued that in an upper-middle-class environment where children are increasingly regarded as commodities, genetic testing raises expectations among parents that they can "choose" to have a "perfect" baby (Browner and Press 1996; Press and Browner 1995; Corea 1985; Rothman 1986). A more complex scenario emerges when women of diverse class, racial, religious, and national backgrounds who were offered prenatal testing were interviewed (Rapp 1999). Whatever their cultural background, most pregnant women and their supporters are concerned not so much with perfection, but seek basic health and "normalcy," recognizing the limits of the material circumstances within which they undertake mothering. Indeed, some were willing to live with a range of disabling conditions if they could manage it practically and if the child could enjoy life. Nonetheless, most were frightened by the stigmatizing conditions that the test might predict, about which they knew almost nothing, and whose consequences they could only imagine (Rapp 1999). Such conflicted responses are not surprising, given that the survival of disabled infants has escalated dramatically thanks to improvements in infant surgery, antibiotics, and life-support technologies. At the same time, the knowledge of what is entailed in caring for such children remains absent from mainstream discourse, underscoring a sense of social segregation and stigma. On the genetic frontier, where the use of prenatal diagnostic technologies is rapidly becoming routine, a gap exists between the medical diagnosis of a fetal anomaly and social knowledge about life with a child who bears that condition. In this gap, the use of amniocentesis and selective abortion becomes perfectly rational. This tendency to marginalize and segregate disability issues will continue, legal progress and expanded public consciousness notwithstanding, until the conditions of care are less privatized and the social fund of knowledge is increased. It is this disjunction, then, between neighboring fields of social knowledge that animates the narrative urgency of those compelled to tell what might be termed their *unnatural histories*, as they struggle to represent the difference that disability makes in the domain of kinship.

CHANGING CULTURAL SCRIPTS

The cultural dialectic between perfectibility and inclusion has often animated the work of the activist individuals, families, and groups who are the crucial link between the intimate domain of kinship and the broader public sphere. The utopian promise of perfectible children has had a long-standing hold on the American cultural imagination and is particularly powerful under current techno-scientific regimes. At the same time, the ideal of equality has been the touchstone of a range of social movements that demand inclusion for those excluded on the basis of differences coded as biological deficiencies. Over the last twenty-five years, they have helped to catalyze policy initiatives that offer a potentially radical challenge to the boundaries of citizenship and the relations of obligation between (temporarily) able-bodied and dependent people across the life cycle. The IDEA, or Individuals with Disabilities Education Act (1975), followed by the ADA, or Americans with Disabilities Act (1990), are the two key pieces of postwar federal legislation that have established the framework for the civil rights for Americans with disabilities. These accomplishments have dramatically transformed both the institutional and intimate frameworks within which American families operate.

The responses of what Oe calls "disabled families" have shaped and been shaped by these historically shifting conditions. In the 1950s and 1960s, for example, many middle-class parents were commonly advised to institutionalize "non-normal" children whose survival rate was rising due to aggressive medical innovations, erasing their presence from the household and muffling their voices in family stories. Since the 1970s, however, deinstitutionalization and early-intervention programs have increasingly supported families in keeping disabled children at home. Responding to these changed circumstances, some families have begun to articulate new and public versions of domestic life with disabled children in an effort to reconfigure the discursive space defining these social fields. At the same time, a combination of forces—the *Roe v. Wade* decision legalizing abortion in 1973; the international development of prenatal genetic testing; and the rise of second-wave feminism, with its advocacy of broad-based options for women's public and private lives—increasingly medicalized and individualized the cultural salience of reproductive choice. Twenty years on, the dilemmas of such "choices" have become a staple of public debate, as powerful medical, genetic, and prosthetic technologies extend and enable fragile lives even as prenatal screening technologies give prospective parents the option to terminate an anomalous pregnancy. Citizens of this "republic of choice" (after Friedman 1990) face contradictory options that exceed the extant frameworks for ethical deliberation. In the contemporary scenario, it is women in particular who have thus been cast as moral pioneers. These anxiety-provoking circumstances generate and are reflected in contemporary public testimony about disability, whether in the work of accomplished writers such as the Nobel Prize-winning Oe or in less prominent forms of cultural production. Such narrative engagements with unanticipated difference within the intimate culture of the family can be understood as interventions into the public sphere. They work to subvert the hegemonic discourse of perfectibility disseminated by such sites as obstetric medicine, middle-class parenting literature, and, more generally, contemporary U.S. models of personhood that valorize celebrity and individual will.

The cultural activity of rewriting life stories and kinship narratives around the fact of disability, whether in memoir, film, or everyday storytelling, enables families to comprehend (in both senses) this anomalous experience, not only because of the capacity of stories to make meaning, but also because of their dialogical relationship with larger social arenas. Indeed, the transformation of both emotional and technical knowledge developed in kin groups with disabled family members can foster networks of support from which activism may emerge. In other words, the way that family members articulate changing experiences and awareness of disability in the domain of kinship not only provides a model for the body politic as a whole, but also helps to constitute a broader understanding of citizenship in which disability rights are understood as civil rights (Asch 1989; Bérubé and Lyon 1998; Kittay 1999; Linton 1998).

MEDIATING DISABILITY

The creation of kinship ties between non-disabled and disabled people requires the imagining, for many families, of an unanticipated social landscape. This sense of reorientation to a place of possibility, as opposed to disappointment, is evident in the text of a flyer authored by Emily Kingsley (see below) posted prominently often without attribution in many American pediatric wards. It offers families of chronically ill and disabled children a parable of an unexpected journey to an unknown world, a counternarrative of hope in the face of the sense of crisis experienced by many families with hospitalized offspring:

WELCOME TO HOLLAND
by Emily Perl Kingsley
I am often asked to describe the experience of raising a child with a disability - to try to help people who have not shared that unique experience to understand it, to imagine how it would feel. It's like this … When you're going to have a baby, it's like planning a fabulous vacation trip—to Italy. You buy a bunch of guide books and make your wonderful plans. The Coliseum. The Michelangelo David. The gondolas in Venice. You may learn some handy phrases in Italian. It's all very exciting. After months of eager anticipation, the day finally arrives. You pack your bags and off you go. Several hours later, the plane lands. The stewardess comes in and says, "Welcome to Holland." "Holland?!?" you say. "What do you mean Holland?? I signed up for Italy! I'm supposed to be in Italy. All my life I've dreamed of going to Italy." But there's been a change in the flight plan. They've landed in Holland and there you must stay. The important thing is that they haven't taken you to a horrible, disgusting, filthy place, full of pestilence, famine and disease. It's just a different

place. So you must go out and buy new guide books. And you must learn a whole new language. And you will meet a whole new group of people you would never have met. It's just a different place. It's slower-paced than Italy, less flashy than Italy. But after you've been there for a while and you catch your breath, you look around … and you begin to notice that Holland has windmills … and Holland has tulips. Holland even has Rembrandts. But everyone you know is busy coming and going from Italy … and they're all bragging about what a wonderful time they had there. And for the rest of your life, you will say "Yes, that's where I was supposed to go. That's what I had planned." And the pain of that will never, ever, ever, ever go away… because the loss of that dream is a very, very significant loss. But … if you spend your life mourning the fact that you didn't get to Italy, you may never be free to enjoy the very special, the very lovely things … about Holland.

There is often a direct relationship between the initial efforts of families to reimagine their narratives and the more public actions they undertake to help rescript narratives of inclusion at a broader cultural level. But the call to rethink kinship enacted in the posting of the Blue Tulips flyer is relatively recent and very much the product of the activism of families who have struggled against the categories imposed by medical and bureaucratic regimes.

The example of Down syndrome can illustrate the negotiation of such a category. Until the 1970s, many U.S. doctors would not treat the esophageal and heart problems for which newborns with DS are at increased risk, although the procedures for repair were increasingly well known. Parents of such children were encouraged to "let go," and often had no source of knowledge with which to dispute medical experts. The result was passive infanticide, or what medical historian Martin Pernick (1996) has called the "Black Stork." For children who survived, institutionalization was common; removal from their families was considered the responsible action to take for their care. Children with DS were regarded as incapable of emotional attachment or education. It is only since the 1970s that the conjunction of the deinstitutionalization movement, the creation of early-intervention programs for developmentally delayed infants and toddlers, and the passage of federal and state laws protecting the civil rights of the disabled have provided a social environment in which most families of DS children are now able to take them home at birth. This remarkable shift in biomedical, legal, and familial discourse and practice can be attributed in part to the direct activism of parents' groups such as the Association for Retarded Children (now the Arc) as well as to the indirect impact of writings by the kin of DS people and eventually by affected individuals themselves—particularly in the form of memoir. Such rescriptings present an alternative world of kinship based on a shared difference, a phenomenon common to many disability support networks (Rapp, Heath, and Taussig 2001). The following quote from two authors who recently became disability activists on behalf of their child clearly acknowledges an indebtedness to those whose narratives have created a sense of kinship that spans generations and crosses biological family lines:

> Like all parents of children with Down syndrome, we owe a great deal to the authors of books like *Count Us In*—themselves young men with Down's syndrome—and their families for having transformed the social meaning of Down's syndrome by helping to develop what's now called "early intervention for infants with disabilities." But we also find ourselves the unwitting heirs of people and movements *we never knew we were related to*. We saunter with our Jamie publicly largely thanks to Dale Evans who, in 1953, wrote *Angel Unaware*, a best selling memoir of her daughter Robin who was born with Down's syndrome and died at age two. (Bérubé and Lyon 1998: 274, emphasis added)

Despite the progress that has been made since the publication *of Angel Unaware*, bringing a child with DS home is still an act of personal assertion in the United States; in New York state and many other places, the mother of a newborn diagnosed in the hospital is always offered fosterage or adoption placement. Although this practice is shockingly offensive to many new mothers, we should point out that it developed with "the best interests of the child" in mind. Hospital personnel know that disabled babies are at high risk of being abandoned; as they grow older and more difficult to care for, they also grow harder to place in a good home. As newborns are the easiest babies to place, social workers offer information on adoption right away. But the practice has an unintended consequence. The task of composing a normalizing narrative that can create a space of inclusion for the DS child within the family circle is immediately thrust upon the mother, who has to justify to medical personnel the otherwise unproblematic action of taking her newborn home with her.

Constructing such a normalizing narrative is an ongoing process. Down syndrome affects the full spectrum of class and ethnic differences in the United States, and parents of DS children pursue a correspondingly wide variety of strategies for expanding the reach and support of their children's lives. The established script of Down syndrome is being rewritten across a range of sites in a way that opens up a supportive universe for disabled people and their kin. The Special Olympics; infant stimulation programs; consciousness-raising and other sorts of events organized by the disability rights community; and Internet chat groups are all examples of sites that can help reconfigure community for dubious family members.

These forms of positive public mediation of disabled people play an important role in refiguring the cultural landscape for new generations of families engaging with the social fact of disability. The activism of one parent, Emily Kingsley, a scriptwriter for the children's television program *Sesame Street*, is exemplary of this process. Kingsley was told that her son "would never have a single meaningful thought" when Jason was born and diagnosed with Down syndrome. She was counseled to institutionalize Jason immediately and to "try again" (Kingsley and Levitz 1994: 3). Instead, she wrote him into the script of *Sesame Street*, where he appeared throughout his childhood. Contrary to the dire predictions for his intelligence, at age six he was "counting in Spanish for the cameras" (1994: 4). The Kingsleys' cultural activism opened the door for people with other disabilities—people using wheelchairs, braces, and seeing-eye dogs—to appear as part of the quotidian world of mass media that is now an integral part of the public sphere of most postindustrial countries. Jason himself went on to coauthor the aforementioned book, *Count Us In*, with his friend Mitchell Levitz, who also has DS. Later, his mother scripted a prime-time docudrama based on her family's experiences, entitled *Kids Like These* (CBS, 1991). Of course, this ability to work in (and have access to) such media venues is not simply a matter of individual achievement, but also of the cultural capital of activist families. As Bérubé and Lyon (1998: 282) point out: "Their fame . . . depends on their good fortune: not only were they born into extremely supportive families that contested the medical wisdom of their day, but they were born into families well-positioned for activism." Another mother, Gail Williamson, whose son Blair has DS and has also appeared on television, was moved to establish Hollywood's first talent agency for disabled actors in the entertainment industry (Gray 1999).

Many Americans met their first person with Down syndrome in the late 1980s through the virtual presence in their living rooms of Chris Burke, who became a teen star in ABC's *Life Goes On*. Introduced by cast members singing the Beatles' popular song, "Ob-La-Di, Ob-La-Da, Life Goes On," the show provided a realistic depiction of disability as part of everyday family life, while indexing, as the theme song's lyrics do, an optimistic message of possibility. But Chris's story is not only about his heroic triumph over adversity as an individual (Burke and McDaniel 1991). It is imbricated in the complex nexus of changing contexts sketched above that have radically altered the biomedical, familial, practical, and legal narratives structuring disability in America over the last three decades.

Inevitably, the advertising industry was quick to follow the lead of *Life Goes On*, recognizing the potential for growth, not only in direct sales to market niches ranging from psychotropic pharmaceuticals to adaptive technologies, but also in a more indirect appeal to the loyalty of families with disabled members, through the inclusion of DS kids and teens in commercials for McDonald's, Benetton, and even in popular advertising circulars. Such efforts have been subject to criticism from some activists for reducing issues of citizenship to consumption. Yet the presence of people with visible disabilities in the landscape of popular and commercial culture has been embraced enthusiastically by many families as a sign of the growing public incorporation of this historically stigmatized difference. It speaks as well to the erasure of disabled characters that continues to prevail in the popular media since the appearance of such figures, even in advertising, is still regarded as exceptional.

"WHAT ARE YOU STARING AT?"

Whatever progress has been made, there are still relatively few televisual spaces for children that regularly feature kids with disabilities talking about their own lives (as opposed to what some disabled children refer to as "models in wheelchairs"). The shows discussed above are salient exceptions, as is the Nickelodeon children's cable network's magazine program, *Nick News*. "What Are You Staring At?" was an innovative special produced by *Nick News* that aired repeatedly during 1999. The half-hour program featured a group of kids and teens with a range of disabilities—DS, hearing and visual impairments, cerebral palsy, polio, burn injuries—talking about their lives with celebrity crips, journalist John Hockenberry and actor Christopher Reeve. The anecdote that follows, an account of one youngster's experience of this show, may be read as an illustration of the way that such public interventions can help to create an alternative horizon of kinship extending beyond the nuclear family.

In the summer of 1999 in New York City, ten-year-old Samantha Myers surfed onto "What Are You Staring At?" and was riveted. When the final credits ended, she announced to her mother that she wanted to talk about her disability on television. Samantha's disorder, Familial Dysautonomia (FD),[6] is an extremely rare condition of the involuntary nervous system that affects all forms of body regulation, including temperature, blood pressure, swallowing, and respiration. With some adult assistance, she found the Web site for the Make-A-Wish Foundation, a group that grants "wishes" to children with life-threatening diseases. She e-mailed them, explaining that her wish was to go on *Nick News* and talk about her life with FD. Within two weeks, she was working with a friend and a Make-A-Wish volunteer, making a pitch book with color photos and handwritten text about her life and disability. Sam's inventory of her life included police-style pictures she took of all her medical equipment, as well as photos of her dog, friends, and relatives.

By her eleventh birthday, she was working with a producer from *Nick News* to make a five-minute segment that she narrated, replete with footage of her school, doctor, friends, and some whimsical computer animation to make it kid-friendly. In late April 2000, the show was broadcast; as a result, over the next few months, Sam was invited to show her tape and talk to a number of groups. Of greatest significance to Sam was that so many FD kids were able to see another child like them on television. She was deluged with e-mail from families with FD children around the country who were thrilled to see an image and story that for once included their experience. Many, like Sam, went on to use copies of the tape to help teachers and classmates understand the particular issues that kids with FD face on a daily basis.

MEDIATED KINSHIP

The media world into which Sam surfed at the end of the twentieth century is evidence of a transforming public culture in which disability is becoming a more visible presence in daily life. This anecdotal evidence—Sam's immediate sense of kinship with the disabled kids she saw and heard on television and her desire to join that process—suggests how significant such imagery can be to those who do not see themselves regularly in dominant forms of representation. Indeed, much of the early writing in disability studies focused not only on the need for changes in civil rights legislation, but also on the absence of disabled people from literature and popular media—or, where present, the negativity of their portrayal, citing the legacy of freak shows, circuses, and asylums (Bogdan 1988; Thomson 1997). Others were working actively to alter the media landscape itself. Along with parent-activists who worked in the mainstream media, such as Emily Kingsley, there were people

like Mary Johnson and Cass Irvin, who in 1980 founded the alternative journal *The Disability Rag* (Shaw 1994). Nowadays, the work of activists in visual media is increasingly evident in the plethora of photography shows and film and video festivals devoted in part or entirely to the topic of disability. And, of course, the Web sites, e-lists, and chat groups of the Internet have dramatically expanded the range of sites at which images of disability are being negotiated.

The circulatory reach of electronic media is the key factor in the creation of what we call *mediated kinship*. Emerging as a neighboring—and sometimes overlapping—field to the formal, institutionalized discourse of disability rights, mediated kinship offers a critique of normative American family life that is embedded within everyday cultural practice. Across many genres, a common theme is an implicit rejection of the pressure to produce "perfect families through the incorporation of difference under the sign of love and intimacy in the domain of kinship relations. We suggest that these mediated spaces of public intimacy—talk shows, on-line disability support groups, Web sites, and so on—are crucial for building a social fund of knowledge more inclusive of the fact of disability. These media practices provide a counterdiscourse to the naturalized stratification of family membership that for so long has marginalized, in particular, those disabled from birth. It is not only the acceptance of difference within families, but also the embrace of relatedness that such models of inclusion present to the body politic that makes these spaces potentially radical in their implications. As sites of information and free play of imagination, these cultural forms help to create a new social landscape.

The struggle to form inclusive familial units takes place within an increasingly complex discursive world, a terrain in which the so-called genetic revolution—and the part played within it by prenatal testing—cannot be ignored. One suggestive source of images by which that revolution is imagined is via a classic trope of science fiction: the neoeugenic dystopia, as portrayed in books such as *The Handmaid's Tale* (Atwood 1986) and in films such as *Gattaca* (Andrew Niccol, 1997); these are stories of monstrous kinship. But a more common discursive field is the science or business page of the newspaper, where advances in scientific knowledge, especially genetic technologies, are regularly reported, yet the social dilemmas they index go largely undiscussed.

These dilemmas beg questions about who is entitled to make interventions into reproduction, the capacity of kinship to encompass difference, and the social location of care. Although these are experienced as private, family matters, they cannot be contained within domestic domains. Caretaking is perhaps the most naturalized of these, conventionally attached to the unpaid labor of women in the home. Yet, in the United States, it is rapidly becoming a politicized arena in a privatizing economy in which families are expected to be "always on call," as Carol Levine argues in her book of that title, to care for disabled kin (Levine 2000; see also Nussbaum 2001). If paid, the labor of family caregivers would cost about $200 billion a year (Langone 2000). Nevertheless, while health insurance increasingly covers the routinization of new reproductive technologies (NRTs) and the costs of neonatal intensive care units (NICUs), most home-based personal assistance—a need estimated at 21 billion hours yearly—goes unpaid by public funds, despite the demonstrable bodily, emotional, and economic benefits of deinstitutionalizing support (Johnson 2000: 14; Linton 1998; Russell 1998). This is a skeletal sketch of the political economy of health care and assisted living "choices" that affects all Americans. Yet it is a barely visible landscape to most people unless and until their own or a family member's disability reveals its limitations on a practical, daily level.[7]

These revelations of the limits of kinship-based caretaking and the need for broader social recognition and resources for people with disabilities fuel the narrative urgency we have described throughout, beginning with Oe's compelling story of a "healing family," offering stories of familial inclusion that can serve as models of social inclusion as well. Additionally, progress in legal arenas has problematized the presumption of American citizenship as the exclusive entitlement of a normative, able-bodied, non-dependent, wage-earning individual. At best, this model of personhood describes only a portion of the normal human life cycle. At worst, it systematically erases the rights of the disabled and their caretakers to have their fundamental needs addressed in the public arena.

Although we have focused here on the nexus of disability rights and reproductive decision-making as highlighted in the parent–child relationship, kinship and disability—as instantiated by congenital difference, accident, illness, infancy, or old age—remain entwined throughout the life cycle. Thus, the disjunction between the aspiration for democratic inclusion and the fantasy of bodily perfectibility through technological intervention has energized much popular cultural expression, creating a growing sense of public intimacy with experiences of disability. In this gap, disability narratives offer what we have called *unnatural histories*, visions of lives lived against the grain of normalcy. It is here, we have argued, that the relations of kinship have the capacity to enable disability, giving narrative shape and cultural imagination to efforts to form a more perfect union.

NOTES

We have many people to thank, first and foremost our children, who have opened our eyes to worlds more exotic than we ever imagined we would encounter as anthropologists. We thank Carol A. Breckenridge, Candace Vogler, and the editorial board of *Public Culture* for helpful comments, and Barbara Abrash and Simi Linton for their constructive engagement with the final draft.

1. Oe's writings point to the impossibility of individual solutions—even at the level of narrative—to what are cultural and social dilemmas. In a kind of parallel process, Oe has also written movingly on the aftermath of Hiroshima, an assignment he began the same year Hikari was born. This project enabled him to cope with the incomprehensibility of his son's condition by placing it in an even more inexplicable context of social suffering.

2. For example, national attention was riveted on the upper-middle-class Kelso family of suburban Philadelphia in December 1999, when they abandoned their ten-year-old son, Steven, with his diapers, medications, toys, and medical records at the Du Pont Hospital for Children in Wilmington, Delaware. Their nursing schedule had fallen apart over the holidays, and the parents claimed they could no longer cope with the intensity of their child's needs. While stories of abandonment are not uncommon, this one made public headlines in part because the mother had been a prominent volunteer on the Pennsylvania Developmental Disabilities Council.

3. The recent explosion of U.S. writing on disability, building on the groundbreaking work of scholars/activists who have been writing since the 1970s, is reflected in such developments as the dramatic growth of the Society for Disability Studies, the launching of book series such as Corporealities: Discourses of Disability (edited by David T. Mitchell and Sharon L. Snyder for the University of Michigan Press), and the creation of university-based disabilities studies programs, such as the one at the University of Illinois at Chicago. All are founded on a commitment to the centrality of disabled people both as researchers and subjects (see e.g., Charlton 1998, *Nothing about Us without Us*). In anthropology, the efforts of pioneers such as Robert Edgerton (1993, first published 1967) and Henri-Jacques Stiker (1999, first published 1982) ave been joined by an emerging scholarship focusing on issues ranging from stigma (Ingstad and Whyte 1995), to cultural communities of difference (Groce 1985), to the phenomenology of differently abled bodies (Frank 2000; Murphy 1987).

4. Of course, fathers have frequently been deeply involved and committed to this kind of labor and have played exemplary public roles as well (e.g., Oe 1995; Bérubé 1996). However, the high divorce rates in families with disabled children is one indication that such fathers might be more the exception than the rule. We also note the gendered nature of caretaking and the professions associated with it, such as nursing, home health care, special education, and occupational and physical therapy.

5. Rayna Rapp first heard this parable, attributed to Emily Kingsley, at a Down syndrome parents' support group in 1985. It was plastered on the walls of the pediatric ward Faye Ginsburg occupied with her daughter for most of 1989. More elaborate versions have since appeared in print, at sites as diverse as the Brooklyn waiting room of a school board Committee on Special Education and the back of a newsletter for parents of disabled children.

6. Information on FD is readily accessible at two Web sites: www.FamilialDysautonomia.org and www.FDVillage.org.

7. In the United States and throughout much of the world, the tasks of caretaking continue to be naturalized in the domain of unpaid domestic labor. Increasingly, however, challenges to this situation are emerging as a result of the expanding needs of caretaking over the life cycle. The increased rate of survival among such formerly high-risk groups as low-birth-weight babies, the chronically ill, and the elderly make claims on public resources, usually mediated through their kin. Advocacy groups such as the growing movement for Independent Living seek public support for personal assistance, a policy that, they argue, "would relieve an enormous amount of stress on families and, over time . . . would begin to alter the public perception toward significantly disabled people and the people who relate to them" (Marca Bistro, head of the National Council on Disability, quoted in Johnson 2000: 14).

REFERENCES

Asch, Adrienne. 1989. Reproductive technology and disability. In *Reproductive laws for the 1990's*, edited by Sherrill Cohen and Nadine Taub. Clifton, N.J.: Humana.

Atwood, Margaret. 1986. *The handmaid's tale.* Boston: Houghton-Mifflin.

Beck, Martha N. 1999. *Expecting Adam: A true story of birth, rebirth, and everyday magic.* New York: Times Books.

Berlant, Lauren. 1998. Intimacy: A special issue. *Critical Inquiry* 24: 281–88.

Bérubé, Michael. 1996. *Life as we know it: A father, a family, and an exceptional child*. New York: Pantheon.

Bérubé, Michael, and Janet Lyon. 1998. Living on disability: Language and social policy in the wake of the ADA. In *The visible woman: Imaging technologies, gender, and science*, edited by Paula. A. Treichler, Lisa Cartwright, and Constance Penley. New York: New York University Press.

Blair, John. 2000. Online deliveries lighten burden for the disabled. *New York Times*, 5 September, B1, 5.

Blumberg, Lisa. 1998. The bad baby blues: Reproductive technology and the threat to diversity. *The Ragged Edge*, July/August, 12–14, 16.

Bogdan, Robert. 1988. *Freak show: Presenting human oddities for amusement and profit*. Chicago: University of Chicago Press.

Brewster, Arlene. 1984. After hours: A patient's reaction to amniocentesis. *Obstetrics and Gynecology* 67: 443–44.

Browner, Carol H., and Nancy Ann Press. 1996. The production of authoritative knowledge in American prenatal care. *Medical Anthropology Quarterly* 10: 141–56.

Burke, Chris, and Jo Beth McDaniel. 1991. *A special kind of hero: Chris Burke's own story*. New York: Doubleday.

Charlton, James. 1998. *Nothing about us without us: Disability oppression and empowerment*. Berkeley: University of California Press.

Corea, Gena. 1985. *The mother machine: Reproductive technologies from artificial insemination to artificial wombs*. New York: Harper and Row.

Edgerton, Robert B. 1993. *The cloak of competence: Stigma in the lives of the mentally retarded*. 1967. Reprint, Berkeley: University of California Press.

Evans, Dale. 1953. *Angel unaware*. Westwood, N.J.: Revell.

Featherstone, Helen. 1980. *A difference in the family: Life with a disabled child*. New York: Basic Books.

Finger, Anne. 1990. *Past due: A story of disability, pregnancy, and birth*. Seattle: Seal.

Frank, Gelya. 2000. *Venus on wheels: Two decades of dialogue on disability, biography, and being female in America*. Berkeley: University of California Press.

Friedman, Lawrence. 1990. *Republic of choice: Law, authority and culture*. Cambridge: Harvard University Press.

Fries, Kenny, ed. 1997. *Staring back: The disability experience from the inside out*. New York: Plume.

Ginsburg, Faye, and Rayna Rapp. 1999. Fetal reflections: Confessions of two feminist anthropologists as mutual informants. In *Fetal subject, feminist positions*, edited by Lynn M. Morgan and Meredith W. Michaels. Philadelphia: University of Pennsylvania Press.

Goffman, Erving. 1963. *Stigma: Notes on the management of spoiled identity*. Englewood Cliffs, N.J.: Prentice-Hall.

Gray, Barbara. 1999. They're her all-star kids. *Family Circle*, 13 July, 15–18.

Green, Rose. 1992. Letter to a genetic counselor. *Journal of Genetic Counseling* 1: 55–70.

Groce, Nora. 1985. *Everyone here spoke sign language: Hereditary deafness on Martha's Vineyard*. Cambridge: Harvard University Press.

Handler, Lowell. 1998. *Twitch and shout: A Tourreter's tale*. New York: Dutton.

Hardacre, Helen. 1997. *Marketing the menacing fetus in Japan*. Berkeley: University of California Press.

Hirschman, Albert O. 1977. *The passions and the interests: Political arguments for capitalism before its triumph*. Princeton, N.J.: Princeton University Press.

Hockenberry, John. 1995. *Moving violations: War zones, wheelchairs, and declarations of independence*. New York: Hyperion.

Ingstad, Benedicte, and Susanne Reynolds Whyte, eds. 1995. *Disability and culture*. Berkeley: University of California Press.

Jablow, Martha Moraghan. 1982. *Cara: Growing with a retarded child*. Philadelphia: Temple University Press.

Johnson, Mary. 2000. The "care" juggernaut. *The Ragged Edge*, November/December: 10–12, 14.

Kingsley, Jason, and Mitchell Levitz. 1994. *Count us in: Growing up with Down syndrome*. New York: Harcourt Brace.

Kittay, Eva Feder. 1999. *Love's labor: Essays on women, equality, and dependency*. New York: Routledge.

Kolker, Aliza, and Meredith Burke. 1993. Grieving the wanted child. *Health Care for Women International* 14: 513–26.

Kuusisto, Stephen. 1998. *Planet of the blind: A memoir*. New York: Delta.

Landsman, Gail. 1999. Does God give special kids to special parents? Personhood and the child with disabilities as gift and as giver. In *Transformative motherhood: On giving and getting in a consumer culture*, edited by Linda L. Layne. New York: New York University Press.

——. 2000. "Real motherhood": Class and children with disabilities. In *Ideologies and technologies of motherhood: Race, class, sexuality, nationalism*, edited by France Winddance Twine and Heléna Ragoné. New Brunswick, N.J.: Rutgers University Press.

Langone, John. 2000. When friends and family fill most of a patient's medical needs. *New York Times*, 12 October, F6.

Layne, Linda. 1996. "How's the baby doing?": Struggling with narratives of progress in a neonatal intensive care unit. *Medical Anthropological Quarterly* 10: 624–56.

Levine, Carol, ed. 2000. *Always on call: When illness turns families into caregivers.* New York: United Hospital Fund of New York.

Linton, Simi. 1998. *Claiming disability: Knowledge and identity.* New York: New York University Press.

Mairs, Nancy. 1996. *Waist-high in the world: A life among the non-disabled.* Boston: Beacon.

McGee, Glenn. 1997. *The perfect baby: A pragmatic approach to genetics.* Lanham, Md.: Rowman and Littlefield.

Murphy, Robert. 1987. *The body silent.* New York: Henry Holt.

Nussbaum, Martha. 2001. Disabled lives: Who cares? *New York Review of Books* 48: 34–37.

O'Connell, Linda G., and Lisa G. Foster. 2000. Uncommon children. *Mt. Holyoke Alumnae Quarterly*, spring, 13–18.

Oe, Kenzaburo. 1995. *A healing family*, edited by S. Shaw and translated by Stephen Snyder. Tokyo: Kodansha International.

Parens, Erik, and Adrienne Asch, eds. 2000. *Prenatal testing and disability rights.* Washington, D.C.: Georgetown University Press.

Pernick, Martin S. 1996. *The black stork: Eugenics and the death of "defective" babies in American medicine and motion pictures since 1915.* New York: Oxford University Press.

Press, Nancy Ann, and Carol H. Browner. 1995. The normalization of prenatal diagnostic screening. In *Conceiving the new world order: The global politics of reproduction*, edited by Faye D. Ginsburg and Rayna Rapp. Berkeley: University of California Press.

Rapp, Rayna. 1999. *Testing women, testing the fetus: The social impact of amniocentesis in America.* New York: Routledge.

Rapp, Rayna, Deborah Heath, and Karen Sue Taussig. 2001. Genealogical disease: Where hereditary abnormality, biomedical explanation, and family responsibility meet. In *Relative matters: New directions in the study of kinship*, edited by Sarah Franklin and Susan MacKinnon. Durham, N.C.: Duke University Press.

Rothman, Barbara Katz. 1986. *The tentative pregnancy: Prenatal diagnosis and the future of motherhood.* New York: W. W. Norton.

Russell, Marta. 1998. *Beyond ramps: Disability at the end of the social contract: A warning from an uppity crip.* Monroe, Maine: Common Courage.

Seligman, Milton, and Rosalyn Benjamin Darling. 1989. *Ordinary families, special children: A systems approach to childhood disability.* New York: Guilford.

Shaw, Barrett. 1994. *The ragged edge: The disability experience from the pages of the first fifteen years of The Disability Rag.* Louisville, Ky.: Advocado.

Stiker, Henri-Jacques. 1999. *A history of disability*, translated by William Sayers. Ann Arbor: University of Michigan Press.

Thomson, Rosemarie Garland. 1997. *Extraordinary bodies: Figuring physical disability in American culture and literature.* New York: Columbia University Press.

CHAPTER 15

Aesthetic Nervousness

Ato Quayson

WHAT IS AESTHETIC NERVOUSNESS?

Let me begin formulaically: Aesthetic nervousness is seen when the dominant protocols of representation within the literary text are short-circuited in relation to disability. The primary level in which it may be discerned is in the interaction between a disabled and nondisabled character, where a variety of tensions may be identified. However, in most texts aesthetic nervousness is hardly ever limited to this primary level, but is augmented by tensions refracted across other levels of the text such as the disposition of symbols and motifs, the overall narrative or dramatic perspective, the constitution and reversals of plot structure, and so on. The final dimension of aesthetic nervousness is that between the reader and the text. The reader's status within a given text is a function of the several interacting elements such as the identification with the vicissitudes of the life of a particular character, or the alignment between the reader and the shifting positions of the narrator, or the necessary reformulations of the reader's perspective enjoined by the modulations of various plot elements and so on. As I shall show throughout this study, in works where disability plays a prominent role, the reader's perspective is also affected by the short-circuiting of the dominant protocols governing the text—a short-circuit triggered by the representation of disability. For the reader, aesthetic nervousness overlaps social attitudes to disability that themselves often remain unexamined in their prejudices and biases. The reader in this account is predominantly a nondisabled reader, but the insights about aesthetic nervousness are also pertinent to readers with disabilities, since it is the construction of a universe of apparent corporeal normativity both within the literary text and outside it whose basis requires examination and challenge that is generally at issue in this study. The various dimensions of aesthetic nervousness will be dealt with both individually and as parts of larger textual configurations in the works of Samuel Beckett, Toni Morrison, Wole Soyinka, and J. M. Coetzee. The final chapter, on the history of disability on Robben Island in South Africa, will be used to refocus attention from the literary-aesthetic domain to that of the historical intersection between disability, colonialism, and apartheid. This will help us see what extensions might be possible for the concept of aesthetic nervousness beyond the literary-aesthetic field.

There are two main sources for the notion of aesthetic nervousness that I want to elaborate here. One is Rosemarie Garland

Thomson's highly suggestive concept of the normate, which we have already touched on briefly, and the other is drawn from Lennard Davis's and Mitchell and Snyder's reformulations of literary history from a disability studies perspective. As Thomson (1997) argues in a stimulating extension of some of Erving Goffman's (1959) insights about stigma, first-time social encounters between the nondisabled and people with disabilities are often short-circuited by the ways in which impairments are interpreted. She puts the matter in this way:

> In a first encounter with another person, a tremendous amount of information must be organized and interpreted simultaneously: each participant probes the explicit for the implicit, determines what is significant for particular purposes, and prepares a response that is guided by many cues, both subtle and obvious. When one person has a visible disability, however, it almost always dominates and skews the normate's process of sorting out perceptions and forming a reaction. The interaction is usually strained because the nondisabled person may feel fear, pity, fascination, repulsion, or merely surprise, none of which is expressible according to social protocol. Besides the discomforting dissonance between experienced and expressed reaction, a nondisabled person often does not know how to act toward a disabled person: how or whether to offer assistance; whether to acknowledge the disability; what words, gestures, or expectations to use or avoid. Perhaps most destructive to the potential for continuing relations is the normate's frequent assumption that a disability cancels out other qualities, reducing the complex person to a single attribute.
>
> (Thomson 1997, 12)

To this we should quickly recall Mitchell and Snyder's remark concerning the degree to which Brueghel's paintings succeeded in disrupting and variegating the visual encounter between bodies in painting. Clearly, disruption and variegation are also features of real-world encounters between the nondisabled and persons with disabilities. Thomson proposes the notion of the "normate" to explicate the cluster of attitudes that govern the nondisabled's perception of themselves and their relations to the various "others" of corporeal normativity. As she persuasively shows, there are complex processes by which forms of corporeal diversity acquire cultural meanings that in their turn undergird a perceived hierarchy of bodily traits determining the distribution of privilege, status, and power. In other words, corporeal difference is part of a structure of power, and its meanings are governed by the unmarked regularities of the normate. However, as the paragraph quoted above shows, there are various elements of this complex relationship that do not disclose themselves as elements of power as such, but rather as forms of anxiety, dissonance, and disorder. The common impulse toward categorization in interpersonal encounters is itself part of an ideal of order that is assumed as implicit in the universe, making the probing of the explicit for the implicit part of the quest for an order that is thought to lie elsewhere. It is this, as we noted in the previous section, that persistently leads to the idea that the disabled body is somehow a cipher of metaphysical or divine significance. Yet the impairment is often taken to be the physical manifestation of the exact opposite of order, thus forcing a revaluation of that impulse, and indeed, of what it means to be human in a world governed by a radical contingency. The causes of impairment can never be fully anticipated or indeed prepared for. Every/body is subject to chance and contingent events. The recognition of this radical contingency produces features of a primal scene of extreme anxiety whose roots lie in barely acknowledged vertiginous fears of loss of control over the body itself (Grosz 1996; Wasserman 2001; Lacan 1948, 1949).[1] The corporeal body, to echo the sonnet

"Death Be Not Proud" by John Donne, is victim to "Fate, chance, kings, and desperate men" and subject to "poison, warre, and sicknesse" as well. The dissonance and anxiety that cannot be properly articulated via available social protocols then define the affective and emotional economy of the recognition of contingency. In other words, the sudden recognition of contingency is not solely a philosophical one—in fact, it hardly ever is at the moment of the social encounter itself—but is also and perhaps primarily an emotional and affective one. The usefulness of the social model of disability is precisely the fact that it now forces the subliminal cultural assumptions about the disabled out into the open for examination, thus holding out the possibility that the nondisabled may ultimately be brought to recognize the sources of the constructedness of the normate and the prejudices that flow from it.

Since the world is structured with a particular notion of unmarked normativity in mind, people with disabilities themselves also have to confront some of these ideas about contingency in trying to articulate their own deeply felt sense of being (Murphy 1990, 96–115). At a practical and material level, there are also the problems of adjustment to a largely indifferent world. As Wood and Bradley (1978, 149) put it: "On a material plane the disabled individual is . . . less able to adapt to the demands of his environment: he has reduced power to insulate himself from the assaults of an essentially hostile milieu. However, the disadvantage he experiences is likely to differ in relation to the nature of the society in which he finds himself." Contradictory emotions arise precisely because the disabled are continually located within multiple and contradictory frames of significance within which they, on the one hand, are materially disadvantaged, and, on the other, have to cope with the culturally regulated gaze of the normate. My use of the word "frames"

in this context is not idle. Going back to the Scope poster, it is useful to think of such frames in the light of physical coordinates, as if thinking of a picture frame. The frames within which the disabled are continually placed by the normate are ones in which a variety of concepts of wholeness, beauty, and economic competitiveness structure persons with disability and place them at the center of a peculiar conjuncture of conceptions.

Thomson's notion of the relations between the normate and the disabled derives ultimately from a symbolic interactionism model. To put it simply, a symbolic interactionism model of interpretation operates on the assumption that "people do not respond to the world directly, but instead place social meanings on it, organize it, and respond to it on the basis of these meanings" (Albrecht 2002, 27). The idea of symbolic interactionism is pertinent to the discussion of literary texts that will follow because not only do the characters organize their perceptions of one another on the basis of given symbolic assumptions, but as fictional characters they are themselves also woven out of a network of symbols and interact through a symbolic relay of signs. Furthermore, as I shall show incrementally in different chapters and in a more situated form in the chapter on J.M. Coetzee (chapter 6 [original volume]), symbolic interactionism also implies the presence of an implied interlocutor with whom the character or indeed real-life person enters into a series of dialogical relationships, thus helping to shape a horizon of expectations against which versions of the self are rehearsed. Following Thomson's lead, the first aspect of aesthetic nervousness that I want to specify is that it is triggered by the implicit disruption of the frames within which the disabled are located as subjects of symbolic notions of wholeness and normativity. Disability returns the aesthetic domain to an active ethical core that serves to disrupt the surface of representation. Read from a perspective of disability studies, this active ethical core becomes manifest because the disability representation is seen as having a direct effect on social views of people with disability in a way that representations of other literary details, tropes, and motifs do not offer. In other words, the representation of disability has an efficaciousness that ultimately transcends the literary domain and refuses to be assimilated to it. This does not mean that disability in literature can be read solely via an instrumentalist dimension of interpretation; any intervention that might be adduced for it is not inserted into an inert and stable disability "reality" that lies out there. For, as we have noted, disability in the real world already incites interpretation in and of itself. Nevertheless, an instrumentalist dimension cannot be easily suspended either. To put the matter somewhat formulaically: the representation of disability oscillates uneasily between the aesthetic and the ethical domains, in such a way as to force a reading of the aesthetic fields in which the disabled are represented as always having an ethical dimension that cannot be easily subsumed under the aesthetic structure. Ultimately, aesthetic nervousness has to be seen as coextensive with the nervousness regarding the disabled in the real world. The embarrassment, fear, and confusion that attend the disabled in their everyday reality is translated in literature and the aesthetic field into a series of structural devices that betray themselves when the disability representation is seen predominantly from the perspective of the disabled rather than from the normative position of the nondisabled.

In his essay entitled "Who Put the *The* in The Novel?" Lennard Davis (2002) explores the links that have largely been taken for granted in literary history between the novel form, an *English* nation, and the various destabilizations of the social status of character that help to define the essential structure of the novel in the eighteenth and nineteenth centuries. The realist novels of the two centuries were based on the construction of the "average" citizen. This average citizen was nonheroic and middle class. But the average citizen was also linked to the concept of "virtue." As Davis notes, "Virtue implied that there was a specific and knowable moral path and stance that a character could and should take. In other words, a normative set of behaviours was demanded of characters in novels" (94). Entangled with these dual notions of the average citizen and of virtue were implicit ideas of wholeness, with no major protagonist in the entire period marked by a physical disability. Undergirding the novel's rise then is a binary opposition between normal/abnormal, with this binary generating a series of plots. Essentially, the key element of such plots is the initial destabilization of the character's social circumstances, followed by their efforts to rectify their loss and return, perhaps chastened, to their former position. Crucially, however, as the nineteenth century progresses the negative or immoral gets somatized and represented as a disability (95–98). One of the conclusions Davis draws from his discussion is that plot functions in the eighteenth and nineteenth centuries "by temporarily deforming or disabling the fantasy of nation, social class, and gender behaviors that are constructed norms" (97).

In taking forward Davis's argument, there are a number of qualifications I want to register. Distinctive in his account is the link he persuasively establishes between nation, the average citizen, virtue, and specific forms of novelistic emplotment. That cannot be questioned. However, it is not entirely accurate that the binary of normal/abnormal starts with the eighteenth- and nineteenth-century novels or indeed that they inaugurate the plots of the deformation of social status. On the contrary, as can be shown from an examination of folktales from all over the world, the plot of physical and/or social deformation is actually one of the commonest starting points of most story plots (see Propp 1958; Zipes 1979), so much so that it is almost as if the deformation of physical and/or social status becomes the universal starting point for the generation of narrative emplotment as such. As Davis points out, in agreement with established scholarship on the novel, the crucial term that is introduced in the eighteenth and nineteenth century is "realism," the notion that somehow the novelistic form refracts a verisimilar world outside of its framework. But realism is itself a cultural construction, since for the Greeks their myths were also a form of realism. What needs to be taken from Davis's account is the effect that the collocation of the social imaginary of the nation and the production of a specific form of bodily and sexual realism had on the way the novel was taken to represent reality. In each instance, the assumed representation of reality depended upon unacknowledged views of social order deriving not just from an understanding of class relations but from an implicit hierarchization of corporeal differences. Even though Davis is not the only one to have noted the peculiar place of the disabled in the eighteenth- and nineteenth-century novel (see Holmes 2000, for example), it is in clarifying the status of the disabled body as *structurally constitutive* to the maintenance of the novel's realism that he makes a distinctive contribution to literary history.

However, in trying to extend the significance of the constitutive function of deformation from the novel to other literary forms, we also have to note that "deformation" can no longer be limited solely to that of social or class position, as Davis suggests in his discussion. From the novels of the early twentieth century onward, the deformations emerge from the intersection of a variety of vectors including gender, ethnicity, sexuality, urban identity, and particularly disability, these providing a variety of *constitutive points for the process of emplotment.* Indeed, Davis himself notes in another context the reiteration of disability in the works of Conrad. A similar view can be expressed of the work of Joyce (*Ulysses, Finnegans Wake*), Virginia Woolf (*Mrs. Dalloway*), Thomas Mann (*The Magic Mountain*), and T. S. Eliot's "The Waste Land," among others. I choose the phrase "constitutive points" as opposed to "starting points" to signal the fact that the social deformation does not always show itself at the beginning of the plot. In much of the work we will look at, from Beckett and Soyinka through Morrison and Coetzee, there are various articulations of a sense of social deformation. However, the deformation is not always necessarily revealed as inaugural or indeed placed at the starting point of the action or narrative as such. It is often revealed progressively or in fragments in the minds of the characters, or even as flashbacks that serve to reorder the salience of events within the plot. The varied disclosures of social deformation are also ultimately linked to the status of disability as a trigger or mechanism for such plot review and disclosure. In that sense, the range of literary texts we shall be exploring is not undergirded exclusively by the binary opposition of normal/abnormal, but by the *dialectical interplay* between unacknowledged social assumptions and the reminders of contingency as reflected in the body of the person with disability.

The notion of dialectical interplay is crucial to my model of interpretation, because one of the points I will repeat throughout the study is that a dialectical interplay can be shown to affect all levels of the literary text, from the perspectival modulations of the narrator (whether first or third person) and the characters to the temporal sequencing and ordering of leitmotifs and symbolic discourses that come together to structure the plotlines. Even though, as Davis rightly notes, the plots of social deformation dominated the eighteenth- and nineteenth-century novel, this view cannot be limited solely to novelistic discourse. Following the point I made a moment ago about the near universality of such plots, I want to suggest that we consider the plot of social deformation as it is tied to some form of physical or mental deformation to be relevant for the discussion of *all* literary texts. This is a potentially controversial point, but given the ubiquity of the role of the disabled in texts from a range of cultures and periods it is difficult to shake off the view that disability is a marker of the aesthetic field as such. Disability teases us out of thought, to echo Keats, not because it resists representation, but because in being represented it automatically restores an ethical core to the literary-aesthetic domain while also invoking the boundary between the real and the metaphysical or otherworldly. Along with the category of the sublime, it inaugurates and constitutes the aesthetic field as such. And like the sublime, disability elicits language and narrativity even while resisting or frustrating complete comprehension and representation and placing itself on the boundary between the real and the metaphysical. When I state that disability "inaugurates" the aesthetic domain, it is not to privilege the "firstness" or "primariness" of first-time encounters between the disabled and nondisabled characters, even though this has been implied in my reliance on Thomson. Rather, I intend the term "inaugurate" in the sense of the setting of the contours of the interlocking vectors of representation, particularly in narrative and drama, which are the two literary forms that will feature mainly in this study. My position overlaps with Davis's but extends his insights to accommodate a more variegated methodology for understanding the status of disability in literary writing.

The analogy between the inaugural status of the sublime and of disability serves to open up a number of ways in which the structurally constitutive function of disability to literary form might be explored. In the *Critique of Judgment*, Kant follows his discussion of the beautiful and its relation to purposelessness or autonomy with the discussion of the sublime and its inherent link to the principle of disorder. For Kant, "*Beauty* is an object's form of purposiveness insofar as it is perceived in the object *without the presentation of purpose*" (1987, 31), the idea here being that only the lack of a determinate or instrumental end allows the subjective feeling of beauty to occur. The sublime, on the other hand, is an aspect of understanding in confrontation with something ineffable that appears to resist delimitation or organization. It exposes the struggle between Imagination and Reason: "[What happens is that] our imagination strives to progress toward infinity, while our reason demands absolute totality as a real idea, and so [the imagination,] our power of estimating the magnitude of things in the world of sense, is inadequate to that idea. Yet this inadequacy itself is the arousal in us of the feeling that we have within us a supersensible power" (108; translator's brackets). Even while generative of representation, the sublime transcends the imaginative capacity to represent it. As Crockett (2001, 75) notes in glossing the nature of this struggle, "the sublime is contra-purposive, because it conflicts with one's purposeful ability to represent it." The implicit dichotomy in the *Critique of Judgment* between the sublime and the beautiful has been explored in different directions by scholars in the intervening three hundred and fifty years since its formulation, but what has generally been agreed upon is the idea of the resistance of the sublime to complete representation, even if this resistance is then incorporated into a motivation for representation as such.[2] What the representation of disability suggests, which both overlaps and distinguishes itself from the sublime as a conceptual category, is that even while also producing a contradictory semiotics of inarticulacy and articulation, it is quite directly and specifically tied to forms of social hierarchization. For disability, the semiotics of articulation/inarticulation that may be perceived within the literary domain reflect difficulties regarding its salience for the nondisabled world. This, as can be gleaned from the Whyte and Ingstad collection already referred to, cuts across cultures. Thus even if the ambivalent status of disability for literary representation is likened to that of the sublime, it must always be remembered that, unlike the effects of the sublime on literary discourse, disability's ambivalence manifests itself within the real world in socially mediated forms of closure. We might then say that disability is an analogue of the sublime in literary-aesthetic representation (ineffability/articulation) yet engenders attempts at social hierarchization and closure within the real world.

Disability might also be productively thought of as being on a continuum with the sublime in terms of its oscillation between a pure abstraction and a set of material circumstances and conditions. Considered in this way, we can think of the sublime as occupying one end of the spectrum (being a pure abstraction despite generating certain psychological effects of judgment and the impulse to represent it in material forms) and disability occupying the other end and being defined by a different kind of oscillation between the abstract and the material. For unlike the sublime, disability oscillates between a pure process of abstraction (via a series of discursive framings,

metaphysical transpositions, and socially constituted modalities of [non]response, and so forth) and a set of material conditions (such as impairment, accessibility and mobility difficulties, and economic considerations). It is not to be discounted also that many impairments also involve living with different levels of pain, such that the categories of pain and disability not infrequently imply each other. It is disability's rapid oscillation between a pure process of abstraction and a set of material conditions that ensures that the ethical core of its representation is never allowed to be completely assimilated to the literary-aesthetic domain as such. Disability serves then to close the gap between representation and ethics, making visible the aesthetic field's relationship to the social situation of persons with disability in the real world. This does not necessarily mean that we must always read the literary representation in a directly instrumental way. As noted earlier, the intervention of the literary representation is an intervention into a world that already situates disability within insistent framings and interpretations. The literary domain rather helps us to understand the complex *processes* of such framings and the ethical implications that derive from such processes.

Finally, it is to Mitchell and Snyder's book *Narrative Prosthesis* (2003) that I wish to turn in elaborating what I mean by aesthetic nervousness. Mitchell and Snyder follow David Wills (1995) in trying to define literary discourse as essentially performing certain prosthetic functions. Among these prosthetic functions are the obvious ones of using the disabled as a signal of moral disorder such that the nondisabled may glean an ethical value from their encounter with persons with disabilities. Since Mitchell and Snyder are also keen to situate narrative prosthesis as having significance for the lived experience of disability, they also assign an inherently pragmatic orientation to what they describe as textual prosthesis: "Whereas an actual prosthesis is always somewhat discomforting, a textual prosthesis alleviates discomfort by removing the unsightly from view. . . . [T]he erasure of disability via a "quick fix" of an impaired physicality or intellect removes an audience's need for concern or continuing vigilance" (8). They make these particular remarks in the context of films and narratives in which persons with disabilities somehow manage to overcome their difficulties and live a happy life within the realm of art. In such instances, the representation of disability serves a pragmatic/cathartic function for the audience and the reader. More significantly, however, they also note that even while disability recurs in various works as a potent force to challenge cultural ideas about the normal and the whole, it also *operates as the textual obstacle that causes the literary operation of open-endedness to close down or stumble*" (50).

This last observation brings their discussion of narrative prosthesis very close to my own notion of aesthetic nervousness, except that they proceed to expound upon this blocking function in what can only be nonaesthetic terms. This is how they put it:

> This "closing down" of an otherwise permeable and dynamic narrative form demonstrates the historical conundrum of disability. [Various disabled characters from literature] provide powerful counterpoints to their respective cultures' normalizing Truths about the construction of deviance in particular, and the fixity of knowledge systems in general. Yet each of these characterizations also evidences that the artifice of disability binds disabled characters to a programmatic (even deterministic) identity.
>
> (Mitchell and Snyder 2003, 50)

Thus Mitchell and Snyder's idea of the shutting down or stumbling of the literary operation is extrinsic to the literary field itself and is to be determined by setting the literary representations of disability against socio-cultural understandings. While agreeing with them that the ultimate test of the salience of a disability representation are the various social and cultural contexts within which they might be thought to have an effect, I want to focus my attention on the devices of aesthetic collapse that occur *within* the literary frameworks themselves. Also, I would like to disagree with them on their view of the programmatic identity assigned to the disabled, because, as I will try to show by reading the disabled character within the wider discursive structure of relations among different levels of the text, we find that even if programmatic roles were originally assigned, these roles can shift quite suddenly, thus leading to the "stumbling" they speak of. I choose to elaborate the textual "stumbling" in terms of aesthetic nervousness.

When it comes to their specific style of reading, Mitchell and Snyder are inspired by Wills to elaborate the following provisional typology:

> Our notion of narrative prosthesis evolves out of this specific recognition: a narrative issues to resolve or correct—to "prostheticize" in David Wills's sense of the term—a deviance marked as improper to a social context. A simple schematic of narrative structure might run thus: first, a deviance or marked difference is exposed to the reader; second, a narrative consolidates the need for its own existence by calling for an explanation of the deviation's origins and formative consequences; third, the deviance is brought from the periphery of concerns to the center of the story to come; and fourth, the remainder of the story rehabilitates or fixes the deviance in some manner. The fourth step of the repair of the deviance may involve an obliteration of the difference through a "cure," the rescue of the despised object from social censure, the extermination of the deviant as a purification of the social body, or the revaluation of an alternative mode of being.

... Narratives turn signs of cultural deviance into textually marked bodies.

(53–54)

Again, their method is defined by an assumption of narrative pragmatism or instrumentalism; that is to say, the literary text aims solely to resolve or correct a deviance that is thought to be improper to a social context. Unlike them, I will be trying to show that this prostheticizing function is bound to fail, not because of the difficulties in erasing the effects of disability in the real world, but because the aesthetic domain itself is short-circuited upon the encounter with disability. As mentioned earlier, disability joins the sublime as marking the constitutive points of aesthetic representation. Aesthetic nervousness is what ensues and can be discerned in the suspension, collapse, or general short-circuiting of the hitherto dominant protocols of representation that may have governed the text. To my mind, in this paragraph Mitchell and Snyder are attempting to define processes of representation that may occur separately (i.e., across individual and distinguishable texts) as well as serialized within a particular text. One of my central points is precisely the fact that even when the disabled character appears to be represented programmatically, the restless dialectic of representation may unmoor her from the programmatic location and place her elsewhere as the dominant aesthetic protocols governing the representation are short-circuited.

To establish the central parameters of aesthetic nervousness, then, a number of things have to be kept in mind. First is that in literature, the disabled are fictional characters created out of language. This point is not made in order to sidestep the responsibility to acknowledge language's social efficaciousness. Rather, I want to stress that as linguistic creations, the disabled in literature may trade a series of features with the nondisabled, thus transferring some of their significations to the nondisabled and vice versa. Furthermore, I want to suggest that when the various references to disability and to disability representation are seen within the broad range of an individual writer's work, it helps to foreground hitherto unacknowledged dimensions of their writing and, in certain cases, this can even lead to a complete revaluation of critical emphasis. Consider in this regard Shakespeare's *Richard III*, for instance, which is of course very widely discussed in disability studies. However, in Shakespeare disability also acts as a metaphor to mark anomalous social states such as those involving half-brothers and bastards. Indeed, there is a studied pattern in Shakespeare where bastards are considered to be internally deformed and villainous, their bastardy being directly correlated to a presumed moral deficit. And so we have the elemental and almost homicidal competition between half-brothers that reappears in conflicts between Robert Falconbridge and his bastard brother Philip in *King John*, between Don John and Don Pedro in *Much Ado About Nothing*, between Edmund and Edgar in *King Lear*, and between Richard III and Edward in *Richard III*. This last play is of course grounded on the resonance of jealousy and brotherhood, as well as on the Machiavellianism of a deformed protagonist. There the disability is placed at the foreground of the action from the beginning and brings together various threads that serve to focalize the question of whether Richard's deformity is an insignia of or indeed the cause of his villainy.[3] Thus to understand Richard III properly, we would have to attend equally to his disability and his bastardy in the wider scheme of Shakespeare's work. Once this is done, we find that our interpretation of the character has to be more complicated than just recognizing his villainy, which of course is the dominant invitation proffered by the play.

The choice of Beckett, Soyinka, Morrison, and Coetzee is partly meant to serve this function of establishing the interrelations between disability and other vectors of representation among the wide oeuvre of each writer. However, comparisons and contrasts within the work of individual writers or indeed between them will not be made chronologically or with the suggestion of evolution and change in the representation of disability. Rather, I shall be focusing on thematic clusterings and on making links between apparently unrelated characters and scenes across the various texts to show how the parameters of aesthetic nervousness operate within individual texts as well as across various representations. Also, the writers will be used as nodal points from which to make connections to the work of other writers. Thus each chapter, though focusing predominantly on the individual writer in question, will also provide a gateway for connecting these writers to various others that have had something to say about disability. Each chapter is conceived of as comparative both in terms of the relations among the works of the main writers in the study and between these and the many other representations of disability that will be touched upon over the course of the discussions.

I want to emphasize my view that to properly establish the contours of aesthetic nervousness, we have to understand disability's resonance on a multiplicity of levels simultaneously; disability acts as a threshold or focal point from which various vectors of the text may be examined. Thus, as we shall see with respect to Toni Morrison, though her physically disabled female characters seem to be strong and empowered, there is often a contradiction between the levels of narratorial perspective, symbolic implication, and the determinants of the interactions among the characters themselves that ends up unsettling the unquestioned sense of strength that we might get from just focusing on what the disabled women in her texts do or do not do. With Beckett, on the other hand, we find that as he proliferates devices by which to undermine the stability of ontological categories, he ends up also undermining the means by which the many disabilities that he frequently represents in his texts may be interpreted. As can be seen from the vast scholarship on Beckett, it is very rare that his impaired characters are read as disabled, even though their disabilities are blatant and should be impossible to ignore. Rather, the characters are routinely assimilated by critics to philosophical categories and read off as such. This is due to the peculiarly self-undermining structures of his works, both the novels and the plays. Beckett is also unusual among the writers in this study in that he seems to fulfill a central feature of what Sandblom (1997) describes as the inextricable link between disease and creativity. Pertinent to the discussion of Beckett's work is that he himself suffered endless illnesses ranging from an arrhythmic heartbeat and night sweats to cysts and abscesses on his fingers, the palm of his left hand, the top of his palate, his scrotum and, most painfully later in life, his left lung. Often these cysts and abscesses had to be lanced or operated upon, leading to great and regular discomfort. It is not for nothing then that the deteriorating and impaired body held a special fascination for him. He used the disabled, maimed, and decaying body as a multiple referent for a variety of ideas that seem to have been at least partially triggered by encounters with others and his own personal experience of pain and temporary disability. This is something that has passed largely unremarked in the critical writings on Beckett, and I propose to center on it to discuss the peculiar status he assigns to disability and pain in works such as *Endgame* and *Molloy*, both of which should to all intents and purposes be "painfull" but are not.

In a way, Wole Soyinka's work is quite different from that of the other three in the study. His writing focuses more securely on a set of ritual dispositions drawn from a traditional Yoruba and African cultural sensibility. This sensibility is then combined with an intense political consciousness, such that each of his plays may be read as partial allegories of the Nigerian and African postcolonial condition. The combination of the ritualistic with the political is something for which Soyinka has become notably famous. What I shall show with regard to his work are the ways in which disability acts as a marker of both ritual and the political, but in ways that interrupt the two domains and force us to rethink the conceptual movement between the two. The final chapter, on Robben Island, will be used to bring to conclusion a particular vector of interpretation that will have been suggested in the chapter on Beckett, given further elaboration in the discussions of Morrison and Soyinka, and picked up and intensified in the one on Coetzee. I shall discuss this in various guises, but they will all come together under the conceptual rubric of the *structure of skeptical interlocution*. In essence, the idea derives from Bakhtin's proposition of the inherent dialogism of speech acts, that anticipation of an interlocutor even when the context of communication does not seem to explicitly denominate one. The choice of the plays of Beckett and Soyinka allows a certain salience to the idea of the (skeptical) interlocutor, since as dramatic texts they incorporate dialogue as an explicit feature of dialogism. But what I have in mind in relation to the structure of skeptical interlocution is a little bit more complicated than can be captured solely in dramatic texts. Rather, I mean to suggest that there is always an anticipation of doubt within the perceptual and imagined horizon of the disabled character in literature, and that this doubt is incorporated into their rep-

resentation. This is so whether the character is represented in the first person, as we see in Beckett's Molloy, or in the third person, as we see in Coetzee's *Life and Times of Michael K.* The chapter on Coetzee will be used to focus on the difference between speech and the elective silence of autistic characters and on the ways in which these raise peculiar problems for the status of the skeptical interlocutor in literary writing. Autism features in that chapter not just as a dimension of disability but as a theoretical paradigm for raising questions about narrativity as such. However, it is when we come to the chapter on Robben Island that the structure of skeptical interlocution will be allowed to take life (literally and metaphorically, as will be demonstrated). The structure of interlocution with regard to the history of Robben Island will help to shed light on how aesthetic nervousness might be extended from discussions of the literary-aesthetic domain to an analysis of historical personages and real-life events.

I should like to address a point of potential confusion that may have arisen in this introduction. So far I have proceeded as though the literary representation of disabled persons and the aesthetic nervousness that attends such representation can be taken as an analogue to the real-life responses toward people with disabilities by society at large. This fusion of levels is only partially intended. For, as I noted earlier, there is no doubt that literary representation of disability somewhat subtends real-life treatment of disabled people in a variety of ways. However, I also want to note that the aesthetic nervousness of the literary-aesthetic domain cannot by any means be said to be equivalent to the responses to disabled persons in reality. To say that the literary model provides an analogue to reality does not mean that it is the same as that reality. The epistemological effect of representation is quite different from the emotional effects of misunderstanding and stereotyping in the real world. Thus the first may be used to illuminate aspects of the second but must not be taken to have exhausted or replaced it. Our commitment must ultimately be to changing the world and not merely reading and commenting on it.

It is important also to state at the outset that central to the ways in which I propose to establish the parameters of aesthetic nervousness is the device of close reading. This seems to me necessary in order to be able to do full justice to the subtle cues by which the literary text "stumbles" (to return to Mitchell and Snyder) and by which the literary representation reveals the parameters of aesthetic nervousness. Apart from Morrison, none of the writers in this study has previously been read from the perspective of disability studies. Part of my task will involve the rather boring process of taxonomizing the disability representations we find in the works in question. This will be done to provide a map of the varied uses to which the writers put the disabled in order to allow us to discern patterns that are elaborated upon or repeated across the works. It is a happy coincidence that all four writers are Nobel Prize winners and thus likely to be widely taken up in literary curricula. My choice of them was not informed by this fact, however (in fact, Coetzee was part of my study long before his Nobel Prize). I settle on them because of my years of teaching and thinking about their work in different contexts and the fact that they enable us to see a full range of discourses regarding disability and other details of literary representation. I wish to see students and other readers being able to pay close attention to all the subtle details of literary representation well beyond the focus on disability, even if that is their

starting point. The focus on disability is thus meant to achieve two related effects: One is to make more prominent the active ethical core that is necessarily related to disability and that hopefully helps to restore a fully ethical reading to literature. The other is that from using disability to open up the possibility of close reading, I hope to encourage us to lift our eyes from the reading of literature to attend more closely to the implications of the social universe around us.

NOTES

1. On first considering this point about the vertiginous fears of the nondisabled regarding disability I focused primarily on Lacan's discussion of the mirror phase and his exploration of the *imagos* of dismemberment that come up for people under psychic stress. From this, I elaborated what I termed the primal scene of the encounter between the disabled and the nondisabled, which, as I argued, was riven by constitutive emotional ambiguities. Even though I still find that perspective persuasive, in the current discussion I want to leave the contours of the psychoanalytic interpretation to one side and instead invoke the work of philosophers and disability writers who have thought and written about this matter. For my earlier argument, see "Disability and Contingency" in *Calibrations: Reading for the Social* (2003). At any rate, though I didn't know it then, the argument about Lacan and the primal scene of disability had already been quite persuasively put by Lennard Davis (1995, 140–142) and so will not be reprised here.

2. For the discussions of the sublime and the beautiful that I have drawn upon, see Allison (2001), Crockett (2001), Ashfield and de Bolla (1996), Caruth (1988), and de Man (1990). The issue of whether the sublime triggers an ethical recognition or not is a contentious one and not yet settled on either side, but Ashfield and de Bolla provide a good account of how the ethical debates on the sublime have unfolded in British literary history from the eighteenth century onward.

3. For particularly insightful readings of *Richard III* from a disability studies perspective, see Mitchell and Snyder (2000, 95–118) and Lennard Davis.

CHAPTER 16

The Social Model of Disability

Tom Shakespeare

INTRODUCTION

In many countries of the world, disabled people and their allies have organised over the last three decades to challenge the historical oppression and exclusion of disabled people (Driedger, 1989; Campbell and Oliver, 1996; Charlton, 1998). Key to these struggles has been the challenge to over-medicalized and individualist accounts of disability. While the problems of disabled people have been explained historically in terms of divine punishment, karma or moral failing, and post-Enlightenment in terms of biological deficit, the disability movement has focused attention onto social oppression, cultural discourse, and environmental barriers.

The global politics of disability rights and deinstitutionalisation has launched a family of social explanations of disability. In North America, these have usually been framed using the terminology of minority groups and civil rights (Hahn, 1988). In the Nordic countries, the dominant conceptualisation has been the relational model (Gustavsson et al., 2005). In many countries, the idea of normalisation and social role valorisation has been inspirational, particularly amongst those working with people with learning difficulties (Wolfensburger, 1972). In Britain, it has been the

social model of disability which has provided the structural analysis of disabled people's social exclusion (Hasler, 1993).

The social model emerged from the intellectual and political arguments of the *Union of Physically Impaired Against Segregation* (UPIAS). This network had been formed after Paul Hunt, a former resident of the Lee Court Cheshire Home, wrote to *The Guardian* newspaper in 1971, proposing the creation of a consumer group of disabled residents of institutions. In forming the organization and developing its ideology, Hunt worked closely with Vic Finkelstein, a South African psychologist, who had come to Britain in 1968 after being expelled for his anti-apartheid activities. UPIAS was a small, hardcore group of disabled people, inspired by Marxism, who rejected the liberal and reformist campaigns of more mainstream disability organisations such as the Disablement Income Group and the Disability Alliance. According to their policy statement (adopted December 1974), the aim of UPIAS was to replace segregated facilities with opportunities for people with impairments to participate fully in society, to live independently, to undertake productive work and to have full control over their own lives. The policy statement defined disabled people as an oppressed group and highlighted barriers:

> We find ourselves isolated and excluded by such things as flights of steps, inadequate public and personal transport, unsuitable housing, rigid work routines in factories and offices, and a lack of up-to-date aids and equipment.
>
> (UPIAS Aims paragraph 1)

Even in Britain, the social model of disability was not the only political ideology on offer to the first generation of activists (Campbell and Oliver, 1996). Other disabled-led activist groups had emerged, including the Liberation Network of People with Disabilities. Their draft Liberation Policy, published in 1981, argued that while the basis of social divisions in society was economic, these divisions were sustained by psychological beliefs in inherent superiority or inferiority. Crucially, the Liberation Network argued that people with disabilities, unlike other groups, suffered inherent problems because of their disabilities. Their strategy for liberation included: developing connections with other disabled people and creating an inclusive disability community for mutual support; exploring social conditioning and positive self-awareness; the abolition of all segregation; seeking control over media representation; working out a just economic policy; encouraging the formation of groups of people with disabilities.

However, the organization which dominated and set the tone for the subsequent development of the British disability movement, and of disability studies in Britain, was UPIAS. Where the Liberation Network was dialogic, inclusive and feminist, UPIAS was hard-line, male-dominated, and determined. The British Council of Organisations of Disabled People, set up as a coalition of disabled-led groups in 1981, adopted the UPIAS approach to disability. Vic Finkelstein and the other BCODP delegates to the first Disabled People's International World Congress in Singapore later that year, worked hard to have their definitions of disability adopted on the global stage (Driedger, 1989). At the same time, Vic Finkelstein, John Swain and others were working with the Open University to create an academic course which would promote and develop disability politics (Finkelstein, 1998). Joining the team was Mike Oliver, who quickly adopted the structural approach to understanding disability, and was to coin the term "social model of disability" in 1983.

WHAT IS THE SOCIAL MODEL OF DISABILITY?

While the first UPIAS Statement of Aims had talked of social problems as an added burden faced by people with impairment, the Fundamental Principles of Disability discussion document, recording their disagreements with the reformist Disability Alliance, went further.

> In our view, it is society which disables physically impaired people. Disability is something imposed on top of our impairments, by the way we are unnecessarily isolated and excluded from full participation in society. Disabled people are therefore an oppressed group in society.
>
> (UPIAS, 1975)

Here and in the later development of UPIAS thinking are the key elements of the social model: the distinction between disability (social exclusion) and impairment (physical limitation) and the claim that disabled people are an oppressed group. Disability is now defined, not in functional terms, but as

> the disadvantage or restriction of activity caused by a contemporary social organisation which takes little or no account of people who have physical impairments and thus excludes them from participation in the mainstream of social activities.
>
> (UPIAS, 1975)

This redefinition of disability itself is what sets the British social model apart from all other socio-political approaches to disability, and what paradoxically gives the social model both its strengths and its weaknesses.

Key to social model thinking is a series of dichotomies:

1. Impairment is distinguished from disability. The former is individual and private, the latter is structural and public. While doctors and professions allied to medicine seek to remedy impairment, the real priority is to accept impairment and to remove disability. Here there is an analogy with feminism, and the distinction between biological sex (male and female) and social gender (masculine and feminine) (Oakley, 1972). Like gender, disability is a culturally and historically specific phenomenon, not a universal and unchanging essence.

2. The social model is distinguished from the medical or individual model. Whereas the former defines disability as a social creation—a relationship between people with impairment and a disabling society—the latter defines disability in terms of individual deficit. Mike Oliver writes:

> Models are ways of translating ideas into practice and the idea underpinning the individual model was that of personal tragedy, while the idea underpinning the social model was that of externally imposed restriction.
> (Oliver, 2004, 19)

Medical model thinking is enshrined in the liberal term "people with disabilities," and in approaches that seek to count the numbers of people with impairment, or to reduce the complex problems of disabled people to issues of medical prevention, cure or rehabilitation. Social model thinking mandates barrier removal, anti-discrimination legislation, independent living and other responses to social oppression. From a disability rights perspective, social model approaches are progressive, medical model approaches are reactionary.

3. Disabled people are distinguished from non-disabled people. Disabled people are an oppressed group, and often non-disabled people and organisations—such as professionals and charities—are the causes or contributors to that oppression. Civil rights, rather than charity or pity, are the way to solve the disability problem. Organisations and services controlled and run by disabled people provide the most appropriate solutions. Research accountable to, and preferably done by, disabled people offers the best insights.

For more than ten years, a debate has raged in Britain about the value and applicability of the social model (Morris, 1991; Crow, 1992; French, 1993; Williams, 1999; Shakespeare and Watson, 2002). In response to critiques, academics and activists maintain that the social model has been misunderstood, misapplied, or even wrongly viewed as a social theory. Many leading advocates of the social model approach maintain that the essential insights developed by UPIAS in the 1970s still remain accurate and valid three decades later.

STRENGTHS OF THE SOCIAL MODEL

As demonstrated internationally, disability activism and civil rights are possible without adopting social model ideology. Yet the British social model is arguably the most powerful form which social approaches to disability have taken. The social model is simple, memorable, and effective, each of which is a key requirement of a political slogan or ideology. The benefits of the social model have been shown in three main areas.

First, the social model, called "the big idea" of the British disability movement (Hasler, 1993), has been effective *politically* in building the social movement of disabled people. It is easily explained and understood, and it generates a clear agenda for social change. The social model offers a straightforward way of distinguishing allies from enemies. At its most basic, this reduces to the terminology people use: "disabled people" signals a social model approach, whereas "people with disabilities" signals a mainstream approach.

Second, by identifying social barriers to be removed, the social model has been effective *instrumentally* in the liberation of disabled people. Michael Oliver argues that the social model is a "practical tool, not a theory, an idea or a concept" (2004, 30). The social model demonstrates that the problems disabled people face are the result of social oppression and exclusion, not their individual deficits. This places the moral responsibility on society to remove the burdens which have been imposed, and to enable disabled people to participate. In Britain, campaigners used the social model philosophy to name the various forms of discrimination which disabled people (Barnes, 1991), and used this evidence as the argument by which to achieve the 1995 Disability Discrimination Act. In the subsequent decade, services, buildings and public transport have been required to be accessible to disabled people, and most statutory and voluntary organizations have adopted the social model approach.

Third, the social model has been effective *psychologically* in improving the self-esteem of disabled people and building a positive sense of collective identity. In traditional accounts of disability, people with impairments feel that they are at fault. Language such as "invalid" reinforce a sense of personal deficit and failure. The focus is on the individual, and on her limitations of body and brain. Lack of self-esteem and self-confidence is a major obstacle to disabled people participating in society. The social model has the power to change the perception of disabled people. The problem of disability is relocated from the individual, to the barriers and attitudes which disable her. It is not the disabled person who is to blame, but society. She does not have to change, society does. Rather than feeling self-pity, she can feel anger and pride.

WEAKNESSES OF THE SOCIAL MODEL

The simplicity which is the hallmark of the social model is also its fatal flaw. The social model's benefits as a slogan and political ideology are its drawbacks as an academic account of disability. Another problem is its authorship by a small group of activists, the majority of whom had spinal injury or other physical impairments and were white heterosexual men. Arguably, had UPIAS included people with learning difficulties, mental health problems, or with more complex physical impairments, or more representative of different experiences, it could not have produced such a narrow understanding of disability.

Among the weaknesses of the social model are:

1. The neglect of impairment as an important aspect of many disabled people's lives. Feminists Jenny Morris (1991), Sally French (1993), and Liz Crow (1992) were pioneers in this criticism of the social model neglect of individual experience of impairment:

> As individuals, most of us simply cannot pretend with any conviction that our impairments are irrelevant because they influence every aspect of our lives. We must find a way to integrate them into our whole experience and identity for the sake of our physical and emotional well-being, and, subsequently, for our capacity to work against Disability.
>
> (Crow, 1992, 7)

The social model so strongly disowns individual and medical approaches, that it risks implying that impairment is not a problem. Whereas other socio-political accounts of disability have developed the important insight that people with impairments are disabled by society as well as by their bodies, the social model suggests that people are disabled by society not by their bodies. Rather than simply opposing medicalization, it can be interpreted as rejecting medical prevention, rehabilitation or cure of impairment, even if this is not what either UPIAS, Finkelstein, Oliver, or Barnes intended. For individuals with static impairments, which do not degenerate or cause medical complications, it may be possible to regard disability as entirely socially created. For those who have degenerative conditions which may cause premature death, or any condition which involves pain and discomfort, it is harder to ignore the negative aspects of impairment. As Simon Williams has argued,

> . . . endorsement of disability solely as social oppression is really only an option, and an erroneous one at that, for those spared the ravages of chronic illness.
>
> (Williams, 1999, 812)

Carol Thomas (1999) has tried to develop the social model to include what she calls "impairment effects," in order to account for the limitations and difficulties of medical conditions. Subsequently, she suggested that a relational interpretation of the social model enables disabling aspects to be attributed to impairment, as well as social oppression:

> once the term "disability" is ring-fenced to mean forms of oppressive social reactions visited upon people with impairments, there is no need to deny that impairment and illness cause some restrictions of activity, or that in many situations both disability and impairment effects interact to place limits on activity.
>
> (2004, 29)

One curious consequence of the ingenious reformulation is that only people with impairment who face oppression can be called disabled people. This relates to another problem:

2. The social model assumes what it needs to prove: that disabled people are oppressed. The sex/gender distinction defines gender as a social dimension, not as oppression. Feminists claimed that gender relations *involved* oppression, but did not define gender relations *as* oppression. However, the social model defines disability as oppression. In other words, the question is not whether disabled people are oppressed in a particular situation, but only the extent to which they are oppressed. A circularity enters into disability research: it is logically impossible for a qualitative researcher to find disabled people who are not oppressed.

3. The analogy with feminist debates about sex and gender highlights another problem: the crude distinction between impairment (medical) and disability (social). Any researcher who does qualitative research with disabled people immediately discovers that in everyday life it is very hard to distinguish clearly between the impact of impairment, and the impact of social barriers (see Watson, 2002; Sherry, 2002). In practice, it is the interaction of individual bodies and social environments which produces disability. For example, steps only become an obstacle if someone has a mobility impairment: each element is necessary but not sufficient for the individual to be disabled. If a person with multiple sclerosis is depressed, how easy is it to make a causal separation between the effect of the impairment itself; her reaction to having an impairment; her reaction to being oppressed and excluded on the basis of having an impairment; other, unrelated reasons for her to be depressed? In practice, social and individual aspects are almost inextricable in the complexity of the lived experience of disability.

Moreover, feminists have now abandoned the sex/gender distinction, because it implies that sex is not a social concept. Judith Butler (1990) and others show that what we think of as sexual difference is always viewed through the lens of gender. Shelley Tremain (2002) has claimed similarly that the social model treats impairment as an unsocialized and universal concept, whereas, like sex, impairment is always already social.

4. The concept of the barrier-free utopia. The idea of the enabling environment, in which all socially imposed barriers are removed, is usually implicit rather than explicit in social model thinking, although it does form the title of a major academic collection (Swain et al., 1993). Vic Finkelstein (1981) also wrote a simple parable of a village designed for wheelchair users to illustrate the way that social model thinking turned the problem of disability on its head. Yet despite the value of approaches such as Universal Design, the concept of a world in which people with impairments were free of environmental barriers is hard to operationalize.

For example, numerous parts of the natural world will remain inaccessible to many disabled people: mountains, bogs, beaches are almost impossible for wheelchair users to traverse, while sunsets, birdsong, and other aspects of nature are difficult for those lacking sight or hearing to experience. In urban settings, many barriers can be mitigated, although historic buildings often cannot easily be adapted. However, accommodations are sometimes incompatible because people with different impairments may require different solutions: blind people prefer steps and defined curbs and indented paving, while wheelchair users need ramps, dropped curbs, and smooth surfaces. Sometimes, people with the same impairment require different solutions: some visually impaired people access text in Braille, others in large

print, audio tape or electronic files. Practicality and resource constraints make it unfeasible to overcome every barrier: for example, the New York subway and London Underground systems would require huge investments to make every line and station accessible to wheelchair users. A copyright library of five million books could never afford to provide all these texts in all the different formats that visually impaired users might potentially require. In these situations, it seems more practical to make other arrangements to overcome the problems: for example, Transport for London have an almost totally accessible fleet of buses, to compensate those who cannot use the tube, while libraries increasingly have arrangements to make particular books accessible on demand, given notice.

Moreover, physical and sensory impairments are in many senses the easiest to accommodate. What would it mean to create a barrier free utopia for people with learning difficulties? Reading and writing and other cognitive abilities are required for full participation in many areas of contemporary life in developed nations. What about people on the autistic spectrum, who may find social contact difficult to cope with: a barrier free utopia might be a place where they did not have to meet, communicate with, or have to interpret other people. With many solutions to the disability problem, the concept of addressing special needs seems more coherent than the concept of the barrier free utopia. Barrier free enclaves are possible, but not a barrier free world.

While environments and services can and should be adapted wherever possible, there remains disadvantage associated with having many impairments which no amount of environmental change could entirely eliminate. People who rely on wheelchairs, or personal assistance, or other provision are more vulnerable and have fewer choices than the majority of able-bodied people. When Michael Oliver claims that

> An aeroplane is a mobility aid for non-flyers in exactly the same way as a wheelchair is a mobility aid for non-walkers.
>
> (Oliver, 1996, 108)

his suggestion is amusing and thought provoking, but cannot be taken seriously. As Michael Bury has argued,

> It is difficult to imagine any modern industrial society (however organised) in which, for example, a severe loss of mobility or dexterity, or sensory impairments, would not be 'disabling' in the sense of restricting activity to some degree. The reduction of barriers to participation does not amount to abolishing disability as a whole.
>
> (Bury, 1997, 137)

Drawing together these weaknesses, a final and important distinction needs to be made. The disability movement has often drawn analogies with other forms of identity politics, as I have done in this chapter. The disability rights struggle has even been called the "Last Liberation Movement" (Driedger, 1989). Yet while disabled people do face discrimination and prejudice, like women, gay and lesbian people, and minority ethnic communities, and while the disability rights movement does resemble in its forms and activities many of these other movements, there is a central and important difference. There is nothing intrinsically problematic about being female or having a different sexual orientation, or a different skin pigmentation or body shape. These other experiences are about wrongful limitation of negative freedom. Remove the social discrimination, and women and people of color and gay and lesbian people will be able to flourish and participate. But disabled people face both discrimination and intrinsic limitations. This claim has three implications. First, even if social barriers are removed as far as practically possible, it will remain disadvantageous to have many forms of impairment. Second, it is harder to celebrate disability than it is to celebrate Blackness, or Gay Pride, or being a woman. "Disability pride" is problematic, because disability is difficult to recuperate as a concept, as it refers either to limitation and incapacity, or else to oppression and exclusion, or else to both dimensions. Third, if disabled people are to be emancipated, then society will have to provide extra resources to meet the needs and overcome the disadvantage which arises from impairment, not just work to minimize discrimination (Bickenbach et al., 1999).

BEYOND THE SOCIAL MODEL?

In this chapter, I have tried to offer a balanced assessment of the strengths and weaknesses of the British social model of disability. While acknowledging the benefits of the social model in launching the disability movement, promoting a positive disability identity, and mandating civil rights legislation and barrier removal, it is my belief that the social model has now become a barrier to further progress.

As a researcher, I find the social model unhelpful in understanding the complex interplay of individual and environmental factors in the lives of disabled people. In policy terms, it seems to me that the social model is a blunt instrument for explaining and combating the social exclusion that disabled people face, and the complexity of our needs. Politically, the social model has generated a form of identity politics which has become inward looking and separatist.

A social approach to disability is indispensable. The medicalization of disability is inappropriate and an obstacle to effective analysis and policy. But the social model is only one of the available options for theorizing disability. More sophisticated and complex approaches are needed, perhaps building on the WHO initiative to create the

International Classification of Functioning, Disability and Health. One strength of this approach is the recognition that disability is a complex phenomenon, requiring different levels of analysis and intervention, ranging from the medical to the socio-political. Another is the insight that disability is not a minority issue, affecting only those people defined as disabled people. As Irving Zola (1989) maintained, disability is a universal experience of humanity.

BIBLIOGRAPHY

Barnes, C. (1991). *Disabled People in Britain and Discrimination.* London: Hurst and Co.

Bickenbach, J. E., Chatterji, S., Badley, E. M., and Ustun, T. B. (1999). "Models of Disablement, Universalism and the International Classification of Impairments, Disabilities and Handicaps." *Social Science and Medicine*, 48: 1173–1187.

Bury, M. (1997). *Health and Illness in a Changing Society.* London: Routledge.

Butler, J (1990). *Gender Trouble: Feminism and the Subversion of Identity.* New York: Routledge.

Campbell, J. and Oliver, M. (1996). *Disability Politics: Understanding Our Past, Changing Our Future.* London: Routledge.

Charlton J (1998). *Nothing About Us Without Us: Disability, Oppression and Empowerment.* Berkeley: University of California Press.

Crow, L. (1992). "Renewing the Social Model of Disability." *Coalition*, July: 5–9.

Dreidger, D. (1989). *The Last Civil Rights Movement.* London: Hurst.

Finkelstein, V. (1981). "To Deny or Not to Deny Disability." In *Handicap in a Social World*, edited by A Brehin et al. Sevenoaks: OUP/Hodder and Stoughton.

Finkelstein, V. (1998). "Emancipating disability studies." In *The Disability Reader: Social Science Perspectives*, edited by T. Shakespeare. London: Cassell.

French, S. (1993). "Disability, Impairment or Something in Between." In *Disabling Barriers, Enabling Environments*, edited by J. Swain, S. French, C. Barnes, C. Thomas. London: Sage, 17–25.

Gustavsson, A., Sandvin, J., Traustadóttir, R. and Tossebrø, J (2005). *Resistance, Reflection and Change: Nordic disability Research.* Lund, Sweden: Studentlitteratur.

Hahn, H. (1988). "The Politics of Physical Differences: Disability and Discrimination." *Journal of Social Issues*, 44 (1) 39–47.

Hasler, F. (1993). "Developments in the Disabled People's Movement." In *Disabling Barriers, Enabling Environments*, edited by J. Swain, S. French, C. Barnes, C. Thomas et al. London: Sage.

Morris, J. (1991). *Pride Against Prejudice.* London: Women's Press.

Oakley, A. (1972). *Sex, Gender and Society.* London: Maurice Temple Smith.

Oliver, M. (1996). *Understanding Disability: From Theory to Practice.* Basingstoke: Macmillan.

Oliver, M. (2004). "The Social Model in Action: If I Had a Hammer." In *Implementing the Social Model of Disability: Theory and Research*, edited by C. Barnes and G. Mercer: Leeds: The Disability Press.

Shakespeare, T. and Watson, N. (2001). "The Social Model of Disability: An Outdated ideology?" In *Exploring Theories and Expanding Methodologies: Where Are We and Where Do We Need to Go? Research in Social Science and Disability volume 2*, edited by S. Barnarrt and B. M. Altman. Amsterdam: JAI.

Sherry, M. (2002). "If Only I Had a Brain." Unpublished PhD dissertation, University of Queensland.

Swain, J., Finkelstein, V., French, S. and Oliver, M. eds. (1993). *Disabling Barriers, Enabling Environments.* London: OUP/Sage.

Thomas, C. (1999). *Female Forms.* Buckingham: Open University Press.

Thomas, C. (2004). "Developing the Social Relational in the Social Model of Disability: A Theoretical Agenda." In *Implementing the Social Model of Disability: Theory and Rresearch*, edited by C. Barnes and G. Mercer. Leeds: The Disability Press.

Tremain, S. (2002). "On the Subject of Impairment." In *Disability/Postmodernity: Embodying Disability Theory*, edited by M. Corker and T. Shakespeare, pp. 32–47. London: Continuum.

Union of the Physically Impaired Against Segregation (1974/5). Policy Statement, available at http://www.leeds.ac.uk/disability-studies/archiveuk/archframe.htm; accessed August 10, 2005.

Union of the Physically Impaired Against Segregation (1975). Fundamental Principles, available at http://www.leeds.ac.uk/disability-studies/archiveuk/archframe.htm; accessed August 10, 2005.

Watson, N. (2002). "Well, I Know This Is Going to Sound Very Strange to You, But I Don't See Myself as a Disabled Person: Identity and Disability." *Disability and Society*, 17, 5: 509–528.

Williams, S. J. (1999). "Is Anybody There? Critical Realism, Chronic Illness, and the Disability Debate." *Sociology of Health and Illness*, 21, 6: 797–819.

Wolfensberger, W. (1972). *The Principle of Normalization in Human Services.* Toronto: National Institute on Mental Retardation.

Zola, I. K. (1989). "Towards the Necessary Universalizing of a Disability Policy." *The Milbank Quarterly*, 67, suppl.2, Pt. 2: 401–428.

CHAPTER 17

Narrative Prosthesis

David Mitchell and Sharon Snyder

LITERATURE AND THE UNDISCIPLINED BODY OF DISABILITY

This chapter prefaces the close readings to come [in *Narrative Prosthesis*] by deepening our theory of narrative prosthesis as shared characteristics in the literary representation of disability. We demonstrate one of a variety of approaches in disability studies to the "problem" that disability and disabled populations pose to all cultures. Nearly every culture views disability as a problem in need of a solution, and this belief establishes one of the major modes of historical address directed toward people with disabilities. The necessity for developing various kinds of cultural accommodations to handle the "problem" of corporeal difference (through charitable organizations, modifications of physical architecture, welfare doles, quarantine, genocide, euthanasia programs, etc.) situates people with disabilities in a profoundly ambivalent relationship to the cultures and stories they inhabit. The perception of a "crisis" or a "special situation" has made disabled people the subject of not only governmental policies and social programs but also a primary object of literary representation.

Our thesis centers not simply upon the fact that people with disabilities have been the object of representational treatments, but rather that their function in literary discourse is primarily twofold: disability pervades literary narrative, first, as a stock feature of characterization and, second, as an opportunistic metaphorical device. We term this perpetual discursive dependency upon disability *narrative prosthesis*. Disability lends a distinctive idiosyncrasy to any character that differentiates the character from the anonymous background of the "norm." To exemplify this phenomenon, the opening half of this chapter analyzes the Victorian children's story *The Steadfast Tin Soldier* in order to demonstrate that disability serves as a primary impetus of the storyteller's efforts. In the second instance, disability also serves as a metaphorical signifier of social and individual collapse. Physical and cognitive anomalies promise to lend a "tangible" body to textual abstractions; we term this metaphorical use of disability the *materiality of metaphor* and analyze its workings as narrative prosthesis in our concluding discussion of Sophocles' drama *Oedipus the King*. We contend that disability's centrality to these two principal representational strategies establishes a conundrum: while stories rely upon the potency of disability as a symbolic figure, they rarely take up disability as an experience of social or political dimensions.

While each of the chapters that follow [in *Narrative Prosthesis*] set out some of the key cultural components and specific historical contexts that inform this history of disabled representations, our main objective addresses the development of a representational or "literary" history. By "literary" we mean to suggest a form of writing that explicitly values the production of what narrative theorists such as Barthes, Blanchot, and Chambers have referred to as "open-ended" narrative.[1] The identification of the open-ended narrative differentiates a distinctively "literary" component of particular kinds of storytelling: those texts that not only deploy but explicitly foreground the "play" of multiple meanings as a facet of their discursive production. While this definition does not overlook the fact that all texts are inherently "open" to a multiplicity of interpretations, our notion of literary narrative identifies works that *stage* the arbitrariness of linguistic sign systems as a characterizing feature of their plots and commentaries. Not only do the artistic and philosophical works under discussion here present themselves as available to a multiplicity of readings, they openly perform their textual *inexhaustibility*. Each shares a literary objective of destabilizing sedimented cultural meanings that accrue around ideas of bodily "deviance." Thus, we approach the writings of Montaigne, Nietzsche, Shakespeare, Melville, Anderson, Dunn, and an array of post-1945 American authors as writers who interrogate the objectives of narrative in general and the corporeal body in particular as discursive products. Their narratives all share a self-reflexive mode of address about their own textual production of disabled bodies.

This textual performance of ever-shifting and unstable meanings is critical in our interpretive approach to the representation of disability. The close readings that follow hinge upon the identification of disability as an ambivalent and mutable category of cultural and literary investment. Within literary narratives, disability serves as an interruptive force that confronts cultural truisms. The inherent vulnerability and variability of bodies serves literary narratives as a metonym for that which refuses to conform to the mind's desire for order and rationality. Within this schema, disability acts as a metaphor and fleshly example of the body's unruly resistance to the cultural desire to "enforce normalcy."[2] The literary narratives we discuss all deploy the mutable or "deviant" body as an "unbearable weight" (to use Susan Bordo's phrase) in order to counterbalance the "meaning-laden" and ethereal projections of the mind. The body's weighty materiality functions as a textual and cultural other—an object with its own undisciplined language that exceeds the text's ability to control it.

As many theorists have pointed out, this representational split between body and mind/text has been inherited from Descartes (although we demonstrate that disability has been entrenched in these assumptions throughout history). Keeping in mind that the perception of disability shifts from one epoch to another, and sometimes within decades and years, we want to argue that the disabled body has consistently held down a "privileged" position with respect to thematic variations on the mind/body split. Whether a culture approaches the body's materiality as a denigrated symbol of earthly contamination (such as in early Christian cultures), or as a perfectible *technē* of the self (as in ancient Athenian culture), or as an object of medical interpretation (as in Victorian culture), or as specular commodity in the age of electronic media (as is the case in postmodernism), disability perpetually serves as the symbolical symptom to be interpreted by discourses on the body. Whereas the "able" body has no definitional core (it poses as transparently "average" or "normal"), the disabled body surfaces as any body capable of being narrated as "outside the norm." Within such a representational schema, literary narratives revisit disabled bodies as a reminder of the "real" physical limits that "weigh down" transcendent ideals of the mind and knowledge-producing disciplines. In this sense, disability serves as the *hard kernel* or recalcitrant corporeal matter that cannot be deconstructed away by the textual operations of even the most canny narratives or philosophical idealisms.[3]

For our purposes in [*Narrative Prosthesis*], the representation of disability has both allowed an interrogation of static beliefs about the body and also erupted as the unseemly *matter* of narrative that cannot be textually undone. We therefore forward readings of disability as a narrative device upon which the literary writer of "open-ended" narratives depends for his or her disruptive punch. Our phrase *narrative prosthesis* is meant to indicate that disability has been used throughout history as a crutch upon which literary narratives lean for their representational power, disruptive potentiality, and analytical insight. Bodies show up in stories as dynamic entities that resist or refuse the cultural scripts assigned to them. While we do not simply extol these literary approaches to the representation of the body (particularly in relation to recurring tropes of disability), we want to demonstrate that the disabled body represents a potent symbolic site of literary investment.

The reasons for this dependency upon disability as a device of characterization and interrogation are many, and our concept of narrative prosthesis establishes a variety of motivations that ground the narrative deployment of the "deviant" body. However, what surfaces as a theme throughout these chapters is the paradoxical impetus that makes disability into both a destabilizing sign of cultural prescriptions about the body *and* a deterministic vehicle of characterization for characters constructed as disabled. Thus, in works as artistically varied and culturally distinct as Shakespeare's *Richard III*, Montaigne's "Of Cripples," Melville's *Moby-Dick*, Nietzsche's *Thus Spoke Zarathustra*, Anderson's *Winesburg, Ohio*, Faulkner's *The Sound and the Fury*, Salinger's *The Catcher in the Rye*, Lee's *To Kill a Mockingbird*, Kesey's *One Flew Over the Cuckoo's Nest*, Dunn's *Geek Love*, Powers's *Operation Wandering Soul*, and Egoyan's *The Sweet Hereafter*, the meaning of the relationship between having a physical disability and the nature of a character's identity comes under scrutiny. Disability recurs in these works as a potent force that challenges cultural ideals of the "normal" or "whole" body. *At the same time, disability also operates as the textual obstacle that causes the literary operation of open-endedness to close down or stumble.*

This "closing down" of an otherwise permeable and dynamic narrative form demonstrates the historical conundrum of disability. Characters such as Montaigne's "les boiteux," Shakespeare's "hunchback'd king," Melville's "crippled" captain, Nietzsche's interlocutory "throng of cripples," Anderson's storied "grotesques," Faulkner's "tale told by an idiot," Salinger's fantasized commune of deaf-mutes, Lee's racial and cognitive outsiders, Kesey's ward of acutes and chronics, Dunn's chemically altered freaks, and Power's postapocalyptic wandering children provide powerful counterpoints to their respective cultures' normalizing Truths about the construction of deviance in particular, and the fixity of knowledge systems in general. Yet each of these characterizations also evidences that the artifice of disability binds disabled characters to a programmatic (even deterministic) identity. Disability may provide an explanation for the origins of a character's identity, but its deployment usually proves either too programmatic or unerringly "deep" and mysterious. In each work analyzed in [*Narrative Prosthesis*], disability is used to underscore, in the words of Richard Powers, adapting the theories of Lacan, that the body functions "like a language" as a dynamic network of misfirings and arbitrary adaptations (*Goldbug* 545). Yet, this defining corporeal unruliness consistently produces characters who are indentured to their biological programming in the most essentializing manner. Their disabilities surface to explain everything or nothing with respect to their portraits as embodied beings.

All of the above examples help to demonstrate one of the central assumptions undergirding [*Narrative Prosthesis*]: *disability is foundational to both cultural definition and to the literary narratives that challenge normalizing prescriptive ideals.* By contrasting and comparing the depiction of disability across cultures and histories, one realizes that disability provides an important barometer by which to assess shifting values and norms imposed upon the body. Our approach in the chapters that follow [in ibid.] is to treat disability as a narrative device—an artistic prosthesis—that reveals the pervasive dependency of artistic, cultural, and philosophical discourses upon the powerful alterity assigned to people with disabilities. In short, disability characterization can be understood as a prosthetic contrivance upon which so many of our cultural and literary narratives rely.

THE (IN)VISIBILITY OF PROSTHESIS

The hypothesis of this *discursive dependency* upon disability strikes most scholars and readers at first glance as relatively insubstantial. During a recent conference of the Herman Melville Society in Volos, Greece, we met a scholar from Japan interested in representations of disability in American literature. When asked if Japanese literature made use of disabled characters to the same extent as American and European literatures, he honestly replied that he had never encountered any. Upon further reflection, he listed several examples and laughingly added that of course the Nobel Prize winner Kenzaburo Oë wrote almost exclusively about the subject. This "surprise" about the pervasive nature of disabled images in national literatures catches even the most knowledgeable scholars unaware. Without developed models for analyzing the purpose and function of representational strategies of disability, readers tend to filter a multitude of disability figures absently through their imaginations.

For film scholarship, Paul Longmore has perceptively formulated this paradox, asking why we screen so many images of disability and simultaneously screen them out of our minds. In television and film portraits of disability, Longmore argues, this screening out occurs because we are trained to compartmentalize impairment as an isolated and individual condition of existence. Consequently, we rarely connect together stories of people with disabilities as evidence of a wider systemic predicament. This same phenomenon can be applied to other representational discourses.

As we discussed in our introduction to *The Body and Physical Difference*, our current models of minority representations tend to formulate this problem of literary/critical neglect in the obverse manner (5). One might expect to find the argument in the pages to come that disability is an ignored, overlooked, or marginal experience in literary narrative, that its absence marks an ominous silence in the literary repertoire of human experiences. In pursuing such an argument one could rightly redress, castigate, or bemoan the neglect of this essential life experience within discourses that might have seen fit to take up the important task of exploring disability in serious terms. Within such an approach, disability would prove to be an unarticulated subject whose real-life counterparts could then charge that their own social marginality was the result of an attendant representational erasure outside of medical discourses. Such a methodology would theorize that disability's absence proves evidence of a profound cultural repression to escape the reality of biological and cognitive differences.

However, what we hope to demonstrate in [*Narrative Prosthesis*] is that disability has an unusual literary history. Between the social marginality of people with disabilities and their corresponding representational milieus, disability undergoes a different representational fate. While racial, sexual, and ethnic criticisms have often founded their critiques upon a pervasive absence of their images in the dominant culture's literature, we argue that images of disabled people abound in history.[4] Even if we disregard the fact that entire fields of study have been devoted to the assessment, cataloging, taxonomization, pathologization, objectification, and rehabilitation of disabled people, one is struck by disability's prevalence in discourses outside of medicine and the hard sciences. Once a reader begins to seek out representations of disability in our literatures, it is difficult to avoid their proliferation in texts with which one believed oneself to be utterly familiar. Consequently, as in the discussion of images of disability in Japanese literature mentioned above, the representational prevalence of people with disabilities is far from absent or tangential. As we discussed in *Narrative Prosthesis,* scholarship in the humanities study of disability has sought to pursue previously unexplored questions of the utility of disability to numerous discursive modes, including literature. Our hypothesis in *Narrative Prosthesis* is a paradoxical one: disabled peoples' social invisibility has occurred in the wake of their perpetual circulation throughout print history. This question is not simply a matter of stereotypes or "bad objects," to borrow Naomi Schor's phrase.[5] Rather, the interpretation of representations of disability strikes at the very core of cultural definitions and values. What is the significance of the fact that the earliest known cuneiform tablets catalog 120 omens interpreted from the "deformities" of Sumerian fetuses and irregularly shaped sheep's and calf's livers? How does one explain the disabled gods, such as the blind Hod, the one-eyed Odin, the one-armed Tyr, who are central to Norse myths, or Hephaestus, the "crook-footed god," in Greek literature? What do these modes of representation reveal about cultures as they forward or suppress physical differences? Why does the "visual" spectacle of so many disabilities become a predominating trope in the nonvisual textual mediums of literary narratives?

SUPPLEMENTING THE VOID

What calls stories into being, and what does disability have to do with this most basic preoccupation of narrative? Narrative prosthesis (or the dependency of literary narratives upon disability) forwards the notion that all narratives operate out of a desire to compensate for a limitation or to reign in excess. This narrative approach to difference identifies the literary object par excellence as that which has become extraordinary—a deviation from a widely accepted norm. Literary narratives begin a process of explanatory compensation wherein perceived "aberrancies" can be rescued from ignorance, neglect, or misunderstanding for their readerships. As Michel de Certeau explains in his well-known essay "The Savage 'I,' " the new world travel narrative in the fifteenth and sixteenth centuries provides a model for thinking about the movement of all narrative. A narrative is inaugurated "by the search for the strange, which is presumed different from the place assigned it in the beginning by the discourse of the culture" from which it originates (69). The very need for a story is called into being when something has gone amiss with the known world, and, thus, the language of a tale seeks to comprehend that which has stepped out of line. In this sense, stories compensate for an unknown or unnatural deviance that begs an explanation.

Our notion of narrative prosthesis evolves out of this specific recognition: a narrative issues to resolve or correct—to "prostheticize" in David Wills's sense of the term—a deviance marked as improper to a social context. A simple schematic of narrative structure might run thus: first, a deviance or marked difference is exposed to a reader; second, a narrative consolidates the need for its own existence by calling for an explanation of the deviation's origins and formative consequences; third, the deviance is brought from the periphery of concerns to the center of the story to come; and fourth, the remainder of the story rehabilitates or fixes the deviance in some manner. This fourth step of the repair of deviance may involve an obliteration of the difference through a "cure," the rescue of the despised object from social censure, the extermination of the deviant as a purification of the social body, or the revaluation of an alternative mode of being. Since what we now call disability has been historically narrated as that which characterizes a body as deviant from shared norms of bodily appearance and ability, disability has functioned throughout history as one of the most marked and remarked upon differences that originates the act of storytelling. Narratives turn signs of cultural deviance into textually marked bodies.

In one of our six-year-old son's books entitled *The Steadfast Tin Soldier,* this prosthetic relation of narrative to physical dif-ference is exemplified. The story opens with a child receiving a box of tin soldiers as a birthday gift. The twenty-five soldiers stand erect and uniform in every way, for they "had all been made from the same tin spoon" (Campbell 1). Each of the soldiers comes equipped with a rifle and bayonet, a blue and red outfit signifying membership in the same regiment, black boots, and a stern military visage. The limited omniscient narrator inaugurates the conflict that will propel the story by pointing out a lack in one soldier that mars the uniformity of the gift: "All of the soldiers were exactly alike, with the exception of one, who differed from the rest in having only one leg" (2). This unfortunate blemish, which mars the otherwise flawless ideal of the soldiers standing in unison, becomes the springboard for the story that ensues. The incomplete leg becomes a locus for attention, and from this imperfection a story issues forth. The twenty-four perfect soldiers are quickly left behind in the box for the reason of their very perfection and uniformity—the "ideal" or "intended" soldier's form promises no story. As Barbara Maria Stafford points out, "there [is] only a single way of being healthy and lovely, but an infinity of ways of being sick and wretched" (284). This infinity of ways helps to explain the pervasive dependency of literary narratives upon the trope of disability. Narrative interest solidifies only in the identification and pursuit of an anomaly that inaugurates the exceptional tale or the tale of exception.

The story of *The Steadfast Tin Soldier* stands in a prosthetic relation to the missing leg of the titular protagonist. The narrative in question (and narrative in a general sense) rehabilitates or compensates for its "lesser" subject by demonstrating that the outward flaw "attracts" the storyteller's— and by extension the reader's—interest. The act of characterization is such that narrative must establish the exceptionality of its subject matter to justify the telling of a story. A subject demands a story only in relation to the degree that it can establish its own extraordinary circumstances.[6] The normal, routine, average, and familiar (by definition) fail to mobilize the storytelling effort because they fall short of the litmus test of exceptionality. The anonymity of normalcy is no story at all. Deviance serves as the basis and common denominator of all narrative. In this sense, the missing leg presents the aberrant soldier as the story's focus, for his physical difference exiles him from the rank and file of the uniform and physically undifferentiated troop. Whereas a sociality might reject, isolate, institutionalize, reprimand, or obliterate this liability of a single leg, narrative embraces the opportunity that such a "lack" provides—in fact, wills it into existence—as the impetus that calls a story into being. Such a paradox underscores the ironic promise of disability to all narrative.

Display demands difference. The arrival of a narrative must be attended by the "unsightly" eruption of the anomalous (often physical in nature) within the social field of vision. The (re)mark upon disability begins with a stare, a gesture of disgust, a slander or derisive comment upon bodily ignominy, a note of gossip about a rare or unsightly presence, a comment upon the unsuitability of deformity for the appetites of polite society, or a sentiment about the unfortunate circumstances that bring disabilities into being. This ruling out-of-bounds of the socially anomalous subject engenders an act of violence that stories seek to 'rescue" or "reclaim" as worthy of narrative attention. Stories always perform a compensatory function in their efforts to renew interest in a previously denigrated object. While there exist myriad inroads to the identification of the anomalous—femininity, race, class, sexuality—disability services this narrative appetite for difference as often as any other constructed category of deviance.

The politics of this recourse to disability as a device of narrative characterization demonstrates the importance of disability to storytelling itself. Literary narratives support our appetites for the exotic by posing disability as an "alien" terrain that promises the revelation of a previously uncomprehended experience. Literature borrows the potency of the lure of difference that a socially stigmatized condition provides. Yet the reliance upon disability in narrative rarely develops into a means of identifying people with disabilities as a disenfranchised cultural constituency. The ascription of absolute singularity to disability performs a contradictory operation: a character "stands out" as a result of an attributed blemish, but this exceptionality divorces him or her from a shared social identity. As in the story of *The Steadfast Tin Soldier*, a narrative disability establishes the uniqueness of an individual character and is quickly left behind as a purely biological fact. Disability marks a character as "unlike" the rest of a fiction's cast, and once singled out, the character becomes a case of special interest who retains originality to the detriment of all other characteristics. Disability cannot be accommodated within the ranks of the norm(als), and, thus, the options for dealing with the difference that drives the story's plot is twofold: a disability is either left behind or punished for its lack of conformity.

In the story of *The Steadfast Tin Soldier* we witness the exercise of both operations on the visible difference that the protagonist's disability poses. Once the soldier's incomplete leg is identified, its difference is quickly nullified. Nowhere in the story does the narrator call attention to a difficult negotiation that must be attempted as a result of the missing appendage. In fact, like the adventurer of de Certeau's paradigmatic travel narrative, the tin figure undergoes a series of epic encounters without further reference to his limitation: after he falls out of a window, his bayonet gets stuck in a crack; a storm rages over him later that night; two boys find the figure, place him into a newspaper boat, and sail him down the gutter into a street drain; he is accosted by a street rat who poses as gatekeeper to the underworld; the newspaper boat sinks in a canal where the soldier is swallowed by a large fish; and finally he is returned to his home of origin when the family purchases the fish for dinner and discovers the one-legged figure in the belly. The series of dangerous encounters recalls the epic adventure of the physically able Odysseus on his way home from Troy; likewise, the tin soldier endures the physically taxing experience without further remark upon the incomplete leg in the course of the tale. The journey and ultimate return home embody the cyclical nature of all narrative (and the story of disability in particular)— the deficiency inaugurates the need for a story but is quickly forgotten once the difference is established.

However, a marred appearance cannot ultimately be allowed to return home unscathed. Near the end of the story the significance of the missing leg returns when the tin soldier is reintroduced to his love—the paper maiden who pirouettes upon one leg. Because the soldier mistakes the dancer as possessing only one leg like himself, the story's conclusion hinges upon the irony of an argument about human attraction based upon shared likeness. If the maiden shares the fate of one-leggedness, then, the soldier reasons, she must be meant for him. However, in a narrative twist of deus ex machina the blemished soldier is inexplicably thrown into the fire by a boy right at the moment of his imagined reconciliation with the "one-legged" maiden. One can read this ending as a punishment for his willingness to desire someone physically perfect and therefore unlike himself. Shelley's story of Frankenstein (discussed in chapter

5 [of *Narrative Prosthesis*]) ends in the monster's anticipated obliteration on his own funeral pyre in the wake of his misinterpretation as monstrous, and the tin soldier's fable reaches its conclusion in a similar manner. Disability inaugurates narrative, but narrative inevitably punishes its own prurient interests by overseeing the extermination of the object of its fascination.

THE PHYSIOGNOMY OF DISABILITY

What is the significance of disability as a pervasive category of narrative interest? Why do the convolutions, distortions, and ruptures that mark the disabled body's surface prove seductive to literary representation? What is the relationship of the external evidence of disability's perceived deviances and the core of the disabled subject's being? The disabled body occupies a crossroads in the age-old literary debate about the relationship of form to content. Whereas the "unmarred" surface enjoys its cultural anonymity and promises little more than a confirmation of the adage of a "healthy" mind in a "healthy" body, disability signifies a more variegated and sordid series of assumptions and experiences. Its unruliness must be tamed by multiple mappings of the surface. If form leads to content or "embodies" meaning, then disability's disruption of acculturated bodily norms also suggests a corresponding misalignment of subjectivity itself.

In *Volatile Bodies* Elizabeth Grosz argues that philosophy has often reduced the body to a "fundamental continuity with brute, inorganic matter" (8). Instead of this reductive tendency, Grosz calls for a more complex engagement with our theorizations of the body: "the body provides a point of mediation between what is perceived as purely internal and accessible only to the subject and what is external and publicly observable, a point from which to rethink the opposition between the inside and the outside" (20). Approaching the body as a mediating force between the outside world and internal subjectivity would allow a more thoroughgoing theory of subjectivity's relationship to materiality. In this way, Grosz argues that the body should not be understood as a receptacle or package for the contents of subjectivity, but rather plays an important role in the formation of psychic identity itself.

Disability will play a crucial role in the reformulation of the opposition between interior and exterior because physical differences have so often served as an example of bodily form following function or vice versa. The mutability of bodies causes them to change over time (both individually and historically), and yet the disabled body is sedimented within an ongoing narrative of breakdown and abnormality. However, while we situate our argument in opposition to reading physical disability as a one-to-one correspondence with subjecthood, we do not deny its role as a foundational aspect of identity. The disabled subject's navigation of social attitudes toward people with disabilities, medical pathologies, the management of embodiment itself, and daily encounters with "perfected" physicalities in the media demonstrates that the disabled body has a substantial impact upon subjectivity as a whole. The study of disability must understand the impact of the experience of disability upon subjectivity *without simultaneously situating the internal and external body within a strict mirroring relationship to one another.*

In literature this mediating role of the external body with respect to internal subjectivity is often represented as a relation of strict correspondence. Either the "deviant" body deforms subjectivity, or "deviant" subjectivity violently erupts upon the surface of its bodily container. In either instance the corporeal body of disability is represented as manifesting its own internal

symptoms. Such an approach places the body in an automatic physiognomic relation to the subjectivity it harbors. As Barbara Maria Stafford has demonstrated, practices of interpreting the significance of bodily appearances since the eighteenth century have depended upon variations of the physiognomic method.

> Physiognomics was body criticism. As corporeal connoisseurship, it diagnosed unseen spiritual qualities by scrutinizing visible traits. Since its adherents claimed privileged powers of detection, it was a somewhat sinister capability. . . . The master eighteenth-century physiognomist, Lavater, noted that men formed conjectures "by reasoning from the exterior to the interior." He continued: "What is universal nature but physiognomy. Is not everything surface and contents? Body and soul? External effect and internal faculty? Invisible principle and visible end?" (84)

For cultures that operated upon models of bodily interpretation prior to the development of internal imaging techniques, the corporeal surface was freighted with significance. Physiognomy became a paradigm of access to the ephemeral and intangible workings of the interior body. Speculative qualities such as moral integrity, honesty, trustworthiness, criminality, fortitude, cynicism, sanity, and so forth, suddenly became available for scrutiny by virtue of the "irregularities" of the body that enveloped them. For the physiognomist, the body allowed meaning to be inferred from the outside in; such a speculative practice resulted in the ability to anticipate intangible qualities of one's personhood without having to await the "proof" of actions or the intimacy of a relationship developed over time. By "reasoning from the exterior to the interior," the trained physiognomist extracted the meaning of the soul without the permission or participation of the interpreted.

If the "external effect" led directly to a knowledge of the "internal faculty," then those who inhabited bodies deemed "outside the norm" proved most ripe for a scrutiny of their moral or intellectual content. Since disabled people by definition embodied a form that was identified as "outside" the normal or permissible, their visages and bodily outlines became the physiognomist's (and later the pathologist's) object par excellence. Yet, the "sinister capability" of physiognomy proves more complex than just the exclusivity of interpretive authority that Stafford suggests. If the body would offer a surface manifestation of internal symptomatology, then disability and deformity automatically preface an equally irregular subjectivity. Physiognomy proves a deadly practice to a population already existing on the fringes of social interaction and "humanity." While the "authorized" physiognomist was officially sanctioned to interpret the symbology of the bodily surface, the disabled person became every person's Rorschach test. While physiognomists discerned the nuances of facial countenances and phrenologists surveyed protuberances of the skull, the extreme examples offered by those with physical disabilities and deformities invited the armchair psychology of the literary practitioner to participate in the symbolic manipulation of bodily exteriors.

Novelists, dramatists, philosophers, poets, essayists, painters, and moralists all flocked to the site of a physiognomic circus from the eighteenth century on. "Irregular" bodies became a fertile field for symbolists of all stripes. Disability and deformity retained their fascination for would-be interpreters because their "despoiled" visages commanded a rationale that narrative (textual or visual) promised to decipher. Because disability represents that which goes awry in the normalizing bodily schema, narratives sought to unravel the riddle of anomaly's origins. Such a riddle

was inherently social in its making. The physiognomic corollary seemed to provide a way in to the secrets of identity itself. The chapters that follow demonstrate that the problem of the representation of disability is not the search for a more "positive" story of disability, as it has often been formulated in disability studies, *but rather a thoroughgoing challenge to the undergirding authorization to interpret that disability invites*. There is a politics at stake in the fact that disability inaugurates an explanatory need that the unmarked body eludes by virtue of its physical anonymity. To participate in an ideological system of bodily norms that promotes some kinds of bodies while devaluing others is to ignore the malleability of bodies and their definitively mutant natures.

Stafford's argument notwithstanding, the body's manipulation by physiognomic practices did not develop as an exclusively eighteenth-century phenomenon. Our own research demonstrates that while physiognomics came to be consolidated as a scientific ideology in the eighteenth and nineteenth centuries, people with disabilities and deformities have always been subject to varieties of this interpretive practice. Elizabeth Cornelia Evans argues that physiognomic beliefs can be traced back as far as ancient Greece. She cites Aristotle as promoting physiognomic reasoning when he proclaims,

> It is possible to infer character from physique, if it is granted that body and soul change together in all natural affections . . . For if a peculiar affection applies to any individual class, e.g., courage to lions, there must be some corresponding sign for it; for it has been assumed that body and soul are affected together (7).

In fact, one might argue that physiognomics came to be consolidated out of a general historical practice applied to the bodies of disabled peoples. If the extreme evidence of marked physical differences provided a catalog of reliable signs, then perhaps more minute bodily differentiations could also be cataloged and interpreted. In this sense, people with disabilities ironically served as the historical locus for the invention of physiognomy.

As we pointed out earlier, the oldest surviving tablets found along the Tigris River in Mesopotamia and dated from 3000 to 2000 B.C. deployed a physiognomic method to prognosticate from deformed fetuses and irregular animal livers. The evidence of bodily anomalies allowed royalty and high priests to forecast harvest cycles, geographic conditions, the outcomes of impending wars, and the future of city-states. The symbolic prediction of larger cultural conditions from physical differences suggests one of the primary differences between the ancient and modern periods: physical anomalies metamorphosed from a symbolic interpretation of worldly meanings to a primarily individualized locus of information. The movement of disability from a macro to a micro level of prediction underscores our point that disability has served as a foundational category of cultural interpretation. The long-standing practice of physiognomic readings demonstrates that disability and deformity serve as the impetus to analyze an otherwise obscured meaning or pattern at the individual level. In either case the overdetermined symbolism ascribed to disabled bodies obscured the more complex and banal reality of those who inhabited them.

THE MATERIALITY OF METAPHOR

Like Oedipus (another renowned disabled fictional creation), cultures thrive upon solving the riddle of disability's rhyme and reason. When the limping Greek protagonist overcomes the Sphinx by answering "man who walks with a cane" as the concluding answer to her three-part query,

we must assume that his own disability served as an experiential source for this insight. The master riddle solver in effect trumps the Sphinx's feminine otherness with knowledge gleaned from his own experience of inhabiting an alien body. In doing so, Oedipus taps into the cultural reservoir of disability's myriad symbolic associations as an interpretive source for his own riddle-solving methodology. Whereas disability usually provides the riddle in need of a narrative solution, in this instance the experience of disability momentarily serves as the source of Oedipus's interpretive mastery. Yet, Sophocles' willingness to represent disability as a mode of experience-based knowledge proves a rare literary occasion and a fleeting moment in the play's dramatic structure.

While Oedipus solves the Sphinx's riddle in the wake of his own physical experience as a lame interpreter and an interpreter of lameness, his disability remains inconsequential to the myth's plot. Oedipus's disability—the result of Laius's pinning of his infant son's ankles as he sends him off to die of exposure— "marks" his character as distinctive and worthy of the exceptional tale. Beyond this physical fact, Sophocles neglects to explore the relationship of the body's mediating function with respect to Oedipus's kingly subjectivity. Either his "crippling" results in an insignificant physical difference, or the detailing of his difference can be understood to embody a vaguely remembered history of childhood violence enacted against him by his father. The disability remains a physical fact of his character that the text literally overlooks once this difference is established as a remnant of his repressed childhood. Perhaps those who share the stage with Oedipus either have learned to look away from his disability or have imbibed the injunction of polite society to refuse commentary upon the existence of the protagonist's physical difference.

However, without the pinning of Oedipus's ankles and his resulting lameness two important aspects of the plot would be compromised. First, Oedipus might have faltered at the riddle of the Sphinx like others before him and fallen prey to the voracious appetite of the she-beast; second, Sophocles' protagonist would lose the physical sign that literally connects him to an otherwise inscrutable past. In this sense, Oedipus's physical difference secures key components of the plot that allow the riddle of his identity to be unraveled. At the same time, his disability serves as the source of little substantive commentary in the course of the drama itself. Oedipus as a "lame interpreter" establishes the literal source of his ability to solve the baffling riddle and allows the dramatist to metaphorize humanity's incapacity to fathom the dictums of the gods. This movement exemplifies the literary oscillation between micro and macro levels of metaphorical meaning supplied by disability. Sophocles later moves to Oedipus's self-blinding as a further example of how the physical body provides a corporeal correlative to the ability of dramatic myth to bridge personal and public symbology.

What is of interest for us in this ancient text is the way in which one can read its representational strategy as a paradigm for literary approaches to disability. The ability of disabled characters to allow authors the metaphorical "play" between macro and micro registers of meaning-making establishes the role of the body in literature as a liminal point in the representational process. In his study of editorial cartoonings and caricatures of the body leading up to the French Revolution, Antoine de Baecque argues that the corporeal metaphor provided a means of giving the abstractions of political ideals an "embodied" power. To "know oneself" and provide a visual correlative to a political commentary, French cartoonists and essayists deployed the body as a metaphor because the body "succeeds in *connecting* narrative and knowledge, meaning and knowing" most viscerally (5). This form of textual embodiment concretizes an otherwise ephemeral concept within a corporeal essence. To give an abstraction a body allows the idea to simulate a foothold in the material would that it would otherwise fail to procure.

Whereas an ideal such as democracy imparts a weak and abstracted notion of governmental and economic reform, for example, the embodied caricature of a hunchbacked monarch overshadowed by a physically superior democratic citizen proved more powerful than any ideological argument. Instead of political harangue, the body offers an illusion of fixity to a textual effect:

> [Body] metaphors were able simultaneously to describe the event and to make the description attain the level of the imaginary. The deployment of these bodily *topoi*—the degeneracy of the nobility, the impotence of the king, the herculean strength of the citizenry, the goddesses of politics appearing naked like Truth, the congenital deformity of the aristocrats, the bleeding wound of the martyrs—allowed political society to represent itself at a pivotal moment of its history. . . . One must pass through the [bodily] forms of a narrative in order to reach knowledge. (De Baecque 4–5)

Such a process of giving body to belief exemplifies the corporeal seduction of the body to textual mediums. The desire to access the seeming solidity of the body's materiality offers representational literatures a way of grasping that which is most unavailable to them. For de Baecque, representing a body in its specificity as the bearer of an otherwise intangible concept grounds the reality of an ideological meaning. The passage through a bodily form helps secure a knowledge that would otherwise drift away of its own insubstantiality. The corporeal metaphor offers narrative the one thing it cannot possess—an anchor in materiality. Such a process embodies the materiality of metaphor; and literature is the writing that aims to concretize theory through its ability to provide an embodied account of physical, sensory life.

While de Baecque's theory of the material metaphor argues that the attempt to harness the body to a specific ideological program provides the text with an illusory opportunity to embody Truth, he overlooks the fact that the same process embeds the body within a limiting array of symbolic meanings: crippling conditions equate with monarchical immobility, corpulence evidences tyrannical greed, deformity represents malevolent motivation, and so on. Delineating his corporeal catalog, the historian bestows upon the body an elusive, general character while depending for his readings almost exclusively upon the potent symbolism of disabled bodies in particular. Visible degeneracy, impotency, congenital deformity, festering ulcerations, and bleeding wounds in the passage previously quoted provide the contrastive bodily coordinates to the muscular, aesthetic, and symmetrical bodies of the healthy citizenry. One cannot narrate the story of a healthy body or national reform movement without the contrastive device of disability to bear out the symbolic potency of the message. The materiality of metaphor via disabled bodies gives all bodies a tangible essence in that the "healthy" corporeal surface fails to achieve its symbolic effect without its disabled counterpart.

As Georges Canguilhem has pointed out, the body only calls attention to itself in the midst of its breakdown or disrepair (209). The representation of the process of breakdown or incapacity is fraught with political and ideological significance. To make the body speak essential truths, one must give a language to it. Elaine Scarry argues that "there is ordinarily no language for [the body in] pain" (13). However, we would argue that the body itself has no language, since language is something foreign to its nonlinguistic materiality. It must be spoken for if its meanings are to prove narratable. The narration of the disabled body allows a textual body to *mean* through its long-standing historical representation as an overdetermined symbolic surface; the disabled body also offers narrative the illusion of grounding abstract knowledge within a bodily materiality. *If the body is the Other of text, then textual representation seeks access to that which it is least able to grasp.* If the nondysfunctional body proves too uninteresting to narrate, the disabled body becomes a paramount device of characterization. Narrative prosthesis, or the dependency upon the disabled body, proves essential to (even the essence of) the stories analyzed in the chapters to come.

NOTES

1. Many critics have designated a distinctive space for "the literary" by identifying those works whose meaning is inherently elastic and multiple. Maurice Blanchot identifies literary narrative as that which refuses closure and readerly mastery—"to write [literature] is to surrender to the interminable" (27). In his study of Balzac's *Sarrasine*, Roland Barthes characterizes the "plural text" as that which is allied with a literary value whose "networks are many and interact, without any one of them being able to surpass the rest; the text is a galaxy of signifiers, not a structure of signifieds; it has no beginning; it is reversible; we gain access to it by several entrances, none of which can be authoritatively declared to be the main one" (5). Ross Chambers's analysis of oppositionality argues that literature strategically deploys the "play" or "leeway" in discursive systems as a means of disturbing the restrictive prescriptions of authoritative regimes (iv). As our study develops, we demonstrate that the strategic "open-endedness" of literary narrative is paralleled by the multiplicity of meanings bequeathed to people with disabilities in history. In doing so, we argue not only that the open-endedness of literature challenges sedimented historical truths,

but that disability has been one of the primary weapons in literature's disruptive agenda.

2. In his important study *Enforcing Normalcy*, Lennard Davis theorizes the "normal" body as an ideological construct that tyrannizes over those bodies that fail to conform. Accordingly, while all bodies feel insubstantial when compared to our abstract ideals of the body, disabled people experience a form of subjugation or oppression as a result of this phenomenon. Within such a system, we will argue in tandem with Davis that disability provides the contrastive term against which the concepts health, beauty, and ability are determined: "Just as the conceptualization of race, class, and gender shapes the lives of those who are not black, poor, or female, so the concept of disability regulates the bodies of those who are 'normal.' In fact, the very concept of normalcy by which most people (by definition) shape their existence is in fact tied inexorably to the concept of disability, or rather, the concept of disability is a function of a concept of normalcy. Normalcy and disability are part of the same system" (2).

3. Following the theories of Lacan, Slavoj Zizek in *The Sublime Object of Ideology* extracts the notion of the "hard kernel" of ideology. For Zizek, it represents the underlying core of belief that refuses to be deconstructed away by even the most radical operations of political critique. More than merely a rational component of ideological identification, the "hard kernel" represents the irrationality behind belief that secures the interpellated subject's "illogical" participation in a linguistically permeable system.

4. There is an equivalent problem to the representation of disability in literary narratives within our own critical rubrics of the body. The disabled body continues to fall outside of critical categories that identify bodies as the product of cultural constructions. While challenging a generic notion of white, male body as ideological proves desirable in our own moment within trhe realms of race, gender, sexuality, and class, there has been a more pernicious history of literary and critical approaches to the disabled body. In our introduction to *The Body and Physical Difference*, we argue that minority discourses in the humanities tend to deploy the evidence of "corporeal aberrancy" as a means of identifying the invention of an ideologically encoded body: "While physical aberrancy is often recognized as constructed and historically variable it is rarely remarked upon as its own legitimized or politically fraught identity" (5).

5. For Naomi Schor the phrase "bad objects" implies a discursive object that has been ruled out of bounds by the prevailing academic politics of the day, or one that represents a "critical perversion" (xv). Our use of the phrase implies both of these definitions in relation to disability. The literary object of disability has been almost entirely neglected by literary criticism in general until the past few years, when disability studies in the humanites have developed; and "disability" as a topic of investigation still strikes many as a "perverse" interest for academic contemplation. To these two definitions we would also add that the labeling of disability as a "bad object" nonetheless overlooks the fact that disabilities fill the pages of literary interest. The reasons for overabundance of images of disability in literature is the subject [*Narrative Prosthesis*].

6. The title of Thomson's *Extraordinary Bodies: Figuring Disabiltiy in American Culture and Literature* forwards the term extraordinary in order to play off of its multiple nuances. It can suggest the powerful sentimentality of overcoming narratives so often attached to stories about disabled people. It can also suggest those whose bodies are the products of overdetermined social meaning that exaggerate physical differences or perform them as a way of enhancing their exoticness. In addition, we share with Thomson the belief that disabled bodies prove extraordinary in the ways in which they expose the variety and mutable nature of physicality itself.

WORKS CITED

Blanchot, Maurice. *The Space of Literature*. 1955. Trans. Ann Smock. Lincoln: U of Nebraska P, 1982.

Campbell, Katie. *The Steadfast Tin Soldier*. Morris Plains, NJ: Unicorn, 1990.

Chambers, Ross. *Room For Maneuver: Reading the Oppositional in Narrative*. Chicago: U of Chicago P, 1991.

Davis, Lennard. *Enforcing Normalcy: Disability, Deafness, and the Body*. New York: Verso, 1995.

Mitchell, David and Snyder, Susan (eds.) *The Body and Physical Difference: Discourses of Disability*. Ann Arbor: U of Michigan P, 1997.

Schor, Naomi. *Bad Objects: Essays Popular and Unpopular*. Durham, NC: Duke UP, 1995.

Stafford, Barbara Maria. *Body Criticism: Imaging the Unseen in Enlightenment Art and Medicine*. Cambridge, MA: MIT Press, 1994.

Thomson, Rosemarie Garland. *Extraordinary Bodies: Figuring Disability in American Culture and Literature*. New York: Columbia UP, 1997.

Zizek, Slavoj. *The Sublime Object of Ideology*. New York: Verso, 1999.

CHAPTER 18

The Unexceptional Schizophrenic: A Post-Postmodern Introduction

Catherine Prendergast

Postmodern theory has been indispensable to disability studies because it has challenged normativity and destabilized narratives of national progress, social order, and identity. The essay nevertheless contends that crucial texts of postmodern theory have only achieved such destabilizations by holding one identity stable: that of the schizophrenic. These texts base their understanding of schizophrenia (and, by extension, the postmodern condition) on the writing of a few, distinctly exceptional, schizophrenics. An explosion of civic writing in the mid-1990s by writers who mark themselves specifically as non-exceptional schizophrenics, however, interrogates the desire for the stable schizophrenic, easy to recognize and therefore incarcerate, or celebrate, as the occasion demands. Attention to such writing reveals schizophrenics to be an active and growing constituency arguing for their rights in the public sphere. The essay concludes that recognition of this constituency and the multitude of voices it represents could greatly inform future theoretical programs that invoke "the schizophrenic."

Wasn't it because they didn't go far enough in listening to the insane that the great observers who drew up the first classifications impoverished the material they were given—to such an extent it appeared problematic and fragmentary to them?

(Jacques Lacan)

Postmodern theory owes a great debt to schizophrenics—and to cyborgs, border-crossers, and other figures culturally designated as hybrid. But most belatedly, and most significantly to disability studies, the debt is owed to schizophrenics, those people who bear the diagnosis of schizophrenia, along with its legal, social, and rhetorical consequences. Without schizophrenics, postmodernity would struggle to limit its boundaries, for the schizophrenic in postmodern theory marks the point of departure from the modern, the Oedipal, the referential, the old. Postmodern theory has been indispensable to disability studies because it has allowed not only for a challenge to normativity, but also for the destabilizing of narratives of national progress, social order, and identity (Corker and Shakespeare). However, crucial texts of postmodern theory have only achieved these destabilizations by holding one identity stable: that of the schizophrenic.

"Someone asked us if we had seen a schizophrenic—no, no, we have never seen one," Deleuze and Guattari assert in the final pages of *Anti-Oedipus: Capitalism and Schizophrenia* (380). While this claim, on its face, is somewhat unlikely for at least Guattari, the more immediate question is, how do they know? The schizophrenic is imagined here to be immediately recognizable with a disorder visible, and yet, because not seen, at the same time invisible and outside the social order. So distanced from the public domain, the schizophrenic is ripe for appropriation by Deleuze and Guattari who find in this figure their anti-Oedipus. It's a peculiarly honorary position the schizophrenic seems to hold: "The schizophrenic is closest to the beating heart of reality" (87), "the possessor of the most touchingly meager capital" (12). Rosi Braidotti, writing for *The Deleuze Dictionary*, aptly summarizes the importance of the schizophrenic to the anti-Oedipal project: "[T]he image of thought implied by liberal individualism and classical humanism is disrupted in favour of a multi-layered dynamic subject. On this level schizophrenia acts as an alternative to how the art of thinking can be practiced" (239). And yet this dynamic subject, always seemingly in motion, ever demonstrating this new mode of thinking, is nonetheless in Deleuze and Guattari's work to be sharply differentiated from "the schizo," reduced by hospitalization, "deaf, dumb and blind," cut off from reality, "occupying the void" (88). By *A Thousand Plateaus*, the schizophrenic has disappeared almost entirely, metaphorically consumed by the rhizome.

It is probable, that when Deleuze and Guattari proclaimed that "no, no," they had never seen a schizophrenic, they were not expecting to be taken literally. As active readers we might try a thought experiment of our own and replace "schizophrenic" in that phrase with "woman," or the designation for an individual of any racialized group. Such a statement would be so much less likely, because at the time *Anti-Oedipus* was published (originally in 1972, in French), the civil rights movement and the burgeoning women's rights movements would have drained the resulting expression of any ironic value. In the wake of a formerly disadvantaged group's clear entrée into the civic sphere, no purchase can be gained through claiming—even facetiously—never to have met a member of that group. That Deleuze and Guattari can make the claim to mediate schizophrenic experience while never having met a schizophrenic says a great deal about the lack of self-identifying schizophrenics in the public sphere one generation ago.

Deleuze and Guattari are hardly the only postmodern theorists to ground their analysis of the late capitalist order in a stereotypical portrayal of the schizophrenic. Fredric Jameson also delineates the position of the schizophrenic, analogizing the postmodern condition to the breakdown of the signifying chain that characterizes schizophrenic thought: "[T]he schizophrenic is reduced to an experience of pure material signifiers, or, in other words, a series of pure and unrelated presents in time" (27). Jean Baudrillard, similarly, analogizes the experience of postmodern reality to the experience of schizophrenia, correcting modernist notions of the schizophrenic as he does so: "The schizophrenic is not, as generally claimed, characterized by his loss of touch with reality, but by the absolute proximity to and total instantaneousness with things, this overexposure to the transparency of the world" (27). Reality is thus accessible to postmodern theory through the thought patterns of the schizophrenic. What is common in these moments of access is the certitude with which schizophrenics are discussed; the schizophrenic is allowed no change in position or in thinking, and no agenda of her or his own. In the wake of this certainty regarding how schizophrenics think and how they act, Petra Kuppers's comment on her viewing of the work of artist and schizophrenic Martin Ramírez is very refreshing: "I can't know Ramírez—that is the only firm knowledge I can take away from the images and their history of making, storing, display, and criticism" (189).

Postmodern theory has many roots, and in discussing Jameson, Baudrillard, and Deleuze and Guattari, those who have specifically drawn upon schizophrenia to elucidate postmodernity, I am not limiting postmodernism to those entities. Nor do I find reason to challenge the central insights of postmodern theory and their utility to much of disability studies. I do, however, believe that it is productive to consider postmodern attempts to ground the shared postmodern condition in the unshared position of the schizophrenic, and interrogate those attempts within the context of the disability rights and specifically mental disability rights movements. My examination of how one theoretical program can propose to liberate at the same time as it (certainly unwittingly) casts certain identities outside the social order—whether in celebratory fashion, as in Deleuze and Guattari or Jameson, or in pathologizing fashion, as in Baudrillard—draws inspiration from David T. Mitchell and Sharon L. Snyder's recollection in *Narrative Prosthesis* that the identity work conducted by race and sexuality studies historically involved distancing people of color and women from the "real" abnormalities with which they had long been metaphorically associated:

> As feminist, race, and sexuality studies sought to unmoor their identities from debilitating physical and cognitive associations, they inevitably positioned disability as the "real" limitation from which they must escape. . . . Formerly denigrated identities are "rescued" by understanding gendered, racial, and sexual differences as textually produced, distancing them from the "real" of physical

or cognitive aberrancy projected onto their figures. (2–3)

Following Mitchell and Snyder, it is interesting to note that Deleuze and Guattari, to launch their critique of late capitalism, have to distance schizoanalysis from the "real" schizo, stuck in the void. This central displacement is necessary to allow for the metaphorizing of schizophrenia along the exclusively positive channels Deleuze and Guattari allow. However positive, this metaphorizing enacts what Susan Sontag would call a "rhetorical ownership" over schizophrenia. Sontag suggests that the "metaphorical trappings" that attach to diagnoses have very real consequences, in terms of how people seek treatment, or don't, including what kind of treatment they seek. She writes: "it is highly desirable for a specific dreaded illness to come to be seen as ordinary. . . . Much in the way of individual experience and social policy depends on the struggle for rhetorical ownership of the illness: how it is possessed, assimilated in argument and in cliché" (93–94).

Clichés are, by definition, metaphors that have become too stable. The appropriation of the schizophrenic by postmodern theory is a cliché, one that posits continually the rhetorical exceptionalism of schizophrenics. This stability mirrors the medicalized investment, which, as Snyder and Mitchell have observed in "Disability Haunting in American Poetics," finds disability to be "an organic predicament based on the common sense notion that disability status cannot be altered" (2). As a result of this common sense notion, Snyder and Mitchell argue, the disabled are not allowed to enter the history of U.S. social conflict as an active constituency arguing for their rights within the public sphere. Postmodern theory values schizophrenics precisely because it imagines them insulated from civic life. They are to remain

THE UNEXCEPTIONAL SCHIZOPHRENIC: A POST-POSTMODERN INTRODUCTION | 239

the "exceptional, private citizenry" that Snyder and Mitchell identify as typical of the role given to the disabled. There is, however, an increasingly public citizenry of schizophrenics who claim the following: to speak publicly, particularly on issues that affect their lives; to self-identify as schizophrenic without having to embrace the stigma associated with the term nor undersign any medicalized investment; to found and use their own press organs to further their causes (in this way, very much the "bodies with organs"); to be considered in public addresses, and finally, to enjoy a rhetorical position and a life that is not predicated on complete absence of impairment. In short, they claim the right to unexceptional instability, which is not something postmodern theory has readily granted them.

THE MODEL SCHIZOPHRENIC

It is not surprising that the postmodern theory I have reviewed should hold the identity of schizophrenics so constant, because much of it is based on a few, rather exceptional schizophrenics. The history of perhaps the most exceptional I will turn to here: Judge Daniel Paul Schreber. As Rosemary Dinnage observes, Schreber's 1903 *Memoirs of My Nervous Illness*, something of a self-report, is "the most written-about document in all psychiatric literature. . . . Everyone has had something to say about Schreber" (xi). Schreber's writings cannot help but come to us as metaphor, saturated with the resonances of his commentators: Freud, Jung, Lacan, and Deleuze and Guattari, chief among them. Equally exceptional as the reception of his work were Schreber's life and the course of his illness. A prominent German judge, Schreber was the son of Moritz Schreber, an immensely influential though controversial German authority on child-rearing. That Moritz Schreber's

systems for parenting stressed nearly sadistic obedience and control is a fact about which analyzers of Daniel Schreber's pathology make some hay.[1] Also well-noted is that Schreber's schizophrenia did not manifest until he was in his forties in the midst of his career.[2] He recovered from his first breakdown only to be incarcerated for nearly a decade when he was in his fifties. While in the asylum, he recorded his observations of his body and his religious conceptions including those supernatural matters "which cannot be expressed in human language; they exceed human understanding" (Schreber 16). Schreber was keen to publish his manuscript (his family, fearing embarrassment, not so very keen), however, inmates of asylums were not permitted by law to publish their work. In 1902, after a protracted legal battle, Schreber secured his release entering into the public sphere physically, and soon after, rhetorically. His *Memoirs*, published the following year, were quickly recognized as a critical account of psychosis. He had become fully exceptional. Lacan, who analyzed Schreber through his *Memoirs* wrote: "That Schreber was *exceptionally gifted*, as he himself puts it, at observing phenomena of which he is the center and at searching for their truth, makes his testimony incomparably valuable" (233, emphasis Lacan's).

Undeniably, however, what made Judge Schreber most exceptional to modern commentators including Lacan was Freud's 1911 analysis of the Schreber case. Schreber might at first seem an unusual subject for Freud to analyze given that Freud considered schizophrenics unfit subjects for the talking cure. Colin McCabe records, "Any psychotic patient that presented him or herself in Freud's consulting rooms would, by the very nature of their condition, swiftly either refuse treatment or be referred on to a hospital" (ix). McCabe puzzles why Freud did not read Schreber's *Memoirs* until seven years after its publication, even though it had been a topic of great discussion in psychiatric circles. That Freud did eventually turn his attention to the Schreber case McCabe credits to Freud's fear that psychoanalysis, particularly its tenets grounding the relationship between the unconscious and the conscious in sexuality, faced threats from competing biological and social theories of the psyche. Schreber, to Freud, then, was also exceptional; Freud's location of Schreber's psychosis in repressed homosexuality was to be the exception that proved his rule of neurosis.

Freud's defensive and unconvincing analysis of Schreber through the *Memoirs*, ("very unsatisfactory" Jung would deem it),[3] made Schreber the perfect platform from which Deleuze and Guattari could launch their assault on psychoanalytic theory's complicity with the capitalist order. Judge Schreber, along with the also exceptional Antonin Artaud, became their model schizophrenics. But it was Schreber who allowed for the most direct attack on Freud. Deleuze and Guattari declared that Freud had done Schreber a great disservice in his reading of *Memoirs*, cutting off Schreber rhetorically at the kneecaps. "Not one word is retained," they complained, of Schreber's original work in Freud's treatment. Schreber, they wryly remarked, was not only sodomized by rays from heaven (as Schreber in his *Memoirs* describes), but was "posthumously oedipalized by Freud," who, they point out, never met his "patient" *in vivo* (57).

The concern Deleuze and Guattari have for Schreber seems to be one of recuperating his rhetorical position; Schreber, thus rhetorically enabled, can become the agent who can trick Freud in the session that never occurred, breaking through "the simplistic terms and functions of the Oedipal triangle" (14). However, Deleuze and Guattari themselves evince less than total confidence in Schreber's self-account. Their remark, "if we are to believe Judge Schreber's doctrine" (19) suggests that Schreber occupies only a qualified rhetorical position in *Anti-Oedipus*, one that is valuable, but provisional, even on the subject of Schreber's own experience. Deleuze and Guattari find in Schreber's memoirs the seeds of the break from representation, but they can only access it through an act of representation, one that grants Schreber no firmer rhetorical ground than he enjoyed through Freud's text.

Where Deleuze and Guattari find Schreber through Freud, Jameson finds him through Lacan: "I have found Lacan's account of schizophrenia useful here not because I have any way of knowing whether it has clinical accuracy but chiefly because—as description rather than diagnosis—it seems to me to offer a suggestive aesthetic model" (26). Through Jameson's formulation of Schreber's condition, we can understand schizophrenia as that state which enacts disruptions of temporality. Jameson cites as further examples of such disruption the work of John Cage and Samuel Beckett, neither of whom were diagnosed schizophrenics. Cage and Beckett quickly, however, become metaphors of schizophrenia through Jameson's analysis. In the end Jameson leaves us with an aestheticization of the schizophrenic experience. Schizophrenia is always/ already artistic, always/already literary, always/already metaphorical. What might usefully rescue schizophrenia from these metaphoric entrapments is a shift in focus toward a rhetorical exploration, one that examines the circumstances of publication of schizophrenic writing, situating that writing within, as Snyder and Mitchell have suggested, histories of conflict over who may take up space in the public sphere.

NEWS FROM THE VOID

Two publications by schizophrenics entering the public sphere in 1995 form an interesting juxtaposition in this regard. One will be familiar and widely recognizable as exceptional: the publication of Ted Kaczynski's "Industrial Society and its Future" [commonly known as the "Unabomber manifesto"] in *The New York Times*, a 36,000 word rant against modernity Kaczynski would go so far as to kill to see published. The other publication is much less well known. In 1995, Editor-in-Chief Ken Steele released the inaugural edition of *New York City Voices: A Consumer Journal for Mental Health*. To appreciate the profundity of this publication, a short biography of Steele is appropriate. Steele began hearing voices in 1962 when he was fourteen years old. The voices urged him repeatedly to kill himself. After a few failed attempts to follow their orders, Steele ran away from home, and was shortly afterward diagnosed with schizophrenia by a physician. At age seventeen he took off for New York City and was quickly ushered into the world of male hustling. Over the next thirty years he would be homeless, raped, shuttled between several psychiatric hospitals, and he would attempt to end his life several more times. In 1995, then under treatment with a new medication, Ken Steele's voices stopped. Five years later, Steele died of a heart attack, possibly related to obesity that has since been identified as a common side effect of the medication he had been taking.

Significantly, Steele had actually begun engaging in advocacy slightly before the end of his voices. In order to fulfill the mandated "structured activity" as part of his care, he decided to found a voter registration project for the mentally ill. He had become alarmed at growing threats to Social Security Disability and proposed cutbacks to a range of other services the mentally ill rely on: housing, mental health clinics, and research. While he was still coping with his voices, he took a folding table and voter registration cards to homeless shelters and mental health clinics to register mentally ill voters of any party. After his voices stopped, however, he decided not only to help the mentally ill enter the polity via the vote, but also to use rhetoric as a tool to increase their civic presence. He founded *New York City Voices* primarily as a journal to inform about legislative issues, but writing the journal itself served its own enfranchising purposes.

A typical example of a story from *New York City Voices*, written by Steele himself in the July/August 1999 issue, is not rhetorically exceptional in any of the ways postmodern theorists might expect:

> Did you know that only one-half of one percent of those Americans with disabilities presently receiving Social Security Disability Insurance (SSDI) or Supplemental Security Income (SSI) are employed? How many more of us do you think would like to work but cannot, because we would lose cash benefits if we earn over $500 a month and Medicare and Medicaid health coverage if we work more than three years?

What follows is a plea to support the Ticket to Work and Self-Sufficiency Program. There is nothing distinctly disorganized about this opening of rhetorical questions, which lays out the false choice Steele sees between accepting work and accepting health coverage. I would even venture to say that were it not for Steele's self-identification as mentally ill throughout the article (and his invocation of an audience of the mentally ill), there would be nothing to mark Steele as schizophrenic.

Another writer for the journal, Lisa Gibson, in an article advocating for insurance parity in the Jan/Feb 2000 issue, writes that her manic depression has been the most crucial element of her life, exceeding the force of other social categories to which she also belongs. She begins by describing the importance of narrative in self-identification:

Charles Dickens began his book David Copperfield with the words "I am born." If I were to write an autobiography, I would begin with the words "I am born with manic-depression," for this illness has been the single most defining factor of my life and my personality. No other factor—being female, being southern, being the middle child—has had such an impact on me as this disease.

As Steele notes in *The Day the Voices Stopped*:

> Most striking about *New York City Voices* has been the inclusion of personal stories by people with mental illness, written in our own words and under our own bylines (often accompanied by a photograph of the contributor). A bold but necessary move, self-disclosure is a first step toward successfully addressing the stigma associated with being mentally ill. (221)

This self-disclosure is a defining feature of a rhetoric self-conscious of the usual position of the schizophrenic rhetor; typically schizophrenics are considered beings with speech, but speech that is generally treated as an index of sanity or insanity, with referentiality only to diagnostic criteria, and without referentiality to the civic world. Self-disclosure is thus a necessary component of civic rhetoric for these authors, involving the investiture of the previously stigmatizing moniker *schizophrenic* with new meaning. These writers appropriate the term *schizophrenic* in much the same way as the gay community successfully appropriated the previously denigrating term *queer*.

Snyder and Mitchell have identified the 1970s as the moment disability memoirs began to be published *en masse*: "These first person stories interrupted several hundred years of inaccurate disability representation by interested professionals in medicine, rehabilitation, and other caring professions" (9). When we look back at the mid-1990s from a vantage point thirty years hence, we will see it as the moment mental disability narratives began appearing *en masse*—which explains why the most blatant appropriations of the schizophrenic seem to end in the late 1980s. There is little getting around the fact that the explosion of civic rhetoric by schizophrenics corresponds with the advent of atypical antipsychotic medications in the 1990s. The first mass-market magazine authored primarily by schizophrenics, *Schizophrenia Digest*, began in 1994, for example, and continues to this day to chronicle schizophrenics' struggles with social discrimination, limited treatment options, and those medications that may have allowed for certain forms of expression, but with troubling and sometimes life-threatening side-effects. Within the *Digest*'s pages, schizophrenics write of the need to speak in order to break through the assumption of the normative audience that informs most published material. As Vicky Yeung writes of her experience reading personal finance books written from a normative perspective:

> [T]he author assumes I'm not limited by my mind's matter as to how much money I conceivably can make. These writers give tips that are unhelpful for me, like increasing my income through investing in mutual funds, working at several jobs, etc., as if I could do any of those things. Really, they're writing for the "normal healthy mind" audience. (47)

In this passage Yeung elucidates her exclusion from the normative processes of late capitalism, incapable as those processes are of incorporating a non-incarcerated, non-revenue producing, non-exceptional subject. Her quotation marks around "normal healthy mind" indicate that she does not consider herself "exceptional," except that normativity makes her so.

As Daniel Frey, successor to Steele as Editor-in-Chief of *New York City Voices* has observed of the erasure of this non-exceptional subject through the exceptionalizing of schizophrenics:

> The extremes of schizophrenia get the most publicity, like the genius John Nash on the one hand and the subway killer Gary Goldstein on the other. Every day people like me get overlooked even though we compose the vast majority of schizophrenics. The mental health consumer movement is the last great civil rights movement in this country.

Frey asks here for a move away from both pathologized and vaunted genius/artist versions of schizophrenics; he suggests movement toward the vast middle ground of schizophrenics who hold unexceptional jobs, or move through multiple hospitalizations without either killing anyone or winning Nobel prizes. Frey's speech does not ask for leaps of interpretation, does not mark itself as any more "everyday" than he marks himself. He simply heralds the end of the exemplar schizophrenic. He asks that schizophrenics be able to participate in, as well as critique, late capitalism; one wonders what Deleuze and Guattari would have made of schizophrenic Bill MacPhee, publisher of *Schizophrenia Digest* in which Vicky Yeung's critique of capitalism appears, who affirmed that his life was changed in 1994 by the book "101 Ways to Start a Business with Little or No Capital." His business? A magazine for schizophrenics.

To see the "ordinary" schizophrenic is, in short, to give up the stable schizophrenic. The identity of being a schizophrenic, because it is tied to a history of having been diagnosed with the condition, may remain constant, but impairments fluctuate in time. As Kuppers notes, "Mental health is a contested terrain: on the one hand, mental normalcy is a problematic concept given the malleability and changing nature of human mental and emotional states. On the other hand, certain permutations of

mentality are severely policed and bracketed off into deviancy" (59). The public seemingly only desires the stable schizophrenic, easy to incarcerate, or easy to celebrate as the occasion requires. The public does not want to allow for fluctuation between states, and even less for the possibility that both states exist at once. A genuinely postmodern perspective would not insist that schizophrenic rhetoric be fixed, but rather would allow for Bill MacPhee, Lisa Gibson, Vicki Yeung, and Daniel Frey to continue to engage in civic rhetoric, while being schizophrenic. It would allow them to occupy the contested public sphere, bringing to it the force of their narratives.

The narrative power of fluctuations between mental states is perhaps best captured by Richard MacLean's memoir *Recovered, not Cured*. MacLean begins the work on a past moment of impairment, set off in space and time:

> Another World, August 1994. I am crouching in an alleyway. They can't see me here, so for a moment I am safe. There must be hundreds of loudspeakers projecting secret messages, and umpteen video cameras tracking every move I make (xi).

The book ends in "The Present":

> Nowadays, I say that I am recovered, not cured. I have a job as a graphic designer and illustrator, I have a band in which I do vocals and guitar, I have my friends and my family. I pay my taxes and do the dishes; I'm independent. I have achieved a sense of normality and live with the knowledge that a couple of pills a day will keep me slightly lethargic yet "sane" at the same time. I can live with that. (174)

The actual structure of MacLean's text belies the sense of progression that these two time points imply. Interspersed through MacLean's narrative are his own illustrations, many created "years ago," as well as numerous emails from schizophrenics he has received since beginning a life of public advocacy. This structure enacts a merging of all states in the present, a time when "sane" appears only in quotation marks. MacLean acknowledges in a section entitled "A Kind of Closure":

> If I had my way, of course, all this would never have happened. However, I hoped that by writing about it I might be able to seal off all the chaos I had experienced; seal it up with sealing wax, put it in a cupboard or throw it to the sea. It hasn't worked out quite so simply. To this day, although my illness is at a manageable level, I am residually delusional and sometimes read odd meanings into things. (172)

There is, MacLean asserts, no definitive closure for him.

I would like to return, in only provisional closing then, to the quote from Lacan I selected for the epigraph, a reflection on schizophrenic voice: "Wasn't it because they didn't go far enough in listening to the insane that the great observers who drew up the first classifications impoverished the material they were given—to such an extent it appeared problematic and fragmentary to them?" Lacan suggests that schizophrenics had not been listened to except metaphorically. The problem according to Lacan is that these great observers thought that what schizophrenics were saying could not really be what they were actually saying. It would have to be something else. Lacan was, ironically, talking about the much-observed Schreber, who died in an asylum four years after the publication of the *Memoirs*. Let us change Lacan's "it," though, so it no longer stands simply for the utterances of one schizophrenic at one moment in time. Let us have "it" stand in for all schizophrenic utterances at all points in time. That "it"

should appear problematic. It should appear fragmentary. But it should appear, and once appearing, be considered unexceptional.[4]

NOTES

1. See, for example, *Soul Murder* by Schatzman.
2. Schreber was not diagnosed schizophrenic during his life (the diagnosis not then being in use), however, Deleuze and Guattari, typical of his modern commentators, ascribe him that condition.
3. Jung's response quoted in Dinnage, and further elaborated in McCabe.
4. Many thanks to the JLD reviewers for their invaluable comments on an earlier version of this essay.

WORKS CITED

Baudrillard, Jean. *The Ecstasy of Communication.* Trans. Bernard Schutze and Caroline Schutze. New York: Semiotext(e), 1988.

Braidotti, Rose. "Schizophrenia." *The Deleuze Dictionary.* Ed. Adrian Parr. New York: Columbia UP, 2005, 237–40.

Corker, Mairian and Tom Shakespeare, ed. *Disability/Postmodernity: Embodying Disability Theory.* New York: Continuum, 2002.

Deleuze, Gilles and Félix Guattari. *A Thousand Plateaus: Capitalism and Schizophrenia.* Trans. Brian Massumi. Minneapolis: U of Minnesota P, 1987.

——. *Anti-Oedipus: Capitalism and Schizophrenia.* Trans. Robert Hurley, Mark Seem, and Helen R. Lane. Minneapolis: U of Minnesota P, 2000.

Dinnage, Rosemary. Introduction. In *Memoirs of My Nervous Illness by Daniel Paul Schreber*, eds. Ida Macalpine and Richard A. Hunter, xi–xxiv. New York: New York Review of Books, 2000.

Freud, Sigmund. *The Schreber Case.* Trans. Andrew Webber. New York: Penguin, 2002.

Frey, Daniel. "First Break: Three Years Later." *New York City Voices*, www.nycvoices.org, posted 2002.

Gibson, Lisa. "Parity Matters to Me." *New York City Voices*, www.nyvoices.org, posted 2000.

Jameson, Frederic. *Postmodernism, or, the Cultural Logic of Late Capitalism.* Durham: Duke UP, 1992.

Kuppers, Petra. *The Scar of Visibility: Medical Performance and Contemporary Art.* Minneapolis: U of Minnesota P, 2007.

Lacan, Jacques. *The Seminar of Jacques Lacan Book III: The Psychoses 1955–1956.* Trans. Russell

Grigg. Ed. Jacques-Alain Miller. New York: Norton, 1997.

MacLean, Richard. *Recovered, Not Cured: A Journey through Schizophrenia.* Crows Nest, Australia: Allen & Unwin, 2003.

McCabe, Colin. Introduction. *The Schreber Case.* By Sigmund Freud, trans. Andrew Webber, vi–xxii. New York: Penguin, 2002.

Mitchell, David T. and Sharon L. Snyder. *Narrative Prosthesis: Disability and the Dependencies of Discourse.* Ann Arbor: U of Michigan P, 2001.

Schatzman, Morton. *Soul Murder: Persecution in the Family.* New York: Random House, 1973.

Schreber, Daniel Paul. *Memoirs of My Nervous Illness.* Trans. Ida Macalpine and Richard A. Hunter. New York: New York Review of Books, 2000.

Snyder, Sharon L. and David T. Mitchell. "Disability Haunting in American Poetics." *Journal of Literary Disability* 1.1 (2007): 1–12.

Sontag, Susan. *Aids and Its Metaphors.* New York: Farrar, Straus, and Giroux, 1988.

——. *Illness as Metaphor.* New York: Farrar, Straus and Giroux, 1978.

Steele, Ken and Claire Berman. *The Day the Voices Stopped.* New York: Basic Books, 2002.

Yeung, Vicky. "Born with a Gift and a Purpose." *Schizophrenia Digest* 5.3 (2007): 47.

CHAPTER 19

Deaf Studies in the 21st Century: "Deaf-Gain" and the Future of Human Diversity

H-Dirksen L. Bauman and Joseph J. Murray

DEAF-GAIN: COGNITIVE, CULTURAL, AND CREATIVE DIVERSITY

Given the threats posed to the signing Deaf community by the medical and educational institutions of normalization, the Deaf community and Deaf Studies scholars find themselves cornered into the fundamental existential question: Why should deaf people continue to exist? Indeed, on what grounds can one argue for the preservation of what most consider a disability? As Burke (2006) notes, such bioethical arguments hinge on the demonstration of the intrinsic and extrinsic value of Deaf communities and their languages. Intrinsic arguments seek to prove the worth of deaf people and sign languages for their own good, whereas extrinsic arguments demonstrate the useful contributions of deaf people and their languages for the greater good of humanity. Although intrinsic arguments have long been made (i.e., Deaf culture and sign languages should be preserved because they are as valid as other cultures and languages), extrinsic arguments have not yet been fully developed or understood. Future directions in the field of Deaf Studies may be thought of as the vigorous exploration and demonstration of the important extrinsic value of Deaf communities and their languages.

While having to argue for the most basic right of all—the right to exist—Deaf Studies is put on the defensive. However, scholars are beginning to recognize that the most vigorous response would be to cease arguing against medical and educational institutions of normalization, and instead, go on the offensive by reframing representations of deafness from sensory lack to a form of sensory and cognitive diversity that offers vital contributions to human diversity. Within the frame of human diversity, Deaf Studies scholars are inquiring into the insights that may be gleaned from deaf people whose highly visual, spatial, and kinetic structures of thought and language may shed light into the blindspots of hearing ways of knowing.

The overarching extrinsic value of Deaf communities and their languages, then, may best be explained by the emerging discipline of biocultural diversity, a field that has arisen as an area of transdisciplinary research concerned with investigating the links between the world's linguistic, cultural, and biological diversity as manifestations of the diversity of life. The impetus for the emergence of this field came from the observation that all three diversities are under threat by some of the same forces, and from the perception that loss of diversity at all levels spells dramatic consequences for humanity and the earth (Maffi, 2005). A body of research has begun to link the decreases in biocultural and linguistic diversity, noting that when an indigenous language dies, the unique knowledge of the local environment, developed over centuries, dies with it (Harmon, 2002; Maffi, 2005; Skutnabb-Kangas, 2000). Most predictions suggest that within the next century, half of the world's 6,000 spoken languages will disappear, which is at the rate of a language death every two weeks (Crystal, 2002). There are currently no statistics about the number of signed languages in the world, and clearly, when a signed language dies, there may not be the same amount of biological and environmental knowledge lost with it. However, in the same vein, Deaf Studies scholars may begin to add to the notions of linguistic and biodiversity new categories of diversity foregrounded by signed languages—namely, cognitive, cultural, and creative diversity.

Once we place Deaf communities and their languages within the framework of biocultural diversity, a new frame emerges. The task of Deaf Studies in the new century is to ask a fundamental question: How does being Deaf reorganize what it means to be human? Indeed, what dramatic consequences would arise from the (neo)eugenic drive toward normalization? Embracing deaf people and their languages will invariably lead toward a deeper understanding of the human proclivity for adaptation. In the face of sensory loss, we may better appreciate the dynamic and pliable nature of the mind and the human will to communicate and to form community. In this light, deafness is not so much defined by a fundamental lack, as in *hearing loss*, but as its opposite, as a means to understand the plenitude of human being, as *Deaf-gain*.[1]

Deaf-gain, as we explore later, is the notion that the unique sensory orientation of Deaf people leads to a sophisticated form of visual-spatial language that provides opportunities for exploration into the human character. In this spirit, Gallaudet University's Vision Statement commits to promoting "the recognition that deaf people and their sign languages are vast resources with significant contributions to the cognitive, creative, and cultural dimensions of human diversity" (http://www.gallaudet.edu/mission.xml). In what follows, contemporary and future directions for each of these forms of human diversity and "Deaf-gain" will be discussed as emerging and future trajectories of the field of Deaf Studies that collectively demonstrate the value of Deaf Studies to the academy and Deaf communities to humanity.

COGNITIVE DIVERSITY AND DEAF-GAIN: REDEFINING THE NATURE OF LANGUAGE

The prime example of the extrinsic value of deaf people and their languages is the wholesale redefinition of language that has come about as a result of sign language studies. Just as we once thought the flat Earth to be at the center of the universe, we once assumed that language could only take the form of speech. Now that we know the brain may just as easily develop a signed as a spoken language, we must reconfigure our understanding of language, in all its complexities. Four decades of sign language research has now deepened our awareness of the nature of language—from language acquisition, structure, and more. We now know that the fundamental character of the brain is plasticity and flexibility (Petitto, Zatorre, Gauna, Nikelski, Dostie, & Evans, 2000). This redefining would not have come about without the study of signed languages, and may be seen as the initial instance of Deaf-gain. Due to the existence of signing communities, linguists and anthropologists have been able to peer into the development of language, revealing insights into the debates over the innateness or social origins of language acquisition (Sandler, Meir, Padden, & Aronoff, 2005). In addition, sign languages have also provided insight into new and revived theories of the origins of language (Armstrong, 2002; Armstrong & Wilcox, 2007; Armstrong, Wilcox, & Stokoe, 1995; Corballis, 2003; Stokoe, 2001). The implications of these discoveries extend into the core of what it means to be human, but have yet to be applied to Deaf education. As Stokoe (2001, p. 16) wrote, "the status of deaf people, their education, their opportunities in life, and the utilization of their potential—all these could be much enhanced if we understood the way deaf people still make language may be the way the whole human race became human." As a result of the natural human proclivity to sign, hearing parents are increasingly using sign language, with results that suggest increased linguistic, cognitive, and social development.

COGNITIVE DIVERSITY AND DEAF-GAIN: VISUAL LANGUAGE/ VISUAL LEARNING

Another significant area of future research in the area of Deaf-gain is the particular, highly developed visual ways of being in the world brought about by the unique sensory orientation of deaf individuals and communities (Bahan, 2008; Marschark, 2003). The link between enhanced visuospatial abilities and use of sign languages has been documented in studies of speed in generating mental images (Emmorey & Kosslyn, 1996; Emmorey, Kosslyn, & Bellugi, 1993), mental rotation skills (Emmorey, Klima, & Hicock, 1998), increased facial recognition skills (Bettger, Emmorey, McCullough, & Bellugi, 1997), increased peripheral recognition skills (Bavelier, Tomann, Hutton, Mitchell, Corina, Liu, & Neville, 2000),

and increased spatial cognition (Bellugi, O'Grady, Lillio-Martin, O'Grady Hynes, Van Hoek, & Corina, 1989). We may take these indications of increased visual-spatial cognition and develop them into future research into practices of visual learning for all sighted individuals. The benefits may be far reaching, for as Stokoe recognized, "vision may have an advantage, for it is neurologically a richer and more complex physiological system than hearing. Sight makes use of much more of the brain's capacity than does hearing" (p. 20). Given the drive to diversify education along the lines of "multiple intelligences" (Gardner, 1993), it would only makes sense that the most visually oriented of all humans would take the lead toward future experimentation in visual learning.

As testimony to the promises of the field of visual language and visual learning, the National Science foundation recently funded a Science of Learning Center at Gallaudet University to "gain a greater understanding of the biological, cognitive, linguistic, sociocultural, and pedagogical conditions that influence the acquisition of language and knowledge through the visual modality" (VL2, 2008; http://vl2.gallaudet.edu/). Given the immense amount of information processed visually[2] (for sighted people), it is not surprising that learning may be enhanced when pedagogies focus on transmitting visual information (Gardner, 1993; Moore & Dwyer, 1994). This project goes beyond the Deaf education model of addressing alternative (read: remedial) ways of teaching deaf people, to ask how deaf people's visual orientation to the world may be able to offer hearing people new ways of learning, even in fields traditionally dominated by an auditory/phonetic orientation, such as literacy development. Indeed, as textuality in the 21st century is becoming increasingly visual and digital, there is a trend away from traditional print-based texts to video and multimedia texts. Insights from the world's most visually acute people may provide insights on how we may all process information visually.

If this is the case, then future directions of Deaf Studies and Deaf education may have less to do with audiological loss than Deaf-gain—that is, a bilingual, visual learning environment could be so rich in processing information in multiple channels that hearing parents would want their children to go to sign language schools. In this scenario, Deaf education would give way to dual-language education, open to all who desire such a learning environment. Two examples of these types of bilingual sign language schools are P.S. 47: The ASL–English Bilingual School in New York City and The Cassato School, near Torino, Italy. Indeed, before such a paradigm shift were to take root in a systematic way, the status of sign languages as academic languages would have to be reconceived.

COGNITIVE DIVERSITY AND DEAF-GAIN: SIGN LANGUAGES AND ACADEMIC DISCOURSE

Traditionally, signed languages have been seen as, essentially "oral" languages as they have no written form.[3] Common wisdom holds that writing is an essential element to the development of literacy, as essential as water is to swimming. The word "literacy," after all, derives from the Greek *littere*, or "written letter." However, as Kuntze (2008) has suggested, just as definitions of language have changed in the wake of the validation of sign languages, so may the definition of literacy. Kuntze shows how one may demonstrate characteristics of literate thought in written, signed, and visual modalities. One such characteristic, notes Kuntze, is inference making. Whether the information that an individual receives "is expressed in written language or in a different language such as ASL or in a different

mode like film, the act of inference making will be necessary if one is to achieve a richer interpretation of the content" (p. 150). Clearly, one may exercise inference and other critical thinking strategies using a nonwritten language such as ASL or through watching silent films.

Evolving definitions of literacy are happening in tandem with emerging video technologies that allow greater ease of producing academic texts in ASL. Once video journals such as the *Deaf Studies Digital Journal* (dsdj.gallaudet.edu) mature, standards for academic publishing in signed languages will develop. The significance of academic discourse in ASL may be most prominent if the visual, spatial, and kinetic dimensions of the language are explored for their greatest rhetorical power. For example, imagine how precisely an ASL-fluent biology professor would describe the process of cell mitosis, using ASL's rich classifier system to indicate pairs of chromosomes splitting and cell walls dividing, so that students may witness the linguistic reenactment of a physical process, or the precise description of the French philosopher Michel Foucault's notion of the "microphysics of power," which would be shown as a dispersion of multiple sites of power throughout society, rather than a more traditional top-down model of power. The point here is that sign languages are rich in what Taub (2001) calls "metaphoric iconicity," in which complex ideas are demonstrated through visual-spatial metaphors. Such a language does not lack in abstraction, but gains in clarity of the concrete representation of complex ideas.

This unique advantage of sign languages was originally articulated by the early 19th-century teacher of the deaf, Auguste Bebian, who believed that "sign language has a superior capacity for expressing mental operations" (1984, p. 151). The difference, Bebian explains, is that spoken language is fundamentally arbitrary, but discourse in sign language, would "frequently acquire a self-evident certainty or become a manifest absurdity to all" (p. 151). Indeed, the speaking biology student could say, "the chromosomes split," whereas the signing biology student would reveal the internal mental images of her conception of how the chromosomes split visually and spatially. Similarly, the philosophy student would reveal the degree of precision of his understanding of Foucault's unique conception of "power" through the spatial arrangement of his description. Clearly, the validity of such observations about the unique qualities of intellectual discourse in sign language now lay before the fields of Deaf education, Deaf Studies, and linguistics to explore this vein of potential Deaf-gain.

CREATIVE DIVERSITY AND DEAF-GAIN: FILM LANGUAGE/SIGN LANGUAGE

Comparisons have often been made between the film language and sign languages (Bahan, 2006; Bauman, 2006; Sacks, 1990). In addition to a traditional linguistic means of describing sign languages through phonology, morphology, and syntax, one may also see fluent signers as everyday filmmakers, a skill that is heightened in the literary and dramatic uses of sign language. Indeed, when seen through lens of film grammar (Arijon, 1991), sign languages present a constant tableau of close-up and distant shots, replete with camera movements and editing techniques. Given such an intimate, cognitive relationship with cinematic grammar, we must wonder what innovations might emerge if we were to invest in the cinematic education of the next generation of deaf children. Again, no research has been conducted to this point about the potential innovations that would emerge from Deaf filmmakers, but such exploration is clearly an important trajectory for Deaf Studies to explore the poten-

tial of Deaf-gain in this area. A rigorous educational film program in deaf schools would have the added benefit of inserting a deaf public voice into popular media.

CREATIVE DIVERSITY AND DEAF-GAIN: DEAF SPACE AND THE BUILT ENVIRONMENT

Although Deaf Studies is inherently interdisciplinary, one may not immediately think of architecture as an important area of creative exchange. However, in 2005, Gallaudet University hosted a two-day "Deaf Space" workshop, which resulted in what has grown into a series of Deaf Studies courses, the Gallaudet University Deaf Space Design Guide, and the incorporation of some key Deaf Space principles in the Sorenson Language and Communication Center at Gallaudet.

The Deaf Space project does not focus on issues of accommodation, but rather on Deaf cultural aesthetics that are embodied in the built environment. In the original workshop in 2005, a common aesthetic emerged that was described as organic, curvilinear, and bathed in light. Since that time, students and faculty have researched core issues, such as the qualities of lighting, proxemics of signers, and the tension between open, visually accessible spaces and privacy. Although the notion of Deaf space generates from designing the optimal environment for Deaf signers, the basic precept is that Deaf space principles would create exceptional buildings for everyone, regardless of audiological status.

Further study of Deaf space and planning in the future of Deaf Studies may also lead toward an understanding of the urgency that Deaf communities may be strengthened by gaining control over the spaces where deaf individuals live. As deaf individuals are born into a dispersion among hearing families, they are subject to a diasporic condition from the onset (Allen, 2007). Indeed, one of the primary differences between the linguistic minority of sign language users and other language groups is that deaf people have never occupied a homeland. They may have congregated at residential schools, but these spaces were designed on 19th-century asylum architecture—hardly the autochthonous creation of a group with deep ties to the land. From schools to Deaf clubs, Deaf spaces have generally reflected the design of hearing architects. On a personal level, however, deaf people have a long tradition of home renovations that bear similarities—such as increasing the visual reach throughout a house—that permit greater visual communication, as well as a sense of connection (Malzkuhn, 2007). The cultural significance of home renovations and the deaf relationship to place cannot be underestimated, for as Findley (2005, p. 5) notes, "not having control of the space one is occupying is in some way demoralizing." For this reason, Deaf people have always felt the need to dream of a homeland, from Jacob Flournoy's 19th-century proposals for a Deaf state (Krentz, 2000) to the recent proposal for Laurent, South Dakota (Willard, n.d.) as just such a homeland. Indeed, as. Le Corbusier wrote, "the occupation of space is the first proof of existence" (Findley, 2005, p. 5). As such, Deaf people may find architecture and. community planning an integral element to linguistic and cultural revitalization. Such a future exploration would result in diversity of the design and qualities of living spaces.

DEAF-GAIN AND CREATIVE DIVERSITY: SIGN LANGUAGE LITERATURE

Just as the validation of sign language revolutionized the study of language, so too must the nature of literature be reconsidered from the ground up. The unique visual and spatial properties of sign language make it a particularly rich medium for poetic image and metaphor (Bauman, 2008; Bauman, Nelson, & Rose, 2006; Davidson, 2008; Taub, 2001; Wilcox, 2000). For centuries, writers have been seeking to extend both the visual and performative aspects of literature, resulting in various experimental forms, from the unity of painting and poetry in the works of William Blake to concrete poetry, slam, and performance poetry. Sign poetry extends both the performative and visual traditions of literature into new forms. Sign language poetic practice has become increasingly innovative in its use of visual textual forms, as sign language poets have experimented with the interaction of the components of film language—camera movement, editing, visual prosody, *mise en scene*—and sign language. Ella Mae Lentz's collaboration with Lynette Taylor (Lentz, 1996), and Dutch poets Wim Emmerik and Giselle Meyer's collaboration with Anja Hiddinga and Lendeert Pot (Hiddinga et al., 2005) represent the creative potential of a blending cinematic techniques with sign language poetry. In addition to experimentation with visual textuality, sign language poetry extends the embodied, performative tradition, exemplified by the Beat generation's spoken word poetry. Allen Ginsberg, for one, recognized the enormous potential of sign language performance when he participated in a gathering of Deaf and hearing poets in Rochester, New York. When he asked Deaf poets to translate the phrase "hydrogen jukebox" from his poem, "Howl," Patrick Graybill responded with a translation that led Ginsberg to exclaim, "that is exactly it, what I have been trying to convey, the hard clear image of it" (Cohn, 1999; Cook, 2006).

Similarly, the history of theater reveals an enduring human desire for nonverbal, visual spectacle. The history of mime and theatrical tableau, and explorations in experimental visual theater by directors and writers like Antonin Artaud and Robert Wilson, indicate that theater yearns to draw particular attention to the spatial and kinetic modalities. Golden (2009) suggests that Deaf/sign language theater and the practice of visual theater engage in an exchange to the mutual benefit of each practice. Clearly, the highly visual nature of Deaf theater, Golden suggests, may enhance the genre of visual theater.

CULTURAL DIVERSITY AND DEAF-GAIN: TRANSNATIONAL DEAF COMMUNITY

The tools of cultural studies that have served Deaf Studies so well in earlier eras have now also changed. Scholars have called into question the old anthropology of culture, with its language of bounded cultural entities, cultural contact, and cross-cultural communication. The dangers of essentialism have gained increasing urgency, especially among scholars of South Asia, who see the results of religious essentialism in the violent clashes on the Indian subcontinent (Appadurai, 2006). Deaf Studies has begun to encompass a cosmopolitan, transnational perspective that moves outside the phase of legitimization of the category of Deaf and into a critical inquiry into the nature of being deaf, how ways of understanding and living as deaf have shaped the material and ideological worlds of Deaf and hearing people. In fact, the very trope of "Deaf worlds" and "hearing worlds" is being understood as a product of a particular set of historical conditions (Murray, 2007).

There is a small, but growing, body of work that explores how deaf people interact across national boundaries (Breivik, Haualand, & Solvang, 2002; Murray, 2007; Nakamura, 2006). Transnational contact between deaf people existed since the early 19th century, emerging at a series of Parisian Deaf-mute banquets, and a tran-

snational Deaf public sphere developed alongside a series of international congresses of Deaf people from 1873 onward (Ladd, 2003; Murray, 2007). This sphere created a shared discursive field in which deaf people could articulate common strategies on living as visual minorities in societies governed by auditory principles. Taking a transnational orientation to deaf people's lives foregrounds the commonality of Deaf ways of being, but paradoxically also heightens our understanding of deaf people as intimately tied to local discursive constructions of nation and society. The physical assemblage of large numbers of deaf people often brings with it a reorganization of physical space according to Deaf norms, as deaf people temporarily colonize portions of a city at large-scale quadrennial events such as World Federation of the Deaf Congresses or Deaflympic sporting competitions. A complete understanding of the spatial reorganization that occurs and its implication in terms of "Deaf-gain" have yet to be realized. However, by viewing deaf peoples' lives in different national contexts, we also understand how integrated deaf people are into their national and social contexts. There are many ways to be Deaf, because deaf people are not isolated from the societies in which they live (Monaghan, Schmaling, Nakamura, & Turner, 2003).

An expanded frame of reference will naturally include the global South, which will have an increasingly prominent role in transnational Deaf communities of the future, especially if current demographic analyses regarding developed countries trend as predicted (Johnston, 2006). Economic disparities between the North and South have resulted in lesser rates of cochlear implantation, less use of genetic testing, and hindrances in the prevention of childhood illnesses, all of which have the result of expanding the population of deaf children and potential native signers. These factors will likely not persist, but what they mean for the present generation of deaf people is that the demographic imbalance between deaf people in developing and developed countries will likely become even more prominent, with the rate of sign language use presumably shifting to developing countries as well. The central loci of Deaf Studies may well shift from Western countries to the global South, from discretely bounded national communities to a more fluid array of affinitive networks of various sizes and forms, existing in both physical and virtual space (Breivik, 2007; Kusters, 2007).

CULTURAL DIVERSITY AND DEAF-GAIN: INTERNATIONAL SIGN AND SIGNED LANGUAGES

Communication at international meetings of Deaf individuals often occurs in International Sign (IS), a form of cross-national communication that emerges when signers from different signed languages come into contact. Most research on IS to date has studied its linguistic properties. Although this research is still developing, early conclusions indicate that IS has more language-like properties than pidgins, another form of communication that emerges when two or more languages come into contact (Supalla & Webb, 1995). There is evidence of IS being used as far back as the early 19th century (Ladd, 2003), when it was used for political discourse at international meetings, as well as in informal interactions between Deaf travelers (Murray, 2007). The ability of signing deaf people to meet and interact across linguistic boundaries—without sharing a common language beforehand—has existed for at least two centuries. Some of this is no doubt due to the common experience of being Deaf in nondeaf societies. One author attributes this ease of understanding to a shared theory of mind among Deaf people, the term referring to the ability to "inhabit and intuit" another person's consciousness (Fox, 2008, pp. 80–81). Fox notes that semantically related signs for mental processes (think, decide, believe) are located at or near the head in ASL and European signed languages (Fox, 2008, p. 82), thus possibly assisting users of one signed language in understanding another signed language. The study of IS is still in its early stages and questions remain. If international signed communication has existed for two centuries, has there been continuity in lexical or other structural properties of IS in this period? Can we characterize "it" as an "it," or were there many versions of IS throughout the decades? A community of users has existed, but was there generational transmission and if so, what does this tell us about the language-like properties of IS? Beyond a focus on IS as a distinct entity are questions IS raises by its very existence. At the very least, IS calls into question the inevitability of linguistic dissimilarities, with its apparatus of interpretation, and raises larger questions on the histories and modalities of communication between linguistically distinct groups of people.

The study of IS is part of a body of work going beyond the study of sign languages under national markers—ASL, Danish Sign Language—to a realization that signing exists in a diverse array of situations and communities. Scholars have seen a sign language being born in Nicaragua (Senghas, 1995, 2003) and are studying the use of signing among a Bedouin community in Israel (Fox, 2007; Sandler et al., 2005), one of many communities around the world where both hearing and deaf people sign (Groce, 1985; Johnson, 1994; Marsaja, 2008). There are obvious benefits to scholars in seeing linguistic phenomena take place in the field: scholars have never witnessed a spoken language being created, and the study of Nicaraguan sign language allows linguists the opportunity to see if their theories are correct. Think of astrophysicists being able to witness the Big Bang. Beyond this, the existence—and persistence—of sign languages allows us to understand the diversity of human ways of being and communicating, and offers a direct challenge to conceptions of normalcy that would peg all humans into a phonocentric square hole.

CULTURAL DIVERSITY AND DEAF-GAIN: DEAF COLLECTIVIST CULTURE AND THE FUTURE OF COMMUNITY

A growing body of research points toward the dissolution of a sense of community and civic engagement. Robert Putnam's *Bowling Alone: The Collapse and Revival of American Community* points to the factors of work, television, computers, suburban life, and family structures as having contributed to this decline. Other studies confirm Putnam's observations, noting that social networks and people's sense of connectedness have taken a precipitous decline in the past three decades (McPherson, Smith-Lovin, & Brashears, 2006). As a culture that exhibits a high degree of collectivism (Mindess, 2006), Deaf cultural relations may offer insights and examples to understand, if not emulate. The circular proxemics of deaf people as they align themselves to be seen are the structural embodiment of nonhierarchical relations. Although Derrida (1973) has highlighted the significance of "hearing oneself speak" as a prime source of deriving a sense of presence, deaf individuals can neither hear themselves speak nor fully see themselves sign (Bauman, January, 2008). Granted that signers may see their own hand movements from their vantage, they will never be able to see their own faces, which are so vital to the linguistic and emotional content of sign language expression. The sense of presence conveyed through the system of hearing oneself speak is radically altered through the self-awareness of one's own signing. The sense of presence for signers, then, is derived through the presence of the *other*. This constant confirmation of presence through the face of the other may partially explain the prevalence of collectivism of Deaf cultures. Although the significance of prolonged face-to-face engagement and eye contact over a lifetime cannot be underestimated, little research has been done to understand the psychological implications of Deaf ways of being together.

One study is currently under way to examine the nature of human contact in the example of the "Deaf walk" as opposed to the hearing walk (Sirvage, forthcoming). As two hearing individuals engage in discussion while walking, they simply need to ensure that they are close enough and speak loudly enough for the other to hear. There is no need for eye contact. Significantly, when deaf people walk, however, they engage in constant eye contact, and more significantly, they must take care of the other person, extending their peripheral vision to ensure that the other person does not walk into any objects. Although this may seem a minor point, there is a larger lesson about the nature of Deaf collectivist relations. Signers take care of each other, whether strangers or intimate friends, when engaged in a peripatetic conversation. Future studies should inquire into expanding the notion of the Deaf walk to larger cultural ways of being that may have lessons for an increasingly isolated society.

SUMMARY AND CONCLUSIONS: MEDIA PRODUCTION AND THE DEAF PUBLIC VOICE

This brief discussion of human diversity and Deaf-gain has little to do with a critique of audism, or any other defensive posture that has largely characterized late 20th-century and early 21st-century Deaf Studies. The critique of power relations that forms a principal activity of all cultural studies is implicit in pointing out what has been lost in the oversight of sign languages and Deaf communities as having intrinsic and extrinsic value to human diversity. By taking advantage of the unique Deaf ways of being, forms of cultural production may provide new areas of experimentation and insight, left hidden in the phonocentric blindspots within the ways that cultural practices and disciplines have evolved.

Commerson (2008) suggested that such a reframing of human diversity and Deaf Studies would be more likely to take place if there is a strong visual presence in media. If deafness is reframed from lack to gain, then the sense of gain may be embodied through characters in film, television, video, Internet sites, newspapers, and other forms of public discourse. Given the existential threats to Deaf communities and their languages, the 21st-century practice of Deaf Studies must move from a defensive posture to one that actively seeks to redefine public perception—and do so quickly.

As 21st-century Deaf Studies argues for both intrinsic and extrinsic value, it must be careful to make the point that this argument is not simply for the preservation of deaf people and sign languages for the sake of scientific exploration of the human character. Instead, Deaf Studies may want to take the counterintuitive position that all individuals would be enriched by become a bit more Deaf. By that we mean society would do well to become more acutely aware of the nuances of communication, more engaged with eye contact and tactile relations, more fluent in a language rich in embodied metaphor, more aware of the role of being a member of close-knit communities, and if nothing else, more appreciative of human diversity, so that

we ate constantly reminded that the bedrock of reality may be just as diaphanous as any other social construction. As Sandel (2007) argues in *The Case Against Perfection,* human diversity teaches us the value of moving from an ethic of molding individuals to beholding them in their extraordinarily rich ways of being.

NOTES

1. The notion of "Deaf-gain" was originally articulated by the British performance artist, Aaron Williamson, who, when presenting to Dirksen Bauman's graduate class, "Enforcing Normalcy," stated that while all his doctors told him that he was losing his hearing, not one told him that he was gaining his deafness.

2. As Stokoe (2001) described, "The nerves connecting eyes and brain outnumber by far all the brain connections to the other sensory organs, the ears included. Visual processing involves so much of the brain that a visual field may convey an enormous amount of information simultaneously, whereas language sounds have to reach the ear sequentially, one by one, until the whole message is received and can be interpreted."

3. Despite no widely accepted written form, there have been many attempts throughout history. One of the earliest is August Bebian's Mimography (Renard, 2004), the most well-known is probably Sign Writing (http://www.signwriting.org/), and a promising new form is being developed by Arnold (2007).

REFERENCES

Akamatsu, C. T., Musselman, C., & Zweibel, A. (2000). Nature versus nurture in the development of cognition in deaf people. In P. Spencer, C. Erting, & M. Marschark (Eds.), *The deaf child in the family and at school.* (pp. 255–274). Mahwah, NJ: Lawrence Erlbaum Associates.

Allen, S. (2007). *A deaf diaspora: Exploring underlying cultural yearnings for a deaf home.* Master's thesis, Gallaudet University, Washington, DC.

Appadurai, A. (2006). *Fear of small numbers: An essay on the geography of anger.* Durham, NC: Duke University Press.

Arijon, D. (1991). *Grammar of the film language.* Los Angeles: Silman-James Press.

Armstrong, D. (2002). *Original signs: Gesture, sign, and the sources of language.* Washington, DC: Gallaudet University Press.

Armstrong, D., & Wilcox, S. (2007). *The gestural origins of language.* Cambridge: Cambridge University Press.

Armstrong, D., Wilcox S., & Stokoe, W. (1995). *Gesture and the nature of language.* Cambridge: Cambridge University Press.

Arnold, R. (2007). *Proposal for a written form of American Sign Language.* Unpublished master's thesis, Gallaudet University, Washington, DC, United States of America.

Arnos, K. (2003). The implications of genetic testing for deafness. *Ear and Hearing, 24,* 324–331.

Bahan, B. (2006). Face-to-face tradition in the American deaf community: Dynamics of the teller, the tale and the audience. In Bauman, H.-D., Nelson, J., & Rose, H. (2006). *Signing the body poetic: Essays on American Sign Language literature.* (pp. 21–50). Berkeley: University of California Press.

Bahan, B. (2008). On the formation of a visual variety of the human race. In Bauman, H.-D. (Ed.) (2008). *Open your eyes: Deaf studies talking.* (pp. 83–99). Minneapolis: University of Minnesota Press.

Bauman, H.-D. (in press). *Gallaudet university deaf and diverse campus design guide.* Washington, DC: Gallaudet University institutional document.

Bauman, H.-D. (2006). Getting out of line: Toward a visual and cinematic poetics of ASL. In Bauman, H.-D., Nelson, J., & Rose, H. (2006). *Signing the body poetic: Essays on American Sign Language literature.* (pp. 95–117). Berkeley: University of California Press.

Bauman, H.-D. (2008). Body/text: Sign language poetics and spatial form in literature. In K. Lindgren, D. DeLuca, & D. J. Napoli (Eds.), *Signs and voices: Deaf culture, language, identity, and arts.* (pp. 163–176). Washington, DC: Gallaudet University Press.

Bauman, H.-D. (2008). Listening to phonocentrism with deaf eyes: Derrida's mute philosophy of (sign) language. *Essays in Philosophy, 9*(1). Retrieved October 22, 2009 from http://www.humboldt.edu/~essays/bauman.html

Bauman, H.-D., Nelson, J., & Rose, H. (2006). *Signing the body poetic: Essays on American Sign Language literature.* Berkeley: University of California Press.

Bavelier, D., Tomann, A., Hutton, C., Mitchell, T. V., Corina, D. P., Liu, G., & Neville, H. J. (2000). Visual attention to the periphery is enhanced in congenitally deaf individuals. *Journal of Neuroscience, 20,* 1–6.

Baynton, D. C. (1996). *Forbidden signs: American culture and the campaign against sign language.* Chicago: University of Chicago Press.

Baynton, D. C. (2000). Disability and the justification of inequality in American history. In P. Longmore & L. Umansky (Eds.), *The new disability history: American perspectives* (pp. 33–57). New York: New York University Press.

Bebian, A. (1984). Essay on the deaf and natural language, or introduction to a natural classification of ideas with their proper signs. In H. Lane (Ed.), *The Deaf experience: Classics in language and education.* Trans. F. Philip. Cambridge, MA: Harvard University Press.

Bell, A. G. (1883). *Memoir upon the formation of a deaf variety of the human race.* Washington, DC: Volta Bureau.

Bellugi, U., O'Grady, L., Lillio-Martin, D., O'Grady Hynes, M., Van Hoek, K., & Corina, D. (1989). In V. Volterra & C. Erting (Eds.), *Enhancement of spatial cognition in deaf children: Gesture to language in hearing children* (pp. 278–298). New York: Springer-Verlag.

Bettger, J. G., Emmorey, K., McCullough, S. H., & Bellugi, U. (1997). Enhanced facial discrimination: Effects of experience with American Sign Language. *Journal of Deaf Studies and Deaf Education, 2,* 223–233.

Biesold, H. (1999). *Crying hands: Eugenics and deaf people in Nazi Germany.* Washington, DC: Gallaudet University Press.

Breivik, J. K. (2007). *Dov identitet i endring-lokale liv-globale bevegelser.* Oslo: Universitetsforlaget.

Breivik, J. K., Haualand, H., & Solvang, P. (2002). *Rome—a temporary deaf city!* Deaflympics 2001. Bergen, Norway: Rokkansentret Working Paper 2–2003.

Brownstein, Z., & Avraham, K. B. (2006). Future trends and potential for treatment of sensorineural hearing loss. *Seminars in Hearing, Genetics and Hearing Loss, 27* (3), 193–204.

Bryan, A. (November 22, 2007). Parliament: Deaf embryo selection to be made illegal. [Blog entry]. Retrieved November 20, 2008, from http://www.grumpyoldeafies.com/2007/11/parliament_deaf_embroyo_select.html

Burch, S. (2002). *Signs of Resistance: American Deaf Cultural History, 1900 to World War II.* New York: New York University Press.

Burke, T. B. (2006). Bioethics and the deaf community. In K. Lindgren, D. DeLuca, & D. J. Napoli (Eds.), *Signs and voices: Deaf culture, identity, language, and arts* (pp. 63–74). Washington, DC: Gallaudet University Press.

Burke, T. B. (December 5, 2007). British bioethics and the human fertilisation and embryology bill. [Blog entry]. Retrieved November 20, 2008, from http://www.deafdc.com/blog/teresa-blankmeyer-burke/2007-l2-05/british-bioethics-and-the-human-fertilisation-and-emhryology-bill/

Carty, B. (2006). Comments on "w(h)ither the deaf community?" *Sign Language Studies 6* (2), 18l–l89.

Chorost, M. (2005). *Rebuilt: How becoming part computer made me more human.* Boston. MA: Houghton Mifflin Harcourt.

Cohn, J. (1999). *Sign mind: Studies in American Sign Language poetics.* Boulder, CO: Museum of American Poetics Publications.

Commerson, R. (2008). *Media, power and ideology: Re-presenting DEAF.* Master's thesis, Gallaudet University, Washington, DC. Retrieved from http://mosinternational.com/

Cook, P. (Author and Signer). (2006). Hydrogen jukebox [ASL story on DVD]. In Bauman, H.-D., Nelson, J., & Rose, H. *Signing the body poetic: Essays in American Sign Language literature.* Berkeley: University of California Press.

Corballis, M. (2003). *From hand to mouth: On the origins of language.* Princeton, NJ: Princeton University Press.

Cripps, J., & Small, A. (2004). *Case report re: Provincial service delivery gaps for deaf children 0–5 years of age.* Mississauga, ON: Ontario Cultural Society of the Deaf.

Crystal, D. (2002). *Language death.* Cambridge: Cambridge University Press.

Davidson, M. (2008). Tree-tangled in tree: Re-siting poetry through ASL. In K. Lindgren, D. DeLuca, & D. J. Napoli (Eds.), *Signs and voices: Deaf culture, identity, language and arts.* (pp. 177–188). Washington, DC: Gallaudet University Press.

Davis, L. (1995). *Enforcing normalcy: Deafness, disability and the body.* London: Verso Press.

Davis, L. (2006). Constructing normalcy: The bell curve, the novel, and the invention of the disabled body in the nineteenth century. In L. Davis (Ed.), *The disability studies reader* (pp. 3–16). New York: Taylor & Francis.

Derrida, J. (1973). Of grammatology. Trans. G. Spivak. Baltimore: Johns Hopkins University Press.

Emmorey, K., Klima, S. L., & Hickok, G. (1998). Mental rotation within linguistic and non-linguistic domains in users of American Sign Language. *Cognition, 68,* 221–226.

Emmorey, K., & Kosslyn, S. (1996). Enhanced image generation abilities in deaf signers: A right hemisphere effect. *Brain and Cognition, 32,* 28–44.

Emmorey, K., Kosslyn, S., & Bellugi, U. (1993). Visual imagery and visual-spatial language: Enhanced visual imagery abilities in deaf and hearing ASL signers. *Cognition, 46,* 139–181.

Erting, C. J., Johnson, R. C., Smith, D. L., & Snider, B. C. (1993). *The deaf way: Perspectives from the international conference on deaf culture.* Washington DC: Gallaudet University Press.

Findley, L. (2005). *Building change: Architecture, politics and cultural agency.* New York: Routledge.

Foucault, M. (1990). *History of sexuality Vol. 1. The will to knowledge.* New York: Vintage Press.

Fox, M. (2008). *Talking hands: What sign language reveals about the mind.* New York: Simon & Schuster.

Frontrunners Weekly Reports. (2005, September 30). Interviews on genocide. *Frontrunners.* Retrieved November 29, 2008, from http://frl.frontrunners.dk/Weekly%20Reports/weeklyreports.htm

Furman, N., Goldberg, D., & Lusin, N. (November 13, 2007). Foreign language enrollments in united states institutions of higher education, fall 2006. *Modern Language Association.*

Retrieved November 23, 2009, from http://www.mla.org/2006_flenrollmentsurvey

Gardner, H. (1993). *Frames of mind: The theory of multiple intelligences.* New York: Basic Books.

Generic Evaluation of Congenital Hearing Loss Expert Panel. (2002). Genetics evaluation guidelines for the etiologic diagnosis of congenital hearing loss. *Genetics of Medicine, 4* (3), 162–171.

Golden, J. (2009). *Deaf ASL and visual theatre: Connections and opportunities.* Unpublished master's thesis, Gallaudet University, Washington, DC.

Gray, R. (2008, April 13). Couples could win right to select deaf baby. *Telegraph.co.uk.* Retrieved (November 29, 2008, from http://www.telegraph.co.uk/news/uknews/1584948/Couples-could-win-right-to-select-deaf-baby.html (Reader comments at: http://www.telegraph.co.uk/news/yourview/1584973/How-far-should-embryo-selection-go.html)

Groce, N. (1985). *Everyone here spoke sign language: Hereditary deafness on Martha's Vineyard.* Cambridge, MA: Harvard University Press.

Hall, S. (1973). *Encoding and decoding in television discourse.* Birmingham, AL: Birmingham Centre for Cultural Studies.

Harmon, D. (2002). *In light of our differences: How diversity in nature and culture makes us human.* Washington, DC: Smithsonian Institution Press.

Haualand, H. (Writer), & Otterstedt, L. (Director). (2007). *Arven etter frankenstein.* [Theatrical Production]. Oslo, Norway: Theater Manu.

Hiddinga, A., Pot, L. (Filmmakers); Emmerik, W, & Meyer, G. (Poets). (2005). *Motioning.* Amsterdam, Holland: Geelprodukt Productions.

Hoggart, R. (1957). *The uses of literacy in everyday life.* London: Chatto & Windus.

Hyde, M., Power, D. J., & Lloyd, K. (2006). Comments on "W(h)ither the deaf community?" *Sign Language Studies, 6* (2), 190–201.

Johannsen, K. (2008). Electronic mail communication received December 29, 2008.

Johnson, R. (1994). *Sign language and. the concept of deafness in a traditional Yucatec Mayan village.* In C. Erting, R. Johnson, D. Smith, & B. Sniden (Eds.), *The deaf way: Perspectives from the international conference on deaf culture* (pp. 102–109). Washington, DC: Gallaudet University Press.

Johnston, T. (2004). W(h)ither the deaf community? Population, genetics, and the future of Australian Sign Language. *American Annals of the Deaf, 148* (5). Reprinted in (2006) *Sign Language Studies, 6* (2), 137–173.

Kochhar, A., Hildebrand, M. S., & Smith, R. J. (2007). Clinical aspects of hereditary hearing loss. *Genetics in Medicine, 9* (7), 393–408.

Krentz, C. (2000). *A mighty change: An anthology of deaf American writing, 1816–1864.* Washington, DC: Gallaudet University Press.

Kuntze, M. (2008). Turning literacy on its head. In H.-D. Bauman (Ed.), *Open your eyes: Deaf studies talking.* Minneapolis: University of Minnesota Press.

Kusters, A. (2007). *"Reserved for the handicapped?" Deafhood on the lifeline of Mumbai.* Unpublished master's thesis, University of Bristol.

Ladd, P. (2003). *Understanding deaf culture: In search of deafhood.* Clevedon, UK: Multicultural Matters.

Lane, H. (1984). *When the mind hears: A history of the deaf.* New York: Random House.

Lane, H. (1992). *The mask of benevolence: Disabling the deaf community.* New York: Alfred A. Knopf.

Lane, H., & Fischer, R. (1993). Looking back: A reader on the history of deaf communities and their sign languages. *International Studies on Sign Language and Communication of the Deaf, 20.* Hamburg: Signum Verlag.

Lane, H., Hoffmeister, R., & Bahan, B. (1996). *Journey into the deaf world.* San Diego: Dawn Sign Press.

Lentz, E. (Poet), & Taylor, L. (Filmmaker). (1996). *The treasure* [Signed Poetry]. Berkeley, California: InMotion Press.

Maffi, L. (2005). Linguistic, cultural, and biological diversity. *Annual Review of Anthropology, 34,* 599–617.

Malzkuhn, M. (2007). *Home customization: Understanding deaf ways of being.* Unpublished master's thesis, Gallaudet University, Washington, DC.

Marsaja, I. G. (2008). *Desa Kolok: A deaf village and its sign language in Bali, Indonesia.* Nijmegen, the Netherlands: lshara Press.

Marschark, M. (2003). Cognitive functioning in deaf adults and children. In M. Marschark & P. Spencer (Eds.), *Oxford handbook of deaf studies, language, and education.* Oxford: Oxford University Press.

McPherson, M., Cinith Lovin, L., & Braohoaro, M. E. (2006). Social isolation in America: Changes in core discussion networks over two decades. *American Sociological Review, 71,* 353–375.

Mindess, A. (2006). *Reading between the signs. Intercultural communication for sign language interpreters,* 2nd edition. Boston: Intercultural Press.

Monaghan, L., Schmaling, C., Nakamura, K., & Turner, G. H. (2003). *Many ways to be deaf: International variation in deaf communities.* Washington, DC: Gallaudet University Press.

Moore, D., & Dwyer, F. (1994). *Visual literacy: A spectrum of visual learning.* Englewood Cliffs, NJ: Educational Technology Publications.

Morton, C. C, & Nance, W. E. (2006). Newborn hearing screening—a silent revolution. *New England Journal of Medicine, 354* (20), 2151–2164.

Mundy, L. (2002, March 31). A world of their own. *The Washington Post,* pp. W22.

Murray, J. (2002). True love and sympathy: The deaf-deaf marriages debate in transatlantic perspective. In J. V. Van Cleve (Ed.), *Genetics, disability, and deafness.* (pp. 42–71). Washington, DC: Gallaudet University Press.

Murray, J. (2006). Genetics: A future peril facing the global deaf community. In H. Goodstein (Ed.), *The Deaf way II reader: Perspectives from the Second International Conference on Deaf Culture* (pp. 351–356). Washington, DC: Gallaudet University Press.

Murray, J. (2007). *A touch of nature makes the whole world kin: The transnational lives of deaf Americans.* Unpublished doctoral dissertation, University of Iowa.

Nakamura, K. (2006). *Deaf in Japan: Signing and the politics of identity.* Ithaca, NY: Cornell University Press.

Noble, T. (2003, July 11). Deafness-test embryo fails to take. *The Age.* Retrieved November 23, 2009, from http://www.theage.com.au/articles/2003/07/10/1057783282446.html

Office of Public Sector Information. (2008). *The National Archives.* Retrieved January 2009, from http://www.opsi.gov.uk/acts/acts2008/ukpga_20080022_en_2#ptl-pb5-1lgl4

Padden, C., & Humphries, T. (1988). *Deaf in America: Voices from a culture.* Cambridge, MA: Harvard University Press.

Potitto, L. A., Zatorro, R., Gauna, K., Nikolski, F. J., Dostie, D., & Evans, A. (December 5, 2000). Speech-like cerebral activity in profoundly deaf people while processing signed languages: Implications for the neural basis of human language. *Proceedings of the National Academy of Sciences, 97* (25), 13961–13966.

Putnam, R. (2000). *Bowling alone: The collapse and revival of American community.* New York: Simon & Schuster.

Renard, M. (2004). *Ecrire les signes. La mimographie d'Auguste Bébian et les notations contemporaines. [Escribir las señas. La Mimografía de Auguste Bébian y las notaciones contemporáneas].* Paris: Editions du Fox.

Sacks, O. (1990). *Seeing voices: Journey into the deaf world.* Berkeley: University of California Press.

Salmi, E., & Laakso, M. (2005). *Maahan lämpimäänn: Suomen viittomakielisten historia.* Helsinki: Kuurojen Liittory.

Sandel, M. (2007). *The case against perfection: Ethics in the age of genetic engineering.* Cambridge, MA: Havard University Press.

Sandler, W., Meir, I., Padden, C., & Aronoff, M. (2005). The emergence of grammar in a new sign language. *Proceedings of the National Academy of Sciences, 102* (7), 2661–2665.

Senghas, A. (1995). Conventionalization in the first generation: A community acquires a language. *USD Journal of Contemporary Legal Issues, 6,* Spring, 1995.

Senghas, A. (2003). Intergenerational influence and ontogenetic development in the emergence of spatial grammar in Nicaraguan Sign Language. *Cognitive Development, 18,* 511–531.

Sirvage, R. (forthcoming). *Walking signers: An investigation on proxemics.* Unpublished master's thesis. Gallaudet University, Washington, DC.

Skutnabb-Kangas, T. (2000). *Linguistic genocide in education—or worldwide diversity and human rights?* Mahwah, NJ: Lawrence Erlbaum Associates.

Snoddon, K. (2008). "American Sign Language

and early intervention." *Canadian Modern Language Review, 64* (4). June (pp. 581–604).

Stokoe, W. (2001). *Language in hand: Why sign came before speech.* Washington, DC: Gallaudet University Press.

Supalla, T., & Webb, R. (1995). The grammar of international sign: A new look at pidgin languages. In K. Emmorey & J. S. Reilly (Eds.), *Language, gesture, and space* (pp. 333–351). Hillsdale, NJ: Lawrence Erlbaum Associates.

Sutton, V. (2008). Retrieved November 20, 2008 from www.signwriting.org

Taub, S. (2001). *Language from the body: Iconicity and metaphor in American Sign Language.* Cambridge: University of Cambridge Press.

Van Cleve, J. V. (1993). *Deaf history unveiled: Interpretations from the new scholarship.* Washington, DC: Gallaudet University Press.

Van Cleve, J. V., & Crouch, B. A. (1989). *A place of their own: Creating the deaf community in America.* Washington, DC: Gallaudet University Press.

VL2. (2008). Visual language and visual learning website introduction. Retrieved November 20, 2008, from http://vl2.gallaudet.edu/

Wallvik, B. (1997). . . . *ett folk uten land* . . . Borgå: Finland: Döva och hörselskadade barns stödforening r.f.

Welles, E. B. (2004). Foreign language enrollments in United States institutions of higher education. *ADFL Bulletin, 35* (2–3).

Wilcox, P. (2000). *Metaphor in American Sign Language.* Washington, DC: Gallaudet University Press.

Willard, T. (n.d.). Special Report: Laurent, SD in Deafweekly. Deafweekly electronic mailing list. Retrieved November 20, 2008, from http://www.deafweekly.com/backissues/laurent.htm

Williams, R. (1958). *Culture and society, 1780–1950.* London and New York: Columbia University Press.

Williams, R. (1961). *The long revolution.* London and New York: Columbia University Press.

PART V

*I*dentities and Intersectionalities

CHAPTER 20

The End of Identity Politics: On Disability as an Unstable Category

Lennard J. Davis

There are times when the black man is locked into his body. Now, "for a being who has acquired consciousness of himself and of his body, who has attained the dialectic of subject and object, the body is no longer a cause of the structure of consciousness, it has become an object of consciousness."

—Frantz Fanon, citing Merleau-Ponty,
Black Skin, White Masks

At times we might look back nostalgically to the moment when identity was relatively simple, when it was possible to say that one *was* black or white, male or female, "Indian" or not. It might once have been possible to answer the question that James Weldon Johnson's narrator in *The Autobiography of an Ex-Colored Man* asks his mother "Are you white?" with her clear reply, "No, I am not white . . ." (8). But the issue of identity by race, gender, or sexual orientation, particularly in America, has become more clouded, fuzzier, grainier than it used to be. And so, the issue of a disability identity has begun to enter murkier grounds.

When I discussed the idea of clouding the issue of disability identity, a prominent disability scholar advised me not to pursue this line of thinking. "We're not ready to dissolve disability identity. We're just beginning to form it." While I agree that there is a strategic kind of identity politics one

might want to pursue, especially early on in an academic or political movement, I also think that ignoring the current seismic shifts in identity politics would be equally disastrous and could lead to major instability in the near future. If disability studies were to ignore the current intellectual moment and plow ahead using increasingly antiquated models, the very basis for the study of the subject could be harmed by making its premises seem irrelevant, shoddily thought through, and so on.

In effect, we do have to acknowledge that, unlike race, class, gender, sexual preference, and the like, disability is a relatively new category. Although the category has existed for a long time, its present form as a political and cultural formation has only been around since the 1970s, and has come into some kind of greater visibility since the late 1980s. The political and academic movement around disability is at best a first- or second-wave enterprise. The first wave of any struggle involves the establishment of the identity against the societal definitions that were formed largely by oppression. In this first phase, the identity—be it blackness, or gayness, or Deafness—is hypostasized, normalized, turned positive against the negative descriptions used by the oppressive regime. Thus "Black is Beautiful," "Gay Pride," and "Deaf Power" might be seen as mere reappropriations of a formerly derogatory discourse. The first phase also implies a pulling together of forces, an agreement to agree for political ends and group solidarity, along with the tacit approval of an agenda for the establishment of basic rights and prohibitions against various kinds of discrimination and ostracism.

In a second wave, a newer generation of people within the identity group, ones who have grown up with the libratory models well in place, begin to redefine the struggle and the subject of study. They no longer seek group solidarity since they have a firm sense of identity. In a second wave, the principals are comfortable about self-examining, finding diversity within the group, and struggling to redefine the identity in somewhat more nuanced and complex ways. Often this phase will produce conflict within a group rather than unity. We've seen this most dramatically in the feminist movement when second-wave thinkers like Judith Butler have critiqued earlier essentialist notions that pulled the movement together initially. The conflict can come from differences that have been suppressed for the sake of maintaining a unified front so that the group could emerge in the first place and resist the formerly oppressive categorization and treatment.

Disability studies is, as I have said, a relatively new field of study. Its earliest proponents were writing in the 1970s and 1980s. The second wave of disability writing can be seen as emerging in the 1990s. Both the first and second waves have had a strong interest in preserving the notion of a distinct and clear entity known variously as "people with disabilities" (PWDs) or "Deaf people." In the case of PWDs, the interest has been in creating a collectivity where before there had been disunity. In the past, people with disabilities did not identify as such. Medical definitions of im-

pairments were developed with no need to create unity among diverse patient groups. Wheelchair users saw no commonality with people with chronic fatigue syndrome or Deaf people. Given the American ethic of individuality and personal achievement, there would have been little incentive for PWDs to identify with the "handicaps" of other people. Rather, the emphasis would have been on personal growth, or overcoming the disability, and normalization through cure, prosthesis, or medical interventions. With the return of veterans from the Vietnam war, a movement grew up around civil rights for people with disabilities, which culminated in the Americans with Disabilities Act of 1990. By the beginning of the millennium disability activism, consciousness, and disability studies is well established, although many areas of the ADA are being rolled back in the courts and in the legislature.[1]

To begin with, one might want to point out the obvious point that history repeats itself. As Marx wrote about the failed revolution in France, people tend to model political movements on those of the past. For people with disabilities the civil rights model was seen as more progressive and better than the earlier charity and medical models. In the earlier versions, people with disabilities were seen variously as poor, destitute creatures in need of the help of the church or as helpless victims of disease in need of the correction offered by modern medical procedures. The civil rights model, based on the struggles of African Americans in the United States, seemed to offer a better paradigm. Not plagued by God nor beset by disease, people with disabilities were seen as minority citizens deprived of their rights by a dominant ableist majority.

Along with this model went the social model, which saw disability as a constructed category, not one bred into the bone. This social model is in dialogue with what is often referred to as the British model, which sees a distinction between impairment and disability. Impairment is the physical fact of lacking an arm or a leg. Disability is the social process that turns an impairment into a negative by creating barriers to access. The clearest example of this distinction is seen in the case of wheelchair users. They have impairments that limit mobility, but are not disabled unless they are in environments without ramps, lifts, and automatic doors. So, as long as the minority and/or social model held fast, this model seems to have worked pretty well, or at least as well as the civil rights model itself worked.

Enter postmodernity. The postmodern critique is one that destabilizes grand, unifying theories, that renders problematic desires to unify, to create wholes, to establish foundations. One could fill archives with what has been said or written about the culture wars, the science wars, and whatever other wars. In terms of identity, there has been an interesting and puzzling result. The one area that remained relatively unchallenged despite the postmodern deconstructionist assault was the notion of group identity. Indeed, the postmodern period is the one that saw the proliferation of multiculturality. One could attack the shibboleths of almost any ground of knowledge, but one could never attack the notion of being, for example, African American, a woman, or gay. To do so would be tantamount to being part of the oppressive system that created categories of oppressed others. One could interrogate the unity of the novel, science, even physics, but one could not interrogate one's right to be female, of color, or queer. Given this resistant notion of identity, the disability movement quite rightly desired to include disability as part of the multicultural quilt. If all the identities were under the same tent, then disability wanted to be part of the academic and cultural solidarity that

being of a particular, oppressed minority represented.

Yet, within that strong notion of identity and identity politics, a deconstructive worm of thought began its own parasitic life. That worm targeted "essentialism." Just as no one wants to be a vulgar Marxist, no one wanted to be an essentialist. Essentialists—and there were fewer and fewer of them very soon after we began to hear the word—were putatively accused of claiming in a rather simple-minded way that being a woman or an ethnic minority was somehow rooted in the body. That identity was tied to the body, written on the body. Rather, the way out of this reductionist mode was to say that the body and identities around the body were socially constructed and performative. So while postmodernism eschewed the whole, it could accept that the sum of the parts made up the whole in the form of the multicultural, rainbow quilt of identities [2] Social constructionism and performativity seemed to offer the way out of the problem caused by the worm of essentialism, but it also created severe problems in shaping notions of identity. [3] If all identities are socially constructed or performative, is there a core identity there? Is there a there?

Disability offers us a way to rethink some of these dilemmas, but in order to do so, I think we need to reexamine the identity of disability, and to do so without flinching, without hesitating because we may be undoing a way of knowing. As with race, gender, and sexual orientation, we are in the midst of a grand reexamination. Disability, as the most recent identity group on the block, offers us the one that is perhaps least resistant to change or changing thoughts about identity. And, most importantly, as I will argue, disability may turn out to be the identity that links other identities, replacing the notion of postmodernism with something I want to call "dismodernism."

I am arguing that disability can be seen as the postmodern subject position for several reasons. But the one I want to focus on now is that these other discourses of race, gender, and sexuality began in the mid-nineteenth century, and they did so because that is when the scientific study of humans began. The key connecting point for all these studies was the development of eugenics.[4] Eugenics saw the possible improvement of the race as being accomplished by diminishing problematic peoples and their problematic behaviors—these peoples were clearly delineated under the rubric of feeble-mindedness and degeneration as women, people of color, homosexuals, the working classes, and so on. All these were considered to be categories of disability, although we do not think of them as connected in this way today. Indeed, one could argue that categories of oppression were given scientific license through these medicalized, scientificized discourses, and that, in many cases, the specific categories were established through these studies.

Postmodernity along with science now offers us the solvent to dissolve many of these categories. In the area of race, we now know, for example, that there is no genetic basis to the idea that race, in its eugenic sense, exists. Thus far, no one has been able to identify a person as belonging to a specific "race" through DNA analysis. In fact, DNA analysis lets us understand that the category of race does not exist in physiological terms. Further, DNA analysis tells us that there is more genetic variation within a group we have called a race than within the entire human gene pool. Indeed, no one is even able to tell us how many races there are, and fine distinctions between phenotypes tend to dissolve the notion of categorical racial identities even further. The Human Genome Project offered up the possibility of mapping with certainty the complete sequence of approximately 3.2 billion pairs of nucleotides that make us human. But the project has left us with more questions than it has answered. For example, scientists are puzzling over the relatively low count of genes in the human genome. It had been estimated that humans would have approximately 100,000 genes, but the study yielded a mere 30,000, putting Homo sapiens on par with the mustard cress plant (25,000 genes) in terms of genetic complexity.[5] More annoying and less known is the fact that the two groups who analyzed the genome, the privately owned Celera group and the government-financed consortium of academic centers, have come up with only 15,000 that they jointly agree on. Fifteen thousand more genes do not overlap in either analysis.[6] Considerable doubt exists as to whether these genes are "real."

More to the point, there is considerable confusion over race in relation to genetics. On the one hand, we are told that the mapped human genome, taken from the DNA of one or two individuals, is the same for all humans. We are further informed that there is relatively little diversity in our genetic makeup. But we are also told that various "races" and ethnic groups have differing genetic markers for disability, defect, and disease. The contradiction is one that has been little explored, and those who have pursued the point have come under criticism for racializing genetics.[7] Central to the confusion is the category of race itself. If we say, on the one hand, that there is no genetic way to ascertain race, and we also say that we have examined certain racial groups and discovered a greater chance of finding a particular gene, then we have indeed mixed our scientific categories.[8]

If we step back from the genetic level, we might want to investigate identity questions at the cellular level. Here, tellingly, we could investigate the HeLa cells widely used in laboratories and schools in what is called an "immortal cell line," much like the lines developed currently for stem-cell research. These cells all derive from an African American woman named Henrietta Lacks who died in 1951 of cervical cancer. The cells were taken without the permission of Ms. Lacks, and became so widespread as to be ubiquitous. For the point of view of this discussion, the cells were presumed to be universal until 1967, when a geneticist named Stanley Gartler announced that at least eighteen other cell lines had been contaminated by the HeLa cells. He determined this by insisting that the presence of G6PD (glucose-6-phosphate dehydrogenase), an enzyme which is a factor in red blood cell production, had been a marker in all these lines and that this type of enzyme "has been found only in Negroes" (61).[9] Thus, during the early period of genetic research previously universal cells were racialized at the cellular level. But the appearance of race at the cellular level is no longer possible or relevant. The markers thought to be of a specific racial group have no validity for that identificatory purpose.

The issue of race is also complicated by the use of in vitro fertilization in a recent case of "scrambled eggs," in which a fertility doctor implanted in a woman's womb not only her own fertilized embryo but that of another couple as well. The resulting birth was of fraternal twins, one white and the other black.[10] Such complications of reproductive technologies will certainly lead to other kinds of choices being made by parents and physicians, intentional as well as unintentional, with the effect of rendering even more complex racial or even gender identity.[11] Finally, the patrolled area of "mixed race" is being interrogated. The fact that multiracial identifications have been prohibited on national censuses is now being challenged. The reasons for keeping single-race checkoff boxes is itself a highly politicized and tactical arena in which, understandably, oppressed groups have gained redress and power by creating a unified subject. Where censuses allow a mixed-race checkoff, the statistical stronghold of race may well become weakened with questionable results.

In the area of gender, we are also seeing confusions in otherwise fixed categories. A culture of transgendered peoples is now being more widely permitted and the right to be transgendered is being actively fought for. The neat binaries of male and female are being complicated by volition, surgery, and the use of pharmaceuticals. Intersexuals, formerly known as hermaphrodites, were routinely operated upon at birth to assign them a specific gender. That move is now being contested by groups of adult intersexuals. Some feel they were assigned the wrong gender, and others feel that they would have liked to remain indeterminate. Transsexuals now routinely occupy various locations along a gender continuum, demarcating their place by clothing and other style-related choices, surgical corrections, and hormonal therapy. Even on the genetic level, females who are genetically male and males who are genetically female are a naturally occurring phenomenon. The gender determination is suppressed or enhanced in these cases of "Turner Syndrome" or "Klinefelter Syndrome," so that the genetic markers do not express the expected sexual phenotypes.[12]

Likewise, ethnicity is increasingly seen as problematic. Indeed, writers like Benedict Anderson have shown us that the idea of the nation is formed out of the suppression of ethnicities, although those ethnicities can end up forming new national consciousnesses. Steven Steinberg asserts that ethnicity is only one generation deep, and that all citizens become Americans after that generation, with only a thin veneer of food choices or other accoutrements of their ethnic origin to hold onto.[13]

Sexual orientation, which in the heyday of identity politics had a fairly definitive hold on defining a self, is now being questioned by many under the rubric of "queer studies." Whereas once the choice of sexual partner indicated who one was—gay, lesbian, heterosexual, or bisexual—now, in an era of dissolving boundaries, sexual orientation has become strangely unhinged, especially with the advent of transgender politics. When a male-to-female transsexual marries a person who defines herself as a woman, should that relationship be called lesbian? If an intersexual person chooses a person of either gender, or another intersexual, how do we define the relationship? In such cases, sexual orientation becomes the only option that does not define the person in all ways as fitting into a discrete category. The change from the expression "sexual preference" to "sexual orientation" serves to indicate something hardwired into a person's identity.

There has been some suggestion that there exists a "gay" gene, which, if it could be found definitively, would somehow settle the issue of gayness. But what we are seeing in the development of the Human Genome Project is that genetics is not the court of last resort in the story of life. No one gene determines the course of a human life. At this moment, while much good science has gone into the project of genetics, there is still no gene therapy that works. In addition, the low number of genes in the recent mapping indicates that genes alone will not tell the story. Further, even where genes are shown to contribute to disease, as in for example the case of Jewish women of Eastern European origin who carry a marker for a type of breast cancer, there is no good explanation for why only one-third of all such women will eventually develop breast cancer. If genes were the uncomplicated set of instructions that we are told they are, in a process of scientific grandiosity sometimes referred to as "geno-hype," there would be a one-for-one correspondence between the incidence of markers and the occurrence of disease.

Ultimately, if the grounds for an essentialist view of the human body are being challenged, so are the notions that identity is socially constructed. Most coherent of these critiques is Ian Hacking's *The Social Construction of What?* Hacking shows, to my satisfaction at least, that the idea of social constructionism, while very useful in many regards, is itself tremendously underdeveloped theoretically and methodologically. And it has reached the end of its shelf life. Once shocking and daring, now it has simply become a way of saying that objects in the world have a history of shifting feelings, concepts, and durations. In addition, Walter Benn Michaels has recently said at a public presentation at the University of Illinois at Chicago in March 2001, that if we agree that there is no biological basis for race, then how does it make sense to say there is a social construction of it? Michaels gives the example that if we agree there is no scientific basis for the existence of unicorns, does it make sense to say let's talk about the social construction of the unicorn?

So, if we follow this line of thinking, joining forces with the major critique of identity, we find ourselves in a morass in terms of identity politics and studies. There are various tactics one can take in the face of this conceptual dead end. One can object vehemently that X does indeed exist, that people have suffered for being X, and still do. Therefore, while there may be no basis in theory for being X, large numbers of people are nevertheless X and suffer even now for being so. Or one can claim that although no one has been able to prove the biological existence of X, they will be able to do so someday. In the gap between then and now, we should hold onto the idea of being X. Or one could say that despite the fact that there is no proof of the existence of X, one wants to hold to that identity because it is, after all, one's identity. Finally, we can say that we know X isn't really a biologically valid identity, but we should act strategically to keep the category so that we can pass laws to benefit groups who have been discriminated against because of the pseudo-existence of this category.

All these positions have merit, but are probably indefensible rationally. The idea of maintaining a category of being just because oppressive people in the past created it so they could exploit a segment of the population, does not make sense. To say that one wants to memorialize that category based on the suffering of people who occupy it makes some sense, but does the memorialization have to take the form of continuing the identity?[14] Even attempts to remake the identity will inevitably end up relying on the categories first used to create the oppression. Finally, strategic essentialism, as it is called, is based on several flawed premises, most notably the idea that we can keep secret our doubts so that legislators and the general public won't catch on. This Emperor's New Clothes approach is condescending to all parties, including the proponents of it.

Let us pause for a moment here to take into consideration the concept of disability as a state of injury, to use Wendy Brown's term. One of the central motivations for the Human Genome Project is the elimination of "genetic defects." The argument is based on a vision of the "correct" or "real" genome being one without errors or mistakes. Somewhere, in some empyrean there exists the platonic human genome. This genome is a book or text made up of letters sequenced in the right order without "mistakes." As such, it is in fact a sacred text and our correct reading of it is not unlike the vision that the fundamentalist has that his or her sacred text is infallible. However, the problem is that, as it stands now, the human genome is in need of fixing to make it perfect. Errors of transcription have ruined the primal perfection of the text. The problem is related to exegesis and amanuensis.

Thus, people with genetic diseases have "birth defects" and are "defective."

This explanation, like most, is partial and error-laden. It is based on a pre-postmodern definition of human subjects as whole, complete, perfect, self-sustaining. This is the neoclassical model of Pico della Mirandola, Descartes, Locke, Hume, Kant, and so on. But if we think of cystic fibrosis or sickle cell anemia as "defects" in an otherwise perfect and whole human subject, are we making a grand mistake? Clearly, the people who have such genetic conditions are in grave peril. Few, if any, will live to a ripe old age. Each will have health issues. It would be in the interest of both those people and their physicians to heal their illnesses. Since there is no cure for these diseases at the present time, it seems reasonable to think that we can eliminate the defect by means of genetic medicine. So the idea that one would want to fix these genetic defects seems more than logical.

Yet the model involved in the idea of birth "defect" comes to us direct and unaltered from a eugenic model of the human body. Words like "fit," "normal," "degenerate," "feeble," "defect," and "defective" are all interlaced. Their roots lie directly in the "scientific" study of humans that reached its liminal threshold in the middle of the nineteenth century. We now openly repudiate eugenics, mainly because of the Nazis' use of "negative eugenics," that is, the direct elimination of "defectives" from the human race. This seems so horrendous to us that the term is no longer used. But organizations in the United States and England have simply morphed their names into ones that use the term "genetics," preserving the Latin linguistic root in both eugenic and genetic. Now eugenics (or genetics) is carried out through two avenues—prenatal screening, which works some of the time, and genetic engineering, which has not worked on humans so far. In both cases, the aim is to improve the human stock and to remove genetic defects. With the advent of the Human Genome and genetic sequencing projects, the illusion is that single genes will be discovered that can be "fixed" with an improved consequence. There is, of course, the problem of the "single gene" hypothesis, now being hotly debated in the context of the latest claim that there is a single gene for speech.[15]

Many would claim that for behaviors like speech, sexual orientation, or intelligence, there can be no single gene or genetic causality. So the premise that we can fix a single gene is itself a problem. Further, the idea of a "mistake" is also problematic. Take the examples I have given of sickle-cell anemia and cystic fibrosis. The genetic markers for both these are recessive, which means that a great number of the population will have genetic information (or misinformation) for these diseases. It turns out that people who carry the trait are resistant to malaria (in the case of sickle-cell anemia) and cholera (in the case of cystic fibrosis). If we posit that other "defects" are also protective against pandemic diseases, we can see that the simple elimination of such defects might be a complicated process with a possibly dubious result. What we are discussing is an algorithm of collective protectivity through genetic diversity versus harm to select individuals. I'm not arguing for a trade-off, but I think evolution has made that trade-off and our genes contain the history of humans and pandemics.

The use of genetic testing to avoid giving birth to children with genetic defects is itself problematic. On a simple statistical level, it can probably only be done in relatively wealthy countries and among middle- and upper-class people. Paradoxically, the effect of doing so may actually serve to increase the incidence of the condition because each time a person is born with the disease, two of the inherited traits end with the person upon his or her death. By bypassing this draconian form of genetic regulation, we may actually be contributing to the increased distribution of the trait in the gene pool, particularly in developing countries. The effect shows us that the simple answer of fixing the defect itself is not simple. Further, we may be tampering with the ability of humans to survive pandemics that we know about and others that we don't know about. How many people, for example, are now protected against developing active AIDS because they carry a trait for a "defect"?

Another aspect of this "defect" scenario is that a new issue is beginning to arise in the courts—the right not to be born. French courts upheld this idea in regard to women who did not receive genetic testing and who gave birth to children who were, for example, born without an arm. The courts endorsed compensatory payments to such children who had the right to not be born and whose parents were not able to exercise that right because of lack of information. The legislature in a subsequent act voided the court's ruling. Nevertheless, here indeed is a slippery slope, which many people with disabilities have regarded with suspicion. They rightly claim that their parents might have aborted them had they known of their upcoming impairment as children. On the other side of the disability divide, Deaf parents and parents of small stature have the ability to screen for the birth of a hearing child or a normal-sized child and to abort. And, of course, in countries like India and China, genetic testing is used to abort female fetuses. In the United States, the American Society for Reproductive Medicine, which sets the standards for most fertility clinics, officially stated that it is sometimes acceptable for couples to choose the sex of their children by selecting either male or female embryos and discarding the rest.[16] These cases begin to blur the notion of what a "defect" is and is not. Designer babies, as foreseen in the film *Gattaca*, can begin to be seen as those who will not contain, for example, genes for breast cancer or high blood pressure. The possibilities are limitless.

Some of the issues I've outlined here are the result of a destabilization of the categories we have known concerning the body. The body is never a single physical thing so much as a series of attitudes toward it. The grand categories of the body were established during the Renaissance and the Enlightenment, and then refined through the use of science and eugenics. Postmodernism along with science has assaulted many of these categories of self and identity. What we need now is a new ethics of the body that acknowledges the advances of science but also acknowledges that we can't simply go back to a relatively simple notion of identity. Genetics offers the way back, without, thus far, being able to deliver on that promise.

What I would like to propose is that this new ethics of the body begin with disability rather than end with it. To do so, I want to make clear that disability is itself an unstable category. I think it would be a major error for disability scholars and advocates to define the category in the by-now very problematic and depleted guise of one among many identities. In fact I argue that disability can capitalize on its rather different set of definitions from other current and known identities. To do this, it must not ignore the instability of its self-definitions but acknowledge that their instability allows disability to transcend the problems of identity politics. In setting up this model we must also acknowledge that not only is disability an unstable category but so is its doppelgänger—impairment.

In the social model, disability is presented as a social and political problem that turns an impairment into an oppression either by erecting barriers or by refusing to create barrier-free environments (where barrier is used in a very general and metaphoric sense). But impairment is not a neutral and easily understood term. It relies heavily on a medical model for the diagnosis of the impairment. For example, is Asperger's Syndrome or hysteria an impairment or the creation of the *folie à deux* of the observing physician and the cooperating patient?[17] Is anorexia or ADD an impairment or a disability? Particularly with illnesses that did not exist in the past, the plethora of syndromes and conditions that have sprouted in the hearts and minds of physicians and patients—conditions like attention deficit disorder, fugue states, pseudoneurotic schizophrenia, or borderline psychosis—we have to question the clear line drawn between the socially constructed "disability" and the preexistent and somatic "impairment." Ian Hacking, in *Mad Travelers: Reflections on the Reality of Transient Mental Illnesses*, points out that fidgety children were not considered to have impairments until ADD began. Is the impairment bred into the bone, or can it be a creation of a medical—technological—pharmaceutical complex?

Further, it is hard if not impossible to make the case that the actual category of disability really has internal coherence. It includes, according to the Americans with Disabilities Act of 1990, conditions like obesity, attention deficit disorder, diabetes, back pain, carpal tunnel syndrome, severe facial scarring, chronic fatigue syndrome, skin conditions, and hundreds of other conditions. Further, the law specifies that if one is "regarded" as having these impairments, one is part of the protected class.

The perceived legal problem is that the protected class is too large, and that is one of the reasons there is a perceived backlash in the United States against the ADA. In response to initial concerns that too many people with minor conditions were qualifying as disabled, the federal courts have issued very narrow interpretations of disability.[18] While we must deplore the fact that approximately 95 percent of cases brought before the courts are currently decided in favor of employers, we may also understand that some of this backlash is generated by a fear of creating a protected class that is too large. As with affirmative action, there is also general resentment among the populace that certain minority groups have special rights and privileges with regard to college admissions, job hiring, and so on. I want to be clear that I am not arguing against the protection of historically oppressed groups, as I will explain further. But I am calling attention to the increasingly ineffective means of achieving a goal of equality and equity in housing, jobs, and public accommodations.

Indeed, the protected class will only become larger as the general population ages. With the graying of the baby boomers, we will see a major increase in the sheer numbers of people with disabilities. As noted in the Introduction, the World Health Organization (WHO) predicts that by the year 2020, there will be more than 690 million people over the age of sixty-five, in contrast with today's 380 million. Two-thirds of the elderly will be in developing and under-developed nations. The increase in the elderly population will cause a major change in the disease patterns of these countries. There will be increasing rates of cancer, kidney failure, eye disease, diabetes, mental illness, and other chronic, degenerative illnesses such as cardiovascular disease. Although we may want to call all these senior citizens people with disabilities, what will that mean? Will we have to start making decisions about who is disabled and who is not? What Occam's razor will we use to hone the definition then? And how will this majority of older people redefine disability, since they did not grow up with a disability or acquire one early in life? Who will get to claim the definition of disability or the lack of one?

Complicating the issue of disability identity is the notion of cure. Just as people can slip into disability in the blink of an eye or the swerve of a wheel, so too can people be cured. Indeed, although we don't expect this in the near future, it is possible to imagine a world in which disability decreases from 15 to 20 percent of the population to just 2 or 3 percent. Just as we saw a major reduction in infectious diseases in the West over the previous century, so too may we see a decrease in disabilities. Gene therapy, colossally unsuccessful up until this point, could have a major although unlikely breakthrough and become the treatment of choice for many illnesses. Stem cell research could lead to the regeneration of many tissues that are the cause of degenerative and traumatic diseases and conditions. And technological fixes may become much more sophisticated, so that, for example, cochlear implants, now very problematic even if you believe in the concept, could become foolproof. Indeed, this specter is rather terrifying and offensive to many Deaf people, and with good reason. Advances in biotechnology could create natural and effective gaits for paraplegics or useful prostheses that might be virtually indistinguishable from human limbs. Indeed, political issues aside, the possibility does exist of cures for many impairments that now define a group we call "people with disabilities." We must recall though, that cures will of course only be available to people with means in wealthy countries.

What we are discussing is the instability of the category of disability as a subset of the instability of identity in a postmodern era. It would be understandable if one responded to what I've suggested by saying that, notwithstanding this instability, the category must be left alone. It must be maintained for all the reasons I had suggested earlier. Or, as one of my students responded, "What will happen to the handicapped parking space, if what you advocated happens?" True, but I want to propose that the very rationale for disability activism and study is good enough, indeed better than good enough, rationale for many people—people other than those we now call People with Disabilities. Rather than ignore the unstable nature of disability, rather than try to fix it, we should amplify that quality to distinguish it from other identity groups that have, as I have indicated, reached the limits of their own projects. Indeed, instability spells the end of many identity groups; in fact it can create a dismodernist approach to disability as a neoidentity.

What characterizes the limitations of the identity group model is its exclusivity (which contains the seeds of its own dissolution through the paradox of the proliferation of identity groups). Indeed, you have to be pretty *unidentified* in this day and age to be without an identity. So the very criticism of the category of disability as being too large, as containing too big a protected class, is actually a *fait accompli* with the notion of identity in general. We should not go on record as saying that disability is a fixed identity, when the power behind the concept is that disability presents us with a malleable view of the human body and identity.

Enlightenment thought would have it that the human is a measurable quantity, that all men are created equal, and that each individual is paradoxically both the same and different. Or perhaps, as Kierkegaard put it, "the single individual is the particular that has its *telos* in the universal."[19] In the past much of the paradoxical attitude toward citizens with disabilities arose from the conflict between notions of the equality of universal rights and the inequality of particular bodies.[20]

For all the hype of postmodern and deconstructive theory, these intellectual attempts made little or no impression on identity politics. Rather, those who pushed identity had very strong Enlightenment notions of the universal and the individual.

The universal subject of postmodernism may be pierced and narrative-resistant but that subject was still whole, independent, unified, self-making, and capable. The dismodern era ushers in the concept that difference is what all of us have in common. That identity is not fixed but malleable. That technology is not separate but part of the body. That dependence, not individual independence, is the rule. There is no single clockmaker who made the uniform clock of the human body. The watchword of dismodernism could be: Form follows dysfunction.

What dismodernism signals is a new kind of universalism and cosmopolitanism that is reacting to the localization of identity. It reflects a global view of the world. To accomplish a dismodernist view of the body, we need to consider a new ethics of the body. We may take Kierkegaard's by-now naïve belief in the universal and transform it, knowing that this new universalism cannot be a return to Enlightenment values. Rather it must be a corrective to the myths not only of the Enlightenment but of postmodernism as well.

A new ethics of the dismodernist body consists of three areas: The first concerns the official stance—care *of* the body is now a requirement for existence in a consumer society. We are encouraged and beseeched to engage in this care; indeed, it is seen as a requirement of citizenship. This care of the body involves the purchase of a vast number of products for personal care and grooming, products necessary to having a body in our society. Although we are seen as self-completing, the contemporary body can only be completed by means of consumption. This is the official stance: that the contemporary human body is incomplete without deodorant, hair gel, sanitary products, lotions, perfumes, shaving creams, toothpastes, and so on.[21] In addition, the body is increasingly becoming a module onto which various technological additions can be attached. The by-now routine glasses, contact lenses, and hearing aids are supplemented by birth-control implants, breast implants, penile implants, pacemakers, insulin regulators, monitors, and the like. Further work will also intimately link us to more sophisticated cybertechnology. All this contributes to what Zygmund Bauman calls "the privatization of the body," which he sees as the "primal scene of postmodern ambivalence." The aim and goal, above all, is to make this industrial-modeled, consumer-designed body appear "normal." And even people with disabilities have to subscribe to this model and join the ranks of consumers.[22]

Another official area pertains to care *for* the body, an area that also links the economy with the body. Here we must confront an entire industry devoted to caring for the human body. We are discussing the healthcare industry and the dependent care industry. Included here are physicians' private practices, clinics, medical insurance companies, medical laboratories, hospitals, extended-care facilities, hospitals, hospices, nursing homes, in-home caregivers, pharmacies, manufacturers of assistive devices, and organizations that promote the research, development, and care of certain kinds of illnesses and conditions. In most countries, this industry makes up the largest sector of the economy. There are obviously huge economic advantages to the creation and maintenance of the disability industry. It is important to recall that since huge financial commitments are being made to the abnormal body, the ethics involved in the distribution of resources and the shaping of this industry is a major part of our approach to an ethical society. By and large, this industry is controlled and dominated by people who are not people with disabilities.

Finally, to secure a dismodernist ethics, in opposition or in some cases in alliance with the official stance, we need to discuss caring *about* the body. This is the area I would most like to emphasize. If we care about the body, that is to say care about the issues I have raised, we finally begin to open up and develop a dismodernist discourse of the body and the uses of bodies. This area begins with attention paid to human rights and civil rights that have to be achieved to bring people with disabilities to the awareness of other identity groups. Here we must discuss the oppression of so-called abnormal bodies, and the treatment of the poor with disabilities. Class again becomes an issue in identity. We must focus on the poor, since by all estimates the majority of people with disability are poor, unemployed, and undereducated. In the United States, only one-third of people with disabilities are employed, versus upward of 70 percent of "normal" workers. Indeed, many people with disabilities end up in prisons—particularly those with cognitive and affective disabilities. A *New York Times* article (August 7, 2000) pointed out that one in ten death row inmates are mentally retarded. Since the majority of people in the United States become quadriplegic or paraplegic from gunshot wounds, a disproportionate number of African American males are so impaired. And therefore a large number of these males with disabilities are also in prisons, often without adequate accommodations.

On an international level, land mines create impairments on a daily basis, and this fact combined with other technologies of war and extremely poor working conditions in sweatshop environments creates a level of disability in so-called developing countries that requires attention and thought. The treatment of women and female babies—including the abortion of female fetuses, the use of clitorectomies, the oppression of gay, lesbian, bisexual, and transgendered people—often intersects in familiar and unfamiliar ways with the mechanisms of disablement. It can be said that the most oppressed person in the world is a disabled female, Third World, homosexual, woman of color. In addition, the absence of adequate wheelchairs in poor countries, along with inadequate street and public accommodation facilities create a virtually inaccessible world for people with mobility impairments.

My point is that with a dismodernist ethic, you realize that caring *about* the body subsumes and analyzes care *of* and care *for* the body. The latter two produce oppressive subjection, while the former gives us an ethic of liberation. And the former always involves the use of culture and symbolic production in either furthering the liberation or the oppression of people with disabilities.

An ethics of the body provides us with a special insight into the complex and by now dead end of identity politics. The problem presented to us by identity politics is the emphasis on an exclusivity surrounding a specific so-called identity. Writers like Kenneth Warren, K. Anthony Appiah, Paul Gilroy, Wendy Brown, Walter Benn Michaels, Thomas Holt, and others are now critiquing the notion of a politics based on specific identities and on victim status. Disability studies can provide a critique of and a politics to discuss how all groups, based on physical traits or markings, are selected for disablement by a larger system of regulation and signification. So it is paradoxically the most marginalized group—people with disabilities—who can provide the broadest way of understanding contemporary systems of oppression.

This new way of thinking, which I am calling dismodernism, rests on the operative notion that postmodernism is still based on a humanistic model. Politics have been directed toward making all identities equal under a model of the rights of the dominant, often white, male, "normal" subject. In a dismodernist mode, the ideal is not a hypostatization of the normal (that is, dominant) subject, but aims to create a new category based on the partial, incomplete subject whose realization is not autonomy and independence but dependency and interdependence. This is a very different notion from subjectivity organized around wounded identities; rather, *all* humans are seen as wounded. Wounds are not the result of oppression, but rather the other way around. Protections are not inherent, endowed by the creator, but created by society at large and administered to all. The idea of a protected class in law now becomes less necessary since the protections offered to that class are offered to all. Thus, to belatedly answer my student, normal parking becomes a subset of handicapped parking.

The dismodernist subject is in fact disabled, only completed by technology and by interventions. Rather than the idea of the complete, independent subject, endowed with rights (which are in actuality conferred by privilege), the dismodernist subject sees that metanarratives are only "socially created" and accepts them as that, gaining help and relying on legislation, law, and technology. It acknowledges the social and technological to arrive at functionality. As the quadriplegic is incomplete without the motorized wheelchair and the controls manipulated by the mouth or tongue, so the citizen is incomplete without information technology, protective legislation, and globalized forms of securing order and peace. The fracturing of identities based on somatic markers will eventually be seen as a device to distract us from the unity of new ways of regarding humans and their bodies to further social justice and freedom.

We can thus better understand how the by now outdated postmodern subject is a ruse to disguise the hegemony of normalcy. Foucault is our best example. His work is, as Edward Said has noted, in *Power, Politics and Culture: Interview with Edward W. Said*, a homage to power, not an undermining of it. Said calls Foucault a "scribe" of power because of his fascination with the subject. For Foucault the state is power and citizens are docile bodies. This overtly sadomasochistic model is one that is part of a will-to-power, a fantasy of utter power and utter subjection. That model appeared to be postmodern, but was in fact the nineteenth century of Freud, Sacher-Masoch, and imperialism writ large. Instead, dismodernism doesn't require the abjection of wounds or docility to describe the populace, or the identity groups within. Rather it replaces the binary of docility and power with another—impairment and normalcy. Impairment is the rule, and normalcy is the fantasy. Dependence is the reality, and independence grandiose thinking. Barrier-free access is the goal, and the right to pursue happiness the false consciousness that obscures it. Universal design becomes the template for social and political designs.

The rhizomatic vision of Deleuze's solution to the postmodernist quandary presented by power, with its decentered, deracinated notion of action, along with the neorationalist denial of universals, leaves us with a temporary, contingent way of thinking about agency and change. The dismodernist vision allows for a clearer, more concrete mode of action—a clear notion of expanding the protected class to the entire population; a commitment to removing barriers and creating access for all. This includes removing the veil of ideology from the concept of the normal, and denying the locality of identity. This new ethic permits, indeed encourages, cosmopolitanism, a new kind of empire, to rephrase Hardt and Negri, that relies on the electronic senses as well as the neoclassical five. It moves beyond the fixity of the body to a literally constructed body, which can then be reconstructed with all the above goals in mind.

Clearly, what I am describing is the beginning of a long process. It began with the efforts of various identities to escape oppression based on their category of oppression. That struggle is not over and must continue. While there is no race, there is still racism. But dismodernism argues for a commonality of bodies within the notion of difference. It is too easy to say, "We're all disabled." But it is possible to say that we are all disabled by injustice and oppression of various kinds. We are all nonstandard, and it is under that standard that we should be able to found the dismodernist ethic.

What is universal in life, if there are universals, is the experience of the limitations of the body. Yet the fantasy of culture, democracy, capitalism, sexism, and racism, to name only a few ideologies, is the perfection of the body and its activities. As Paul Gilroy writes, "The reoccurrence of pain, disease, humiliation, grief, and care for those one loves can all contribute to an abstract sense of human similarity powerful enough to make solidarities based on cultural particularity appear suddenly trivial."[23] It is this aspect of experience, a dismodern view, that seems suddenly to be, at the beginning of the twenty-first century, about the only one we can justify.

NOTES

1. For more on this, see a special issue of the *Berkeley Journal of Employment and Labor Law* 22:1 (2000), and also Leslie Francis and Anita Silvers, eds., *Americans with Disabilities: Exploring Implications of the Law for Individuals and Institutions* (New York: Routledge, 2000).

2. I have written more about this aspect of identity and disability in chapter 5 of *Bending Over Backwards: Disability, Dismodernism and Other Difficult Positions* (New York: New York University Press, 2002).

3. See Ian Hacking, *The Social Construction of What?* (Cambridge: Harvard UP, 1999; rpt. 2001).

4. I have made this point elsewhere. See Lennard J. Davis, *Enforcing Normalcy: Disability, Deafness, and the Body* (London: Verso, 1995) for greater exposition.

5. Let us not even consider the further problem that in order to locate a gene, we have to cordon off "good DNA" from "junk" DNA may have a role to play in "influencing" the good DNA. Thus the exact science of genetics begins to resemble other explanatory systems requiring influence based on humors, astrological causes, and so on. Indeed, many human traits are polygenic, involving several different genes working in coordination with each other and with other processes.

6. Raymond Bonniet and Sarah Rimer, *New York Times* (August 24, 2001), A13

7. See Steve Olsen, "The Genetic Archeology of Race," *Atlantic Monthly* (April 2001).

8. See works like Tukufu Zuberi, *Thicker than Blood: An Essay on How Racial Statistics Lie* (Minneapolis: University of Minnesota Press, 2001).

9. For the most complete discussion of HeLa cells in regard to racial politics, see Hannah Landecker, "Immortality, In Vitro: A History of the HeLa Cell Line," in *Biotechnology and Culture: Bodies, Anxieties, Ethics*, ed. Paul E. Brodwin (Bloomington: Indiana UP, 2000), 53–72.

10. Dwight Garner, *New York Times Sunday Magazine* (March 25, 2001).

11. Although, as Dorothy Roberts has pointed out, prenatal technology is still very much a site of racial discrimination. See her "Race and the New Reproduction," *Hastings Law Journal* 47: 4 (1996).

12. For more on this subject, see Leslie Feinberg, *Transgender Warriors: Making History from Joan of Arc to Dennis Rodman* (Boston: Beacon Press, 1996). Also see Bob Beale, "New Insights into the X and Y Chromosomes," *The Scientist* (July 23, 2001) 15 (15): 18.

13. Steven Steinberg, *The Ethnic Myth* (Boston: Beacon Press, 2001).

14. See Wendy Brown, *States of Injury: Power and Freedom in Late Modernity* (Princeton: Princeton UP, 1995).

15. Nicholas Wade, *New York Times* (October 4 2001

16. Gina Kolata, *New York Times* (September 28, 2001), A14.

17. See Ian Hacking's discussion of transient mental illnesses in *Mad Travelers: Reflections on the Reality of Transient Mental Illnesses* (Charlottesville: University of Virginia, 1998).

18. For an extensive discussion of the legal issues around disability, see a special issue of the *Berkeley Journal of Employment and Labor Law* 21: 1 (2000). For background on many of these issues, see Ruth O'Brien, *Crippled Justice: The History of Modern Disabiltiy Policy in the Workplace* (Chicago: U of Chicago P, 2001).

19. Søren Kierkegaard, *Fear and Trembling*, trans. Alastair Hanney (London: Penguin, 1985), 83

20. See my chapter, "Introduction, Disability, Normality and Power," in this volume.

21. As an assignment, I ask my students to tally up the cost of all the products they buy for their bodies. The annual cost is astounding.

22. Magazines like *We* and *Poz* generate income by selling trendy and sexy wheelchairs and other equipment for people with disabilities. Of course, the routine body care products are called for here as well.

23. Paul Gilroy, *Against Race: Imagining Political Culture beyond the Color Line* (Cambridge: Harvard UP, 2000), 17.

CHAPTER 21

Disability and the Theory of Complex Embodiment—For Identity Politics in a New Register

Tobin Siebers

THE IDEOLOGY OF ABILITY

We seem caught as persons living finite lives between two sets of contradictory ideas about our status as human beings. The first contradiction targets our understanding of the body itself. On the one hand, bodies do not seem to matter to who we are. They contain or dress up the spirit, the soul, the mind, the self. I am, as Descartes explained, the thinking part. At best, the body is a vehicle, the means by which we convey who we are from place to place. At worst, the body is a fashion accessory. We are all playing at Dorian Gray, so confident that the self can be freed from the dead weight of the body, but we have forgotten somehow to read to the end of the novel. On the other hand, modern culture feels the urgent need to perfect the body. Whether medical scientists are working on a cure for the common cold or the elimination of all disease, a cure for cancer or the banishment of death, a cure for HIV/AIDS or control of the genetic code, their preposterous and yet rarely questioned goal is to give everyone a perfect body. We hardly ever consider how incongruous is this understanding of the body—that the body seems both inconsequential and perfectible.

A second but related contradiction targets the understanding of the human being in time. The briefest look at history reveals that human beings are fragile. Human life confronts the overwhelming reality of sickness, injury, disfigurement, enfeeblement, old age, and death. Natural disasters, accidents, warfare and violence, starvation, disease, and pollution of the natural environment attack human life on all fronts, and there are no survivors. This is not to say that life on this earth is wretched and happiness nonexistent. The point is simply that history reveals one unavoidable truth about human beings—whatever our destiny as a species, we are as individuals feeble and finite. And yet the vision of the future to which we often hold promises an existence that bears little or no resemblance to our history. The future obeys an entirely different imperative, one that commands our triumph over death and contradicts everything that history tells us about our lot in life. Many religions instruct that human beings will someday win eternal life. Science fiction fantasizes about aliens who have left behind their mortal sheath; they are superior to us, but we are evolving in their direction. Cybernetics treats human intelligence as software that can be moved from machine to machine. It promises a future where human beings might be downloaded into new hardware whenever their old hardware wears out. The reason given for exploring human cloning is to defeat disease and aging. Apparently, in some future epoch, a quick trip to the spare-parts depot will cure what ails us; people will look better, feel healthier, and live three times longer. Finally, the human genome project, like eugenics before it, places its faith in a future understanding of human genetics that will perfect human characteristics and extend human life indefinitely.

However stark these contradictions, however false in their extremes, they seem credible in relation to each other. We are capable of believing at once that the body does not matter and that it should be perfected. We believe at once that history charts the radical finitude of human life but that the future promises radical infinitude. That we embrace these contradictions without interrogating them reveals that our thinking is steeped in ideology. Ideology does not permit the thought of contradiction necessary to question it; it sutures together opposites, turning them into apparent complements of each other, smoothing over contradictions, and making almost unrecognizable any perspective that would offer a critique of it. In fact, some cultural theorists claim to believe that ideology is as impenetrable as the Freudian unconscious—that there is no outside to ideology, that it can contain any negative, and that it sprouts contradictions without suffering them (see Goodheart 1996; Siebers 1999). I argue another position: ideology creates, by virtue of its exclusionary nature, social locations outside of itself and therefore capable of making epistemological claims about it. The arguments that follow here are based on the contention that oppressed social locations create identities and perspectives, embodiments and feelings, histories and experiences that stand outside of and offer valuable knowledge about the powerful ideologies that seem to enclose us.

This book pursues a critique of one of these powerful ideologies—one I call the ideology of ability. The ideology of ability is at its simplest the preference for able-bodiedness. At its most radical, it defines the baseline by which humanness is determined, setting the measure of body and mind that gives or denies human status to individual persons. It affects nearly all of our judgments, definitions, and values about human beings, but because it is discriminatory and exclusionary, it creates social locations outside of and critical of its purview, most notably in this case, the perspective of disability. Disability defines the invisible center around which our contradictory ideology about human ability revolves. For the ideology of ability makes us fear disability, requiring that we imagine our bodies are of no consequence while dreaming at the same time that we might perfect them. It describes disability as what we flee in the past and hope to defeat in the future. Disability identity stands in uneasy relationship to the ideology of ability, presenting a critical framework that disturbs and critiques it.

One project of this book is to define the ideology of ability and to make its workings legible and familiar, despite how imbricated it may be in our thinking and practices, and despite how little we notice its patterns, authority, contradictions, and influence as a result. A second and more important project is to bring disability out of the shadow of the ideology of ability, to increase awareness about disability, and to illuminate its kinds, values, and realities. Disability creates theories of embodiment more complex than the ideology of ability allows, and these many embodiments are each crucial to the understanding of humanity and its variations, whether physical, mental, social, or historical. These two projects unfold slowly over the course of my argument for the simple reason that both involve dramatic changes in thinking.

The level of literacy about disability is so low as to be nonexistent, and the ideology of ability is so much a part of every action, thought, judgment, and intention that its hold on us is difficult to root out. The sharp difference between disability and ability may be grasped superficially in the idea that disability is essentially a "medical matter," while ability concerns natural gifts, talents, intelligence, creativity, physical prowess, imagination, dedication, the eagerness to strive, including the capacity and desire to strive—in brief, the essence of the human spirit. It is easy to write a short list about disability, but the list concerning ability goes on and on, almost without end, revealing the fact that we are always dreaming about it but rarely thinking critically about why and how we are dreaming.

I resort at the outset to the modern convention of the bullet point to introduce the ideology of ability as simply as possible. The bullet points follow without the thought of being exhaustive or avoiding contradiction and without the full commentary that they deserve. Some of the bullets are intended to look like definitions; others describe ability or disability as operators; others still gather stereotypes and prejudices. The point is to begin the accumulation of ideas, narratives, myths, and stereotypes about disability whose theory this book seeks to advance, to provide a few small descriptions on which to build further discussion of ability as an ideology, and to start readers questioning their own feelings about ability and disability:

- Ability is the ideological baseline by which humanness is determined. The lesser the ability, the lesser the human being.
- The ideology of ability simultaneously banishes disability and turns it into a principle of exclusion.
- Ability is the supreme indicator of value when judging human actions, conditions, thoughts, goals, intentions, and desires.
- If one is able-bodied, one is not really aware of the body. One feels the body only when something goes wrong with it.
- The able body has a great capacity for self-transformation. It can be trained to do almost anything; it adjusts to new situations. The disabled body is limited in what it can do and what it can be trained to do. It experiences new situations as obstacles.
- Disability is always individual, a property of one body, not a feature common to all human beings, while ability defines a feature essential to the human species.
- Disability can be overcome through will power or acts of the imagination. It is not real but imaginary.
- "Disability's no big deal," as Mark O'Brien writes in his poem, "Walkers" (1997, 36).
- It is better to be dead than disabled.
- Nondisabled people have the right to choose when to be able-bodied. Disabled people must try to be as able-bodied as possible all the time.
- Overcoming a disability is an event to be celebrated. It is an ability in itself to be able to overcome disability.
- The value of a human life arises as a question only when a person is disabled. Disabled people are worth less than nondisabled people, and the difference is counted in dollars and cents.
- Disabilities are the gateway to special abilities. Turn disability to an advantage.
- Loss of ability translates into loss of sociability. People with disabilities are bitter, angry, self-pitying, or selfish. Because they cannot see beyond their own pain, they lose the ability to consider the feelings of other people. Disability makes narcissists of us all.
- People who wish to identify as disabled are psychologically damaged. If they could think of themselves as able-bodied, they would be healthier and happier.

To reverse the negative connotations of disability apparent in this list, it will be necessary to claim the value and variety of disability in ways that may seem strange to readers who have little experience with disability studies. But it is vital to show to what extent the ideology of ability collapses once we "claim disability" as a positive identity (Linton 1998). It is equally vital to understand that claiming disability, while a significant political act, is not only political but also a practice that improves quality of life for disabled people. As documented in the case of other minority identities, individuals who identify positively rather than negatively with their disability status lead more productive and happier lives. Feminism, the black and red power movements, as well as gay and disability pride—to name only a few positive identity formations—win tangible benefits for their members, freeing them not only from the violence, hatred, and prejudice directed toward them but also providing them with both shared experiences to guide life choices and a community in which to prosper.

Some readers with a heightened sense of paradox may object that claiming disability as a positive identity merely turns disability into ability and so remains within its ideological horizon. But disability identity does not flounder on this paradox. Rather, the paradox demonstrates how difficult it is to think beyond the ideological horizon of ability and how crucial it is to make the attempt. For thinking of disability as ability, we will see, changes the meaning and usage of ability.

MINORITY IDENTITY AS THEORY

Identity is out of fashion as a category in critical and cultural theory. While it has been associated by the Right and Left with self-victimization, group think, and political correctness, these associations are not the real reason for its fall from grace. The real reason is that identity is seen as a crutch for the person who needs extra help, who is in pain, who cannot think independently. I use the word "crutch" on purpose because the attack on identity is best understood in the context of disability.

According to Linda Martin Alcoff's extensive and persuasive analysis in *Visible Identities*, the current rejection of identity has a particular philosophical lineage, one driven, I believe, by the ideology of ability (2006, 47–83). The line of descent begins with the Enlightenment theory of rational autonomy, which represents the inability to reason as the sign of inbuilt inferiority. Usually, the defense of reason attacked non-Europeans as intellectually defective, but because these racist theories relied on the idea of biological inferiority, they necessarily based themselves from the start on the exclusion of disability. "The norm of rational maturity," Alcoff makes clear, "required a core self stripped of its identity. Groups too immature to practice this kind of abstract thought or to transcend their ascribed cultural identities were deemed incapable of full autonomy, and their lack of maturity was often 'explained' via racist theories of the innate inferiority of non-European peoples" (2006, 22). The Enlightenment view then descends to two modern theories, each of which sees dependence on others as a form of weakness that leads to oppressive rather than cooperative behavior. The first theory belongs to Freud, for whom strong identity attachments relate to pathological psychology and figure as symptoms of ego dysfunction. In psychoanalysis, in effect, a lack lies at the heart of identity (2006, 74), and those unable to overcome this lack fall into patterns of dependence and aggression. Second, in Sartre's existential ontology, identity is alienated from the real self. Identity represents for Sartre a social role, linked to bad faith and motivated by moral failing and intellectual weakness, that tempts the self with inauthentic existence, that is, an existence insufficiently free from the influence of others (2006, 68).

Dossier No. 1 *The Nation* November 6, 2006

Show Him the Money

By Katha Pollitt

I wanted to admire *The Trouble with Diversity*, Walter Benn Michaels's much-discussed polemic against identity politics and economic inequality. Like him, I'm bothered by the extent to which symbolic politics has replaced class grievances on campus, and off it too: the obsessive cultivation of one's roots, the fetishizing of difference, the nitpicky moral one-upmanship over language. Call an argument "lame" on one academic-feminist list I'm on and you'll get—still!—an electronic earful about your insensitivity to the disabled . . . .

These two strains of thinking, despite their differences, support the contemporary distrust of identity. Thus, for Michel Foucault and Judith Butler—to name two of the most influential theorists on the scene today— identity represents a "social necessity that is also a social pathology" (Alcoff 2006, 66); there supposedly exists no form of identity not linked ultimately to subjugation by others. In short, contemporary theorists banish identity when they associate it with lack, pathology, dependence, and intellectual weakness. Identity in their eyes is not merely a liability but a disability.

Notice, however, that identity is thought defective only in the case of minorities, whereas it plays no role in the critique of majority identifications, even among theorists who assail them. For example, no one attacks Americanness specifically because it is an identity. It may be criticized as an example of nationalism, but identity receives little or no mention in the critique. Identity is attacked most frequently in the analysis of minority identity—only people of color, Jews, Muslims, gay, lesbian, bisexual, and transgendered people, women, and people with disabilities seem to possess unhealthy identities. It is as if identity itself occupied a minority position in present critical and cultural theory—for those who reject identity appear to do so only because of its minority status, a status linked again and again to disability.

Moreover, the rejection of minority identity repeats in nearly every case the same psychological scenario. The minority identity, a product of damage inflicted systematically on a people by a dominant culture, is rearticulated by the suffering group as self-affirming, but because the identity was born of suffering, it is supposedly unable to shed its pain, and this pain soon comes to justify feelings of selfishness, resentment, bitterness, and self-pity—all of which combine to justify the oppression of other people. Thus, J. C. Lester (2006) complains that "the disabled are in danger of being changed," because of disability studies, "from the proper object of decent voluntary help, where there is genuine need, into a privileged and growing interest group of oppressors of more ordinary people." Nancy Fraser also points out that identity politics "encourages the reification of group identities" and promotes "conformism, intolerance, and patriarchalism" (2000, 113, 112). Even if this tired scenario were credible—and it is not because it derives from false ideas about disability—it is amazing that so-called politically minded people are worried that a few minority groups might somehow, some day, gain the power to retaliate for injustice, when the wealthy, powerful, and wicked are actively plundering the globe in every conceivable manner: the decimation of nonindustrial countries by the industrial nations, arms-trafficking, enforcement of poverty to maintain the circuit between cheap labor and robust consumerism, global warming, sexual trafficking of women, industrial pollution by the chemical and oil companies, inflation of costs for drugs necessary to fight epidemics, and the cynical failure by the wealthiest nations to feed their own poor, not to mention starving people outside their borders.

My argument here takes issue with those who believe that identity politics either springs from disability or disables people for viable political action. I offer a defense of identity politics and a counterargument to the idea, embraced by the Right and Left, that identity politics cannot be justified because it is linked to pain and suffering. The idea that suffering produces weak identities both enforces the ideology of ability and demonstrates a profound misunderstanding of disability: disability is not a pathological condition, only analyzable via individual psychology, but a social location complexly embodied. Identities, narratives, and experiences based on disability have the status of theory because they represent locations and forms of embodiment from which the dominant ideologies of society become visible and open to criticism. One of my specific tactics throughout this book is to tap this theoretical power by juxtaposing my argument with dossier entries detailing disability identities, narratives, images, and experiences. The dossier is compiled for the most part from news stories of the kind that appear in major newspapers across the country every day, although I have avoided the feel-good human-interest stories dominating the news that recount how their disabled protagonists overcome their disabilities to lead "normal" lives. Rather, the dossier tends to contain testimony about the oppression of disabled people, sometimes framed in their own language, sometimes framed in the language of their oppressors. At first, the dossier entries may have no particular meaning to those untutored in disability studies, but my hope is that they will grow stranger and stranger as the reader progresses, until they begin to invoke feelings of horror and disgust at the blatant and persistent prejudices directed against disabled people. The dossier represents a deliberate act of identity politics, and I offer no apology for it because identity politics remains in my view the most practical course of action by which to address social injustices against minority peoples and to apply the new ideas, narratives, and experiences discovered by them to the future of progressive, democratic society.

Identity is neither a liability nor a disability. Nor is it an ontological property or a state of being. Identity is, properly defined, an epistemological construction that contains a broad array of theories about navigating social environments. Manuel Castells calls identity a collective meaning, necessarily internalized by individuals for the purpose of social action (1997, 7), while Charles Taylor argues, "My identity is defined by the commitments and identifications which provide the frame or horizon within which I can try to determine from case to case what is good, or valuable, or what ought to be done, or what I endorse or oppose" (1987, 27). Alcoff explains that "identity is not merely that which is given to an individual or group, but is also a way of inhabiting, interpreting, and working through, both collectively and individually, an objective social location and group history" (2006, 42). We do well to follow these writers and to consider identity a theory-laden construction, rather than a mere social construction, in which knowledge for social living adheres—though not always and necessarily the best knowledge. Thus, identity is not the structure that creates a person's pristine individuality or inner essence but the structure by which that person identifies and becomes identified with a set of social narratives, ideas, myths, values, and types of knowledge of varying reliability, usefulness, and verifiability. It represents the means by which the person, qua individual, comes to join a particular social body. It also represents the capacity to belong to a collective on the basis not merely of biological tendencies but symbolic ones—the very capacity that distinguishes human beings from other animals.

While all identities contain social knowledge, mainstream identities are less critical, though not less effective for being so, because they are normative. Minority identities acquire the ability to make epistemological claims about the society in which they hold liminal positions, owing precisely to their liminality. The early work of Abdul JanMohamed and David Lloyd, for example, privileges the power of the minor as critique: "The study—and production—of minority discourse requires, as an inevitable consequence of its mode of existence, the transgression of the very disciplinary boundaries by which culture appears as a sublimated form with universal validity. This makes it virtually *the* privileged domain of cultural critique" (1987, 9). The critique offered by minority identity is necessarily historical because it relies on the temporal contingency of its marginal position. Different groups occupy minority positions at different times, but this does not mean that their social location is any less objective relative to their times. Nor does it suggest that structures of oppression differ in the case of every minority identity. If history has taught us anything, it is that those in power have the ability to manipulate the same oppressive structures, dependent upon the same prejudicial representations, for the exclusion of different groups. The experiences of contemporary minority people, once brought to light, resound backward in history, like a reverse echo effect, to comment on the experiences of past minority peoples, while at the same time these past experiences contribute,

one hopes, to an accumulation of knowledge about how oppression works.

Minority identity discovers its theoretical force by representing the experiences of oppression and struggle lived by minority peoples separately but also precisely as minorities, for attention to the similarities between different minority identities exposes their relation to oppression as well as increases the chance of political solidarity. According to the definition of Gary and Rosalind Dworkin, minority identity has recognizable features that repeat across the spectrum of oppressed people. "We propose," Dworkin and Dworkin write, "that a minority group is a group characterized by four qualities: identifiability, differential power, differential and pejorative treatment, and group awareness" (1976, 17). These four features form the basis of my argument about minority identity as well, with one notable addition—that minority status also meet an ethical test judged both relative to society and universally. These features require, each one in turn, a brief discussion to grasp their collective simplicity and power and to arrive at a precise and universal definition of minority identity on which to base the elaboration of disability identity, to describe its relation to minority identity in general, and to defend identity politics as crucial to the future of minority peoples and their quest for social justice and inclusion.

1. Identifiability as a quality exists at the heart of identity itself because we must be able to distinguish a group before we can begin to imagine an identity. Often we conceive of identifiability as involving visible differences connected to the body, such as skin color, gender traits, gestures, affect, voice, and body shapes. These physical traits, however, are not universal with respect to different cultures, and there may be actions or cultural differences that also figure as the basis of identifiability. Note as well that identifiability exists in time,

and time shifts its meaning. As a group is identified, it acquires certain representations, and the growth of representations connected to the group may then change how identifiability works. For example, the existence of a group called disabled people produces a general idea of the people in the group—although the existence of the group does not depend on every disabled person fitting into it—and it then becomes easier, first, to identify people with it and, second, to shift the meaning of the group definition. Fat people are not generally considered disabled at this moment, but there are signs that they may be in the not too distant future (Kirkland 2006). Deaf and intersex people have resisted being described as disabled; their future relation to the identity of disabled people is not clear.

Two other obvious characteristics of identifiability need to be stressed. First, identifiability is tied powerfully to the representation of difference. In cases where an existing minority group is not easily identified and those in power want to isolate the group, techniques will be used to produce identifiability. For example, the Nazis required that Jews wear yellow armbands because they were not, despite Nazi racist mythology, identifiably different from Germans. Second, identity is social, and so is the quality of identifiability. There are many physical differences among human beings that simply do not count for identifiability. It is not the fact of physical difference that matters, then, but the representation attached to difference—what makes the difference identifiable. Representation is the difference that makes a difference. We might contend that there is no such thing as private identity in the same way that Wittgenstein claimed that private language does not exist. Identity must be representable and communicable to qualify as identifiable. Identity serves social purposes, and a form of identity not representable in society would be incomprehensible and ineffective for these purposes.

Of course, people may identify themselves. Especially in societies where groups are identified for differential and pejorative treatment, individuals belonging to these groups may internalize prejudices against themselves and do on their own the work of making themselves identifiable. Jim Crow laws in the American South counted on people policing themselves—not drinking at a white water fountain if they were black, for example. But the way in which individuals claim identifiability also changes as the history of the group changes. A group may be singled out for persecution, but as it grows more rebellious, it may work to preserve its identity, while transforming simultaneously the political values attached to it. The American military's policy, "Don't ask, don't tell" in the case of gay soldiers, tries to stymie the tendency of individuals to claim a positive minority identity for political reasons.

2. Differential power is a strong indicator of the difference between majority and minority identity; in fact, it may be the most important indicator because minority status relies on differential power rather than on numbers. The numerical majority is not necessarily the most powerful group. There are more women than men, and men hold more political power and have higher salaries for the same jobs. Numerical advantage is significant, but a better indicator is the presence of social power in one group over another. Dworkin and Dworkin mention the American South in the 1950s and South Africa under apartheid as good examples of differential power located in a nonnumerical majority (12). Minorities hold less power than majority groups.

3. A central question is whether the existence of differential treatment already implies pejorative treatment. Allowing that differential treatment may exist for legitimate reasons—and it is not at all certain

that we should make this allowance—the addition of pejorative treatment as a quality of minority identity stresses the defining connection between oppression and minority status. Differential and pejorative treatment is what minority group members experience as a consequence of their minority position. It affects their economic standing, cultural prestige, educational opportunities, and civil rights, among other things. Discrimination as pejorative treatment often becomes the focus of identity politics, those concerted attempts by minorities to protest their inferior and unjust status by forming political action groups.

The emergence of identity politics, then, relies on a new epistemological claim. While it is not necessarily the case that a group will protest against discrimination, since there is a history of groups that accept inferior status and even fight to maintain it, the shift to a protest stance must involve claims different from those supporting the discriminatory behavior. A sense of inequity comes to pervade the consciousness of the minority identity, and individuals can find no reasonable justification for their differential treatment. Individuals in protest against unjust treatment begin to develop theories that oppose majority opinion not only about themselves but about the nature of the society that supports the pejorative behavior. They develop ways to represent the actions used to perpetuate the injustice against them, attacking stereotypes, use of violence and physical attack, and discrimination. Individuals begin to constitute themselves as a minority identity, moving from the form of consciousness called internal colonization to one characterized by a new group awareness.

4. Group awareness does not refer to group identifiability but to the perception of common goals pursued through cooperation, to the realization that differential and pejorative treatment is not justified by actual qualities of the minority group, and to the conviction that majority society is a disabling environment that must be transformed by recourse to social justice. In other words, awareness is not merely self-consciousness but an epistemology that adheres in group identity status. It is the identity that brings down injustice initially on the individual's head. This identity is constructed in such a way that it can be supported only by certain false claims and stereotypes. Resistance to these false claims is pursued and shared by members of the minority identity through counterarguments about, and criticism of, the existing state of knowledge. Thus, minority identity linked to group awareness achieves the status of a theoretical claim in itself, one in conflict with the mainstream and a valuable source of meaningful diversity. Opponents of identity politics often argue that identity politics preserves the identities created by oppression: these identities are born of suffering, and embracing them supposedly represents a form of self-victimization. This argument does not understand that new epistemological claims are central to identity politics. For example, societies that oppress women often assert that they are irrational, morally depraved, and physically weak. The minority identity "woman," embraced by feminist identity politics, disputes these assertions and presents alternative, positive theories about women. Identity politics do not preserve the persecuted identities created by oppressors because the knowledge claims adhering in the new identities are completely different from those embraced by the persecuting groups.

Opponents of identity politics are not wrong, however, when they associate minority identity with suffering. They are wrong because they do not accept that pain and suffering may sometimes be resources for the epistemological insights of minority identity. This issue will arise whenever we consider disability identity, since it is the identity most associated with pain, and a great deal of discrimination against people with disabilities derives from the irrational fear of pain. It is not uncommon for disabled people to be told by complete strangers that they would kill themselves if they had such a disability. Doctors often withhold treatment of minor illnesses from disabled people because they believe they are better off dead—the doctors want to end the suffering of their patients, but these disabled people do not necessarily think of themselves as in pain, although they must suffer discriminatory attitudes (Gill 2000; Longmore 2003, 149–203). Nevertheless, people with disabilities are not the only people who suffer from prejudice. The epistemological claims of minority identity in general are often based on feelings of injustice that are painful. Wounds received in physical attacks may pale against the suffering experienced in the idea that one is being attacked because one is unjustly thought inferior—and yet suffering may have theoretical value for the person in pain. While there is a long history of describing pain and suffering as leading to egotism and narcissism—a metapsychology that plays an ancillary role in the evolution of the ideology of ability—we might consider that the strong focus given to the self in pain has epistemological value.[1] Suffering is a signal to the self at risk, and this signal applies equally to physical and social situations. The body signals with pain when a person is engaged in an activity that may do that person physical harm. Similarly, consciousness feels pain when the individual is in social danger. Suffering has a theoretical component because it draws attention to situations that jeopardize the future of the individual, and when individuals who suffer from oppression gather together to share their experiences, this theoretical component may be directed toward political ends.

By suggesting that suffering is theory-laden—that is, a sensation evaluative of states of reality—I am trying to track how and why minority identity makes epistemological claims about society. All identity is social theory. Identities are the theories that we use to fit into and travel through the social world. Our identities have a content that makes knowledge claims about the society in which they have evolved, and we adjust our identities, when we can, to different situations to improve our chances of success. But because mainstream identities so robustly mimic existing social norms, it is difficult to abstract their claims about society. Identities in conflict with society, however, have the ability to expose its norms. Minority identity gains the status of social critique once its content has been sufficiently developed by groups that unite to protest their unjust treatment by the society in which they live.

5. In addition to the four qualities proposed by Dworkin and Dworkin, groups claiming minority identity need to meet an ethical test. Minority identities make epistemological claims about the societies in which they hold liminal positions, but not all theories are equal in ethical content, especially relative to minority identity, since it begins as a product of oppression and acquires the status of social critique. While matters ethical are notoriously difficult to sort out, it is nevertheless worth pausing briefly over how ethics relates to minority identity because ethical content may serve to check fraudulent claims of minority status. For example, in South Africa of recent date, the ideology of apartheid represented the majority position because it held power, identified the nature of minority identity, and dictated differential and pejorative treatment of those in the minority. Today in South Africa, however, the apartheidists are no longer in the majority. Applying the theory of Dworkin and Dworkin, they might be construed as

having a minority identity: they are identifiable, they have differential power, they are treated pejoratively, and they possess group awareness—that is, they present a set of claims that actively and consciously criticize majority society. They also believe themselves to be persecuted, and no doubt they feel suffering about their marginal position.

Why are the apartheidists not deserving of minority status? The answer is that the theories contained in apartheidist identity do not pass an ethical test. The contrast between its ethical claims and those of the majority are sufficiently striking to recognize. The apartheidists propose a racist society as the norm to which all South African citizens should adhere. Relative to South African social beliefs and those of many other countries, apartheid ideology is unacceptable on ethical grounds because it is biased, violent, and oppressive. Consequently, the apartheidists fail to persuade us with their claims, and we judge them not a minority group subject to oppression but a fringe group trying to gain unlawful advantage over others.

To summarize, the definition embraced here—and used to theorize disability identity—does not understand minority identity as statistical, fixed in time, or exclusively biological but as a politicized identity possessing the ability to offer social critiques. There are those who attack minority identities precisely because they are politicized, as if only minorities made political arguments based on identity and politicized identity in itself were a species of defective attachment. But many other examples of politicized identity exist on the current scene—Democrats, Republicans, Socialists, the Christian Coalition, the American Nazi Party, and so on. In fact, any group that forms a coalition to make arguments on its own behalf and on the behalf of others in the public forum takes on a politicized identity. Arguments to outlaw minority political action groups merely because they encourage politicized identities would have to abolish other political groups as well.

DISABILITY AND THE THEORY OF COMPLEX EMBODIMENT

Feminist philosophers have long argued that all knowledge is situated, that it adheres in social locations, that it is embodied, with the consequence that they have been able to claim that people in marginal social positions enjoy an epistemological privilege that allows them to theorize society differently from those in dominant social locations (Haraway 1991, 183–201; Harding 1986). Knowledge is situated, first of all, because it is based on perspective. There is a difference between the knowledge present in a view of the earth from the moon and a view of the earth from the perspective of an ant. We speak blandly of finding different perspectives on things, but different perspectives do in fact give varying conceptions of objects, especially social objects. Nevertheless, situated knowledge does not rely only on changing perspectives. Situated knowledge adheres in embodiment. The disposition of the body determines perspectives, but it also spices these perspectives with phenomenological knowledge—lifeworld experience—that affects the interpretation of perspective. To take a famous example from Iris Young, the fact that many women "throw like a girl" is not based on a physical difference. The female arm is as capable of throwing a baseball as the male arm. It is the representation of femininity in a given society that disables women, pressuring them to move their bodies in certain, similar ways, and once they become accustomed to moving in these certain, similar ways, it is difficult to retrain the body. "Women in sexist society are physically handicapped," Young explains. "Insofar as we learn to live out our existence in accordance with the definition that patriarchal culture assigns to us, we are physically inhibited, confined, positioned, and objectified" (2005, 171). It is possible to read the differential and pejorative treatment of women, as if it were a disability, on the surface of their skin, in muscle mass, in corporeal agility. This form of embodiment is also, however, a form of situated knowledge about the claims being made about and by women in a given society. To consider some positive examples, the particular embodiment of a woman means that she might, after experiencing childbirth, have a new and useful perception of physical pain. Women may also have, because of menstruation, a different knowledge of blood. Female gender identity is differently embodied because of women's role in reproductive labor. The presence of the body does not boil down only to perspective but to profound ideas and significant theories about the world.

Embodiment is, of course, central to the field of disability studies. In fact, a focus on disability makes it easier to understand that embodiment and social location are one and the same. Arguments for the specificity of disability identity tend to stress the critical nature of embodiment, and the tacit or embodied knowledge associated with particular disabilities often justifies their value to larger society. For example, George Lane's body incorporates a set of theoretical claims about architecture that the Supreme Court interprets in its ruling against the State of Tennessee, finding that Lane's inability to enter the Polk County Courthouse reveals a pattern of discrimination against people with disabilities found throughout the American court system. Chapter 5 [in the original volume] explores disability passing not as avoidance of social responsibility or manipulation for selfish interests but as a form of embodied knowledge—forced into usage by prejudices against disability— about the relationship between the social

environment and human ability. The young deaf woman who tries to pass for hearing will succeed only if she possesses significant knowledge about the informational potential, manners, physical gestures, conversational rituals, and cultural activities that define hearing in her society. Disabled people who pass for able-bodied are neither cowards, cheats, nor con artists but skillful interpreters of the world from whom we all might learn.

Dossier No. 2   *New York Times Online*
November 15, 2006

Officials Clash over Mentally Ill in Florida Jails

By Abby Goodnough

MIAMI, Nov. 14—For years, circuit judges here have ordered state officials to obey Florida law and promptly transfer severely mentally ill inmates from jails to state hospitals. But with few hospital beds available, Gov. Jeb Bush's administration began flouting those court orders in August. . . .

"This type of arrogant activity cannot be tolerated in an orderly society," Judge Crockett Farnell of Pinellas-Pasco Circuit Court wrote in an Oct. 11 ruling.

State law requires that inmates found incompetent to stand trial be moved from county jails to psychiatric hospitals within 15 days of the state's receiving the commitment orders. Florida has broken that law for years, provoking some public defenders to seek court orders forcing swift compliance. . . .

Two mentally ill inmates in the Escambia County Jail in Pensacola died over the last year and a half after being subdued by guards, according to news reports. And in the Pinellas County Jail in Clearwater, a schizophrenic inmate gouged out his eye after waiting weeks for a hospital bed, his lawyer said. . . .

The problem is not unique to Florida, although it is especially severe in Miami-Dade County, which has one of the nation's largest percentages of mentally ill residents, according to the National Alliance for the Mentally Ill, an advocacy group. . . .

In Miami, an average of 25 to 40 acutely psychotic people live in a unit of the main county jail that a lawyer for Human Rights Watch, Jennifer Daskal, described as squalid after visiting last month. . . . Ms. Daskal said that some of the unit's 14 "suicide cells"— dim, bare and designed for one inmate—were holding two or three at a time, and that the inmates were kept in their cells 24 hours a day except to shower. . . .

But embodiment also appears as a bone of contention in disability studies because it seems caught between competing models of disability. Briefly, the medical model defines disability as a property of the individual body that requires medical intervention. The medical model has a biological orientation, focusing almost exclusively on disability as embodiment. The social model opposes the medical model by defining disability relative to the social and built environment, arguing that disabling environments produce disability in bodies and require interventions at the level of social justice. Some scholars complain that the medical model pays too much attention to embodiment, while the social model leaves it out of the picture. Without returning to a medical model, which labels individuals as defective, the next step for disability studies is to develop a theory of complex embodiment that values disability as a form of human variation.

The theory of complex embodiment raises awareness of the effects of disabling environments on people's lived experience of the body, but it emphasizes as well that some factors affecting disability, such as chronic pain, secondary health effects, and aging, derive from the body. These last disabilities are neither less significant than disabilities caused by the environment nor to be considered defects or deviations merely because they are resistant to change. Rather, they belong to the spectrum of human variation, conceived both as variability between individuals and as variability within an individual's life cycle,

and they need to be considered in tandem with social forces affecting disability.[2] The theory of complex embodiment views the economy between social representations and the body not as unidirectional as in the social model, or nonexistent as in the medical model, but as reciprocal. Complex embodiment theorizes the body and its representations as mutually transformative. Social representations obviously affect the experience of the body, as Young makes clear in her seminal essay, but the body possesses the ability to determine its social representation as well, and some situations exist where representation exerts no control over the life of the body.

As a living entity, the body is vital and chaotic, possessing complexity in equal share to that claimed today by critical and cultural theorists for linguistic systems. The association of the body with human mortality and fragility, however, forces a general distrust of the knowledge embodied in it. It is easier to imagine the body as a garment, vehicle, or burden than as a complex system that defines our humanity, any knowledge that we might possess, and our individual and collective futures. Disability gives even greater urgency to the fears and limitations associated with the body, tempting us to believe that the body can be changed as easily as changing clothes. The ideology of ability stands ready to attack any desire to know and to accept the disabled body in its current state. The more likely response to disability is to try to erase any signs of change, to wish to return the body magically to a past era of supposed perfection, to insist that the body has no value as human variation if it is not flawless.

Ideology and prejudice, of course, abound in all circles of human existence, labeling some groups and individuals as inferior or less than human: people of color, women, the poor, people with different sexual orientations, and the disabled confront the intolerance of society on a daily basis. In nearly no other sphere of existence, however, do people risk waking up one morning having become the persons whom they hated the day before. Imagine the white racist suddenly transformed into a black man, the anti-Semite into a Jew, the misogynist into a woman, and one might begin to approach the change in mental landscape demanded by the onset of disability. We require the stuff of science fiction to describe these scenarios, most often for comic effect or paltry moralizing. But no recourse to fiction is required to imagine an able-bodied person becoming disabled. It happens every minute of every day.

The young soldier who loses his arm on an Iraqi battlefield wakes up in bed having become the kind of person whom he has always feared and whom society names as contemptible (Corbett 2004). Given these circumstances, how might we expect him to embrace and to value his new identity? He is living his worst nightmare. He cannot sleep. He hates what he has become. He distances himself from his wife and family. He begins to drink too much. He tries to use a functional prosthetic, but he loathes being seen with a hook. The natural prosthetic offered to him by Army doctors does not really work, and he prefers to master tasks with his one good arm. He cannot stand the stares of those around him, the looks of pity and contempt as he tries to perform simple tasks in public, and he begins to look upon himself with disdain.

The soldier has little chance, despite the promise of prosthetic science, to return to his former state. What he is going through is completely understandable, but he needs to come to a different conception of himself, one based not on the past but on the present and the future. His body will continue to change with age, and he may have greater disabling conditions in the future. He is no different in this regard from any other human being. Some disabilities can be approached by demanding changes in how people with disabilities are perceived, others-bychangesinthebuiltenvironment. Some can be treated through medical care. Other disabilities cannot be approached by changes in either the environment or the body. In almost every case, however, people with disabilities have a better chance of future happiness and health if they accept their disability as a positive identity and benefit from the knowledge embodied in it. The value of people with disabilities to themselves does not lie in finding a way to return through medical intervention to a former physical perfection, since that perfection is a myth, nor in trying to conceal from others and themselves that they are disabled. Rather, embodiment seen complexly understands disability as an epistemology that rejects the temptation to value the body as anything other than what it was and that embraces what the body has become and will become relative to the demands on it, whether environmental, representational, or corporeal.

INTERSECTIONAL IDENTITY COMPLEXLY EMBODIED

The ultimate purpose of complex embodiment as theory is to give disabled people greater knowledge of and control over their bodies in situations where increased knowledge and control are possible. But the theory has side benefits for at least two crucial debates raging on the current scene as well. First, complex embodiment makes a contribution to influential arguments about intersectionality—the idea that analyses of social oppression take account of overlapping identities based on race, gender, sexuality, class, and disability.[3] While theorists of intersectionality have never argued for a simple additive model in which oppressed identities are stacked one upon another, a notion of disability embodiment helps to resist the temptation of seeing some identities as more pathological than others, and it offers valuable advice about how to conceive the standpoint of others for the purpose of understanding the prejudices against them. This is not to suggest that the intersection of various identities produces the same results for all oppressed groups, since differences in the hierarchical organization of race, gender, sexuality, class, and disability do exist (Collins 2003, 212). Rather, it is to emphasize, first, that intersectionality as a theory references the tendency of identities to construct one another reciprocally (Collins 2003, 208); second, that identities are not merely standpoints where one may stand or try to stand but also complex embodiments; and, third, that the ideology of ability uses the language of pathology to justify labeling some identities as inferior to others.[4]

For example, theorists of intersectional identity might find useful the arguments in disability studies against disability simulation because they offer a view of complex embodiment that enlarges standpoint theory. The applied fields of occupational therapy and rehabilitation science sometimes recommend the use of disability simulations to raise the consciousness of therapists who treat people with disabilities. Instructors ask students to spend a day in a wheelchair or to try navigating classroom buildings blindfolded to get a better sense of the challenges faced by their patients. The idea is that students may stand for a time in the places occupied by disabled people and come to grasp their perspectives. Disability theorists have attacked the use of simulations for a variety of reasons, the most important being that they fail to give the student pretenders a sense of the embodied knowledge contained in disability identities. Disability simulations of this kind fail because they place students in a time-one position of disability, before knowledge about disability is acquired,

usually resulting in emotions of loss, shock, and pity at how dreadful it is to be disabled. Students experience their body relative to their usual embodiment, and they become so preoccupied with sensations of bodily inadequacy that they cannot perceive the extent to which their "disability" results from social rather than physical causes. Notice that such games focus almost entirely on the phenomenology of the individual body. The pretender asks how his or her body would be changed, how his or her personhood would be changed, by disability. It is an act of individual imagination, then, not an act of cultural imagination. Moreover, simulations tempt students to play the game of "What is Worse?" as they experiment with different simulations. Is it worse to be blind or deaf, worse to lose a leg or an arm, worse to be paralyzed or deaf, mute, and blind? The result is a thoroughly negative and unrealistic impression of disability.

The critique of disability simulation has applications in several areas of intersectional theory. First, the practice of peeling off minority identities from people to determine their place in the hierarchy of oppression is revealed to degrade all minority identities by giving a one-dimensional view of them. It also fails to understand the ways in which different identities constitute one another. Identities may trump one another in the hierarchy of oppression, but intersectional identity, because embodied complexly, produces not competition between minority identities but "outsider" theories about the lived experience of oppression (see Collins 1998). Additionally, coming to an understanding of intersecting minority identities demands that one imagine social location not only as perspective but also as complex embodiment, and complex embodiment combines social and corporeal factors. Rather than blindfolding students for a hour, then, it is preferable to send them off wearing sunglasses and carrying a white cane, in the company of a friend, to restaurants and department stores, where they may observe firsthand the spectacle of discrimination against blind people as passersby avoid and gawk at them, clerks refuse to wait on them or condescend to ask the friend what the student is looking for, and waiters request, usually at the top of their lungs and very slowly (since blind people must also be deaf and cognitively disabled), what the student would like to eat.[5]

It is crucial to resist playing the game of "What Is Worse?" when conceiving of intersectional identity, just as it is when imagining different disabilities. Asking whether it is worse to be a woman or a Latina, worse to be black or blind, worse to be gay or poor registers each identity as a form of ability that has greater or lesser powers to overcome social intolerance and prejudice. Although one may try to keep the focus on society and the question of whether it oppresses one identity more than another, the debate devolves all too soon and often to discussions of the comparative costs of changing society and making accommodations, comparisons about quality of life, and speculations about whether social disadvantages are intrinsic or extrinsic to the group. The compelling issue for minority identity does not turn on the question of whether one group has the more arduous existence but on the fact that every minority group faces social discrimination, violence, and intolerance that exert toxic and unfair influence on the ability to live life to the fullest (see Asch 2001, 406–7).

SOCIAL CONSTRUCTION COMPLEXLY EMBODIED

Second, the theory of complex embodiment makes it possible to move forward arguments raging currently about social construction, identity, and the body. Aside from proposing a theory better suited to the experiences of disabled people, the goal is to advance questions in identity and body theory unresponsive to the social construction model. Chapters 3, 4, and 6 [original volume] make an explicit adjustment in social construction theory by focusing on the realism of identities and bodies. By "realism" I understand neither a positivistic claim about reality unmediated by social representations, nor a linguistic claim about reality unmediated by objects of representation, but a theory that describes reality as a mediation, no less real for being such, between representation and its social objects.[6] Rather than viewing representation as a pale shadow of the world or the world as a shadow world of representation, my claim is that both sides push back in the construction of reality. The hope is to advance discourse theory to the next stage by defining construction in a radical way, one that reveals constructions as possessing both social and physical form. While identities are socially constructed, they are nevertheless meaningful and real precisely because they are complexly embodied. The complex embodiment apparent in disability is an especially strong example to contemplate because the disabled body compels one to give concrete form to the theory of social construction and to take its metaphors literally.

Consider an introductory example of the way in which disability complexly embodied extends the social construction argument in the direction of realism. In August 2000 a controversy about access at the Galehead hut in the Appalachian Mountains came to a climax (Goldberg 2000). The Appalachian Mountain Club of New Hampshire had just constructed a rustic thirty-eight bed lodge at an elevation of thirty-eight hundred feet. The United States Forest Service required that the hut comply with the Americans with Disabilities Act (ADA) and be accessible to people with disabilities, that it have a wheelchair ramp and grab bars in larger toilet stalls. The Appalachian Mountain Club had to pay an extra $30,000 to $50,000 for a building already costing $400,000 because the accessible features were late design changes. Its members ridiculed the idea that the building, which could be reached only by a super-rugged 4.6 mile trail, would ever be visited by wheelchair users, and the media tended to take their side.

At this point a group from Northeast Passage, a program at the University of New Hampshire that works with people with disabilities, decided to make a visit to the Galehead hut. Jill Gravink, the director of Northeast Passage, led a group of three hikers in wheelchairs and two on crutches on a twelve-hour climb to the lodge, at the end of which they rolled happily up the ramp to its front door. A local television reporter on the scene asked why, if people in wheelchairs could drag themselves up the trail, they could not drag themselves up the steps into the hut, implying that the ramp was a waste of money. Gravink responded, "Why bother putting steps on the hut at all? Why not drag yourself in through a window?"

The design environment, Gravink suggests pointedly, determines who is able-bodied at the Galehead lodge. The distinction between the disabled and non-disabled is socially constructed, and it is a rather fine distinction at that. Those who are willing and able to climb stairs are considered able-bodied, while those who are not willing and able to climb stairs are disabled. However, those who do climb stairs but are not willing and able to enter the building through a window are not considered disabled. It is taken for granted that nondisabled people may choose when to be able-bodied. In fact, the built environment is full of technologies that make life easier for those people who possess the physical power to perform tasks without these technologies. Stairs, elevators, escalators, washing machines, leaf and snow blowers, eggbeaters, chainsaws, and other tools help to relax physical standards for performing certain tasks. These tools are nevertheless viewed as natural extensions of the body, and no one thinks twice about using them. The moment that individuals are marked as disabled or diseased, however, the expectation is that they will maintain the maximum standard of physical performance at every moment, and the technologies designed to make their life easier are viewed as expensive additions, unnecessary accommodations, and a burden on society.

The example of the Galehead hut exposes the ideology of ability—the ideology that uses ability to determine human status, demands that people with disabilities always present as able-bodied as possible, and measures the value of disabled people in dollars and cents. It reveals how constructed are our attitudes about identity and the body. This is a familiar point, and usually social analysis comes to a conclusion here, no doubt because the idea of construction is more metaphorical than real. The implication seems to be that knowledge of an object as socially constructed is sufficient to undo any of its negative effects. How many books and essays have been written in the last ten years, whose authors are content with the conclusion that x, y, or z is socially constructed, as if the conclusion itself were a victory over oppression?

Far from being satisfied with this conclusion, my analysis here will always take it as a point of departure from which to move directly to the elucidation of embodied causes and effects. Oppression is driven not by individual, unconscious syndromes but by social ideologies that are embodied, and precisely because ideologies are embodied, their effects are readable, and must be read, in the construction and history of societies. When a Down syndrome citizen tries to enter a polling place and is turned away, a social construction is revealed and must be read. When wheelchair users are called selfish if they complain about the inaccessibility of public toilets, a social construction is revealed and must be read (Shapiro 1994, 126–27). When handicapped entrances to buildings are located in the rear, next to garbage cans, a social construction is revealed and must be read. When a cosmetic surgeon removes the thumb on a little boy's right hand because he was born with no thumb on his left hand, a social construction is revealed and must be read (Marks 1999, 67). What if we were to embrace the metaphor implied by social construction, if we required that the "construction" in social construction be understood as a building, as the Galehead hut for example, and that its blueprint be made available? Not only would this requirement stipulate that we elaborate claims about social construction in concrete terms, it would insist that we locate the construction in time and place as a form of complex embodiment.

Whenever anyone mentions the idea of social construction, we should ask on principle to see the blueprint—not to challenge the value of the idea but to put it to practical use—to map as many details about the construction as possible and to track its political, epistemological, and real effects in the world of human beings. To encourage this new requirement, I cite three familiar ideas about social construction, as currently theorized, from which flow—or at least should—three methodological principles. These three principles underlie the arguments to follow, suggesting how to look for blueprints and how to begin reading them:

- Knowledge is socially situated—which means that knowledge has an objective and verifiable relation to its social location.
- Identities are socially constructed—which means that identities contain complex theories about social reality.
- Some bodies are excluded by dominant

social ideologies—which means that these bodies display the workings of ideology and expose it to critique and the demand for political change.

NOTES

1. The nature of pain and the methodology of its study are diverse because they involve the definition of emotion and consciousness. Aydede collects a strong sampling of contemporary views about pain; one of which, the perceptual theory, appeals to the idea that pain has the capacity to signal changes in states of reality (59–98).

2. Snyder and Mitchell express this view powerfully throughout *Cultural Locations of Disability*. For example: "As Darwin insisted in *On the Origin of Species*, variation serves the good of the species. The more variable a species is, the more flexible it is with respect to shifting environmental forces. Within this formulation, one that is central to disability studies, variations are features of biological elasticity rather than a discordant expression of a 'natural' process gone awry" (2006, 70).

3. The literature on intersectionality is now vast. Some key texts relating to disability include Barbee and Little; Beale; Butler and Parr; Fawcett; Hayman and Levit; Ikemoto; Jackson-Braboy and Williams; Martin; O'Toole (2004); and Tyjewski.

4. While not aware of disability studies per se, Johnny Williams provides an excellent intersectional analysis of stereotypical conflations of race and class, arguing that American society explains the social and economic failures of minority groups in terms of personal "inabilities," while maintaining the belief that "social arrangements are fundamentally just" (221).

5. Catherine Kudlick proposed, on the DS-HUM listserve, an exercise similar to this one to replace traditional and biased disability simulations often used by classroom instructors. I am indebted to her discussion.

6. Philosophical realism has a number of varieties. The particular lineage of interest to me focuses on Hilary Putnam in philosophy and Richard Boyd in the philosophy of science. Satya P. Mohanty imports Boyd's ideas into the humanities in general and critical theory in particular, putting the concept of realism in the service of minority studies in novel and convincing ways. Other important figures in philosophical realism working in the humanities include Linda Martin Alcoff, Michael Hames-Garcia, Paula M. L. Moya, and Sean Teuton.

REFERENCES

Alcoff, Linda Martin. *Real Knowing: New Versions of Coherence Theory.* Ithaca, N.Y.: Cornell University Press, 1996.

——. "Who's Afraid of Identity Politics?" *Reclaiming Identity: Realist Theory and the Predicament of Postmodernism.* Ed. Paula M. L. Moya and Michael R. Hames-Garcia. Berkeley and Los Angeles: University of California Press, 2000. Pp. 312–44.

——. *Visible Identities: Race, Gender and the Self.* New York: Oxford University Press, 2006.

Alcoff, Linda Martin, Michael Hames-Garcia, Satya P. Mohanty, and Paula M. L. Moya, eds. *Identity Politics Reconsidered.* New York: Palgrave Macmillan, 2006.

Asch, Adrienne, and Harilyn Rousso. "Therapists with Disabilities: Theoretical and Clinical Issues." *Psychiatry* 48 (1985): 1–12.

Asch, Adrienne, and Michelle Fine. *Women with Disabilities: Essays in Psychology, Culture, and Politics.* Philadelphia: Temple University Press, 1988.

Asch, Adrienne. "Critical Race Theory, Feminism, and Disability: Reflections on Social Justice and Personal Identity." *Ohio State Law Journal* 62.1 (2001): 391–423.

Castells, Manuel. *The Power of Identity.* 2nd ed. Oxford: Blackwell, 1997 (2004).

Collins, Patricia Hill. "Some Group Matters: Intersectionality, Situated Standpoints, and Black Feminist Thought." *A Companion to African-American Philosophy.* Ed. Tommy L. Lott and John P. Pittman. Malden: Blackwell, 2003. Pp. 205–29.

——. "Learning from the Outsider within Revisited." *Fighting Words: Black Women and the Search for Justice.* Minneapolis: University of Minnesota Press, 1998. Pp. 3–10.

Corbett Sara. "The Permanent Scars of Iraq." *New York Times Magazine,* 15 February 2004: 34–41, 58, 60, 66.

Dworkin, Anthony Gary, and Rosalind J. Dworkin, eds. *The Minority Report: An Introduction to Racial, Ethnic, and Gender Relations.* New York: Praeger, 1976.

Fraser, Nancy. "Rethinking Recognition." *New Left Review* 3 (May–June 2000): 107–20.

Gill, Carol J. "Health Professionals, Disability, and Assisted Suicide: An Examination of Relevant Empirical Evidence and Reply to Batavia." *Psychology, Public Policy, and Law* 6.2 (2000): 526–45.

Goldberg, Carey. "For These Trailblazers, Wheelchairs Matter. *New York Times Online,* August 17, 2000. Available at http://query.nytimes.com/gst/fullpage. html.res9EoCE3DA173EF934A2575BCoA9669C8B 63&sec=health&spon=&pagewanted=all (accessed December 22, 2006).

Goodheart, Eugene. *The Reign of Ideology.* New York: Columbia University Press, 1996.

Haraway, Donna J. *Simians, Cyborgs, and Women: The Reinvention of Nature.* New York: Routledge, 1991.

Harding, Sandra. *The Science Question in Feminism.* Ithaca, N.Y.: Cornell University Press, 1986.

JanMohamed, Abdul, and David Lloyd. "Introduction: Minority Discourse—What Is to Be Done?" *Cultural Critique* 7 (1987): 5–17.

Kirkland, Anna. "What's at Stake in Fatness as a Disability?" *Disability Studies Quarterly* 26.1, (2006). Available at www.dsq-sds.org/_articles_htmlJ2006/ winter/kirkland.asp (accessed November 17, 2006).

Lester, J. C. "The Disability Studies Industry." *Libertarian Alliance,* September 26, 2002. Available at www.la-articles.org.uk/dsi.htm (accessed November 11, 2006).

Linton, Simi. *Claiming Disability: Knowledge and Identity.* New York: New York University Press, 1998.

Linton, Simi, Susan Mello, and John O'Neill. "Disability Studies: Expanding the Parameters of Diversity." *Radical Teacher* 47 (1995): 4–10.

Longmore, Paul. *Why I Burned My Book and Other Essays on Disability.* Philadelphia: Temple University Press, 2003.

Marks, Deborah. *Disability: Controversial Debates and Psychosocial Perspectives.* London: Routledge, 1999.

O'Brien, Mark. "On Seeing a Sex Surrogate." *The Sun* 174 (May), 1990. Available at www.pacificnews. org/marko/sex-surrogate.html (accessed April 29, 2005).

——. *The Man in the Iron Lung.* Berkeley, Calif.: Lemonade Factory, 1997.

——. N.d. "Questions I Feared the Journalist Would Ask." Mark O'Brien Papers, BANC MSS 99/247 c. Bancroft Library, University of California, Berkeley.

O'Brien, Mark, with Gillian Kendall. *How I Became a Human Being: A Disabled Man's Quest for Independence.* Madison: University of Wisconsin Press, 2003.

Shapiro, Joseph. *No Pity: People with Disabilities Forging a New Civil Rights Movement.* New York: Three Rivers Press, 1993.

——. "Disability Policy and the Media: A Stealth Civil Rights Movement Bypasses the Press and Defies Conventional Wisdom." *Policy Studies Journal* 22.1 (1994): 123–32.

Siebers, Tobin. *Morals and Stories.* New York: Columbia University Press, 1992.

——. "Kant and the Politics of Beauty." *Philosophy and Literature* 22.1 (1998): 31–50.

——. "My Withered Limb." *Michigan Quarterly Review* 37.2 (1998): 196–205.

——. *The Subject and Other Subjects: On Ethical, Aesthetic, and Political Identity.* Ann Arbor: University of Michigan Press, 1998.

——. "*The Reign of Ideology* by Eugene Goodheart." *Modern Philology* 96.4 (1999): 560–63.

——. *The Mirror of Medusa.* Rev. ed. Christchurch, New Zealand: Cybereditions, 2000.

——. "What Can Disability Studies Learn from the Culture Wars?" *Cultural Critique* 55 (2003): 182–216.

Taylor, Charles. *Sources of the Self: The Making of Modern Identity.* Cambridge, Mass.: Harvard University Press, 1987.

Young, Iris. *On Female Body Experience: "Throwing Like a Girl" and Other Essays.* Cambridge, Mass.: Oxford University Press, 2005.

CHAPTER 22

Defining Mental Disability

Margaret Price

NAMING AND DEFINITION

Who am I talking about? So far I've used a variety of terms to denote impairments of the mind, and I haven't yet exhausted the list. Contemporary language available includes *psychiatric disability, mental illness, cognitive disability, intellectual disability, mental health service user* (or *consumer*), *neurodiversity, neuroatypical, psychiatric system survivor, crazy,* and *mad.* "No term in the history of madness is neutral," Geoffrey Reaume argues, "not *mental illness, madness,* or any other term" (182). Moreover, as Ian Hacking has pointed out, particular names may thrive in a particular "ecological niche"—for instance, the intersection of the diagnosis "neurasthenia" with nineteenth-century French stories of the "Wandering Jew" (2, 120) or the diagnosis "drapetomania," applied to African American slaves who attempted to escape (Jackson 4). Keeping this dynamism in mind, the following analysis does not aim to accept some terms and discard others. Rather, I want to clarify the different areas they map and show that each does particular kinds of cultural work in particular contexts. Although I use *mental disability* as my own term of choice, I continue to use others as needed, and my overall argument is for deployment of language in a way that

operates as inclusively as possible, inviting coalition, while also attending to the specific texture of individual experiences. In doing so, I follow the urging of Tanya Titchkosky, who argues that the aim of analyzing language about disability should not be to mandate particular terms but rather "to examine what our current articulations of disability are saying in the here and now" ("Disability" 138). The problem of naming has always preoccupied DS scholars,[1] but acquires a particular urgency when considered in the context of disabilities of the mind, for often the very terms used to name persons with mental disability have explicitly foreclosed our status *as* persons. Aristotle's famous declaration that man is a rational animal (1253a; 1098a) gave rise to centuries of insistence that to be named mad was to lose one's personhood.

Mad is a term generally used in non-U.S. contexts, and has a long history of positive and person-centered discourses. MindFreedom International, a coalition of grassroots organizations, traces the beginning of the "Mad Movement" to the early 1970s, and reports on "Mad Pride" events that continue to take place in countries including Australia, Ghana, Canada, England, and the United States. MindFreedom and other groups organize activist campaigns, sponsor exhibits and performances, and act as forums and support networks for their thousands of members. *Mad* is less recognizable in the United States, which can be to its advantage, since its infrequency helps detach it from implication in medical and psychiatric industries. In addition, *mad* achieves a broad historical sweep. Psychiatry, with its interest in brains, chemistry, and drugs, arose only in the last couple of centuries; however, writings on madness can be found in pre-Socratic discourse, and their historical progression through centuries spans medicine, philosophy, and literature, as Allen Thiher shows in *Revels in Madness: Insanity in Medicine and Literature.*

> The center of our discourses on madness has had many names: *thymos, anima*, soul, spirit, self, the unconscious, the subject, the person. Whatever be the accent given by the central concept, access to the entity afflicted with madness is obtained through a language game in which these concepts or names play a role, organizing our experience of the world even as the world vouchsafes criteria for correct use of these notions.
>
> (3)

Thiher does not discuss at length his choice of *mad*, but it is evident from the far-reaching scope of his study that this term achieves a flexibility that *mental illness* and *cognitive disability* do not: it unites notions of that "central concept" through time and across cultures. As with *queer*, the broad scope of *mad* carries the drawback of generality but also the power of mass.

Many persons in the mad movement identify as psychiatric system survivors. According to MindFreedom, psychiatric system survivors are "individuals who have personally experienced human rights violations in the mental health system." A more inclusive term is *consumer/survivor/ex-patient* (*c/s/x*). Drawing upon the work of Linda J. Morrison, Bradley Lewis argues that this term "allows a coalition among people with diverse identification" while also indicating that the relationship between the three positions is neither exclusive nor linear (157). Lewis goes on to suggest that we might add *patient* as well, making the abbreviation into a quatrad (p/c/s/x), to represent the fact that some persons within the psychiatric system are forced into this objectified and passive role (157).

When I first encountered the term *survivor*, I felt hesitant. It seemed to have unsettling similarities to "cure": a survivor, I thought, implicitly had *had* a traumatic experience and come out the other side. This doesn't describe my experience. I make regular use of the psychiatric system, and I consider myself the agent and director of my treatments; for example, I interviewed and discarded psychiatrists until I found one who agrees with my approach to my bodymind.[2] However, there is no avoiding the fact that he, not I, wields the power of the prescription pad. In addition, I possess the economic and cultural privilege that permits me to try out and reject various caregivers, a privilege not open to many in the c/s/x group. And finally, like any "patient," I am subject to my caregivers' power over information. For example, when my psychiatrist and my therapist conferred and arrived at one of my diagnoses, they chose not to share that diagnosis with me until some months later (their stated reason being that I had been in the midst of a crisis and was not ready to process the information). As it happens, I think they made an appropriate decision, but the fact remains that regardless of what I thought, the outcome would have been the same; I had no say in the matter.

In her ethnographic study *Talking Back to Psychiatry*, Linda J. Morrison interviewed activists in the c/s/x movement, which she defines as "people who have been diagnosed as mentally ill and are engaged in different forms of 'talking back' to psychiatry and the mental health system," as well as allies including "dissident mental health professionals, lawyers, advocates, and family members" (ix). Morrison found that they made use of the term *survivor* in various ways, and that a "heroic survivor narrative" is deeply influential in the movement, both through published accounts (such as Kate Millett's *The Loony-Bin Trip*) and in individuals' processes of identity formation vis-à-vis psychiatric discourse (101). Participants' survivor narratives "exist in a range of intensity, from high drama to muted skeptical observations" (129), but the narrative as a whole, Morrison argues, plays a crucial role in the movement, helping to build solidarity and empower resistant voices. Significantly, this narrative, and the term *survivor*, have also been singled out for denigration by critics (Morrison 152–53).

My own thinking on *psychiatric system survivor* was deepened when I discussed it with my colleague Petra Kuppers. One evening at a conference, sitting on the bed in her hotel room and chewing over my thoughts, I said that I didn't feel I "survived" the psychiatric system so much as worked within it, negotiating and resisting as I went. "But," Petra said simply, "that *is* survival." Her insight has shifted my view of the term: rather than thinking of a survivor as one who has undergone and emerged from some traumatic experience (such as incarceration in a mental institution), it can also denote one who is actively and resistantly involved with the psychiatric system on an ongoing basis.

Mental illness introduces a discourse of wellness/unwellness into the notion of madness; its complement is *mental health*, the term of choice for the medical community as well as insurance companies and social support services. This well/unwell paradigm has many problems, particularly its implication that a mad person needs to be "cured" by some means. One mate-

rial consequence of this view is that mental health insurance operates on a "cure" basis, demanding "progress" reports from therapists and social workers, and cutting off coverage when the patient is deemed to have achieved a sufficiently "well" state. For instance, although the American Psychiatric Association recommends that persons with my diagnoses remain in long-term talk therapy, my insurance company (CIGNA) determined in 2006 that I was "well enough" and terminated my mental-health coverage, except for brief pharmaceutical consultations with my psychiatrist. During a months-long battle with the "physician reviewer" employed by CIGNA, my therapist's and psychiatrist's requests for continued coverage (which, according to ClGNA's rules, I was not permitted to make directly) were repeatedly turned down. Ultimately, my therapist was informed that the decision would stand unless I "actually attempt[ed] suicide," at which point I would be deemed unwell enough to resume therapy. This "well/unwell" paradigm reflects the larger tendency of American medical systems to intervene in "problems" rather than practice a more holistic form of care.

However, an advantage of *mental illness* is that it can be allied with the substantial—and sometimes contentious—conversation within DS on the intersections between illness and disability. In a 2001 *Hypatia* article, "Unhealthy Disabled: Treating Chronic Illnesses as Disabilities," Susan Wendell points out that activists in the disability rights movement in the United States have often sought to "distinguish themselves from those who are ill" (18). This has led to a schism between those she calls the "healthy disabled," whose impairments "are relatively stable and predictable for the foreseeable future" (19), and those who are chronically ill. Because those with chronic illnesses are often exhausted, in pain, or experiencing mental confusion, their very identities as activists come into question:

> Fluctuating abilities and limitations can make people with chronic illnesses seem like unreliable activists, given the ways that political activity in both disability and feminist movements are structured. . . . Commitment to a cause is usually equated to energy expended, even to pushing one's body and mind excessively, if not cruelly.
>
> (25)

Wendell acknowledges that "healthy disabled" and "unhealthy disabled" are blurry categories: a person with cerebral palsy, for example, may also experience exhaustion, pain, or mental confusion; indeed, a person with a physical impairment may also have a chronic illness. Usually, however, "disabled" implicitly means "healthy disabled," and full inclusion of the unhealthy disabled must involve "changes in the structure, culture, and traditions of political activism," with new attitudes toward "energy and commitment, pace and cooperation" (Wendell 26). As yet, such changes are largely unrealized. Consider the last conference you attended: did events run from 9:00 a.m. until late at night? Consider the "tenure clock," or activist efforts that call for attendance in public places for hours at a time: do such occasions assume each participant will have the ability to meet people, interact, and function for hours on end? Consider the persons who did not attend. Do you know who they are?

Andrea Nicki's theory of psychiatric disability picks up Wendell's point about energy and health, but reshapes it to critique the implicitly rational mind of the "good" disabled person—or, as Quintilian might have put it, the "good disabled person speaking well" (see Brueggemann, *Lend*). Not only must this person be of rational mind, Nicki argues; he must also adhere to a "cultural demand of cheerfulness," which is particularly insidious

because in some cases—for a person with depression, for example—this would involve not just an attitude *toward* his illness but a direct erasure *of* his illness (94). Like Wendell, Nicki calls for redesign of our social and work environments, emphasizing the importance of interdependence as a means to achieve this goal. Anne Wilson and Peter Beresford have argued that the project will be difficult, and will involve not just surface-level changes, but a full reworking of the social model of disability (145).

One part of this reworking will be the acknowledgment that, although discursive alliances can be drawn between physical and mental illness, important differences exist as well. For example, while members of the disability rights movement, including myself, proudly call ourselves "disabled," many members of the c/s/x movement view the term *disabled* with more suspicion. In the view of the c/s/x movement, when psychiatry assigns a diagnosis of "mental illness" to a person, that person is marked as permanently damaged, and as one whose rights may be taken away—unless, of course, she complies with psychiatry's requirements for "care," which may include medication, incarceration, or electroshock. Morrison makes this point by contrasting psychiatric diagnosis with the diagnosis of a cold:

> In modern psychiatry, a person who has been diagnosed with a serious and persistent mental illness (SPMI) is rarely considered "cured" or completely free of illness. The implied expectation is that mental illnesses are chronic. They may remit but they are likely to recur. Compare, for example the yearly cold symptoms with congestion and cough that many people experience, followed by recovery to a "normal" state. In psychiatric illness, recovery from the symptoms would not be considered the end of the problem. The likelihood of a return to a symptomatic state, with resultant need for

medical intervention, would be assumed ... [A] former patient is always expected to become a future patient and the sick role is ongoing. In fact, if a patient believes otherwise, this can be considered a symptom of exacerbated illness.

(5)

This paradox, in which belief of one's own wellness may *in itself* be considered evidence of unwellness, lies at the heart of psychiatric diagnosis. To accept the psychiatric profession's definition of oneself as sick is considered a key move toward getting well; the technical term for acceptance of a psychiatric label is "insight." Although members of the c/s/x movement occupy a range of perspectives, generally the movement resists psychiatry's efforts to place its "patients" into the "sick role." Like Deaf activists, c/s/x activists have much in common with disability activists, but strong differences as well—one of which is the issue of whether or not to self-identify as *disabled.*

One thing c/s/x and disability activists agree upon, however, is the deeply problematic nature of modern psychiatric discourse. Working in concert with the gigantic forces of for-profit insurance companies and the pharmaceutical industry, mainstream psychiatry places ever-increasing emphasis on a biological and positivist definition of mental illness, all while claiming to remain "theory-neutral" (Lewis 97). However, dissident voices can be heard within psychiatry as well. As Morrison shows, some medical professionals are members of the c/s/x movement. Groups that bring together critical psychologists and psychiatrists and the c/s/x movement have proliferated since the 1990s, and include the Critical Psychiatry Network; Psychology, Politics and Resistance; the Mental Health Alliance; and Radical Psychology Network. This resistant strain of psychiatry is sometimes called *postpsychiatry*, a theory/practice that views

"mind" philosophically and socially as well as biologically.

Postpsychiatrist medical philosophers Patrick Bracken and Philip Thomas argue that, once Descartes had established the now-conventional body/mind split (as well as valorization of the individual subject), subsequent theories of mind continued to perpetuate this belief, extending into nineteenth- and twentieth-century psychiatry, which expanded its effects still further. Bracken and Thomas identify three outcomes of this philosophy: the beliefs that "madness is internal"; that madness can be explained neurologically and treated (solely) with pharmaceuticals; and that psychiatrists have the "right and responsibility" to coerce their patients ("Postpsychiatry" 725). Postpsychiatry offers an alternative path, Bracken and Thomas suggest, not by replacing old techniques with new ones, but rather by "open[ing] up spaces in which other perspectives can assume a validity previously denied them"—especially the perspectives of those labeled "mentally ill" ("Postpsychiatry" 727). In addition to centering the agency of mad people, Bracken and Thomas argue for replacing the conventional separation of body and mind with an emphasis on social context, ethical as well as technical (chemical) modes of care, and an end to the claim that coercive "treatments" are applied for "objective" or "scientific" reasons. In a later, briefer article, Bracken and Thomas clarify the relationship of Cartesian dualism to postpsychiatry: human mental life, they argue, is not "some sort of enclosed world residing inside the skull," but is constructed "by our very presence and through our physical bodies" ("Time to Move" 1434).

Bradley Lewis offers an in-depth account of postpsychiatry in *Moving Beyond Prozac, DSM, & the New Psychiatry: The Birth of Postpsychiatry.* Describing himself as a "hybrid academic," Lewis holds both an

M.D. in psychiatry and a Ph.D. in inter-disciplinary humanities (ix). From this unusual position, Lewis makes a call for postpsychiatry that is both pragmatic and theoretical: cyborg theory, neurophysiology, and the governing structure of the APA all occupy significant parts of his attention. *Moving Beyond Prozac* describes "a theorized postpsychiatry," which would "take seriously the role of language and power" as well as "work without the pseudo-foundations and pseudo-certainties of modernist science and reason" (17). Lewis does not wish to do away with psychiatrists and clinics, but rather to reform them. The reformed "clinical encounter," for example, would include "not only the modernist values of empirical diagnosis and rational therapeutics but also additional clinical values like ethics, aesthetics, humor, empathy, kindness and justice" (17; see also Lewis, "Narrative Psychiatry"). While pragmatic, Lewis's argument is not individualistic, but aimed at discourses and structures of power. Individual psychiatrists and practices do need to change, Lewis suggests, but the core project is revision of the psychiatric profession to become more democratic, less positivist, less capitalistic, and to include the voices and concerns of *all* its stakeholders, including the c/s/x group.

Neuroatypical and *neurodiverse* mark a broader territory than psychiatric discourse: these terms include all whose brains position them as being somehow different from the neurotypical run of the mill. *Neuroatypical* is most often used to indicate persons on the autism spectrum, including those with Asperger's syndrome (AS), but has also been used to refer to persons with bipolar disorder (Antonetta) and traumatic brain injuries (Vidali). In her "bipolar book" (13) *A Mind Apart*, Susanne Antonetta argues that neurodiversity acts a positive force in human evolution, enabling alternative and creative ways of thinking, knowing, and apprehending the world.

A potential problem with the rhetoric of neurodiversity is that it can read as overly chipper (like a "Celebrate Diversity!" bumper sticker); its optimism can flatten individual difference. However, it also carries a complement, *neurotypical* (or NT), which destabilizes assumptions about "normal" minds and can be used to transgressive effect (Brownlow). For example, Aspies For Freedom has used NT to parody the rhetoric of "cure" propagated by the organization Fighting Autism. Until very recently, Fighting Autism published and maintained a graphic called the "autism clock" which purported to record the "incidence" of autism for persons aged three to twenty-two and the supposed economic "cost" of this incidence.[3] In response, Aspies For Freedom published a parody of the autism clock, which pathologizes neurotypicals and suggests that for the onrush of diagnoses ("1 every minute"), there will be "2 to take them."

While Fighting Autism viewed autism as a disease that must be battled and cured, Aspies For Freedom takes the stance that autism is a form of neurodiversity, that is, of difference, not something that should be eradicated. Although public opinion of autism tends to be dominated by the disease/cure model, resistant voices of neurodiversity have proliferated, especially through web-based communities, blogs, and webtexts (see, for example, Yergeau, "Aut(hored)ism").

Some DS scholars, including Cynthia Lewiecki-Wilson, have called for a coalition of those with psychiatric and cognitive disabilities; she suggests that the term *mental disability* can be used to denote the rhetorical position of both groups:

> For the purposes of this paper, I group mental illness and severe mental retardation under the category *mental disabilities*. Despite the varieties of and differences among mental impairments, this collective category

focuses attention on the problem of gaining rhetoricity to the mentally disabled: that is, rhetoric's received tradition of emphasis on the individual rhetor who produces speech/writing, which in turn confirms the existence of a fixed, core self, imagined to be located in the mind.

(157)

In other words, according to Lewiecki-Wilson, the notion that one's disability is located in one's mind unites this category, not because such a thing is inherently true, but because persons labeled with these kinds of disabilities share common experiences of disempowerment as rhetors. My own struggles for adequate terminology follow Lewiecki-Wilson's call for coalition politics. Although it is important to note the differences between specific experiences, in general I believe we need *both* local specificity *and* broad coalitions for maximum advantage. Persons with impaired bodyminds have been segregated from one another enough.

For a while, I used the term *psychosocial disability.* I like its etymology, the fact that it bumps *psych* (soul) against social context; I like its ability to reach toward both mind and world. Its emphasis on social context calls attention to the fact that psychosocial disabilities can be vividly, and sometimes unpredictably, apparent in social contexts. Although it's common to describe psychosocial disabilities as "invisible," or "hidden," this is a misnomer. In fact, such disabilities may become vividly manifest in forms ranging from "odd" remarks to lack of eye contact to repetitive stimming.[4] Like queerness, psychosocial disability is not so much invisible as it is apparitional, and its "disclosure" has everything to do with the environment in which it dis/appears.[5] *Psychosocial disability* announces that it is deeply intertwined with social context, rather than buried in an individual's brain.

Although *psychosocial* has been used

in narrow ways that comply with a medical model of disability, it also has considerable traction within disability studies. In her introduction to a 2002 special issue of *Disability Studies Quarterly*, Deborah Marks argues that a psychosocial perspective can "challenge the disciplinary boundary between psychological and social paradigms." Taking up her point, Patrick Durgin has amplified the term's radical possibilities:

A "psycho-social formulation" is, in short, the none-of-the-above option in the diagnostic pantheon. It is the excluded middle or liminal space where impairment meets world to become disability. To use clinical language, it does not "present" clinically because it resists being given diagnostic surmise; and yet it won't "pass" as normal.

(130)

Durgin goes on to argue that, although *psychosocial* may seem a kind of "golden mean" between medical and social paradigms, it too must undergo critical examination; not least, I would add, because this term can and has been used in medicalized and positivist projects. For example, in the third and fourth editions of the *Diagnostic and Statistical Manual of Mental Disorders*, the authors have made a great show of considering social factors in their new classification of "mental disorders," and also of having involved a broad base of patients and clinicians in developing the manual. Yet, as Lewis points out, that show is largely illusory; the central developers of the landmark DSM-III (and inventors of its categories) numbered just *five persons*, and the overarching rationale for the manual is increasingly positivist and biological. Despite this history, I value the potential of *psychosocial* for reappropriation. In a sense, Durgin is saying to the authors of the DSM, "You want social? We'll give you social."

My appreciation of *psychosocial* has

been affirmed by philosopher Cal Montgomery, who pointed out its usefulness in terms of sensory as well as cognitive disabilities, saying, "I do think we need a way of talking inclusively about people for whom access to human interaction is problematic." However, having spent the last couple of years trying this term out—on the page, in conference presentations, at dinner with friends—I've become increasingly uncomfortable with it, because in most cases if seems to provoke puzzlement rather than connection. Explaining my experiences to Cal, I wrote: "I've been using the term 'psychosocial disability' in various settings for over a year—at conferences, in casual conversations, in my writing, etc.—and it seems that, *unless* I'm writing an article where I can fully explain what I'm getting at, people just kind of go blank when I use the term. I have started to feel like, what's the point of using a term that no one gets but me?" Put simply, in most social contexts, *psychosocial* failed to *mean*.

So I have taken another tack. Following Lewiecki-Wilson, these days I'm using *mental disability*. As Lewiecki-Wilson argues, this term can include not only madness, but also cognitive and intellectual dis/abilities of various kinds. I would add that it might also include "physical" illnesses accompanied by mental effects (for example, the "brain fog" that attends many autoimmune diseases, chronic pain, and chronic fatigue). And, as Cal suggests, we should keep in mind its potential congruence with sensory and other kinds of disabilities—that is, its commonalities with "people for whom access to human interaction is problematic."

Finally, while I respect the concerns of those who reject the label *disabled*, I have chosen to use a term that includes *disability* explicitly. In my own experience, claiming disability has been a journey of community, power, and love. Over the last twenty years, I have migrated from being a person who spent a lot of time in hospitals, who was prescribed medications and prodded by doctors, to a person who inhabits a richly diverse, contentious, and affectionate disability community. Let me tell a story to explain this migration: On a December day in 2008, I arrived in a fluorescent-lit hotel room in San Francisco to listen to a panel of scholars talk about disability. I had recently made a long airplane journey and felt off-balance, frightened, and confused. I sat beside disability activist and writer Neil Marcus, and when he saw my face, he opened his arms and offered me a long, hard-muscled hug. That hug, with arms set at awkward angles so we could fit within his wheelchair, with chin digging info scalp and warm skin meeting skin—that, to me, is disability community. Neil may or may not know what it is like to wake with night terrors at age forty, I may or may not know what it feels like to struggle to form words, but the reaching across those spaces is what defines disability for me. We write, we question and disagree, we are disabled. Simi Linton has said of the term *disability* that "We have decided to reassign meaning rather than choose a new name" (31).

And so, in naming myself a crazy girl, neuroatypical, mentally disabled, psychosocially disabled—in acknowledging that I appear (as a colleague once told me) "healthy as a horse" yet walk with a mind that whispers in many voices—I am trying to reassign meaning. In the best of all possible worlds I would refuse to discard terms, refuse to say which is best. I believe in learning the terms, listening to others' voices, and naming myself pragmatically according to what the context requires. I believe that this is language.

NOTES

1. See Christensen; Dajani; Linton, chap. 2; Titchkosky, "Disability"; Trent, introduction; and Zola.

2. I use the term *bodymind* to emphasize that although "body" and "mind" usually occupy separate conceptual and linguistic territories, they are deeply intertwined. This theory is drawn in part from Babette Rothschild's *The Body Remembers.* Although Rothschild's usage refers to persons who have experienced trauma, I believe it can be usefully applied to persons with mental disabilities of all kinds, for—as I argue throughout this book—our problems are in no sense "all in our minds." If it weren't so unwieldy, I would be tempted to use something like *psychobiosocialpoliticalbodymind.*

3. Just as this book was going to press, the autism clock was removed from the website. When I wrote to inquire, I received a notice that it has "been brought to our attention that the autism clock was offensive to some members of the autism community." In addition, the domain name of the website was changed from fightingautism.org to thoughtfulhouse.org. While limited, these measures indicate that the hard work of neurodiverse activists is being noticed.

4. *Stimming,* short for "self-stimulating," is a self-soothing repetitive activity that may be practiced by persons with a variety of disabilities, including autism, obsessive-compulsive disorder, or anxiety.

5. For more on the apparitional nature of mental disabilities, see Montgomery, "Critic of the Dawn" and "A Hard Look at Invisible Disability," and Samuels. For more on the apparitional nature of disability and illness generally, see Myers, "Coming Out" and Siebers, "Disability as Masquerade."

WORKS CITED

American Psychiatric Association. *Diagnostic and Statistical Manual of Mental Disorders.* Text revision. 4th ed. Arlington, VA: APA, 2000.

Antonetta, Susanne. *A Mind Apart: Travels in a Neurodiverse World.* New York: Penguin, 2005.

Aristotle. *The Complete Works of Aristotle.* Jonathan Barnes, ed. and trans. Bollingen Series LXXI: 1–2. Princeton, NJ: Princeton UP, 1984.

Aristotle. *The Nicomachean Ethics.* Trans. J. A. K. Thomson. Rev. Hugh Tredennick. Intro. Jonathan Barnes. New York: Penguin, 2004.

Bracken, Patrick, and Philip Thomas. "Postpsychiatry: A New Direction for Mental Health." *British Medical Journal* 322 (2001): 724–27.

Bracken, Patrick, and Philip Thomas. "Time to Move Beyond the Mind-Body Split." *British Medical Journal* 325 (2002): 1433–34.

Brownlow, Charlotte. "Re-presenting Autism: The Construction of 'NT Syndrome.'" *Journal of Medical Humanities* 31 (2010): 243–55.

Brueggemann, Brenda Jo. *Lend Me Your Ear: Rhetorical Constructions of Deafness.* Washington, DC: Gallaudet P, 1999.

Christensen, Carol. "Disabled, Handicapped or Disordered: What's in a Name?" *Disability and the Dilemmas of Education and Justice.* Ed. Carol Christensen and Fazal Rizvi. Buckingham: Open UP. 63–77.

Dajani, Karen Finlon. "What's in a Name? Terms Used to Refer to People with Disabilities." *Disability Studies Quarterly* 21.3 (2001).

Durgin, Patrick F. "Psychosocial Disability and Post-Ableist Poetics: The 'Case' of Hannah Weiner's *Clairvoyant Journals.*" *Contemporary Women's Writing* 2:2 (2008): 131–54.

Hacking, Ian. *Mad Travelers: Reflections on the Reality of Transient Mental Illness.* Cambridge, MA: Harvard UP, 1998.

Jackson, Vanessa. "In Our Own Voice: African-American Stories of Oppression, Survival and Recovery in Mental Health Systems." MFI Portal. April 4, 2009. http://www.mindfreedom.org/kb/mental-health-abuse/Racism/InOurOwn-Voice/vie.

Lewiecki-Wilson, Cynthia. "Rethinking Rhetoric through Mental Disabilities." *Rhetoric Review* 22.2 (2003): 156–67.

Lewis, Bradley. *Moving Beyond Prozac, DSM, & the New Psychiatry.* Ann Arbor: U of Michigan P, 2006.

Lewis, Bradley. "Narrative Psychiatry." *Comprehensive Textbook of Psychiatry,* 9th ed. Ed. Benjamin J. Saddock and Virginia A. Sadock. Philadelphia: Lippincott, 2009. 2934–39.

Linton, S. *Claiming Disability: Knowledge and Identity.* New York: New York UP, 1998.

Marks, Deborah. "Introduction: Counselling, Therapy and Emancipatory Praxis." *Disability Studies Quarterly* 22.3 (2002).

Millet, Kate. *The Loony-Bin Trip.* New York: Simon and Schuster, 1990.

Montgomery, Cal. "Critic of the Dawn." *Ragged Edge Online* 22.3 (May 2001). http://www.ragged-edge-mag.com/0501/0501cov.htm.

Montgomery, Cal. "A Hard Look at Invisible Disability." *Ragged Edge Online* 22.2 (March 2001). http://www.ragged-edge-mag.com/0301/0301ft1.htm.

Morrison, Linda J. *Talking Back to Psychiatry: The Psychiatric Consumer/Survivor/Ex-Patient Movement.* New York: Routledge, 2005.

Myers, Kimberly R. "Coming Out: Considering the Closet of Illness." *Journal of Medical Humanities* 25.4 (2004): 255–70.

Nicki, Andrea. "The Abused Mind: Feminist Theory, Psychiatric Disability, and Trauma." *Hypatia* 16.4 (2001): 80–104.

Reaume, Geoffrey. "Mad People's History." *Radical History Review* 94 (2006): 170–82.

Rothschild, Babette. *The Body Remembers: The Psychophysiology of Trauma and Trauma Treatment.* New York: Norton, 2000.

Samuels, Ellen. "My Body, My Closet: Invisible Disability and the Limits of Coming-out Discourse." *GLQ* 9.1 (2003): 233–55.

Siebers, Tobin. "Disability as Masquerade." *Literature and Medicine* 23.1 (2004): 1–22.

Thiher, Allen. *Revels in Madness: Insanity in Medicine and Literature.* Ann Arbor: U of Michigan P, 2004.

Titchkosky, Tanya. "Disability: A Rose by Any Other Name? 'People-First' Language in Canadian Society." *Canadian Review of Sociology and Anthropology* 38.2 (2001): 125–40.

Trent, James W. Jr. *Inventing the Feeble Mind: A History of Mental Retardation in the United States.* Berkeley: U of California P, 1994.

Vidali, Amy. "Rhetorical Hiccups: Disability Disclosure in Letters of Recommendation." *Rhetoric Review* 28.2 (2009): 185–204.

Wendell, Susan. "Unhealthy Disabled: Treating Chronic Illnesses as Disabilities." *Hypatia* 16.4 (2001): 17–33.

Zola, Irving Kenneth. "Self, Identity and the Naming Question: Reflections on the Language of Disability." *Social Science and Medicine* 36.2 (1993): 167–73.

CHAPTER 23

Disability and Blackness

Josh Lukin

In 2005 the Modern Language Association's Committee on Disability Issues in the Professsion wrote, "The future of Disability Studies is Black indeed." Their prophecy expressed a determination to begin a long-overdue discussion of black issues and artists in the context of Disability Studies, and vice-versa. Committee member Robert McRuer, of George Washington University, noted that, with few exceptions, Disability Studies silently assumes whiteness in its practitioners and subjects. McRuer recalled how, twenty-four years earlier, the endless repetition of the phrase "blacks and women," as though the two were mutually exclusive categories, had provoked the creation of the volume, *All the Women Are White, All the Blacks Are Men, but Some of Us Are Brave: Black Women's Studies.* That emphasis on where identities intersect, and the need to create more complex concepts of identity that could accommodate that intersectionality, transformed feminism: McRuer and his allies hoped for a similarly deep transformation in Disability Studies.

To understand this state of affairs, we need to look back. The disability rights movement gained widespread recognition in the 1970s; the academic field of Disability Studies is associated with the founding of the Society for Disability Studies [SDS] in the 1980s; and humanities scholars at

the MLA have been working in the field since the early 1990s. Rosemarie Garland-Thomson's 1996 *Extraordinary Bodies*, a pioneering study of disability in literature, addressed depiction of disability in the work of black writers such as Audre Lorde, Ann Petry, and Toni Morrison. Although African Americans constitute twelve percent of the population in general, they make up eighteen percent of Americans with disabilities; so one might reasonably ask why the appearance of Black Disability Studies has taken so long considering that a greater percentage of black people appear to be disabled? And what role can literary scholars have in developing black disability studies? The answers to those two questions are connected, and relate to the tensions between black activism and disability advocacy going back to the earlier days of the disability movement.

I. ACTIVISM

Black disabled activist Johnnie Lacy, in a 1998 interview for UC Berkeley's oral history archive, recounted several decades of experience trying to negotiate her minority identities. As early as 1960, Lacy was exquisitely conscious of the power that even those who might oppose race and sex discrimination felt they could wield in oppressing people with disabilities. She recalls the San Francisco State University professor who successfully organized a movement to stop her from studying in his department because he saw no place in his profession for wheelchair-users.

> ... my final and departing shot to him was that if I were just a woman, he could not do this to me; if I were only a person of color, he would not be able to do this to me; and ... the only reason that—the only way that you [are] able to take this unfair advantage is because I have a disability.

Although the analogy between racist and ableist discrimination is evident in Lacy's protest, she did not see that analogy being widely understood. At the time, and well into the early Seventies, her interaction with her fellow black activists led her to believe that the black community shared the larger society's prejudices against the disabled:

> I believe that African Americans see disability in the same way that everybody else sees it—[perceiving people with disabilities as] worthless, mindless—without realizing that this is the same attitude held by others toward African Americans. This belief in effect cancels out the black identity they share with a disabled black person, both socially and culturally, because the disability experience is not viewed in the same context as if one were only black, and not disabled. Because of this myopic view, I as a black disabled person could not share in the intellectual dialogue viewed as exclusive to black folk. In other words, I could be one or the other but not both.

Although the black community acknowledged the existence of disability, Lacy felt that it did not recognize the possibility of people with disabilities having a group identity. "I also discovered ... that many African-Americans consider being black as having a disability, and so they didn't really identify with disability as a disability but just as one other kind of inequity that black people had to deal with."

With the late Seventies came the "504 Demonstration," the Stonewall Inn of the disability rights movement. The Rehabilitation Act of 1973 had contained a provision making it illegal for any federally funded institution or activity to discriminate against the disabled; but this passage, like the lines in the 1964 Civil Rights Act prohibiting sex discrimination, was not taken seriously by the federal government. Like the women's movement of a decade earlier, and the desegregation movement before that, the disability movement took to direct action to compel the state to keep its promise. For twenty-five days, disability activists occupied the San Francisco offices of the Department of Health, Education, and Welfare, ultimately prompting HEW to grant their demands that the anti-discrimination law be enforced with no exceptions.

Johnnie Lacy was among the many disabled citizens who gained a new understanding of the position of the disabled in society, realizing that a newly self-aware minority was no longer going to ask meekly for the favor of equal opportunity:

> I saw disabled people demanding things ... that should have been theirs ... and I immediately made the connection ... I had worked in the anti-poverty program before, and poor [Black and Latino] people were given the same kinds of lack of respect and the same kinds of treatment.

At this point, Lacy did not feel she had to deny or disavow her other identities to accept her newly affirmed status as a member of the disability community: the education she received in and around the 504 Demonstrations gave her,

> a sense of pride as a disabled person, not as a black person and not as a woman. But

it . . . brought the three together for the first time to me. And sort of made me feel like a whole person . . . I could identify myself with a whole group of people that I never identified and that I didn't really know existed. It was like sharing my experiences as a disabled person for the first time, sharing my insights . . . It was like being with a group of people who saw themselves as people, not as objects of pity . . . people, like I say, were being empowered and they were not blaming themselves.

As an activist in the new movement, working at Berkeley's Center for Independent Living and similar institutions, Lacy found herself on the other side of the divide: instead of feeling frustrated with the black community's limited understanding of disability culture, she became a kind of ethnographic guide to the largely white disability community, trying to educate its members who had no clue as to how to approach the black community. Although she quickly taught her white colleagues to avoid openly condescending behavior, she had more difficulty with their ignorance of cultural difference:

It's just that they came from backgrounds where . . . they just didn't have that much exposure to people of color, and they truly did not know how to outreach with these folks. They just felt that if you're disabled, that's the only thing, you know, that's important.

She struggled to explain how many minority cultures had different attitudes toward community and family than did the independence-minded white professional class, and how those differences were relevant to the Independent Living Movement. Ultimately the movement's minority outreach resources improved with the recruitment of more activists of color who had received and given training in the "504 group."

The obstacles to recognition and understanding between the two movements, black and disabled, are discussed further by blind black activist Donald Galloway in the Berkeley oral history archive. Working at the Center for Independent Living in 1973, he was punished for advocating a larger minority presence:

I was the only black, and I started bringing black people into the center as drivers and attendants, and bringing in professional types . . . I went to the board of directors at the center, and said, we're going to start a black caucus to make sure we get our voice heard. That went over like a lead balloon . . . because the attitude was that we were all one, and there's no need for it . . . I got kicked off the board because of my position.

But while the disability movement took some time to perceive the need for attention to race, Galloway recalls Bay Area black leaders who were responsive to the needs of the disabled in the Seventies. He was among those who brought the Black Panther Party into an alliance with the 504 demonstrators and persuaded the black elected officials of Berkeley to support the Center for Independent Living (see Schweik for a detailed account of the other individuals involved in that alliance).

Yet, despite his personal successes in connecting with black organizations on specific issues, Galloway ultimately shared Lacy's feeling that there was a gap in mutual understanding between the movements:

To be realistic about it, the black community, even now, the organized black community did not really identify with the struggle of people with disabilities in the same way. I think that we, as disabled people, identify with the black movement. But the black movement . . . did not want to include people with disabilities in the movement . . . In fact, Senator Humphrey, during the 1973 debate . . . when the Civil Rights Act of 1964 came up to be voted on, he wanted to include people with disabilities, and the black organized community said, "No . . ."

Only in the Nineties, when a broad coalition was required to save the Civil Rights Act, did Galloway see a mutually respectful alliance forming. His description of it is telling:

> We came in and basically helped to bail—not to bail—to help them, to help us to—it's hard to call them and us, because I'm a part of both groups, so I'm bouncing back and forth, so you understand when I said them and us. We had to go in and help support the reauthorization of it. It was successful. And now they are beginning to understand that we needed to support each other . . . It's that kind of awareness that's beginning to happen between the different groups. The women's movement went through the same thing.

II. SCHOLARSHIP

The issues behind Galloway's struggle over which group to call "them" and "us" are illuminated by a recollection Johnnie Lacy has of a Community Action agency meeting in the Sixties:

> I can remember one manager standing up and declaring very loudly that he didn't see a difference between disabled people and black people, because he was black, and he felt just as disabled as a disabled person. And I think he got a big support for that statement. And I think it clearly was a dividing point, between the way blacks saw disability and the way that black disabled people saw disability. There was a difference.

That "difference" is central to the conflict between the two movements—whenever one group said "We are the same," the other group said, with some insight, "No. You are exploiting my group's experience just so that you can have a metaphor for your own." And individuals who occupied both groups at once were caught in the crossfire. The tension created by one group feeling that its experience was being reduced to a metaphor still occurs in situations where people with disabilities seek representation alongside racial and ethnic minorities.

The manager whose analogy elicited Lacy's objection was using rhetoric familiar to students of disability. Characters with disabilities in novels are always symbols of something or other. Very rarely do we see what a person with a disability interacting with the world experiences—a descriptive goal that is taken for granted in stories about characters from other historically marginalized groups. Readers now are sensitive to racial and gender metaphors. But, as critic Michael Bérubé has observed, it still takes a rare sensibility to notice that the lawyer in *Native Son* presents disability as a moral failing when he shouts, "Your philanthropy was as tragically blind as your sightless eyes!" (569).

Hence, in its rhetorical use of disability, the manager's claim that he feels just like a disabled person because he is black comes as no surprise. But in historical terms, it is a novel connection—traditionally, African Americans have been extremely averse to race/disability analogies; when scholars seek to include disability alongside race and ethnicity in a multicultural curriculum, objections still arise from representatives of racial minorities who take offense at the suggestion that they could have anything in common with the disabled. Jennifer James, a literary scholar at George Washington University, has researched the historical reasons for this aversion.

Simply put, from the beginnings of the United States, the claim that "Blackness is like disability" was not used as an expression of how black Americans suffered but as a tool of their oppression. During the American Revolution, James explains, "the Continental Congress decided not to enlist 'Negroes, Boys unable to bear Arms nor Old men unfit to endure the Fatigues of the Campaign,' . . . New Hampshire refused to accept 'lunatics, idiots and Negros,' implying blackness was a similar mental deficiency." The very fact of blackness was regarded as a deformity or disability, even by white Americans sympathetic to the cause of civic equality. In the 1860s, "Abolitionist Thomas Wentworth Higginson, who commanded . . . the first African American regiment officially raised for the Civil War, issued this progress report on his black subordinates: they 'were growing more like white men—less grotesque.'" These associations naturally influenced black writers' priorities: James argues that in

> post-Civil War African American literature particularly, it was imperative that the black body and the black mind be portrayed as uninjured . . . in order to disprove one of the main anti-black arguments that surfaced after emancipation—that slavery had made blacks 'unfit' for citizenship.

The same rhetorical issues were at work in the integration struggles that followed World War II: as postwar civil rights agitations grew, the stakes surrounding public portrayals of blackness also increased. To aid the struggle, image brokers sought cultural products that highlighted the tragedy of white oppression and the reliability of black dignity. In practice, this meant excluding portrayals of black Americans that would suggest sexuality, childishness, or disability, all of which were associated with the history of anti-black stereotypes. The ironies are painful here—black soldiers were disproportionately punished for infractions of discipline during the war, and those with war-derived physical and mental disabilities were often denied discharge, and sometimes subjected to beatings and torture in the guise of "therapy." But the pressure to convey the public message that "The Negro is just like you," with "you" being an imagined able-bodied, empowered, white audience who could aid in the liberation struggle, led to strange

silences and distortions on the subject of disabled black veterans. It was in this context, James says, that John Oliver Killens censured his fellow black novelist Ralph Ellison for depicting psychologically disabled black veterans.

James finds tools for understanding this problem in recent disability scholarship, especially that of Henri-Jacques Stiker. People disabled by wartime injury or by work-related accidents, Stiker explains, have for the past century or more been the object of attempts to reintegrate them into society. Such efforts assume that "integration" is desirable and "society" is something everyone wants to be part of. To James, John Oliver Killens' complaint is part of a "black politics of rehabilitation" that requires black bodies to prove their "sameness" before Black people can be fully integrated into the national community. For people with disabilities, "readjustment must be to society as society is presently constituted." Society promises the benefits of sameness, luring the "other" to accept rehabilitation. The idea that "society" requires radical change, and the idea that the forces *creating* marginalized groups and minorities outside the norm must be fought, form no part of this rehabilitative model.

The argument that demanding to be "like everybody else" attributes a greater value to "everybody else" than "everybody else" may possess is of course a commonplace of black activism from the Sixties onward, beginning with James Baldwin's asking, in the context of his demand for immense transformations in Western societies, "Do I really *want* to be integrated into a burning house?" But Jennifer James finds that even in the Fifties, there was one literary voice consistently and repeatedly defying the pressure to engage in "damage control," and possessing none of the "hesitance to offer graphic descriptions of a black body wounded by warfare" that she sees informing most postwar black literature. This author, who presented unashamed depictions of unrehabilitated black male bodies, was the poet and novelist Gwendolyn Brooks. In her 1944 "Soldier Sonnets" (retitled "gay chaps at the bar"), her 1949 volume *Annie Allen*, and her 1953 novel *Maud Martha*, Brooks breaks with a tradition of black American war writers who evaded the issue of bodily injury; she seeks to give voice to various "non-heroic" bodies using prose and verse structures that mirror their broken forms. The argument that "we are like other people" does appear in such sonnets as "the white troops had their orders but the Negroes looked like men," but these "men" are not idealized figures of empowerment: they lose their limbs, faces, blood, and lives in a war that offers little glory. Brooks' project, James believes, is to force socially produced disability into view and to show that society, rather than the individual, is in dire need of rehabilitation.

The head of Temple University's Institute on Disabilities, Diane Bryen, in 1996 summarized the central precepts of Disability Studies and the movements that gave rise to it. They include

- An opposition to "cureism," the belief that the goal of people with disabilities should be focused on eliminating their disability.
- An opposition to the depiction of people with disabilities as helpless, pitiful, and powerless victims of their impairments.
- An opposition to the "Supercrip" myth of the disabled person who pulls himself up by his bootstraps to become an Inspiration to Us All.
- Perception of the "problem of disability" as a social (not a medical) problem that can be minimized by eliminating barriers in the environment.
- The belief that people with disabilities have shared histories, cultures, and interests, and a desire for full citizenship, encompassing social and political self-determination.
- The insistence, exemplified in the slogan "Nothing about us without us," that people with disabilities and their perspectives be included in accounts of disability and the formation of disability policy.

These dogmas have been powerful tools for uniting people with similar goals, values, and experiences. But some of them suffer from the problems inherent in any attempt to make broad generalizations that define a culture or an identity.

While Jennifer James's work shows how black voices and Disability Studies critiques converge, Anna Mollow, another participant in the Black Disability Studies panel, focuses on how black perspectives can shake up and complicate the conventional wisdom of the Disability Studies world. She urges that,

> in examining intersections of forms of oppression, we guard against the dangers of a 'disability essentialism,' in which the experiences, needs, desires, and aims of all disabled people are assumed to be the same and those with 'different' experiences are accommodated only if they do not make claims that undermine the movement's foundational arguments.

Mollow's work on Meri Nana-Ama Danquah shows how a narrative in many ways at odds with the standards of the approach Bryen outlined: for Danquah, the fight is not to get out of a system that unjustly stigmatizes her as ill, or to combat stereotypes about triumph and inspiration, but to get into a system that unjustly denies the reality of her illness and the resources she needs to recover.

There have been several positive developments both in intersectional activism and in academic analysis since the prediction opening this essay, including the rise of the National Black Disability Coalition and the publication of Chris Bell's *Blackness and Disability* anthology. In the Bay Area, still a disability activism mecca, black performance artist Leroy Moore is a leader both in social justice organizing and in the arts, with such projects as Krip Hop Nation, which supports and raises public awareness of musicians with disabilities. The University of Michigan Press has published Terry Rowden's *The Songs of Blind Folk: African American Musicians and the Cultures of Blindness* as part of its disability studies series; the journal *MELUS* has published an issue on "Race, Ethnicity, Disability, and Literature." Education scholar Nirmala Erevelles has been writing groundbreaking work at the intersection of disability studies and critical race theory, analyzing the creation of disability in people disadvantaged by class and race, the oppression of disabled people of color, and he ideological use disability to justify racial, gender, ethnic, and national oppression. There is a growing body of work of activist women of color in the blogosphere and on the academic conference circuit that is increasing awareness of disability movement struggles and insights.

The theme running through the work of all of these writers is the need to listen to black voices and consider distinctively black experiences when tracing the history of disability and its artistic representation. Their insights can help us make sense of the dilemmas and obstacles described by African Americans with disabilities and indeed could help to reduce the misunderstandings and ignorance encountered by Lacy, Galloway, and others in their position. Simi Linton has written that the "Disability Studies' project is to weave disabled people back into the fabric of society, thread by thread, theory by theory. It aims to expose the ways in which disability has been made exceptional and to work to naturalize disabled

people—remake us as full citizens whose rights and privileges are intact, whose history and contributions are recorded, and whose often distorted representations in art, literature, film, theater, and other forms of artistic expression are fully analyzed" (522). It is imperative that those threads and theories, and that "fabric of society," not be imagined as all white.

WORKS CITED

Bell, Christopher M., ed. *Blackness and Disability: Critical Examinations and Cultural Interventions.* East Lansing: Michigan State University Press, 2011. Print.

Bérubé, Michael. "Disability and Narrative." *PMLA* 120.2 (2005). 518–522. Print.

Bryen, Diane N. and Sieglinde A. Shapiro. "Disability Studies: What Is It and Why Is It Needed?" Temple University *Faculty Herald* February 1996. *Temple University Institute on Disabilities.* Web. 3 March 2012.

Danquah, Meri Nana-Ama. *Willow Weep for Me: A Black Woman's Journey Through Depression.* New York: Norton, 1998.

Erevelles, Nirmala, Anne Kanga, and Renee Middleton. "How Does It Feel to Be a Problem? Race, Disability, and Exclusion in Educational Policy." In Brantlinger, Ellen, ed. *Who Benefits from Special Education? Remediating [Fixing] Other People's Children.* London: Routledge, 2005. Print.

Erevelles, Nirmala, and Andrea Minear. "Unspeakable Offenses: Untangling Race and Disability in Discourses of Intersectionality." *Journal of Literary & Cultural Disability Studies* 4.2 (2010). 127–145. Print.

Erevelles, Nirmala, and Ivan Eugene Watts. "These Deadly Times: Reconceptualizing School Violence by Using Critical Race Theory and Disability Studies." *American Educational Research Journal* 41.2 (2004). 271–299. Print.

Fiedler, Leslie. *Freaks: Myths and Images of the Secret Self.* New York: Simon and Schuster, 1978.

——. *Tyranny of the Normal: Essays on Bioethics, Theology, & Myth.* Boston: Godine, 1996.

Galloway, Donald. "Blind Services and Advocacy and the Independent Living Movement in Berkeley." Interviews conducted by Sharon Bonney and Fred Pelka. 2000–2002. *Disability Rights and Independent Living Movement Oral History Series.* UC Berkeley, 2004. Web. 3 March 2012.

Garland-Thomson, Rosemarie. *Extraordinary Bodies: Figuring Physical Disability in American Culture and Literature.* New York: Columbia UP, 1996. Print.

Hull, Gloria T., Patricia Bell-Scott, and Barbara Smith. *All the Women Are White, All the Blacks Are Men, but Some of Us Are Brave.* Old Westbury, NY: Feminist Press, 1982. Print.

James, Jennifer C. *A Freedom Bought with Blood: African American War Literature from the Civil War to World War II.* Chapel Hill: UNC Press, 2007. Print.

Lacy, Johnnie. "Director, Community Resources For Independent Living: An African-American Woman's Perspective on The Independent Living Movement in The Bay Area, 1960s–1980s." Interview conducted by David Landes. 1998. *Disability Rights and Independent Living Movement Oral History Series.* UC Berkeley, 2000. Web. 3 March 2012.

——. "Minority vs. Disability Identity." *Disability Rights and Independent Living Movement Oral History Series.* UC Berkeley, 2000. Web. 3 March 2012.

Linton, Simi. "What Is Disability Studies?" *PMLA* 120.2 (2005). 518–522. Print.

Lukin, Josh. "The Black Panther Party." In *Encyclopedia of American Disability History,* ed. Susan Burch. New York: Facts on File, 2009. Print.

Rowden, Terry. *The Songs of Blind Folk: African American Musicians and the Cultures of Blindness.* Ann Arbor: University of Michigan Press, 2009. Print.

Schweik, Susan. "Lomax's Matrix: Disability, Solidarity, and the Black Power of 504." *Disability Studies Quarterly* 31.1 (2011). Web. 3 March 2012.

Stiker, Henri-Jacques. A History of Disability. 1982 (as *Corps infirmes et societés*). Trans. William Sayres. Ann Arbor: University of Michigan Press, 1999.

Wu, Cynthia and Jennifer C. James, eds. *Melus* 31.3 (2006): *Race, Ethnicity, Disability, and Literature.* Print.

CHAPTER 24

My Body, My Closet: Invisible Disability and the Limits of Coming Out

Ellen Samuels

THE LIMITS OF ANALOGY

A story: On a breezy afternoon one April I met with "Samantha," a student in an undergraduate course on literature and disability, to talk about her paper on cultural images of burn survivors. After showing me her draft, she remained, eager to talk about issues of disability and visibility, about her own experience as a person who appears "normal" until one looks closely enough to see the scars on her jaw and neck, the puckered skin that disappears under the neck of her T-shirt and reappears on her arm and wrist. Since I almost always look "normal" despite my disabling chronic illness, I sympathized with her struggle over how and when to come out about her disability identity. "My parents don't understand why I would call myself disabled," Samantha said matter-of-factly; then she added with a mischievous grin, "In fact, there are two basic things my family just doesn't want to accept: that my cousin is gay and that I'm disabled. So we're going to take a picture of ourselves at a gay pride march next month and send it to them."

The moral: I admire Samantha's wit and intelligence. I am also struck by the convergence of many themes in her story: the shifting and contested meanings of disability; the uneasy, often self-destroying tension between appearance and identity; the social scrutiny that refuses to accept statements of identity without "proof"; and, finally, the discursive and practical connections between coming out—in all the meanings of the term—as queer and as disabled. Thus I begin with Samantha's story to frame a discussion not only of analogies between queerness and disability but of the specifics of coming out in each context as a person whose bodily appearance does not immediately signal one's own sense of identity. In the first section of this essay I consider the complicated dynamics inherent in the analogizing of social identities, with specific reference to feminist, queer, and disability studies. In the second section I turn to the politics of visibility and invisibility, drawing on autobiographical narratives as well as social theory to explore constructions of coming out or passing in a number of social contexts. In the third section I further explore these issues through a focus on two "invisible" identities: lesbian-femme and nonvisible disability.[1] Thus each section seeks to "queer" disability in order to develop new paradigms of identity, representation, and social interaction.

A number of disability theorists suggest that disability has more in common with sexual orientation than with race, ethnicity, or gender—other categories often invoked analogically to support the social model of disability.[2] One argument for this connection is that most people with disabilities, like most queers, do not share their identity with immediate family members and often have difficulty accessing queer or crip culture.[3] The history of an oppressive medical model for homosexuality and the nature-nurture and assimilation-transformation debates in the modern LGBT civil rights movement offer additional areas of potential common ground with disability activism. Haunting such arguments, however, is the vexed issue of analogy itself, which cannot be extracted from the tangled history of the use and misuse of such identity analogies in past liberation movements.

In particular, most current analogies between oppressed social identities draw in some fashion on the sex-race analogy that emerged from the women's liberation movement of the 1970s. This analogy was used primarily by white women to claim legitimacy for feminist political struggle by analogizing it to the struggle of African Americans for civil rights. The sex-race analogy has been extensively critiqued, most importantly by feminists of color, and has by now been renounced by most white feminists. The gist of such a critique is suggested by the title of Tina Grillo and Stephanie M. Wildman's article "Obscuring the Importance of Race: The Implications of Making Comparisons between Racism and Sexism (or Other Isms)," and is summarized by Lisa Maria Hogeland:

> First, in its use of *race*, it represents a fantastic vision of African-American identity, community, and politics—uncontested, uncontradictory, unproblematic—that is shaped by a simultaneous nostalgia for and forgetting of the Civil Rights Movement, as if identity, community, and politics had never been the subjects of struggle. Second, the analogy attempts to forge out of that nostalgia and forgetting an equally fantastic vision of a self-evident identity, community, and politics of

> *sex*, whether construed as gender or as sexuality. Third, implicit in the setting together of the two is a fantasy of coalition . . . [which] sidesteps the processes and practices that would make such coalition possible.[4]

Despite the validity of this critique, Hogeland observes that the sex-race analogy continues to function in feminist theory and has also emerged strongly in queer theory (45).

My own investigation of the analogies regarding disability, however, suggests that their use has transformed from a comparison between *similar* oppressions to a strategic *contrasting* of identities to elucidate a particular aspect of the primary identity under discussion. Such a transformation accords with the classic definition of analogy as based on "a similarity or resemblance of relations, in which the resemblance lies in the qualities of two or more objects that are essentially dissimilar."[5] In practice, such analogies often both create and rely on artificial dichotomies that not only produce inequality between the terms of comparison but exclude or elide anomalous experiences that do not fit easily within their terms.

For John Swain and Colin Cameron, strategic contrasting supports the claim that disability and sexual "preference" are both social labels that are "usually self-referent from only one side," so that, unlike dual or multiple labels such as male and female, and black, Asian, Latina, and white, the labels of nondisabled and heterosexuality are always already presumed "unless otherwise stated." Swain and Cameron conclude: "There is a coming out process for gay men and lesbian women which has no real equivalent in gender and race categorizations," and "there is a similar coming out process for disabled people."[6] In this argument, the identities of gayness and disability are stabilized and opposed to those of gender and race. Such an analogy not only relies on an overly restrictive, unilateral view of gender and race but implies false equations between the two identities on each side of the opposition (gay = disabled; gender = race), thereby invoking the original sex-race analogy in a renewed form. While this analogy claims for sexual oppression the same legitimacy as that (supposedly) achieved for racial oppression—my experience is *like* your experience—contrasting analogies such as that employed by Swain and Cameron claim for gay or disabled oppression a different valence than that of gender or race: my experience is *different* from yours. Yet both analogies have the same goal—to persuade the listener of the validity and urgency of the speaker's original experience—and thus both implicitly devalue the other term of comparison.

An important difference between the analogies of sex-race and sexual orientation-disability is that the former relates to oppressions, while the latter describes processes of liberation and self-actualization, in this case, "coming out." Perhaps analogies between liberatory practices are less problematic than those between oppressions, since they claim a sameness not of experience but of resistance. This argument has a certain logic; however, it does not address the deeper issue of the presumption of sameness that produces oversimplified "mapping analogies." As Eve Tavor Bannet explains, the mapping analogy represents a historical mutation of analogy that, by "stressing resemblance over difference to make different entities more or less alike[,] transformed analogy into an equivalence—a rule of presumed resemblance, structural isomorphism, or homology between domains. The moment of essential difference which distinguishes analogy from identity, and different entities from each other, was flattened into a moment of proportional representation."[7] Clearly, the sex-race analogy suffers from the endemic flaws of the mapping analogy itself, yet all language functions in a sense through analogy, and so it remains an inescapable part of the communicative realm. Certainly, the tendency to make analogies between identities and liberation movements is pervasive and often persuasive, and so I suggest not that we attempt to escape from analogy but that we seek to employ it more critically than in the past.

Bannet examines a particular means of destabilizing and evolving mapping analogies through her discussion of Wittgenstein, for whom

> analogy is not just an image, an extended simile, or the juxtaposition of objects of comparison. . . . analogy in Wittgenstein's sense is a traditional method of reasoning from the known to the unknown, and from the visible to the speculative, by carrying familiar terms, paradigms, and images across into unfamiliar territory.[8]

I find this model of analogy especially useful, both because of its acknowledgment of the instability of its terms and because of its foregrounding of the issue of visibility as a key component of analogical language. Indeed, when we consider that "theories and practices of identity and subject formation in Western culture are largely structured around the logic of visibility, whether in the service of science (Victorian physiognomy), psychoanalysis (Lacan's mirror stage), or philosophy (Foucault's reading of the Panopticon)," it becomes apparent that the speculative or "invisible" has generally functioned as the subordinate term in analogical equations to this date.[9] Thus a central premise of this essay is that it behooves us to refocus our endeavors from the visible signs of these identities to their invisible manifestations. The focus on specularity and visible difference that permeates much disability theory creates a dilemma not only for nonvisibly disabled people who wish to enter the conversation but for the overarching concepts of disability and normalization themselves.[10] Passing, closeting, and coming out become vexed issues that strain at the limitations of the discourse meant to describe them.

THE LIMITS OF VISIBILITY

> Coming out, then, for disabled people, is a process of redefinition of one's personal identity through rejecting the tyranny of the *normate,* positive recognition of impairment and embracing disability as a valid social identity. Having come out, the disabled person no longer regards disability as a reason for self-disgust, or as something to be denied or hidden, but rather as an imposed oppressive social category to be challenged and broken down. . . . Coming out, in our analysis, involves a political commitment. Acceptance of a medical model of disability and being categorized by others as disabled does not constitute coming out as disabled.
>
> —Swain and Cameron, "Unless Otherwise Stated"

One of the limitations of Swain and Cameron's analogy between coming out as gay or lesbian and coming out as disabled is their one-sided definition of coming out itself. For these writers, coming out refers specifically to accepting one's "true" identity and must entail identification with the political analysis of the marginalized group. In both queer and disabled contexts, however, coming out can entail a variety of meanings, acts, and commitments. The dual meanings most crucial to my argument can be signified grammatically: to "come out to" a person or group usually refers to a specific revelatory event, while to "come out" (without an object) usually refers to the time that one first realized and came to terms with one's own identity. When *coming out* is considered as a self-contained phrase, as in Swain and Cameron's article, we may grant some validity

to the observation that "people with hidden impairments are sometimes less likely to 'come out' as disabled, and move to a positive acceptance of difference and a political identity, because it is easier to maintain a 'normal' identity."[11] However, when we add the preposition *to* to the phrase, the above statement becomes almost an oxymoron: the narratives of people with "hidden impairments," like those of people with other nonvisible social identities, are suffused with themes of coming out, passing, and the imperatives of identity.

Nor is coming out a static and singular event, as Swain and Cameron imply, an over-the-rainbow shift that divides one's life before and after the event. Certainly, there must be some people who experience such momentous comings out, but I believe that the majority of us find that, even after our own internal shift, and even after a dozen gay pride marches, we must still make decisions about coming out on a daily basis, in personal, professional, and political contexts. In *Dress Codes,* Noelle Howey's memoir about her father's transition from male to female, she describes four separate moments of her father's coming out: when he told her mother, when her mother told her, when the family threw a party for Noelle's father to come out as female to friends and coworkers, and when Noelle's father came out to her years later as a lesbian.[12] Eli Clare writes of coming out as a complex convergence of identities and desires: "My coming out wasn't as much about discovering sexual desire and knowledge as it was about dealing with gender identity. Simply put, the disabled, mixed-class tomboy who asked her mother, 'am I feminine?' didn't discover a sexuality among dykes but rather a definition of woman large enough to be comfortable for many years."[13]

When we look at narratives of disabled people about their own coming-out processes, we see that the language of coming out is used liberally but often carries very different meanings. While many of these stories emphasize connections with a disability community, much as Swain and Cameron suggest, they also demonstrate the various methods and implications that coming out entails for different individuals. Rosemarie Garland-Thomson, who calls her book *Extraordinary Bodies* "the consequence of a coming-out process," describes how she had long thought of her congenital disability as a "private matter" and did not identify with disability culture or disabled people, although she did feel a special connection with disabled characters in the literature she studied.[14] Deciding to focus her scholarly work on disability was both a cause and a consequence of her coming to identify with the disability community. Similarly, Nomy Lamm, born with one leg, did not come out as disabled until late in her teens, when, through her involvement in queer and feminist activism, she met two other "freaky crip girls" and transitioned fairly quickly from "I'm not really disabled, and even if I am, nobody notices" to "I am a foxy one-legged dyke, and you will love it, or else."[15]

Not all coming-out processes are so straightforward. Carolyn Gage writes: "Did I come out? Not at first. I told my friends I had CFIDS [chronic fatigue immune dysfunction syndrome], but I did not really tell them what that meant. . . . When I did go places with friends, I passed for able-bodied as much as I could."[16] For Gage, coming out did not take place until nearly a decade after she first fell ill, and it took the form of a letter to her friends that explicitly spelled out her disability, her limitations, and what she needed in terms of accommodation and support. Perhaps because of the nonvisible, contingent, and fluctuating nature of chronic illness, as opposed to the disabilities of Garland-Thomson and Lamm, Gage's coming-out process was not primarily focused on claiming the label of "disability." Rather, it required her to construct a specific narrative explaining her body to a skeptical, ignorant, and somewhat hostile audience. Susan Wendell, who also has CFIDS, speaks of the difficulty of convincing people to take her word for it regarding her abilities: "Some people offer such acceptance readily, others greet every statement of limitation with skepticism, and most need to be reminded from time to time."[17]

What is notable in Gage's and Wendell's accounts is that coming out is primarily portrayed as the process of revealing or explaining one's disability *to* others, rather than as an act of self-acceptance facilitated by a disability community. I would suggest that the nonvisible nature of Gage's and Wendell's disabilities means that, for them, the primary meaning of coming out includes the term *to* and connotes the daily challenge of negotiating assumptions about bodily appearance and function. This dynamic is not limited to those with chronic illnesses but can also be found in narratives by people with a range of nonvisible disabilities, especially sensory disabilities.[18] Megan Jones, a deaf-blind woman, writes of her response to the ubiquitous question "So, how bad is your vision and hearing anyway? I mean, you seem to get around pretty good as far as I can tell."[19] Jones admits that she once felt obliged to respond with an extended narrative explaining exactly the permeability of her cornea and the sound frequencies she could detect. Georgina Kleege writes about her need "to identify [her] blindness in public," particularly in the classroom, so that her students will understand why she cannot see them raising their hands. Kleege also writes of situations in which she chooses *not* to mention her blindness, such as social settings and a previous job, largely to avoid patronizing reactions or the suspicion of fraud but also simply because her "blindness was an irrelevant fact that they did not need to know about me, like my religion or political affiliation."[20]

Kleege's account points to the flip side of having to come out to be recognized as disabled: the ability to pass. Like racial, gender, and queer passing, the option of passing as nondisabled provides both a certain level of privilege and a profound sense of misrecognition and internal dissonance. Kleege reflects ruefully on a circumstance in which, during a flight on which nondisabled passengers and flight attendants were ignoring or complaining about a wheelchair-using passenger, she did not come out: "Because my disability was invisible to them, it allowed them to assume I felt about the disabled as they did, that I would have behaved as they had."[21] Even though Kleege and her husband were the only passengers who assisted the wheelchair user, and Kleege came out to *her* as blind, she still expresses profound guilt that she failed to identify herself as a member of the woman's community to the airline staff and other passengers.

This dilemma can be even more complicated for those with a disability whose symptoms and severity fluctuate widely. Wendell writes:

> Because my disability is no longer readily apparent, and because it is an illness whose symptoms vary greatly from day to day, I live between the world of the disabled and the non-disabled. I am often very aware of my differences from healthy, non-disabled people, and I often feel a great need to have my differences acknowledged when they are ignored. . . . On the other hand, I am very aware of how my social, economic, and personal resources, and the fact that I can "pass" as non-disabled among strangers, allow me to live a highly assimilated life among the non-disabled.[22]

Wendell then emphasizes that, even when she herself passes as nondisabled, she makes a point of identifying herself with the disability community and working for disability rights. Thus she complicates the assumption of a direct relationship between visible impairment and political identification with disability rights, as well as crucially undermining the related claim that passing as "normal" is by definition a form of negative disability identity.[23]

Nevertheless, the perception persists that nonvisibly disabled people prefer to pass and that passing is a sign and product of assimilationist longings: "By passing as non-disabled, by minimizing the significance of their impairments within their own personal and social lives . . . people with hidden impairments often make an effort to avoid the perceived stigma attached to a disabled identity." Even when passing is acknowledged as a valid strategy for negotiating certain situations, it is portrayed as an undesirable response: "If . . . disabled people pursue normalization too much, they risk denying limitations and pain for the comfort of others and may edge into the self-betrayal associated with 'passing.'"[24] I do not deny that some nonvisibly disabled people may wish to assimilate or choose to pass; however, I believe that such an overall negative perception of passing exceeds the reality and must be interpreted in the context of other forms of bodily passing in Euro-American culture. As Lisa Walker observes: "Traditionally, passing (for straight, for white) has been read as a conservative form of self-representation that the subject chooses in order to assume the privileges of the dominant identity. Passing is the sign of the sell out" and of the victim.[25]

Such condemnations of passing often conflate two dynamics: passing deliberately (as implied by the term *hidden)* and passing by default, as it were. I certainly do not make any effort to appear "heterosexual" or "nondisabled" when I leave the house in the morning; those are simply the identities usually derived from my appearance by onlookers. While there are a number of queer accoutrements, such as buttons, stickers, jewelry, and T-shirts, that I could (and often do) choose to wear to signal my lesbian identity, a very different cultural weight is placed on any attempt to signal a disabled identity, as suspicions of fraud attach to any visible sign of disability that is not functionally essential. The analogy between coming out as queer and coming out as disabled breaks down as the different meanings and consequences of such acts come into consideration.

My quandary is not unique, nor is my search for a nonverbal sign. Deborah Peifer observes that "I don't look blind, so strangers, sisters, don't realize that I'm not seeing them. After so many years of being defiantly out of the closet as a lesbian, I am, in some ways, passing as sighted. Other than wearing a 'Yes, I am legally blind' sign, I don't know of any way to provide that information to strangers." Jones became so frustrated with strangers not believing in her visual and hearing impairments, and so oppressed by their refusal to respect her assistance dog's status, that she began to use a white cane she did not need: "I find that when I use a cane people leave me alone. . . . people go right into their Blind-Person-With-A-Cane-And-Guide-Dog Red Alert mode." Kleege also mentions that "I now carry a white cane as a nonverbal sign that I don't see as much as I seem to. But like a lot of blind people who carry canes and employ guide dogs, these signs are not always understood, and the word still needs to be spoken."[26] These writers each contend with cultural assumptions that the identity they wish to signal exists only as visible physical difference. Since race, in Euro-American culture, is also assumed to be immediately visible and intelligible, Toi Derricotte, a light-skinned African American woman, writes of wishing for "a cross, a star, some sign of gold to wear so that, before they wonder or ask, I can present a dignified response to the world's interrogations."[27] In this case, coming out as disabled appears to have more in common with racial discourses of coming out or passing than with queer discourse, since the contingent (non)visibility of queer identity has produced a variety of nonverbal and/or spoken means to signal that identity, while the assumed visibility of race and disability has produced an absence of nonverbal signs and a distrust of spoken claims to those identities.

In the absence of recognized nonverbal signs, we often resort to the "less dignified" response of claiming identity through speech. The complex longing, fear of disbelief, and internal dissonance caused by coming out in this form resound through the narratives of all people who pass by default. Passing subjects must cope with a variety of external social contexts, few of which welcome or acknowledge spontaneous declarations of invisible identity. Derricotte writes that "for several years I wore my identity like a banner. 'Hello, I'm Toi Derricotte, I'm black.'" The awkwardness of such revelations is amplified in Peifer's account of how she chose to voice her lesbian identity after blindness prevented her from participating in the subtle visual signals with which queer people in public often acknowledge each other: "They now know at the grocery store ('As a lesbian, I wish to buy these peaches') and the drugstore ('As a lesbian, I wish to explain that the yeast infection for which I am purchasing this ointment was the result of taking antibiotics, not heterosexual intercourse')."[28] Clearly, simply voicing one's identity in any and all situations is a far-from-perfect solution to the dilemmas presented by invisibility. In addition, the general cultural prejudice against such statements means that embarrassment may be the least disturbing negative response they evoke.

Suspicions of fraud often greet declarations of nonvisible identity. As Amanda

Hamilton writes, people with nonvisible disabilities "are in a sense forced to pass, and the same time assumed to be liars." Adrian Piper, a light-skinned African American, also writes of the catch-22 of remaining silent versus speaking up: "For most of my life I did not understand that I needed to identify my racial identity publicly and that if I did not I would be inevitably mistaken for white. I simply didn't think about it. But since I also made no special effort to hide my racial identity, I often experienced the shocked and/or hostile reactions of whites who discovered it after the fact." Piper adds that "some whites simply can't take my avowed racial affiliation at face value, and react to what they see rather than what I say."[29] It takes tremendous chutzpah for nonvisibly disabled people to assert our disabilities in public settings or to ask for accommodation; denial, mockery, and silent disapproval are some of the cultural mechanisms used to inhibit us. While nonvisibly disabled people are usually required to produce medical documentation of our impairments, people who pass racially, like Derricotte and Piper, face semantic battles, interrogations about their ancestry, and challenges to their dedication to the African American community.[30]

Derricotte's memoir, *The Black Notebooks*, is an expanded meditation on race, passing, and the self. In the chapter "Diaries at an Artist's Colony" she describes hearing a racist comment on her first night at the colony and not confronting the speaker. Later, in a section of that chapter called "Coming Out," she concedes that "I [was] afraid to come out as a black person, to bear that solitude, that hatred, that invisibility."[31] Here Derricotte locates invisibility *not* as equivalent to passing but as the alienating consequence of coming out in a hostile context. When she does come out later to a white woman, the woman's resistance ironically foregrounds the white colonists' own anxiety about race:

She said, "There aren't any black people here. I haven't seen any." "Yes there are," I said, smiling.

"Who?"

"You're looking at one."

"You're not really black. Just an eighth or something." . . .

A woman at the table said, "Did you read that article in *The New York Times* that said if they were strict about genetics, sixty percent of the people in the United States would be classified as black?"

I looked around the table; I was laughing. The others were not. They were worried about how black I was and they should have been worrying about how black *they* were. (145)

Derricotte's story can be read as a narrative enactment of Elaine Ginsberg's observation that "passing forces reconsideration of the cultural logic that the physical body is the site of identic intelligibility."[32] Derricotte reverses the terms of the racial dichotomy black/white to refocus racial anxiety onto whiteness as an artificial cultural construct, in a move that reflects Wittgenstein's reversal of analogy to lead us "from what we suppose *is* the case everywhere to what *might* happen otherwise in particular cases."[33] While Derricotte's coming out was necessary for the scene to unfold, her passing provided the foundational meaning of the exchange. Thus we see how passing can become a subversive practice and how the passing subject may be read not as an assimilationist victim but as a defiant figure who, by crossing the borders of identities, reveals their instability.[34]

THE LIMITS OF SUBVERSION

A story: When a friend of mine read the story of Samantha with which this essay opens, she asked why Samantha would identify as disabled. I did not have a concrete answer for her. Faced with that question, many of us might point to our Social

Security status, our medical records, our neurological test results, or the signs of difference on our bodies. I cannot tell you where Samantha would point. I can only observe the pride with which she claims her identity, the eagerness with which she seeks to communicate it to others. I can only conclude that, for Samantha, "being disabled" means being not a victim, not a special case, but a member of a proud and fierce community.

Her attitude is refreshing. It demonstrates the usefulness of analogizing concepts of pride between queer and disability contexts. As I continue in this section to investigate the complex dynamics of passing and visibility by examining two contemporary identities—lesbian-femme and nonvisible disability issues of pride, resistance, and subversion come to the fore. While I myself claim both identities, that is not the main reason I chose them. When reading about coming out and queer identity, I found that writings that questioned the politics of visibility largely focused on the controversial category of lesbian-femme. Similarly, in both the disability community and the field of disability studies, the question of nonvisible disability is emerging as a highly vexed, profoundly challenging concern. Embodying both identities as I do, I naturally notice connections between the experiences they produce; at the same time, I am also aware of the significant differences and contradictions between those experiences.[35] To begin with, we may briefly examine some of the interesting correspondences and contrasts between these identities. Considering Joan Nestle's suggestion that "if the butch deconstructs gender, the femme constructs gender," what useful trains of thought can we set into motion by analogizing *butch/femme* and *gender* to *visibly/nonvisibly disabled* and *ability,* and what are the inherent problems of such an analogy?[36]

Both femme lesbians and people with nonvisible disabilities present what Marjorie Garber calls a "category crisis."[37] In the dominant cultural discourse, as well as in lesbian and disability subcultures, certain assumptions about the correlation between appearance and identity have resulted in an often exclusive focus on visibility as both the basis of community and the means of enacting social change. Discourses of coming out and passing are central to visibility politics, in which coming out is generally valorized while passing is seen as assimilationist. Thus vigilant resistance to external stereotypes of disability and lesbianism has not kept our subcultures from enacting dynamics of exclusion and surveillance over their members. Nor does a challenge to those dynamics necessarily imply a wish on my part to discard visibility politics or a rejection of the value and importance of visibility for marginalized communities. As Walker observes:

> The impulse to privilege the visible often arises out of the need to reclaim signifiers of difference which dominant ideologies have used to define minority identities negatively. But while this strategy of reclamation is often affirming, it can also replicate the practices of the dominant ideologies which use visibility to create social categories on the basis of exclusion. The paradigm of visibility is totalizing when a signifier of difference becomes synonymous with the identity it signifies. In this situation, members of a given population who do not bear that signifier of difference or who bear visible signs of another identity are rendered invisible and are marginalized within an already marginalized community.[38]

Moreover, people with nonvisible disabilities not only are marginalized in disability communities but walk an uneasy line between those communities and the dominant culture, often facing significant discrimination because our identities are unrecognized or disbelieved.

The history of femme identity in Euro-American culture, much like that of nonvisible disabilities, is one of indeterminacy and ambiguity: "The femme woman has been the most ambiguous figure in lesbian history; she is often described as the nonlesbian lesbian, the duped wife of the passing woman, the lesbian who marries."[39] Extending Terry Castle's analysis of the "apparitional lesbian," Walker suggests that "the feminine lesbian . . . perhaps more than any other figure for same-sex desire, 'haunts the edges of the field of vision.'" The sexologists who first named lesbianism in the early twentieth century had difficulty describing femmes except as dupes of the masculine "inverts" on whom their theories centered, since "the feminine lesbian produces a collapse at the intersection of the systems of marking and visibility that underpin the theory of inversion."[40] During the rise of lesbian feminism in the 1970s and 1980s, femme lesbians were shunned for supposedly copying heterosexual roles and buying into misogynist beauty standards. In the early 1990s, with the publication of Nestle's groundbreaking anthology, *The Persistent Desire*, many femme writers and activists began to speak out in defense of their identities and to protest "the penalties we have had to pay because we look like 'women'—from straight men, from so-called radical feminists, and from some lesbian separatists who, because of their anger at the social construction of femininity, cannot allow us to even exist." Yet Rebecca Ann Rugg, a member of the generation following Nestle's, still describes facing "two constant problems for a nineties femme: invisibility as a dyke and how to authenticate herself as one despite doubt and rudeness from others."[41]

Rugg's comment also rings true for the experiences of many people with nonvisible disabilities, who face not only uneasy inclusion in the disability community but a daily struggle for accommodation and benefits that reflects the dominant culture's insistence on visible signs to legitimate impairment. The very diversity of nonvisible disabilities, which include a wide range of impairments, such as chronic and terminal illness, sensory impairment, learning and cognitive differences, mental illness, and repetitive strain injuries, presents a category crisis. While I do not claim to present a comprehensive range of impairments among the authors I cite, a reading of numerous narratives across impairments suggests a common experience structured by the disbelieving gaze of the normate (much as theorists such as Garland-Thomson and Lennard J. Davis argue that disability is constructed via the normate's stare confronted by people with visible disability).[42]

In an intriguing twist, Cal Montgomery rejects the distinction between visible and nonvisible disabilities and instead points to contradictions between "tools," behaviors, and social expectations:

> The person who uses a white cane when getting on the bus, but then pulls out a book to read while riding; the person who uses a wheelchair to get into the library stacks, but then stands up to reach a book on a high shelf; the person who uses a picture-board to discuss philosophy; the person who challenges the particular expectations of *disability* that other people have is suspect. "I can't see what's wrong with him," people say, meaning, "He's not acting the way I think he should." "She's invisibly disabled," they say, meaning, "I can't see what barriers she faces."[43]

Montgomery's examples illustrate the category crisis evoked by invisible and nonvisible disabilities. These contradictions among appearance, behavior, and social expectations are, of course, embodied as well in the figure of the femme: "Women who look and act like girls and who desire girls. We're just the queerest of the queers."[44]

Yet there are significant differences between nonvisible disability and femme identity. Nestle writes of the "bitter irony" that while "in the straight world, butches bear the brunt of the physical and verbal abuse for their difference, in the lesbian-feminist world, femmes have had to endure a deeper attack on their sense of self-worth."[45] This remark highlights an important distinction, for it appears that femme lesbians are marginalized primarily in lesbian subculture, while people with nonvisible disabilities write more often of the frustration and discrimination they face in the dominant culture. Thus passing and coming out take on different valences with regard to these different identities. However, as we have seen, these different valences are translated into the theoretical fields based on those identities, that is, queer theory and disability studies, in intriguingly similar fashions.

The difficulty of circulating in the dominant culture as a femme is largely produced by unwanted attention from men and by the general assumption that one is heterosexual. Combined with denigration and misrecognition in the lesbian community, these dynamics can cause significant frustration and alienation for femmes: "Femme is *loquería* ['the crazies']. Having your identity constantly under question, who wouldn't risk losing their mind, and their identity along the way?"[46] Nevertheless, there appears to be a wide difference between that alienation and the harassment, discrimination, and economic repercussions experienced by non-visibly disabled people in the culture at large. Many write of being denied benefits and accommodations because their nonvisible disabilities are perceived as minor or imaginary.[47] Nonvisibly disabled people who use disabled parking permits are routinely challenged and harassed by strangers.[48] Recently, a sympathetic nondisabled friend of mine told me that a colleague of hers had reported triumphantly her detection of someone using a disabled parking permit illegally. The colleague's conclusion was based on the fact that the woman she saw getting out of the car was young and "well-groomed" and had no sign of a limp. In addition, the colleague continued, she had followed the woman closely as they entered the building and had ascertained that she was breathing "normally" and so could have no respiratory impairments. Such constant and invasive surveillance of non-visibly disabled bodies is the result of a convergence of complicated cultural discourses regarding independence, fraud, malingering, and entitlement; the form it takes almost always involves a perceived discontinuity between appearance, behavior, and identity.

It is useful here to consider Foucault's interpretation of the Panopticon as a cultural mechanism that, among its other uses, functions to "distinguish 'laziness and stubbornness'" and "to put beggars and idlers to work." Foucault invokes the Panopticon, a nineteenth-century prison design in which a central watchtower is surrounded by individual windowed cells, as the metaphoric basis for contemporary surveillance of and by individual members of society. The Panopticon's power is to "induce in the inmate a state of conscious and permanent visibility that assures the automatic functioning of power."[49] Thus the Panopticon-like surveillance promoted by cultural myths of fraud ensures that, just as "the Other named as invisible is unseen as an individual, while simultaneously [it is] hyper-visible as a stereotype," the nonvisibly disabled subject is rendered hypervisible through social scrutiny and surveillance.[50] Thus many nonvisibly disabled people may feel that our choice is between passing and performing the dominant culture's stereotypes of disability:

Many people are more comfortable relating to me and accommodating me if they can be absolutely certain that I am who I say I am, a deaf-blind person. And they are not absolutely certain that I am that person until I bump into a wall or shape my hands into what is to them an incomprehensible language. In other words, I must make myself completely alien to these people in order for them to feel that they understand me.[51]

In contrast to this general cultural reaction to nonvisible disability, the disability community, while still largely structured around visible disabilities, is increasingly cognizant and welcoming of nonvisibly disabled people. There are certainly exceptions, which often seem to arise in connection with questions of access to disability-centered events, such as conferences.[52] Nevertheless, a large body of writing criticizing the disability community for excluding those with non-visible disabilities simply does not exist. In contrast, the vast majority of twentieth-century American writings on femme identity make some reference to feeling excluded, ignored, or belittled in the larger lesbian community. I have already discussed the history of the lesbian feminist movement's rejection of femme identity, as well as the contemporary response. Both Rugg and Walker suggest that queer theory, which challenges categories of gender and desire, may have indirectly contributed an epistemological basis for the latest devaluing of femme identity: Rugg writes that "femme circulates as a term of derision" in many dyke spaces, particularly in the "pomo dyke scene," which emphasizes gender bending and androgyny.[53] Similarly, I would suggest that, while disability studies has presented profound challenges to dominant cultural conceptions of the body, social identity, and independence, it has not provided the theoretical basis on which to critique and transform the equation of appearance with ability.

Instead, its focus on the visual continues to render nonvisible disabilities *invisible* while reinforcing the exact cultural reliance on visibility that oppresses all of us.

Walker suggests that "the femme can be read as the 'blind spot' in [Judith] Butler's notion of gender as a performance."[54] I have often felt a similar gap in disability studies texts, even as I have benefited hugely from many of their insights. Their focus on visuality and the "gaze" sometimes leads me to question if my extremely limiting and life-changing health condition really qualifies as a disability according to the social model. Such anxieties open up larger questions regarding the shifting definition of disability and the need to resist hierarchies of oppression.

In a phrase that echoes the experiences of people with nonvisible disabilities, Rugg observes that "daily lives lived femme constantly require negotiating problems of visibility," but she subverts the victimizing potential of this observation with its conclusion: "Thus, there are innumerable examples of radical and subversive performances of femme in every imaginable context."[55] Mykel Johnson also argues for an interpretation of femme as subversive performance:

> It seems to me that femme dykes, as well as butch dykes, fuck with gender. We are not passing as straight women. Lesbian femme is not the same as "feminine." . . . a femme dyke is not trying to be discreet. There is something in femme, in fact, that is about creating a display. A femme dyke displays the erotic power of her beauty. She is bold enough to claim that power in a culture that has maintained a tyranny of "beauty norms" that may or may not include her. . . . A femme dyke is not domesticated but wild.[56]

It is challenging, however, to imagine nonvisible disability as a subversive display. While many markers of femme identity carry erotic significance and are linked to a fundamental discourse of desire, markers of nonvisible disability tend to carry medical significance and be linked to fundamental discourses of illness. However, it is possible for nonvisibly disabled people, like femme lesbians, to choose to ally ourselves with individuals visibly marked by their shared identity; as Rugg insists, "Those of us perceived as acceptable by an assimilationist politics must constantly show our alliance to people marked as stereotypical."[57]

Furthermore, some clues may be given for the possibility of such subversive performance from the narratives of people with multiple identities, including femme and disabled. Mary Frances Platt writes of her struggle to reclaim femme identity after becoming disabled as an adult:

> The more disabled I became, the more I mourned the ways my sexual femme self had manifested through the nondisabled me. . . . It's been five years now since I began using a wheelchair. I am just awakening to a new reclamation of femme. . . . An outrageous, loud-mouthed femme who's learning to dress, dance, cook, *and* seduce on wheels; finding new ways to be gloriously fucked by handsome butches and aggressive femmes. I hang out more with the sexual outlaws now—you know, the motorcycle lesbians who see wheels and chrome between your legs as something exciting, the leather women whose vision of passion and sexuality doesn't exclude fat, disabled me.[58]

Like Platt, Sharon Wachsler found a new source of "femmeness" in herself after being forced to relinquish many external signifiers and behaviors of femme:

> Because of my chemical sensitivities, I had to throw out all my personal-care products, including perfume, hair-styling aids and cosmetics. . . . Now that I could no longer attend those [queer] events or wear the clothing, makeup and accessories that went with them, was I still femme? Where is the meaning in being femme if I'm absent from the queer women's community and have lost the markers of femme identity?

Since becoming disabled, Wachsler has learned to value aspects of herself that she once considered "too femme," such as accepting help from others. By creating accessible spaces in which to enact her new femme identity, Wachsler has reconnected with its meaning: "I carry my femmeness inside me like a red satin cushion. It comforts me. It gives me a place to rest. It sets me aglow with color. And I know that when it can, my femme flare will emerge glittering."[59]

Platt's and Wachsler's transformations indicate a merging of femme and disability identities that produces a third identity, "disabled femme," one intriguing example of "disability queered." This identity can be understood as well through Gloria Anzaldúa's concept of "*mestiza* consciousness": "The work of *mestiza* consciousness is to break down the subject-object duality that keeps her [the *mestiza*] a prisoner and to show in the flesh and through the images in her work how duality is transcended."[60] Gaby Sandoval, a Chicana nondisabled femme, draws on Anzaldúa's work when she revises passing into a positive strategy by suggesting that her experience as a Chicana who grew up "passing the border" between the United States and Mexico gave her the skills to negotiate the ambiguities of mixed-race and femme identity:

> I am at home in my discomfort. I am a queer child; never quite fitting in, but always passing. I am a femme who exploits the confines of gender perceptions. . . . These abilities are definitely telling of a life lived on the border, with all of its contradictions and confusions.[61]

Similarly, Willy Wilkinson, a disabled Asian American transperson, writes of a merging of border identities that inform and empower one another:

The thing about mixed [race] people is that, like transgendered people, we are stealth. You don't always see us coming, and you can't be so sure about what you're dealing with. . . . I'm accustomed to cultural conflict and surprise with the same intimacy that I know the terrain of my features and the hues of my skin. . . . How fitting to become disabled with an illness [CFIDS] rife with ambiguity and complexity, one whose very realness is questioned. It's the story of my life.[62]

In each of these cases, *mestiza* consciousness emerges not simply as a combination of factors but as a praxis of embodied identities that occupies the border as homeland. Femme identity and nonvisible disability can both benefit from such examples, which urge us to find subversion at the meeting points between our bodies and our chosen communities, between our voices and the resistant audiences of power. In addition, by queering disability in these ways, we offer the larger fields of queer and disability studies new possibilities beyond simple analogizing as we explore "unfamiliar territory" together.

The moral: Recently, I met with Samantha to show her a draft of this essay, to see if my memory and representation of our encounter matched her own recollection. After reading my words, she showed me prints of the photo-essay she is constructing for her senior thesis: black-and-white shots of the gnarled skin of her hands juxtaposed against other landscapes: cypress bark, deep-sea sponges, the surface of San Francisco Bay. These images will be juxtaposed with head shots of disabled and nondisabled people covering their faces with their hands, hiding their identities behind their smooth skin. In a way, Samantha is my opposite: her disability lives on the skin, while mine hides beneath it. But as we work toward one another, I begin to believe that the skin, the bound-ary between us, can be our homeland, our shared definition.

NOTES

For feedback and support through several versions of this essay, I am grateful to Alison Kafer, Robert McRuer, Meagan Rosser, Susan Schweik, Stefanie Stroup, and Abby L. Wilkerson.

1. In current disability discourse, the terms *invisible disability* and *nonvisible disability* are often used interchangeably. Yet while the term *invisible* may be used in a literal sense to signify an unmarked social identity, the metaphor of invisibility has long been used to indicate the marginality or oppression of a social group. Thus disability discourse (like queer theory and other liberatory movements) also employs metaphorics of visibility that are unmoored from any question of marked or unmarked bodies. To minimize confusion in this essay, I employ *nonvisible* to indicate the condition of unmarked identity and *invisible* to indicate social oppression and marginality. However, I also seek to investigate how the two meanings and conditions intersect, since nonvisible disabilities remain largely invisible, both in disability discourse and in the culture at large.

2. For a prominent example of the disability/sexual orientation analogy see John Swain and Colin Cameron, "Unless Otherwise Stated: Discourses of Labelling and Identity in Coming Out," in *Disability Discourse*, ed. Mairian Corker and Sally French (Philadelphia: Open University Press, 1999), 68–78. Tom Shakespeare analogizes disability to gender, sexual orientation, and race in "Disability, Identity, and Difference," in *Exploring the Divide: Illness and Disability*, ed. Colin Barnes and Geof Mercer (Leeds: Disability, 1996), 94–113. Rosemarie Garland-Thomson and Susan Wendell both make frequent analogies between disability and gender. See Garland-Thomson, *Extraordinary Bodies: Figuring Physical Disability in American Culture and Literature* (New York: Columbia University Press, 1997); and Wendell, *The Rejected Body: Feminist Philosophical Reflections on Disability* (New York: Routledge, 1996). Garland-Thomson also argues for a view of disability as ethnicity, but she invokes sexual orientation only with regard to nonvisible disability, which, "much like a homosexual identity, always presents the dilemma of whether or when to come out or to pass" (14). Lennard J. Davis, however, defines

disability both in analogies to race, gender, and class and in contrast to them in *Enforcing Normalcy: Disability, Deafness, and the Body* (London: Verso, 1995), xvi, 2.

3. See Shakespeare, "Disability, Identity, and Difference," 105; and Wendell, *Rejected Body*, 82.

4. Tina Grillo and Stephanie M. Wildman, "Obscuring the Importance of Race: The Implications of Making Comparisons between Racism and Sexism (or Other Isms)," in *Critical White Studies: Looking behind the Mirror*, ed. Richard Delgado and Jean Stefancic (Philadelphia: Temple University Press, 1997), 619–26; Lisa Maria Hogeland, *"Invisible Man* and Invisible Women: The Sex/Race Analogy of the 1970s," *Women's History Review* 5 (1996): 46.

5. Nilli Diengott, "Analogy As a Critical Term: A Survey and Some Comments," *Style* 19 (1985): 228.

6. Swain and Cameron, "Unless Otherwise Stated," 68. The example of "black, Asian, Latina, and white" is one that I have extrapolated from Swain and Cameron's article rather than one that they themselves offer.

7. Eve Tavor Bannet, "Analogy As Translation: Wittgenstein, Derrida, and the Law of Language," *New Literary History* 28 (1997): 658.

8. Ibid., 655.

9. Linda Schlossberg, introduction to *Passing: Identity and Interpretation in Sexuality, Race, and Religion*, ed. María Carla Sánchez and Linda Schlossberg (New York: New York University Press, 2001), 1.

10. Davis writes that "disability is a specular moment" and argues that all disability, even mental illness, "shows up as a disruption in the visual field" *(Enforcing Normalcy,* xvi, 11–15, 129–42). Garland-Thomson also focuses on the "stare" that constructs the category of disability *(Extraordinary Bodies,* 26); Kenny Fries uses a similar focus *(Staring Back: The Disability Experience from the Inside Out* [New York: Plume, 1997], 1).

11. Tom Shakespeare, Kath Gillespie-Sells, and Dominic Davies, *The Sexual Politics of Disability: Untold Desires* (New York: Cassell, 1996), 55. These authors clearly share Swain and Cameron's definition of coming out, as seen in their summary on page 58.

12. From a private conversation with Noelle Howey, July 2001. Howey further discusses her experiences in *Dress Codes: Of Three Girlhoods— My Mother's, My Father's, and Mine* (New York: Picador, 2002).

13. Eli Clare, *Exile and Pride: Disability, Queerness,*

and Liberation (Cambridge, Mass.: South End, 1999), 133.

14. Garland-Thomson, *Extraordinary Bodies*, ix.

15. Nomy Lamm, "Private Dancer: Evolution of a Freak," in *Restricted Access: Lesbians on Disability*, ed. Victoria A. Brownworth and Susan Raffo (Seattle: Seal, 1999), 160–61.

16. Carolyn Gage, "Hidden Disability: A Coming Out Story," in Brownworth and Russo, *Restricted Access*, 203. CFIDS is a debilitating systemic illness that primarily affects the neurological, immune, and muscular systems. It is also known as myalgic encephalomyelitis. For more detail see Peggy Munson, ed., *Stricken: Voices from the Hidden Epidemic of Chronic Fatigue Syndrome* (New York: Haworth, 2000).

17. Wendell, *Rejected Body*, 4.

18. This dynamic can be found as well in the writings of people with visible disabilities who ponder whether to "come out" textually, thus revealing their absent bodies much as nonvisibly disabled people who come out are revealing some aspect of their health or mental status. As Nancy Mairs reflects in *Waist-High in the World: A Life among the Nondisabled* (Boston: Beacon, 1996), "I might have chosen to write in such a way as to disregard or deny or disguise the fact that I have MS" (10).

19. Megan Jones, "'Gee, You Don't *Look* Handicapped . . .': Why I Use a White Cane to Tell People That I'm Deaf," *Electric Edge*, July–August 1997, accessed on 10 July 2002 at www.ragged-edge-mag.com/archive/look.htm.

20. Georgina Kleege, *Sight Unseen* (New Haven: Yale University Press, 1999), 11–12.

21. Ibid., 38–39.

22. Wendell, *Rejected Body*, 76.

23. See Shakespeare, "Disability, Identity, and Difference," 100.

24. Swain and Cameron, "Unless Otherwise Stated," 76; Garland-Thomson, *Extraordinary Bodies*, 13.

25. Lisa Walker, *Looking Like What You Are: Sexual Style, Race, and Lesbian Identity* (New York: New York University Press, 2001), 8.

26. Deborah Peifer, "Seeing Is Be(liev)ing," in Brownworth and Russo, *Restricted Access*, 34; Jones, "'Gee, You Don't *Look* Handicapped . . .'"; Kleege, *Sight Unseen*, 39.

27. Toi Derricotte, *The Black Notebooks: An Interior Journey* (New York: Norton, 1997), 112.

28. Ibid., 111; Peifer, "Seeing Is Be(live)ing," 34.

29. Amanda Hamilton, "Oh the Joys of Invisibility!" letter to the editor, *Electric Edge*, July–August 1997, accessed on 10 July 2002 at www.ragged-edge-mag.com/archive/look.htm; Adrian Piper, "Passing for White, Passing for Black," in *Passing and the Fictions of Identity*, ed. Elaine K. Ginsberg

(Durham: Duke University Press, 1996), 256–57, 266.

30. Derricotte, *Black Notebooks*, 145, 160, 182; Piper, "Passing for White, Passing for Black," 234–38, 256–57, 262–64.

31. Derricotte, *Black Notebooks*, 142.

32. Ginsberg, *Passing*, 4.

33. Bannet, "Analogy As Translation," 663.

34. This dynamic may also be observed from the role of passing in transgender contexts, in which the ability to pass for a new or different gender, or to present an ambiguous gender, is often experienced as a validation of radical identity rather than as assimilation or misrecognition.

35. To locate myself in my analysis, I refer to both femmes and people with nonvisible disabilities with the pronoun *we* throughout this section; however, I do not mean to imply that I speak for all femmes or all nonvisibly disabled people or that all people who share these identities think alike.

36. Joan Nestle, ed., *The Persistent Desire: A Femme-Butch Reader* (Boston: Alyson, 1992), 16.

37. Cited in Ginsberg, *Passing*, 8.

38. Walker, *Looking Like What You Are*, 209–10.

39. Nestle, *Persistent Desire*, 15–16.

40. Walker, *Looking Like What You Are*, 11, 5.

41. Nestle, *Persistent Desire*, 18; Rebecca Ann Rugg, "How Does She Look?" in *Femme: Feminists, Lesbians, and Bad Girls*, ed. Laura Harris and Elizabeth Crocker (New York: Routledge, 1997), 175.

42. See the pages referenced in note 10 for a discussion of this argument. One further distinction to be made here, however, is that the disbelieving gaze structuring the experience of the nonvisibly disabled subject may come not only from the normate but also from other disabled subjects. See Cal Montgomery, "A Hard Look at Invisible Disability," *Ragged Edge*, no. 2 (2001): 16.

43. Ibid., 16.

44. Madeline Davis, "Epilogue: Nine Years Later," in Nestle, *Persistent Desire*, 270.

45. Nestle, *Persistent Desire*, 15.

46. Gaby Sandoval, "Passing *Loquería*," in Harris and Crocker, *Femme*, 173. Sandoval adapts Gloria Anzaldúa's description of being a lesbian of color as making for *"loquería*, the crazies" (*Borderlands*, 2d ed. [San Francisco: Aunt Lute, 1999], 19).

47. Jones, a graduate student, once received a letter from her university, responding to her request for funds for assistance, "which essentially said, 'We do not understand what you mean when you refer to yourself as "deaf-blind." When you were in the office the other day you seemed to function just fine'" ("'Gee, You Don't *Look* Handicapped . . .'"). It took Jones a year of procuring letters from every authority imaginable to receive the necessary funding. This dynamic is not unusual, but it is brought up frequently in conversations among people with nonvisible disabilities. As Hamilton observes, responding to Jones's story, many students with nonvisible disabilities are forced to "'pass' as 'normal' students, making sophisticated compensation strategies in order to complete our requirements and research, at which point, when we hit barriers . . . sure enough, we aren't disabled enough—thanks to the success of previous compensation efforts" ("Oh the Joys of Invisibility!").

48. I have experienced this harassment many times, as has every nonvisibly disabled person with a parking permit I have asked about it.

49. Michel Foucault, *Discipline and Punish: The Birth of the Prison*, trans. Alan Sheridan (New York: Vintage, 1995), 203–5, 201.

50. Hogeland, "*Invisible Man* and Invisible Women," 36.

51. Jones, "'Gee, You Don't *Look* Handicapped . . .'"

52. Montgomery observes that "although [the disability community] may understand disability differently than others do, we have not, as a group, abandoned the suspicion of people who may not be 'really' disabled, who may be 'slacking' or 'faking' or encroaching on 'our' movement and 'our' successes. And we respond to people who challenge *our* ideas of what disabled people are 'really like' just as nondisabled people do: with suspicion" ("Hard Look at Invisible Disability," 16).

53. Rugg, "How Does She Look?" 176.

54. Walker, *Looking Like What You Are*, 203. Furthermore, "Butler's genealogy rests on deconstructing the normative paradigm that figures a correspondence between sex, gender, and sexuality. In turn, this rests on an inner/outer distinction that 'stabilizes and consolidates the coherent subject.' This binary locates the 'self' within the body and reads the body as reflection of the 'truth' of that self. . . . In a strategy of destabilization which relies on the visual performance of difference, the fact that no distinction between 'inner' and 'outer' identities is made visible on the surface of the femme's body as it is on the drag queen's and the butch's bodies marginalizes the femme" (204–5). For more on Butler's original claims see Judith Butler, *Bodies That Matter: On the Discursive Limits of "Sex"* (New York: Routledge, 1993).

55. Rugg, "How Does She Look?" 176.

56. Mykel Johnson, "Butchy Femme," in Nestle, *Persistent Desire*, 397–98.

57. Rugg, "How Does She Look?" 180.

58. Mary Frances Platt, "Reclaiming Femme . . . Again," in Nestle, *Persistent Desire*, 388–89.

59. Sharon Wachsler, "Still Femme," in Brownworth and Russo, *Restricted Access*, 111–12, 114.

60. Anzaldúa, *Borderlands*, 102. I use the term *mestiza* with acute awareness of its racial and cultural references. While many of the authors I refer to are white or Anglo, Anzaldúa's term appears to be an appropriate and accurate description of the consciousness that they reveal, and the application of her theoretical terms to disability seems a logical extension of her own compelling interest in the "magical," boundary-crossing potential of "abnormality and so-called deformity" (41).

61. Sandoval, "Passing *Loquería*," 170–71.

62. Willy Wilkinson, "Stealth," in Munson, *Stricken*, 81.

CHAPTER 25

Integrating Disability, Transforming Feminist Theory

Rosemarie Garland-Thomson

DISABILITY STUDIES AND FEMINIST STUDIES

Over the last several years, disability studies has moved out of the applied fields of medicine, social work, and rehabilitation to become a vibrant new field of inquiry within the critical genre of identity studies that has developed so productively in the humanities over the last twenty or so years. Charged with the residual fervor of the civil rights movement, women's studies and race studies established a model in the academy for identity-based critical enterprises that followed, such as gender studies, queer studies, disability studies, and a proliferation of ethnic studies, all of which have enriched and complicated our understandings of social justice, subject formation, subjugated knowledges, and collective action.

Even though disability studies is now flourishing in disciplines such as history, literature, religion, theater, and philosophy in precisely the same way feminist studies did twenty-five years ago, many of its practitioners do not recognize that disability studies is part of this larger undertaking that can be called identity studies. Indeed, I must wearily conclude that much of current disability studies does a great deal of wheel reinventing. This is largely due to the fact that many disability studies scholars simply don't know either feminist theory or the institutional history of women's studies. All too often the pronouncements in disability studies of what we need to start addressing are precisely issues that feminist theory has been grappling with for years. This is not to say that feminist theory can be transferred wholly and intact over to the study of disability studies, but it is to suggest that feminist theory can offer profound insights, methods, and perspectives that would deepen disability studies.

Conversely, feminist theories all too often do not recognize disability in their litanies of identities that inflect the category of woman. Repeatedly, feminist issues that are intricately entangled with disability—such as reproductive technology, the place of bodily differences, the particularities of oppression, the ethics of care, the construction of the subject—are discussed without any reference to disability. Like disability studies practitioners unaware of feminism, feminist scholars are often simply unacquainted with disability studies perspectives. The most sophisticated and nuanced analyses of disability, in my view, come from scholars conversant with feminist theory. And the most compelling and complex analyses of gender intersectionality take into consideration what I call the ability/disability system—along with race, ethnicity, sexuality, and class.

I want to give the omissions I am describing here the most generous interpretation I can. The archive, Foucault has shown us, determines what we can know. There has been no archive, no template for understanding disability as a category of analysis and knowledge, as a cultural trope and an historical community. So just as the now widely recognized centrality of gender and race analyses to all knowledge was unthinkable thirty years ago, disability is still not an icon on many critical desktops now. I think, however, that feminist theory's omission of disability differs from disability studies' ignorance of feminist theory. I find feminist theory and those familiar with it quick to grasp the broad outlines of disability theory and eager to consider its implications. This, of course, is because feminist theory itself has undertaken internal critiques and proved to be porous and flexible. Disability studies is news, but feminist theory is not. Nevertheless, feminist theory is still resisted for exactly the same reasons that scholars might resist disability studies: the assumption that it is narrow, particular, and has little to do with the mainstream of academic practice and knowledge (or with themselves). This reductive notion that identity studies are intellectual ghettos limited to a narrow constituency demanding special pleading is the persistent obstacle that both feminist theory and disability studies must surmount.

Disability studies can benefit from feminist theory and feminist theory can benefit from disability studies. Both feminism and disability studies are comparative and concurrent academic enterprises. Just as feminism has expanded the lexicon of what we imagine as womanly, has sought to understand and destigmatize what we call the subject position of woman, so has disability studies examined the identity disability in the service of integrating disabled people more fully into our society. As such, both are insurgencies that are becoming institutionalized underpinning inquiries outside and inside the academy. A feminist disability theory builds on the strengths of both.

FEMINIST DISABILITY THEORY

My title here, "Integrating Disability, Transforming Feminist Theory," invokes and links two notions, integration and transformation, both of which are fundamental to the feminist project and to the larger civil rights movement that informed it. Integration suggests achieving parity by fully including that which has been excluded and subordinated. Transformation suggests reimagining established knowledge and the order of things. By alluding to integration and transformation, I set my own modest project of integrating disability into feminist theory in the politicized context of the civil rights movement in order to gesture toward the explicit relation that feminism supposes between intellectual work and a commitment to creating a more just, equitable, and integrated society.

This essay aims to amplify feminist theory by articulating and fostering feminist disability theory. In naming feminist disability studies here as an academic field of inquiry, I am sometimes describing work that is already underway, some of which explicitly addresses disability and some which gestures implicitly to the topic. At other times, I am calling for study that needs to be done to better illuminate feminist thought. In other words, this essay in part sets an agenda for future work in feminist disability theory. Most fundamentally, though, the goal of feminist disability theory, as I lay it out in this essay, is to augment the terms and confront the limits of the ways we understand human diversity, the materiality of the body, multiculturalism, and the social formations that interpret bodily differences. The fundamental point

I will make here is that integrating disability as a category of analysis and a system of representation deepens, expands, and challenges feminist theory.

Academic feminism is a complex and contradictory matrix of theories, strategies, pedagogies and practices. One way to think about feminist theory is to say that it investigates how culture saturates the particularities of bodies with meanings and probes the consequences of those meanings. Feminist theory is a collaborative, interdisciplinary inquiry and a self-conscious cultural critique that interrogates how subjects are multiply interpellated: in other words, how the representational systems of gender, race, ethnicity, ability, sexuality, and class mutually produce, inflect, and contradict one another. These systems intersect to produce and sustain ascribed, achieved, and acquired identities, both those that claim us and those that we claim for ourselves. A feminist disability theory introduces the ability/disability system as a category of analysis into this diverse and diffuse enterprise. It aims to extend current notions of cultural diversity and to more fully integrate the academy and the larger world it helps shape.

A feminist disability approach fosters more complex understandings of the cultural history of the body. By considering the ability/disability system, feminist disability theory goes beyond explicit disability topics such as illness, health, beauty, genetics, eugenics, aging, reproductive technologies, prosthetics, and access issues. Feminist disability theory addresses such broad feminist concerns as the unity of the category "woman," the status of the lived body, the politics of appearance, the medicalization of the body, the privilege of normalcy, multiculturalism, sexuality, the social construction of identity, and the commitment to integration. To borrow Toni Morrison's notion that blackness is an idea that permeates American culture, disability too is a pervasive, often unarticulated, ideology informing our cultural notions of self and other (Playing in the Dark 19). Disability—like gender—is a concept that pervades all aspects of culture: its structuring institutions, social identities, cultural practices, political positions, historical communities, and the shared human experience of embodiment.

Integrating disability into feminist theory is generative, broadening our collective inquires, questioning our assumptions, and contributing to feminism's multiculturalism. Introducing a disability analysis does not narrow the inquiry, limit the focus to only women with disabilities, or preclude engaging other manifestations of feminisms. Indeed, the multiplicity of foci we now call feminisms is not a group of fragmented, competing subfields, but rather a vibrant, complex conversation. In talking about "feminist disability theory," I am not proposing yet another discrete "feminism," but suggesting instead some ways that thinking about disability transforms feminist theory. Integrating disability does not obscure our critical focus on the registers of race, sexuality, ethnicity, or gender, nor is it additive (to use Gerda Lerner's famous idea). Rather, considering disability shifts the conceptual framework to strengthen our understanding of how these multiple systems intertwine, redefine, and mutually constitute one another. Integrating disability clarifies how this aggregate of systems operate together, yet distinctly, to support an imaginary norm and structure the relations that grant power, privilege, and status to that norm. Indeed, the cultural function of the disabled figure is to act as a synecdoche for all forms that culture deems nonnormative.

We need to study disability in a feminist context to direct our highly honed critical skills toward the dual scholarly tasks of unmasking and reimagining disability, not only for people with disabilities but for everyone. As Simi Linton puts it, studying disability is "a prism through which one can gain a broader understanding of society and human experience" (1998, 118). It deepens the understanding of gender and sexuality, individualism and equality, minority group definitions, autonomy, wholeness, independence, dependence, health, physical appearance, aesthetics, the integrity of the body, community, and ideas of progress and perfection in every aspect of culture. A feminist disability theory introduces what Eve Sedgwick has called a "universalizing view" of disability that will replace an often persisting "minoritizing view." Such a view will cast disability as "an issue of continuing, determinative importance in the lives of people across the spectrum" (1990, 1). In other words, understanding how disability operates as an identity category and cultural concept will enhance how we understand what it is to be human, our relationships with one another, and the experience of embodiment. The constituency for a feminist disability theory is all of us, not only women with disabilities: disability is the most human of experiences, touching every family and—if we live long enough—touching us all.

THE ABILITY/DISABILITY SYSTEM

Feminist disability theory's radical critique hinges on a broad understanding of disability as a pervasive cultural system that stigmatizes certain kinds of bodily variations. At the same time, this system has the potential to incite a critical politics. The informing premise of feminist disability theory is that disability, like femaleness, is not a natural state of corporeal inferiority, inadequacy, excess, or a stroke of misfortune. Rather, disability is a culturally fabricated narrative of the body, similar to what we understand as the fictions of race and gender. The disability/ability system produces subjects by differentiating and marking bodies. Although this comparison of bodies is ideological rather than biological, it nevertheless penetrates into the formation of culture, legitimating an unequal distribution of resources, status, and power within a biased social and architectural environment. As such, disability has four aspects: first, it is a system for interpreting and disciplining bodily variations; second, it is a relationship between bodies and their environments; third, it is a set of practices that produce both the able-bodied and the disabled; fourth, it is a way of describing the inherent instability of the embodied self. The disability system excludes the kinds of bodily forms, functions, impairments, changes, or ambiguities that call into question our cultural fantasy of the body as a neutral, compliant instrument of some transcendent will. Moreover, disability is a broad term within which cluster ideological categories as varied as sick, deformed, abnormal, crazy, ugly, old, feebleminded, maimed, afflicted, mad, or debilitated—all of which disadvantage people by devaluing bodies that do not conform to cultural standards. Thus the disability system functions to preserve and validate such privileged designations as beautiful, healthy, normal, fit, competent, intelligent—all of which provide cultural capital to those who can claim such status, who can reside within these subject positions. It is, then, the various interactions between bodies and world that materialize disability from the stuff of human variation and precariousness.

A feminist disability theory denaturalizes disability by unseating the dominant assumption that disability is something that is wrong with someone. By this I mean, of course, that it mobilizes feminism's highly developed and complex critique of gender, class, race, ethnicity, and sexuality as exclusionary and oppressive systems rather than as the natural and appropriate order of things. To do this, feminist disability theory engages several of the fundamental premises of critical theory: 1) that representation structures reality; 2) that the margins define the center; 3) that gender (or disability) is a way of signifying relationships of power; 4) that human identity is multiple and unstable; 5) that all analysis and evaluation have political implications.

In order to elaborate on these premises, I discuss here four fundamental and interpenetrating domains of feminist theory and suggest some of the kinds of critical inquiries that considering disability can generate within these theoretical arenas. These domains are: 1) representation; 2) the body; 3) identity; 4) activism. While I have disentangled these domains here for the purposes of setting up a schematic organization for my analysis, these domains are, of course, not discrete in either concept or practice, but rather tend to be synchronous.

REPRESENTATION

The first domain of feminist theory that can be deepened by a disability analysis is representation. Western thought has long conflated femaleness and disability, understanding both as defective departures from a valued standard. Aristotle, for example, defined women as "mutilated males." Women, for Aristotle, have "improper form;" we are "monstrosit[ies]" (1944, 27–8; 8–9). As what Nancy Tuana calls "misbegotten men," women thus become the primal freaks in western history, envisioned as what we might now call congenitally deformed as a result of their what we might now term a genetic disability (1993, 18). More recently, feminist theorists have argued that female embodiment is a disabling condition in sexist culture. Iris Marion Young, for instance, examines how enforced feminine comportment delimits women's sense of embodied agency, restricting them to "throwing like a girl" (1990b, 141). Young asserts that, "Women

in a sexist society are physically handicapped" (1990b, 153). Even the general American public associates femininity and disability. A recent study on stereotyping showed that housewives, disabled people, blind people, so-called retarded people, and the elderly were judged as being similarly incompetent. Such a study suggests that intensely normatively feminine positions—such as a housewife—are aligned with negative attitudes about people with disabilities (Fiske 2001).[1]

Recognizing how the concept of disability has been used to cast the form and functioning of female bodies as non-normative can extend feminist critiques. Take, for example, the exploitation of Saartje Bartmann, the African woman exhibited as a freak in nineteenth-century Europe (Fausto Sterling 1995; Gilman 1985). Known as the Hottentot Venus, Bartmann's treatment has come to represent the most egregious form of racial and gendered degradation. What goes unremarked in studies of Bartmann's display, however, is the ways that the language and assumptions of the ability/disability system were implemented to pathologize and exoticize Bartmann. Her display invoked disability by presenting as deformities or abnormalities the characteristics that marked her as raced and gendered. I am not suggesting that Bartmann was disabled, but rather that the concepts of disability discourse framed her presentation to the western eye. Using disability as a category of analysis allows us to see that what was normative embodiment in her native context became abnormal to the western mind. More important, rather than simply supposing that being labeled as a freak is a slander, a disability analysis presses our critique further by challenging the premise that unusual embodiment is inherently inferior. The feminist interrogation of gender since Simone de Beauvoir has revealed how women are assigned a cluster of ascriptions, like Aristotle's, that mark us as Other. What is less widely recognized, however, is that this collection of interrelated characterizations is precisely the same set of supposed attributes affixed to people with disabilities.

The gender, race, and ability systems intertwine further in representing subjugated people as being pure body, unredeemed by mind or spirit. This sentence of embodiment is conceived of as either a lack or an excess. Women, for example, are considered castrated,—or to use Marge Piercy's wonderful term—"penis-poor" (1969). They are thought to be hysterical, or to have overactive hormones. Women have been cast as alternately having insatiable appetite in some eras and as pathologically self-denying in other times. Similarly, disabled people supposedly have extra chromosomes or limb deficiencies. The differences of disability are cast as atrophy, meaning degeneration, or hypertrophy, meaning enlargement. People with disabilities are described as having aplasia, meaning absence or failure of formation, or hypoplasia, meaning underdevelopment. All these terms police variation and reference a hidden norm from which the bodies of people with disabilities and women are imagined to depart.

Female, disabled, and dark bodies are supposed to be dependent, incomplete, vulnerable, and incompetent bodies. Femininity and race are the performance of disability. Women and the disabled are portrayed as helpless, dependent, weak, vulnerable, and incapable bodies. Women, the disabled, and people of color are always ready occasions for the aggrandizement of benevolent rescuers, whether strong males, distinguished doctors, abolitionists, or Jerry Lewis hosting his Telethons. For example, an 1885 medical illustration of a pathologically "love deficient" woman who fits the cultural stereotype of the ugly woman or perhaps the lesbian suggests how sexuality and appearance slide into the terms of disability.

This illustration shows the language of deficiency and abnormality used to simultaneously devalue women who depart from the mandates of femininity by equating them with disabled bodies. Such an interpretive move economically invokes the subjugating effect of one oppressive system to deprecate people marked by another system of representation.

Subjugated bodies are pictured as either deficient or as profligate. For instance, what Susan Bordo describes as the too-muchness of women also haunts disability and racial discourses, marking subjugated bodies as ungovernable, intemperate, or threatening (1993). The historical figure of the monster, as well, invokes disability, often to serve racism and sexism. Although the term has expanded to encompass all forms of social and corporeal aberration, *monster* originally described people with congenital impairments. As departures from the normatively human, monsters were seen as category violations or grotesque hybrids. The semantics of monstrosity are recruited to explain gender violations such as Julia Pastrana, for example, the Mexican Indian "bearded woman," whose body was displayed in nineteenth-century freak shows both during her lifetime and after her death. Pastrana's live and later embalmed body spectacularly confused and transgressed established cultural categories. Race, gender, disability, and sexuality augmented one another in Pastrana's display to produce a spectacle of embodied otherness that is simultaneously sensational, sentimental, and pathological (Thomson 1999). Furthermore much current feminist work theorizes figures of hybridity and excess such as monsters, grotesques, and cyborgs to suggest their transgressive potential for a feminist politics (Haraway 1991; Braidotti 1994; Russo 1994). However, this metaphorical invocation seldom acknowledges that these figures often refer to the actual bodies of people with disabilities.

Erasing real disabled bodies from the history of these terms compromises the very critique they intend to launch and misses an opportunity to use disability as a feminist critical category.

Such representations ultimately portray subjugated bodies not only as inadequate or unrestrained but at the same time as redundant and expendable. Bodies marked and selected by such systems are targeted for elimination by varying historical and cross-cultural practices. Women, people with disabilities or appearance impairments, ethnic others, gays and lesbians, and people of color are variously the objects of infanticide, selective abortion, eugenic programs, hate crimes, mercy killing, assisted suicide, lynching, bride burning, honor killings, forced conversion, coercive rehabilitation, domestic violence, genocide, normalizing surgical procedures, racial profiling, and neglect. All these discriminatory practices are legitimated by systems of representation, by collective cultural stories that shape the material world, underwrite exclusionary attitudes, inform human relations, and mold our senses of who we are. Understanding how disability functions along with other systems of representation clarifies how all the systems intersect and mutually constitute one another.

THE BODY

The second domain of feminist theory that a disability analysis can illuminate is the investigation of the body: its materiality, its politics, its lived experience, and its relation to subjectivity and identity. Confronting issues of representation is certainly crucial to the cultural critique of feminist disability theory. But we should not focus exclusively on the discursive realm. What distinguishes a feminist disability theory from other critical paradigms is that it scrutinizes a wide range of material practices involving the lived body. Perhaps because women and the disabled are cultural signifiers for the body, their actual bodies have been subjected relentlessly to what Michel Foucault calls "discipline" (1979). Together, the gender, race, ethnicity, sexuality, class, and ability systems exert tremendous social pressures to shape, regulate, and normalize subjugated bodies. Such disciplining is enacted primarily through the two interrelated cultural discourses of medicine and appearance.

Feminist disability theory offers a particularly trenchant analysis of the ways that the female body has been medicalized in modernity. As I have already suggested, both women and the disabled have been imagined as medically abnormal—as the quintessential "sick" ones. Sickness is gendered feminine. This gendering of illness has entailed distinct consequences in everything from epidemiology and diagnosis to prophylaxis and therapeutics.

Perhaps feminist disability theory's most incisive critique is revealing the intersections between the politics of appearance and the medicalization of subjugated bodies. Appearance norms have a long history in western culture, as is witnessed by the anthropometric composite figures of ideal male and female bodies made by Dudley Sargent in 1893. The classical ideal was to be worshiped rather than imitated, but increasingly in modernity the ideal has migrated to become the paradigm which is to be attained. As many feminist critics have pointed out, the standardization of the female body that the beauty system mandates has become a goal to be achieved through self-regulation and consumerism (Wolf 1991; Haiken 1997). Feminist disability theory suggests that appearance and health norms often have similar disciplinary goals. For example, the body braces developed in the 1930s to "correct" scoliosis, discipline the body to conform to the dictates of both the gender and the ability systems by enforcing standardized female form similarly to the nineteenth-century corset, which, ironically, often disabled female bodies. Although both devices normalize bodies, the brace is part of medical discourse while the corset is cast as a fashion practice.

Similarly, a feminist disability theory calls into question the separation of reconstructive and cosmetic surgery, recognizing their essentially normalizing function as what Sander L. Gilman calls "aesthetic surgery" (1998). Cosmetic surgery, driven by gender ideology and market forces, now enforces feminine body standards and standardizes female bodies toward what I have called the "normate"—the corporeal incarnation of culture's collective, unmarked, normative characteristics (1997, 8). Cosmetic surgery's twin, reconstructive surgery, eliminates disability and enforces the ideals of what might be thought of as the normalcy system. Both cosmetic and reconstructive procedures commodify the body and parade mutilations as enhancements that correct flaws so as to improve the psychological well being of the patient. The conception of the body as what Susan Bordo terms "cultural plastic" increasingly through surgical and medical interventions pressures people with disabilities or appearance impairments to become what Michel Foucault calls "docile bodies." (1993, 246; 1979, 135). The twin ideologies of normalcy and beauty posit female and disabled bodies, particularly, as not only spectacles to be looked at, but as pliable bodies to be shaped infinitely so as to conform to a set of standards called "normal" and "beautiful."

Normal has inflected beautiful in modernity. What is imagined as excess body fat, the effects of aging, marks of ethnicity such as "jewish" noses, bodily particularities thought of as blemishes or deformities, and marks of history such as scarring and impairments are now expected to be surgically erased to produce an unmarked body. This visually unobtrusive body may then pass unnoticed within the milieu of anonymity that is the hallmark of social relations beyond the personal in modernity. The point of aesthetic surgery, as well as the costuming of power, is not to appear unique—or to "be yourself," as the ads endlessly promise—but rather not to be conspicuous, not to look different. This flight from the nonconforming body translates into individual efforts to look normal, neutral, unmarked, to *not* look disabled, queer, ugly, fat, ethnic, or raced. For example, beauty is set out comparatively and supposedly self-evidently in an 1889 treatise called *The New Physiogomy* which juxtaposed a white, upper-class English face called "Princess Alexandra" with a stereotypical face of an Irish immigrant, called "Sally Muggins" in a class and ethnic-based binary of apparently self-evident beauty and ugliness. Beauty, then, dictates corporeal standards that create not distinction but utter conformity to a bland look that is at the same time unachievable so as to leash us to consumer practices that promise to deliver such sameness. In the language of contemporary cosmetic surgery, the unreconstructed female body is persistently cast as having abnormalities that can be corrected by surgical procedures which supposedly improve one's appearance by producing ostensibly natural looking noses, thighs, breasts, chins, and so on. Thus, our unmodified bodies are presented as unnatural and abnormal while the surgically altered bodies are portrayed as normal and natural. The beautiful woman of the twenty-first century is sculpted surgically from top to bottom, generically neutral, all irregularities regularized, all particularities expunged. She is thus non-disabled, deracialized, and de-ethnicized.

In addition, the politics of prosthetics enters the purview of feminism when we consider the contested use of breast implants and prostheses for breast cancer survivors. The famous 1993 *New York Times* cover photo of the fashion model, Matushka, baring her mastectomy scar or Audre Lorde's account of breast cancer in *The Cancer Journals* challenge the sexist assumption that the amputated breast must always pass for the normative, sexualized one either through concealment or prosthetics (1980). A vibrant feminist conversation has emerged about the politics of the surgically altered, the disabled, breast. Diane Price Herndl challenges Audre Lorde's refusal of a breast prosthesis after mastectomy and Iris Marion Young's classic essay "Breasted Experience" queries the cultural meanings of breasts under the knife (2002; 1990a).

Another entanglement of appearance and medicine involves the spectacle of the female breast, both normative and disabled. In January 2000, the San Francisco-based Breast Cancer Fund mounted "Obsessed with Breasts," a public awareness poster campaign showing women boldly displaying mastectomy scars. The posters parodied familiar commercial media sites—a Calvin Klein perfume ad, a Cosmopolitan magazine cover, and a Victoria Secret catalog cover—that routinely parade women's breasts as upscale soft porn. The posters replace the now unremarkable eroticized breast with the forbidden image of the amputated breast. In doing so, they disrupt the visual convention of the female breast as sexualized object for male appropriation and pleasure. The posters thus produce a powerful visual violation by exchanging the spectacle of the eroticized breast, which has been desensationalized by its endless circulation, with the medicalized image of the scarred breast, which has been concealed from public view. The Breast Cancer Fund used these remarkable images to challenge both sexism in medical research and treatment for breast cancer as well as the oppressive representational practices that make everyday erotic spectacles of women's breasts while erasing the fact of the amputated breast.

Feminist disability theory can press far its critique of the pervasive will-to-normalize the non-standard body. Take two related examples: first, the surgical separation of conjoined twins and, second, the surgical assignment of gender for the intersexed, people with ambiguous genitalia and gender characteristics. Both these forms of embodiment are regularly—if infrequently—occurring, congenital bodily variations that spectacularly violate sacred ideologies of western culture. Conjoined twins contradict our notion of the individual as discrete and autonomous—actually, quite similarly to the way pregnancy does. Intersexed infants challenge our insistence that biological gender is unequivocally binary. So threatening to the order of things is the natural embodiment of conjoined twins and intersexed people that they are almost always surgically normalized through amputation and mutilation immediately after birth (Clark and Myser 1996; Dreger 1998a; Kessler 1990; Fausto-Sterling 2000). Not infrequently, one conjoined twin is sacrificed to save the other from the supposed abnormality of their embodiment. Such mutilations are justified as preventing suffering and creating well adjusted individuals. So intolerable is their insult to dominant ideologies about who patriarchal culture insists that we are that the testimonies of adults with these forms of embodiment who say that they do not want to be separated is routinely ignored in establishing the rationale for "medical treatment." (Dreger 1998b). In truth, these procedures benefit not the affected individuals, but rather they expunge the kinds of corporeal human variations that contradict the ideologies the dominant order depends upon to anchor truths it insists are unequivocally encoded in bodies.

I do not want to oversimplify here by suggesting that women and disabled people should not use modern medicine to improve their lives or help their bodies function more fully. But the critical issues are complex and provocative. A feminist disability theory should illuminate and explain, not become ideological policing or set orthodoxy. The kinds of critical analyses I'm discussing here offer a counter logic to the overdetermined cultural mandates to comply with normal and beautiful at any cost. The medical commitment to healing, when coupled with modernity's faith in technology and interventions that control outcomes, has increasingly shifted toward an aggressive intent to fix, regulate, or eradicate ostensibly deviant bodies. Such a program of elimination has often been at the expense of creating a more accessible environment or providing better support services for people with disabilities. The privileging of medical technology over less ambitious programs such as rehabilitation has encouraged the cultural conviction that disability can be extirpated, inviting the belief that life with a disability is intolerable. As charity campaigns and telethons repeatedly affirm, cure rather than adjustment or accommodation is the overdetermined cultural response to disability (Longmore 1997). For instance, a 1949 March of Dimes poster shows an appealing little girl stepping out of her wheelchair into the supposed redemption of walking: "Look, I Can Walk Again!" the text proclaims while at once charging the viewers with the responsibility of assuring her future ambulation. Nowhere do we find posters suggesting that life as a wheelchair user might be full and satisfying, as many people who actually use them find their lives to be. This ideology of cure is not isolated in medical texts or charity campaigns, but in fact permeates the entire cultural conversation about disability and illness. Take, for example, the discourse of cure in get well cards. A 1950 card, for instance, urges its recipient to "snap out of it." Fusing racist, sexist, and ablist discourses, the card recruits the Mammy figure to insist on cure. The stereotypical racist figure asks, " Is you sick, Honey?" and then exhorts the recipient of her care to "jes hoodoo all dat illness out o you."

The ideology of cure directed at disabled people focuses on changing bodies imagined as abnormal and dysfunctional rather than on exclusionary attitudinal, environmental and economic barriers. The emphasis on cure reduces the cultural tolerance for human variation and vulnerability by locating disability in bodies imagined as flawed rather than social systems in need of fixing. A feminist disability studies would draw an important distinction between prevention and elimination. Preventing illness, suffering, and injury is a humane social objective. Eliminating the range of unacceptable and devalued bodily forms and functions the dominant order calls disability is, on the other hand, a eugenic undertaking. The ostensibly progressive socio-medical project of eradicating disability all too often is enacted as a program to eliminate people with disabilities through such practices as forced sterilization, so-called physician-assisted suicide and mercy killing, selective abortion, institutionalization, and segregation policies.

A feminist disability theory extends its critique of the normalization of bodies and the medicalization of appearance to challenge some widely held assumptions about reproductive issues as well. The cultural mandate to eliminate the variations in form and function that we think of as disabilities has undergirded the reproductive practices of genetic testing and selective abortion (Saxton 1998; Parens and Asch 2000; Rapp 1999). Some disability activists argue that the "choice" to abort fetuses with disabilities is a coercive form of genocide against the disabled (Hubbard

1990). A more nuanced argument against selective abortion comes from Adrienne Asch and Gail Geller, who wish to preserve a woman's right to choose whether to bear a child, but who at the same time object to the ethics of selectively aborting a wanted fetus because it will become a person with a disability (1996). Asch and Geller counter the quality-of-life and prevention-of-suffering arguments so readily invoked to justify selective abortion, as well as physician-assisted suicide, by pointing out that we cannot predict or—more precisely—control in advance such equivocal human states as happiness, suffering, or success. Neither is any amount of prenatal engineering going to produce the life that any of us desire and value. Indeed, both hubris and a lack of imagination characterize the prejudicial and reductive assumption that having a disability ruins lives. A vague notion of suffering and its potential deterrence drives much of the logic of elimination that rationalizes selective abortion (Kittay 2000). Life chances and quality are simply far too contingent to justify prenatal prediction.

Similarly, genetic testing and applications of the Human Genome Project as the key to expunging disability are often critiqued as enactments of eugenic ideology, what the feminist biologist Evelyn Fox Keller calls a "eugenics of normalcy" (1992). The popular utopian notion that all forms of disability can be eliminated through prophylactic manipulation of genetics will only serve to intensify the prejudice against those who inevitably will acquire disabilities through aging and encounters with the environment. In the popular celebrations of the Human Genome Project as the quixotic pinnacle of technological progress, seldom do we hear a cautionary logic about the eugenic implications of this drive toward what Priscilla Wald calls "Future Perfect" (2000, 1). Disability scholars have entered the debate over so-called

physician-assisted suicide, as well, by arguing that oppressive attitudes toward disability distort the possibility of unbiased free choice (Battin et al. 1998). The practices of genetic and prenatal testing as well as physician-administered euthanasia, then, become potentially eugenic practices within the context of a culture deeply intolerant of disability. Both the rhetoric and the enactment of this kind of disability discrimination create a hostile and exclusionary environment for people with disabilities that perhaps exceeds the less virulent architectural barriers that keep them out of the workforce and the public sphere.

Integrating disability into feminism's conversation about the place of the body in the equality and difference debates produces fresh insights as well. Whereas liberal feminism emphasizes sameness, choice, and autonomy, cultural feminism critiques the premises of liberalism. Out of cultural feminism's insistence on difference and its positive interpretation of feminine culture comes the affirmation of a feminist ethic of care. This ethic of care contends that care giving is a moral benefit for its practitioners and for humankind. A feminist disability studies complicates both the feminist ethic of care and liberal feminism in regard to the politics of care and dependency.

A disability perspective nuances feminist theory's consideration of the ethics of care by examining the power relations between the givers and receivers of care. Anita Silvers has argued strongly that being the object of care precludes the equality that a liberal democracy depends upon and undermines the claim to justice as equality that undergirds a civil rights approach used to counter discrimination (1995). Eva Kittay, on the other hand, formulates a "dependency critique of equality" (1999, 4), which asserts that the ideal of equality under liberalism repudiates the fact of human dependency, the need for mutual care, and the asymmetries of care relations. Similarly, Barbara Hillyer has called attention to dependency in order to critique a liberal tendency in the rhetoric of disability rights (1993). Disability itself demands that human interdependence and the universal need for assistance be figured into our dialogues about rights and subjectivity.

IDENTITY

The third domain of feminist theory that a disability analysis complicates is identity. Feminist theory has productively and rigorously critiqued the identity category of woman, on which the entire feminist enterprise seemed to rest. Feminism increasingly recognizes that no woman is ever *only* a woman, that she occupies multiple subject positions and is claimed by several cultural identity categories (Spelman 1988). This complication of *woman* compelled feminist theory to turn from an exclusively male/female focus to look more fully at the exclusionary, essentialist, oppressive, and binary aspects of the category woman itself. Disability is one such identity vector that disrupts the unity of the classification woman and challenges the primacy of gender as a monolithic category.

Disabled women are, of course, a marked and excluded—albeit quite varied—group within the larger social class of women. The relative privileges of normative femininity are often denied to disabled women (Fine and Asch 1988). Cultural stereotypes imagine disabled women as asexual, unfit to reproduce, overly dependent, unattractive—as generally removed from the sphere of true womanhood and feminine beauty. Women with disabilities must often struggle to have their sexuality and rights to bear children recognized (Finger 1990). Disability thus both intensifies and attenuates the cultural scripts of femininity. Aging is a form of disablement that disqualifies older women from the limited power allotted fe-

males who are young and meet the criteria for attracting men. Depression, anorexia, and agoraphobia are female-dominant, psycho-physical disabilities that exaggerate normative gendered roles. Feminine cultural practices such as foot binding, clitorectomies, and corsetting, as well as their less hyperbolic costuming rituals such as stiletto high heels, girdles, and chastity belts—impair women's bodies and restrict their physical agency, imposing disability on them.

Banishment from femininity can be both a liability and a benefit. Let me offer—with some irony—an instructive example from popular culture. Barbie, that cultural icon of femininity, offers a disability analysis that clarifies both how multiple identity and diversity are commodified and how the commercial realm might offer politically useful feminist counterimages. Perhaps the measure of a group's arrival into the mainstream of multiculturalism is to be represented in the Barbie pantheon. While Barbie herself still identifies as ablebodied—despite her severely deformed body—we now have several incarnations of Barbie's "friend," Share-A-Smile Becky. One Becky uses a cool hot pink wheelchair; another is Paralympic Champion Becky, brought out for the 2000 Sydney Olympics in a chic red-white-and-blue warm-up suit with matching chair. Most interesting however is Becky, the school photographer, clad in a preppy outfit, complete with camera and red high-top sneakers. As she perkily gazes at an alluring Barbie in her camera's viewfinder, this Becky may be the incarnation of what one scholar has called "Barbie's queer assessories" (Rand 1995).

A disabled, queer Becky is certainly a provocative and subversive fusion of stigmatized identities, but more important is that Becky challenges notions of normalcy in feminist ways. The disabled Becky, for example, wears comfortable clothes: pants with elastic-waists no doubt, sensible shoes, and roomy shirts. Becky is also one of the few dolls who has flat feet and legs that bend at the knee. The disabled Becky is dressed and poised for agency, action, and creative engagement with the world. In contrast, the prototypical Barbie performs excessive femininity in her restrictive sequined gowns, crowns, and push-up bras. So while Becky implies on the one hand that disabled girls are purged from the feminine economy, on the other hand Becky also suggests that disabled girls might be liberated from those oppressive and debilitating scripts. The last word on Barbies comes from a disability activist who quipped that he'd like to outfit a disabled doll with a power wheelchair chair and a briefcase to make her a civil rights lawyer who enforces the Americans with Disabilities Act. He wants to call her "Sue-Your-Ass-Becky."[2] I think she'd make a very good role model.

The paradox of Barbie and Becky, of course, is that the ultra-feminized Barbie is a target for sexual appropriation both by men and beauty practices while the disabled Becky escapes such sexual objectification at the potential cost of losing her sense of identity as a feminine sexual being. Some disabled women negotiate this possible identity crisis by developing alternate sexualities, such as lesbianism (Brownsworth and Raffo 1999). However, what Harlan Hahn calls the "asexual objectification" of people with disabilities complicates the feminist critique of normative sexual objectification (1988). Consider the 1987 *Playboy* magazine photos of the paraplegic actress Ellen Stohl. After becoming disabled, Stohl wrote to editor Hugh Hefner that she wanted to pose nude for *Playboy* because "sexuality is the hardest thing for disabled persons to hold onto." ("Meet Ellen Stohl," 68.) For Stohl, it would seem that the performance of excessive feminine sexuality was necessary to counter the social interpretation that disability cancels

out sexuality. This confirmation of normative heterosexuality was then for Stohl no Butlerian parody, but rather was the affirmation she needed as a disabled woman to be sexual at all.

Ellen Stohl's presentation by way of the sexist conventions of the porn magazine illuminates the relation between identity and the body, an aspect of subject formation that disability analysis can offer. Although binary identities are conferred from outside through social relations, these identities are nevertheless inscribed on the body as either manifest or incipient visual traces. Identity's social meaning turns on this play of visibility. The photos of Stohl in *Playboy* both refuse and insist on marking her impairment. The centerfold spread—so to speak—of Stohl nude and masturbating erases her impairment to conform to the sexualized conventions of the centerfold. This photo expunges her wheelchair and any other visual clues to her impairment. In other words, to avoid the cultural contradiction of a sexual disabled woman, the pornographic photos must offer up Stohl as visually nondisabled. But to appeal to the cultural narrative of overcoming disability that sells so well, seems novel, and capitalizes on sentimental interest, Stohl must be visually dramatized as disabled at the same time. So *Playboy* includes several shots of Stohl that mark her as disabled by picturing her in her wheelchair, entirely without the typical porn conventions. In fact, the photos of her using her wheelchair invoke the asexual poster child. Thus, the affirmation of Stohl's sexuality she sought by posing nude in the porn magazine came at the expense of denying through the powerful visual register her identity as a woman with a disability, even while she attempted to claim that identity textually.

Another aspect of subject formation that disability confirms is that identity is always in transition. Disability reminds us that the body is, as Denise Riley asserts, "an unsteady mark, scarred in its long decay" (Riley 1999, 224). As Caroline Walker Bynum's intriguing work on werewolf narratives suggests, the body is in a perpetual state of transformation (1999). Caring for her father for over twenty years of Alzheimer's disease prompted Bynum to investigate how we can understand individual identity as continuous even though both body and mind can and do change dramatically, certainly over a lifetime and sometimes quite suddenly. Disability invites us to query what the continuity of the self might depend upon if the body perpetually metamorphoses. We envision our racial, gender, or ethnic identities as tethered to bodily traits that are relatively secure. Disability and sexual identity, however, seem more fluid, although sexual mutability is imagined as elective where disability is seldom conceived of as a choice. Disability is an identity category that anyone can enter at any time, and we will all join it if we live long enough. As such, disability reveals the essential dynamism of identity. Thus, disability attenuates the cherished cultural belief that the body is the unchanging anchor of identity. Moreover, it undermines our fantasies of stable, enduring identities in ways that may illuminate the fluidity of all identity.

Disability's clarification of the body's corporeal truths suggests as well that the body/self materializes—in Judith Butler's sense—not so much through discourse, but through history (1993). The self materializes in response to an embodied engagement with its environment, both social and concrete. The disabled body is a body whose variations or transformations have rendered it out of sync with its environment, both the physical and the attitudinal environments. In other words, the body becomes disabled when it is incongruent both in space and the milieu of expectations. Furthermore, a feminist disability theory presses us to ask what kinds of knowledge might be produced through having a body radically marked by its own particularity, a body that materializes at the ends of the curve of human variation. For example, an alternative epistemology that emerges from the lived experience of disability is nicely summed up in Nancy Mairs' book title, *Waist High in the World*, which she irreverently considered calling "cock high in the world." What perspectives or politics arise from encountering the world from such an atypical position? Perhaps Mairs' epistemology can offer us a critical positionality called sitpoint theory, a neologism I can offer that interrogates the ableist assumptions underlying the notion of standpoint theory (Harstock 1983).

Our collective cultural consciousness emphatically denies the knowledge of bodily vulnerability, contingency, and mortality. Disability insists otherwise, contradicting such phallic ideology. I would argue that disability is perhaps the essential characteristic of being human. The body is dynamic, constantly interactive with history and environment. We evolve into disability. Our bodies need care; we all need assistance to live. An equality model of feminist theory sometimes prizes individualistic autonomy as the key to women's liberation. A feminist disability theory, however, suggests that we are better off learning to individually and collectively accommodate the body's limits and evolutions than trying to eliminate or deny them.

Identity formation is at the center of feminist theory. Disability can complicate feminist theory often quite succinctly by invoking established theoretical paradigms. This kind of theoretical intertextuality inflects familiar feminist concepts with new resonance. Let me offer several examples: the idea of "compulsory ablebodiedness," which Robert McRuer has coined, extends Adrienne Rich's famous analysis of "compulsory heterosexuality" (2001, 1986). Joan

Wallach Scott's germinal work on gender is recruited when we discuss disability as "a useful category of analysis" (1988, 1). The feminist elaboration of the gender system informs my use of the disability system. Lennard Davis suggests that the term *normalcy studies* supplant the name *disability studies*, in the way that *gender studies* sometimes succeeds *feminism* (1995). The oft invoked distinction between sex and gender clarifies a differentiation between impairment and disability, even though both binaries are fraught. The concept of performing disability, cites (as it were) Judith Butler's vigorous critique of essentialism (1990). Reading disabled bodies as exemplary instances of "docile bodies" invokes Foucault (1979). To suggest that identity is lodged in the body, I propose that the body haunts the subject, alluding to Susan Bordo's notion regarding masculinity that "the penis haunts the phallus" (1994, 1). My own work has complicated the familiar discourse of the gaze to theorize what I call the stare, which I argue produces disability identity. Such theoretical shorthand impels us to reconsider the ways that identity categories cut across and redefine one another, pressuring both the terms *woman* and *disabled*.

A feminist disability theory can also highlight intersections and convergences with other identity-based critical perspectives such as queer and ethnic studies. Disability coming-out stories, for example, borrow from gay and lesbian identity narratives to expose what previously was hidden, privatized, medicalized in order to enter into a political community. The politicized sphere into which many scholars come out is feminist disability studies, which enables critique, claims disability identity, and creates affirming counter narratives. Disability coming-out narratives raise questions about the body's role in identity by asking how markers so conspicuous as crutches, wheelchairs, hearing aides, guide dogs, white canes, or empty sleeves could ever have been closeted.

Passing as nondisabled complicates ethnic and queer studies' analyses of how this seductive but psychically estranging access to privilege operates. Some of my friends, for example, have measured their regard for me by saying, "But I don't think of you as disabled." What they point to in such a compliment is the contradiction they find between their perception of me as a valuable, capable, lovable person and the cultural figure of the disabled person whom they take to be precisely my opposite: worthless, incapable, and unlovable. People with disabilities themselves routinely announce that they don't consider themselves as disabled. Although they are often repudiating the literal meaning of the word *disabled*, their words nevertheless serve to disassociate them from the identity group of the disabled. Our culture offers profound disincentives and few rewards to identifying as disabled. The trouble, of course, with such statements is that they leave intact without challenge the oppressive stereotypes that permit, among other things, the unexamined use of disability terms such as *crippled, lame, dumb, idiot, moron* as verbal gestures of derision. The refusal to claim disability identity is in part due to a lack of ways to understand or talk about disability that are not oppressive. People with disabilities and those who care about them flee from the language of *crippled* or *deformed* and have no other alternatives. Yet, the civil rights movement and the accompanying Black-is-beautiful identity politics have generally shown white culture what is problematic with saying to Black friends, "I don't think of you as Black." Nonetheless, by disavowing disability identity, many of us learned to save ourselves from devaluation by a complicity that perpetuates oppressive notions about ostensibly "real" disabled people. Thus, together we help make the alternately menacing and pathetic cultural figures who rattle tin cups or rave on street corners, ones we with impairments often flee from more surely than those who imagine themselves as nondisabled.

ACTIVISM

The final domain of feminist theory that a disability analysis expands is activism. There are many arenas of what can be seen as feminist disability activism: marches, protests, the Breast Cancer Fund poster campaign I discussed above, action groups such as the Intersex Society of North America (ISNA), and Not Dead Yet, who oppose physician-assisted suicide, or the American Disabled for Accessible Public Transit (ADAPT). What counts as activism cuts a wide swath through U.S. society and the academy. I want to suggest here two unlikely, even quirky, cultural practices that function in activist ways but are seldom considered as potentially transformative. One practice is disabled fashion modeling and the other is academic tolerance. Both are different genres of activism from the more traditional marching-on-Washington or chaining-yourself-to-a-bus modes. Both are less theatrical, but perhaps fresher and more interestingly controversial ways to change the social landscape and to promote equality, which I take to be the goal of activism.

The theologian and sociologist, Nancy Eiesland, has argued that in addition to legislative, economic, and social changes, achieving equality for people with disabilities depends upon cultural "resymbolization" (1994, 98). Eiesland asserts that the way we imagine disability and disabled people must shift in order for real social change to occur. Whereas Eiesland's work resymbolizes our conceptions of disability in religious iconography, my own examinations of disabled fashion models do similar cultural work in the popular sphere, introducing some interesting complications into her notion of resymbolization.

Images of disabled fashion models in the media can shake up established categories and expectations. Because commercial visual media are the most widespread and commanding source of images in modern, image-saturated culture, they have great potential for shaping public consciousness—as feminist cultural critics are well aware. Fashion imagery is the visual distillation of the normative, gilded with the chic and the luxurious to render it desirable. The commercial sphere is completely amoral, driven as it is by the single logic of the bottom line. As we know, it sweeps through culture seizing with alarming neutrality anything it senses will sell. This value-free aspect of advertising produces a kind of pliable potency that sometimes can yield unexpected results.

Take, for example, a shot from the monthly fashion feature in *WE Magazine*, a *Cosmopolitan* knock-off targeted toward the disabled consumer market. In this conventional, stylized, high fashion shot, a typical female model—slender, white, blond, clad in a black evening gown—is accompanied by her service dog. My argument is that public images such as this are radical because they fuse two previously antithetical visual discourses—the chic high fashion shot and the earnest charity campaign. Public representations of disability have traditionally been contained within the conventions of sentimental charity images, exotic freak show portraits, medical illustrations, or sensational and forbidden pictures. Indeed, people with disabilities have been excluded most fully from the dominant, public world of the marketplace. Before the civil rights initiatives of the mid-twentieth century began to transform the public architectural and institutional environment, disabled people were segregated to the private and the medical spheres.

Until recently, the only available public image of a woman with a service dog that shaped the public imagination was street-corner beggar or a charity poster. By juxtaposing the elite body of a visually normative fashion model with the mark of disability, this image shakes up our assumptions about the normal and the abnormal, the public and the private, the chic and the desolate, the compelling and the repelling. Introducing a service dog—a standard prop of indigents and poster children—into the conventional composition of an upscale fashion photo forces the viewer to reconfigure assumptions about what constitutes the attractive and the desirable.

I am arguing that the emergence of disabled fashion models is inadvertent activism without any legitimate agent for positive social change. Their appearance is simply a result of market forces. This both troubling and empowering form of entry into democratic capitalism produces a kind of instrumental form of equality: the freedom to be appropriated by consumer culture. In a democracy, to reject this paradoxical liberty is one thing; not to be granted it is another. Ever straining for novelty and capitalizing on titillation, the fashion advertising world promptly appropriated the power of disabled figures to provoke responses. Diversity appeals to an upscale liberal sensibility these days, making consumers feel good about buying from companies that are charitable toward the traditionally disadvantaged. More important, the disability market is burgeoning. At 54 million people and growing fast as the baby boomers age, their spending power was estimated to have reached the trillion-dollar mark in 2000 (Williams 1999).

For the most part, commercial advertising that features disabled models are presented the same as nondisabled models, simply because all models look essentially the same. The physical markings of gender, race, ethnicity, and disability are muted to the level of gesture, subordinated to the overall normativity of the models' appearance. Thus, commercial visual media cast disabled consumers as simply one of many variations that compose the market to which they appeal. Such routinization of disability imagery—however stylized and unrealistic it may be—nevertheless brings disability as a human experience out of the closet and into the normative public sphere. Images of disabled fashion models enable people with disabilities, especially those who acquire impairments as adults, to imagine themselves as a part of the ordinary, albeit consumerist, world rather than as in a special class of excluded untouchables and unviewables. Images of impairment as a familiar, even mundane, experience in the lives of seemingly successful, happy, well-adjusted people can reduce the identifying against oneself that is the overwhelming effect of oppressive and discriminatory attitudes toward people with disabilities. Such images, then, are at once liberatory and oppressive. They do the cultural work of integrating a previously excluded group into the dominant order—for better or worse—much like the inclusion of women in the military.

This form of popular resymbolization produces counterimages that have activist potential. A clearer example of disability activism might be Aimee Mullins, who is a fashion model, celebrity, champion runner, a Georgetown University student, and double amputee. Mullins was also one of *People Magazine*'s 50 Most Beautiful people of 1999. An icon of disability pride and equality, Mullins exposes—in fact calls attention to—the mark of her disability in most photos, refusing to normalize or hide her disability in order to pass for nondisabled. Indeed, her public version of her career is that her disability has been a benefit: she has several sets of legs, both cosmetic and functional, and so is able to choose how tall she wants to be. Photographed in her prosthetic legs, she embodies the sexualized jock look that demands women be both slender and fit. In her cosmetic legs, she captures the look of the high fashion beauty in the controversial shoot by Nick Knight called "Accessible," showcasing outfits created by designers such as Alexander McQueen. But this is high fashion with a difference. In the jock shot her functional legs are brazenly displayed, and even in the voguishly costumed shot, the knee joints of her artificial legs are exposed. Never is there an attempt to disguise her prosthetic legs; rather the entire photos thematically echo her prostheses and render the whole image chic. Mullins' prosthetic legs—whether cosmetic or functional—parody, indeed proudly mock, the fantasy of the perfect body that is the mark of fashion, even while the rest of her body conforms precisely to fashion's impossible standards. So rather than concealing, normalizing, or erasing disability, these photos use the hyperbole and stigmata traditionally associated with disability to quench postmodernity's perpetual search for the new and arresting image. Such a narrative of advantage works against oppressive narratives and practices usually invoked about disabilities. First, Mullins counters the insistent narrative that one must overcome an impairment rather than incorporating it into one's life and self, even perhaps as a benefit. Second, Mullins counters the practice of passing for non-disabled that people with disabilities are often obliged to enact in the public sphere. So Mullins uses her conformity with beauty standards to assert her disability's violation of those very standards. As legless and beautiful, she is an embodied paradox, asserting an inherently disruptive potential.

What my analysis of these images reveals is that feminist cultural critiques are complex. On the one hand, feminists have rightly unmasked consumer capitalism's appropriation of women as sexual objects for male gratification. On the other hand, these images imply that the same capitalist system in its drive to harvest new markets can produce politically progressive counter images and counternarratives, however fraught they may be in their entanglement with consumer culture. Images of disabled fashion models are both complicit and critical of the beauty system that oppresses all women. Nevertheless, they suggest that consumer culture can provide the raw material for its own critique.

The concluding version of activism I offer is less controversial and more subtle than glitzy fashion spreads. It is what I call academic activism—the activism of integrating education—in the very broadest sense of that term. The academy is no ivory tower but rather it is the grass roots of the educational enterprise. Scholars and teachers shape the communal knowledge and the archive that is disseminated from kindergarten to the university. Academic activism is most self-consciously vibrant in the aggregate of interdisciplinary identity studies—of which women's studies is exemplary—that strive to expose the workings of oppression, examine subject formation, and offer counter-narratives for subjugated groups. Their cultural work is building an archive through historical and textual retrieval, canon reformation, role modeling, mentoring, curricular reform, and course and program development.

A specific form of feminist academic activism I elaborate here can be deepened through the complication of a disability analysis. I call it the methodology of intellectual tolerance. By this I don't mean tolerance in the more usual sense of tolerating each other—although that would be useful as well. What I mean is the intellectual position of tolerating what has previously been thought of as incoherence. As feminism has embraced the paradoxes that have emerged from its challenge to the gender system, it has not collapsed into chaos, but rather it developed a methodology that tolerates internal conflict and contradiction. This method asks difficult questions, but accepts provisional answers. This method recognizes the power of identity at the same time that it reveals identity as a fiction. This method both seeks equality, and it claims difference. This method allows us to teach with authority at the same time that we reject notions of pedagogical mastery. This method establishes institutional presences even while it acknowledges the limitations of institutions. This method validates the personal but implements disinterested inquiry. This method both writes new stories and recovers traditional ones. Considering disability as a vector of identity that intersects gender is one more internal challenge that threatens the coherence of woman, of course. But feminism can accommodate such complication and the contradictions it cultivates. Indeed the intellectual tolerance I am arguing for espouses the partial, the provisional, the particular. Such an intellectual habit can be informed by disability experience and acceptance. To embrace the supposedly flawed body of disability is to critique the normalizing, phallic fantasies of wholeness, unity, coherence, and completeness. The disabled body is contradiction, ambiguity, and partiality incarnate.

My claim here has been that integrating disability as a category of analysis, a historical community, a set of material practices, a social identity, a political position, and a representational system into the content of feminist—indeed into all—inquiry can strengthen the critique that is feminism. Disability, like gender and race, is everywhere, once we know how to look for it. Integrating disability analyses will enrich and deepen all our teaching and scholarship. Moreover, such critical intellectual work facilitates a fuller integration of the sociopolitical world—for the benefit of everyone. As with gender, race, sexuality, and class: to understand how disability operates is to understand what it is to be fully human.

NOTES

1. Interestingly, in Fiske's study, feminists, businesswomen, Asians, Northerners, and Black professionals were stereotyped as highly competent, thus envied. In addition to having very low competence, housewives, disabled people, blind people, so-called retarded people, and the elderly were rated as warm, thus pitied.
2. Personal conversation with Paul Longmore, San Francisco, CA, June 2000.

WORKS CITED

Americans with Disabilities Act of 1990. Retrieved 15 August 2002, from http://www.usdoj.gov/crt/ada/pubs/ada.txt.

Aristotle. 1944. *Generation of Animals*. Trans. A.L. Peck. Cambridge: Harvard UP.

Asch, Adrienne, and Gail Geller. 1996. "Feminism, Bioethics and Genetics." In *Feminism, Bioethics: Beyond Reproduction*, ed. S.M. Wolf, 318–50. Oxford: Oxford UP.

Battin, Margaret P., Rosamond Rhodes, and Anita Silvers, eds. 1998. *Physician Assisted Suicide: Expanding the Debate*. New York: Routledge.

Bordo, Susan. 1994. "Reading the Male Body." In *The Male Body*, ed. Laurence Goldstein, 265–306. Ann Arbor: U of Michigan P.

———. 1993. *Unbearable Weight: Feminism, Western Culture and the Body*. Berkeley: U of California P.

Braidotti, Rosi. 1994. *Nomadic Subjects: Embodiment and Sexual Difference in Contemporary Feminist Thought*. New York: Columbia UP.

Brownsworth, Victoria A., and Susan Raffo, eds. 1999. *Restricted Access: Lesbians on Disability*. Seattle: Seal Press.

Butler, Judith. 1993. *Bodies that Matter*. New York: Routledge.

———. 1990. *Gender Trouble*. New York: Routledge.

Bynum, Caroline Walker. 1999. "Shape and Story: Metamorphosis in the Western Tradition." Paper presented at NEH Jefferson Lecture. 22 March, at Washington, DC.

Clark, David L., and Catherine Myser. 1996. "Being Humaned: Medical Documentaries and the Hyperrealization of Conjoined Twins." In *Freakery: Cultural Spectacles of the Extraordinary Body*, ed. Rosemarie Garland Thomson, 338–55. New York: New York UP.

Davis, Lennard. 1995. *Enforcing Normalcy: Disability, Deafness, and the Body*. New York: Verso.

De Beauvoir, Simone. (1952) 1974. *The Second Sex*. Trans. H.M. Parshley. New York: Vintage Press.

Dreger, Alice Domurat. 1998a. *Hermaphrodites and the Medical Invention of Sex*. Cambridge: Harvard UP.

——. 1998b. "The Limits of the Individuality: Ritual and Sacrifice in the Lives and Medical Treatment of Conjoined Twins." In *Freakery: Cultural Spectacles of the Extraordinary Body*, ed. Rosemarie Garland–Thomson, 338–55. New York: New York UP.

Eiesland, Nancy. 1994. *The Disabled God: Toward a Liberatory Theology of Disability*. Nahsville: Abingdon Press.

Fausto-Sterling, Anne. 2000. *Sexing the Body: Gender Politics and the Construction of Sexuality*. New York: Basic Books.

——. 1995. "Gender, Race, and Nation: The Comparative Anatomy of Hottentot Women in Europe, 1815–1817." In *Deviant Bodies: Cultural Perspectives in Science and Popular Culture*, eds. Jennifer Terry and Jacqueline Urla, 19–48. Bloomington: Indiana UP.

Fine, Michelle, and Adrienne Asch, eds. 1988. *Women with Disabilities: Essays in Psychology, Culture, and Politics*. Philadelphia: Temple UP.

Finger, Anne. 1990. *Past Due: A Story of Disability, Pregnancy, and Birth*. Seattle: Seal Press.

Fiske, Susan T., Amy J. C. Cuddy, and Peter Glick. 2001. "A Model of (Often Mixed) Stereotype Content: Competence and Warmth Respectively Follow from Perceived Status and Competition." Unpublished study.

Foucault, Michel. 1979. *Discipline and Punish: The Birth of the Prison*. Trans. Alan M. Sheridan-Smith. New York: Vintage Books.

Garland–Thomson, Rosemarie. 1999. "Narratives of Deviance and Delight: Staring at Julia Pastrana, 'The Extraordinary Lady.'" In *Beyond the Binary*, ed. Timothy Powell, 81–106. New Brunswick: Rutgers UP.

Gilman, Sander L. 1999. *Making the Body Beautiful*. Princeton: Princeton UP.

——. 1998. *Creating Beauty to Cure the Soul*. Durham: Duke UP.

——. 1985. *Difference and Pathology: Stereotypes of Sexuality, Race, and Madness*. Ithaca: Cornell UP.

Hahn, Harlan. 1988. "Can Disability Be Beautiful?" *Social Policy* 18 (Winter): 26–31.

Haiken, Elizabeth. 1997. *Venus Envy: A History of Cosmetic Surgery*. Baltimore: Johns Hopkins UP.

Haraway, Donna. 1991. *Simians, Cyborgs, and Women*. New York: Routledge.

Harstock, Nancy. 1983. "The Feminist Standpoint: Developing the Ground for a Specifically Feminist Historical Materialism." In *Discovering Reality*, eds. Sandra Harding and Merrell Hintikka, 283–305. Dortrecht, Holland: Reidel Publishing.

Herndl, Diane Price. 2002. "Reconstructing the Post-human Feminist Body: Twenty Years after Audre Lorde's *Cancer Journals*." In *Disability Studies: Enabling the Humanities*, eds. Sharon Snyder, Brenda Brueggemann, and Rosemarie Garland-Thomson, 144–55. New York: MLA Press.

Hillyer, Barbara. 1993. *Feminism and Disability*. Norman: U of Oklahoma P.

Hubbard, Ruth. 1990. "Who Should and Who Should Not Inhabit the World?" In *The Politics of Women's Biology*, 179–98. New Brunswick: Rutgers UP.

Keller, Evelyn Fox. 1992. "Nature, Nurture and the Human Genome Project." In *The Code of Codes: Scientific and Social Issues in the Human Genome Project*, eds. Daniel J. Kevles and Leroy Hood, 281–99. Cambridge: Harvard UP.

Kessler, Suzanne J. 1990. *Lessons from the Intersexed*. New Brunswick: Rutgers UP.

Kittay, Eva Feder. 1999. *Love's Labor: Essays on Women, Equality, and Dependency*. New York: Routledge.

Kittay, Eva, with Leo Kittay. 2000. "On the Expressivity and Ethics of Selective Abortion for Disability: Conversations with My Son." In *Prenatal Testing and Disability Rights*, eds. Erik Parens and Adrienne Asch, 165–95. Georgetown: Georgetown UP.

Linton, Simi. 1998. *Claiming Disability: Knowledge and Identity*. New York: New York UP.

Longmore, Paul K. 1997. "Conspicuous Contribution and American Cultural Dilemmas: Telethon Rituals of Cleansing and Renewal." In *The Body and Physical Difference: Discourses of Disability*, eds. David Mitchell and Sharon Snyder, 134–58. Ann Arbor: U of Michigan P.

Lorde, Audre. 1980. *The Cancer Journals*. San Francisco: Spinsters Ink.

Mairs, Nancy. 1996. *Waist High in the World: A Life Among the Disabled*. Boston: Beacon Press.

McRuer, Robert. 1999. "Compulsory Able-Bodiedness and Queer/Disabled Existence." Paper presented at MLA Convention, 28 December, at Chicago, IL.

"Meet Ellen Stohl." 1987. *Playboy*. July: 68–74

Morrison, Toni. 1992. *Playing in the Dark: Whiteness and the Literary Imagination*. Cambridge: Harvard UP.

Parens, Erik, and Adrienne Asch. 2000. *Prenatal Testing and Disability Rights*. Georgetown: Georgetown UP.

Piercy, Marge. 1969. "Unlearning Not to Speak." In *Circles on Water*, 97. New York: Doubleday.

Rand, Erica. 1995. *Barbie's Queer Accessories*. Durham: Duke UP.

Rapp, Rayna. 1999. *Testing Women, Testing the Fetus:*

The Social Impact of Amniocentesis in America. New York: Routledge.

Rich, Adrienne. 1986. "Compulsory Heterosexuality and Lesbian Existence." In *Blood, Bread, and Poetry*, 23–75. New York: Norton.

Riley, Denise. 1999. "Bodies, Identities, Feminisms." In *Feminist Theory and the Body: A Reader*, eds. Janet Price and Margrit Shildrick, 220–6. Edinburgh, Scotland: Edinburgh UP.

Russo, Mary. 1994. *The Female Grotesque: Risk, Excess, and Modernity.* New York: Routledge.

Saxton, Marsha. 1998. "Disability Rights and Selective Abortion." In *Abortion Wars: A Half Century of Struggle (1950-2000)*, ed. Ricky Solinger, 374–93. Berkeley: U of California P.

Scott, Joan Wallach. 1988. "Gender as Useful Category of Analysis." In *Gender and the Politics of History*, 29–50. New York: Columbia UP.

Sedgwick, Eve Kosofsky. 1990. *Epistemology of the Closet.* Berkeley: U of California P.

Silvers, Anita. 1995. "Reconciling Equality to Difference: Caring (f)or Justice for People with Disabilities." *Hypatia* 10(1): 30–55.

Spelman, Elizabeth, V. 1988. *Inessential Woman: Problems of Exclusion in Feminist Thought.* Boston: Beacon Press.

——. 1997. *Extraordinary Bodies: Figuring Physical Disability in American Culture and Literature.* New York: Columbia UP.

Tuana, Nancy. 1993. *The Less Noble Sex: Scientific, Religious and Philosophical Conceptions of Woman's Nature.* Indianapolis: Indiana UP.

Wald, Priscilla. 2000. "Future Perfect: Grammar, Genes, and Geography." *New Literary History* 31(4): 681–708.

Williams, John M. 1999. "And Here's the Pitch: Madison Avenue Discovers the 'Invisible Consumer.'" *WE Magazine*, July/August: 28–31.

Wolf, Naomi. 1991. *The Beauty Myth: How Images of Beauty Are Used Against Women.* New York: William Morrow and Co.

Young, Iris Marion. 1990a. "Breasted Experience." In *Throwing Like a Girl and Other Essays in Feminist Philosophy and Social Theory*, 189–209. Bloomington: Indiana UP.

——. 1990b. "Throwing Like a Girl." In *Throwing Like a Girl and Other Essays in Feminist Philosophy and Social Theory*, 141–59. Bloomington: Indiana UP.

CHAPTER 26

Unspeakable Offenses: Untangling Race and Disability in Discourses of Intersectionality

Nirmala Erevelles and Andrea Minear

The Literature of Critical Race Feminist Theory approaches disability as an expression of intersectional identity wherein devalued social characteristics compound stigma resulting in so-called spirit murder. Three diverging practices of intersectionality are identified as guiding scholarship on the constitutive features of multiply minoritizing identities: (1) anticategorical frameworks that insist on race, class, and gender as social constructs/fictions; (2) intracategorical frameworks that critique merely additive approaches to differences as layered stigmas; and (3) constitutive frameworks that describe the structural conditions within which social categories in the above models are constructed by (and intermesh with) each other in specific historical contexts. In being true to Critical Race Feminist Theory approaches, the article draws on two other narratives, one historical and one contemporary, to describe how individuals located perilously at the intersections of race, class, gender, *and* disability are constituted as non-citizens and (no)bodies by the very social institutions (legal, educational, and rehabilitational) that are designed to protect, nurture, and empower them.

On October 29, 1984, Eleanor Bumpurs, a 270 pound, arthritic, sixty-seven year old woman was shot to death while resisting eviction from her apartment in the Bronx. She was $98.85, or one month, behind in her rent. New York City mayor Ed Koch and police commissioner Benjamin Ward described the struggle preceding her demise as involving two officers with plastic shields, one officer with a restraining hook, another officer with a shotgun, and at least one supervising officer. All the officers also carried service revolvers. According to Commissioner Ward, during the course of the attempted eviction Eleanor Bumpurs escaped from the restraining hook twice and wielded a knife that Commissioner Ward said was "bent" on one of the plastic shields. At some point, Officer Stephen Sullivan, the officer positioned furthest away from her aimed and fired his shotgun. It is alleged that the blast removed half of her hand so that, according to the Bronx district attorney's office, "it was anatomically impossible for her to hold the knife." The officer pumped his gun and shot again, making his mark completely the second time around.

(Williams, 271)

In her essay, "Spirit Murdering the Messenger," Critical Race Feminist (CRF) Patricia Williams describes the brutal murder of a poor, elderly, overweight, disabled, black woman by several heavily armed police officers. Trapped at the intersections of multiple oppressive contexts, Eleanor Bumpurs's tattered body was quite literally torn apart by her multiple selves—being raced, classed, gendered, and disabled. In the essay, Williams reads this murder as an unambiguous example of "racism [experienced] as . . . an offense so painful and assaultive as to constitute . . . 'spirit murder'" (230). Toward the end of the essay Williams struggles to fathom why the officer who fired the fatal shots saw such an "'immediate threat and endangerment to life'. . . . [that he] could not allay his need to kill a sick old lady fighting off hallucinations with a knife" (234). In this quote, Williams recognizes Eleanor Bumpurs's disability when invoking her arthritis and possible mental illness. However, Williams deploys disability merely as a descriptor, a difference that is a matter of "magnitude" or "context," what another CRF scholar, Angela Harris, has described as "nuance theory" (14). According to Harris, "nuance theory constitutes black women's oppression as only an intensified example of (white) women's oppression" and is therefore used as the "ultimate example of how bad things [really] are" for all women (15).

While we agree with the critique of nuance theory in feminist analyses that ignore the real experiences of black women, we argue that CRF scholars deploy a similar analytical tactic through their unconscious non-analysis of disability as it intersects with race, class, and gender oppression. Disability, like race, offers not just a "nuance" to any analysis of difference. For example, one could argue that the outrage emanating from a heaving, black body wielding a knife sent a nervous (and racist) police officer into panic when confronted by his own racialized terror of otherness. But what about the other ideological terrors that loomed large in this encounter? Could the perception of Eleanor Bumpurs as a dangerous, obese, irrational, black woman also have contributed to her construction as criminally "insane" (disability) because her reaction to a "mere" legal matter of eviction (class) was murderous rage? And did our socially sanctioned fears of the mentally ill and our social devaluation of disabled (arthritic and elderly) bodies of color justify the volley of shots fired almost instinctively to protect the public from the deviant, the dangerous, and the disposable? We, therefore, argue that in the violent annihilation of Eleanor Bumpurs's being, disability as it intersects with race, class, and gender served more than just a "context" or "magnifier" to analyze the oppressive conditions that caused this murder.

In this article, we demonstrate how the omission of disability as a critical category in discussions of intersectionality has disastrous and sometimes deadly consequences for disabled people of color caught at the violent interstices of multiple differences. In the first section, we will theorize intersectionality as first proposed by Crenshaw and explore the different ways in which it can be utilized by both Critical Race Theory and Disability Studies to analyze the experiences of people located at the interstices of multiple differences. Next, true to CRT tradition, we draw on two other narratives, one historical and one contemporary, to describe how individuals located perilously at the interstices of race, class, gender, *and* disability are constituted as non-citizens and (no) bodies by the very social institutions (legal, educational, and rehabilitational) that are designed to protect, nurture, and empower them.

INTERSECTIONALITY AT THE CROSSROADS: THEORIZING MULTIPLICATIVE DIFFERENCES

With the deconstruction of essentialism, the challenge of how to theorize identity in all its complex multiplicity has preoccupied feminist scholars of color.[1] Kimberle Crenshaw, one of the key proponents of the theory of intersectionality, has argued that "many of the experiences black women face are not subsumed within the traditional boundaries of race or gender oppression as these boundaries are currently understood" (358). Part of the problem of "relying on a static and singular notion of being or of identity" (Pastrana, 75) is that the single characteristic that is foregrounded (e.g. female or black) is expected to explain all of the other life experiences of the individual or the group. Additionally, Crenshaw points out that social movements based on a single identity politics (e.g. the Feminist Movement, Black Power Movement, GLBT and the Disability Rights Movement) have historically conflated or ignored intragroup differences and this has sometimes resulted in growing tensions between the social movements themselves.

Feminists of color have, therefore, had the difficult task of attempting to theorize oppression faced at the multiple fronts of race, class, gender, sexuality, and disability.[2] Thus, if one is poor, black, elderly, disabled, and lesbian, must these differences be organized into a hierarchy such that some differences gain prominence over others? What if some differences coalesce to create a more abject form of oppression (e.g. being poor, black, and disabled) or if some differences support both privilege/invisibility within the same oppressed community (e.g. being black, wealthy, and gay)? What happens if we use "race" as a stable register of oppression against which other discriminations gain validity through their similarity and difference from that register? (Arondekar).

In the face of this theoretical challenge, intersectionality has been set up as the most appropriate analytical intervention expected to accomplish the formidable task of mediating multiple differences. For example, Patricia Hill Collins writes that "[a]s opposed to examining gender, race, class, and nation as separate systems of oppression, intersectionality explores how these systems mutually construct

one another . . ." (63). CRF Adrien Wing writes:

> We, as black women, can no longer afford to think of ourselves as merely the sum of separate parts that can be added together or subtracted from, until a white male or female stands before you. The actuality of our experience is multiplicative. Multiply each of my parts together, WE X WE X WE X WE X I, and you have *one* indivisible being. If you divide one of these parts from one you still have one.
>
> (31)

But this is all much easier said than done. Attempts to deploy intersectionality as an analytical tool in academic research have taken on different forms with varying analytical outcomes—some more useful than others. McCall, in an overview of how intersectionality has been utilized in women studies' scholarship, has identified three different modes of theorizing intersectionality. The first mode uses an *anticategorical* framework based on the poststructuralist argument that social categories like race, gender, sexuality, and disability are merely social constructions/fictions. CRF scholars are, however, unwilling to completely do away with the social categories that constitute identity in the first place. As Crenshaw explains:

> To say that a category such as race and gender is socially constructed is not to say that the category has no significance in our world. On the contrary, a large and continuing project for subordinated people . . . is thinking about the way in which power is clustered around certain categories and is exercised against others.
>
> (375)

As a result, feminists of color are more apt to use an *intracategorical* framework that focuses on "particular social groups at neglected points of intersection of multiple master categories" (McCall, 1780). As Crenshaw explains:

[I]ntersectionality provides a basis for reconceptualizing race as a coalition between men and women of color ... Intersectionality may provide the means for dealing with other marginalizations as well. For example, race can also be a coalition of straight and gay people of color, and thus serve as a basis for critique of churches and other cultural institutions that reproduce heterosexism.

(377)

The intracategorical framework is especially promising to CRF scholars because it validates the reality of racism as it intersects with sexism and other social categories of difference (e.g. heterosexism; classism) in the everyday lives of women of color. However, Yuval-Davis, while producing a list of possible differences (potentially incomplete) that includes "'race'/skin color; ethnicity; nation/state; class, culture; ability; age; sedentariness/origin; wealth; North-South; religion, stage of social development" (203), asks if it is even conceivable to address all these possible social categories intersecting with a common master category (e.g. race or gender) at any given time? Do some differences acquire greater prominence than others (e.g. sexuality)? Are some "other" differences just added on to merely complicate and "nuance" this intersectional analysis (e.g. disability)?

If the intracategorical framework rejects merely tacking on another difference to its litany of categories (e.g. disability), it would have to, in effect, reject the additive approach to multiple differences and instead utilize what Yuval-Davis has described as the constitutive approach to multiple differences. This approach, while foregrounding the actual experiences of women of color at the intersection of multiple social categories, also describes the structural conditions within which these social categories are constructed by, and intermeshed with each other in specific historical contexts. McCall calls this third approach to theorizing intersectionality the *intercategorical* framework. Yuval-Davis explains:

> The point of intersectional analysis is not to find "several identities under one".... This would reinscribe the fragmented, additive model of oppression and essentialize specific social identities. Instead the point is to analyse the differential ways by which social divisions are concretely enmeshed and constructed by each other and how they relate to political and subjective constructions of identities.
>
> (205)

Therefore, rather than merely adding disability to nuance an intersectional analysis, we will foreground the historical contexts and structural conditions within which the identity categories of race and disability intersect.

POINTS OF CONTACT: AT THE INTERSECTION OF CRT AND DISABILITY STUDIES

In educational contexts, the association of race with disability has resulted in large numbers of students of color (particularly African American and Latino males) being subjected to segregation in so-called special-education classrooms through sorting practices such as tracking and/or through labels such as mild mental retardation and/or emotional disturbance.[3] The PBS film, *Beyond Brown: Pursuing the Promise* (Haddad, Readdean, & Valadez) substantiates these claims with the following statistics.

- Black children constitute 17 percent of the total school enrollment, but 33 percent of those labeled "mentally retarded."
- During the 1998–1999 school year more than 2.2 million children of color in U.S. schools were served by special education. Post-high school outcomes

for these students were striking. Among high school youth with disabilities, about 75 percent of African Americans, compared to 39 percent of whites, are still not employed three to five years out of school. In this same time period, the arrest rate for African Americans with disabilities is 40 percent, compared to 27 percent for whites.

- States with a history of legal school segregation account for five of the seven states with the highest overrepresentation of African Americans labeled mentally retarded. They are Mississippi, South Carolina, North Carolina, Florida, and Alabama.
- Among Latino students, identification for special education varies significantly from state to state. Large urban schools districts in California exhibit disproportionately large numbers of Latino English-language learners represented in special education classes in secondary schools.
- Some 20 percent of Latino students in grades 7 through 12 had been suspended from school according to statistics from 1999 compared with 15 percent of white students and 35 percent of African American students.

The association of race with disability has been extremely detrimental to people of color in the U.S.—not just in education, but also historically where associations of race with disability have been used to justify the brutality of slavery, colonialism, and neo-colonialism. Unfortunately, rather than nurturing an alliance between race and disability, CRT scholars (like other radical scholars) have mistakenly conceived of disability as a biological category, as an immutable and pathological abnormality rooted in the "medical language of symptoms and diagnostic categories" (Linton, 8). Disability studies scholars, on the other hand, have critiqued this "deficit" model of disability and have described disability as a socially constructed category that derives meaning and social (in)significance from the historical, cultural, political, and economic structures that frame social life.

Thus, at the first point of contact, both CRT and disability scholars begin with the critical assumption that race and disability are, in fact, social constructs. Thus, Haney Lopez explains "Biological race is an illusion. . . . Social race, however, is not. . . . Race has its genesis and maintains its vigorous strength in the realm of social beliefs" (172). Similarly, Garland-Thomson describes disability as "the attribution of corporeal deviance—not so much a property of bodies [but rather] . . . a product of cultural rules about what bodies should be or do" (6). At their second point of contact, race and disability are both theorized as relational concepts. Thus, CRT scholars argue that "[r]aces are constructed relationally against one another, rather than in isolation" (Haney Lopez, 168) such that the privileges that Whites enjoy are linked to the subordination of people of color (Harris). Similarly, Lennard Davis points out that "our construction of the normal world is based on a radical repression of disability" (22) because "without the monstrous body to demarcate the borders of the generic . . . and without the pathological to give form to the normal, the taxonomies of bodily value that underlie political, social and economic arrangements would collapse" (Garland-Thomson, 20). Finally, at the third point of contact, both perspectives use stories and first-person accounts to foreground the perspectives of those who have experienced victimization by racism and ableism first-hand (Espinoza and Harris; Angela Harris; Ladson-Billings and Tate IV; Parker, Deyhle, and Villenas; Linton; Connor).

In building on these alliance possibilities, disability-studies scholars have argued that disability is, in fact, constitutive of most social differences, particularly race (Baynton; Erevelles; James and Wu). One example to support the above claim lies in the historical narrative of eugenics as a program of selective breeding to prevent the degeneration of the human species. Colonial ideologies conceiving of the colonized races as intrinsically degenerate sought to bring these "bodies" under control via segregation and/or destruction. Such control was regarded as necessary for the public good. The association of degeneracy and disease with racial difference also translated into an attribution of diminished cognitive and rational capacities of non-white populations. Disability related labels such as feeble-mindedness and mental illness were often seen as synonymous with bodies marked oppressively by race (Baynton; Gould). Fearing that such characteristics could be passed down from generation to generation and further pose a threat to the dominant white race, "protective" practices such as forced sterilizations, rigid miscegenation laws, residential segregation in ghettoes, barrios, reservations and other state institutions and sometimes even genocide (e.g. the Holocaust) were brought to bear on non-white populations under the protected guise of eugenics. However, constructing the degenerate "other" was not just an ideological intervention to support colonialism. In the more contemporary context of transnational capitalism, Erevelles argues that:

> the 'ideology' of disability is essential to the capitalist enterprise because it is able to regulate and control the unequal distribution of surplus through invoking biological difference as the 'natural' cause of all inequality, thereby successfully justifying the social and economic inequality that maintains social hierarchies ... [D]isability ... is [therefore] the organizing grounding principle in the construction of the categories of gender, race, class, and sexual orientation.
>
> (526)

It is easy to dismiss eugenics as a relic of a bygone era, but the continued association of race and disability in debilitating ways necessitates that we examine how eugenic practices continue to reconstitute social hierarchies in contemporary contexts via the deployment of a hegemonic ideology of disability that have real material effects on people located at the intersections of difference. To illustrate the argument, we will now draw on the narratives of two protagonists, Junius Wilson and Cassie Smith.

THE "UNSPEAKABLE" LIFE OF JUNIUS WILSON

The first narrative, the story of Junius Wilson, poignantly told in Susan Burch and Hannah Joyner's book, *Unspeakable: The Life of Junius Wilson,* occurred at the intersection of disability, race, gender, and class. Born in 1908 to Sidney and Mary Wilson in the predominantly African American community of Castle Hayne on the outskirts of Wilmington, North Carolina, Junius Wilson became deaf as a toddler. The tensions of raising a deaf child in poverty conditions within a political context of racial violence caused Sidney Wilson to desert his family, forcing his wife Mary to send the young Wilson to the residential North Carolina School for the Colored Blind and Deaf in Raleigh. In the segregated school in Raleigh, Wilson was initiated into a "black deaf community" and "Raleigh signs" that were specific to the school and that had almost no currency elsewhere—a fact that would later contribute to Wilson's social isolation in both the deaf and the black communities. Additionally, in line with racist ideologies of African American students' low mental capacities, the school encouraged vocational work over traditional classroom work, so while Wilson could write his name out, he was unable to read and write anything else. Then, in 1924, Wilson was expelled from the school because of a minor infraction and forced to return home.

Returning home from Raleigh, Wilson's habits of "touching or holding people, stamping feet and waving arms" (33) constructed him as a threatening figure in a society ruled by Jim Crow laws—habits that could compromise the safety of himself, his familiy, and his community. It was perhaps for all these reasons and in an effort to protect his family and his community that Arthur Smith, the family friend, accused the 17-year-old Junius Wilson of assaulting and attempting to rape his young wife, Lizzie. Thus, in August, 1925, Junius Wilson was arrested and taken to New Hanover County jail. Unable to communicate with Wilson, the court held a lunacy hearing where it was concluded that Wilson was both "feeble-minded" and dangerous, and was therefore committed to the criminal ward of the North Carolina State Hospital for the Colored Insane in Goldsboro that housed epileptics, "idiots," and other "mental defectives" and exerted institutional control rather than practices of healing.

With eugenics ideologies dominant in the early twentieth century, one means of social control was castration, the surgical removal of the testicles. Thus, in 1932, Wilson was castrated and henceforth was no longer perceived as a danger because he became "a submissive black man . . . [with] eyes downcast, silent, and reserved . . . a gentle childlike patient" (49). Seen now as a potentially useful worker, Wilson was sent to work in the Farm Colony (the farm attached to the hospital) and was leased to private farmers till his retirement in 1970, where he was transferred to a geriatric ward. Even though all charges against him were dropped by then, he continued to be incarcerated for another twenty years because it was conceived of as "the most benevolent course of action" (1).

In the 1970s, in response to the Civil Rights of Institutionalized Persons Act, Carolina Legal Assistance (CLA), a group of attorneys in Raleigh, found scores of African American men and women "dumped in hospitals, abandoned by communities, and otherwise mislabeled as feebleminded" (124), one of whom was Junius Wilson. After several years of lawsuits and the involvement of advocates and family members, Wilson was moved out to a cottage on the grounds of the hospital on February 4, 1994. He died on March 17, 2001. Hovering precipitously at the boundaries of race, class, gender, *and* disability, Wilson had been held in the isolating confines of the institution for more than three quarters of his life. Overwhelmed by the enormity of the crime committed against Wilson, Burch and Joyner (2007) ask, "How should a society—indeed, how can a society—make amends for past misdeeds?" (3).

But society seldom makes amends for past misdeeds. On the contrary, it is often apt to repeat them. Junius Wilson's story took place in the early twentieth century. Our second narrative, Cassie Smith's story, takes place in the present, almost a century later. The terrifying aspect of Cassie's story is that it continues Wilson's narrative, in effect becoming its sequel by once again foregrounding the violence that lies at the intersection of race, class, gender, *and* disability.

HER TIME IS UP! CASSIE GOTTA GO! EXCLUSION AT THE INTERSECTIONS

One of the authors of this article, Andrea, had met Cassie two years ago at the home school cooperative, DAWN, which she ran for students like Cassie who did not seem to "fit" in public school. Cassie's mother, Aliya Smith, a single mother on disability for the last 15 years, lives in public housing with her daughter Cassie and her six-year-old son Charles in a small southern town.

Cassie's father lives close by but has been mostly absent from her life. She had been very close to her grandmother who passed away a year ago.

On her first day at DAWN, Cassie tried desperately to fit in with the other eight adolescent girls at the school. She was dressed neatly. But she had severe eczema on her skin and was eyed suspiciously by the other girls as if her rash was contagious. Her hair was braided stylishly, but her braids were already loosening and falling out because she picked at her head continuously. Her big toothy grin gave way to raucous laughter, much louder than the children in the small school were used to. She tried so hard to be friendly, but she was met with wariness.

After barely less than a day of observation and evaluation, Andrea realized that Cassie could not read—a fact that she had successfully hidden from even her closest friends. When asked to write a journal entry, her sentences contained a string of three letter words that made little sense such as "pig as you as zoo cat by as no as dog pig as zoo no by you as zoo as cat red." Cassie "pretended" very well, opening her book, following along and even reading "along with" someone, saying a word immediately after the other person began the word. Because she did not read, she had limited knowledge of other subject areas. She could barely add and could not subtract. She recognized some coins, but could not figure money. Andrea realized with dismay that twelve-year-old Cassie was functionally illiterate.

When we interviewed Cassie and her mother, her turbulent and tragic educational history was slowly revealed. We learned to our horror that Cassie had been bounced around to a different school every year of her school life; two schools in some years. As a toddler, Cassie spent a lot of time with her grandmother because of Aliya's poor health. At age four, Cassie started out in a private preschool program at the Holy Trinity Baptist School. Without the benefit of records or first-hand knowledge, we wonder whether the fact that Cassie was an economically disadvantaged black child in an all-white school caused her to appear "behind" and uncontrollable. Aliya recalls, "She used to get temper tantrums and they told me if I couldn't get her straightened up, she gotta go!" Aliya moved Cassie to the Head Start program and then to her neighborhood school for kindergarten:

> And then they [the school personnel] said that she needed help (Cassie interjects: "No, I don't!"). So we had to go through evaluations, meetings, and stuff. They tried to say that she was mentally retarded. (Cassie interjects, "I am not MR!") . . . [Aliya continues in response to Cassie] But she was then. So they sent her to "Sally's Corner."

In this small southern town, "Sally's Corner" was touted as the haven for kids with severe emotional and behavioral problems. In its mission statement the school claimed to offer treatment based on "an interdisciplinary approach with psychology, education, nursing, psychiatry, social work and counseling comprising the professions that impact each client's treatment." The website also included several testimonials from parents and one child that described "Sally's Corner" very positively. Cassie's memories of "Sally's Corner," however, were very dark:

> Cassie: ["Sally's Corner"] is like a bad place. They put you there when you get in trouble. They restrain you. They put your arms like this . . . sit on you kinda and put you in a room where no windows at and a little time out room by yourself. . . . And they come and look at you. And I say, "Let me out" and kick the door. . . .

NE: What is it that that gets you really angry?

Cassie: When somebody tries to fight with me and pull my hair

NE: But the teachers don't try to fight with you, do they?

Cassie: Oh I'll still fight you the big ole fat ole . . . sit on me . . . Half ton white folks.

By Cassie's own admission, we can understand that she was no easy client, and it is reasonable to assume that Cassie was in need of some kind of program that would help manage her fits of rage so she could also learn. And surely, they had all that expertise from the multi-disciplinary team to do something for her. But again, we do not really know what happened there except for this explanation from Aliya about why she wanted Cassie to leave "Sally's Corner" after only a couple of months there:

> They locked you up all the time. They had this jail cell. She had spit on the wall while she was in there. They called my mama [Cassie's grandmother]. I was sick at that time. My mama and my sister-in-law went. My mama was so mad when she went out there. She told them, "Open the door. Let that child outta there!" My mama did not understand. Actually she did not care. Like she [Cassie] was being treated like a dog or something . . . And then they said that before she left she had to scrub the room. My mama said, "Get that child outta there!" And they said she could not leave before she did that. So my mom told Cassie what were the spots that she spit at. And to clean just them. They wanted her to clean the whole room! Then she got to get ready to go. . . . It was time for her to go. . . . Kept on trying to get her out. . . . They finally agreed and I got her to go to Woodberry Gardens.

Once again, while we acknowledge that we have only one side of the story, there are aspects that still puzzle us. Surely "a model treatment program" had more options for a small, angry five-year-old African American girl with anger-management issues than being thrown into a "jail cell"? What was it about that tiny enraged black body that terrified the staff so much that they threw all their knowledge out of the window, opting instead for the behavioral strategy of "imprisonment"?

This was the educational legacy that Cassie would carry forward with her as she moved into the first grade at her new elementary school, Woodberry Gardens. After two good years she was inexplicably moved to Spartan Elementary and once again to Nottingham. Each time, as Aliya put it, they told her that "It was time for her to leave there . . . Her time was up."

Apparently, at this time, Cassie no longer held the label "mental retardation." Still, when asked, her mother just says, "She acted crazy!" She was now thrown into a regular program at Nottingham Elementary with no supports. Once again her academic and behavioral problems were exacerbated. Once again she was teased and called names by her peers. Once again she fought back— she cut a classmate's hair. And once again she suffered the consequences of her negative behavior. Less than two months before her graduation from elementary school, Cassie was transferred to her eighth school, Athena Elementary. Aliya was livid:

> You talking about somebody was mad. No! I could never understand why they sent her to Athena. I went over there and met with the teacher. . . . It had something to do with her learning. There was a month and half to graduate and they sent her to Athena. Then that teacher was up there ill-treating her. . . . They wanted her to graduate with her Athena [special education] class. And I said, "I didn't spend all that money and time at Nottingham for this. I was so mad. I told them that I would have her out of school if they would not let me take her out [of Athena]. Then they listened. When they figured out that I was not playing with them, they got

those papers. Like they couldn't get them fast enough. They just moved them in the office. And I took her to Nottingham and she was there was for three days so that she could graduate with her class. And they did it [the graduation ceremony] in such a way, that she had to be escorted. Like she was such a bad child. Like she was coming from prison. Her last two teachers had to walk with her side by side. She was the last one to walk.

Thus, after being in eight schools in eight years, Cassie came to DAWN, the home-school cooperative, as a sixth grader with a plethora of problems. In this supportive context, Cassie made great leaps in her social behavior and even made some academic headway. However, Andrea was forced to close DAWN at the end of the year for financial reasons, and so Cassie prepared to re-enter public school in the next fall.

Eager to learn, but receiving very little help in school, Cassie soon got frustrated and into fights again. She was sent to the Alternative School which ironically she actually liked because of the structure and individual attention. But then, even this realm of contentment vanished one day— the day of the "incident." One spring day, six students (four boys and two girls) were left without supervision in a classroom for a few minutes while one of the teachers walked a student to his car to speak to his mother. The boys teased and taunted the girls making rude, sometimes vulgar, suggestions and then laughing them off. One of the boys told Cassie, "So-and-so thinks you're pretty. He wants you to suck his dick." And so she went behind the cubbies and obliged.

By the next day, word spread all over the school. As the rumor gathered momentum, more and more people became aware, including the school counselor and the assistant principal. However, neither the classroom teacher, nor the parents of the perpetrators were notified for nearly two

or three weeks. According to the Assistant Principal, there was an ongoing investigation and then a meeting was called with the Building Based Special Team (BBST) and the parent to discuss what they called a "manifestation determination." The question of the day: Was it Cassie's "learning disability" that caused her to have oral sex with a boy in her class or was this done on her own volition? Following "procedure" each member concurred that her "learning disability" could not have caused her to perform oral sex. She knew what she was doing. Therefore she was GUILTY. Under the zero-tolerance policy, this called for expulsion.

Not once did the committee even bother to look at Cassie's painful history of exclusion, segregation, incarceration, and negation. It was lucky that Andrea was there. Aliya was a poor advocate for her child. Intimidated, angry, confused, and defensive, she often ended up blaming her daughter for the "stupid thing she did." It was Andrea who saved the day. Drawing on her experiences as a former special education teacher, Andrea brought up Cassie's educational history of social isolation and low self-esteem that were the by-products of her "learning disability" and that may have influenced her decision to perform a sexual act that garnered her some form of warped recognition/respect/visibility among her peers. In addition, Andrea had to spell out the possible legal ramifications of leaving students unsupervised in a locked and isolated classroom for even a short period of time. We believe that it was the last statement that sealed the deal. It was not the history of educational abuse, but the threat of legal ramifications that made the committee decide that they would not recommend expulsion. Cassie would have another chance at school. But whether she would have the support that she needed to make it through another school year was still an open question.

The process of narrating Cassie's educational history during the interviews inadvertently produced an unpredictable benefit for Aliya. In a marked difference from the "professionals" who were reviewing Cassie's case, it was Aliya, confused, angry, troubled, and yet still hopeful, who was able to see how the different disruptive, demeaning, and punitive experiences that began early in Cassie's life were now responsible for the risky, sullen, and disorderly behaviors of her teenage daughter. Now with the gift of hindsight, and therefore conscious of her own disempowerment in the process, Aliya poignantly reflected:

> If I had known the system better, I would not have put her there ["Sally's Corner"]. But at that time I did not know the system. It seemed that they were trying to hurt me, rather than help me.

"UNSPEAKABLE OFFENSES": AN INTERCATEGORICAL ANALYSIS OF INTERSECTIONALITY

Just like Junius Wilson, Cassie is also located at the boundaries of race, class, gender, *and* disability. Each of their stories brings to the forefront several questions: How does racism in its interaction with the inauspicious combination of class, gender, *and* disability oppression cohere to locate Wilson and the Smiths beyond the pale of appropriate interventions by the very institutions (legal, rehabilitative, and educational) that were designed to nurture and empower them? At which point did disability trump race? When did class become the critical influential factor? At what point did gender become the only perceivable threat? In each of the stories, it is very difficult to unravel and isolate the strands that played an integral part in weaving the violent tapestry of their broken lives.

For Junius Wilson, it was the socio-political context of racial terror and abject poverty in the Jim Crow South that constituted his deafness as "dangerous" difference that could only be contained within the institutional confines of a segregated residential school for the "Colored" deaf. Ironically, this confinement provided Wilson with a cultural community of other deaf students of color while it at the same time alienated him from his community outside the school. Additionally, unlike white deaf students, being black and deaf located him at the lowest rungs of the social hierarchy of the time, providing him with an inferior education that would also play a part in his continued social isolation. On returning home, his disability cast a shadow on his race and gender and contributed to his construction as the dangerously virile young black male—images that led to the false accusation of sexual assault, his incarceration, and ultimately to the final violent act of his castration. During that time, he was put to work in the farm colony as part of the surplus population being utilized to produce profits for the institution. Without financial resources and other social supports, his family could do little to intervene on his behalf, which resulted in him languishing in an institution for 76 years. The institution's refusal to release him even after all charges were dropped against him was justified under a mantle of benevolence. It was this same benevolence that allowed the institution to justify the unequal and oppressive conditions in the institution by arguing that "the lack of facilities are not due to racial biases but the fact [that] Negro patients are willing to accept what is provided to them, 'which is more than they have at home'" (Burch & Joyner, 74).

In an earlier section of this article, we wrote that Cassie Smith provided Junius Wilson's story with its unwelcome sequel. At first glance, this assertion may seem far-fetched in the contemporary historical context of the New South where Jim Crow (re)appears as only a distant and shameful memory. Yet, Cassie's story foregrounds an interesting twist to the continuing saga of racial segregation in the New South. In place of Jim Crow, Cassie's ever-changing labels of MR, LD, and ADHD were used as the justification for her continued segregation in an effort to protect the mainstream from a dangerous racialized Other—the economically disadvantaged disabled African American girl. Here, class and race also played a significant role in maintaining this segregation. As educators, we have known privileged white students with similar behavioral problems whose parents were able to corral the school's best resources, were able to access professional help outside the school, and, in the worst case scenario, were able to transfer their child to a private school. Aliya Smith's economic and social disadvantages did not permit her these luxuries. Instead, her disadvantages proved to be a further liability, a signal to the school professionals that there was really no need to "fight" for her daughter Cassie. As a result, even though Cassie had an IEP replete with individualized goals to improve both her behavior and her learning, she never met most of those goals, and nobody cared. This was apparent in her seventh grade report card that listed her as earning As and Bs, even though she was still functionally illiterate and still had little behavior control.

Finally, perhaps most telling is how disability as a "social" not a "clinical" condition was used to establish the benevolence of the special education bureaucracy and in doing so masked the violence that became an inextricable part of Cassie's educational career. Cassie was first MR, then ADHD, and then LD—labels that ebbed and flowed with the passing tides in different contexts. Clearly, given its temporality, "mental retardation" cannot be a robust category. So, could it then be that the educational gatekeepers, when confronted with an allegedly undisciplined, economically disadvantaged, African American girl, fearfully sought the protection of the label "mental retardation"—a label that would justify her incarceration at the tender age of five years old and continue to support her social isolation as it made its punitive march on the successive legs of her young educational career?

We argue here that an intercategorical analysis of intersectionality enables us to foreground the structural context where the social categories of race, class, gender, *and* disability are (re) constituted within the two narratives of Junius Wilson and Cassie Smith. First, we identify disability as the organizing ideological force that is deployed in both narratives as the means to organize the social hierarchies in their respective historical contexts. Here, we describe disability as the very embodiment of the disruption of normativity that is, in turn, symbolic of efficient and profitable individualism and the efficient economic appropriation of those profits produced within capitalist societies. In the early twentieth century, Jim Crow and eugenics served as the two principal mechanisms that patrolled the boundaries of society in order to identify those individuals/communities who were seen as a threat to the normative social order (the status quo) within an incipient capitalist society. The New South replaced those outmoded mechanisms of segregation with more modern systems that were more appropriately in keeping with the times. Thus, for example, in educational contexts the special education bureaucracy with its complex machinery of pseudo-medical evaluations, confusing legal discourses, and overwhelming paperwork administered by a body of intimidating professionals now performs tasks that are not very different from Jim Crow and eugenic ideologies. To put it more simply, special education, instead of being used to individualize education programs to meet the special needs of students, is instead used to segregate students who disrupt the "normal" functioning of schools. Moreover, on the few occasions when Cassie's mother sought to confront them, they invoked their complicated bureaucracy (e.g. using phrases like *manifestation determination)* to further confuse and intimidate her. While we do not deny that Cassie did have significant problems, we argue that the only intervention that was sought by the special education bureaucracy as the most effective was segregation and ultimately incarceration (alternative school and later a very real possibility of prison). Cassie is, no doubt, difficult to manage and perhaps even challenging to care about enough to help her conquer her barriers. But it is her *right* that she *not* be made dispensable.

"SPIRIT MURDER" AND THE "NEW" EUGENICS: CRITICAL RACE THEORY MEETS DISABILITY STUDIES

The three stories of Eleanor Bumpurs, Junius Wilson, and Cassie and Aliya Smith, however poignant they may appear to be, are not unique. Police brutality, false imprisonment, and educational negligence are commonplace in the lives of people of color—especially those who are located at the margins of multiple identity categories. So common are these practices that CRF scholar Patricia Williams has argued that these kinds of assaults should not be dismissed as the "odd mistake" but rather be given a name that associates them with criminality. Her term for such assaults on an individual's personhood is "spirit murder," which she describes as the equivalent of body murder.

> One of the reasons I fear what I call spirit murder, or disregard for others whose lives qualitatively depend on our regard, is

that its product is a system of formalized distortions of thought. It produces social structures centered around fear and hate, it provides a timorous outlet for feelings elsewhere unexpressed ... We need to see it as a cultural cancer; we need to open our eyes to the spiritual genocide it is wreaking on blacks, whites, and the abandoned and abused of all races and ages. We need to eradicate its numbing pathology before it wipes out what precious little humanity we have left.

(234)

Clearly, in our educational institutions there are millions of students of color, mostly economically disadvantaged and disabled, for whom spirit murder is the most significant experience in their educational lives. In fact, it is this recognition of spirit murder in the everyday lives of disabled students of color that forges a critical link between disability studies and CRT/F through the intercategorical analysis of intersectionality. In other words, utilizing an intercategorical analysis from the critical standpoint of disability studies will foreground the structural forces in place that constitute certain students as a surplus population that is of little value in both social and economic terms. That most of these students are poor, disabled, and of color is critical to recognize from within a CRT/F perspective. By failing to undertake such an analysis, we could miss several political opportunities for transformative action.

NOTES

1. See e.g. bell hooks; Angela Davis; Audre Lorde; Gloria Anzaldúa; Gloria Hull, Patricia Bell Scott, and Barbara Smith.
2. For examples, consult Gloria Anzaldúa; Kimberlé Crenshaw; Angela Harris; Adrien Wing; and Audre Lorde.
3. Artiles; Artiles, Harry, Reschly, and Chinn; Connor and Ferri; Reid and Knight; Watts and Erevelles.

WORKS CITED

Anzaldúa, Gloria. *Making Face Making Soul: Haciendo Caras: Creative and Critical Perspectives of Women of Color.* San Francisco: Aunt Lute Books, 1990.

Arondekar, Anjali. "Border/Line Sex: Queer Positionalities, or How Race Matters Outside the United States." *Interventions* 7.2 (2005): 236–50.

Artiles, Alfredo J. "The Dilemma of Difference: Enriching the Disproportionality Discourse with Theory and Content." *Journal of Special Education* 32.1 (1998): 32–7.

Artiles, Alfredo J., Beth Harry, Daniel J. Reschly and Philip C. Chinn. "Over-Identification of Students of Color in Special Education: A Critical Overview." *Multicultural Perspectives* 4.1 (2002): 3–10.

Baynton, Douglas. "Disability in History." *Perspectives* 44.9 (2006): 5–7.

Beyond Brown: Pursuing the Promise. Dir. Lulie Haddad, Cyndee Readdean and John J. Valadez. PBS, 2004.

Burch, Susan and Hannah Joyner. *Unspeakable: The Life of Junius Wilson.* Chapel Hill: U of North Carolina P, 2007.

Connor, David J. *Urban Narratives: Portraits in Progress—Life at the Intersections of Learning Disability, Race, and Class.* New York: Peter Lang, 2007.

Connor, David J. and Beth A. Ferri. "Integration and Inclusion—A Troubling Nexus: Race, Disability, and Special Education." *The Journal of African American History* 90.1/2 (2005): 107–27.

Crenshaw, Kimberlé. "Mapping the Margins: Intersectionality, Identity Politics, and Violence against Women." *Critical Race Theory: The Key Writings that Formed the Movement.* Ed. Kimberlé Crenshaw, Neil Gotanda, Gary Pellar, and Kendall Thomas. New York: New Press, 1996. 357–83.

Davis, Angela.Y. *Women, Race, and Class.* New York: Vintage, 1983.

Davis, Lennard J. *Enforcing Normalcy: Disability, Deafness, and the Body.* New York: Verso, 1995.

Erevelles, Nirmala. "(Im)Material Citizens: Cognitive Disability, Race and the Politics of Citizenship." *Disability, Culture, and Education* 1.1 (2002): 5–25.

Erevelles, Nirmala. "Disability and the Dialectics of Difference." *Disability and Society* 11.4 (1996): 519–37.

Espinoza, Leslie and Angela. P. Harris. "Afterword: Embracing the Tar-Baby—LatCrit Theory and the Stick Mess of Race." *California Law Review* 88.5 (1997): 499–559.

Garland-Thomson, Rosemarie. *Extraordinary Bodies: Figuring Physical Disability in American Culture and Literature.* New York: Columbia UP, 1997.

Gould, Stephen. J. *The Mismeasure of Man.* New York: Norton, 1981.

Haney Lopez, Ian. F. "The Social Construction of Race." *Critical Race Theory: The Cutting Edge.* Ed. Richard Delgado and Jean Stefancic. Philadelphia: Temple UP, 2007. 163–75.

Harris, Angela. "Race and Essentialism in Feminist Legal Theory." *Critical Race Feminism.* Ed. Adrien. K. Wing. New York: New York UP, 1997. 11–26.

Harris, Cheryl I. "Whiteness as Property." *Critical Race Theory: Key Writings that Formed the Movement.* Ed. Kimberlé Crenshaw, Neil Gotanda, Gary Pellar, and Kendall Thomas. New York: New P, 1995. 276–91.

Hill Collins, Patricia. "It's All in the Family: Intersections of Gender, Race, and Nation." *Hypatia* 13.3 (1998): 62–82.

hooks, bell. *Feminist Theory: From Margin to Center.* Cambridge, MA: South End P, 1985.

Hull, Gloria. T., Patricia Bell Scott and Barbara Smith. *All the Women Are White, All the Men Are Black, But some of Us Are Brave.* New York: The Feminist P at CUNY, 1982.

James, Jennifer. C. and Cynthia Wu. "Editors' Introduction: Race, Ethnicity, Disability, and Literature: Intersections and Interventions." *MELUS* 31.3 (2003): 3–13.

Ladson-Billings, Gloria and William F. Tate IV. "Toward a Critical Race Theory of Education." *Teachers College Record* 97.1 (1995): 47–68.

Linton, Simi. *Claiming Disability: Knowledge and Identity.* New York: New York UP, 1998.

Lorde, Audre. *Sister Outside: Essays and Speeches.* Berkeley, CA: The Crossing P Feminist Series, 1984.

McCall, Leslie. "The Complexity of Intersectionality." *Signs: Journal of Women in Culture and Society* 30.3 (2005): 1771–1800.

Parker, Laurence, Donna Deyhle, and Sofia Villenas. *Race Is . . . Race Isn't: Critical Race Theory and Qualitative Studies in Education.* Boulder, CO: Westview P, 1999.

Pastrana, Antonio. "Black Identity Constructions: Inserting Intersectionality, Bisexuality, and (Afro-) Latinidad into Black Studies." *Journal of African American Studies* 8.1–2 (2004): 74–89.

Reid, D. Kim and Michelle G. Knight. "Disability Justifies Exclusion of Minority Students: A Critical History Grounded in Disability Studies." *Educational Researcher* 35.6 (2006): 18–33.

Watts, Ivan and Nirmala Erevelles. "These Deadly Times: Reconceptualizing School Violence by using Critical Race Theory and Disability Studies." *American Educational Research Association* 41.2 (2004): 271–99.

Williams, Patricia. J. "Spirit Murdering the Messenger: The Discourse of Fingerpointing as the Law's Response to Racism." *Critical Race Feminism: A Class Reader.* Ed. Adrien. K. Wing. New York: New York UP, 1997. 229–42.

Wing, Adrien. "Brief Reflections toward a Multiplicative Theory and Praxis of Being." *Critical Race Feminism: A Reader.* Ed. Adrien K. Wing. New York: New York UP, 1997. 27–34.

Yuval-Davis, Nira. "Intersectionality and Feminist Politics." *European Journal of Women's Studies* 13.3 (2006): 193–203.

Compulsory Able-Bodiedness and Queer/Disabled Existence

Robert McRuer

CONTEXTUALIZING DISABILITY

In her famous critique of compulsory heterosexuality Adrienne Rich opens with the suggestion that lesbian existence has often been "simply rendered invisible" (178), but the bulk of her analysis belies that rendering. In fact, throughout "Compulsory Heterosexuality and Lesbian Existence," one of Rich's points seems to be that compulsory heterosexuality depends as much on the ways in which lesbian identities are made visible (or, we might say, comprehensible) as on the ways in which they are made invisible or incomprehensible. She writes:

> Any theory of cultural/political creation that treats lesbian existence as a marginal or less "natural" phenomenon, as mere "sexual preference," or as the mirror image of either heterosexual or male homosexual relations is profoundly weakened thereby, whatever its other contributions. Feminist theory can no longer afford merely to voice a toleration of "lesbianism" as an "alternative life-style," or make token allusion to lesbians. A feminist critique of compulsory heterosexual orientation for women is long overdue. (178)

The critique that Rich calls for proceeds not through a simple recognition or even valuation of "lesbian existence" but rather through an interrogation of how the system of compulsory heterosexuality utilizes that

existence. Indeed, I would extract from her suspicion of mere "toleration" confirmation for the idea that one of the ways in which heterosexuality is currently constituted or founded, established as the foundational sexual identity for women, is precisely through the deployment of lesbian existence as always and everywhere supplementary—the margin to heterosexuality's center, the mere reflection of (straight and gay) patriarchal realities. Compulsory heterosexuality's casting of some identities as alternatives ironically buttresses the ideological notion that dominant identities are not really alternatives but rather the natural order of things.[1]

More than twenty years after it was initially published, Rich's critique of compulsory heterosexuality is indispensable, the criticisms of her ahistorical notion of a "lesbian continuum" notwithstanding.[2] Despite its continued relevance, however, the realm of compulsory heterosexuality might seem to be an unlikely place to begin contextualizing disability.[3] I want to challenge that by considering what might be gained by understanding "compulsory heterosexuality" as a key concept in disability studies. Through a reading of compulsory heterosexuality, I want to put forward a theory of what I call compulsory able-bodiedness. The Latin root for *contextualize* denotes the act of weaving together, inter-weaving, joining together, or composing. This chapter thus contextualizes disability in the root sense of the word, because I argue that the system of compulsory able-bodiedness that produces disability is thoroughly interwoven with the system of compulsory heterosexuality that produces queerness, that—in fact—compulsory heterosexuality is contingent on compulsory able-bodiedness and vice versa. And, although I reiterate it in my conclusion, I want to make it clear at the outset that this particular contextualizing of disability is offered as part of a much larger and collective project of unraveling and decomposing both systems.[4]

The idea of imbricated systems is, of course, not new—Rich's own analysis repeatedly stresses the imbrication of compulsory heterosexuality and patriarchy. I would argue, however, as others have, that feminist and queer theories (and cultural theories generally) are not yet accustomed to figuring ability/disability into the equation, and thus this theory of compulsory able-bodiedness is offered as a preliminary contribution to that much-needed conversation.[5]

ABLE-BODIED HETEROSEXUALITY

In his introduction to *Keywords: A Vocabulary of Culture and Society*, Raymond Williams describes his project as

> the record of an inquiry into a *vocabulary*: a shared body of words and meanings in our most general discussions, in English, of the practices and institutions which we group as *culture* and *society*. Every word which I have included has at some time, in the course of some argument, virtually forced itself on my attention because the problems of its meaning seemed to me inextricably bound up with the problems it was being used to discuss. (15)

Although Williams is not particularly concerned in *Keywords* with feminism or gay and lesbian liberation, the processes he describes should be recognizable to feminists and queer theorists, as well as to scholars and activists in other contemporary movements, such as African American studies or critical race theory. As these movements have developed, increasing numbers of words have indeed forced themselves on our attention, so that an inquiry into not just the marginalized identity but also the dominant identity has become necessary. The problem of the meaning of masculinity (or even maleness), of whiteness, of heterosexuality has increasingly been understood as inextricably bound up with the problems the term is being used to discuss.

One need go no further than the *Oxford English Dictionary* to locate problems with the meaning of heterosexuality. In 1971 the *OED Supplement* defined *heterosexual* as "pertaining to or characterized by the normal relations of the sexes; opp. to *homosexual*." At this point, of course, a few decades of critical work by feminists and queer theorists have made it possible to acknowledge quite readily that heterosexual and homosexual are in fact not equal and opposite identities. Rather, the ongoing subordination of homosexuality (and bisexuality) to heterosexuality allows for heterosexuality to be institutionalized as "the normal relations of the sexes," while the institutionalization of heterosexuality as the "normal relations of the sexes" allows for homosexuality (and bisexuality) to be subordinated. And, as queer theory continues to demonstrate, it is precisely the introduction of normalcy into the system that introduces compulsion: "Nearly everyone," Michael Warner writes in *The Trouble with Normal: Sex, Politics, and the Ethics of Queer Life*, "wants to be normal. And who can blame them, if the alternative is being abnormal, or deviant, or not being one of the rest of us? Put in those terms, there doesn't seem to be a choice at all. Especially in America where [being] normal probably outranks all other social aspirations" (53). Compulsion is here produced and covered over, with the appearance of choice (sexual preference) mystifying a system in which there actually is no choice.

A critique of normalcy has similarly been central to the disability rights movement and to disability studies, with—for example—Lennard Davis's overview and critique of the historical emergence of normalcy or Rosemarie Garland-Thomson's introduction of the concept of the "normate" (Davis, 23–49; Thomson, 8–9). Such scholarly and activist work positions us to locate the problems of able-bodied identity, to see the problem of the meaning of able-bodiedness as bound up with the problems it is being used to discuss. Arguably, able-bodied identity is at this juncture even more naturalized than heterosexual identity. At the very least, many people not sympathetic to queer theory will concede that ways of being heterosexual are culturally produced and culturally variable, even if and even as they understood heterosexual identity itself to be entirely natural. The same cannot be said, on the whole, for able-bodied identity. An extreme example that nonetheless encapsulates currently hegemonic thought on ability and disability is a notorious *Salon* article by Norah Vincent attacking disability studies that appeared online in the summer of 1999. Vincent writes, "It's hard to deny that something called normalcy exists. The human body is a machine, after all—one that has evolved functional parts: lungs for breathing, legs for walking, eyes for seeing, ears for hearing, a tongue for speaking and most crucially for all the academics concerned, a brain for thinking. This is science, not culture."[6] In a nutshell, you either have an able body, or you don't.

Yet the desire for definitional clarity might unleash more problems than it contains; if it's hard to deny that something called normalcy exists, it's even harder to pinpoint what that something is. The

OED defines *able-bodied* redundantly and negatively as "having an able body, i.e. one free from physical disability, and capable of the physical exertions required of it; in bodily health; robust." Able bodiedness, in turn, is defined vaguely as "soundness of health; ability to work; robustness." The parallel structure of the definitions of ability and sexuality is quite striking: first, to be able-bodied is to be "free from physical disability," just as to be heterosexual is to be "the opposite of homosexual." Second, even though the language of "the normal relations" expected of human beings is not present in the definition of able-bodied, the sense of "normal relations" is, especially with the emphasis on work: being able-bodied means being capable of the normal physical exertions required in a particular system of labor. It is here, in fact, that both able-bodied identity and the *Oxford English Dictionary* betray their origins in the nineteenth century and the rise of industrial capitalism. It is here as well that we can begin to understand the compulsory nature of able-bodiedness: in the emergent industrial capitalist system, free to sell one's labor but not free to do anything else effectively meant free to have an able body but not particularly free to have anything else.

Like compulsory heterosexuality, then, compulsory able-bodiedness functions by covering over, with the appearance of choice, a system in which there actually is no choice. I would not locate this compulsion, moreover, solely in the past, with the rise of industrial capitalism. Just as the origins of heterosexual/homosexual identity are now obscured for most people so that compulsory heterosexuality functions as a disciplinary formation seemingly emanating from everywhere and nowhere, so too are the origins of able-bodied/disabled identity obscured, allowing what Susan Wendell calls "the disciplines of normality" (87) to cohere in a system of compulsory able-bodiedness that similarly emanates from everywhere and nowhere. Able-bodied dilutions and misunderstandings of the minority thesis put forward in the disability rights movement and disability studies have even, in some ways, strengthened the system: the dutiful (or docile) able-bodied subject now recognizes that some groups of people have chosen to adjust to or even take pride in their "condition," but that recognition, and the tolerance that undergirds it, covers over the compulsory nature of the able-bodied subject's own identity.[7]

Michael Bérubé's memoir about his son Jamie, who has Down syndrome, helps exemplify some of the ideological demands currently sustaining compulsory able-bodiedness. Bérubé writes of how he "sometimes feel[s] cornered by talking about Jamie's intelligence, as if the burden of proof is on me, official spokesman on his behalf." The subtext of these encounters always seems to be the same: "*In the end, aren't you disappointed to have a retarded child? [. . .] Do we really have to give this person our full attention?*" (180). Bérubé's excavation of this subtext pinpoints an important common experience that links all people with disabilities under a system of compulsory able-bodiedness—the experience of the able-bodied need for an agreed-on common ground. I can imagine that answers might be incredibly varied to similar questions—"In the end, wouldn't you rather be hearing?" and "In the end, wouldn't you rather not be HIV positive?" would seem, after all, to be very different questions, the first (with its thinly veiled desire for Deafness not to exist) more obviously genocidal than the second. But they are not really different questions, in that their constant repetition (or their presence as ongoing subtexts) reveals more about the able-bodied culture doing the asking than about the bodies being interrogated. The culture asking such questions assumes in advance that we all agree: able-bodied

identities, able-bodied perspectives are preferable and what we all, collectively, are aiming for. A system of compulsory able-bodiedness repeatedly demands that people with disabilities embody for others an affirmative answer to the unspoken question, Yes, but in the end, wouldn't you rather be more like me?

It is with this repetition that we can begin to locate both the ways in which compulsory able-bodiedness and compulsory heterosexuality are interwoven and the ways in which they might be contested. In queer theory, Judith Butler is most famous for identifying the repetitions required to maintain heterosexual hegemony:

> The "reality" of heterosexual identities is performatively constituted through an imitation that sets itself up as the origin and the ground of all imitations. In other words, heterosexuality is always in the process of imitating and approximating its own phantasmatic idealization of itself—*and failing*. Precisely because it is bound to fail, and yet endeavors to succeed, the project of heterosexual identity is propelled into an endless repetition of itself. ("Imitation," 21)

If anything, the emphasis on identities that are constituted through repetitive performances is even more central to compulsory able-bodiedness—think, after all, of how many institutions in our culture are showcases for able-bodied performance. Moreover, as with heterosexuality, this repetition is bound to fail, as the ideal able-bodied identity can never, once and for all, be achieved. Able-bodied identity and heterosexual identity are linked in their mutual impossibility and in their mutual incomprehensibility—they are incomprehensible in that each is an identity that is simultaneously the ground on which all identities supposedly rest and an impressive achievement that is always deferred and thus never really guaranteed. Hence Butler's queer theories of gender performativity could be easily extended to disability studies, as this slightly paraphrased excerpt from *Gender Trouble* might suggest (I substitute, by bracketing, terms having to do literally with embodiment for Butler's terms of gender and sexuality):

> [Able-bodiedness] offers normative . . . positions that are intrinsically impossible to embody, and the persistent failure to identify fully and without incoherence with these positions reveals [able-bodiedness] itself not only as a compulsory law, but as an inevitable comedy. Indeed, I would offer this insight into [able-bodied identity] as both a compulsory system and an intrinsic comedy, a constant parody of itself, as an alternative [disabled] perspective. (122)

In short, Butler's theory of gender trouble might be resignified in the context of queer/disability studies to highlight what we could call "ability trouble"—meaning not the so-called problem of disability but the inevitable impossibility, even as it is made compulsory, of an able-bodied identity.

QUEER/DISABLED EXISTENCE

The cultural management of the endemic crises surrounding the performance of heterosexual and able-bodied identity effects a panicked consolidation of hegemonic identities. The most successful heterosexual subject is the one whose sexuality is not compromised by disability (metaphorized as queerness); the most successful able-bodied subject is the one whose ability is not compromised by queerness (metaphorized as disability). This consolidation occurs through complex processes of conflation and stereotype: people with disabilities are often understood as somehow queer (as paradoxical stereotypes of the asexual or oversexual person with disabilities would suggest), while queers are often understood as somehow disabled (as

ongoing medicalization of identity, similar to what people with disabilities more generally encounter, would suggest). Once these conflations are available in the popular imagination, queer/disabled figures can be tolerated and, in fact, utilized in order to maintain the fiction that able-bodied heterosexuality is not in crisis. As lesbian existence is deployed, in Rich's analysis, to reflect back heterosexual and patriarchal "realities," queer/disabled existence can be deployed to buttress compulsory able-bodiedness. Since queerness and disability both have the potential to disrupt the performance of able-bodied heterosexuality, both must be safely contained—embodied—in such figures.

In the 1997 film *As Good As It Gets*, for example, although Melvin Udall (Jack Nicholson), who is diagnosed in the film as obsessive-compulsive, is represented visually in many ways that initally position him in what Martin F. Norden calls "the cinema of isolation" (i.e., Melvin is represented in ways that link him to other representations of people with disabilities), the trajectory of the film is toward able-bodied heterosexuality. To effect the consolidation of heterosexual and able-bodied norms, disability and queerness in the film are visibly located elsewhere, in the gay character Simon Bishop (Greg Kinnear). Over the course of the film, Melvin progressively sheds his own sense of inhabiting an anomalous body, and disability is firmly located in the non-heterosexual character, who is initially represented as able-bodied, but who ends up, after he is attacked and beaten by a group of burglars, using a wheelchair and cane for most of the film. More important, the disabled/queer figure, as in many other contemporary cultural representations, facilitates the heterosexual romance: Melvin first learns to accept the differences Simon comes to embody, and Simon then encourages Melvin to reconcile with his girlfriend, Carol Connelly (Helen Hunt).

Having served their purpose, Simon, disability, and queerness are all hustled off-stage together. The film concludes with a fairly traditional romantic reunion between the (able-bodied) male and female leads.[8]

CRITICALLY QUEER, SEVERELY DISABLED

The crisis surrounding heterosexual identity and able-bodied identity does not automatically lead to their undoing. Indeed, as this brief consideration of *As Good As It Gets* should suggest, this crisis and the anxieties that accompany it can be invoked in a wide range of cultural texts precisely to be (temporarily) resolved or alleviated. Neither gender trouble nor ability trouble is sufficient in and of itself to unravel compulsory heterosexuality or compulsory able-bodiedness. Butler acknowledges this problem: "This failure to approximate the norm [. . .] is not the same as the subversion of the norm. There is no promise that subversion will follow from the reiteration of constitutive norms; there is no guarantee that exposing the naturalized status of heterosexuality will lead to its subversion" ("Critically Queer," 22; quoted in Warner, "Normal and Normaller" 168–169, n. 87). For Warner, this acknowledgment in Butler locates a potential gap in her theory, "let us say, between virtually queer and critically queer" (Warner, "Normal and Normaller," 168–169, n. 87). In contrast to a virtually queer identity, which would be experienced by anyone who failed to perform heterosexuality without contradiction and incoherence (i.e., everyone), a critically queer perspective could presumably mobilize the inevitable failure to approximate the norm, collectively "working the weakness in the norm," to use Butler's phrase ("Critically Queer," 26).[9]

A similar gap could be located if we appropriate Butler's theories for disability studies. Everyone is virtually disabled, both in the sense that able-bodied norms are "intrinsically impossible to embody" fully, and in the sense that able-bodied status is always temporary, disability being the one identity category that all people will embody if they live long enough. What we might call a critically disabled position, however, would differ from such a virtually disabled position; it would call attention to the ways in which the disability rights movement and disability studies have resisted the demands of compulsory able-bodiedness and have demanded access to a newly imagined and newly configured public sphere where full participation is not contingent on an able body.

We might, in fact, extend the concept and see such a perspective not as critically disabled but rather as severely disabled, with *severe* performing work similar to the critically queer work of *fabulous*. Tony Kushner writes:

> *Fabulous* became a popular word in the queer community—well, it was never *un*-popular, but for a while it became a battle cry of a new queer politics, carnival and camp, aggressively fruity, celebratory and tough like a streetwise drag queen: *"FAAAAABULOUS!"* [. . .] *Fabulous* is one of those words that provide a measure of the degree to which a person or event manifests a particular, usually oppressed, subculture's most distinctive, invigorating features. (vii)

Severe, though less common than *fabulous*, has a similar queer history: a severe critique is a fierce critique, a defiant critique, one that thoroughly and carefully reads a situation—and I mean reading in the street sense of loudly calling out the inadequacies of a given situation, person, text, or ideology. "Severely disabled," according to such a queer conception, would reverse the able-bodied understanding of severely disabled bodies as the most marginalized, the most excluded from a privileged and always elusive normalcy, and would instead suggest that it is precisely those bodies that are best positioned to refuse "mere toleration" and to call out the inadequacies of compulsory able-bodiedness. Whether it is the "army of one-breasted women" Audre Lorde imagines descending on the Capitol; the Rolling Quads, whose resistance sparked the independent living movement in Berkeley, California; Deaf students shutting down Gallaudet University in the Deaf President Now action; or ACT UP storming the National Institutes of Health or the Food and Drug Administration, severely disabled/critically queer bodies have already generated ability trouble that remaps the public sphere and reimagines and reshapes the limited forms of embodiment and desire proffered by the systems that would contain us all.[10]

Compulsory heterosexuality is intertwined with compulsory able-bodiedness; both systems work to (re)produce the able body and heterosexuality. But precisely because these systems depend on a queer/disabled existence that can never quite be contained, able-bodied heterosexuality's hegemony is always in danger of being disrupted. I draw attention to critically queer, severely disabled possibilities to further an incorporation of the two fields, queer theory and disability studies, in the hope that such a collaboration (which in some cases is already occurring, even when it is not acknowledged or explicitly named as such) will exacerbate, in more productive ways, the crisis of authority that currently besets heterosexual/able-bodied norms. Instead of invoking the crisis in order to resolve it (as in a film like *As Good As It Gets*), I would argue that a queer/disability studies (in productive conversations with disabled/queer movements outside the academy) can continuously invoke, in order to further the crisis, the inadequate resolutions that compulsory heterosexuality and compulsory able-bodiedness offer us.

And in contrast to an able-bodied culture that holds out the promise of a substantive (but paradoxically always elusive) ideal, a queer/disabled perspective would resist delimiting the kinds of bodies and abilities that are acceptable or that will bring about change. Ideally, a queer/disability studies—like the term *queer* itself—might function "oppositionally and relationally but not necessarily substantively, not as a positivity but as a positionality, not as a thing, but as a resistance to the norm" (Halperin, 66). Of course, in calling for a queer/disability studies without a necessary substance, I hope it is clear that I do not mean to deny the materiality of queer/disabled bodies, as it is precisely those material bodies that have populated the movements and brought about the changes detailed above. Rather, I mean to argue that critical queerness and severe disability are about collectively transforming (in ways that cannot necessarily be predicted in advance) the substantive uses to which queer/disabled existence has been put by a system of compulsory able-bodiedness, about insisting that such a system is never as good as it gets, and about imagining bodies and desires otherwise.

NOTES

1. In 1976, the Brussels Tribunal on Crimes against Women identified "compulsory heterosexuality" as one such crime (Katz, 26). A year earlier, in her important article "The Traffic in Women: Notes on the 'Political Economy' of Sex," Gayle Rubin examined the ways in which "obligatory heterosexuality" and "compulsory heterosexuality" function in what she theorized as a larger sex/gender system (179, 198; cited in Katz, 132). Rich's 1980 article, which has been widely cited and reproduced since its initial publication, was one of the most extensive analyses of compulsory heterosexuality in feminism. I agree with Jonathan Ned Katz's insistence that the concept is redundant because "any society split between heterosexual and homosexual is compulsory" (164), but I also acknowledge the historical and critical usefulness of the phrase. It is easier to

understand the ways in which a society split between heterosexual and homosexual is compulsory precisely because of feminist deployments of the redundancy of compulsory heterosexuality. I would also suggest that popular queer theorizing outside of the academy (from drag performances to activist street theater) has often employed redundancy performatively to make a critical point.

2. In an effort to forge a political connection between all women, Rich uses the terms "lesbian" and "lesbian continuum" to describe a vast array of sexual and affectional connections throughout history, many of which emerge from historical and cultural conditions quite different from those that have made possible the identity of lesbian (192–199). Moreover, by using "lesbian continuum" to affirm the connection between lesbian and heterosexual women, Rich effaces the cultural and sexual specificity of contemporary lesbian existence.

3. The incorporation of queer theory and disability studies that I argue for here is still in its infancy. It is in cultural activism and cultural theory about AIDS (such as John Nguyet Erni's *Unstable Frontiers* or Cindy Patton's *Fatal Advice*) that a collaboration between queer theory and disability studies is already proceeding and has been for some time, even though it is not yet acknowledged or explicitly named as such. Michael Davidson's "Strange Blood: Hemophobia and the Unexplored Boundaries of Queer Nation" is one of the finest analyses to date of the connections between disability studies and queer theory.

4. The collective projects that I refer to are, of course, the projects of gay liberation and queer studies in the academy and the disability rights movement and disability studies in the academy. This chapter is part of my own contribution to these projects and is part of my longer work in progress, titled *Crip Theory: Cultural Signs of Queerness and Disability.*

5. David Mitchell and Sharon Snyder are in line with many scholars working in disability studies when they point out the "ominous silence in the humanities" on the subject of disability (1). See, for other examples, Simi Linton's discussion of the "divided curriculum" (71–116), and assertions by Rosemarie Garland-Thomson and by Lennard Davis about the necessity of examining disability alongside other categories of difference such as race, class, gender, and sexuality (Garland-Thomson, 5; Davis, xi).

6. Disability studies is not the only field Vincent has attacked in the mainstream media; see her article "The Future of Queer: Wedded to Orthodoxy," which mocks academic queer theory. Neither being disabled nor being gay or lesbian in and of itself guarantees the critical consciousness generated in the disability rights or queer movements, or in queer theory or disability studies: Vincent herself is a lesbian journalist, but her writing clearly supports both able-bodied and heterosexual norms. Instead of a stigmaphilic response to queer/disabled existence, finding "a commonality with those who suffer from stigma, and in this alternative realm [learning] to value the very things the rest of the world despises" (Warner, *Trouble,* 43), Vincent reproduces the dominant culture's stigmaphobic response. See Warner's discussion of Erving Goffman's concepts of stigmaphobe and stigmaphile (41–45).

7. Michel Foucault's discussion of "docile bodies" and his theories of disciplinary practices are in the background of much of my analysis here (135–169).

8. The consolidation of able-bodied and heterosexuality identity is probably most common in mainstream films and television movies about AIDS, even—or perhaps especially—when those films are marketed as new and daring." The 1997 Christopher Reeve-directed HBO film *In the Gloaming* is an example. In the film, the disabled/queer character (yet again, in a tradition that reaches back to *An Early Frost* [1985]), is eliminated at the end but not before effecting a healing of the heteronormative family. As Simon Watney writes about *An Early Frost,* "The closing shot [. . .] shows a 'family album' picture. [. . .] A traumatic episode is over. The family closes ranks, with the problem son conveniently dispatched, and life getting back to normal" (114). I am focusing on a non-AIDS-related film about disability and homosexuality, because I think the processes I theorize here have a much wider currency and can be found in many cultural texts that attempt to represent queerness or disability. There is not space here to analyze *As Good As It Gets* fully; for a more comprehensive close reading of how heterosexual/able-bodied consolidation works in the film and other cultural texts, see my article "As Good As It Gets: Queer Theory and Critical Disability." I do not, incidentally, think that these processes are unique to fictional texts: the MLA's annual *Job Information List,* for instance, provides evidence of other locations where heterosexual and able-bodied norms support each other while ostensibly allowing for tolerance of queerness and disability. The recent high visibility of queer studies and disability studies on university press lists, conference

proceedings, and even syllabi has not necessarily translated into more jobs for disabled/queer scholars.

9. See my discussion of Butler, Gloria Anzaldua, and critical queerness in *The Queer Renaissance: Contemporary American Literature and the Reinvention of Lesbian and Gay Identities* (149–153).

10. On the history of the AIDS Coalition to Unleash Power (ACT UP), see Douglas Crimp and Adam Rolston's *AIDS DemoGraphics*. Lorde recounts her experiences with breast cancer and imagines a movement of one-breasted women in *The Cancer Journals*. Joseph P. Shapiro recounts both the history of the Rolling Quads and the Independent Living Movement and the Deaf President Now action in *No Pity: People with Disabilities Forging a New Civil Rights Movement* (41–58; 74–85). Deaf activists have insisted for some time that deafness should not be understood as a disability and that people living with deafness, instead, should be seen as having a distinct language and culture. As the disability rights movement has matured, however, some Deaf activists and scholars in Deaf studies have rethought this position and have claimed disability (that is, disability revalued by a disability rights movement and disability studies) in an attempt to affirm a coalition with other people with disabilities. It is precisely such a reclaiming of disability that I want to stress here with my emphasis on severe disability.

WORKS CITED

As Good As It Gets. Dir. James L. Brooks. Perf. Jack Nicholson, Helen Hunt, and Greg Kinnear. TriStar, 1997.

Berube, Michael. *Life As We Know It: A Father, a Family, and an Exceptional Child*. New York: Vintage-Random House, 1996.

Butler, Judith. "Critically Queer." *GLQ: A Journal of Lesbian and Gay Studies* 1.1 (1993): 17–32

———. *Gender Trouble: Feminism and the Subversion of Identity*. New York: Routledge, 1990.

———. "Imitation and Gender Insubordination." In *Inside/Out: Lesbian Theories, Gay Theories*, edited by Diana Fuss, (13–31). New York: Routledge, 1991.

Crimp, Douglas, and Adam Rolston. *AIDS DemoGraphics*. Seattle: Bay Press, 1990.

Davidson, Michael. "Strange Blood: Hemophobia and the Unexplored Boundaries of Queer Nation." In *Beyond the Binary: Reconstructing Cultural Identity in a Multicultural Context*, edited by Timothy Powell (39–60). New Brunswick: Rutgers UP, 1999.

Davis, Lennard J. *Enforcing Normalcy: Disability, Deafness, and the Body*. London: Verso, 1995.

Erni, John Nguyet. *Unstable Frontiers: Technomedicine and the Cultural Politics of "Curing" AIDS*. Minneapolis: U of Minnesota P, 1994.

In the Gloaming. Dir. Christopher Reeve. Perf. Glenn Close, Robert Sean Leonard, and David Strathairn. HBO, 1997.

Foucault, Michel. *Discipline and Punish: The Birth of the Prison*. Translated by Alan Sheridan. New York: Vintage-Random House, 1977.

Garland-Thomson, Rosemarie. *Extraordinary Bodies: Figuring Physical Disability in American Culture and Literature*. New York: Columbia UP, 1997.

Halperin, David, *Saint Foucault: Toward a Gay Historiography*, Oxford: Oxford UP, 1995.

Katz, Jonathan Ned. *The Invention of Heterosexuality*. New York: Dutton, 1995.

Kushner, Tony. "Foreword: Notes Toward a Theater of the Fabulous." In *Staging Lives: An Anthology of Contemporary Gay Theater*, edited by John M. Clum, vii–ix. Boulder: Westview Press, 1996.

Linton, Simi. *Claiming Disability: Knowledge and Identity*. New York: NYU Press, 1998.

Lorde, Audre. *The Cancer Journals*. San Francisco: Aunt Lute Books, 1980.

McRuer, Robert. "As Good As It Gets: Queer Theory and Critical Disability." *GLQ: A Journal of Lesbian and Gay Studies* 9.1–2 (2003): 79–105.

———. *Crip Theory: Cultural Signs of Queerness and Disability*. New York: NYU Press, 2006.

———. *The Queer Renaissance: Contemporary American Literature and the Reinvention of Lesbian and Gay Identities*. New York: NYU Press, 1997.

Mitchell, David T., and Sharon L. Snyder. "Introduction: Disability Studies and the Double Bind of Representation." In *The Body and Physical Difference: Discourses of Disability*, edited by Mitchell and Snyder, 1–31. Ann Arbor: U of Michigan P, 1997.

Norden, Martin F. *The Cinema of Isolation: A History of Physical Disability in the Movies*. New Brunswick: Rutgers UP, 1994.

Patton, Cindy. *Fatal Advice: How Safe-Sex Education Went Wrong*. Durham: Duke UP, 1997.

Rich, Adrienne. "Compulsory Heterosexuality and Lesbian Existence." In *Powers of Desire: The Politics of Sexuality*, edited by Ann Snitow, Christine Stansell, and Sharon Thompson, 177–205. New York: Monthly Review Press, 1983.

Rubin, Gayle. "The Traffic in Women: Notes on the 'Political Economy' of Sex." In *Toward an Anthropology of Women*, edited by Rayna R. Reiter, 157–210. New York: Monthly Review Press, 1975. .

Shapiro, Joseph P. *No Pity: People with Disabilities Forging a New Civil Rights Movement.* New York: Times Books-Random House, 1993.

Vincent, Norah. "Enabling Disabled Scholarship." *Salon.* Aug. 18, 1999. Available at http://www.salon.com/books/it/1999/08/18/disability

——. "The Future of Queer: Wedded to Orthodoxy." *The Village Voice* 22 Feb. 2000: 16.

Warner, Michael. "Normal and Normaller: Beyond Gay Marriage." *GLQ: A Journal of Lesbian and Gay Studies* 5.2 (1999): 119–171.

——. *The Trouble with Normal: Sex, Politics, and the Ethics of Queer Life.* New York: The Free Press, 1999.

Watney, Simon. *Policing Desire: Pornography, AIDS, and the Media.* 2nd ed. Minneapolis: U of Minnesota P, 1989.

Wendell, Susan. *The Rejected Body: Feminist Philosophical Reflections on Disability.* New York: Routledge, 1996.

Williams, Raymond. *Keywords: A Vocabulary of Culture and Society.* Rev. ed. New York: Oxford UP, 1983.

PART VI

*D*isability and Culture

Cripping Heterosexuality, Queering Able-Bodiedness: *Murderball, Brokeback Mountain* and the Contested Masculine Body

Cynthia Barounis

INTRODUCTION

At the 2006 Academy Awards, *Brokeback Mountain* took home three Oscars and the independent film *Murderball*, which chronicled the lives of a group of quadriplegic rugby players, was nominated for best documentary feature. The aesthetic elevation of these two particular films reveals much about how contemporary cultural anxieties regarding queerness and physical disability are negotiated through visual culture. It's not uncommon, of course, to see films that deal with disability and homosexuality at the Oscars. What was out of the ordinary, however, was the extent to which *Murderball* and *Brokeback Mountain* each harnessed the normalizing powers of masculinity, presenting a narrative of gender that helped to generate mainstream appeal in the box office and, more importantly, mainstream approval of a stigmatized social identity. In these narratives, disability and queer sexuality are not just shown to be compatible with masculinity; they are, more fundamentally, celebrated as the logical extension of masculinity's excess. But the emphasis on masculinity that these two films share is also the source of their antagonism. Indeed, a close reading of these two films exposes masculinity as the visual mechanism through which

disability and homosexuality distance themselves from one another, each identity to some extent disciplining the other. Such mutual regulation, however, is not arbitrary and I will argue that it is precisely the various historical linkages between queerness and disability—their continual status as uneasy bedfellows—that bring us to this reactionary cultural moment where able-bodiedness is queered and heterosexuality is defiantly "cripped."

Recently, critics have begun to explore the ways in which a queer theoretical approach might deepen our engagement with disability studies.[1] Robert McRuer's recent book *Crip Theory: Cultural Signs of Queerness and Disability* opens up some exciting possibilities for this dialogue. McRuer examines queerness and disability as parallel sites of oppression; the homosexual body and the disabled body are each regulated by a system of compulsory identity that privilege, respectively, heterosexuality and able-bodiedness. Thus disability studies, McRuer suggests, has much to gain by borrowing from the vocabulary and framework of queer theory. "Cripping" a text, for example, may begin to serve the same function for disability studies that "queering" did for gay and lesbian studies. McRuer makes clear, however, that systems of heterosexual and able-bodied privilege share more than just a family resemblance; not merely parallel, they are deeply intertwined. Thus "compulsory heterosexuality" and "compulsory able-bodiedness" are often wedded together in a mutual effort to both conflate and regulate disability and homosexuality. McRuer's analyses proceed from this assumption, and through a set of diverse cultural readings, he locates the places where able-bodied and heterosexual privilege join forces. While McRuer details several rich sites of cultural resistance, most of his mainstream examples suggest that "heteronormative epiphanies are repeatedly, and often necessarily, able-bodied ones" (McRuer, 2006: 13).[2] What such epiphanic moments of able-bodied heteronormativity require, he suggests, are bodies that are flexible enough to make it through a crisis. And more often than not, it's the heterosexual and able body that is brought out of this crisis, usually at the expense of a disabled character who has been queered or a queer character who has been "cripped."

In what follows, I will explore how the terms of this struggle have—in a short time—become radically reversed. In *Brokeback Mountain* and *Murderball*, systems of heterosexuality and able-bodiedness do not combine in order to produce a stigmatized disabled/queer subjectivity. Instead, these two films set up a world where the mainstreaming of homosexuality stigmatizes disability and where claiming an in-your-face crip subjectivity relies on successful heterosexual conquest. It is a universe where heteromasculine epiphanies are never able-bodied ones, and a queer male subjectivity forms in fundamental opposition to disability. Here, bodies are not flexible, but resolute and resistant to change. It is the very stubbornness of these bodies—their resistance to a traditional narrative arc of character growth—that enables the visual rhetoric of masculinity to do the work that it does in

both films, carrying the characters through an apparent transition that turns out to be no transition at all.

If these films turn McRuer's formulation inside out, however, it is only because they are reacting against the representational history that he has so thoroughly exposed—one in which queerness and disability are made to appear as two components of the same identity. Cinematic history had been permeated with such figures: medicalized images of the homosexual who is either psychologically or physically diseased, spiritualized idealizations of the desexualized disabled person, and nightmares of the injured heterosexual man whose acquired disability castrates him. Thus it is films like *Born on the Fourth of July* and *Philadelphia* that constitute the cultural unconscious of both films. This is the representational history that both films attempt to disavow, even as they structure themselves around it. But there may be a folly in too quickly dismissing those histories in which queerness and disability were intertwined. Confronting and critically showcasing that past, I'd like to propose, may ultimately be what offers us our most effective strategies for cultural critique.

REHABILITATING HETEROMASCULINITY

To suggest that *Murderball* (2005), a recent documentary chronicling the lives of a set of quadriplegic wheelchair rugby athletes, is invested in heteromasculinity more than likely states the obvious to anyone who has seen the film. The key players featured throughout are rugged, athletic—and occasionally tattooed—trash-talking men whose ultimate goal is to crush the competition and come home from the Paralympics with a gold medal. The documentary eschews sentimentality in favor of a more hard-edged realism that foregrounds its subjects as ordinary specimens of a male sports world. When they're not giving (or getting) a beating on the court, they're drinking and having sex with women, or bragging about drinking and having sex with women. Indeed, the film's emphasis on the heterosexual potency of quadriplegic men is one of its most provocative features, and one that has received widespread praise from reviewers.[3]

On a basic level, then, the film's popularity can be considered a success for disability cultural activism. It is an authentic portrayal of a disabled subculture that avoids the traditional narrative traps of many mainstream disability films.[4] The viewer is immediately directed to check his or her well-intentioned sympathies at the door, along with any preconceived notions about the fragility of the disabled body. And disabled sexuality, a taboo and uncomfortable territory for many non-disabled viewers, is reclaimed with a vengeance.[5] Indeed, one of the difficulties in analyzing *Murderball* is that its most radical features are simultaneously its most conventional. Thus, while non-disabled viewers may find their assumptions and stereotypes challenged by the masculine sexual bravado of *Murderball*'s quadriplegic rugby players, there may be a simultaneous sense of relief at ironclad endurance of male heterosexual privilege. Heterosexuality no longer functions as evidence that a disabled masculinity has finally been "cured"; instead, it's the masculinization of disability that holds the power to rehabilitate heteronormativity from its own gender trouble.

Far from the typical narrative arc of a heteromasculinity lost through injury and reclaimed through rehabilitation, the documentary figures disability as not only reflecting but, in fact, amplifying a deeply constant heterosexual masculine selfhood. Revisiting the night of his injury, for example, Mark Zupan explains doing "shots with the girls" at a local bar to celebrate a soccer win before passing out in the back of his best friend's truck; his friend, unaware of Zupan's presence in the vehicle, drove home drunk and had an accident in which Zupan was thrown into nearby canal where he held onto a branch for fourteen hours before anyone discovered him. It's a story that mixes ordinary masculinity with extraordinary toughness and endurance. Explaining the origins of their disabilities, the rugby players relate similar tales of risky behavior associated with conventions of "tough guy," "daredevil," or even just normative "frat boy" modes of masculinity. Scott Hogsett was thrown off of a balcony during a fistfight; Keith Cavill was injured while attempting a set of dangerous motorcycle stunts; and while Bob Lubjano explains that his amputated limbs are the effect of a "rare blood disease," the back of the DVD release puts on a slightly different spin, characterizing his impairment as the result of an encounter with "rogue bacteria." This act of anthropomorphosis endows the simple act of getting sick with a quality of combat, aggressivity, and risk and is characteristic of much of the rhetoric surrounding the film and the sport in general.[6]

This is not the first time that the language of combat has been used to redescribe disability through a lens of masculinity. In "Fighting Polio Like a Man," Daniel Wilson analyzes a set of interviews that were done with male polio survivors during the Cold War Era. Their narratives of rehabilitation were highly gendered:

> Ironically, the very cultural values that initially emasculated the paralyzed polio survivor also provided the means by which a young male could construct a sense of masculinity consistent with society's values and expectations . . . Recovery from polio could be easily construed as a battle or contest against the virus, against the doctors and therapists, even against one's damaged body and sense of self . . . This new sense of manhood was constructed, or reconstructed,

not on school athletic fields or on fields of battle but in the rehabilitation facilities.

(Wilson, 2004: 121)

In this narrative, the illness provides the opportunity for the reassertion of masculinity, but only insofar as illness is made into the obstacle which the subject must overcome in order to access normative categories of gender and sexuality. But while these earlier accounts framed disability as the foe to be vanquished, *Murderball* to the contrary claims disability as a weapon to be wielded *against* one's foe. While Wilson observes that the polio survivor's narratives "perform masculinity by demonstrating how these men . . . became men by the way they fought polio" (Wilson, 2004: 131), we find here that the *Murderball* athletes became men not by fighting their injuries but, to the contrary, by acquiring an injury that enabled them to fight.

Indeed, if honorable combat is positioned as that which put the players in the wheelchair, then it's the chair itself that that opens up larger, more mythic opportunities to accumulate battle scars. One reviewer admires the fact the rugby chairs resemble "chariots of war"—a point that is in no subtle way driven home by one interviewee who explains how the chairs are made: "What we do is we take these wheelchairs and turn them into a gladiator, a battling machine, a *Mad Max* wheelchair that can stand knocking the living daylights out of each other." In this respect, the film's opening sequence, characterized by Zupan himself as "preparing for battle," is worth examining. As the film begins, an uncomfortable silence accompanies our only glimpse of Zupan's vulnerability as he slowly and painstakingly pulls his pants down and off of his immobile legs. The camera sweeps erotically across his bare chest and limbs, eventually settling on the black tattoo that takes up the greater part of his shin. Zupan pulls on a pair of work-out shorts, removes his shirt, and wheels out of the room. In the DVD director commentary that accompanies this moment, Rubin and Shapiro discuss the "Clark Kent" logic underlying the scene: "He's about to transform into the rugby guy. There will be the phone booth moment coming—you'll see when the garage door opens." But while Clark Kent's transformation always seemed to involve a stripping down—his nylon suit showing through his bourgeois dress shirt, his glasses always a discardable accessory—Zupan's transformation is shown as a welding on of new parts.[7]

The moment that the camera zooms in on Zupan's tattoo is the moment that the man becomes more than mere flesh. And it is precisely at that point that the intimacy and vulnerability of the scene's opening is eclipsed by a prosthetic remaking of the body—an elaborate new technology of gender.[8] We hear and see the rip of duct tape, the whirring of the wheel, and the clanging of metal. Later, we will watch an animated clip in which metal screws are incorporated into the skeletal drawing of a spine; the image gradually fades into a shot of the actual scars that mark one player's neck. Thus both man and chair are visually constructed as the product of custom-built state-of-the-art manufacturing. If, according to the logic of the film, it was the amplification of ordinary masculinity that led to Zupan's injury, then this extraordinarily refashioned machinic masculinity is nothing less than mythic.

In a recent issue of *Narrative*, Rosemarie Garland-Thomson has described the players featured in *Murderball* as "[c]yborgs composed of steel fused with flesh," arguing that that, in the documentary, "[d]isability provides an unanticipated opportunity for boys to come into themselves as athletes and men" (Garland-Thomson, 2007: 115).[9] Garland-Thomson generously concludes, however, that rather than reconstructing heteronormative masculinity, *Murderball* provides us with "what Judith Halberstam calls an alternative masculinity," one which is "non-phallic" (Garland-Thomson, 2007: 116). But to redefine disability through masculinity, as the documentary certainly does, is not necessarily to redefine masculinity itself. Though the film does present us with multiple images of the male cyborg, these images seem to fall short of approximating Haraway's feminist technoscience or Halberstam's technotopic body.[10] Indeed, Haraway's cyborg myth contests both the legitimacy of the masculinist cyborg and the overall male monopoly on technoculture. Repudiating narratives of origin, cyborgs and technotopic bodies are not aimed at helping "boys to come into themselves as athletes and as men" but, rather, at creating alternative queer temporalities in which boys sometimes become something other than men, and girls sometimes become something other than women.

Additionally, Garland-Thomson's claim that *Murderball* creates an "innovative, non-phallic, alternative sexuality," (Garland-Thomson, 2007: 116) focuses on a single reference to cunnilingus while overlooking the dynamic staging that privileges heterosexual phallic penetration as the measurement of the players' masculinity. While Mark Zupan certainly mentions that most wheelchair athletes "like to eat pussy," it is important to point out that this comment is embedded within a sentence that begins with Zupan gesturing downwards and reassuring the viewer: "That still works." In another scene, the ability to have an erection is somewhat taken for granted as an essential feature of quadriplegia. After reassuring an attractive able-bodied woman that the three players sitting at the table are all fully functional, Scott Hogsett relates the following story:

> When I first got injured, I was in intensive care, and, uh, everyone was curious how I was gonna be, how much function I was gonna have when I came out of my coma that I was in, and I was about ready to wake up, and the nurses decided to give me a bed-bath in the bed, and the one nurse got so excited that I got a woody, she ran outside and got my mom and showed her my, uh, erection.

What is significant about this exchange is the swiftness with which the image of the impotent quadriplegic is replaced by the image of the quadriplegic whose erection is being celebrated by the community of women surrounding him. While the woman's question might well have opened up a conversation about alternative sexual practices that don't privilege phallic potency, the response ultimately ends up both creating a heteronormatively functional elite among the disabled while simultaneously generalizing the situation of that elite to the entire quadriplegic community.

There is, however, at least one "alternative masculinity" present in *Murderball*. Following an exchange in which an American player accuses former U.S. Coach Joe Soares of "betray[ing] his country" by leaving to coach team Canada, the camera cuts to an evening scene in the hotel room where all four of the featured U.S. players, along with two or three others, play a game of modified poker. The circular movement of the camera and its various close-ups on individual players' faces as they banter back and forth creates a tightly sealed homosocial space within which this "alternative masculinity" is rigidly disciplined. Within the confusion of a lively dialogue, we witness a lanky, long-haired teammate named Sam defend Soares's decision to coach the Canadian team. The dialogue runs as follows:

Sam: On a professional level, I don't think there's anything wrong with it.

Andy: That's number two on the list of most stupid things I've ever heard at this camp. I heard Sam say that he doesn't like big tits and he'd dump a girl with big tits, if everything was perfect—but, if she has big tits, [imitating Sam] "it's over, they get in the way"

Sam: I like athletic girls. That's what I said all along that night when they asked me.

Zupan: You knew you weren't going to live that one down.

Sam: I'm okay with my sexuality. I can say that. I don't like big tits.

Zupan: You like shoes though.

Sam: I do like shoes.

At this point, everyone laughs and the camera pans to the mechanical card shuffler that happens to be in motion. This is one of the most revealing scenes in the film because it invokes multiple vectors of the gender trouble that the film is careful to guard against. On the one hand, it immediately solidifies the link between heteromasculinity and patriotism. As I have argued, physical disability has been positioned within the film as the manly consequence of both heteromasculinity and honorable combat. This is why Sam's moral defense of a known "traitor" leads the players to move abruptly into an interrogation of Sam's heteronormativity. Though there's nothing homosexual about a man who "like[s] athletic girls," there is something queer, according the film's logic, about a man who lacks desire for the appropriate object choice—in this case, "a girl with big tits." "Big tits" are, of course, functioning here as a metonym of idealized femininity, with all of its attendant associations of passivity, nurturance and non-athleticism.[11] Sam's interest in "athletic girls" thus feminizes (and arguably queers) him to the extent that it's framed as a desire for masculinity (albeit a masculinity that is attached to a female body).[12] While this sequence opens up some fascinating tensions, the soft roar of the mechanical card shuffler has the

last word, and Sam—along with his anti-normative desires—are silenced for the remainder of the film.

I have thus far suggested that in both the film and its reception, excessive hetero-masculinity is celebrated as the originary moment out of which disability is generated as the inevitable consequence. But where does this leave disabled women, and the ideological status of femininity more generally? By coding disability as a property of heterosexual masculinity, *Murderball* simultaneously codes able-bodiedness as a property of heterosexual femininity. Within the logic of the film, it's the gender-normative able-bodied woman who reinforces heteromasculine potency.[13] Such women, in fact, are central to the film's network of associations, serving a specific and limited purpose—to humanize the disabled players by occupying their traditional role in the narrative of heterosexual conquest. Thus we see women in various contexts, but they are always feminine, always heterosexual, and always engaging in activities that support and reinforce the heterosexual masculinity of the players. They are featured as friendly nurses, cheering sections at games, concerned mothers, and most importantly, proof that whatever other effects the injury has had on their body, the men's ability to engage in heterosexual, penetrative sex is not compromised.[14]

But because the film has polarized disability as a property of athletic heteromasculinity and able-bodiedness as a property of heterosexual, non-athletic femininity, there is no longer a viable space for the physically disabled athletic woman; her body is not only rendered unintelligible but becomes a palpable threat to the narrative glue that holds masculinity, disability, and heteronormativity firmly together. Wendy Seymour has suggested that the same logic that masculinizes the quadriplegic or paraplegic man also functions to both masculinize and desexualize the quadriplegic or paraplegic woman (Seymour, 1998: 120). This brings up a set of thorny issues involving whether or not disabled women's exclusion from the structures of conventional heterosexual femininity can open up other liberatory possibilities, even as such exclusions simultaneously police and regulate their sexuality.[15] While a thorough negotiation of these issues is beyond the scope of this paper, the fact remains that *Murderball* explores neither side of the debate. Disabled women, and particularly disabled female athletes, are not celebrated as having been liberated from oppressive conventions of gender. Nor are they given access to normative femininity; visually, they are never made into objects of the voyeuristic male gaze that, after Laura Mulvey's classic 1975 article, has become common currency in discussions of cinematic spectatorship. Neither, interestingly, are they victims of "the stare," a visual dynamic coined by Garland-Thomson to encapsulate the revulsion of the able-bodied viewer whose lengthy hostile gaze at a "freakishly" embodied other is emptied of sexual desire (Garland-Thomson, 1997: 26). Indeed the few images of disabled women that the documentary presents function more as a set of fleeting and brief snapshots that, while easy to miss, do momentarily interrupt the temporal, and often verbal, logic through which these "boys" become "men." These more or less static images haunt the film's perimeter, a subtle threat to the coherence of a narrative that celebrates quadriplegia as the natural outcome of the hypermasculine male body.

Indeed, even the most attentive viewer might, on a first viewing, miss the few glimpses that are to be had of disabled female athletics. The first opportunity isn't until just before the final dramatic showdown between the U.S. and Canada at the 2004 Paralympics. In a brief montage that showcases a variety of Paralympic sports, there is a two-second clip of female leg amputees playing volleyball. Significantly, they are all low to the ground, and filmed (perhaps unavoidably) from above. Not only does the angle diminish their size and power, but also they are absent of any type of prosthesis or equipment and none of them are using wheelchairs. Given that prosthetics and wheelchair technology have earlier in the film been powerfully deployed to signify and naturalize disabled masculinity, and given that this clip is sandwiched between clips of Paralympic male sports (all of them requiring varying levels of prosthesis), it may be plausible to argue that the framing of these female athletes functions to neutralize any threat to disabled masculinity that their presence might pose.

The only other scene in which disabled women are presented in an athletic capacity is during the documentary's final scene, as the players teach a group of newly disabled Iraq War veterans how to play the game. Between clips, we see two young women, though very briefly and in a limited context. Early in the scene, the camera abruptly cuts to a young woman standing with a basketball under one arm—her other arm visibly absent. The shot—lasting for no more than two seconds—catches her from the neck down; in fact we are only able to identify her as female because her white sports bra is visible underneath her white t-shirt. Because she is decapitated by the frame, we are unable to establish any filmic identification with her. Simultaneously, her disability and her desexualized wardrobe prevent the viewer from establishing her as an object of desire via conventional modes of cinematic spectatorship. Unlike the able-bodied girlfriends of the quad rugby players, or even the Paralympic volleyball players, this female body becomes visually unintelligible within the logic of the film.[16]

Later in the scene, the camera pans upwards from the feet of an individual wearing one prosthetic leg. As the frame reaches her chest, and then her face, we realize that it is a young, female veteran. Her shirt showcases the American flag and her gaze is intently fixed on something outside the frame. She's attractive and her demeanor exudes fortitude. In a sense, we have finally met the "athletic girl" whose specter was both invoked and repressed during the earlier poker scene.[17] This one, however, is not quite so quick to be dispelled. The camera quickly cuts to two male amputees who are wearing similar leg prostheses. While the purpose of this moment was no doubt to establish the effect that the Iraq War continues to have on American bodies, it serves simultaneously to establish a solid identification between the disabled woman and her male counterparts. The entire progression lasts only eight seconds, so it's easy to miss. But, I want to suggest, these eight seconds are what the rest of the documentary labors to repress. While most of the documentary features women only in conventional, able-bodied roles that reify masculinity by performing its opposite, this moment confronts the viewer with an unapologetic assertion of another type of "alternative masculinity," one that is attached to a female body.

But, although this moment lasts longer than any other depiction of a disabled woman in the film, it too is quickly redirected and contained by the dominant narrative of male heteromasculinity at work in the film. From here, the film dives quickly into the central tension of the scene. Masculine athleticism has once more found its proper object as a young man in a wheelchair expresses doubt in his ability to throw the ball. This first throw fails to reach its intended target, but after some hearty encouragement from the old pros, his second attempt is a success. The girl we have just seen is cut sporadically into this narrative, and in these brief half-second clips she appears to be actively involved in (and indeed taking delight from) a game of quad rugby. But interestingly, the chair that she's using, though present by implication, is rendered invisible in these clips—we see her only from the elbows up. If the logic of the film has transformed the rugby chair into a metonym for a heteronormative masculinity that is reserved only for male bodies, then her temporary use of it becomes an appropriation that cannot be accommodated by the documentary's visual economy. The deconstructive potential of her participation is ultimately contained as the scene's primary drama resumes. The young male veteran finally throws a successful pass, establishing that masculinity has ultimately been returned to a male body. But while most of the documentary functions to contain the presence of the disabled female athlete, the film's epilogue ultimately lays bare some of this tension when it features Bob Lubjano kissing (albeit chastely) his girlfriend, who is identified as a Paralympic swimmer. We would do well to take this moment, as well as the others that preceded it, as an opportunity to reflect on and draw out the gender trouble that complicates not only the film, but also the cultural past that has conflated queerness and disability.

"GETTIN' OUT WHILE I STILL CAN WALK"

In some ways, the only thing that *Murderball* (2005) and *Brokeback Mountain* (2005) have in common is their release date. *Murderball* is about traveling the world to represent one's country; *Brokeback Mountain* is about spending a lifetime *in* the country. *Murderball* embraces the urban technologized body; *Brokeback Mountain*'s rural naturalism makes even the telephone look like technological excess. What the films do share, however, is a strategic deployment of masculinity that normalizes a historically marginalized population. But if *Murderball*'s celebration of quadriplegia is rooted in a narrative of heteronormative masculinity that disciplines and represses queerness, then *Brokeback Mountain* is conversely invested in particularly able-bodied masculinity that normalizes homo-sexuality by simultaneously disciplining disability.

It would be difficult to dispute the fact that Jack and Ennis emblematize a particular brand of frontier masculinity, one that has been until now historically off-limits in mainstream cinematic representations of homosexuality. But what *Brokeback Mountain* did was more than simply suggest that cowboys can be gay too; it implied that cowboys are gay precisely *because* they're cowboys.[18] Gay male sexuality in the film seems to spring directly from an inborn aggression and competitive instinct. It is figured as a natural corollary to male horseplay—the violent, almost primitive, crashing together of two male bodies. And above all else, it is organic.[19] Thus in the original story, we find Ennis in his first sexual encounter with Jack drawing upon what appears to be a physically innate drive: this was "nothing he'd done before, but no instruction manual needed" (Proulx, 1999: 259). Unlike the machinic heteromasculinity glorified in *Murderball*, this homosexual manliness is born directly out of the earth.

This organicism partially explains the able-bodied ideologies that underpin Jack and Ennis's masculinity. The stubbornness of their genders becomes to some extent the stubbornness of their physical bodies themselves. The Darwinian logic of the traditional frontier narrative places the male body in harsh conditions; it is the fittest who survive, the ablest bodies that endure. Thus the same excessive masculinity that *Murderball* celebrates as the cause of disability becomes, in *Brokeback Mountain*, the skill for keeping one's spine intact. Upon their first trip back to the mountain, the first thing that Jack and Ennis do is strip off their clothes and jump from a peak into the stream below. But on Brokeback Mountain, the water is never too shallow and getting thrown from a horse leaves only some minor bruising.[20]

Part of Jack and Ennis's talent for remaining able-bodied, however, is tied directly to gay male sexuality. In several scenes, Ennis is presented with what ultimately becomes a choice between either facing harsh (and potentially debilitating) natural conditions or putting himself in a position that could lead to a homosexual encounter. Indeed on several occasions, the desire to remain able-bodied sends Ennis directly into Jack's arms. Thus the first sex scene unfolds out of Jack's concern for Ennis's health. Having had too much to drink, Ennis decides to sleep outdoors despite Jack's warning, "Freeze your ass off when that fire dies down. Better off sleepin' in the tent." But it is only when Jack's prediction comes true and Ennis seems on the verge of frostbite that he finally acquiesces; the two men share a blanket and their physical proximity quickly leads to their first sexual encounter. On another occasion, a storm breaks out, and Jack and Ennis can be observed shouting to one another in the entry flap of the tent. "Them sheep will drift if I don't get back up there tonight!" yells Ennis. Jack replies, "You'll get pitched off your mount in a storm like this. You'll wish you hadn't tried it! It's too cold! Close it up!" Thus Ennis's masculinity lies in his frontier brand of self-discipline, expressed through his avoidance of unnecessary risk and his knowledge of his own limitations in the face of nature. If his masculinity is of the earth, then his respect for natural law is what causes him ultimately to listen to Jack's advice. Having decided to keep Ennis's body out of danger, the two men close the tent flap, and presumably spend the night having sex. Thus the rugged homosexual masculinity of the expansive outdoors appears to carry sort of curative power that keeps male bodily integrity firmly intact.

But while Jack and Ennis constantly encounter and avoid threats from the wilderness they spend the summer inhabiting, the real threat of sickness, contamination, and disability comes from the world of heterosexual domesticity that lies below the mountain. Thus Joe Aguirre travels up the mountain to deliver news of Jack's sick uncle down below, on his deathbed as a result of pneumonia. "Bad news," Jack replies, "There ain't nothin' I can do about it up here, I guess." Aguirre responds, "There's not much you can do about it down there, neither. Not unless you can cure pneumonia." Aguirre's reply is no doubt designed to emphasize Aguirre's position as an unsympathetic boss and foreground Jack's exploitation as a working-class laborer. But it simultaneously emphasizes the contagion that spreads "down there" in the realm of rural domesticity, and the exposure to illness that Jack and Ennis avoid in the able-bodied "up here" of male homosexual freedom.

Thus the progression that starts off Jack and Ennis's descent from the mountain evokes multiple images of Jack and Ennis's newly vulnerable bodies. Jack mentions the possibility that the draft will prevent him from working on the mountain the following summer. The expansive sky that seemed unlimited on the mountain peak is claustrophobically framed by the walls of the alley where Ennis doubles over, retching in grief at his separation from Jack. Ennis's married life consists of a domestic routine that involves caring for his daughters' runny noses and coughs. In an effort to convince Ennis to move the family to more densely populated area of the town, Ennis's wife Alma argues, "I'm scared for Jenny, scared if she has another one of 'em bad asthma spells." To top it off, Ennis's coworker delivers a monologue in which he explains, "My old lady's tryin' to get me

to quit this job. She says I'm gettin' too old to be breakin' my back shovelin' asphalt." Thus, the "up here" that Jack refers to in his conversation with Aguirre is the place where stubborn gay male bodies contend with the elements and, thanks to the balm of same-sex desire, emerge from this face-off intact. "Down there" is the heterosexual domestic space where male bodies are subject to pneumonia, vulnerable to the Vietnam draft, stricken with attacks of debilitating grief, responsible for asthmatic children, and exposed to literally "back-breaking" labor. Indeed, it becomes impossible to find an able-bodied domesticity anywhere in the film.[21] While domesticity is certainly framed as heterosexual, it is also a site that is implicated in the production of both disability and femininity (Ennis and his wife produce only daughters) and is thus no place for the able body of hypermasculine gay cowboy.

It should, of course, be pointed out that the acts of caring for asthmatic children, hearing about sick uncles, and working in physically taxing occupations never actually threaten to render Ennis literally disabled, and neither would any of the women who inhabit Ennis's heteronormative working class household identify themselves as a person with a disability. Indeed, by invoking these images of sickness and injury, I am gesturing less towards the presence of a concrete disabled identity within the film and more towards Jack and Ennis's construction as able-bodied subjects who are haunted by specters of corporeal fragility, specters that originate from the outside—and in their case, the heterosexual landscape. In this sense, I am actively following McRuer's suggestion that we "attempt to crip disability studies, which entails taking seriously the critique of identity that has animated other progressive theoretical projects, notably queer theory" (McRuer, 2006: 35). McRuer suggests that, like the "gender trouble" that underlies heterosexuality, we might similarly understand "ability trouble" as "not so much the problem of disability but the inevitable impossibility, even as it is made compulsory, of an able-bodied identity" (McRuer, 2006: 10). Just as my previous reading of *Murderball* suggested that it was not homosexuality but rather the heterosexual Sam and the disabled female athlete who held the power to queer the film's heteromasculine narrative, so too in *Brokeback Mountain* it is not disability *per se* but a set of failed performances of health and physical integrity that mark the hetero-domestic sphere as a threatening site of "ability trouble."

The threat that heterosexual domesticity levels against masculine able-bodiedness is perhaps most explicit in Jack and Ennis's first conversation after having reunited following a four year separation. After having sex at a motel, they discuss their new roles as husbands and fathers. Jack explains, "Went down to Texas for rodeoin'. That's how I met Lureen." When Ennis asks, "Army didn't get you?" Jack replies, "No, too busted up. And rodeoin' ain't what it was in my daddy's day. Got out while I could still walk." This process of getting "busted up" receives an even more elaborate treatment in the original story. In the same scene, when Ennis asks if the "army got [Jack]," Proulx has Jack reply:

> They can't get no use out a me. Got some crushed vertebrates. And a stress fracture, the arm bone here, you know how bullridin you're always levern it off your thigh?—she give a little ever time you do it. Even if you tape it good you break it a little goddamn bit at a time. Tell you what, hurts like a bitch afterwards. Had a busted leg. Busted in three places... Bunch a other things, fuckin busted ribs, sprains and pains, torn ligaments... I'm gettin out while I still can walk.
>
> (Proulx, 1999: 266)

When making argument about a film, it can be risky to draw evidence from the literary text upon which the film is based. However, because of the film's uncommon faithfulness to the short story—almost all of the dialogue in the film is taken word-for-word from the story and there's barely a single scene left out—such analysis seem justified. In a film that runs over two hours, it makes sense that the screenwriters might have cut some of the dialogue that merely extends a point that could be made more concisely. Thus what becomes clear when we trace this conversation back to the original source is the extreme threat that heterosexual domesticity poses to the able body of the gay cowboy. The rodeo to some extent functions as an extension of heterosexuality. It's where Jack met his wife, and it is, at the beginning at least, the way he has been financially supporting his family. But it also might break his back. The stakes are raised when Jack, explaining that he "don't got the bones a keep getting wrecked," proposes that he and Ennis settle down "in a little ranch together" (Proulx, 1999: 268). Indeed, this is where the short story sets up an ultimatum much like the ones I outlined earlier; a choice must be made between a future of disabled heterosexuality or a future of able-bodied homosexuality.

At the same time, however, Jack's sexuality occasionally complicates the able-bodied queer masculinity that the film attempts to naturalize. In particular, when Jack travels south of the border to engage in what one might consider "risky" anonymous sex with a male prostitute, the viewer might be reminded of one association that the film labors to repress—the historical connections between gay culture and the AIDS epidemic.[22] It is worth noting here that AIDS has been culturally constructed as a disease originating not only from homosexual men, but also as an "immigrant infection" that, originating from the outside, threatens to infiltrate and contaminate the United States population.

Subjected to mandatory HIV testing during the Regan era, immigrants joined gay men as one of the largest projected menaces to public health. This scapegoating of immigrants and queers functioned to externalize the threat of HIV infection, making it easy for officials to ignore the more important issues of prevention, treatment, and anti-discrimination (Brier, 2001: 253–270). While Jack's illicit encounter with the Mexican prostitute takes place before the start of the AIDS epidemic, and while the prostitute himself is not attempting to emigrate to the United States, the scene on some level still resonates with the cultural meanings that have conflated the tightly sealed national body with the healthy body—a seal that Jack breaks when he crosses back and forth over the border.[23] If we are to read this encounter with racial otherness as metaphoric of the "infected" national body, then this becomes a moment when the narrative becomes haunted by its own future. And it is a future in which the representational linkage between male homosexuality and AIDS—a linkage, in other words, between queerness and disability—will loom large.

In this context, it's worth noting that *Brokeback Mountain* has been repeatedly hailed as the first "mainstream gay movie from Hollywood" since Brian Demme's 1992 film *Philadelphia* and in numerous reviews the film's detachment from AIDS discourse is celebrated (Ehrenstein, 2006: 41). Thus *Brokeback* emerges from a queer filmic tradition in which the associations between homosexuality and AIDS have been largely figured and can, in this context, be read as participating in a representational backlash against homosexuality's place in the AIDS narrative.[24] The film escapes these associations by a feat of geographical and temporal dislocation, as the narrative ends just before the AIDS outbreak in the United States. In this context, barebacking loses its association with threats to

public health, transformed instead into a life-affirming practice structured around a principle of rural able-bodied masculinity. But because *Brokeback* seems so powerfully invested in disavowing the political legacy of AIDS activism, along with the historical process by which the epidemic has imprinted the queer community with the stigma of disability, some of those repressed elements do surface from time to time within the narrative, particularly through Jack in the moments I have just discussed.

I'd like to conclude this section by tentatively pointing to a verbal/visual divide similar to the one that I referenced in my discussion of *Murderball's* narrative performances of heteromasculinity and the static images of the disabled female body that momentarily stall those narratives. Though I have largely relied on verbal examples to describe the strategies thorough which the film constructs its ethos of able-bodiedness, the moments that most powerfully "crip" that narrative are generally mute, relying instead on the transmission of visual cues. When Jack visits Mexico, his encounter with the prostitute is markedly silent; and while Lureen's monotone rehearsal of the official narrative of Jack's death accompanies Ennis's entirely different visual reconstruction of the scene, the images of hate crime violence that confront the viewer in this clip are entirely absent of sound, and differently filmed, playing like a grainy home video without audio. The intrusion of these brief images gestures toward a queer-crip cultural past that cannot, ultimately, be spoken.

But why not take such moments as opportunities to critically consider, and perhaps occasionally even claim, those histories, both representational and material, in which queerness and disability are brought into uneasy proximity? What, ultimately, is to be gained by the current cultural impulse to dissolve this complicated, though albeit troubled, partnership? While critics of both films are certainly justified in celebrating the strategies through which newer films are defiantly cutting the ties that have historically bound queerness to disability, I want to suggest that we remain wary of accepting discourses that celebrate one marginal identity at the expense of another, and that we continue to ask who gets left out of this framework completely. While male homosexuality and male disability may be regulating one another in these films, what is perhaps most perplexing is that it is not the able-bodied gay man whose existence is disavowed *Murderball* but the physically disabled woman. And it is not entirely the heterosexual man who is linked to a disabling domesticity in *Brokeback Mountain*, but primarily the heterosexual woman. Transgender identity is meanwhile rendered unthinkable and race is dealt with problematically, at best. Of course, there is undoubtedly something productive happening when mainstream films begin to challenge the stereotype of the feminized or asexual male quadriplegic, or when those same films acknowledge that male homosexuality is not intrinsically bound up in illness. But these liberatory representations are accompanied by a set of political limitations that demand greater scrutiny. Rather than replace one regime of normalcy with another, we would do well to transform this uncomfortable representational history into an opportunity for continuing the difficult work of coalition building. Only then can we really achieve the cyborg myth of breaking with our origins to fashion new and unthinkable futures.

NOTES

My thanks to Lennard Davis for his feedback on as well as support for this essay.

1. While the relationship between disability and gender has often been theorized, many of these accounts have grown out of a feminist concern for the representations of disabled women and the linkages between femininity and illness. Indeed, many of the early canonical texts of feminist literary criticism focus on relationship between femininity, authorship and mental health, Sandra Gilbert and Susan Gubar's *The Mad Woman in the Attic* being perhaps the most well-known example. More recently, however, scholars like Rosemarie Garland-Thomson have prioritized the physical disability, as opposed to mental illness, in their analysis as well and brought race to bear on these issues in important ways.

2. McRuer does, however, provide a notable counterexample in his observations regarding ableist rhetoric in the popular television show *Queer Eye For the Straight Guy*.

3. Matthew Leyland, for example, offers the following praise in *Sight and Sound*: "Dispelling misconceptions in an unfussy fashion, Shapiro and Rubin . . . venture into taboo territory with an X-rated debate about quad sex. As well as answering questions most disability movies are afraid to ask, the sequence is very funny. 'The more pitiful I am, the more [women] like me,' one wheelchair user chirps unapologetically'" (Leyland, 2005: 70).

4. In *The Cinema of Isolation*, Martin Norden identifies one such narrative trap as the tendency for Hollywood to put well-known, able-bodied actors in disabled roles. Like a straight-identified actor playing a gay role, the casting of able-bodied stars in disabled roles becomes an opportunity for the able-bodied actor to demonstrate superior Oscar-quality acting skills by successfully impersonating what the public would view as extreme difference or otherness (Norden, 1994: 2).

5. In his comparative reading of the armless Venus de Milo and a quadriplegic woman, Pam Herbert, Lennard Davis draws our attention to the able-bodied assumptions underlying Western standards of physical beauty. Thus Davis explores "how people with disabilities are seen and why, by and large, they are de-eroticized" (Davis, 1995: 128). The film's intense eroticization of quadriplegic men can then be read as a radical reclaiming of that which has long been denied to disabled people; that this is accomplished through heteronormative masculinization and at the expense of disabled people whom are further "queered" by the logic of the film, however, is a tension that this section explores in greater detail.

6. In her magazine piece "Seat of Power," Melissa Davis Haller quotes James Gumbert (the coach

for Team USA) as pointing out that "Most of these guys didn't get into their chairs because they were timid . . . They were daredevils." The player featured in the piece agrees: " 'We're true athletes,' he says. 'We have the same rivalries and passion about our sport as anyone'" (Haller, 2005: 22).

7. The celebration of the prosthetic dimensions of Zupan's masculinity also constitutes a subversion of previous stereotypes. Norden points out the common villainization of disabled male figures who are "aided by . . . high tech prostheses" and "whose many battle injuries have transformed him into a walking wonderland of bionic effects . . . more machine than man" (Norden, 1994: 293).

8. Perhaps picking up on the prosthetic dimensions of the sport equipment, one reviewer has remarked upon a quad rugby player who "handles the ball as if it were a part of his body" (Bennett, 2000: 60).

9. My thanks to Megan V. Davis for this reference.

10. Examining the work of three different visual artists, Halberstam defines this technotopic body as "a body situated in an immediate and visceral relation to technologies—guns, scalpel, cars, paintbrushes—that have marked, hurt, changed, imprinted, and brutally reconstructed it" and notes that "in all three instances, the impact of technological intervention is to disrupt gender stability . . . [suggesting that] we should locate femaleness not as the material with which we begin nor as the end product of medical engineering but as a stage and indeed as fleshly place of production" (Halberstam, 2005: 116–117). The men of *Murderball* are certainly "situated in an immediate and visceral relation to technologies that have marked" each of them. But while for Halberstam the technotopic body "disrupts gender stability" and showcases anatomical sex as neither the "material with which we begin nor as the end product of medical engineering," the technologized masculinity of the quad rugby athletes is visually framed within a narrative of continuity that privileges the anatomical origin of maleness and the technologically enhanced final product of heteronormative masculinity. What might have become a radical celebration of technology's roles in producing alternative or queer modes of embodiment here collapses into a reification of gender difference.

11. In *The Gender of Desire*, Michael Kimmel has argued that hegemonic masculinity is fundamentally rooted in a homophobic impulse to simultaneously deny and desire the feminine. If a boy is to access patriarchy, his successful identification with his father must be accompanied by a disavowal of the feminine within himself, a punishment of effeminacy in other men, and a willingness to turn his mother into an object of desire (Kimmel, 2005: 34). If *Murderball* follows the traditional narrative of masculinity that Kimmel has outlined, the players' masculinity ultimately depends on the sexual acquisition of the girl whose "big tits" prove that she's everything that he's not.

12. Interestingly, the player commentary not only conflates Sam's queer object choice with feminization but also with a lack of sexual potency, and a general inability to engage in phallocentric penetrative sex. While watching the poker scene with the commentary function turned on, one hears the players add: "We tried to get Sammy laid the whole year, but he's just not a closer. He's had some opportunities but Sammy cuddles." Sam's decision to not be a "closer" simultaneously resists the narrative *closure* that protectively bounds heteromasculine sexuality in the film.

13. This argument is not an entirely new one; in the context of disabled veteran films, Martin Norden argues that "Movies continue to depend heavily on the idea of women acting as remasculinizing agents to facilitate the protagonists' Oedipal adventures, particularly those featuring embittered veterans" (322). Other films didn't necessarily rely on woman per se, but resolved similar tensions by situating the character among "advancements in science and technology in the form of highly potent prosthesis" (322). Both features, however, appear to be at play in *Murderball*.

14. To this effect, one reviewer celebrates the "lusty montage" which illuminates the "intriguing reasons why some women are particularly attracted to quadriplegic men." In another scene, the viewer is able to appreciate—and perhaps envy—Zupan's ability to attract an able-bodied, conventionally feminine woman who is featured in a black bikini on the side of a pool. Her interview portions in the film mainly function to emphasize the ways in which partnership with a quadriplegic man brings out the "mothering instinct" in women, a quality that she suggests could be what "attracts a lot of girls to quadriplegics." Cut alongside of a clip that features her tying Zupan's shoes, the implication is clear.

15. For a more thorough analysis of these issues, see Rosemarie Garland-Thomson's "Integrating Disability, Transforming Feminist Theory."

16. One analysis that I am omitting here, which is

beyond the scope of this paper, is the similarly problematic image of the disabled black man who shares the frame with this woman. While the frame catches her from the neck down, it simultaneously catches only the top right quadrant of his face in the bottom left corner of the frame. The only other exposure that the viewer has to African-American disabled masculinity are two entirely out-of-context interviews in which a disabled black man (whose name, team affiliation, and general relationship to the sport we never learn) describes some of the tensions he encounters when trying to pick up girls and elaborates upon the "modified doggy-style" that he has perfected during sex. The relative absence of African-American male quadriplegics from the film suggests that the players' disabled masculinity is not only invested in heterosexuality but in whiteness. The brief airtime given to African-American masculinity functions only to rhetorically infuse the sexuality of the featured (white) quadriplegic men with the primitive potency stereotypically projected onto African-American masculinity. That this particular African-American man happens to be describing the "doggy-style" position only exaggerates and exploits the dangerous cultural stereotypes that link African American sexuality to animalism and aggressivity. Thus, while this moment might be read as a sensitive inclusion of a non-white voice in dialogue about male quadriplegia and sexuality, I would argue that it ulitmately collapses into merely another rhetorical building block in the construction and maintenance of the white heteromasculinity.

17. To this effect, it is striking how quickly the players, while appearing on Larry King Live, pass over the related inquiry of a female caller. While all of the other calls lasted several minutes, this particular seemed over as soon as it began. The entire dialogue runs as follows:

Woman: "Being from Alaska, where is [sic] the closest teams and how many are there, and is [sic] there any female teams?"

Bob: "There are women that play rugby, it's a co-ed sport."

Larry King: "And so women can be on *your* team?"

Mark: "Yeah, it's a co-ed sport."

Larry King: "Any in Alaska?"

Scott: "No, the closest team I'd say is in Seattle."

Larry King: "So you have to go to Seattle."

18. In this article, my use of the term "gay" should be read as a shorthand for male same-sex desire and homosexual erotic expression. By employing it in this context, I am by no means making an identity claim about Jack and Ennis—indeed, in both the film and the short story, both men make it clear that they don't self-identify as "queer." It is important, however, to acknowledge the impact that this film has had on members of the gay community, many of whom have identified with and claimed the characters, as well the effect it has had on mainstream understandings of the gay community. Thus by referring to "gay" masculinity or "gay" sexuality, I am referring to the representation of a behavior that has had a significant impact on the cultural understandings of a constructed identity category and the communities that have been formed around that category.

19. If *Murderball* follows a Freudian narrative in which a disavowal of the feminine in the self entails the transformation of women into objects of desire, then in *Brokeback Mountain*, the disavowal of the feminine in the self involves no such transformation; in *Brokeback Mountain*, to embody frontier masculinity is to disavow the feminine, period. Reviewer Constantine Hoffman puts it well when he points out that "*Brokeback* forced us to face the fact that the more 'manly' a man is the more he will enjoy the company of other manly men" (Hoffman, 2006: 26). Indeed, if twenty-five years ago, Adrienne Rich argued that lesbianism was the natural expression of "woman-identification"—a state from which women were coercively exiled by a system of "compulsory heterosexuality"— then *Brokeback Mountain* applies the same logic male same-sex desire. For a feminist disability critique of Rich's article, see Alison Kafer's "Compulsory Bodies: Reflections on Heterosexuality and Able-Bodiedness."

20. While the rodeo, which I will later discuss in more depth, is linked to both heterosexuality and disability, the scene where Ennis is thrown from his horse functions as its able-bodied queer counterpoint: Ennis is barely injured by the incident, able even to immediately chase the horse and mules who have run off. Additionally, upon their first trip back to the mountain after their long separation, the first thing we see Jack and Ennis do is strip off their clothes and jump from a tall cliff into the water below. We might productively compare this scene to the Spanish film *The Sea Inside* where a similar jump off of a similar cliff results in extreme quadriplegic impairment.

21. Robert McRuer's arguments about hetero-sexuality and able-bodied domesticity seem worth addressing in this context. McRuer argues that "[t]he ideological reconsolidation of the home as a site of intimacy and heterosexuality was also the reconsolidation of the home as a site for the redevelopment of able-bodied identities, practices, and relations." Thus an "inability to imagine a queer domesticity" becomes also the "inability to imagine a disabled domesticity" (McRuer, 2006: 89). While McRuer's argument is entirely valid within the context of his examples, *Brokeback Mountain* appears to signal a drastic resignification of these concepts, forcefully undoing the associational link between heterosexual domesticity and able-bodied ideologies.

22. Interestingly, in this respect, Jack emblematizes both the "cult of ability" that McRuer has identified as "the Good Gays who are capable of sustaining a marriage, who are not stigmatized by AIDS, and who went to Washington in 2000 for the Millennium March" and the "cultures of disability" that are made up of participants in "AIDS activism and the lesbian feminist traditions of health care activism that preceded it" (McRuer, 2006: 86).

23. We might consider this moment alongside of the scene that occurs directly after Jack convinces Ennis to spend the night with him in the tent during the hailstorm. What appears to be a decision on the side of able-bodied homo-sexuality turns out to result in another racial contamination—without Ennis there to shepherd them, Aguirre's flock has gotten mixed together with a flock of South American sheep. It is, of course, not at all my intention here to conflate Mexico and South America. However, their geographical proximity and their relationship to Hispanic racial identity does function to link them within the logic of the film.

24. Ironically, these associations were often accompanied by a different understanding of queer masculinity, one that, according to Tim Edwards, saw gay public sex cultures not only as a site of contamination but also as outgrowth of an aggressive and "unnatural" hypermasculine sex drive. If the urban manifestations of gay sexuality appeared to many to link hypermasculinity to sexual excess, indulgence, and disease then Ennis's rural brand of stoic masculinity, founded on an ethic of discipline and restraint, invests his homosexuality with the virtues of health, organicism, and able-bodiedness.

25. For a thorough treatment of cultural understandings of barebacking, see Gregory Tomso's "Bug Chasing, Barebacking, and the Risks of Care." Of course, on another level, the film might be said to constitute the realistic portrait of queer rural masculinities between 1960 and 1980. By no means is my intention to consolidate a grand narrative that privileges urban queer cultures at the exclusion of rural queer manifestations. The film does indeed help us to revise our assumptions about the proper "time and place" for queer sexualities (Halberstam, 2005). I would suggest, however, that in its intense disavowal of all things urban and disabled, *Brokeback Mountain* in fact lends remarkable authority to those representational histories that tied queerness to urban sex cultures and disability.

WORKS CITED

Bennett, R. (2000) "Rugby", *WeMedia* 4(5): pp. 60.

Brier, J. (2001) "The Immigrant Infection: Images of Race, Nation and Contagion in Public Debates on AIDS and Immigration." *Modern American Queer History*. Edited by Allida M. Black. Philadelphia: Temple University Press.

Davis, L. J. (1995) *Enforcing Normalcy: Disability, Deafness, and the Body*. New York: Verso Books.

Edwards, T. (1994) *Erotics & Politics: Gay Male Sexuality, Masculinity, and Feminism*. London: Routledge.

Ehrenstein, D. (2006) "Fun with Harv and George?", *Advocate*, February, p. 41.

Garland-Thomson, R. (1997) *Extraordinary Bodies: Figuring Physical Disability in American Culture and Literature*. New York: Columbia University Press.

Garland-Thomson, R. (2004) "Integrating Disability, Transforming Feminist Theory", in B.G. Smith and B. Hutchison (eds) *Gendering Disability*, pp. 73–104. New Brunswick, NJ: Rutgers University Press.

Garland-Thomson, R. (2007) "Shape Structures Story: Fresh and Feisty Stories about Disability", *Narrative*, 15(1): pp. 113–123.

Gilbert, S. and Gubar, S. (1979) *The Mad Woman in the Attic: The Woman Writer and the Nineteenth Century Literary Imagination*. New Haven, CT: Yale University Press.

Halberstam, J. (2005) *In a Queer Time and Place: Transgender Bodies, Subcultural Lives*. New York: New York University Press.

Haller, M.D. (2005) "Seat of Power", *Cincinnati Magazine*, October, 39(1): pp. 20, 22.

Haraway, D. (1991) *Simians, Cyborgs and Women: The Reinvention of Nature*. New York: Routledge.

Hoffman, C. (2006) "Memo From the Front: It's Just a Manly Thing", *Brandweek*, May, 47(18): p. 26.

Kafer, A. (2003) "Compulsory Bodies: Reflections on Heterosexuality and Able-Bodiedness", *Journal of Women's History*, 15(3): pp. 77–89.

Kimmel, M. S. (2005) *The Gender of Desire: Essays on Male Sexuality*. New York: State University of New York Press.

Lee, A. (2006) *Brokeback Mountain*. Universal Studios.

Leyland, M. (2005) "Murderball", *Sight and Sound*, 15(11): pp. 70–71.

McRuer, R. (2006) *Crip Theory: Cultural Signs of Queerness and Disability*. New York: New York University Press.

Mulvey, L. (1975) "Visual Pleasure and Narrative Cinema", *Screen* 16(3): pp. 6–18.

Norden, M. F. (1994) *The Cinema of Isolation: A History of Physical Disability in the Movies*. New Brunswick, NJ: Rutgers University Press.

Proulx, A. (1999) *Close Range: Wyoming Stories*. New York: Scribners.

Seymour, W. (1998) *Remaking the Body: Rehabilitation and Change*. London: Routledge.

Shapiro, D. A., Mandel, J. and Rubin, H. A. (2005) *Murderball*. THINKFilm and MTV Films.

Tomso, G. (2004) "Bug Chasing, Barebacking, and the Risks of Care", *Literature and Medicine*, 23(1): pp. 88–111.

Wilson, D. J. (2004) "Fighting Polio Like a Man: Intersections of Masculinity, Disability and Aging", in B. G. Smith and B. Hutchison (eds) *Gendering Disability*, pp. 119–133. New Brunswick, NJ: Rutgers University Press.

CHAPTER 29

Sculpting Body Ideals: *Alison Lapper Pregnant* and the Public Display of Disability

Ann Millett-Gallant

In 2005, artist Alison Lapper was thrust into fame when her 11.5 foot tall, 13 ton sculptural portrait, *Alison Lapper Pregnant*, was unveiled on the fourth plinth of Trafalgar Square [see cover image]. Lapper agreed to being cast in the nude by British artist Marc Quinn when she was 7 months pregnant and to be placed on public display; many have called the piece a collaboration. The controversial sculpture has brought widespread attention to the model's body and her life story. Lapper, born without arms and with shortened legs, is an alumnus of British institutions for disabled children and programs for disabled artists, a now single mother, and an artist who makes work about her embodied experiences as a disabled woman. Carved from precious Italian marble and placed on a pedestal among statues of naval captains, Lapper has been called a contemporary heroine of cultural diversity, while the work has also been regarded as a tasteless publicity stunt for Quinn. The exposure of Lapper's body transcends the fact that she is nude, for Lapper grew up in insolated environments of public intuitions and had limited interactions with public life; for Lapper, the work is a true coming out. *Alison Lapper Pregnant* makes a public statement about this disabled woman's right to be represented as a productive social subject *and* a reproductive sexual being and her right to represent others.

This essay will interrogate the sculpture's representation of disability within the contexts of Trafalgar Square, the genre of Public Art, as well as in comparisons with Quinn's previous series of sculptural amputees, *The Complete Marbles* (2002), and, foremost, with Lapper's self-representations. I will argue that *Alison Lapper Pregnant* significantly responds to, as well as transforms, the history of its particular space and interacts with the populations who inhabit that space. Rather than displaying trite political correctness or simple shock value, as much of its criticism wages, the work plays monumental roles in the histories of both disability representation and art. As a public spectacle, it recycles, and I will argue contemporizes, the representation of disability as both heroic and freakish. Further, Lapper's photography and her recently published memoir are key components of such discussions, as they provide perspectives by and a voice to the disabled subject on display. By weaving together these contexts of and reactions to Quinn's and Lapper's works, this essay underscores the necessity of placing the works of disabled and non-disabled artists in dialogues with one another and with larger histories of visual culture.

Public art raises issues of social and artistic representation and the visibility and invisibility of certain members of society. Public space and its monuments have been gendered male and raced white traditionally, and public space is largely ableist in attitude, not to mention accessibility (or lack thereof). Public art, when the most effective, creates dialogues about the role of art in society and whom is included and excluded in the notion of the "public." By honoring individuals marginalized and erased by dominant values and the structures which personify them, many more contemporary public art projects have explicitly protested the status quo. These public art forms, in which I contextualize *Alison Lapper Pregnant*, embody cultural battles for and of representation.

The sculpture produces Lapper as a representative of the historically under-represented. Lapper has positioned the work at the forefront of such initiatives, stating: 'I regard it as a modern tribute to femininity, disability and motherhood . . . The sculpture makes the ultimate statement about disability—that it can be as beautiful and valid a form of being as any other." She acknowledges how her body becomes a monument to bodies and identities that have been socially devalued, shamed, and excluded from public life historically. Lapper goes on to note: "It is so rare to see disability in everyday life—let alone naked, pregnant and proud. The sculpture makes the ultimate statement about disability—that it can be as beautiful and valid a form of being as any other."[1] Here, she characterizes her body as a form of anti-monument, for it represents the "other" to traditional subjects of public monuments, as well as an anti-ideal. Positive feedback about the sculpture also champions it as a liberating anti-ideal.[2] The work may function to force the viewer to question their perceptions of the "ideal," while also questioning whose ideals Lapper is purported to represent.

The work functions visually on confusions between the ideal and anti-ideal. Quinn's work is specifically a quotation of 18th- and 19th-century Neoclassicism. Neoclassical figurative painting, sculpture, and architectural programs taught lessons on heroism and moral virtue, often by depicting the deeds of great and powerful men.[3] In Western culture from the Renaissance to today, this Neoclassical form is characteristically employed for public statues of religious and political heroes. Neoclassicism and its Classical heritage communicate philosophical and political ideals through mathematically constructed aesthetics, specifically, in "whole" bodies.

Quinn subverts the signification of Neoclassical form as the ideal "whole" in *Alison Lapper Pregnant* (2005) and in his series of life size, marble sculptures of amputees, *The Complete Marbles* (2002), which adopt particularly Roman qualities of portrait likeness. By using many high profile disabled models, such as artist Peter Hull and the confrontational "freak" performer and punk rock musician, Matt Fraser, Quinn produces depictions of recognizable subjects and celebrities. Titled with the subjects' proper names, these works challenge how the viewer perceives the body in art, as well as in everyday life, as whole and/or broken.[4] Quinn titled this series *The Complete Marbles* strategically. *The Elgin Marbles* are precious Classical sculptures appropriated from the Parthenon in Greece (produced c. 438–423 BCE). *The Elgin Marbles*, many broken and missing limbs and heads, were amputated from their architectural base (the Parthenon); they are fragments of profoundly aesthetic "wholes," for the Parthenon remains a cultural icon today for its integrated, carefully orchestrated balance and proportion and its intense, methodical control of aesthetics. Extracted from the Temple to Athena, the marbles both fragment and "stand" (or symbolize) one of the greatest symbols of power and wealth in Western history—specifically one famous for its ideal wholeness. Quinn's title for the series, *The Complete Marbles*, places contemporary disabled bodies in these historical legacies, and they are designated as "whole" by their own counter-conventional body standards and disarming beauty.

Quinn's artistic procedures and materials are central to the significances of his works. Like all of the pieces in *The Complete Marbles*, *Alison Lapper Pregnant* was sculpted in Quinn's studio in Pietrasenta, Italy, the center for Carrara marble—the same marble sought by Michelangelo and many Neoclassical sculptors. *Alison Lapper Pregnant* took 10 months to craft from the stubborn substance, which contains exalted histories and symbolic significances. Quinn is quite particular about the material, as he literally goes out of his way to use it, and he prefers this marble for its "intrinsic and metaphoric content."[5] Carrara marble provides a luminosity that makes his amputees shine and radiate, like works from the Greek Hellenistic period.

Many critics deem Quinn's art historical references as subversive, specifically because he focuses on disabled bodies. For example, art writer for the *Sunday Times*, Waldemar Januszczak, states the following about *Allison Lapper Pregnant*:

> By carving Allison Lapper out of pristine marble, Quinn is *taking on* the Greeks; he is *disputing* with Phidias, with Michelangelo, with Sir Joshua Reynolds, with every authoritarian with imagination that has ever insisted upon a standard shape for the human in art; he is contradicting 2,000 years of creative *misrepresentation* of what being human means; and he is giving Allison Lapper the same amount of artistic attention that Canova gave the Empress Josephine. As if that were not enough, Quinn is also cheekily rhyming his sculptures with the broken remnants of classical art—the armless Venus, the legless Apollo—that are the staple diet of all collections of the antique. These are serious achievements.[6] (emphasis mine)

My italics here underscore how Januszczak describes Quinn's use of amputees in art historical, specifically Classical and Neoclassical images, as confrontational and revisionist, as if the works are affronts to these traditions because of the amputees featured. This comment suggests that certain social prejudices against amputees function in critical interpretations of Quinn's work. The form of the Lapper sculpture has been the target of much criticism; however, criticisms against the artistic value of *Alison Lapper Pregnant* (the work) may suggest simultaneous rejection of Alison Lapper pregnant (as an embodiment and social subject). Many have charged Quinn with capitalizing on the shock value and taboo nature of disabled bodies in public spaces.[7] The work functions to make such stereotypes visible and open to public debate.

On the other hand (or stump), positive evaluations of the *Alison Lapper Pregnant* further complicate how the sculpture represents disability in the public eye, as they purport Lapper to be a hero. This idea recalls the stereotype of a disabled hero that is premised on sentimentalization of and low expectations for disabled people in society. What kind of hero is Lapper in these descriptions, one who dismantles notions of appropriate versus shocking bodies? Or one who rehashes the stereotype of "overcoming," which functions to ignore social constructs of disability and is based on the problematic notion of disability as an individual "problem"? Framed as the representation of a hero, the sculpture celebrates Lapper's impairments and perhaps also de-politicizes, or literally aestheticizes disability, as a marginalizing social construct, for the public. Or perhaps it redefines our ideas about heroism and makes a disabled figure a role model, in a positive light.

Lapper's heroism may also be problematically tied to her pregnancy, such that motherhood becomes a means for Lapper to "overcome" disability by conforming to standards for women's roles in society, a point which Kim Q. Hall has interrogated. Hall quotes Quinn: "For me, *Alison Lapper Pregnant* is a monument to the future possibilities of the human race as well as the resilience of the human spirit."[8] Hall frames this comment within political propaganda that has imposed the duty upon women historically to reproduce the nation; such dogma is similar to that expressed throughout Trafalgar Square by the national heroes depicted. Hall argues that the sculpture is championed by Quinn and many others because it confounds the taboo nature of disabled bodies in public spaces, as well as patriarchal and heterosexual values that assert that reproduction validates women. Yet, Hall's persuasive arguments reframe how Lapper's presence in the square plays upon traditional gender roles and disability stereotypes only tangentially, for the sculpture's and Lapper's own consistent divergence from convention affirms the work's adamant non-conformity to "family values." Mainstream discourses that breed women for motherhood suggest that a productive female member of the society is a *reproductive* one, specifically within the institution of marriage. Far from glorifying a nuclear family, Lapper was born to a single, working class mother and is herself an unmarried mother, who has benefited from public programs for disabled artists. Many may view Lapper's choices as amoral and her subsistence as a public burden, therefore she hardly acts in the legacy of national heroes.

Lapper's maternal situation defies ideals of both society and of art for women's bodies. Pregnant bodies, seen most often in art history as fertility figures and virginal Madonnas, occupy a liminal status, as both an ideal state of the female motherhood, yet one that contrasts with the conventions for the sexualized nude, particularly for 21st-century eyes. Popular representations have tended to idealize pregnancy socially, yet they also veil the pregnant female body, reinstating its preferred existence within the proverbial home. Pregnancy is glorified and yet stigmatized and indeed often considered a disability. However, images of pregnant women have become trendy lately, particularly among the elite, with the celebrity "baby boom" displayed in the aesthetic "bumps" on otherwise perfect bodies and within the romanticized unions of the Brangelinas and Tom-Kats of the world; Demi Moore, Melania Trump, and most recently, Britney Spears have been featured by mainstream women's magazines as so-called liberated covergirls and centerfolds, revealing their scantily clad and fashionable pregnant bodies. Again, these pregnant bodies are framed specifically within dominant social ideals and values (with perhaps the exception of Spears and the notorious "Fed-Ex"), values to which Alison Lapper could never conform. *Alison Lapper Pregnant* confuses perceptions of the body in art history and popular culture, ultimately because, for many, the work assertively provokes the fear that the disabled body will reproduce another "damaged" child—from a "broken" body and a "broken" home. The work advocates controversial reproductive rights for disabled women and for single women more broadly. Further, any attempt on Lapper's part to fulfill her role to reproduce the next generation may produce a disabled one, which remains a horror rather than a triumph, according to mainstream values and exclusive social standards for quality of life. Lapper's maternal "acts" poignantly fail to service social ideals, as the sculpture becomes pregnant with ambivalent meanings.

Viewers' reactions to the work as shocking and/or inspiring seem polarized, and yet both connote, to varying degrees, the desire to make a lesson out of the disabled body, in order to justify its display. Many who critique the work and Quinn's *The Complete Marbles* series demand explanation about the cause of the models' impairments and the usefulness of such displays to society. Januszczak has also stated: "With a subject as serious as the loss of human limbs, or the birth of a child to a deformed mother, it is absolutely incumbent upon the gallery to cease playing aesthetic games and to make clearer the artist's intentions."[9] This quote expresses viewers' desire for medical diagnosis to make the works more palatable and less sensationalistic. However, the sculpture also provokes some viewers to question their own desires to know "what happened" to the body and assumptions that the disabled body necessarily connotes accident or victimization.

The notion of making the disabled body into a lesson is relevant to the realm of public art specifically, within which the body becomes a monument to instruct, for public art has a duty, in the eyes of many, to educate and inform. The origin of the word "monument" derives from Latin *monere*, meaning "to remind," "to admonish," "warn," "advise," and "instruct."[10] Poignantly, this word origin emerges also in the word "monster," as scholars of the freak show have pointed out, explaining how the disabled body has historically been seen as an indicator of either supernatural foreshadowing or scientific mistake. The use of the disabled body as a lesson has included public exploitation of so-called medical anomalies, practices which have reinforced medical models, crossed genres into freak shows, and staged the disabled body as an instructional object for the non-disabled viewers. The 19th- and early 20th-century freak show entertained and affirmed middle class spectators' senses of "normalcy," which was constructed specifically in binary opposition to the strikingly "abnormal" spectacle.

The freak show is another relevant comparison for considering the role of Lapper's body in a public space, particularly one that serves as a tourist attraction[11]: "She is presented "like some 19th-century fairground exhibit," one critic stated.[12] In the freak show, the disabled and other extraordinary (exotic, minority) bodies were eroticized; the nudity of the sculpture, to which some take offense, is intrinsic to its unashamed display of the pregnant disabled body and its Neoclassical form; it places the work in a both a history of art and a history of displaying the body as spectacle, in the freak show, pornography, and other voyeuristic venues. This context raises a key question: does the sculpture exploit Alison Lapper?

Lapper is benefiting from the attention the work has drawn to her own art and her life, as she recently published a memoir (2005). In it, she relates Quinn's sculpture to her own self-portrait nude photography, with which she expresses comfort in her own skin and challenges her personal history of being considered physically defective and sexually unattractive. Addressing the controversy regarding the nudity of the statue, Lapper has written:

> In most societies, even in Britain today, pregnant women are not considered to have a beautiful shape. On top of that, short people, who are missing both arms, are generally considered even less beautiful. I was someone who currently combined both disadvantages. How could Marc possibly think I was a suitable subject for a sculpture that people would want to look at? Statues are created and exhibited to give pleasure, to be admired. Would anybody be able to admire the statue of a naked, pregnant, disabled woman?[13]

She attributes the controversy of the sculpture to a society that is prudish to nudity in general, as well as to pregnancy and to disability specifically. Many may deem the work amoral, and therefore in direct opposition to Neoclassical, moralistic traditions, and yet, as Lapper articulates, moral judgments are subjective to the eyes of the beholders.

Lapper does not express feeling exploited. Describing her decision to pose, Lapper writes:

> It was January 1999 when I received a phone call from an artist called Marc Quinn. . . . I was extremely suspicious. I thought he might be just another one in the long line of people who have exploited disability and used it for its curiosity and value. However, when we talked, I realized Marc wasn't interested in disability in the way most people wanted to depict it. He wasn't pitying or moralising—I knew it wasn't a freak show or some kind of weird sexual focus that he was aiming at.[14]

Lapper here recognizes the problematic tropes of representing disabled bodies as sentimentalized heroes or freakish spectacles, both of which make the disabled body into a symbol and lesson to be learned by the so-called normal. Poignantly, she ties these tropes together. Yet by collaborating with Quinn, Lapper makes a statement about the need for public education and exposure of/to disability in contemporary society in order to overturn the stereotypes and the status quo.

Trafalgar Square is an ideal place to raise and interrogate these issues. The modern city, and public squares like Trafalgar especially, were built for tourist gazing, urban surveillance, and commercial spectatorship.[15] Trafalgar Square, designed by John Nash and built by Sir Charles Barry in the 1820s and 30s to commemorate British naval captain and famous imperialist Admiral Horatio Nelson (1758–1805), was named after the Spanish Cape Trafalgar where Nelson's last battle was won. Characteristic of 19th-century Roman revival in Britain, the square's architecture and statuary is specifically Neoclassical to portray political ideals. A monument to Lord Nelson became the central vision of the square. This Neoclassical likeness of Nelson stands on a 185 foot tall column, overseeing the public—a tradition which continues today. Nelson's monument, modeled after the triumphant Roman Column of Trajan, and its surroundings place modern Britain in the traditions of Roman imperialism. Surrounding Nelson are other monuments to British military heroes, represented in idealizing Neoclassical forms.[16] Like the design of the square, the Neoclassical monuments display a particular side of British history and society, one whose power depends on the subordination of those rendered invisible.

With her marble, feminine curves and serene posture, *Alison Lapper Pregnant* would seem out of place in such a paternalistic environment[17]—the freakish anti-hero. And yet others see the sculpture as right at home with the other monuments. She has been compared symbolically and corporeally with Admiral Nelson himself, as the work reinterprets notions of disabled and non-disabled heroes and spectacles. For examples, in letters to the editor, Michael Gallagher calls Lapper: "A great Briton in the truest sense of the word. I am sure that Nelson would have recognised her as a kindred spirit," and Jeanette Hart notes: ". . . Nelson only had one arm, and was blind in one eye, and he was just known as a great man; no one labelled him."[18] Nelson was indeed blinded in one eye during the capture of Corsica from French troops in 1794 and lost his arm in a 1797 capture of the Canary Islands. He continued to lead troops with these impairments until his death at the Battle of Trafalgar in 1805, an act which has augmented his status as a national hero. The column is topped by a statue of Nelson posed with his uniform coat sleeve draped along his chest and tucked into his suitcoat, in a conventional pose for leaders, yet his sleeve is empty. This view is not perceptible for the viewer below. Quinn's public display of Alison Lapper and its comparisons to Nelson's Column have illuminated for some that the disabled body is always already present in an existing vision of heroism. Viewing Lapper as a hero reinterprets or expands the image of a heroic body, and perhaps this designation does not simply rehash stereotypes of overcoming, but rather describes the meaning of her body as a public image within a specific location and historical context.

Alison Lapper Pregnant follows in multiple histories of public art that are celebratory of or in protest to their context—a simultaneous monument and anti-monument. All of the submissions for the Fourth Plinth project competition since 1990 have been consciously critical of the square's aristocratic, nationalistic, and paternalistic traditions, both in content and form. As art critic Paul Usherwood describes it, Lapper carries on this contemporary trend of mocking the square's: "macho triumphalism and formality."[19] Lapper's Neo- or post-Classical form embodies also a breaching of boundaries between convention and subversion. And by embodying contradictions, Lapper once again fits right into Trafalgar Square and translates its history to contemporary debates over civil and human rights. The controversial debates surrounding the work continue a long-standing history of Trafalgar Square, which has been wrought with conflict historically (as evidenced by the background stories on the lives of the men honored there). Trafalgar Square has served as the city's most popular rallying point and the site of: political, economic, and religious protests; interventions of military law; class battles; protests for freedom of speech and rights to assemble, for women's suffrage, and for civil rights, liberties, and decolonization; and pro and anti-war, pro and anti-Fascism and Semitism, and pro and anti- communism rallies.[20] Poignantly, all these displays of activism represent multiple and opposing sides of social and political issues since the 19th-century, and, significant, most of these demonstrations have centered on the base of Nelson's column, because of its physical prominence and its symbolic significance. The monuments of Nelson and Lapper both embody multiple significances contextually and over time and have been witnesses to multiplicities of perspectives. Both Nelson's and Lapper's bodies in Trafalgar Square pay tribute to the necessity of public debate.

The sculpture of Alison Lapper and its social and symbolic meanings must be considered within its specific context. The work embodies, transforms, and contemporizes the history of its space. *Alison Lapper Pregnant* carries on the square's traditions by provoking debate and dissent. The controversy and many opposing opinions expressed publicly about the sculpture enact its social work. Lapper's body on display has provoked constructive investigation about the role of art in society and the roles of disabled bodies as heroes and spectacles. It asks us to interrogate our assumptions about what forms of bodies should or should not appear in public spaces and how. The dubious representations of disability the work evokes are both liberating and stereotypical, which is necessary to provoke debate. That Lapper herself has been so vocal in the discussions is key, for her collaboration with Quinn and her public mediation of the work shows how perspectives *of* disability, not just *about* them, are necessary for any productive dialogue.

Comparisons of Quinn's work with Lapper's own body art, which self-narrates her experiences as a disabled woman artist, provide significant dialogues about disability and visual representation. Born in 1965, Lapper grew up in institutional settings and art schools. Although she was always skilled at making art, Lapper remarks on having to prove herself repeatedly to non-disabled people, intellectually, artistically, and sexually, due to assumptions about her so-called "lacking" anatomy. She moved to London at age 19, where she lived independently for the first time, and later attended the University of Brighton, graduated with a degree in fine art at age 28, purchased a home in Southwick, near Brighton, and began her work as an artist. Lapper has been the focus of the BBC1 series *Child of Our Time* program, to which she has returned for annual appearances, and an hour-long documentary by Milton Media for Denmark's TV2, titled *Alison's Baby*, which has been broadcast in many countries and won the Prix Italia and the Prix Leonardo. In 2003, Lapper won the MBE award for service to the arts. Since graduation from Brighton, she has worked fulltime for the Mouth and Foot Painting Artists' Association of England (MFPA). Funding for this program comes from the artists' production of decorative images for card designs, marketed by the MFPA, and Lapper writes that she still enjoys producing such genre scenes and landscapes, along with her self-portrait work.

Lapper's self-portrait body art, in the forms of photography, sculpture, and installation, marks a continuous process of self discovery. At the University of Brighton, an opinionated viewer challenged the nature of Lapper's figurative work of non-disabled bodies, by suggesting that perhaps Lapper had not fully accepted her own body. This moment became a turning point for Lapper, as she began envisioning her own body as a work of art. Inspired by a photograph of the armless or "broken" Greek statue, the *Venus de Milo*, in which she saw her own likeness, Lapper began casting her body in plaster and photographing herself in Venus-like poses. Like arm-free performance artist Mary Duffy, who delivers impassioned speech about her experiences of being medically and socially objectified, while posing in the nude, Lapper adopted the Venus de Milo as her body image. Lapper's graduation exhibit featured an installation the viewer had to enter on hands and knees, at the height of Lapper herself, in order to see photographs and sculpted casts of her full body and body parts. This installation created an environment that removed the viewer from their own comfort zone physically and perceptually. Other disabled artists also employ their embodied perspectives in their work, such as little person Ricardo Gil. Gil photographs his wife and daughter, both little people, from the perspectives at which he views them—literally, in terms of his height, and figuratively, as intimate close-ups that establish affectionate, familial relationships between the subject and the camera's gaze. In *Johann's Kiss*, 1999, Gil features his smiling wife centered in the frame, embraced by an average-sized, kneeling man, whose head is cropped at the top of the photograph. Figures in the background are cut off at mid torso; however, these are not mistakes of an amateur. Here, "normal" size people don't fit in the little woman's privileged, compositional space or in Gil's proud gaze. Lapper's installation, like Gil's photographs, explored the relationships between the viewer's versus the artist's own acts of looking at, judging, and experiencing the disabled body.[21]

Lapper's self-portrait work and her personifications specifically of the armless Venus de Milo (a cultural icon of artistic and feminine beauty), like Duffy's, explore the complicated interactions of disability and sexuality, particularly for women. Lapper's shameless public exposure in a public art display (*Alison Lapper Pregnant*) takes root in a longer artistic and personal process of "coming out" as a sexual, and indeed reproductive woman. In contrast with the mainstream vision of Lapper's often assumed a-sexuality, a bold and seductive body image emerges in Lapper's work. Lapper's

Untitled (2000) features three views of her nude body in Venus-like, s-curve poses. The photographic media articulates her musculature, flesh, and curve of the breast, while aestheticizing equally her upper-arm "stumps." The strong contrasts of the black background with the marble whiteness of her skin create a photographic sculpture in the round. The photograph, like Duffy's performance and Quinn's *The Complete Marbles* series, plays with the viewer's recognition of Classical statuary (particularly a goddess of love and fertility) and the disabled flesh, as well as perceptions of "whole" versus "deficient" bodies. Carving a sculpture "in the round" refers specifically to Classical and Neoclassical methods of producing balanced, proportional "wholes." This symbolic practice was quoted also by feminist performance artist Eleanor Antin in *Carving: A Traditional Sculpture* (July 15, 1972–August 21, 1972), in which Antin documented her body from all sides daily, as it gradually reduced during a crash diet. Antin's photographs are formally clinical in their starkness, referring to the "before" and "after" photographs quite familiar in our makeover-obsessed contemporary culture, while her body becomes a piece of sculpture in characteristic practices of performance art. Particularly to 21st-century eyes, the Antin's images refer to eating disorders and the extents to which women will go to "perfect" their bodies, according to increasingly narrow and impossible social standards for beauty. Lapper's and Antin's photographic sculptures in the round, like Quinn's sculptures, expose the notion of the "ideal" as fabricated. Lapper's work especially presents a certain disruption between artistic and social visions of the ideal and anti-ideal female body.

Art has provided a means for Lapper to interrogate others' and her own images of her body and to reinvent her image in the public eye. These themes continued in a 2000 exhibit at the Fabrica Gallery in Brighton, featuring sculptural works and photographs of Lapper from childhood to adulthood. The photographic collection intentionally crossed genres, by including artistic self-portraits, snapshots taken by friends at key moments in Lapper's life, and early childhood medical photographs, which questioned viewers' assumptions about seeing her body in different visual contexts. The inclusion of medical photographs in particular was meant to disarm the viewer and incorporate, as well as intervene on, Lapper's experiences of feeling like a medical spectacle and specimen. Indeed, Lapper's unique medical history, chronicled in her memoir as a series of objectifying and shameful displays of her body by doctors to "instruct" their peers on deformity and anomaly, connects intimately in the process of her work; Lapper remarks on her extensive history of being measured and cast in plaster particularly, in both medical and artistic contexts. Other works in the show featured Lapper's face in the vintage black-and-white style of classic Hollywood photographs. These images were strategically placed in a frame on the floor and covered in salt crystals. The viewer had to kneel down and brush aside the crystals to see Lapper's face, portrayed in a photographic softness reminiscent of glamour shots and intended to offset the hard-edge format of the medical images. The demand for viewer interaction with these works, as well at their themes of veiling, revealing, and concealing the body, make them performative—another public display of the disabled body.

Lapper strives in this work to showcase the disabled body as artistic and worthy of aestheticized display. She also makes photographic collages with elements such as flowers and angel wings to symbolize her biographical and artistic journeys. In *Angel* (1999), Lapper's head and nude torso, shot in black and white film, project from the right edge of the painted frame. She bears wings and her body thrusts upward, soaring, like the winged messenger god, Hermes, or the confident, yet tragic Icarus, to unforeseen heights of knowledge and to personal vistas. Winged figures, from Classical mythology to contemporary fantasy, transverse the heavens and the earth—the realms of the gods and mortals; they are figures with extraordinary bodies and supernatural abilities for travel. Lapper here incarnates goddess imagery, enacting a re-vision of art history and resurgence of the disabled body in shameless, empowered self display. She appropriates allegorical bodies to present her own body image. In this frame, *Angel* invokes also the winged Nike, the mythical personification of victory, who is sometimes depicted bearing wings in the place of arms (as in the monumental, *Nike of Samothrace*, c.190 CE). Believed to once stand at the helm of a ship, the headless and armless Greek Hellenistic Nike is now a grand attraction at the Louvre Museum in Paris and a relic of Western culture. The Nike form is poignantly a derivative of Athena, the goddess known for her protection of the city of Athens and who is venerated still today at the Parthenon, the original home of the *Elgin Marbles*. Athena, or Minerva as she was known by the Romans, was a single mother and the goddess of wisdom, women's deeds, and the arts—a quite fitting allegory for Lapper to embody. Further, as Marina Warner (1985) describes, Athena shape-shifted to a number of personas and bodies in order to invoke powers and enact deeds. These performative masquerades of the goddess included her strategic exposure and concealment of her body and identity. Like Athena's performances, Lapper's self-portrait works reveal and conceal her body in multiplying references and significances; similarly to *Alison Lapper Pregnant*, Lapper's body work is pregnant with meaning.

Lapper's works, like Quinn's, juxtapose the portrayal of the body as symbolic allegory and as a portrait subject. As an allegorical figure, *Alison Lapper Pregnant* follows in a tradition of staging the female body particularly as a symbol of heroic, virtuous, and largely patriarchal social values. Justice, Prudence, Fortitude, and Temperance, for examples, are values embodied by the female allegory of British history, Britannia, a Neoclassical figure derived from the Roman Minerva (Athena) and featured most prominently in Neoclassical design on Roman-inspired British coins. Classical Roman revival in Britain, which inspired the architecture and figurative program of Trafalgar Square, appealed to traditions of piety, austerity, and humility in British society, social ideals upheld still today across much of Britain's political landscape. *Alison Lapper Pregnant*, as a Neoclassical sculpture in the round, brings to life the corporeal reality of metaphysical, bodily allegories. Lapper's arch defiance of such longstanding conservative ideals, however, radiates from the sparkling surface of her body and tells "other" stories of British citizenship. She both conforms to and reforms stereotypes of disability, as well as of the British "public." Lapper's self-portrait photographs present additionally graphic portrayals of her particularized experiences, while co-opting the powers of infamous female beings. Britannia follows in the legacy of Minerva as the civic goddess and as a symbol of law abiding chastity; as a reincarnation of these goddesses, Lapper gives birth to new histories of the square and the British nation, both by posing for the statue and by producing self-representations.

Lapper's role in the mediation of *Alison Lapper Pregnant* has brought a voice to its depiction of a pregnant amputee woman, as well as of a contemporary artist; Lapper's own work, which has experienced more attention, albeit slowly, contributes to significant dialogues and representations of disability in visual culture, both today and historically. Quinn's and Lapper's images cause the viewer to do a double-take and to perceive bodies on display in different lights and with frameworks outside of the strict conventions of social ideals. These artists call into question the integrity of Neoclassicism and other idealizing and/or disfiguring traditions for displaying the body in art, as well as in everyday life. These juxtapositions also emphasize the necessity of placing the works of disabled and non-disabled artists in dialogues with each other and with larger visual contexts, in order to see art through new eyes and from the perspective *of* disability. In collaboration, such dialogues can forge fresh, multidimensional images of disability in the public eye, and potentially, can sculpt new, liberating body ideals for the public.

NOTES

1. Alison Lapper (with Guy Feldman), *My Life in My Hands* (London; New York: Simon & Schuster UK, Ltd., 2005), 236.

2. For example, Bert Massie, the chairman of the commission, was quoted in *The Guardian* newspaper as stating: "Congratulations to Marc for realising that disabled bodies have a power and beauty rarely recognised in an age where youth and 'perfection' are idolised." This article also states that the Disability Rights Commission welcomed the statue as a source of pride and a blow against the cult of perfection that effectively disables bodies who don't conform to the norm. Others have suggested, like Lapper, that the work's depiction of a specific embodiment largely under-represented in visual life, at least in a positive way, broadens and humanizes notions of beauty, as well as humanizes certain socially stigmatized individuals. For example, see: Adrian Searle, "Arresting, strange and beautiful," *The Guardian* (Friday September 16, 2005).

3. Some of the better known artists of this style are the French painter Jacques-Louis David, as well as British painters Joshua Reynolds and Benjamin West, and the sculptors Antonio Canova and Bertel Thorvaldson. By reviving Classical figures, Neoclassical artists sought to portray eternal beauty and cultural idealism, in balanced, symmetrical, and "able," or extra-able bodies. In Classical traditions, on which Neoclassicism

was based, figures were composed from the most idyllic features of different individuals and mathematically derived proportions in order to create a composite "whole" body ideal.

4. One the few works in *The Complete Marbles* that is not titled with the models' names, *Kiss*, 2002, refers specifically to Impressionist sculptor Auguste Rodin's canonical work *The Kiss*. Quinn's *Kiss* features two life-size amputees cast from live models, standing on one leg and leaning against one another (rather than seated, as in Rodin's original), to embrace passionately. Quinn here showcases a disabled couple in an allegory of romantic love and as contemporary sexual beings, which challenges popular stereotypes of disability as sexually undesirable. *Kiss* and other works in *The Complete Marbles* series are portraits that call for re-visions of art history and social ideals.

5. Preece.

6. Waldemar Januszczak, *The Sunday Times*, "Matter of life and death—Art-Profile—Marc Quinn," Dec. 10, 2000.

7. Quinn has a certain reputation as a "bad boy" among art critics, exacerbated by inclusion in the controversial exhibit of 1991, in which he debuted one of his most famous pieces, *Self* (1991), a self-portrait bust made from 9 pints of Quinn's blood frozen. Some have connected *Alison Lapper Pregnant* with a longer interest in birth in Quinn's work, as exemplified by *Birth* or *Lucas* (2001), a frozen representation of his son Lucas' head made from real placenta, three days old. His work has many bodily and biological themes; has worked with DNA imaging (*DNA Garden* (2002), grid of 77 Petri dishes), test tubes, and silicon preservation. Examples of Quinn's other works that use body fluids and forms are: *Yellow Cut Nervous Breakdown, Invisible Man, No Invisible Means of Escape XI* (formed from cast white rubber resembling flesh), *The Great Escape* (a cast of his body inside pod), *Continuous Present* (2000) (which features a skull that rotates around a reflective cylinder), *Shit Paintings* and *Shit Head* (1997), *Incarnate* (a boiled sausage form with his blood), *Eternal Spring* I and II (1998) (a series featuring Calla lilies suspended in water), and *Garden* (2000) (a glass walled installation of flora and fauna that was deceptively composed of frozen units of silicon). As exemplified by these examples, Quinn's work has repeatedly used blood, placenta, excrement, ice, and flowers. He chooses materials are chosen because of their corporeality and symbolic connotations.

8. Kim Q. Hall, "Pregnancy, Disability and Gendered Embodiment: Rethinking Alison Lapper

Pregnant," lecture delivered at the Society for Disability Studies Conference, Bethesda, MD, June 17, 2006.

9. Januszczak.

10. Charles L. Griswold, "The Vietnam Veterans Memorial and the Washington Mall: Philosophical Thoughts on Political Iconography," in *Critical Issues in Public Art: Content, Context, and Controversy*, Harriet F. Seine and Sally Webster, eds., 71–100 (Washington and London: Smithsonian Institute Press, 1992), 74.

11. Trafalgar Square is a center of tourist and civil exchange. It sits on a tourist path from the Houses of Parliament and Westminster Abbey and at the top of The Mall, which leads to Buckingham Palace. The National Gallery, the Admiralty, and the church of St. Martin in the Fields are also on the square.

12. Alice Thomson of the *Daily Telegraph* was quoted in Cederwell.

13. Lapper, 236.

14. Lapper, 234.

15. Miles.

16. At the south end of the square is an equestrian statue of Charles I in a conventional pose suggesting royalty and conquest, which is based on a famous Roman statue of Marcus Aurelius and was also the favored position of Louis XV and Napoleon to emphasize their military strength and leadership (for example in David's triumphant, Neoclassical portrait *Napoleon Crossing the Alps* (1801), which served as Imperial propaganda). On both sides of Nelson's Column are the bronze statues of Sir Henry Havelock and Sir Charles James Napier, and fronting the north wall of Trafalgar Square are busts of Generals Beatty, Jellicoe, and Cunningham, all famous military leaders. All of the "heroes" are significantly honored for their participation in the colonization of India, Egypt, and the Caribbean, and were known as brutal leaders of mutinous soldiers who were often of the nationality of the countries the generals fought to dominate.

17. This opinion was expressed, for example, in the following newspaper quote: "Roy Hattersley, in the Daily Mail, agreed that while the sculpture was 'a celebration of both courage and motherhood', it was nevertheless 'the wrong statue in the wrong place.' The Trafalgar Square plinth is crying out for 'individual examples of national achievement and British greatness,' he said. Hattersley drew up his own shortlist of likely greats, including Shakespeare, Milton, Elgar, Newton and Wren. 'Most of us will share the view that Lapper is someone to admire . . . but the

simple truth is that Trafalgar Square is meant for something else.' Quoted from Cederwell.

18. Jeanette Hart, Letter to the editor, *The Guardian* (Wednesday September 21, 2005).

19. Paul Usherwood, "The Battle of Trafalgar Square," *Art Monthly* 2. no. 4 (March 2004), 43.

20. Rodney Mace, *Trafalgar Square: Emblem of Empire* (Southampton, UK: The Camelot Press, Ltd., 1976).

21. For more on Gil, see Ann Millett-Gallant, "Little Displays: The Photography of Ricardo Gil," in *The Review of Disability Studies: An International Journal* Issue 2, v.4 (June 2009).

SELECTED BIBLIOGRAPHY

Cederwell, William. "What they said about . . . the fourth plinth," *The Guardian*, Thursday March 18, 2004. Fourth Plinth Project website: http://www.fourthplinth.co.uk/

Gisbourne, Mark. "The Self and Others" in *Contemporary (U.K.)* no. 2 (Feb. 2002): 52–7.

Hall, Kim Q. "Pregnancy, Disability and Gendered Embodiment: Rethinking Alison Lapper Pregnant," lecture delivered at the Society for Disability Studies Conference, Bethesda, MD, June 17, 2006.

Hutchinson, Ray, editor. *Constructions of Urban Space*. Stamford, CT: Jai Press, Inc., 2000.

Januszczak, Waldemar. *The Sunday Times*, "Matter of life and death—Art-Profile—Marc Quinn," Dec. 10, 2000.

Jones, Jonathan. "Bold, graphic, subversive—but bad art," *The Guardian* (Tuesday March 16, 2004).

Kemp, M. and M. Wallace. *Spectacular Bodies: The Art and Science of the Human Body from Leonardo to Now*. London, Hayward Gallery; Los Angeles: University of California Press, 2000.

Kennedy, Maev. "Pregnant and proud: statue of artist wins place in Trafalgar Square," *The Guardian* (Tuesday March 16, 2004).

Lacy, Suzanne, editor. *Mapping the Terrain: New Genre Public Art*. Seattle: Bay Press, Inc., 1995.

Lapper, Alison. *My Life in My Hands*. London; New York: Simon & Schuster UK, Ltd., 2005.

Mace, Rodney. *Trafalgar Square: Emblem of Empire*. Southampton, UK: The Camelot Press, Ltd., 1976.

Miles, Malcolm. *Art, Space, and the City: Public Art and Urban Futures*. London and New York: Routledge, 1997.

Mitchell, David T. and Snyder, Sharon L. *Narrative Prosthesis: Disability and the Dependencies of Discourse*. Ann Arbor: University of Michigan Press, 2001.

Preece, Robert. "Just a Load of Shock? An Interview

with Marc Quinn," *Sculpture* 19, no. 8 (Oct. 2000): 14–19.

Seine, H.F. and Webster, S. editors. *Critical Issues in Public Art: Content, Context, and Controversy.* Washington and London: Smithsonian Institute Press, 1992.

Selwood, Sara. *The Benefits of Public Art: The Polemics of Public Places.* Poole, Dorset UK: Policy Studies Institute Publications, 1995.

Usherwood, Paul. "The Battle of Trafalgar Square," *Art Monthly* 2. no. 4 (March 2004), 43.

Warner, Marina. *Monuments and Maidens: The Allegory of the Female Form.* New York: Atheneum, 1985.

CHAPTER 30

"When *Black* Women Start Going on Prozac. . . .": The Politics of Race, Gender, and Emotional Distress in Meri Nana-Ama Danquah's *Willow Weep for Me*

Anna Mollow

DISABILITY ESSENTIALISM; OR, WHAT COUNTS?

Meri Nana-Ama Danquah's *Willow Weep for Me: A Black Woman's Journey Through Depression* is a first-person narrative by an author who, without identifying as "disabled" or signaling any alliance with the disability rights movement, instead describes the "suffering" her "illness" caused and recounts her "triumph" over it, an overcoming achieved through a combination of "courage," "resilience," prescription drugs, and other medical interventions (237; 18; 262). As such, Danquah's memoir is precisely the kind of text that much disability scholarship in the humanities has taught us to critique. Foundational work in this field has stressed the formation and assertion of positive disability identities. It has also underscored the distinction between illness and disability, describing disability in terms of visible bodily difference rather than sickness or suffering. Moreover, disability scholars have criticized personal narratives that highlight disabled people's courage or show them "overcoming" their impairments; framing disability in terms of an individual's struggle against adversity, they have argued, deflects attention from the political realities of disability oppression.[1] These arguments have

enormous importance. They form the basis of a scholarship that has redefined disability, demonstrating that it is best understood not as a biological given, but rather as a social process requiring sustained intellectual and political attention.

Yet Danquah's memoir, in its deep engagement with the politics of race, gender, class, and mental illness, forces a reconsideration of several of these tenets of disability studies. Most important, *Willow Weep for Me* makes it clear that disability studies, which has tended to define disability as a visual, objectively observable phenomenon, must also carefully attend to the phenomenological aspects of impairment, particularly those that involve suffering and illness. Such attention will necessitate developing more nuanced ways of describing intersections of multiple forms of oppression than have predominated in the most influential disability scholarship. Examining such intersectionality in Danquah's memoir complicates aspects of some disabled people's critiques of the medical or psychiatric model of mental illness; for many Black women with depression, lack of access to health care, rather than involuntary administration of it, is the most oppressive aspect of the contemporary politics of mental illness.[2] Danquah's memoir may also be the basis for a critique of a tendency, within much disability scholarship, to avoid representing impairments in terms of sickness or suffering. The social model's impairment/disability binary, which has often lead to a de-politicization of impairments, cannot be upheld in *Willow Weep for Me*, which illuminates both the suffering that impairments can cause and the role of politics in producing them. But on the other hand, Danquah's narrative also complicates some disability theorists' deconstructions of the impairment-disability distinction. These postmodern analyses of impairment tend to see individuals' reliance upon impairment categories as invariably serving to buttress hegemonic constructions of disability; but Danquah's autopathography demonstrates that such categories can be mobilized in ways that are politically resistant. Finally, *Willow Weep for Me* presents challenges to disability studies' critique of "stories of overcoming"; by highlighting individuals' power in relation to oppressive political and economic structures, Danquah's narrative offers a powerful antidote to despair.

In order apprehend the significance of *Willow Weep for Me*, a critical method that can account for intersections of multiple forms of oppression is crucial. "I am black; I am female; I am an immigrant," Danquah writes. "Every one of these labels plays an equally significant part in my perception of myself and the world around me" (225).[3] Unfortunately, disability studies has been slow to theorize such intersectionality, particularly when it comes to race. While works like Bonnie G. Smith and Beth Hutchinson's 2004 anthology, *Gendering Disability*, testify to a growing interest in exploring connections between gender and disability, many of the most foundational works in disability studies have analyzed race and disability, not in tandem, but in opposition to each other.[4] In their efforts to stake out a claim for disability as worthy of intellectual and political attention, disability scholars often represent the relationship between people with disabilities and other political minorities in hierarchical terms.[5] In a more subtle way, the frequent use of "like race" analogies in disability scholarship may also have the effect of opposing the interests of disabled people and people of color. When Rosemarie Garland-Thomson characterizes disability as a "form of ethnicity," or when Lennard J. Davis compares "the disabled figure" to "the body marked as differently pigmented," it's clear that neither intends to place race or ethnicity in opposition to disability; rather, they each seek to establish a likeness between two categories, and thus to gain recognition of disabled people as members of a political minority (Garland-Thomson, 6; Davis, EN, 80). But as Trina Grillo and Stephanie M. Wildman have argued, "like race" analogies often have the effect of "obscuring the importance of race," enabling the group making the analogy to take "center stage from people of color" (621). Moreover, such analogies assume a false separation between the forms of oppression being compared. As Grillo and Wildman point out in their discussion of analogies between race and gender, "[a]nalogizing sex discrimination to race discrimination makes it seem that all the women are white and all the men are African-American"; thus, they observe, "the experience of women of color . . . is rendered invisible" (623). The dangers of "like race" analogies in disability studies are similar: if race and disability are conceived of as discrete categories to be compared, contrasted, or arranged in order of priority, it becomes impossible to think through complex intersections of racism and ableism in the lives of disabled people of color. This is not, of course, to deny that analogies can be useful; I share Ellen Samuels's sense that rather than attempting "somehow to escape from analogy," we might "seek to employ it more critically than in the past" (4).[6]

These intersections must be understood in ways that are more than merely additive, as Angela P. Harris argues in her critique of "gender essentialism—the notion that a unitary, 'essential' women's experience can be isolated and described independently of race, class, sexual orientation, and other realities of experience" (585). According to an additive model of multiple oppressions, Harris argues, "black women will never be anything more than a crossroads between two kinds of domination, or at the bottom of a hierarchy of oppressions" (589).[7] I would therefore suggest that, in examining intersections of forms of oppression, we guard against the dangers of a "disability essentialism," in which the experiences, needs, desires, and aims of all disabled people are assumed to be the same and those with "different" experiences are accommodated only if they do not make claims that undermine the movement's foundational arguments. Many of these arguments have been developed primarily with physical disability in mind. Cognitive and psychiatric impairments, although they are gaining more attention, nonetheless remain marginalized, both within disability studies and in the broader culture. I was recently reminded of the extent of this marginalization when I mentioned to a colleague that I was writing an essay on Black women and depression; she responded by asking, "Does depression count as a disability?" Her question is crucial. "The short answer," I told my colleague, "is 'yes'." The longer answer would have involved a discussion of the ways in which truly "counting" the experiences of people with mental illness might necessitate revising some of disability studies' most frequently cited claims.

While the necessity of such revisions becomes particularly evident when the politics of race, gender, and mental illness are analyzed together, the arguments that follow should not be taken as part of an unitary account of such intersections: I wish to be clear that I am not suggesting any intrinsic relationship among Blackness, femininity, and mental illness; nor do I propose to read Danquah's memoir as representative of a monolithic "Black women's perspective on depression."[8] I do hope to show, however, that examining the converging effects of multiple forms of oppression can have profound implications for disability studies. Reading *Willow Weep for Me* with such effects in mind will require the rethinking of some of the field's most central tenets: its reluctance to understand disability in terms of sickness or suffering, its tendency to define disability in visual terms, and its resistance to stories of overcoming. If we avoid this critical reevaluation, we risk misreading as naïve or politically disengaged the work of Danquah and others whose perspectives diverge from disability studies' entrenched ideas.

GOING ON PROZAC

Among people with depression, the politics of mental illness are complex and highly contested. In particular, much controversy surrounds questions about whether people who experience emotional distress are sick. Throughout her memoir, Danquah emphasizes that her depression is an "illness"; by doing so, she adopts a strategy that diverges from that of the psychiatric survivor movement (18). Members of this movement define themselves as "survivors," not of mental illness, but rather of institutionalization in psychiatric hospitals.[9] Indeed, they often reject the very category of "mental illness," which they view as a largely meaningless invention of modern psychiatry that serves to enforce conformity to social norms and to derive money and power for mental health "experts." Protesting doctors' excessive control over the lives of people we diagnose as "mentally ill," psychiatric survivors describe incarceration in mental institutions that are often run like prisons, as well as nonconsensual administration of "therapies" that resemble punishments or even torture.[10] Moreover, they note that psychiatrists themselves are unable to define mental illness; that no biological or genetic cause of any putative mental disorder has ever been demonstrated; and that the most common treatments—psychoactive medications, electroconvulsive therapy (ECT), seclusion, and physical restraints—have no proven benefits and cause debilitating side effects, including brain damage.[11] Survivors' testimonies demonstrate the appalling extent to which the label of "mental illness" has been used to deprive people of autonomy, respect, and human rights.[12]

What, then, do we make of Danquah's definition of her depression as a "mental illness" (20)? In what context do we understand her emphasis upon the necessity of taking antidepressant medication? "I have tried to deny my need for medication and stopped taking it," Danquah explains. "Each time, at the slightest provocation, I have fallen, fast and hard, deeper into the depression" (220; 258). However, Danquah does not regard depression as purely a medical phenomenon. "The illness exists somewhere in that ghost space between consciousness and chemistry," she writes (257–58). She takes her Paxil "reluctantly," observing that "there is something that seems really wrong with the fact that Prozac is one of the most prescribed drugs in this country" (258).[13]

But for Danquah, in contrast to members of the psychiatric survivor movement, lack of access to health care, rather than involuntary imposition of it, is the most salient aspect of her interactions with the medical profession. Danquah sees adequate medical treatment for her depression as a necessity, to which poverty, racism, and gender bias have created almost insurmountable barriers. Her obstetrician dismisses one of her first episodes of severe depression as

the effect of "hormones" (36). Years later, she seeks treatment but has great difficulty locating a mental health clinic she can afford. Danquah is able to pay for only one of the medications she is prescribed, Zoloft, an antidepressant. Anxiety is a side effect of Zoloft, so her doctor writes her a prescription for BuSpar, an anxiety controllant. This drug, however, is prohibitively expensive, so Danquah resorts to alcohol to manage the side effects of her antidepressant. Indeed, the Zoloft seems to cause an insatiable craving for alcohol, which disappears when she discontinues the medication (221). Danquah is forced to figure most of this out without any medical supervision. Most of the practitioners at the mental health clinic she goes to are therapists-in-training, and hers leaves abruptly once she has completed her certification process. Rather than being "reassigned" at random to another therapist, Danquah suspends psychotherapy (208).

In addition to economic obstacles, Danquah faces cultural barriers to appropriate health care. Her psychiatrist, Dr. Fitzgerald, is a white man who describes at length his inability to "even fathom" the racism with which she routinely copes (224). Experiences like this are commonplace for African American women seeking mental health care. Julia A. Boyd, an African American psychotherapist, observes that many white mental health practitioners "remain in a passive state of denial concerning the therapeutic needs of black women" ("Ethnic," 232). In addition, people of color, especially African Americans, are less likely to be diagnosed with depression or prescribed medication when they report their symptoms to a doctor; even in studies controlling for income level and health insurance status, the disparities are great.[14]

The contrast between Danquah's experience and that of many members of the psychiatric survivor movement highlights a conundrum facing people with depression or other mental illnesses. The enormous power that the psychiatric profession wields in modern Western societies creates a double bind, in which both diagnosis with a mental illness or, alternatively, the lack of such a diagnosis, brings with it serious negative social consequences for people experiencing emotional distress.[15] Being diagnosed with a mental illness means risking social stigmatization, involuntary institutionalization, and treatment with dangerous medications. On the other hand, those who are not deemed truly mentally ill are often regarded as merely malingering. Depression, Danquah observes, is "not looked upon as a legitimate illness. Most employers really don't give a damn if you're depressed, and neither do landlords or bill collectors" (144).

This lack of social validation and support is exacerbated by racism. The symptoms of depression, Boyd points out, often "mirror the stereotypes that have been projected onto Black women"; before she was diagnosed with the disorder herself, Boyd thought that "being depressed meant that you were crazy, lazy, unmotivated" (8; 15). Moreover, as Danquah notes, depression is "still viewed as a predominantly 'white' illness"; when Black people become depressed, the symptoms and coping strategies usually go unrecognized (184).[16] Pervasive social denial and lack of access to necessary medical care are the political realities that Danquah highlights in her account of her struggles with depression. While these realities are inextricable from the politics of race, I do not wish to suggest that all Black women with depression share Danquah's perspective on the medicalization of emotional distress.[17]

In addition, it is important to remember that the other aspect of the double bind I have described—i.e., diagnosis of a mental illness as the justification for involuntary confinement and forcible "treatment"—also carries additional risks for Black people. While white people are more often diagnosed with depression and prescribed antidepressants, African Americans are diagnosed with schizophrenia at much higher rates and are also given antipsychotic medications more frequently and in higher doses. They are also more often institutionalized involuntarily, in part because racial stereotypes affect psychiatrists' assessments of their "dangerousness."[18] The pathologization of Black people is also built into what Danquah terms "the oppressive nature of the existing language surrounding depression," the commonplace metaphors of depression as darkness and blackness (21–22).[19]

Danquah's critique of the politics of race and mental illness exposes and protests linguistic, social, cultural, and economic barriers that impede Black women with depression from accessing health care. In contrast to the psychiatric survivor movement, her primary focus is on this lack of access, rather than the effects of involuntary treatment. But she shares with psychiatric survivors a profound sense of the importance of self-determination and control over one's own medical treatment. Danquah begins to see significant improvement in her depression when, as she puts it, "I took control of my own healing" (225). Recognizing that her own role in her treatment is more important than that of her psychiatrist, she realizes, "it did not make that much of a difference to me if Dr. Fitzgerald was listening or not, if he cared or not, if he understood or not. *I* was listening. *I* was hearing. *I* was understanding. *I* cared" (225–26).

DISABILITY OR IMPAIRMENT? DEPRESSION AND THE SOCIAL MODEL

Danquah's understanding of her depression as a "disease" not only adds another dimension to the psychiatric survivor movement's critique of the mental health profession, but also complicates what has come to be known as the "social model" of disability. The social model was developed in Britain in the 1970s; a key moment in its emergence occurred in 1976, when the Union of the Physically Impaired Against Segregation (UPIAS) published its *Fundamental Principles of Disability*. Perhaps the most important of these "fundamental principles" was the crucial distinction the document made between "impairment" and "disability":

> In our view it is society which disables physically impaired people. Disability is something imposed on top of our impairments, by the way we are unnecessarily isolated and excluded from full participation in society . . . (3)

UPIAS's differentiation between the bodily (impairment) and the social (disability) formed the basis of what Mike Oliver subsequently presented as the "social model of disability."[20] The social model, like the minority group model that emerged in the United States, has enabled major transformations in the conceptualization of disability; rather than accepting traditional definitions of disability as a personal misfortune, this new paradigm frames disability in terms of social oppression.

What the social model may sacrifice, however, is a way of thinking in political terms about the suffering that some impairments cause. As Liz Crow points out, the social model sometimes has the effect of obscuring the reality that "[P]ain, fatigue, depression and chronic illness are constant facts of life" for many people with disabilities (58). This problem is pervasive not only in applications of Britain's social model, but also in disability studies in the United States, where the "critique of the medical model" is a fundamental principle. Critiquing the medical model does not necessarily preclude recognition of

chronic and terminal illnesses as disabling forms of impairment. However, in practice this critique often functions to differentiate people with disabilities from those who are ill.[21] Arguing for greater inclusion of people with chronic illness in the disability community, Susan Wendell takes issue with Eli Clare's contention that people with disabilities should not be regarded as "sick, diseased, ill people" hoping to be cured (Wendell 18; Clare 105). As Wendell points out, "some people with disabilities *are* sick, diseased, and ill"; moreover, she observes, some disabled people "very much want" to be cured (18). Danquah expresses this wish at the end of her memoir: "I choose to believe that somewhere, somehow, there is a cure for depression" (257).

If the experiences of those who define themselves as ill and hope to be cured are elided in much disability scholarship, this may be due in part to the field's emphasis on visible aspects of disability. Garland-Thomson's definition of disability as a process that emerges through "a complex relation between seer and seen" is of great value in thinking about the "extraordinary bodies" she discusses, but the framing of disability in terms of outward appearance is less useful for analyzing depression and other invisible impairments, particularly those that involve sickness and suffering (136). Similarly, Harlan Hahn's positing of a "correlation between the visibility of disabilities and the amount of discrimination which they might elicit" has little to do with Danquah's experience."[22] Danquah loses friends and jobs precisely because her disability is *not* visible and therefore is not recognized as a "legitimate illness" (144; 30).

Indeed, disability studies' emphasis upon observable manifestations of impairments makes it difficult to know how to begin thinking about a condition like depression, which is primarily a subjective experience. Moreover, it is an experience characterized by suffering: "Suffering . . .

was what depression was all about," Danquah reflects (237).[23] The issue of suffering has been vexed within disability studies. As Bill Hughes and Kevin Paterson observe, "Disabled people . . . feel uncomfortable with the concept of suffering because . . . it seems inextricably bound to a personal tragedy model of disability" (336). As Oliver states, "the social model is not about the personal experience of impairment but the collective experience of disablement" ("Social," 22). However, the strategy of maintaining a focus on social oppression rather than personal suffering—or on "disability" as opposed to "impairment"—risks reifying a dichotomy that does not easily apply to disorders like depression. While impairments ranging from cerebral palsy to blindness, spinal cord injury, or autism do not always cause suffering in and of themselves, it makes little sense for a person to say she is clinically depressed but does not suffer. And whereas it's illuminating, when discussing the politics surrounding mobility impairments, to observe that disability results from inaccessible architectural structures rather than from bodily deficiency, it's difficult to use this paradigm to understand depression. It is true that, to a certain extent, one could apply the impairment/disability distinction to Danquah's experience. Arguably, Danquah's impairment, depression, becomes disabling because of a societal unwillingness to accommodate it: "I lost my job because the temp agencies where I was registered could no longer tolerate my lengthy absences," she recounts (30). "I lost my friends. Most of them found it too troublesome to deal with my sudden moodiness and passivity" (30). These social pressures correspond to UPIAS's definition of "disability" as "something imposed on top of our impairments" (3).

But an analysis of Danquah's text that privileges "the collective experience" of disability over "the personal experience" of impairment would greatly distort her account of her struggles with depression (Oliver, UD, 12). A lack of social validation or understanding, although a persistent facet of her experience, seems to recede into the background of the intense and prolonged suffering in which her depression immerses her. Throughout *Willow Weep for Me*, Danquah describes this suffering in vivid and often metaphorical language, which contrasts with her matter-of-fact reports of lost friends and career opportunities. She writes that her life "disintegrated; first, into a strange and terrifying space of sadness and then, into a cobweb of fatigue" (27). She describes "nails of despair . . . digging . . . deeply into my skin" and "a dense cloud of melancholy [that] hung over my head" (30). As her depression worsens, she writes, "It seemed as if the world was closing in on me, squeezing me dry" (32). She remembers "absolute terror" and "despair [that] cut so deeply, I thought it would slice me in half" (42; 106). As such stark descriptions of suffering make clear, relegating "impairment" to a secondary status within an impairment-disability binary elides the phenomenological aspects of depression as a state of suffering.

Moreover, analyses that privilege disability over impairment deflect attention from the political nature of impairment itself. In Danquah's narrative, the social environment is important less for its imposition of an additional burden "on top of" a pre-existing impairment than for its role in producing her depression (UPIAS, 3). When Danquah is a child, her schoolmates ostracize her, mocking her accent and calling her "the African Monkey" (104). She recalls that the "host of . . . horrid epithets" to which she was subjected "shattered any personal pride I felt and replaced it with uncertainty and self-hatred" (105). When her father abandons the family, Danquah begins to think of herself as "the ugly little girl, the 'monkey,' the fatherless child" (109). In junior high, she is raped by a recent high school graduate she has a crush on (120). When she confides in her stepfather about the incident, he rapes her, too; the sexual abuse continues throughout her adolescence (124). As a young adult, undiagnosed postpartum depression coupled with physical abuse by the father of her child contribute to an episode of serious depression. A subsequent episode is triggered by the "not guilty" verdict in the Rodney King trial: "We, all black people, had just been told that our lives were of no value," Danquah remembers (42).

DISTRESS OR DISEASE? DECONSTRUCTING THE SOCIAL MODEL

As Danquah's story illustrates, the oppression of disabled people is not merely "something imposed on top of" a pre-existing impairment; rather, the production of some impairments is itself a political process (UPIAS, 3). Therefore, *Willow Weep for Me* might at first seem to accord with the arguments of some disability scholars who, deconstructing the impairment/disability binary, claim that impairment is a discursive production.[24] Shelley Tremain argues that a Foucaultian analysis will reveal "that impairment and its materiality are naturalized *effects* of disciplinary knowledge/power" (SI, 34). Locating the origins of modern-day categorizations of bodies as normal or impaired in the nineteenth-century bio-medical discourses whose genealogies Foucault traces, Tremain observes that impairment is neither a "'prediscursive' antecedent" nor a set of "essential, biological characteristics of a 'real' body" (SI, 42).

Indeed, Tremain's theorization of impairment is *à propos* to any discussion of depression, whose constructedness as a disease entity is easily apparent. While the term "melancholy" is as old as ancient Greek medicine, its defining features have been broad and shifting, never corresponding to the present-day disease category of "clinical depression." The instability of depression as a discrete medical phenomenon is further evident in the extent to which those who wish to establish it as such must continually define it by differentiating it from ordinary states of sadness. "Depression isn't the same as ordinary sadness, it is hell," Danquah's friend Scott says (260). Or, as Danquah explains, "We have all, to some degree, experienced days of depression . . . But for some, such as myself, the depression doesn't lift at the end of the day . . . And when depression reaches clinical proportions, it *is* truly an illness" (18).[25]

Moreover, whereas most people in our culture would not question the validity of diseases like diabetes, cancer, or rheumatoid arthritis, skeptics abound when it comes to depression. Eboni, one of several African American woman with whom Boyd engages in a dialogue about depression, says, "look at what our mothers and grandmothers went through in their lives and we don't hear them whining about depression" (CI, 21). Eboni's comments not only underscore the constructedness of depression as a clinical entity, but also raise another set of questions. While it's relatively easy to observe that depression cannot be regarded as a prediscursive bodily or mental "given," what remains unclear are the possible effects of the processes by which it is currently being consolidated as a definable and describable disease. For example, does the construction of depression as an illness enable a potentially emancipatory reinterpretation of behaviors traditionally regarded as moral weakness, such as the "whining" that Eboni dismisses? It is in part to distinguish depression from "a character flaw" that Danquah insists that depression "*is* truly an illness" (18). But Tremain's analysis of the constructedness of impairments raises the possibility that Danquah's self-construction as a "depressive" might have "insidious" effects (Danquah, 18; Tremain, SI, 37). Reliance on biomedicine's constructions of bodily and mental difference, Tremain argues, may only further consolidate the pervasive power of disciplinary regimes (SI, 42).

Tremain's characterization of impairments as discursively produced is cogent and insightful. However, as I will argue, *Willow Weep for Me* demonstrates that impairment categories can be cited in ways that, rather than merely "meet[ing] requirements of contemporary political arrangements," instead also serve to undermine them (Tremain, SI, 42; FG, 10). To elucidate this process, it will be helpful to reflect upon the epistemic shift that Foucault and other historians have documented in late eighteenth- and early nineteenth-century medicine. With the rise of clinical medicine in the nineteenth century, the physical examination and the dissection of corpses supplanted patients' stories as the privileged modes of generating medical knowledge.[26] The dominant medical epistemology became visual rather than narrative: the patient came to be seen as a passive body, manifesting visible signs of disease which could be interpreted by the doctor's detached "gaze."[27] These visible "signs," or objective manifestations of disease, were privileged over "symptoms," which referred to subjective sensations the patient reported (Porter, 313). The sign/symptom binary remains a centerpiece of contemporary medical epistemology, and its continued importance helps explain why depression has not been regarded as a "real" disease in the same way as illnesses such as arthritis or multiple sclerosis, which can be visualized on X-rays or MRIs. Whereas the careful observation of bodily changes, the dissection of cadavers, and eventually the emerging science of bacteriology enabled nineteenth-century physicians to define diseases like tuberculosis as distinct clinical entities, the same cannot

be said of depression. Indeed, the project of solidifying depression as a bona fide medical condition is grounded in the expectation that it will one day be possible to identify specific biological markers of the disorder and thus to demonstrate that depression is an organic disease of the brain.

Because such signs remain elusive, the construction of depression as a disease is presently occurring in ways that differ significantly from the discursive materialization of most of the impairments that receive attention in disability studies; that is, from most visible impairments.[28] Western medicine has obtained significant knowledge about impairments such as cataracts, colitis, and heart disease, all of which manifest visible signs, without much active participation on the part of the patient; but a depressed person, to be understood as such, must be a subject who communicates.[29] Moreover, he or she must have a degree of psychological depth that a patient being examined for signs of a physical ailment need not be recognized as possessing. Instead of simply reporting a pain or displaying a rash, a fever, or a tremor, the depressed patient is most often subjectivized as such through the production of a narrative.[30] It is perhaps for this reason that, as Danquah observes, our culture is so reluctant to recognize depression in Black women. It is "hard," she remarks, "for black women to be seen as . . . emotionally complex" (21).

Yet it would certainly be a mistake to romanticize medicine's inclusion of subjects' accounts of their distress in its process of consolidating depression as a disease entity. The incorporation of patients' stories into medical discourses on depression or other forms of "mental illness" is shaped by a profound power imbalance between doctors and patients. While a diagnosis of depression is rarely made without the participation of the patient as a speaking subject, once one is labeled "mentally ill," one is often treated as less than a full subject, denied the right to choose a course of treatment or decline medical intervention altogether.[31] Moreover, as Anne Wilson and Peter Beresford point out, patients defined as "mentally ill" have little control over the ways in which their words are presented and interpreted in their medical records. Wilson and Beresford, who are themselves psychiatric system survivors, recall that "it can feel as if everything you say or do is being taken down and recorded to be used in evidence against you" (148). In addition, they point out, "as medical records are ineradicable, they also serve to make permanent and immutable the ostensible psychopathological difference or 'disorder' of those diagnosed 'mentally ill'" (149).

This power imbalance between doctors and "mentally ill" subjects exerts itself in more subtle ways as well. Wilson and Beresford relate that "it can be difficult even to begin to make sense of our experience outside of frameworks provided by 'experts,' whose theories and powers may extend to every aspect of our lives, not least our identity as 'mentally ill' (non-)persons" (145). This observation seems to illustrate Foucault's claim that the "individual is an effect of power" (TL, 98). And indeed, Foucault's arguments about subject formation raise questions about the relation of Danquah's narrative to dominant psychiatric discourses. Does Danquah, by defining herself as a "depressive," merely reinscribe the dictates of psychiatric medicine (18)? According to Tremain, "a Foucauldian approach to disability" shows that "the category of impairment . . . in part persists in order to legitimize the disciplinary regime that generated it" (FG,11; SI, 43). Tremain does not explore the possibility, however, that the production of specific impairment categories might have multiple, competing effects, including, paradoxically, the contestation of the assumptions on which these categories are based.

Such a contestation takes shape in Danquah's autopathography, which depends upon biomedicine's construction of depression as a disease entity but at the same time resists the normalizing effects of this construction. Danquah articulates her resistance to the disciplinary uses of depression as a medical category in ways that Foucault's concept of a "reverse discourse" can illuminate. Foucault argues that the nineteenth-century emergence of psychiatric and other discourses that brought into being "the homosexual" as a "species" had the effect, not only of enabling "a strong advance of social controls into this area of 'perversity,'" but also of making "possible the formation of a 'reverse' discourse: homosexuality began to speak on its own behalf, to demand that its legitimacy . . . be acknowledged, often in the same vocabulary, using the same categories by which it was medically disqualified" (HS, 101–02). Danquah's narrative might be understood as participating in a "reverse discourse" regarding depression. As we have seen, it employs the categories of psychiatric medicine in order to demand that depression's "legitimacy . . . be acknowledged" (HS, 101). Depression, Danquah maintains, is "a legitimate illness"; she is not "a flake or a fraud" (144).[32]

Additionally, at the same time that she emphasizes that depression is an authentic medical condition, Danquah also subverts some of psychiatry's most fundamental assumptions about what it means to be mentally ill. If today's "depressive" is "disqualified" in ways analogous to the disqualification of Foucault's nineteenth-century "homosexual," Danquah's narrative perhaps mobilizes a reverse discourse that resists this disqualification while nonetheless retaining the vocabulary and diagnostic categories that enable it. This can be seen in Danquah's emphasis on the imbrication of her illness with political oppression. A common mode of discrediting people with depression effects a discursive separation of symptoms from politics: depression is said to arise from feelings, beliefs, and attitudes which are disproportionately "negative" in relation to the afflicted person's actual circumstances.[33] Indeed, this is Eboni's critique of psychiatric constructions of depression: "I didn't hear where any of those big-time researchers were lookin' at things like racism or sexism," she points out (21). But this, of course, is exactly what Danquah does look at. By showing how the convergence of racism, sexual violence, and poverty literally made her ill, Danquah insists upon the validity of depression as a diagnostic category while at the same time contesting hegemonic accounts of its etiology.

Moreover, even as Danquah accepts the designation of her emotional distress as a "disease," she also undermines one of psychiatric medicine's most fundamental claims (18). As Wilson and Beresford point out, psychiatry's justification as an institution relies in large part upon "its construction of users of mental health services as Other—a separate and distinct group" (144). Interestingly, however, Danquah's gradual process of accepting that she is ill and needs medical treatment paradoxically culminates in her deconstruction of the normal/mentally ill binary upon which psychiatry's authority depends:

> I had always only thought of therapy in stark, clinical terms: an old bespectacled grey-haired white man with a couch in his office listening to the confessions of crazies. . . . What if, I asked myself, those "crazies" are no different than me? What if they are like me, ordinary people leading ordinary lives who woke up one day and discovered they couldn't get out of bed, no matter how much they wanted to or how hard they tried? (167–68)

Danquah decides to enter psychotherapy, then, not because she comes to define herself as "Other," but because she is able to imagine the dissolution of what Wilson and Beresford call psychiatry's "opposition between 'the mad' and 'the not-mad'" (154). Indeed, her sense that the depressive is not a distinct species, but rather a member of a community of "ordinary people," finds echo in Wilson and Beresford's assertion that "the world does not consist of 'normals' and 'the mentally ill'; it consists of *people*" (Danquah 167–68; Beresford and Wilson, 144).

Like the arguments of critics who use Foucaultian paradigms to analyze disability, Danquah's work demands a deconstruction of the impairment/disability distinction, forcing a theorization of impairment as itself a social process. Yet Danquah nonetheless accepts the category of mental illness and makes it integral to her self-conception. For this reason, an application of Tremain's or Wilson and Beresford's analyses of the constructedness of impairment categories might seem to authorize a reading of Danquah's narrative as "naïve," unaware of how the category of impairment operates within what Tremain, following Foucault, calls the "insidious" production of "an ever-expanding and increasingly totalizing web of social control" (SI, 34; 37; FG, 6).[34] But as we have seen, Foucault's understanding of power is more flexible than Tremain's characterization of it here suggests.[35] Rather than "a general system of domination" whose "effects . . . pervade the entire social body," Foucault describes a "multiple and mobile field of force relations, wherein far-reaching, but *never completely stable* effects of domination are produced" (HS, 92; 101–02; emphasis mine). "Discourse," he explains, "reinforces" power "but also undermines and exposes it" (HS, 101).

Foucault's conception of discourse as reversible points to the possibility that individuals might invoke discursive constructions such as "depression" so as to do more than merely, as Tremain puts it, "identify themselves in ways that make them governable" (SI, 37; FG, 6). It is true that, as David Halperin remarks, Foucault is critical "of discursive reversal . . . as a political strategy" in contemporary Western societies (58). Nevertheless, for Foucault a "reverse discourse" can constitute "a significant act of political resistance"; it is by no means "one and the same as the discourse it reverses" (Halperin, 59). Foucault explains that although reverse discourses and other forms of resistance cannot be delployed "outside" of power, "this does not mean that they are only a reaction or rebound . . . doomed to perpetual defeat" (HS, 95; 96).

Tremain accurately observes that the institutionalization of reverse discourses as identity politics movements poses significant dangers.[36] However, I wish to challenge what seems in her argument to be a global suspicion of any and all processes of "iteration and reiteration of regulatory norms and ideals about human function and structure, competency, intelligence and ability" (SI, 42). This suspicion seems to derive in part from Tremain's mapping of Judith Butler's deconstruction of the sex/gender binary onto the social model's distinction between impairment and disability (SI, 38–41). But the "reiteration" that Tremain regards as functioning to "sustain, and even augment, current social arrangements," is precisely the process in which Butler finds potential for revision of cultural norms and identity categories (SI, 42). Butler argues that "'sex'" is materialized "through a forcible reiteration" of "regulatory norms"; however, this process produces "instabilities" and "possibilities for rematerialization," in which "the force of the regulatory law can be turned against itself" (4). This turning of the regulatory law against itself, Butler suggests, might be achieved through what she calls a "citational politics," which entails a "reworking of abjection into political agency" (21).

Butler's discussion of "citational politics" focuses primarily upon instances in which "the public assertion of queerness" has the effect of "resignifying the abjection of homosexuality into defiance and legitimacy" (21). Although Danquah does not treat race, gender, or mental illness in ways that correspond exactly to Butler's description of queerness as performativity, one can nonetheless discern in *Willow Weep for Me* a "reworking of abjection into political agency" (Butler, 21).[37] Throughout her memoir, Danquah foregrounds abjection in the form of "weakness" (20). She observes that although mental illness is often regarded as a sign of "genius" in white men, of hysteria in white women, and of pathology in Black men, "when a black woman suffers from a mental disorder, the overwhelming opinion is that she is weak. And weakness in black women is intolerable" (20).

It is perhaps also unthinkable: "Clinical depression simply did not exist . . . within the realm of possibilities for any of the black women in my world," Danquah explains (18–19). "Emotional hardship is *supposed* to be built into the structure of our lives" (19). Indeed, when Danquah tells a white woman she meets at a dinner party that she's writing a book on Black women and depression, the woman responds sarcastically: "*Black* women and depression? Isn't that kinda redundant? . . . [W]hen *black* women start going on Prozac, you know the whole world is falling apart" (19–20). The foreclosure of depression as a possible diagnosis for Black women, Danquah argues, derives from the "myth" of Black women's "supposed birthright to strength" (19). "Black women are *supposed* to be strong—caretakers, nurturers, healers of other people—any of the twelve dozen variations of Mammy (19).[38]

By linking the image of the strong Black woman to the stereotype of the "mammy," Danquah points to the history of slavery in the United States as one of its possible origins. As Patricia Hill Collins observes, the figure of the "mammy," or the "faithful, obedient domestic servant," was invented in order to "justify the economic exploitation of house slaves" (71). Danquah's contestation of the ideal of an inherently strong Black womanhood thus resists the social demand that Black women deny their own emotional and material needs in order to attend to those of others.[39] As Evelyn C. White writes, "the vulnerability exposed in *Willow Weep for Me* . . . will do much to transform society's image of Black women as sturdy bridges to everyone's healing except their own" (Danquah NP).

Paradoxically, while the notion that Black women are uniquely equipped to endure hardship has historically served as a justification for their oppression, it may also have enabled their survival. "Given the history of black women in this country," Danquah argues, "one can easily understand how this pretense of strength was at one time necessary for survival" (NP). The belief that strength is a legacy of slavery persists in Black communities, Danquah remarks, pointing out that it is not only white people who dismiss Black women's depression. "If our people could make it through slavery, we can make it through anything," Black men and women have told Danquah (21). But what this "stereotypic image of strength . . . requires" of Black women, Danquah emphasizes, "is not really strength at all. It is stoicism. It is denial. It is a complete negation of their pain" (NP).[40]

Because Black women's emotional suffering is generally regarded as normative and unproblematic—"part of the package," as Danquah puts it—rather than symptomatic of a condition in need of a remedy, Danquah's pathologization of her distress cannot be seen as merely an accession to the social norms upon which the category of "mental illness" depends; rather, by defining her suffering as sickness, Danquah

transgresses the expectation that when Black women suffer, they do so silently and stoically (19). Refusing any denial of her pain, Danquah unflinchingly describes the shame and self-loathing that are both symptoms and sources of her depression. She relates that amid a severe episode of depression she stopped bathing and cleaning her house, leaving "a trail of undergarments and other articles of clothing" on the floor, "dishes with decaying food" on "every counter and tabletop" (28). She recalls feeling "truly pitiful," "hating myself so much I wanted to die" (219; 106). "Something had gone wrong with me," she realizes (29).

This conclusion may seem at odds with one of the central messages of the disability rights movement. Oliver's critique of the medical model on the grounds that it "tends to regard disabled people as 'having something wrong with them' and hence [being] the source of the problem" is a tenet of disability studies ("Social," 20). And while I certainly do not wish to reinstall hegemonic constructions of disability as a form of individual weakness or inferiority, I would suggest that in Danquah's narrative it's more complicated than a simple opposition between an individual and a social problem. Rather than imagining a wall of immunity between self and society, Danquah dramatizes the impossibility of ever remaining untouched by all that is wrong in the world (29). And her recognition that something has "gone wrong" with her is neither an indictment of herself as "the source of the problem" nor a cause of shame; instead, it is the impetus for her decision to make "a commitment to being alive" (Oliver, 20; Danquah, 230).

This commitment requires a valuing of herself that contrasts sharply with the "stereotypic image of strength" with which "African American women who are battling depression must, unfortunately, contend" (Danquah NP). The strength that Danquah displays—and it would be impossible to come away from her book without feeling the magnitude of that strength—is neither endurance nor self-sacrifice; rather, it is what Danquah describes as a readiness "to claim the life that I want" (266).

SHALL WE OVERCOME?

Danquah's memoir about depression ends on a hopeful note. "Having lived with the pain," she writes, "I know now that when you pass through it, there is beauty on the other side" (266). Indeed, as her book's subtitle indicates, hers is a "Black woman's journey *through* depression" (emphasis mine). As such, *Willow Weep for Me* could be read as a story of overcoming. The blurb on the back cover of the paperback edition promises "an inspirational story of healing," and Danquah herself employs many of the linguistic conventions associated with overcoming narratives. It takes "courage, devotion, and resilience" to "contend with depression" and to "triumph" over the illness, she writes (262). Such an emphasis on individual strength is at the crux of what many disability scholars critique in narratives of overcoming. As Simi Linton argues, "the ideas embedded in the *overcoming* rhetoric are of personal triumph over a personal condition," rather than a collective demand for "social change" (18). There is enormous value in this observation, and I wholeheartedly concur with Linton's objections to representations of disability that make "the individual's responsibility for her or his own success . . . paramount" (19). But as we have seen, the opposition between disability as personal misfortune and as social problem is not tenable in Danquah's autopathography, which understands depression as inextricably both of these things. And if despair is both a cause and a symptom of depression, then perhaps part of its solution is a hope that is both personal and political.[41] As Danquah explains, "The social and economic realities of women, blacks, single parents, or any combination of the three" make "my chances for a life that is free of depression appear to be slim . . . While I recognize the importance of such information, I regard most of the data as blather and refuse to embrace it" (257). This refusal is not a denial of political realities; rather, it is an unwillingness to accept defeat, an assertion of personal strength amid overwhelming social oppression. As Danquah puts it, it is a "standing up in defiance of those things which had kept me silent and suffering to say that I, an African American woman, have made this journey through depression" (NP).

NOTES

I would like to thank Richard Ingram, Robert McRuer, and Sue Schweik for their feedback on earlier versions of this essay.

1. See Garland-Thomson 135–37; Linton 17–19; and Mitchell and Snyder 9–11. See also note 21 below.
2. Lack of access to health care is tied to the politics of both race and class. Cultural, linguistic, and geographical barriers, as well as racist stereotypes, present specific impediments for African American, Latino/a, Asian American, and Native American people seeking medical treatment for depression, regardless of income level and health insurance status ("Mental"). Access to health care has received less attention in disability studies than in the disability rights movement, where it has often been the focus of organizing.
3. Born in Ghana, Danquah emigrates to the United States when she is six years old (103). Although being an immigrant is of great importance to Danquah's self-definition, this aspect of her identity receives far less attention in her memoir than race, gender, class, or mental illness.
4. A special issue of *GLQ*, *Desiring Disability: Queer Theory Meets Disability Studies* (2003), edited by Robert McRuer and Abby Wilkerson, is devoted to the topic of queerness and disability.
5. In the introduction to *The Body and Physical Difference*, David T. Mitchell and Sharon L. Snyder write that "while literary and cultural studies have resurrected social identities such as gender, sexuality, class, and race from . . . obscurity and neglect . . . disability has suffered a distinctly

different disciplinary fate" (1–2). Barnes and Mercer draw a "sharp contrast" between the reception of disability studies in academia and that of "radical analyses of racism and sexism that quickly won favor" (IS, 4). Recently, leading disability scholars and activists have made similar comparisons between race and disability in their discussions of Clint Eastwood's 2005 film, *Million Dollar Baby* (Drake and Johnson, 1; Davis "Why," 2). And the chairman of Britain's Disability Rights Commission, Bert Massie, recently stated that "neglect and institutionalized exclusion" of disabled people is "more profound" than that of Black people ("Massie," 1).

6. Samuels's suggestion is part of her extended analysis of the dynamics of "passing" and "coming out" for queer people, racial minorities, and people with disabilities. For critiques of the "like race" analogy in queer theory and activism, see Janet E. Halley and Janet R. Jakobsen.

7. For critiques of additive models of racism and sexism, see Barbara Smith and Elizabeth Spelman. An example of an additive representation of intersectionality in disability studies is Davis's assertion that "the most oppressed person in the world is a disabled female, Third World, homosexual, woman of color" (BOB, 29). This formulation, while a useful beginning, leaves untheorized the specific ways in which various forms of oppression come together in individual lives.

8. The Surgeon General reports that "the prevalence of mental disorders for racial and ethnic minorities in the United States is similar to that for whites." These statistics, however, apply only to those "living in the community"; people who are "homeless, incarcerated, or institutionalized" have higher rates of all forms of mental illness ("Mental" 1). According to the American Psychological Association, women are twice as likely as men to suffer from depression; the reasons for this discrepancy remain controversial ("New," 1).

9. Information about the psychiatric survivor movement can be found at the Mind Freedom Support Coalition International Web site: http://www.mindfreedom.org/

10. Courts have long recognized that patients with physical illnesses or disabilities have the right to refuse medical treatment. This constitutional protection, however, has often been denied to people diagnosed with mental illness, who can be committed to mental institutions and treated involuntarily with toxic drugs and other potentially harmful therapies. In many states, involuntary outpatient treatment is also authorized

by the courts. For more on this, see Jackson and Winick.

11. The side effects of ECT can be severe and permanent, as can those of neuroleptics, the medications most commonly prescribed for schizophrenia and other "psychotic" illnesses. The chemical effects of neuroleptic drugs are similar to those produced by lobotomies (Breggin, TP, 68–91).

12. Jeanine Grobe aptly compares the most common modern-day psychiatric practices to medieval treatments for "insanity": "[M]ore often than not, [contemporary psychiatric] 'medicine' is a complete atrocity—comparable only to the history out of which it grew: is four-point restraint—being tied down at the wrists and ankles—an improvement over being bound with chains? Is the cage inhumane whereas the seclusion room is not? Are the deaths that result from the use of neuroleptic drugs better than the deaths that resulted from bloodletting? Is the terror inspired by the passing of electric current through the brain an improvement over the shock of being submerged in ice water?" (103).

13. The back of *Willow Weep for Me* includes the transcript of an interview of Danquah by Dr. Freda C. Lewis-Hall, director of the Lilly Center for Women's Health, which is part of Eli Lilly, the pharmaceutical company that manufactures Prozac. Danquah has also given book tours in conjunction with the National Mental Health Association's Campaign on Clinical Depression, which is funded by Eli Lilly (http://www.psych.org/pnews/98-05-15/nmha.html). This may raise concerns about bias in Danquah's representations of the benefits of psychoactive medications. However, *Willow Weep for Me* can hardly be said to read like an advertisement for antidepressants. As noted, Danquah expresses concern about their widespread use. In addition, she details the debilitating side effects she experienced from taking Zoloft. Most important, Danquah's memoir certainly does not understand depression as simply a biological illness that can be cured with drug therapy. If, as she claims, depression "exists somewhere in that ghost space between consciousness and chemistry," her interest in the former greatly exceeds her attention to the latter; describing only briefly her experiences with various medications, Danquah foregrounds her personal struggles and the political contexts in which they take place. I would like to thank Jonathan Metzl for bringing Danquah's relationship with Eli Lilly to my attention.

14. A 2001 Surgeon General's report on these disparities indicates that "racial and ethnic minorities" in the U.S. receive "less care and poorer

quality of care" than white people ("Mental"). And a 2000 study of the treatment of people already diagnosed with depression—controlled for age, gender, health insurance status, and other factors—found a striking disparity: 44 percent of white patients and 27.8 percent of Black patients were given antidepressant medication (UT, 70).

15. Anne Wilson and Peter Beresford describe this double bind as an "increasing polarization of madness and distress into two categories—of the 'threateningly mad' and the 'worried well'" (153). Reflecting psychiatry's distinction between "psychoses" and "neuroses," these categories "serve both to dismiss and to devalue the experience and distress of those of us not seen as 'ill' enough to require public resources for support, and to reinforce assumptions about a discrete and separate group of mad people that constitutes a threat to the rest of society" (154; 153).

16. For discussions of the misperception of depression as an illness affecting only white people, see Boyd (5–7) and Marano (2).

17. In Rhonda Collins's documentary film, *We Don't Live under Normal Conditions*, people of various races and ethnicities discuss what it means to them to be depressed; most, but not all, see the origins of their distress as primarily social. Most of the depression memoirs published in the last decade in the United States are authored by white people, many of whom describe the benefits of antidepressants. See Styron, Wurtzel, Solomon, and Jamison.

18. See *Unequal Treatment* 611–21. These discrepancies are well documented and alarming. For example, a 1993 study "found that 79 percent of African Americans in a public-sector hospital were diagnosed with schizophrenia, compared with 43 percent of whites" (613). In another study, "28 percent of African Americans in a university hospital emergency room were given such a diagnosis, compared with 20 percent of whites." A 1996 study found that "African American patients seen in an emergency room received 50 percent higher doses of antipsychotic medications than patients of other ethnic groups, while their doctors devoted less time to assessing them" (613). In a 1998 study, researchers asked psychiatrists to provide diagnoses of patients based upon written case histories. The psychiatrists each reviewed identical case histories, but their diagnoses varied widely, depending on what they were told the patients' race and gender were. The diagnosis of "paranoid schizophrenic disorder," which, the authors of the study note, is associated with "violence, suspiciousness, and dangerousness," was applied to patients believed to be Black men at a rate of 43 percent, compared with 6 percent for white men, 10 percent for white women, and 12 percent for Black women (615).

19. An awareness of the medical profession's pathologizing attitudes toward Black people deters many African Americans from seeking health care, especially for symptoms of mental illness. Psychological studies in reputable journals in the 1950s compared average Africans to "the white mental patient," "the lobotomized West European," and the "traditional psychopath" (L.R.C. Haward and W.A. Roland, "Some intercultural differences on the Draw-A-Person Test: Part I, Goodenough scores," *Man* 54 [1954], p. 87, qtd. in Bulhan, 83–84; J.C. Carothers, "The African mind in health and disease," Geneva, World Health Organization, 1953, qtd. in Bulhan, 84). The 1965 Moynihan Report claimed that African American families were disintegrating because of their putatively "matriarchal" structure (Boyd, "Ethnic," 230). In the 1960s and 1970s, respected neurosurgeons and psychiatrists publishing in venues such as the *Journal of the American Medical Association* advocated psychosurgery to treat the "brain disease" they claimed caused "riots and urban violence" (Breggin, WA, 117). In the early 1990s, Frederick Goodwin, the chief scientist at the National Institute of Mental Health, proposed a "violence initiative," which would identify among "inner-city" adolescents—whom Goodwin compared to monkeys in a jungle—those with a genetic predisposition to violence and then subject them to psychiatric interventions (Breggin, WA 8).

20. See Barnes and Mercer (IS, 2) and Oliver (PD, 11). Although the social model's authors intended it to serve primarily as a "heuristic device," rather than a comprehensive theory of disability, its distinction between impairment and disability remains fundamental to disability scholarship in both the UK and the United States (Barnes and Mercer, IS, 3).

21. The concluding chapter of Garland-Thomson's *Extraordinary Bodies* calls for a shift in understanding disability, "From Pathology to Identity." Steven Taylor argues that "a Disability Studies perspective questions the medical model and challenges" the equation of disability with "sickness and pathology" ("Guidelines," 4). Steven E. Brown states that "a person with a disability is not sick" (11). Barnes and Mercer criticize representations of people with disabilities as "sick" or "suffering" (*Disability*, 9; 10). And Simon Brisenden urges a differentiation "between a disability and a disease" (25). Asserting that "disability is not illness," Anita Silvers acknowledges that

chronic illnesses can be disabling but insists that "persons with paradigmatic disabilities—paraplegia, blindness, deafness, and others" must be distinguished from "people suffering from illness" (77). David Pfeiffer also emphasizes that "disability is not sickness" and claims that "for a half to three quarters of the disability community there is no present sickness which disables them" (6). Pfeiffer doesn't make clear, in his estimate of the statistical prevalence of illness among people with disabilities, how he defines the "disability community."

22. See Harlan Hahn, *The Issue of Equality: European Perceptions of Employment Policy for Disabled Persons* [New York: World Rehabilitation Fund, 1984], 14, qtd. in Hahn, "Advertising," 175.

23. This is not to suggest that suffering is the most important aspect of depression for everyone who experiences it. Jane Phillips describes her depression as a "dark and dangerous illness," but also as an experience that "seemed to serve a function," facilitating her emergence "into an utterly new spring" (140–41). I am grateful to Richard Ingram for bringing this passage to my attention.

24. Deconstructions of the social model share similarities with "universalizing" approaches to disability in the United States, which, rather than conceiving of people with disabilities as members of a distinct minority group, instead highlight the fluidity of disability as an identity category and describe bodily difference as existing on a continuum of human variation.

25. Danquah's assertion is tautological (illnesses, by definition, are conditions that "reach clinical proportions"); however, I am concerned here, not with establishing the "truth" or "falsity" of the claim that depression is an illness, but rather with delineating the tactical and strategic uses to which its construction as such is put. I would like to thank Richard Ingram for pointing out to me the tautological nature of Danquah's statement.

26. In the eighteenth century the physical examination was regarded as so unimportant that doctors often practiced medicine by mail, relying on patients' lengthy narratives to make diagnoses (Reiser, 5–6).

27. For detailed accounts of the history of clinical medicine, see Foucault (BC), Ackernecht, and Jewson.

28. There are exceptions to this trend, most of which are also invisible disabilities: "mental illnesses"; some cognitive disabilities; and physical conditions such as chronic fatigue syndrome, repetitive strain injury, environmental illness, and fibromyalgia, which don't produce objectively observable bodily changes. But most of these conditions, like depression, are "controversial"; they will be defined as "syndromes" rather than actual "diseases" until they can be correlated with measurable physiological abnormalities.

29. Disorders such as these illustrate the impossibility of any absolute binary between "visible" and "invisible" disabilities. These conditions may often be invisible to the casual observer, but their signs can be seen on medical tests. Notwithstanding medical technologies that rely on senses other than sight, the visual bias of modern medical epistemology is pronounced; it can be discerned even the word "stethoscope," which combines the Greek words for "chest" and "I view" (Reiser, 25).

30. Nonverbal people with disabilities can also be diagnosed with depression, but the formation of depression as an impairment category has depended in large part upon patients' verbal articulations of their distress.

31. I would like to thank Richard Ingram for pointing this out to me.

32. My comparison between Danquah's political strategy and that of the nineteenth-century "homosexual" Foucault describes illustrates the limits of analogies between different subject positions. Despite the similarities I will discuss, Danquah's desire to be cured contrasts with the nineteenth-century "homosexual"'s demands to be accepted as such. I would like to thank Sue Schweik for pointing this difference out to me.

33. For example, see "Cognitive" (3).

34. While I share Tremain's sense that it is "politically naïve to suggest that the term 'impairment' is value-neutral," I nonetheless hope to show that it is possible to cite impairment categories without merely reinforcing normalizing discourses (SI, 34).

35. This characterization is consistent with the overall thrust of Tremain's argument. In "On the Subject of Impairment" (2002), Tremain touches briefly on Foucault's concept of discursive reversibility, noting that the "disciplinary apparatus of the state . . . brings into discourse the very conditions for subverting that apparatus" (44). She maintains, however, that by "articulating our lived experiences" in ways that "continue to animate the regulatory fictions of 'impairment,'" disabled people risk merely augmenting normalizing and homogenizing social processes (44; 45). Similarly, in one paragraph of her introduction to *Foucault and the Government of Disability* (2005), Tremain notes Foucault's interest in the "strategic reversibility" engendered by hegemonic discourses but nonetheless reiterates the central claims of her earlier essay.

36. I strongly concur with Tremain's argument for a disability theory that will "expose the disciplinary character of . . . identity," rather than "ground[ing] its claims to entitlement in that identity" (SI, 44; FG, 10). In fact, Tremain's criticisms of identity-based movements parallel arguments I make in my essay, "Disability Studies and Identity Politics: A Critique of Recent Theory." I share Tremain's view that identity politics risks reifying identity categories that might better be contested, is almost inevitably exclusionary and productive of hierarchies, and impedes alliances with other political minorities. Indeed, I am trying to make these problems apparent in my discussion of the ways in which entrenched ideas within disability studies exclude experiences such as Danquah describes in her memoir. But I am also attempting to demonstrate that Danquah utilizes her self-definition as a "depressive" in ways that do not replicate these dynamics of identity politics movements (18).

37. This discrepancy again exemplifies the limitations of analogies between different forms of oppression. Butler asks, "When and how does a term like 'queer' become subject to an affirmative resignification for some when a term like 'nigger,' despite some recent efforts at reclamation, appears capable of only reinscribing its pain?" (223). For Danquah, such reinscription is also the inevitable effect of hearing this word repeated. She remembers the first time she was called a 'nigger' to her face, by a high school boy she had asked to dance: "Even now when I hear that word—*nigger*—whether it is spoken by a black person or a white person, it is the simple tone and disgust of that boy's voice that I hear" (43).

38. Boyd also observes that it can be difficult to reconcile "beliefs about being strong Black women" with "having an illness that we've long associated with weakness of the lowest kind" (CI, 5). Similarly, Angela Mitchell observes that "one reason Black women don't get treated for depression is that we often expect to feel sad, tired, and unable to think straight" (47). She reminds her readers that "Black women do not have to be depressed. It is not our lot in life" (47). The perception that depression is a form of weakness that Black women cannot "afford" is addressed on numerous web sites about Black women and depression (Marano, 2). See Rouse, 6.

39. Mitchell also connects the "mammy stereotype," which is "rooted in the history of slavery," to Black women's depression, arguing that this stereotype creates an imperative for Black women to prioritize other others' needs over their own (53; 56).

40. Similarly, bell hooks has asserted that "to be strong in the face of oppression is not the same as overcoming oppression . . . endurance is not be confused with transformation" (qtd. in Mitchell, 69). Mitchell makes this point as well: Black women's endurance of "suffering and hardship," she argues, should not be confused with "strength" (69).

41. Wilson and Beresford describe the damaging repercussions of constructions of mental illness that "leave the holder of the diagnosis feeling utterly hopeless" and create a social expectation that those who have been diagnosed with mental illness "can never fully recover" (150). In addition, numerous African American feminists, activists, and critical race theorists have argued for the importance of hope and optimism, on both an individual and a collective level. Alex Mercedes, an African American woman who is a subject of Collins's documentary, argues that "it's important to focus on the individual . . . because the revolution will not happen overnight . . . so in the meantime, I, as an individual, must walk through this sexist, patriarchal hell." Harris criticizes white feminism for its focus on "victimization and misery" and insists upon women's ability to "shape their own lives" (613). Warning against the danger of a "capitulation to a sense of inevitable doom," Patricia Williams expresses an "optimistic conviction" of the possibility of both "institutional power to make change" and "the individual will to change" (64; 65; 68). And in the introduction to *The Black Women's Health Book*, White is hopeful about Black women's power to "address and overcome the numerous issues that have damaged" their health, in part through individual "resilience and stalwart determination" (xiv; xvi).

WORKS CITED

Ackernecht, Erwin M. *Medicine at the Paris Hospital 1794–1848*. Baltimore: Johns Hopkins University Press, 1976.

Barnes, Colin, and Geof Mercer, eds. *Implementing the Social Model of Disability: Theory and Research*. Leeds, UK: The Disability Press, 2004. Cited within the text as IS.

——. *Disability*. Cambridge, UK: Blackwell, 2003.

Boyd, Julia A. *Can I Get a Witness?: Black Women and Depression*. New York: Penguin, 1999. Cited within the text as CI.

——. "Ethnic and Cultural Diversity in Feminist Therapy: Keys to Power." In *The Black Women's Health Book: Speaking for Ourselves*, edited by Evelyn

C. White, 226–34. Seattle, Washington: Seal Press, 1990. Cited within the text as "Ethnic."

Breggin, Peter R., M.D. *Toxic Psychiatry: Why Therapy, Empathy, and Love Must Replace the Drugs, Electroshock, and Biochemical Theories of the "New Psychiatry."* New York: St. Martin's Press, 1991. Cited within the text as TP.

Breggin, Peter R., M.D., and Ginger Ross Breggin. *The War against Children.* New York: St. Martin's Press, 1994. Cited within the text as WA.

Brisenden, Simon. "Independent Living and the Medical Model." In *The Disability Reader: Social Science Perspectives,* edited by Tom Shakespeare, 20–7. London and New York: Cassell, 1998.

Brown, Steven. "Freedom of Movement: Independent Living History and Philosophy." Independent Living Research Utilization. Available online at http://www.ilru.org/html/publications/bookshelf/freedom_movement.html (1–20).

Bulhan, Hussein Abdilahi. *Frantz Fanon and the Psychology of Oppression.* New York and London: Plenum Press, 1985.

Clare, Eli. *Exile and Pride: Disability, Queerness, and Liberation.* Cambridge, Massachusetts: South End Press, 1999.

Collins, Patricia Hill. *Black Feminist Thought: Knowledge, Consciousness, and the Politics of Empowerment.* New York and London: Routledge, 1991.

Collins, Rhonda, dir. *We Don't Live under Normal Conditions.* Videocassette. Boston, Massachusetts: Fanlight Productions, 2000.

"Cognitive Therapy for Depression." Available online at *Psychology Information Online* http://www.psychologyinfo.com/depression/cognitive.htm#lifeexperiences (1–7). Cited within the text as "Cognitive."

Crow, Liz. "Including All of Our Lives: Renewing the Social Model of Disability." In *Exploring the Divide: Illness and Disability,* edited by Colin Barnes and Geof Mercer, 55–73. Leeds, UK: The Disability Press, 1996.

Danquah, Meri Nana-Ama. *Willow Weep for Me: A Black Woman's Journey Through Depression.* New York: Ballantine, 1998.

Davis, Lennard J.. *Enforcing Normalcy: Disability, Deafness, and the Body.* London and New York: Verso, 1995. Cited within the text as EN.

——. *Bending Over Backwards: Disability, Dismodernism and Other Difficult Positions.* Foreword Michael Bérubé. New York: New York University Press, 2002. Cited within the text as BOB.

——. "Why 'Million Dollar Baby' infuriates the disabled." *The Chicago Tribune.* February 2, 2005. Available online at http://metromix.chicagotribune.com/movies/mmx-0502020017feb02,0,6865906.story (1–3). Cited within the text as "Why."

Drake, Stephen and Mary Johnson. "Movies about disabled keep myths alive." *Chicago Sun-Times.* February 12, 2005. Available online at http://www.suntimes.com/output/otherviews/cst-edt-ref12.html (1–2).

Foucault, Michel. *The Birth of the Clinic: An Archeology of Medical Perception.* Translated by A. M. Sheridan Smith. New York: Random House, 1973. Cited within the text as BC.

——. *The History of Sexuality.* Volume I: An Introduction. Translated by Robert Hurley. New York: Random House, 1978. Cited within the text as HS.

——. "Two Lectures." *Power/Knowledge: Selected Interviews and Other Writings, 1972–1977.* Pantheon Books, 1980. Cited within the text as TL.

Garland-Thomson, Rosemarie. *Extraordinary Bodies: Figuring Physical Disability in American Culture in Literature.* New York: Columbia University Press, 1997.

Grillo, Trina and Stephanie M. Wildman. "Obscuring the Importance of Race: The Implications of Making Comparisons between Racism and Sexism (or Other Isms)." In *Critical White Studies: Looking Behind the Mirror,* edited by Richard Delgado and Jean Stefancic, 619–626. Philadelphia: Temple University Press, 1997.

Grobe, Jeanine, ed. *Beyond Bedlam: Contemporary Women Psychiatric Survivors Speak Out.* Chicago. Third Side Press, 1995.

"Guidelines for Disability Studies: Highlights of a 2004 SDS Listserv Discussion." *Disability Studies Quarterly* 24.4 (Fall 2004). Available online at http://www.dsq-sds.org/_articles_html/2004/fall/dsq_fall04_listserv.asp (1–14). Cited within the text as "Guidelines."

Hahn, Harlan. "Advertising the Acceptably Employable Image: Disability and Capitalism." In *The Disability Studies Reader,* edited by Lennard J. Davis, 172–86. New York: Routledge, 1997. Cited within the text as "Advertising."

Halley, Janet E. "'Like Race' Arguments." In *What's Left of Theory?: New Work on the Politics of Literary Theory,* edited by Judith Butler, John Guillory, and Kendall Thomas, 40–74. New York: Routledge, 2000.

Halperin, David M. *Saint Foucault: Towards a Gay Hagiography.* New York and Oxford: Oxford UP, 1995.

Harris, Angela P. "Race and Essentialism in Feminist Legal Theory." *Stanford Law Review* 42.3 (February, 1990): 581–616.

Hughes, Bill, and Kevin Paterson. "The Social Model of Disability and the Disappearing Body: Towards a Sociology of Impairment." *Disability & Society* 12.3 (1997): 325–40.

Jackson, Grace E., M.D. "The Right to Refuse Treatment." Available online at http://psychrights.org/Articles/rightorefuse.htm

Jakobsen, Janet R. "Queers Are like Jews, Aren't They? Analogy and Alliance Politics." In *Queer Theory and the Jewish Question*, edited by Daniel Boyarin, Daniel Itzkovitz, and Ann Pellegrini, 64–89. New York: Columbia University Press, 2003.

Jamison, Kay Redfield. *An Unquiet Mind: A Memoir of Moods and Madness*. New York: Random House, 1995.

Jewson, N. D. "The Disappearance of the Sick-Man from Medical Cosmology, 1770–1870." *Sociology*. 10.2 (May 1976): 225–244.

Linton, Simi. *Claiming Disability: Knowledge and Identity*. Foreword Michael Bérubé. New York: New York University Press, 1998.

Marano, Hara Estroff. "Race and the Blues." *Psychology Today*. Available online at http://cms.psychologytoday.com/articles/pto-20030930-000001.html

"Massie: Exclusion 'More Profound' for Disabled People." *Ouch!* BBC.co.uk. June 16, 2005. Available online at http://www.bbc.co.uk/ouch/news/btn/massie_exclusion.shtml. Cited within the text as "Massie."

McRuer, Robert and Abby Wilkerson, eds. *GLQ: A Journal of Lesbian and Gay Studies. Desiring Disability: Queer Theory Meets Disability Studies*. 9.1–2 (2003).

"Mental Health: Culture, Race, and Ethnicity Supplement." U.S. Department of Health and Human Services, Office of the Surgeon General. Available online at http://www.mentalhealth.org/cre/execsummary-2.asp (1–4). Cited within the text as "Mental."

Mitchell, Angela. *What the Blues Is All About: Black Women Overcoming Stress and Depression*. With Kennise Herring, Ph.D. New York: Penguin, 1998.

Mitchell, David T. and Sharon L. Snyder, Eds. *The Body and Physical Difference: Discourses of Disability*. Foreword James I. Porter. Ann Arbor: The University of Michigan Press, 1997.

Mollow, Anna. "Disability Studies and Identity Politics: A Critique of Recent Theory." *Michigan Quarterly Review* 43.2 (Spring 2004): 269–96.

"New Report on Women and Depression: Latest Research Findings and Recommendations." Press Release. American Psychological Association. March 15, 2002. Available online at http://www.apa.org/releases/depressionreport.html (1–5). Cited within the text as "New."

Oliver, Michael. *The Politics of Disablement*. London: Macmillan, 1990. Cited within the text as PD.

——. *Understanding Disabilty: From Theory to Practice*. Houndmills, UK: Palgrave, 1996. Cited within the text as UD.

——. "The Social Model in Action: If I Had a Hammer." *Implementing the Social Model of Disability*.

Theory and Research. Ed Colin Barnes and Geof Mercer. Leeds, UK: The Disability Press, 2004. 18–31. Cited within the text as "Social."

Pfeiffer, David. "The ICIDH and the Need for Its Revision." *Disability & Society* 13.4 (September 1998): 503–23.

Phillips, Jane. *The Magic Daughter: A Memoir of Living with Multiple Personality Disorder*. New York: Penguin, 1995.

Porter, Roy. *The Greatest Benefit to Mankind: A Medical History of Humanity*. New York: W. W. Norton & Company, 1997.

Reiser, Stanley Joel. *Medicine and the Reign of Technology*. Cambridge: Cambridge University Press, 1978.

Rouse, Deborah L. "Lives of Women of Color Create Risk for Depression." *Women's ENews*. http://www.womensenews.org/article.cfm/dyn/aid/666, October 1, 2001. 1–6 (web pagination).

Samuels, Ellen. "My Body, My Closet: Invisible Disability and the Limits of Coming-Out Discourse." *GLQ: A Journal of Lesbian and Gay Studies* 9.1–2 (2003): 233–55.

Silvers, Anita. "Formal Justice." In *Disability, Difference, and Discrimination: Perspectives on Justice in Bioethics and Public Policy*, edited by Anita Silvers, David Wasserman, and Mary B. Mahowald, 13–146. Lanham, MD: Rowan & Littlefield, 1998.

Smith, Barbara. "Notes for Yet Another Paper on Black Feminism, or Will the Real Enemy Please Stand Up?" *Conditions* 5 (1979): 123–142.

Smith, Bonnie G., and Beth Hutchinson, Eds. *Gendering Disability*. New Brunswick, New Jersey, and London: Rutgers University Press, 2004.

Solomon, Andrew. *The Noonday Demon: An Atlas of Depression*. New York: Simon & Schuster, 2001.

Spelman, Elizabeth V. *Inessential Woman: Problems of Exclusion in Feminist Thought*. Boston: Beacon Press, 1988.

Styron, William. *Darkness Visible: A Memoir of Madness*. New York: Random House, 1990.

Tremain, Shelley. "On the Subject of Impairment." *Disability/Postmodernity*. Ed. Mairian Corker and Tom Shakespeare. London: Continuum, 2002. 1–24. Cited within the text as SI.

——. "Foucault, Governmentality, and Critical Disability Theory: An Introduction." In *Foucault and the Government of Disability*, edited by Shelley Tremain. Ann Arbor: University of Michigan Press, 2005. Cited within the text as FG.

Unequal Treatment: Confronting Racial and Ethnic Disparities in Health Care. Ed. Brian D. Smedley, Adrienne Y. Stith, and Alan R. Nelson. Committee on Understanding and Ending Racial and Ethnic Disparities in Health Care. Board on the Health Science Policy. Institute of Medicine of the National

Academy. Washington, DC: The National Academy Press, 2003. Cited within the text as UT.

UPIAS. *Fundamental Principles of Disability*. London: Union of Physically Impaired against Segregation, 1976. Available online at http://www.leeds.ac.uk/disability-studies/archiveuk/UPIAS/fundamental%20principles.pdf

Wendell, Susan. "Unhealthy Disabled: Treating Chronic Illnesses as Disabilities." *Hypatia* 16.4 (2001) 17–33.

White, Evelyn C., ed. *The Black Women's Health Book: Speaking for Ourselves*, 226–34. Seattle, Washington: Seal Press, 1990.

Williams, Patricia J. *Seeing a Color-Blind Future: The Paradox of Race*. The 1997 BBC Reith Lectures. New York: Farrar, Straus and Giroux, 1997.

Wilson, Anne and Peter Beresford. "Madness, Distress and Postmodernity: Putting the Record Straight." In *Disability/Postmodernity*, edited by Mairian Corker and Tom Shakespeare, 143–58. London: Continuum, 2002.

Winick, Bruce J. *The Right to Refuse Mental Health Treatment*. Washington, DC: American Psychological Association, 1997.

Wurtzel, Elizabeth. *Prozac Nation: Young and Depressed in America*. Second edition. New York: Riverhead Books, 1995.

CHAPTER 31

The Enfreakment of Photography
David Hevey

Before reading this chapter, I feel I must contextualise what lies ahead for the reader. In many ways, charity advertising as oppressive imagery appears to be the *bête noire* of disabled people. Unfortunately, oppressive as it is, it represents colours of a social order tied to a specific mast. Those colours and constructions also exist in other areas of photographic representation. This is demonstrated in this chapter. I ask the reader to join me on a journey into oppressive disability imagery. At times, particularly in the examination of the work of Diane Arbus, it can be depressing. However this chapter is here because I feel we have to take the fight against constructed oppression (whether by non-access or by representation) into the camp of the oppressors.

Apart from charity advertising, when did you last see a picture of a disabled person? It almost certainly wasn't in commercial advertising since disabled people are not thought to constitute a body of consumers and therefore do not generally warrant inclusion. It might have been within an "in-house" health service magazine, in which disabled people are positioned to enflesh the theories of their oppressors. The stories might range from the successes of a toxic drugs company to the latest body armour for people with cerebral palsy, and some

person with proverbial "disease" will be shown illustrating the solution and its usefulness. It might have been in an educational magazine, in which a non-disabled "facilitator" will regale in words and text the latest prototype "image-workshop," using disabled people as guinea pigs while developing their "educational" ideas. The text brags about the colonization of disabled people's bodies and identities, while the images show how much "the disabled" enjoyed it. Passive and still and "done to," the images bear a bizarre resemblance to colonial pictures where "the blacks" stand frozen and curious, while "whitey" lounges confident and sure. Whitey knows the purpose of this image, the black people appear not to (or at least, perhaps as employees, have no right to record visual dissent).

The "positive" side of their ultra-minority inclusion, then, is that disabled people are there to demonstrate the successes of their administrators.[1] Apart from the above areas, however, disabled people are almost entirely absent from photographic genres or discussion because they are read as socially dead and as not having a role to play. But although the absence is near absolute, the non-representation of disabled people is not quite total. Taking the structured absence as given, I wanted to discover the terms on which disabled people *were* admitted into photographic representation. As Mary Daly once wrote of feminism, the job entails being a full-time, low-paid researcher of your own destiny.[2]

I visited one of the largest photographic bookshops in London and leafed through the publications. Generally disabled people were absent, but there was a sort of presence. Disabled people are represented but almost exclusively as symbols of "otherness" placed within equations which have no engagement to them and which take their non-integration as a natural by-product of their impairment.

I picked books at random. *The Family of Man; Another Way of Telling; Diane Arbus; Figments from the Real World.* There were obviously lateral associations but only one, *Diane Arbus*, I knew to include images of disabled people. In the research for this book, I had begun to uncover sometimes hidden, sometimes open, but always continuous constructions of disabled people as outsiders admitted into culture as symbols of fear or pity. This was particularly true in literature[3] but I wanted to see if it held true in photography, so I picked the books at random. They may have been connected in styles or schools but, as far as I knew, had no connection whatsoever on disability representation. Only Arbus was infamous for having centred disabled people in her work but I felt an uneasy faith that all of them would "use" disabled people somewhere.

The first book examined was entitled *The Family of Man.*[4] The Family of Man exhibition at the Museum of Modern Art, New York, in 1955 is considered the seminal exhibition for humanist-realist photography. It was the photographic height of postwar idealism. It showed the great "positive image" of an unproblematised and noble world—a world from which pain was banished. Where there are images of "working folk," their muscles and their sweat appear to be a part of the great spiritual order of things. Where there are images of black people, the images show poverty; some show harmony, but all are visually poetic. Black life has been harmonised through aesthetics.

However, throughout the catalogue of the show, which contained 503 images show from 68 countries by 273 male and female photographers, there is only one photograph of someone identifiably disabled. This is more than an oversight. Put together ten years after the Second World War, *The Family of Man* was about "positively" forgetting the past and all its misery. Forward into glory, backward into pain! Although this publication and exhibition heralded a brave new world of postwar hope and harmony, on reading it it becomes clear that the inclusion of disabled people—even disabled people tidied up like black people and working people—was not a part of the postwar visual nirvana. Why was this?

The one image of a disabled person appears on the penultimate page of the 192-page publication. It is mixed in among six other images on that page and is part of the final section of the book, which covers children. Children are shown laughing, playing, dancing, crying and so on. Of the thirty-eight images in this section, three buck this trend. The three are all on this penultimate page. In the final section, after five pages of innocent joy, you encounter on the sixth page three that remind you it is not like that always. At the top of these three is a disabled boy who appears to be a below-the-knee amputee. He is racing along the beach with a crutch under his right arm. He is playing and chasing a football. His body tilts to our right as he approaches the ball, while his crutch tilts to our left, to form a shape like an open and upright compass. The ball is situated in the triangle which his left leg and his right-side crutch make on the sand. The triangle shape is completed by a shadow which the boy casts from his right leg to the crutch (and beyond). The ball enters this triangle focusing point but his right leg does not. Its absence is accentuated and impairment here is read as loss. The game he plays is his personal effort to overcome his loss.

The photograph creates a flowing but awkward symmetry and our reading of its flow is continually interrupted by the fact that the triangle's neatness is dependent on the absence of a limb. Two readings occur simultaneously: it is tragic but he is brave. In a book of hope, the disabled person is the symbol of loss. The disabled boy is a reminder that all is not necessarily well in the world but *he* is doing *his* best to sort it out. The image is "positive" in that he is "positively" adjusting to his loss. Because he is "positively" adjusting to his loss, the image is allowed into the exhibition and the catalogue. The image of his disablement has been used not for him but against him. The image's symbolic value is that disability is an issue for the person with an impairment, not an issue for a world being (inaccessibly) reconstructed. In *The Family of Man*, disabled people were almost entirely absented because harmony was seen to rest in the full operation of an idealised working body. The exhibition and catalogue did not admit disabled people (bar one) because it did not see a position for disabled people within the new model army of postwar production or consumption.

Photographically speaking, the decline of this high ground of postwar hope in the "one world, one voice, one leader" humanity was heralded (in historical photographic terms) by an equally influential but far more subversive exhibition, again at the Museum of Modern Art, New York, which was held in 1967. This exhibition was called New Documents and brought into a wide public consciousness reportage portraiture showing the human race as an alienated species bewildered by its existence. New Documents featured the work of Gary Winogrand, Lee Friedlander and Diane Arbus. The importance of these three photographers (and others like Robert Frank) is that their work heralded the breakdown of the universal humanism of *The Family of Man* into a more fragmented, psychic or surrealistic realism. The appalling reverse of the coin is that they anchored the new forms of a fragmented universe (to a greater or lesser extent) in new, even more oppressive images of disabled people.

What is particularly crucial in terms of the representation of disabled people in this photojournalism is a clear (yet still uncritical) emergence of the portrayal of disabled people as the *symbol* of this new (dis)order. Whereas the tucked-away disabled person in *The Family of Man* had been a hidden blemish on the body of humanity, in a world of the Cold War, the Cuban Missile Crisis and Vietnam, disabled people were represented as the inconcealable birthmark of fear and chaos. Diane Arbus was the second photographer whose work I looked at. The monograph that I had pulled from the shelf is from her posthumous retrospective, held at the Museum of Modern Art, New York, in 1972 and entitled *Diane Arbus*.[5]

Of all photographers who have included or excluded disabled people, Diane Arbus is the most notorious. She was born into an *arriviste* family of immigrants, whose money was made in the fur trade. She became a photographer through her husband, Allan Arbus, and worked with him in fashion photography. She moved away from that (and him) into work which still dealt with the body and its surrounding hyperbole but from a very different angle. It was on her own and in her own work that she became known, unwittingly according to her, as "the photographer of freaks." Whether she liked it or not, there can be no doubt that this is how her work has been received. The monograph contains 81 black-and-white images, of which eleven are of disabled people. These eleven can be divided into three quite critical periods of her work. The first is demonstrated in two portraits of "dwarfs"; the second with the portrait of the "Jewish giant"; and the third with the imagery shot just before her death, that of the "retardees" (her term for people with Down Syndrome).

In any of the material on Arbus, including this monograph, Patricia Bosworth's biography of her entitled *Diane Arbus, A Biography*, and Susan Sontag's discussion of her work in *On Photography*, the stages of her oppressive representations of disabled people are never discussed. Moreover, the "factual" recording of disabled people as freaks is accepted totally without question by major critics like Sontag, who says, "Her work shows people who are pathetic, pitiable, as well as repulsive, but it does not arouse any compassionate feelings."[6] Later, she rhetorically adds, "Do they see themselves, the viewer wonders, like *that?* Do they know how grotesque they are?" (her italics). Sontag brings to the disability imagery of Arbus a complete faith in Arbus's images as unproblematic truthtellers. Bosworth also colludes by patronising disabled people, telling us of Arbus's "gentle and patient" way with "them." Neither of these critics, it goes without saying, considered asking the observed what *they* felt about the images in which they figured. Once again, the entire discourse has absented the voice of those at its center—disabled people.

Since there is only one other book on Arbus's work, and that deals with her magazine work,[7] it is safe to say that Bosworth and Sontag represent key parts of the Arbus industry. In their validations of Arbus's work, they both miss a central point. Although she was profoundly misguided (as I demonstrate further on), there can be no doubt that her work paradoxically had the effect of problematising, or opening up, the issue of the representation of disabled people. Her critics and defenders have built a wall around her work (and any discussion of disability in her work) by "naturalising" the content. In this, the images of disabled people have been lumped into one label, that of "freaks." Perhaps this has been done because her work appears to buck the contradictory trend of "compassion" in the portrayal of disabled "victims" practised by other photographers. Although Arbus's work can never be "reclaimed," it has to be noted that her work, and the use of "enfreakment" as message and metaphor, is far more complicated than either her defenders or critics acknowledge. The process of analysis is not to rehabilitate her or her work but to break it down once and for all.

She was a part of the "snapshot aesthetic" which grew up beyond the New Documents exhibition and exhibitors. This form attempted to overturn the sophisticated and high-technique processes of the Hollywood fantasy portrait, as well as rejecting the beautiful toning of much of *The Family of Man*. However, more than any of her peers, she took this aesthetic nearer to its roots in the family photograph or album (indeed she intended to shoot a project entitled Family Album).[8] Arbus had experienced, in her own family, the emotional and psychological cost of wealth in terms of the painful subjectivity and isolation of the individual hidden and silenced within the outward signs of bourgeois upward mobility and success. In terms of disability, however, Arbus read the bodily impairment of her disabled subject as a sign of disorder, even chaos; that is, as a physical manifestation of *her* chaos, *her* horror. Despite her relationships with disabled people (often lasting a decade or more) she viewed these not as social and equal relationships but as encounters with souls from an underworld.

There was nothing new in this pattern of "reading" the visual site of a disabled person away from a personal value into a symbolic value which then seals the representational fate of the disabled person. However, at least in the first period of her disability work, Arbus deviated from the Richard III syndrome by reading this "disorder" as the manifestation of a psychic disorder not in the subject but in society. There is no question of Arbus using her subjects "positively"—it is clear that she always intended them and their relationships to themselves and others to symbolise something other than themselves. She saw herself and her "freaks" as fellow travellers into a living oblivion, a social death. There is a perverse sense in which she was right—disabled people are expected to inhabit a living death—but the crucial thing is that she considered her projection to be more important than their reality. She "normalised" subjects like Morales, *The Mexican Dwarf*,[9] or *The Russian Midget Friends*[10] by specifically placing them in that great site of bourgeois culture and consumption, the home. The "horror" of Arbus's work is not that she has created Frankenstein but that she moved him in next door! What is more, the freak had brought his family! The "shock" for the hundreds of thousands of non-disabled viewers was that these portraits revealed a hinter-land existing in spite of the segregationist non-disabled world view.

For Arbus, the family—her own family— represented an abyss. She saw in the bourgeois promise to the immigrant family, her own family, a Faustian contract. Her Mephistopheles, her threat to the bourgeois privilege, was to move a non-disabled fear that dare not speak its name into the family snap. In a sense, this first period of her work (a period not of time but of understanding) is her least oppressive and in some ways complete. The sitters acknowledge her presence and her camera. They stare out from the picture at the viewer. Far from making apologies for their presence, they are distinctly proud, they are committed to

their identity. Although the disabled people portrayed existed within subcultures (such as the circus), they were clearly not segregated and it is this which shocked the public who flocked to her posthumous retrospective at the Museum of Modern Art in 1972. It is the *conscious dialogue* between Arbus and the subjects which "horrified" and yet fascinated people more used to compassionate victim images of disabled people obligingly subhuman and obligingly institutionalized as "tragic but brave." Morales, the Mexican "dwarf" in *Diane Arbus*, is pictured naked but for a towel over his crutch. He wears a trilby at a rakish angle and his elbow leans casually on to the sideboard, resting just in front of a bottle of liquor. It is not clear quite what went on between Arbus and Morales (though Arbus had previously "spent the night" with another disabled subject, Moondance, as part of his agreement to be photographed) but the eroticism of the image cannot be denied. Not only is the so-called "dwarf" distinctly unfreaky in his three-quarters nakedness, he is positively virile! A constant theme of Arbus's work, not just of her disability work, is the relationship between people's bodies and their paraphernalia. While the attire is crisp and clear, the flesh of the subject has been "zombified." This, however, is not the case with her first pictures of "dwarfs." Morales's body is very much alive.

Arbus had attempted to trace the psychic disorder of consumer society back to a primal state of terror within everyday life. That she believed disabled people to be the visual witness of this primal state is clear. That is, she accepted at the level of "common sense" the non-integration of disabled people. However, much of "the Horror, the Horror"[11] with which Arbus's work has been received is in her location of this disabled terror within non-disabled normality. The disabled subjects themselves, at least in this early "freak" work, are treated reverentially. The camera is close. The camera is engaged. The subject has agreed to the session (but agreed in isolation?). The "horror" of the process for non-disabled society is in her placing a disabled normality within a non-disabled normality. The horror is in how she could even think them equivalent. The horror, I repeat, was in Arbus's recording in her constructions of disabled people a double bind of segregation/non-segregation. The "non-segregation," however (and this is where Arbus's crime really lay) did not lead towards integration—the "Russian midgets" were not living down the road as part of an independent living scheme—but towards transgression. It was a spectacle, not a political dialectic (the disability paradox) that Arbus wanted to ensnare. For this she accepted, indeed depended, on the given segregation of disabled people as "common sense."

Things began to disintegrate for Arbus in the second part of her disability work. This in illustrated in the monograph by the image entitled *A Jewish Giant at Home with his Parents in the Bronx, N.Y. 1970.* Again, we see a cosy family setting of a front room with two comfy chairs and a sofa, two elderly and self-respecting pensioners, a lamp by the drawn curtains, a reproduction classic painting in a tasteful frame, and a giant. The "giant" is not given a name in the title but his name was Eddie Carmel.[12] Again, Arbus did not sneak in and sneak out in this shot but got to know and photograph Eddie Carmel over a period of ten years before printing this one which she considered to work. This image of *A Jewish Giant* with its glaring flash-lit room, its portrayal of "the beast" from the womb of the mother, shows less harmony, even a deliberate asymmetry from that of her "dwarf" images. In *A Jewish Giant* she had created an image which took her beyond the reverence in both form and content of her "dwarf" images. Unlike them, Eddie the Jewish "giant" directs his attention away from the presence of the camera, his only acknowledgement that an

image is being made is by being on his feet like his parents. His body language appears unclear and unsettled. The flash has cast black halos round the bodies of the subjects and they begin to resemble a Weegee as a found specimen of urban horror. The image of the "giant" as he crouches towards his more formal parents is that of a father over two children. The classic family portrait of parents and child is completely reversed by her use of their size relationship. The body language of the "Jewish giant" is more "out of control" (that is, it diverges more from non-disabled body language signs) than that of the "dwarf." It is all the more "threatening" to the non-disabled family snap because his body is situated with that of his "normal" parents. A clash or a confrontation between styles and discourses is occurring. The alchemy, confrontation and visual disorder of the image bring Arbus closer to avenging the control and repression in her own family. This is the key to her use and manipulation of isolated disabled people. During the ten years of their knowing each other, Eddie Carmel told Arbus about his ambitions, about his job selling insurance, about his acting hopes (and his despair at only being offered "monster" roles), and so on. Arbus dismissed this in her representations. She clearly found his actual day-to-day life irrelevant. Indeed, she appears to have disbelieved him, preferring her own projection of a metaphysical decline. His real tragedy is that he trusted Arbus, and she abused that trust outside of their relationship in an area within her total control, that is, photography.

The visual dialogue within the image between herself and the subject in the "dwarf" works, although decreasing in the imagery of Eddie the "giant," was still prevalent and was important precisely because it created a snapshot family album currency within the imagery. The commonness of this form was a part of its communicative power. As a structure it spoke to millions, while its content, Arbus's enfreakment of disabled people,[13] spoke to the able-bodied fear of millions. Were the subject to disengage, to reject the apparent co-conspiracy (in reality a coercion) or contract between themselves and Arbus, the images would move from the genre of family album currency and understanding of millions, to a reportage subgenre position of one specialist photographer. Arbus's work would then be that of an outsider constructing outsiders which need not be internalised by the viewer. The enfreakment in her disability images was internalised by the non-disabled viewers because the disabled subjects, while chosen for their apparent difference, manifested body language and identity traits recognisable to everyone. Arbus was concerned to show the dichotomy, even the pain, between how people projected themselves and how she thought they "really" were. The projection of this "imagined self" by the subject was through the direct gaze to camera (and therefore direct gaze to viewer). The image of *A Jewish Giant*, to Arbus, suggested a higher level of fear and chaos than the "dwarf" work. This higher level of discrepancy between order (the setting is still the family at home) and chaos (Eddie outgrowing that which contained him), than that manifested in the "dwarf" work, is also highlighted by the fact that, although the "giant" is on his feet posing with his parents, his dialogue is as much between him and his parents as between him and Arbus/the viewer.

Arbus was reported to have told a journalist at the *New Yorker* of her excitement over this image, the first one that had worked for her in the ten years of photographing Eddie. "You know how every mother has nightmares when she's pregnant that her baby will be born a monster? I think I got that in the mother's face as she glares up at Eddie, thinking, 'OH MY GOD, NO!'"[14] You could be forgiven for imagining that the mother recoils from her Eddie

much like Fay Ray recoiled from the horror of King Kong, but this is not the case. Arbus betrayed in her excited phone call to the journalist what she wished the image to say, rather than what it actual does say (though, of course, meanings shift). Arbus's comment about "every mother's nightmare" speaks of her nightmare relationship with her own body, which I believe she viewed as the sole site of her power. It was this loss of control of the body which she saw disability/impairment as meaning. Arbus once quoted a person who defined horror as the relationship between sex and death. She also claimed that she never refused a person who asked her to sleep with them. Furthermore, Bosworth hints that Arbus may have been confused about her bi-sexuality. In any event, the clues suggest that while she viewed her body and sexuality as key points of her power, her sexuality was not clear to her, and sex itself probably failed to resolve her feelings of aloneness and fragmentation. She sought the answer to this dilemma in locating bodily chaos in all her subjects (to varying degrees) and felt she'd found it in its perfect form in disabled people. (That major institutions of American representation, like the Museum of Modern Art, promoted her work shows their willingness to cooperate with this oppressive construction of disabled people.)

The "OH MY GOD, NO!" which she attributes to the mother in *A Jewish Giant* is in reality an "OH MY GOD, YES!" victory call that Arbus herself felt. She had made her psychic vision physical, or so she felt. Diane Arbus's daughter, Doon Arbus, has written that her mother wanted to photograph not what was evil but what was *forbidden*.[15] She believed she had pictured a return of the forbidden and repressed within her own remembered family. In her construction, the awkwardness of *A Jewish Giant* hints at the unwieldiness of her vision as a long-term solution to her own needs and begins to hint at this vision's ultimate destructiveness—not only, and obviously, to disabled people, but to the psychic well-being of Arbus herself.

It is here that the third period in her work on disabled people begins. She starts to photograph "retardees" (as she labels people with Down Syndrome). She moves from observing her subjects at home to observing them in a home; that is, an institution. These images of people with Down Syndrome were practically the last she shot before killing herself. They are clustered, six of them, at the end of the book. In the previous work with "dwarfs" and *A Jewish Giant* Arbus had maintained that she did not photograph anybody who did not agree to be photographed. This was undoubtedly so (although coercion is probably truer than agreement), but the images show a decline in conscious frontal participation of the subject. This decline was also mirrored in the growing discordance on the technical side of her work. The beautiful tones of Morales, the "dwarf," give way to a harsh flashlight in the "Jewish giant." There is no doubt that Arbus, as an ex-fashion photographer, knew what she was doing in using technical disharmony as an underwriting of the narrative disharmony. When we come into the third period, her work on "retardees," Arbus continues to pursue technical discordance. She still uses flash-and-daylight to pick up the figures from their landscape, but the focus is clearly weaker than that of the previous work. The subjects are now barely engaged with Arbus/the viewer *as themselves*.

Arbus finds them not in a position to conspire with her projection. The visual dialogue collapses. The dialectic between body and attire which Arbus had pursued is broken. The chaos of their paper and blanket costumes appears, to her, not to challenge their bodies but to match them. Arbus's order-chaos paradoxical projection has not happened. Instead, Arbus sees zombies in another world. To her they

project no illusions of being neighbours to normality. These people are not at home but in a home. The institution of the family give sway to the institution of segregation (in this case, a New Jersey "home" for "retardees"). The people with Down Syndrome are set in a backdrop of large open fields showing only distant woods. For Arbus, their consciousness and activity is arbitrary. She does not know how to make them perform to her psycho-ventriloquist needs. In her career-long attempt to pull the psychic underworld into the physical overworld by manipulating the bodies of disabled people, she has come to the borders in these images. She had met "the limits of her imagination"; she had not found in these images the catharsis necessary for her to continue. Arbus first loved then hated this last work. She entered a crisis of identity because these segregated people with Down Syndrome would not perform as an echo of her despair. Because of this, her despair deepened. In the final image of this series and the final image of her monograph, nine disabled people pass across the view of the camera. Of the nine, only one turns towards the camera. His gaze misses the camera; consequently the possibilities that might have been opened up by a direct gaze are, for Arbus, lost. He joins the rest of this crowd who come into the frame for no purpose. Arbus's camera became irrelevant not only for disabled people, but for Arbus herself. This was her last work before she killed herself.

The next book I looked at was Gary Winogrand's *Figments from the Real World*.[16] Of the 179 black-and-white plates in *Figments from the Real World*, six included the portrayal of disabled people on one level or another. Like Arbus, the inclusion of disabled people, regardless of their role, was that of a significant minority with their oppression unquestioned and constructed as intact. Unlike Arbus's work, however, Winogrand did not produce any images (at least not for public consumption) whose central character was the disabled person or disablement. He did produce bodies of work on women, for example, but where a disabled person appears in the work, it is as a secondary character to the women. Nevertheless, within the "underrepresentation" in *Figments from the Real World*, it becomes clear that, like Arbus and the others from my ersatz list, "the disabled" had a role to play. Nevertheless, Winogrand consciously or otherwise included disabled people with the specific intention of enfreaking disability in order to make available to his visual repertoire a key *destabilising* factor.

With regard to the representation of women by Winogrand, Victor Burgin has critiqued Winogrand's work and has explored the reading of meaning within his imagery and the relationship of this meaning to the wider social and political discourses of his time.[17] Burgin describes and discusses an image of Winogrand from an exhibition in 1976. The image is of four women advancing towards the camera down a city street. The group of women, who are varying degrees of middle age, is the most prominent feature in the right-hand half of the image; equally prominent is a group of huge plastic bags stuffed full of garbage. The introduction to the catalogue of the exhibition makes it clear that this "joke" is intended. The reading of middle-aged women as "old bags" is unavoidable.

Despite the protestations by John Szarkowski in the introduction of *Figments from the Real World* that Winogrand celebrated women (he called the book of this phase of his work, *Women are Beautiful*), it is clear that his construction of women singly or in groups advancing towards the camera from all directions displays an unease, a fear, of what the results of his desire for them might be. Their faces frown by his camera, their eyes bow down to avoid his gaze. Burgin highlighted the dynamics of his "old bag" image. Winogrand's fear at

what he reads as a loss of (female) beauty in ageing is registered by his "old bag" image. It is no coincidence that one of the six disability images (and the only one of two showing a wheelchair user) in *Figments from the Real World* involves an almost identical dynamic to that of the "old bags."

The center of the image is three young women. They are lit by a sun behind them and their sharp shadows converge towards the camera. They dominate the center third of the image and they are walking along a ray of light towards the lends. They are dressed in the fashion of the moment. In their movement is recorded an affecting, perhaps transitional beauty. Their symmetry is, however, broken by the gaze of the woman on the right. The symmetry is further challenged by this woman being a step ahead of the other two as she stares down at the presence, in the shadows, of a crouched wheelchair user. The other two women slightly move their heads towards the wheelchair. All of their eyes are tightened and all of their facial expressions "interpret" the presence of the wheelchair user with degrees of controlled horror.

Unlike Winogrand's dumping of middle-aged women into "old bags," he confronts these young women with a warning. He observes them as beautiful but warns them that their beauty and all its "paraphernalia" is all that separates them from the "grotesque" form they are witnessing. Beauty is warned of the beast. Clearly, Winogrand could not assuage his desire for women, whom he spent years photographically accosting on the street. His work harbours a resentment that they do not respond to his aggressive desire and so he implants warnings. The asymmetry of the imagery is anchored in the non-disabled reading (in this instant, Winogrand's) of disabled people as sites of asymmetrical disharmony. The women's body harmony (as Winogrand desires it) is set against the wheelchair user's disharmony (as Winogrand sees it).

Winogrand's use of the disabled person, again enfreaked, is to bring out of the underworld and into the shadows a symbol of asymmetry *as fear and decay* which challenges the three women's right to walk "beautifully" down the street.

Like Arbus, Winogrand's use of disability is to warn the "normal" world that their assumptions are fragile. This he does by the use of differentness of many disabled people's bodies as a symbol of the profound asymmetry of consumer society, particularly in the United States. Despite the fact that the American President Roosevelt had been disabled, the enfreakment of disabled people in these new practices became the symbol of the alienation of humanity which these new photographers were trying to record.

The Family of Man exhibition had all but excluded disabled people because they did not represent hope in the new order, so the post New Documents practitioners *included* disabled people for precisely the same reasons. The Family of Man and the New Documents exhibitions, constructed within photographic theories as radically separate, are inextricably linked, in that the inclusion of disabled people does not mean progress, but regression. Disabled people increased their presence in the new reportage of these photographers not as a sign of enlightenment and integration, but as a sign of bedlam.

The fourth book picked at random, I realized afterwards, takes us to a European setting. In *Another Way of Telling*,[18] the inevitable inclusion of a disabled subject comes almost at the very beginning. This book deals heavily with photographs of the countryside and the peasantry of various countries and the first photo-text piece sets this agenda. This is a story of Jean Mohr taking photographs of some cows, while the cow owner jokingly chastises him for taking pictures with permission and without payment. This first part very much sets the geographic and political agenda for the whole book, which explores the three-way relationship between the photographer, the photographed and the different meanings and readings taken from the photographs.

In every image or image-sequence, excluding the second one in the book (that of a blind girl in India) the images are more or less openly problematical. That is, the relationship between the image and its apparent informative or communicative value is put to the test. "Only occasionally is an image self-sufficient," says Jean Mohr. From this assertion, Mohr and Berger explore the image-making processes and what can be taken on or used within the process of photography that might work for both the photographer and the subject. The genesis of the book is to question meaning and use-value of imagery from all points, not just that of the photographer.

In Mohr's eighty-page first part, he illuminates different contexts of his own image-making, from shooting running children from a passing train, to shooting and reshooting working people and directing his work according to their expressed wishes. The theme which pervades the whole book is that of the working process. Moreover, the working process that they have chosen to explore visually is that of people working on the land and their lives and communities. The image-sequences, whether of cow-herders or of wood-cutters, begin with labour and its dignity. Clearly, unlike many "concerned" social realist photographers, Mohr is attempting to inhabit the process from the inside, not just to observe it externally. His method is through the voice, feedback and acknowledgement of the person photographed in their work. Their work is the anchor, the base, from which the story unfolds.

At one point and in one sequence, Mohr turns the camera on himself. He puts himself in the picture. He talks about the fear, the anxiety, even the panic which assails many people when they are the subject of the camera. Am I too fat? Am I too skinny? Is my nose too large? He tells us that he finds the process of putting himself in the picture difficult and talks about how he attempts to lose his image through technical disguises, like deliberately moving the camera during an exposure so as to blur the image, and so on. He anchors this process of putting himself in the picture on the quite valid and narcissistic idea that he used to imagine that he looked like Samuel Beckett. After bringing the story home by saying that he was finally forced to view his own image by being the subject matter of *other* people's lens, rather than his own, he finally finishes it by telling us that a student who photographed him felt that he did indeed resemble Beckett.

His work on other people's images and stories and his work on his own image and self are linked because, in grappling with the process of representation of his self or of others, he tells us and attempts to show us that the meaning of images is rooted in the process and context in which they were made. This is an important assertion but not unique. This book was published in 1982 and came at a time when other photographers and theorists, like Victor Burgin, Allan Sekula, Photography Workshop (Jo Spence/Terry Dennett) *et al.*, were questioning and problematising and naturalist truth-telling assumptions underpinning the left's use of social realist photography. *Another Way of Telling*, then, was a part of this "movement."

However, *Another Way of Telling*, and Jean Mohr's opening piece in particular, is clearly anchored in finding another way of using naturalist reportage, not abandoning it altogether. Mohr explains the use-value of the naturalist image to the subject. He tells stories of how this or that peasant wanted the image to show the whole body—of the person, of the cow, of the tree-cutting

process—rather than be "unnaturally" cropped. Naturalism, then, to him, has a purpose *in context*.

Here, we begin to get close to the *purpose* of the blind girl pictures within Jean Mohr's piece and the book as a whole. The realist (time/place) agenda is set in the first image, that of the cowman, but the *underlying agenda of "simple" naturalism* (that is to say, Mohr and Berger's belief in its ability to tell a simple story) is anchored in the hypersimplicity of the blind girl's pleasure. These pictures of a disabled person—a blind Asian girl—form the apex of the book's naturalist thesis that the value of naturalism is in its portrayal of unconscious innocence.

The story is called "The Stranger who Imitated Animals." The "stranger" in question is Jean Mohr. In the 250-odd words which accompany the five images, he tells us of visiting his sister in the university town of Aligarh in India and of his sister's "warning" of the blind girl who comes round and likes to know what is happening. He awakes the next morning unclear of where he is when.

> The young blind girl said Good Morning. The sun had been up for hours. Without reasoning why I replied to her by yapping like a dog. Her face froze for a moment. Then I imitated a cat caterwauling. And the expression on her face behind the netting changed to one of recognition and complicity in my play-acting. I went on to a peacock's cry, a horse whinnying, a large animal growling—like a circus. With each act and according to our mood, her expression changed. Her face was so beautiful that, without stopping our game, I picked up my camera and took some pictures of her. She will never see these photographs. For her I shall simply remain the invisible stranger who imitated animals.[19]

Clearly, despite his simplification of his response ("without reasoning why"), he responded with impersonations precisely because he had observed that she was blind. He objectified her, his first impulse on waking up to see a blind person was to play games with the blindness. Underlying this was the assumption that blind people (whatever the level of visual impairment) have no idea of quantifiable physical reality and would, of course, think that the sound really was of a yapping dog waking up in bed. His joke reveals his disability (un-)consciousness, not hers.

But she responds to this with laughter, she joins in. So, he further objectifies her by again distancing himself. While she laughs along with his imitations, he secretly photographs her, because her laughing but blind face was "so beautiful." Clearly, because she is laughing in his pictures, he presumably continued his imitations while he photographed her. The game for two turned into manipulation by one. The pictures show her leaning against the dark wooden surround of the door. She is framed by this and leans into this frame by pressing her ears to his mimicry. She is kept at a distance and keeps her responses on that surface of the mosquito net which fits into the wooden frame. This framing of her by the door is copied in his framing of her in the camera. Out of the five pictures in the sequence, four clearly show her eyes. Technically, these have been deliberately whitened in the printing to highlight the blindness.

As labour is the anchor in the other series, and as narcissism is the anchor in his self-image series, shooting the whites of her eyes is the anchor in this series. Her blindness is the symbol of innocence and nobility. Her blindness is the anchor of her simplicity. Her blindness is the object of his voyeurism. He has taken and symbolised this disabled person's image, which he says "she will never see" (he obviously didn't consider aural description), as the anchor and beauty of naturalism. The text which accompanies this series of images doesn't quite have the once-upon-a-time-ness of some of the other photo-essays, but it still

serves to push the imagery into the magical or metaphysical. The always-to-be natural images of the blind girl are the only set that have no significant time element to them. His work with the cowman spans days, his work with the wood-cutter is over a period of time (enough for the wood-cutter to give an opinion of the finished prints), but the work with the blind girl of beauty and innocence needs saying once, because it is forever. Again, like *The Family of Man*, like Arbus and Winogrand, Mohr has chosen to absent both the three-dimensional disabled person and their social story because it is incongruous to their own disability (un) consciousness. Their images tell us nothing about the actual lives of disabled people, but they add to the history of oppressive representation.

I have just analysed a random selection of four major photographic books, only one of which I knew to have been involved in disability representation. In the event, all four were. In the final analysis, these books which include disabled people in their field of photographic reference do so on the condition that disabled people are, to use Sontag's term for Diane Arbus's work, "borderline" cases. Sontag meant this term in its common reference to psychic or spiritual disorder. However, disabled people in the representations which I have discussed in this and the previous chapters share a commonality in that they live in different camps beyond the border. Whether beauty or the beast, they are outsiders. The basis for this border in society is real. It is physical and it is called segregation. The social absence of disabled people creates a vacuum in which the visual meanings attributable (symbolically, metaphorically, psychically, etc.) to impairment and disablement appear free-floating and devoid of any actual people. In the absence of disabled people, the meaning in the disabled person and their body is made by those who survey. They attempt to shift the disablement on to the impairment, and the impairment into a flaw. The very absence of disabled people in positions of power and representation deepens the use of this "flaw" in their images. The repression of disabled people makes it more likely that the symbolic use of disablement by non-disabled people is a sinister or mythologist one. Disablement re-enters the social world through photographic representation, but in the re-entry its meaning is tied not by the observed, disabled people, but by the non-disabled observers.

It is here that all the work, picked at random, is linked. Disabled people, in these photographic representations, are positioned either as meaningful or meaningless bodies. They are meaningful only as polarised anchors of naturalist humility or psychic terror. Brave but tragic: two sides of the segregated coin? Disabled people are taken into the themes pursued by Arbus, Winogrand, Mohr, and so on, to illustrate the truth of their respective grand narratives. The role of the body of the disabled person is to enflesh the thesis or theme of the photographer's work, despite the fact that most of the photographers had taken no conscious decision to work "on" disability. It is as if the spirit of the photographer's mission can be summed up in their manipulation of a disabled person's image. "The disabled" emerge, like a lost tribe, to fulfil a role for these photographers but not for themselves.

Disabled people appeared either as one image at a time per book or one role per book. The use of disabled people is the anchor of the weird, that is, the fear within. They are used as the symbol of enfreakment or the surrealism of all society. "Reactionary" users of this notion hunt the "crips" down to validate chaos within their own environment (Arbus); "progressive" users of this notion hunt them down within their own environment to find an essential romantic humanity in their own lives (but no question of access). The US "crip" sym-bol denotes alienation. The impaired body is the site and symbol of all alienation. It is psychic alienation made physical. The "contorted" body is the final process and statement of a painful mind.

While this symbol functions as a "property" of disabled people as viewed by these photographers, it does not function as *the* property of those disabled people observed. Its purpose was not as a role model, or as references for observed people, but as the voyeuristic property of the non-disabled gaze. Moreover, the impairment of the disabled person became the mark, the target for a disavowal, a ridding, of the existential fears and fantasies of non-disabled people. This "symbolic" use of disablement knows no classic political lines, indeed it may be said to become more oppressive the further left you move.[20] The point is clear. If the disability paradox, the disability dialectic, is between impaired people and disabling social conditions, then the photographers we have just examined represent the construction of an "official" history of blame from the disabling society towards disabled people.

The works were selected at random and I fear their randomness proves my point. Wherever I drilled, I would have found the same substance. Were I to continue through modern photographic publications, I have no doubt that the pattern I am describing would continue; the only variation being that some would use disabled people for the purposes described, while others would absent disabled people altogether. A cursory widening of the list, to glance at photographers who have come after those named above, people like Joel-Peter Witkin,[21] Gene Lambert,[22] Bernard F. Stehle,[23] Nicholas Nixon,[24] and others who have all "dealt with" disablement, shows photographers who continued a manipulation of the disability/impairment image but have done so in a manner which depressingly makes the work by, say, Arbus and Mohr (I don't suppose they ever felt they'd be mentioned in the same breath!) seem positively timid! The work of many of the "post New Documentaries" has shifted the ground on the representation of disabled people by making "them" an even more separate category. While the volume of representation is higher, the categorisation, control and manipulation have become deeper. In this sense, the photographic observation of disablement has increasingly become the art of categorisation and surveillance. Also, from a psychological viewpoint, those that appear to have transgressed this commodification of disabled people have only transgressed their own fears of their constructions. The oppression remains the same. The segregated are not being integrated, they are being broken into! The photographic construction of disabled people continues through the use of disabled people in imagery as the site of fear, loss or pity. Those who are prevented by their liberal instincts from "coming out" in their cripple-as-freak, freak-as-warning-of-chaos, circumvent it by attempting to tell the unreconstructed "natural" story of oblivion. Either way, it is a no-win victim position for disabled people within those forms of representation. My intention in this essay is to suggest new forms.

A final note of hope. Diane Arbus was "extremely upset" when she received a reply from "The Little People's Convention" to her request to photograph them. They wrote that, "We have our own little person to photograph us."[25] In terms of disabled people's empowerment, this is the single most important statement in all of the work considered.

NOTES

1. Vic Finkelstein has argued that the "administrative model" of disablement has replaced the "medical model" to the extent that it is now the dominant oppressive one. This model, according to Finkelstein, suggests that the move away from the large "phase-two" institutions (which mirrored heavy industrial production) towards the dispersal of "care in the community" has meant that disablement has shifted from a predominantly cure-or-care issue to an administrative one. There is no doubt in my mind that this shift is being echoed in the production of "positive" images within the UK local authorities. They are similar to the functionalist images of the charities third-stage imagery in their portrayal of the administration of service provision to (grinning) disabled people.

2. *GYN/ecology* (1981), by Mary Daly, London: Women's Press.

3. *Images of the Disabled, Disabling Images* (1987), ed. Alan Gartner and Tom Joe, New York: Praeger.

4. *The Family of Man*, exhibition and publication by the Museum of Modern Art, New York, 1955. (Reprinted 1983.)

5. *Diane Arbus* (1990), London: Bloomsbury Press.

6. *On Photography* (1979), by Susan Sontag, London: Penguin.

7. "Arbus revisited: a review of the monograph," by Paul Wombell, *Portfolio* magazine, no. 10, Spring 1991.

8. Ibid., p. 33.

9. *Diane Arbus*, op. cit., p. 23. The full title of the photograph is *Mexican Dwarf in his Hotel Room in N.Y.C. 1970*.

10. *Diane Arbus*, op. cit., p. 16. The full title for this photograph is: *Russian Midget Friends in a Living Room on 100th St. N.Y.C. 1963*.

11. The death cry of Kurtz on discovering the unpronounceable, in Conrad's *Heart of Darkness*.

12. *Diane Arbus: A Biography* (1984), by Patricia Bosworth, New York: Avon Books, p. 226.

13. It is important to remember that the ability of naturalist photographic practice to "enfreak" its subject is not peculiar to the oppressive portrayal of disabled people. For example, the same process of fragmenting and reconstructing oppressed people into the projection of the photographer is particularly marked in the projection of the working classes. See *British Photography from the Thatcher Years* (book and exhibition) by Susan Kismaric, Museum of Modern Art, New York, 1990.

14. *Diane Arbus: A Biography*, op. cit., p. 227.

15. Ibid., p. 153.

16. *Gary Winogrand* (1988), *Figments from the Real World*, ed. John Szarkowski, New York: Museum of Modern Art.

17. *The End of Art Theory: Criticism and Post-Modernity* (1986), by Victor Burgin, London: Macmillan, p. 63.

18. *Another Way of Telling* (1982), by John Berger and Jean Mohr, London: Writers and Readers.

19. Ibid., p. 11.

20. For the "left" use of disability/impairment as the site of a defense of the welfare state, see "Bath time at St. Lawrence" by Raissa Page in *Ten-8*, nos. 7/8, 1982. Alternatively, for a cross-section of the inclusion of disability imagery within magazines servicing the welfare state, see the King's Fund Centre reference library, London. Finally, see the impairment charity house journals and read the photo credits, i.e., the Spastics Society's *Disability Now*. Network, Format, Report and other left photo agencies regularly supply uncritical impairment imagery.

21. *Masterpieces of Medical Photography: Selections from the Burns Archive* (1987), ed. Joel-Peter Witkin, California: Twelve-tree Press.

22. *Work from a Darkroom* (1985), by Gene Lambert (exhibition and publication), Dublin: Douglas Hyde Gallery.

23. *Incurably Romantic* (1985), by Bernard F. Stehle, Philadelphia: Temple University Press.

24. *Pictures of People* (1988), by Nicholas Nixon, New York: Museum of Modern Art.

25. *Diane Arbus: A Biography* (1984), by Patricia Bosworth, New York: Avon Books, p. 365.

CHAPTER 32

Blindness and Visual Culture:
An Eyewitness Account

Georgina Kleege

In April 2004, I was invited to speak at a conference on visual culture at the University of California, Berkeley. Speakers were asked to respond to an essay by W. J. T. Mitchell titled, "Showing Seeing: A Critique of Visual Culture," which offers a series of definitions of the emergent field of visual studies, distinguishing it from the more established disciplines of art history, aesthetics and media studies. As an admitted outsider to the field of visual studies, I chose to comment on the following statement: "Visual culture entails a meditation on blindness, the invisible, the unseen, the unseeable, and the overlooked" (Mitchell 2002, 170). In my last book, *Sight Unseen*, I attempted to show blindness through my own experience, and a survey of representations of blindness in literature and film. At the same time, I wanted to show seeing, to sketch my understanding of vision, drawn from a lifetime of living among the sighted in this visual culture we share. I started from the premise that the average blind person knows more about what it means to be sighted than the average sighted person knows about what it means to be blind. The blind grow up, attend school, and lead adult lives among sighted people. The language we speak, the literature we read, the architecture we inhabit, were all designed by and for the sighted.

If visual studies entails a meditation on blindness, it is my hope that it will avoid some of the missteps of similar meditations of the past. Specifically, I hope that visual studies can abandon one of the stock characters of the western philosophical tradition—"the Hypothetical Blind Man" (Gitter 2001, 58). The Hypothetical Blind Man—or the Hypothetical as I will call him for the sake of brevity—has long played a useful, though thankless role, as a prop for theories of consciousness. He is the patient subject of endless thought experiments where the experience of the world through four senses can be compared to the experience of the world through five. He is asked to describe his understanding of specific visual phenomena—perspective, reflection, refraction, color, form recognition—as well as visual aids and enhancements—mirrors, lenses, telescopes, microscopes. He is understood to lead a hermit-like existence, so far at the margins of his society, that he has never heard this visual terminology before the philosophers bring it up. Part of the emotional baggage he hauls around with him comes from other cultural representations of blindness, such as Oedipus and the many Biblical figures whose sight is withdrawn by the wrathful God of the Old Testament or restored by the redeemer of the New. His primary function is to highlight the importance of sight and to elicit a frisson of awe and pity which promotes gratitude among the sighted theorists for the vision they possess.

I will not attempt to survey every appearance of the Hypothetical throughout the history of philosophy. It is enough to cite a few of his more memorable performances, and then to suggest what happens when he is brought face-to-face with actual blind people through their own first-hand, eye-witness accounts. Professor Mitchell alludes to the passages in Descartes' *La Dioptrique* where he compares vision to the Hypothetical's use of sticks to grope his way through space. Descartes's references to the Hypothetical are confusing and are often conflated by his readers. In one instance, he compares the way the Hypothetical's stick detects the density and resistance of objects in his path, to the way light acts on objects the eye looks at. In a later passage, Descartes performs a thought experiment, giving the Hypothetical a second stick which he could use to judge the distance between two objects by calculating the angle formed when he touches each object with one of the sticks. Descartes does not explain how the Hypothetical is supposed to make this calculation or how he can avoid running into things while doing so. I doubt that Descartes actually believed that any blind person ever used two sticks in this way. In fact, the image that illustrates his discussion shows the Hypothetical's dog sound asleep on the ground, indicating that the Hypothetical is going nowhere. Even so, Descartes' description of the way a blind person uses one stick reflects a basic misunderstanding. He imagines that the blind use the stick to construct a mental image, or its equivalent, of their surroundings, mapping the location of specifically identified objects. In fact, then as now, a stick or cane is a poor tool for this kind of mental imaging. The stick serves merely to announce the presence of an obstacle,

not to determine if it is a rock or a tree root, though there are sound cues—a tap versus a thud—that might help make this distinction. In many situations, the cane is more of an auditory than a tactile tool. It seems that in Descartes' desire to describe vision as an extension of or hypersensitive form of touch, he recreates the blind man in his own image, where the eye must correspond to the hand extended by one or perhaps two sticks.

The most detailed depiction of the Hypothetical came about in 1693, when William Molyneux wrote his famous letter to John Locke. He proposed a thought experiment where a blind man who had learned to recognize geometric forms such as a cube and a sphere by touch, would have his sight restored through an operation. Would he be able to distinguish the two forms merely by looking at them? The Molyneux question continues to be debated today, even though the history of medicine is full of case studies of actual blind people who have had their sight restored by actual operations. Apparently, Molyneux was married to a blind woman, which has always led me to wonder why he did not pose his hypothetical question about her. Perhaps he knew that others would object that marriage to a philosopher might contaminate the experimental data. There was a risk that the philosopher might prime her answers or otherwise rig the results. Certainly in commentary on actual cases of restored sight, debaters of the Molyneux question are quick to disqualify those who were allowed to cast their eyes upon, for instance the faces of loved ones, before directing their gaze at the sphere and the cube.

Denis Diderot's 1749 "Letter on the Blind for the Use of Those Who See" is generally credited with urging a more enlightened, and humane attitude toward the blind. His blind man of Puiseaux and Nicholas Saunderson, the English mathematician, were both real rather than hypothetical blind men. As he introduces the man from Pui-seaux, Diderot is at pains to supply details of his family history and early life to persuade his reader that this is a real person. Significantly, the man from Puiseaux is first encountered helping his young son with his studies, demonstrating both that he is a loving family man, and capable of intellectual activity. But the questions Diderot poses generally fall under the pervu of the Hypothetical. Certainly, many of his remarks help support Descartes' theory relating vision to touch:

> One of our company thought to ask our blind man if he would like to have eyes. "If it were not for curiosity," he replied, "I would just as soon have long arms: it seems to me my hands would tell me more of what goes on in the moon than your eyes or your telescopes."
> (Diderot 1999, 153)

Diderot praises the blind man's ability to make philosophical surmises about vision, but does not have a high opinion of blind people's capacity for empathy:

> As of all the external signs which raise our pity and ideas of pain the blind are affected only by cries, I have in general no high thought of their humanity. What difference is there to a blind man between a man making water and one bleeding in silence?
> (Diderot 1999, 156)

The phrasing of the question here suggests an afterthought. I imagine Diderot, at his table, conjuring up two men, one pissing, one bleeding. While his visual imagination is practiced in making these sorts of mental images, he is less adept at tuning his mind's ear. He recognizes that for the blood to be spilt at a rate sufficient to create the same sound as the flowing urine, the bleeding man would normally cry out in pain. So he imagines, in effect, a bleeding mute. But he fails to take into account the relative viscosity, not to mention the different odors,

of the two fluids. But Diderot cannot think of everything.

Now I imagine a blind man wandering onto the scene. My blind man is not quite the one Diderot imagines. For one thing he is a bit preoccupied; the philosophers have dropped by again. They talk at him and over his head, bandying about names that are now familiar to him: Locke, Molyneux, Descartes. They question him about his ability to conceptualize various things: windows, mirrors, telescopes—and he responds with the quaint and winsome answers he knows they have come for. Anything to get rid of them. Distracted as he is, the sound of the bleeding mute's plashing blood registers on his consciousness. Lacking Diderot's imagination, however, the thought does not occur to him that this sound emanates from a bleeding mute. His reason opts instead for the explanation that the sound comes from some man relieving his bladder—a far more commonplace phenomenon, especially in the means streets where the blind man resides. It is not that the blind man has no fellow feeling for the mute. Come to think of it, the mute would make a good companion. He could act as a guide and keep an eye out for marauding philosophers, while the blind man could do all the talking. But the blind man does not have enough information to recognize the mute's dilemma. The only hope for the bleeding mute is to find some way to attract the blind man's attention, perhaps by throwing something. But surely, such a massive loss of blood must have affected his aim. While the blind man, living as he does at the margins of his society, is accustomed to being spurned by local homeowners and merchants who find his presence unsightly, and so might flee the bleeding mute's missiles without suspecting that his aid is being solicited.

The blind man quickens his pace as best he can. The mute succumbs at last to his mortal wound. And the philosopher shifts to another topic.

I am wrong to make fun of Diderot, since his treatment of blindness was at once far more complex and far more compassionate than that of other philosophers. And it is not as if his low opinion of the blind's ability to empathize with others' pain has ceased to contribute to attitudes about blindness. Consider this anecdote from recent history. Some weeks after September 11, 2001, the blind musician Ray Charles was interviewed about his rendition of "America the Beautiful," which received a good deal of air time during the period of heightened patriotism that followed that event. The interviewer, Jim Gray, commented that Charles should consider himself lucky that his blindness prevented him from viewing the images of the World Trade Center's collapse, and the Pentagon in flames: "Was this maybe one time in your life where not having the ability to see was a relief?" Like Diderot, the interviewer assumed that true horror can only be evinced through the eyes. Many eyewitness accounts of the event however, were strikingly nonvisual. Many people who were in the vicinity of Ground Zero during and soon after the disaster found it hard to put what they saw into words, in part because visibility in the area was obscured by smoke and ash, and in part because what they were seeing did not correspond to any visual experience for which they had language. People described instead the sound of falling bodies hitting the ground, the smell of the burning jet fuel, and the particular texture of the ankle deep dust that filled the streets. But for the majority of television viewers, eyewitnesses from a distance, those events are recalled as images, indelible, powerful, and eloquent. To many, like the reporter interviewing Ray Charles, it is the images rather than the mere fact of the events that produce the emotional response. The assumption seems to be that because the blind are immune to images they must also be immune to the significance of the events, and therefore must be somehow detached from or indifferent to the nation's collective horror and grief.

It is fortunate for anyone interested in dismantling the image of blindness fostered by the Hypothetical Blind Man that we have today a great many first-hand accounts of blindness. In recent decades, memoirs, essays and other texts by actual blind people attempt to loosen the grip the Hypothetical still seems to hold on the sighted imagination. Thanks to work by disability historians, we are also beginning to have older accounts of blindness drawn from archives of institutions and schools for the blind around the world. One such account is a text written in 1825, by a twenty-two-year-old blind French woman named Thérèse-Adèle Husson. Born in Nancy into a petit bourgeois household, Husson became blind at nine months following a bout of smallpox. Her case attracted the attention of the local gentry who sponsored a convent education for her, and encouraged her to cultivate her interests in literature and music. At the age of twenty she left home for Paris where she hoped to pursue a literary career. Her first text, "Reflections on the Moral and Physical Condition of the Blind" seems to have been written as a part of her petition for aid from the Hôpital des Quinze-Vingts, an institution that provided shelter and financial support to the indigent blind of Paris. For the most part, her text follows the example of comportment and educational manuals of the time, offering advice to parents and caretakers on the correct way to raise a blind child, and to young blind people themselves on their role in society. It is by turns, formulaically obsequious and radically assertive, since she writes from the premise—revolutionary for the time—that her first-hand experience of blindness gives her a level of expertise that equals or surpasses that of the institution's sighted administrators. While it is unlikely that Husson's convent education would have exposed her to the work of Descartes or Diderot, she considers some of the same questions previously posed to the Hypothetical. It is possible that the provincial aristocrats, who took up her education, may have engaged in amateurish philosophizing in her presence. For instance, like Diderot's blind man of Puiseaux, she prefers her sense of touch to the sight she lacks. She recounts how, at the time of her first communion, her mother promised her a dress made of chiffon, then, either as a joke or in an attempt to economize, purchased cheaper percale instead. When the young Husson easily detected the difference through touch, her mother persisted in her deception, and even brought in neighbor women to corroborate. Whether playing along with the joke, or as a genuine rebuke of her mother's attempt to deceive her, Husson retorted:

I prefer my touch to your eyes, because it allows me to appreciate things for what they really are, whereas it seems to me that your sight fools you now and then, for this is percale and not chiffon.

(Husson 2001, 25)

In a later discussion of her ability to recognize household objects through touch, her impatience seems out of proportion, unless we imagine that she frequently found herself the object of philosophical speculation by literal-minded practitioners:

We know full well that a chest of drawers is square, but more long than tall. Again I hear my readers ask what is a square object! I am accommodating enough to satisfy all their questions. Therefore, I would say to them that it is easy enough to know the difference between objects by touching them, for not all of them have the same shape. For example, a dinner plate, a dish, a glass can't begin to be compared with a chest of drawers, for the first two are round, while the other is hollow; but people will probably point out that

it is only after having heard the names of the articles that I designate that it became possible for me to acquire the certainty that they were hollow, round, square. I will admit that they are right, but tell me, you with the eyes of Argus, if you had never heard objects described, would you be in any better position to speak of them than I?

(Husson 2001, 41)

Her emphasis on square versus round objects as well as her tone and her taunt, "You with the eyes of Argus," suggests an irritation that may come from hearing the Molyneux question one too many times. She is also arguing against the notion that such words as "square" and "round" designate solely visual phenomena, to which the blind have no access and therefore no right to use these words.

Almost a century later, Helen Keller gives vent to a similar irritation at literal-minded readers. In her 1908 book, *The World I Live In*, she gives a detailed phenomenological account of her daily experience of deaf-blindness. Early on, she footnotes her use of the verb "see" in the phrase, "I was taken to see a woman":

The excellent proof-reader has put a query to my use of the word "see." If I had said "visit," he would have asked no questions, yet what does "visit" mean but "see" (*visitare*)? Later I will try to defend myself for using as much of the English language as I have succeeded in learning.

(Keller 2003, 19)

Keller makes good use of her Radcliffe education to show that the more one knows about language the harder it is to find vocabulary that does not have some root in sighted or hearing experience. But, she argues, to deny her the use of seeing-hearing vocabulary would be to deny her the ability to communicate at all.

In their 1995 book, *On Blindness*, two philosophers, one sighted and one blind, conduct an epistolary debate that might seem to put to rest all the old hypothetical questions. Unfortunately, Martin Milligan, the blind philosopher, died before the discussion was fully underway. If he had lived, we can assume not only that he and his sighted colleague, Bryan Magee, would have gotten further with their debate, but also that they would have edited some testy quibbles about which terms to use and which translation of Aristotle is more accurate. Milligan, who worked primarily in moral and political philosophy, and was an activist in blind causes in the United Kingdom, forthrightly resists the impulse to allow the discussion to stray far from the practical and social conditions that affect the lives of real blind people. For instance, he cites an incident from his early life, before he found an academic post, when he was turned down for a job as a telephone typist on a newspaper because the employer assumed that he would not be able to negotiate the stairs in the building. He identifies this as one of thousands of examples of the exaggerated value sighted people place on vision. Any thinking person has to recognize that sight is not required to climb or descend stairs. He asserts that the value of sight would be that it would allow him to move around unfamiliar places with greater ease. He concedes that vision might afford him some aesthetic pleasure while viewing a landscape or painting, but insists that he can know what he wants to know about the visible world from verbal descriptions, and that this knowledge is adequate for his needs, and only minimally different from the knowledge of sighted people. He accuses Magee of voicing "visionist"—or what I might call "sightist"—attitudes that the differences between the sighted and the blind must be almost incomprehensibly vast, and that vision is a fundamental aspect of human existence. Milligan says that these statements seem

to express the passion, the zeal of a missionary preaching to the heathen in outer darkness. Only, of course, your "gospel" isn't "good" news to us heathens, for the message seems to be that ours is a "darkness" from which we can never come in—not the darkness of course that sighted people can know, but the darkness of never being able to know *that* darkness, or of bridging the vast gulf that separates us from those who do.

(Magee and Milligan 1995, 46)

This prompts Magee to cite his own early work on race and homosexuality, as proof of his credentials as a liberal humanist. He also speculates, somewhat sulkily, about whether the first eighteen months of Milligan's life when his vision was presumed to be normal, might disqualify him as a spokesman for the blind, since he might retain some vestige of a visual memory from that period. Later, Magee consults with a neurologist who assures him that the loss of sight at such an early age would make Milligan's brain indistinguishable from that of a person born blind. And so the discussion continues.

Along the way, Magee makes some claims about sight that seem to me to be far from universal. For instance, he states:

By the sighted, seeing is felt as a *need*. And it is the feeding of this almost ungovernable craving that constitutes the ongoing pleasure of sight. It is as if we were desperately hungry all the time, in such a way that only if we were eating all the time could we be content—so we eat all the time.

(Magee and Milligan 1995, 104)

Magee asserts that when sighted people are obliged to keep their eyes closed even for a short time, it induces a kind of panic. To illustrate his point, he notes that a common method of mistreating prisoners is to keep them blindfolded, and this mistreatment can lead them to feel anxious and disoriented. I suspect that his example is influenced by traditional metaphors that equate blindness with a tomb-like imprisonment. Surely a blind prisoner, accustomed to the privation of sight, might still have similar feelings of anxiety and disorientation, due to the threat, whether stated or implied, of ponding bodily harm.

To his credit, Magee does allow that some blind experiences are shared by the sighted. Milligan describes how many blind people negotiate new environments, and can feel the presence of large objects even without touching them as "atmosphere-thickening occupants of space." Magee reports that when he

> was a small child I had a vivid nonvisual awareness of the nearness of material objects. I would walk confidently along a pitch black corridor in a strange house and stop dead a few inches short of a closed door, and then put out my hand to grope for the knob. If I woke up in the dark in a strange bedroom and wanted to get to a light-switch on the opposite side of the room I could usually circumnavigate the furniture in between, because I could "feel" where the larger objects in the room were. I might knock small things over, but would almost invariably "feel" the big ones. I say "feel" because the sensation, which I can clearly recall, was as of a feeling-in-the-air with my whole bodily self. Your phrase "atmosphere-thickening occupants of space" describes the apprehension exactly. I suddenly "felt" a certain thickness in the air at a certain point relative to myself in the blackness surrounding me. . . . This illustrates your point that the blind develop potentialities that the sighted have also been endowed with but do not develop because they have less need of them.
> (Magee and Milligan 1995, 97–98)

Here, and in a few other places in the correspondence, Magee and Milligan seem to be moving in a new direction. It is not merely that they discover a shared perceptual experience, but one that is not easy to categorize as belonging to one of the five traditional senses. Here, a "feeling" is not the experience of texture or form through physical contact, but an apprehension, of an atmospheric change, experienced kinesthetically, and by the body as a whole. This seems to point toward a need for a theory of multiple senses where each of the traditional five could be subdivided into a number of discrete sensory activities, which function sometimes in concert with and sometimes in counterpoint to others. Helen Keller identified at least three different aspects of touch that she found meaningful: texture, temperature, and vibration. In fact, she understands sound as vibrations that the hearing feel in their ears while the deaf can feel them through other parts of their bodies. Thus she could feel thunder by pressing the palm of her hand against a windowpane, or someone's footsteps by pressing the soles of her feet against floorboards.

What these blind authors have in common is an urgent desire to represent their experiences of blindness as something besides the absence of sight. Unlike the Hypothetical, they do not feel themselves to be deficient or partial—sighted people minus sight—but whole human beings who have learned to attend to their nonvisual senses in different ways. I have deliberately chosen to limit my discussion here to works by people who became blind very early in life. One of the most striking features of the Hypothetical Blind Man is that he is always assumed to be both totally and congenitally blind. Real blindness, today as in the past, rarely fits this profile. Only about 10–20 percent of people designated as legally blind, in countries where there is such a designation, are without any visual perception at all. It is hard to come by statistics on people who are born totally blind, in part because it only becomes an issue when the child, or her parents, seek services for the blind, which tends to occur only when the child reaches school age. We can assume that more infants were born blind in the past, since some of the most prevalent causes of infantile blindness have been eliminated by medical innovations in the nineteenth and twentieth centuries. Nevertheless, in the past, as now, the leading causes of blindness occur later in life, and often leave some residual vision. Some may retain the ability to distinguish light from darkness, while others may continue to perceive light, color, form, and movement to some degree. Some people may retain the acuity to read print or facial expressions, while lacking the peripheral vision that facilitates free movement through space. And regardless of the degree or quality of residual vision, blind people differ widely in the ways they attend to, use or value these perceptions.

Although the situation of the Hypothetical is rare, his defenders are quick to discount anyone with any residual sight or with even the remotest possibility of a visual memory. In traditional discussions of blindness, only total, congenital blindness will do. In a review of my book *Sight Unseen*, Arthur Danto asserted that I had too much sight to claim to be blind (Danto 1999, 35). He quoted a totally blind graduate student he once knew who said that he could not conceptualize a window, and that he was surprised when he learned that when a person's face is said to glow, it does not in fact emit light like an incandescent light bulb. Danto does not tell us what became of this student or even give his name, using him only as a modern-day version of the Hypothetical. He then goes on to relate the history of the Molyneux question.

If only the totally blind can speak of blindness with authority, should we make the same restriction on those who talk about vision? Is there such a thing as total vision? We know that a visual acuity of 20/20 is merely average vision. There are individuals whose acuity measures better than 20/20, 20/15, or even 20/10. Such individuals can read every line of the familiar Snellan eye chart, or, as in the case of Ted Williams, can read the print on a baseball whizzing toward their bat at a speed close to ninety miles per hour. How many scholars of visual culture, I wonder but won't ask, can claim such a level of visual acuity?

What visual studies can bring to these discussions is an interrogation of the binary opposition between blindness and sight. It is clearly more useful to think in terms of a spectrum of variation in visual acuity, as well as a spectrum of variation in terms of visual awareness or skill. The visual studies scholar, highly skilled in understanding images, who loses some or even all her sight, will not lose the ability to analyze images and to communicate her observations. In his essay, "Showing Seeing," W. J. T. Mitchell describes a classroom exercise in which students display or perform some feature of visual culture as if to an audience that has no experience of visual culture. The exercise assumes that some students will be better at the task, while others might improve their performance with practice, and in all cases their aptitude would have little, if anything, to do with their visual acuity. The skill, as I understand it, is in the telling as much as it is in the seeing—the ability to translate images in all their complexity and resonance into words.

And as we move beyond the simple blindness versus sight binary, I hope we can also abandon the clichés that use the word "blindness" as a synonym for inattention, ignorance, or prejudice. If the goal is for others to see what we mean, it helps to say what we mean. Using the word in this way seems a vestigial homage to the Hypothetical, meant to stir the same uncanny frisson of awe and pity. It contributes on some level to the perception of blindness as a tragedy too dire to contemplate, which contributes in turn to lowered expectations among those who educate and employ the blind. It also contributes to the perception among the newly blind themselves that the only response to their new condition is to retire from view.

I will leave you with a futuristic image of blindness. In Deborah Kendrick's story, "20/20 with a Twist," Mary Seymour, chief administrator of the department of visual equality, looks back on her life from the year 2020. In this blind Utopia, the major handicaps of blindness have been eliminated; private automobiles were phased out a decade earlier and technologies to convert print to Braille or voice had become ubiquitous and transparent. Of course, Mary reflects, it was not always like this. Back in the dark ages of the 1980s and '90s, Braille proficiency had ceased to be a requirement for teachers of blind children, Braille production facilities and radio reading services were shut down, and blind children were no longer being educated at all. Mary and other blind people who had grown up in an earlier, slightly more enlightened period, banded together to lead a nonviolent, visionary rebellion to bring down the oppressive regime. They tampered with the power supply—since darkness is no impediment to blind activity—scrambled computer transmissions and disrupted television broadcasts. All across the country, television screens went blank while the audio continued, interrupted periodically by the revolutionary message: "You, too, can function without pictures."

The rebel leaders were captured, however, and forced to undergo implantation of optic sensors, which, the captors reasoned, would transform them into sighted people who would see the error of their ways and abandon the cause. But the rebels persisted. The power supply was shut down completely. The government fell, and the captured leaders were liberated in triumph.

Significantly, the optic sensors did not transform the revolutionary leaders into sighted people. Rather, each acquired only a facet of visual experience. One gained the ability to perceive color. Another developed a sort of telepathic vision, allowing him to form images of places at great distances. Mary's sensor gave her a kind of literal hindsight, making her able to create a detailed mental picture of a room, only after she had left it. These bits and pieces of vision serve as a badge of the former rebels' heroic past, and allow them to perform entertaining parlor tricks, but are otherwise easy to disregard.

This is a far cry from the Hypothetical. In Deborah Kendrick's image of the future, blindness is a simple physical characteristic rather than an ominous mark of otherness. If the Hypothetical Blind Man once helped thinkers form ideas about human consciousness surely his day is done. He does too much damage hanging around. It is time to let him go. Rest in peace.

REFERENCES

Charles, Ray. Interview. *The Today Show.* NBC Television, October 4, 2001.

Danto, Arthur. 1999. "Blindness and Sight." *The New Republic* 220 (16): 34–36.

Diderot, Denis. 1999. *Thoughts on the Interpretation of Nature and Other Philosophical Works.* Ed. David Adams. Manchester: Clinaman Press.

Gitter, Elisabeth. 2001. *The Imprisoned Guest: Samuel Howe and Laura Bridgman, the Original Deafblind Girl.* New York: Farrar, Straus and Giroux.

Husson, Thérèse-Adèle. 2001. *Reflections: The Life and Writing of a Young Blind Woman in Post-revolutionary France.* Eds. Catherine J. Kudlick and Zina Weygand. New York and London: New York University Press.

Keller, Helen. 2003. *The World I Live In.* Ed. Roger Shattuck. New York: New York Review Books.

Kendrick, Deborah. 1987. 20/20 with a Twist. In *With Wings: An Anthology of Literature by and about Women with Disabilities,* eds. Marsha Saxton and Florence Howe New York: Feminist Press at the City University of New York.

Magee, Bryan and Milligan, Martin. 1995. *On Blindness.* Oxford and New York: Oxford University Press.

Mitchell, W. J. T. 2002. "Showing Seeing: A Critique of Visual Culture." *Journal of Visual Culture* 1 (2):165–181.

CHAPTER 33

Disability, Life Narrative, and Representation

G. Thomas Couser

Disability is an inescapable element of human existence and experience. Although it is as fundamental an aspect of human diversity as race, ethnicity, gender, and sexuality, it is rarely acknowledged as such. This is odd, because in practice disability often trumps other minority statuses. That is, for people who differ from the hegemonic identity in more than one way, certain impairments—such as blindness or deafness—may function as their primary defining characteristic, their "master status." In this sense, disability may be *more* fundamental than racial, ethnic, and gender distinctions. Yet until the recent advent of Disability Studies, it escaped the critical scrutiny, theoretical analysis, and recognition accorded other forms of human variation.

At the same time, disability has had a remarkably high profile in both high and popular culture, both of which are saturated with images of disability. Unlike other marginalized groups, then, disabled people have been *hyper*-represented in mainstream culture; they have not been disregarded so much as they have been subjected to objectifying notice in the form of mediated staring. To use an economic metaphor that is a literal truth, disability has been an extremely valuable cultural commodity for thousands of years. The cultural representation of disability has functioned at the expense of disabled people, in part because they have rarely controlled their own images. In the last several decades, however, this situation has begun to change, most notably in life writing, especially autobiography: in late twentieth century life writing, disabled people have initiated and controlled their own narratives in unprecedented ways and to an extraordinary degree.

Indeed, one of the most significant developments—if not *the* most significant development—in life writing in North America over the last three decades has been the proliferation of book-length accounts (from both first- and third-person points of view) of living with illness and disability. Whereas in the 1970s it was difficult to find *any* representation of most disabling conditions in life writing, today one can find *multiple* representations of many conditions. Equally significant, and more remarkable, one can find *autobiographical* accounts of conditions that would seem to preclude first-person testimony altogether—for example, autism, locked-in syndrome, and early Alzheimer's disease.

A comprehensive history of disability life writing has yet to be written, but it is safe to say that there was not much in the way of published autobiographical literature before World War II. War both produces and valorizes certain forms of disability; not surprisingly, then, disabled veterans produced a substantial number of narratives after the war. Polio generated even more narratives; indeed, polio may be the first disability to have engendered its own substantial autobiographical literature (Wilson). In the 1980s and 1990s, HIV/AIDS and breast cancer provoked significant numbers of narratives; many of these challenge cultural scripts of the conditions (such as that AIDS is an automatic death sentence or that breast cancer negates a woman's sexuality [Couser 1997]). A dramatic example of the generation of autobiographical literature devoted to a particular condition is the advent of autobiographies by people with autism (sometimes referred to as "autiebiographies"). Before 1985 these were virtually nonexistent; since 1985, nearly one hundred have been produced. (This number does not include the many narratives written by parents of autistic children.) Thus, one major post-World War II cultural phenomenon was the generation of large numbers of narratives about a small number of conditions.

A complementary phenomenon has been the production of small numbers of narratives about a large number of conditions, some quite rare and some only recently recognized. Among these conditions are ALS (also known as Lou Gehrig's disease), Alzheimer's, aphasia, Asperger's syndrome, asthma, cerebral palsy, chronic fatigue syndrome, cystic fibrosis, diabetes, disfigurement, Down syndrome, epilepsy, locked-in syndrome, multiple sclerosis, obesity, obsessive-compulsive disorder, stuttering, stroke, and Tourette syndrome. As the twentieth century drew to a close, then, many disabilities came out of the closet into the living room of life writing.

Like life writing by other marginalized groups—women, African Americans, and gays and lesbian—life writing by disabled people is a cultural manifestation of a human rights movement; significantly, the rise in personal narratives of disability has roughly coincided with the disability rights movement, whose major legal manifestation in the United States is the Americans with Disabilities Act, which was passed in 1990 and amended in 2008, but has yet to be fully implemented. The first flowering of disability autobiography is also part of a disability renaissance involving other arts and media. Disability autobiography should be seen, then, not as spontaneous "self-expression" but as a response—indeed a retort—to the traditional misrepresentation of disability in Western culture generally.

This rich body of narrative can be approached in a number of ways. One way of getting at the relation between somatic variation and life narrative is through an everyday phenomenon: the way deviations from bodily norms often provoke a demand for explanatory narrative in everyday life. Whereas the unmarked case—the "normal" body—can pass without narration, the marked case—the scar, the limp, the missing limb, or the obvious prosthesis—calls for a story. Entering new situations, or re-entering familiar ones, people with anomalous bodies are often called upon to account for them, sometimes quite explicitly: they may be asked, "What happened to *you*"? Or, worse, they may be addressed as if their stories are already known. Evidence of this is necessarily anecdotal. Let one compelling example suffice. Harriet McBryde Johnson, a Charleston lawyer and disability rights advocate who had a congenital muscle-wasting disease, reported remarks made by strangers she encountered on the street as she drove her power chair to the office:

"I admire you for being out: most people would give up."
"God bless you! I'll pray for you."

"You don't let the pain hold you back, do you?"

"If I had to live like you, I think I'd kill myself." (2)

One of the social burdens of disability, then, is that it exposes affected individuals to inspection, interrogation, interpretation, and violation of privacy.

In effect, people with extraordinary bodies are held responsible for them, in two senses. First, they are required to account for them, often to complete strangers; second, the expectation is that their accounts will serve to relieve their auditors' discomfort. The elicited narrative is expected to conform to, and thus confirm, a cultural script. For example, people diagnosed with lung cancer or HIV/AIDS are expected to admit to behaviors that have induced the condition in question—to acknowledge having brought it upon themselves. Thus, one fundamental connection between life narrative and somatic anomaly is that to have certain conditions is to have one's life written *for* one. For people with many disabilities, culture inscribes narratives *on* their bodies, willy nilly.

Disability autobiographers typically begin from a position of marginalization, belatedness, and pre-inscription. Yet one can see why autobiography is a particularly important form of life writing about disability: written from inside the experience in question, it involves *self*-representation by definition and thus offers the best-case scenario for revaluation of that condition. Long the objects of others' classification and examination, disabled people have only recently assumed the initiative in representing themselves; in disability autobiography particularly, disabled people counter their historical subjection by occupying the subject position. In approaching this literature, then, one should attend to the politics and ethics of representation, for the "representation" of disability in such narratives is a political as well as a mimetic act—a matter of speaking *for* as well as speaking *about*.

With particularly severe or debilitating conditions, particularly those affecting the mind or the ability to communicate, the very existence of first-person narratives makes its own point: that people with condition "X" are capable of self-representation. The autobiographical act models the agency and self-determination that the disability rights movement has fought for, even or especially when the text is collaboratively produced. One notable example is *Count Us In: Growing Up with Down Syndrome*, a collaborative narrative by two young men with the syndrome in question. Not only is the title cast in the imperative mood—"count us in"—the subtitle puns on "up" and "down," a bit of verbal play that challenges conventional ideas about mental retardation, such as that those with it never really mature. Autobiography, then, can be an especially powerful medium in which disabled people can demonstrate that they have lives, in defiance of others' common sense perceptions of them. Indeed, disability autobiography is often in effect a post-colonial, indeed an anti-colonial, phenomenon, a form of autoethnography, as Mary Louise Pratt has defined it: "instances in which colonized subjects undertake to represent themselves in ways that engage with [read: contest] the colonizer's own terms" (7).

People with disabilities have become increasingly visible in public spaces and open about their disabilities. But their physical presence in public life represents only a rather limited kind of access. Properly conceived and carried out (admittedly, a large qualifier), life narrative can provide the public with controlled access to lives that might otherwise remain opaque or exotic to them. Further, much disability life writing can be approached as "quality-of-life" writing because it addresses questions discussed under that rubric in philosophy, ethics, and especially biomedical ethics. It should be required reading, then, for citizens in a world with enormous technological capability to sustain life and repair bodies in the case of acute illness and injury but with very little commitment to accommodate and support chronic disability. Because disability life narratives can counter the too often moralizing, objectifying, pathologizing, and marginalizing representations of disability in contemporary culture, they offer an important, if not unique, entree for inquiry into one of the fundamental aspects of human diversity.

WORKS CITED

Couser, G. Thomas. *Recovering Bodies: Illness, Disability, and Life Writing*. Madison: U of Wisconsin P, 1997.

Johnson, Harriet McBryde. *Too Late to Die Young: Nearly True Tales from a Life*. New York: Henry Holt, 2005.

Kingsley, Jason and Mitchell Levitz. *Count Us In: Growing Up with Down Syndrome*. New York: Harcourt, 1994.

Pratt, Mary Louise. *Imperial Eyes: Travel Writing and Transculturation*. New York: Routledge, 1992.

Wilson, Daniel J. "Covenants of Work and Grace: Themes of Recovery and Redemption in Polio Narratives." *Literature and Medicine* 13, 1 (Spring 1994): 22–41.

CHAPTER 34

Autism as Culture

Joseph N. Straus

AUTISM AS CULTURE

The Originary Moment

In 1943, Leo Kanner, a child psychiatrist working at Johns Hopkins University, published an article titled, "Autistic Disturbances of Affective Contact." (Kanner 1943). In it, he identified a group of children who shared certain traits: "All of the children's activities and utterances are governed rigidly and consistently by the powerful desire for aloneness and sameness" (249). The children shared an "*inability to relate themselves* in the ordinary way to people and situations" and an "*anxiously excessive desire for the maintenance of sameness,*" and displayed "an *extreme autistic aloneness* that, whenever possible, disregards, ignores, shuts out anything that comes to the child from the outside" (242, 245, italics in original).

At virtually the same moment, separated by an ocean and a world war, the Viennese psychologist, Hans Asperger, published a study of a group of children with remarkably similar characteristics: "The children I will describe all have in common a fundamental disturbance [that] results in severe and characteristic difficulties of social integration. In many cases, the social problems are so profound that they overshadow everything else" (Asperger 1944/1991, 37). Like Kanner, Asperger chose the term "autism," to refer to what he called "a fundamental disturbance of contact" (38):

> Human beings normally live in constant interaction with their environment, and react to it continually. However, "autists" have severely disturbed and considerably limited interaction. The autist is only himself (cf. the Greek word *autos*) and is not an active member of a greater organism which he is influenced by and which he influences constantly (38).[1]

Presumably there have always been people who had the sorts of neurology and behaviors we now label as autistic, but insofar as they were remarked at all, they were parceled out to different categories (most notably various forms of madness, especially schizophrenia, or "feeblemindedness").[2] By creating the new classification of autism, Kanner and Asperger participate in the endless reshaping of the map of psychological disorders, which rise and fall historically, as much in response to cultural and social pressures as to any neutral, scientific observation.[3] Today, autism may appear a secure, natural category, but it is as historically and culturally contingent as neurasthenia, hysteria, and fugue—science-based and neutral medical categories of a previous era—and may someday share their fate (Hacking 1998; Porter 2002; Davis 2008).

The Rise of Autism

In the decades following Kanner and Asperger's discoveries (or creations), autism remained a small, marginal phenomenon within psychiatry and virtually invisible to the general public. During the 1960s and 1970s, the only mention of autism in the DSM (Diagnostic and Statistical Manual: the official diagnostic guidelines of the American Psychiatric Association) lumped it among the criteria for Childhood Schizophrenia. Autism did not enter the DSM on its own until its third edition, in 1980, and the diagnostic criteria were then significantly expanded and loosened in the fourth edition in 1994, when Asperger's Syndrome was also added to the mix as one of several Autism Spectrum Disorders.[4] As a medical diagnosis, then, autism went from being unknown before 1943, to a marginal phenomenon before 1980, to a remarkably common diagnosis today, with some sources claiming that as many as 1% of all children are or should be classified as somewhere on the autism spectrum (Fombonne 2005).[5]

The rise in diagnosis and classification has fueled a dramatic increase in public awareness, which has in turn encouraged additional diagnosis and classification. As one barometer, articles in the *New York Times* mention autism for the first time in 1960, and contain the word in the title only seventeen times before 1990, when a sharp upward trend begins. In 2008 alone, the *New York Times* ran 169 articles on autism, roughly one every other day, and this degree of attention is indicative of what has been happening in all of the popular media, including the Web. Autism has become a major presence in the culture of early twenty-first century America.

Psychiatric disorders are often a pathologically excessive version of some trait that, in its cultural context, is considered socially desirable (anorexia is excessive thinness, neurasthenia is excessive female passivity, fugue is excessive travel, ADHD is excessive energy and activity, obsession is excessive focus and concentration). In this sense, autism might be understood as excessive individuality, autonomy, and self-reliance, normally understood as highly desirable traits. Autism might be understood to represent a pathological excess of what the Western world most prizes—autonomous individuality, with its promise of liberty and freedom—reconfigured as what it most fears—painful solitude, isolation, and loss of community. Autism has thus become an emblematic psychiatric condition of the late twentieth and early twenty-first centuries, simultaneously a medical diagnosis and a cultural force.

THE CONSTRUCTION OF AUTISM: THE MEDICAL AND SOCIAL MODELS

At present, autism is generally conceived within one of two conceptual models and embedded within one of two sorts of cultures: the medical model and the culture of medical science versus the social model and the culture of the social group. The difference centers on a single question: is autism a medical condition (syndrome, disorder, pathology) or is it a social group (an identity, a shared culture)? Although it is common to imagine culture and science as representing opposing principles (objective versus subjective, part of the natural world, and therefore real, or imagined and created), the work that scientists and doctors do is also creative and imaginative, is also historically contingent, is also expressive of the values of a particular time, place, and worldview.

Medical culture—what has been described and vigorously critiqued within Disability Studies as the *medical model*—has certain defining attributes. First, medical culture treats disability as pathology, either a deficit or an excess with respect to some normative standard. Second, the pathology resides inside the individual body in a determinate, concrete location. Third, the goals of the enterprise are diagnosis and cure. If the pathology cannot be cured—if the abnormal condition cannot be normalized—then the defective body should be sequestered lest it contaminate or degrade the larger community. In this, medical culture is an aspect of what Garland-Thomson (2004) calls "the cultural logic of euthanasia": disabled bodies should either be rehabilitated (normalized) or eliminated (either by being sequestered from sight in homes or institutions or by being allowed or encouraged to die).[6]

Since 1943, when the medicalized construction of autism began, the ways of diagnosing autism, the associated medical interventions or cures, and the conception of autism itself have undergone significant changes. In that sense, it might be better to talk about multiple medical models of autism, including Freudian psychotherapy, cognitive psychology, brain science, and genetics (Nadeson 2005). The shift from model to model comes in part in response to observations and discoveries (the scientific method) and in part in response to changes in fashion: medical science is, in part, a cultural phenomenon with its own history. As that history has unfolded, the medical construction of autism has changed and evolved.

A second way of constructing autism involves the social model of disability as it has been described within Disability Studies. In the social model, disability is understood as socially constructed rather than biologically given: the nature of disability, the kinds of conditions that are considered disabling, and the meanings attached to disability all vary with time, place, and context. For the most part, Disability Studies has concerned itself with physical impairments, especially blindness, deafness, and mobility impairments, tracing their histories and systems of signification in art, culture, and society. Disability Studies, and its social model of disability, have been notably less concerned and successful with cognitive impairments and developmental disabilities, like autism. This has had to do in part with the problem of narration: the member of the minoritized social group should be able to resist medicalized discourse by speaking for him or herself, but people with autism communicate in non-standard ways and may lack the ability to narrate their own experiences.[7] A second issue has been the problem of community: a group of people who have problems with communication and social relatedness may find it difficult to forge a social group, and may thus be difficult to constitute as a self-aware community within a social model of disability.

In recent years, however, thanks to the rapid expansion of the autistic community from the handful of children known to Kanner and Asperger to the vast numbers who now are understood, and understand themselves, to inhabit a broad "autism spectrum," and thanks to the profusion of writing, art, and music by people with autism, and thanks to the Internet which permits reclusive people to find meaningful social contact, it has become possible to conceive people with autism as a social group with a distinctive, shared culture. In what follows, I will critique various medical models of autism, and then argue for a social model of autism—one grounded in Disability Studies—in which we see self-aware people claiming autism as a valued political and social identity and celebrating a shared culture of art and everyday life.[8]

AUTISM AND THE CULTURE OF MEDICINE

Locating Autism in the Psyche: Freudian Psychotherapy

Under the medical model, autism—understood as a sort of illness or disease—has been located in many different places within the defective body, and correspondingly many cures or remedies have been proposed. In the years following the Second World War, amid the ascendancy of Freudian psychoanalysis, autism was located *in the psyche* and conceived as a problem of ego differentiation. For Bruno Bettelheim, the preeminent proponent of the psychoanalytical approach to autism, the condition resulted from a child's deliberate if unconscious choice to withdraw from a hostile, rejecting mother. Like a concentration camp inmate—this analogy was specifically proposed by Bettelheim—the child tries to protect itself from a murderous environment by erecting defenses and retreating into the "empty fortress" of autism. The autism is located within the child, but caused by the "refrigerator mother," whose own pathology prevents the child from developing normally. The proposed cure involves removing the child from the mother's care and providing psychoanalytical treatment.[9] While the psychodynamic approach to autism has largely been abandoned in the US, it persists in other countries (especially France) and in the seemingly ineradicable belief that, when it comes to poor outcomes for children, the mother is always to blame (Ladd-Taylor and Umanski 1998; Landsman 1998).

Locating Autism in the Mind: Cognitive Psychology (Central Coherence, Theory of Mind, and Executive Function)

Approaches to autism that emerge from cognitive psychology locate it *in the mind.* The mind is conceived as a kind of information-processing device, like a computer, and autism results from damage to certain of its "modules." There are three widely discussed theories of autism that identify deficits in *central coherence, theory of mind,* and *executive function.*[10] In the first of these theories, autism is a disorder characterized by "weak central coherence"—an atypically weak tendency to bind local details into global percepts.[11] In this view, the deficits in social relatedness (Kanner's "aloneness"), as well as other intellectual deficits associated with autism, are manifestations of an underlying inability to create larger meanings from discrete elements, or larger social patterns from discrete individuals.[12]

A second prevalent theory of autism based on cognitive psychology contends that the central deficit is a lack of "theory of mind": people with autism are deficient in the ability to attribute intentions, knowledge, and feelings to other people.[13] As a result, people with autism have difficulties both with social relatedness and with communication. Limitations in social relatedness and communication create the impression of isolation, as though the person with autism were living in a separate, self-enclosed world.[14] That notion underpins the label "autism" itself and resonates with both Kanner's "aloneness" and Asperger's "fundamental disturbance of contact."

A third prevalent theory of autism relates autistic behavior to deficiencies in the brain's "executive function." According to this theory, the obsessive routines and inflexibility associated with autism (Kanner's "sameness") result from difficulties in planning strategies for achieving goals and in modulating mental focus or shifting attention easily from task to task.[15]

A Triad of Impairments (Social Interaction, Communication and Imagination, Repetitive Behavior)

The Diagnostic and Statistical Manual of Mental Disorders (DSM) is the authoritative source for a medicalized understanding of autism and other "mental illnesses." The most recent fourth edition of the DSM defines "autistic disorder" as involving three sorts of abnormalities, often referred to as a "triad of impairments: 1) "qualitative impairment in social interaction; 2) "qualitative impairments in communication," which may include "abnormal functioning" in "symbolic and imaginative play"; and 3) "restricted, repetitive, and stereotyped patterns of behavior, interests, and activities." Asperger's Disorder or Asperger Syndrome, which didn't enter the DSM until 1994, is generally understood as a less severe form of autism, along what is commonly referred to as "the autism spectrum."[16]

Locating autism in the psyche or the mind presents a challenge for the medical model, committed as it is to diagnosis and cure. There can be no direct observation of the psyche or the mind—all we can do is observe behaviors and make inferences about the sorts of interior processes that might produce them. In the absence of direct observation, Freudian psychoanalysis and cognitive psychology have to rely on analogy and metaphor. As Susan Sontag (1978) observed, the profusion of metaphors is correlated with the poverty of the science—the metaphors rush into areas of ignorance. The murky causality and ineffectual treatments associated with autism lead directly to metaphorical constructs like "mindblindness," "executive function," and "central coherence," not to mention the "ego." The metaphors are needed to bridge the gap between the behaviors we can observe and their hidden source in the mind.[17] Cognitive scientists generally lack the literary flair of Bettelheim, Kanner, and Asperger, but their language is also necessarily figurative, as they attempt to describe what can only be inferred. The figurative nature of their language enhances a sense that autism is, at least in part, an imaginative

creation of those who describe it, a product of culture as much as science.

Locating Autism in the Brain or the Genes

The most recent science-based studies of autism locate it in the brain or the genes, still inside the individual body, but now in locations that are, at least in principle, available to direct observation. Studies of the brain have focused on its chemistry (Anderson 2005) as well as its structure, development, and function, often using structural and functional imaging studies (MRI and fMRI) (Minshew 2005 and Schultz 2005). Genetic studies have attempted to identify a set of "susceptibility genes" that shape the brain (Rutter 2005).[18]

For the most part, research in both of these areas has been slow to show significant results.[19] That slow progress is certainly due in part to the inherent complexity of the processes being studied. But it is due also to the heterogeneity of the population being studied. Our sense of who is autistic has broadened and diversified remarkably since the originary moment of Kanner and Asperger. For Kanner in particular, autism was an extremely rare disorder affecting children (his term was "infantile autism"), characterized above all by extreme aloneness. In more recent years, autism has been extended to people of all ages who fall anywhere on the autism spectrum (have an "autism spectrum disorder") and even to those who show signs of belonging to a "broader phenotype" of autism (Dawson 2002; Pickles 2000). The definition of autism has not only broadened, but has also changed in fundamental ways: Kanner's "extreme autistic aloneness" is no longer even part of the DSM definition, and in fact does not describe what most people now understand as comprised by autism (people with autism are not "alone"—they mostly want social contact, but they seek it in unusual ways). Medical research is thus directed toward a rapidly expanding and constantly shifting target. I suggested earlier that, due to its lack of secure biological basis, autism might eventually follow the path of neurasthenia and hysteria into quaintness and irrelevance.[20] Now I would like to suggest that this process may be hastened by the increasing incoherence of the category. Eventually, perhaps, what we now think of as autism will collapse from its internal contradictions, its contents redistributed to a variety of new categories and classifications. What holds it together at the moment is not so much science, where we find a striking heterogeneity of possible causes, as culture.

Searching for a Cure

So far I have talked mostly about diagnosis, but the medical model places on equal emphasis on cure. If autism is understood as an illness or disease, and one that is particularly complex in nature and therefore hard to diagnose, it comes as no surprise that proposed cures have sprung up like perennials each spring, and just about as often. People with autism can be induced to function better (i.e. more normally) with behavioral approaches: tasks are broken down into discrete steps, which are rehearsed, and successful completion of them is rewarded.[21] The ineffective cures that have been proposed in recent years include psychotherapy, various forms of play therapy, auditory and sensory integration training, numerous nutritional and dietary regimes, hormone and vitamin treatments, holding therapy, animal therapy, chelation, avoidance of vaccines, and facilitated communication. A small number of drugs may help in moderating some of the behaviors associated with autism, but do nothing to address autism directly. Even the much more promising work going on in neuroscience and genetics may

ultimately prove disappointing—we are much more likely to end up with an at best intermittently reliable genetic screening test that will present prospective parents with a reproductive choice than with a way of curing or significantly remediating autism.[22] Another likely outcome is that genetic research will contribute to the splitting of autism into several different categories—it may turn out that we should be speaking of autisms, rather than autism.[23]

Despite sustained effort, medical science has found little to offer by way of cure, or even significant remediation. This sorry record may have to do simply with the medical, neurological, and genetic complexities of autism. But I suspect it may have also to do with a bad fit between autism and the prevailing culture of science-based medicine: in short, there will never be a cure for autism any more than there were cures for fugue or hysteria because these are not diseases. Rather, they are clusters of behaviors, abilities, and attitudes that, under the right cultural conditions, get grouped together and provided with a label. The label appears to confer coherence on the category, but this is a fiction, or rather, a contingent cultural construction.[24]

Critique of the Medical Model

Instead of thinking of autism as a disease, with apprehensible cause, a determinate diagnosis, and a possible cure, it might be more productive to think of it as a "disease entity," which, according to Davis 2008, "allows us to move away from the positivist kind of descriptive categories of disease and to think of diseases not as discrete objects but as ranges of bodily differences and reaction" (22).[25] Along similar lines, we might begin to think of autism in light of what Morris 1998 calls a *biocultural* model, one that discusses illness and disease as emerging from a complex interaction of biology and culture.[26] In this view, diseases and illnesses of all kinds, including psychiatric conditions like autism, are simultaneously fully real, grounded in biology, and also cultural artifacts.

The medical model requires that we locate autism (like any pathology) in the body of the affected individuals—it is their personal problem and it resides inside them. But autism is intrinsically a relational phenomenon, a function of the interaction between people. In that sense, autism is a social/cultural phenomenon, not located within individuals but rather in the connections among individuals in a community. This may appear ironic in light of Kanner's claim that "aloneness" is the essential feature of autism. But that aloneness is not something individuals can achieve on their own, rather it is something constructed in relation to other people. To talk about it meaningfully, then, we have to consider it within the ambient culture and, more specifically, within the distinctive culture that autistic people have begun to construct.

AUTISM CULTURE

As its central project, Disability Studies has proposed supplanting the medical model of disability with a variety of models that shift our attention from biology to culture.[27] As Rosemarie Garland-Thomson has argued, "The meanings attributed to extraordinary bodies reside not in inherent physical flaws, but in social relationships in which one group is legitimated by possessing valued physical characteristics and maintains its ascendancy and its self-identity by systematically imposing the role of cultural or corporeal inferiority on others."[28] Disability has an evident biological basis in relation to which human societies and cultures create elaborate interpretive networks that give it meaning. The naturally occurring variations in human shape, ability, and behavior are configured and reconfigured to maintain a shifting, culturally contingent distinction between the unremarked, normally abled and the stigmatized disabled. Disability is simultaneously real, tangible, measurable, physical and an imaginative creation designed to make sense of the diversity of human morphology, capability, and behavior. In a related minority-group model, people with disabilities are understood to share a distinctive social, cultural, and political identity, conferred by, among other things, a shared experience of oppression.[29]

To bring the discussion back to autism, we might imagine that it is a social construction rather than a medical pathology, and that people labeled as autistic comprise a definable minority group. But if autism is constructed, who does the constructing? And if people with autism comprise a minority group, what gives the group cohesion and identity other than shared medical symptoms? In answer, I would like to shift attention from autism as an abstract category to people who have been identified, or who might plausibly be identified, or who have identified themselves as autistic and to study the culture that these people have communally begun to create. Within a medical model, autism is constructed by professionals—psychiatrists, psychologists, educators—in their articles, books, and clinical practices. Within a social model, autism is constructed by autistic people themselves through the culture they produce (including writing, art, and music), and its shared features give it cohesion and a distinctive identity.[30]

As an identity group, autism is somewhat amorphous, inclusive, and heterogenous (although no more so than other strategically deployed political groups, such as women, gay, or Hispanic). In current thinking, autism lies along a spectrum, a neat linear progression from "low functioning" to "high functioning."

Given the increasing size and diversity of the population classified as autistic, however, it might be better to think of it as an agglomeration, a network of overlapping subgroups, and with the group as a whole defined by boundaries that are notably permeable and porous. As with other "minority groups," one can become autistic in a variety of ways, including medical diagnosis, personal choice and self-identification, and even casual classification by outsiders. I don't think it would be appropriate to impose a litmus test or to require a doctor's note. Instead, I intend the designation "autistic" to be an inclusive one, especially for those who self-identify as autistic, that is, who claim autism.

Using the concept of "neurodiversity" as a point of departure—a belief that autism is not a defect or pathology, but rather an aspect of naturally occurring and inherently desirable human variability—I will explore features of a distinctively autistic cognitive style and creative imagination. I will seek to understand autism as a way of being in the world, a world-view enshrined in a culture: to echo a familiar rallying cry from the disability rights movement, autism is a difference, not a deficit.

The medical model of autism provides a point of departure for a discussion of autistic culture, but in that model, the autistic style and creative imagination are stigmatized as symptoms of a defective body and mind. Aloneness, sameness, deficits in executive function, lack of theory of mind, inadequate drive toward central coherence, impairments in social and communication skills, abnormal functioning in imagination, stereotyped patterns of behavior—all the symptoms of "autistic disorder"—can be reinterpreted and recast as differences rather than deficits. The term *autism* is a medical term with a strongly stigmatizing impact. In what follows, and in keeping with the current impulse to embrace neurological difference, I will attempt to reclaim autism as a term of cultural identification and pride, analogous in this way to *queer* and *crip* (McRuer 2006). My goal is to have autism suggest not a defect but a distinctive and valuable style of thinking and imagining—a vibrant and interesting way of being in the world.[31] In what follows, I suggest three characteristics of the autistic vision, each related to diagnostic categories proposed by clinicians, and then I explore the ways in which this vision is expressed in writing, music, and art by autists. I focus on high autistic culture—writing, music, and art—because here the distinctive autistic sensibility is distilled and presented in the form of durable, public objects. The same traits, however, can be found operating in less sensational ways in the daily lives of people with autism, what I think of as the culture of everyday.

Local Coherence

People with autism are often richly attentive to minute details, sometimes at the expense of the big picture. They have an unusual and distinctive ability to attend to details on their own terms, not subsumed into a larger totality—a propensity to perceive the world in parts rather than as a connected whole. Objects are apprehended in their full discrete and concrete individuality rather than as members or representatives of a larger subsuming abstract category. Autistic cognition involves "detail-focused processing" (Happé 2005, 640); it is based on *local coherence*.[32]

Writing as an insider, a person with autism, Temple Grandin confirms this sense of details perceived in their full individuality without regard to a subsuming context or category:

Unlike those of most people, my thoughts move from video-like, specific images to generalization and concepts. For example, my concept of dogs is inextricably linked to every dog I've ever known. It's as if I have a card catalogue of dogs I have seen, complete with pictures, which continually grows as I add more examples to my video library.... My memories usually appear in my imagination in strict chronological order, and the images I visualize are always specific. There is no generic, generalized Great Dane.

(Grandin 1995, 27–28)

Similarly, Kamran Nazeer, also self-identified as autistic, observes:

Echolalia, or the constant, disconnected use of a particular word or phrase, is one example of rhythmic or repetitive behavior, a trait common among autistic people and often described as the desire for local coherence. This is the preference that autistic people frequently demonstrate for a limited, though immediate, form of order as protection against complexity or confusion.

(Nazeer 2006, 3–4)

One aspect of local coherence is a refusal to subsume perceptions into a hierarchy—individual events are full and complete in themselves, not operating the service of a higher totality (Headlam 2006). As Gunilla Gerland observes,

There was something special about the way I saw things. My vision was rather flat, two-dimensional in a way, and this was somehow important to the way I viewed space and people. I seemed to have to fetch visual impressions from my eyes. Visual impressions did not come to *me*. Nor did my vision provide me with any automatic priority in what I saw—everything seemed to appear just as clearly and with the same sharpness of image. The world looked like a photograph.

(Gerland 1997, 65–66)

Fixity of Focus

In talking about local coherence, Nazeer refers to another characteristic of the autistic cognitive style, namely a preference for repetition.[33] People with autism often have a preference for orderliness, system, and ritual. As Daniel Tammet, self-identified with Asperger Syndrome, says, "I have an almost obsessive need for order and routine which affects virtually every aspect of my life" (Tammet 2006, 1–2). Of course obsession and single-mindedness can be highly desirable traits—human achievement often depends on them—and people with autism often have these traits in a high degree:

In between episodes of compulsive behavior, I yearn for calmness and constancy. When things stay the same it's easier to feel safe, to understand what is expected and to gain a sense of connection.

(Lawson 2000, 2)

Autistic children don't like anything that looks out of place—a thread hanging on a piece of furniture, a wrinkled rug, books that are crooked on the bookshelf. Sometimes they will straighten out the books and other times they will be afraid. . . . When I became interested in something, I rode the subject to death. I would talk about the same thing over and over again. It was like playing a favorite song over and over on the stereo. Teenagers do this all the time, and nobody thinks that it is odd. But autism exaggerates normal behavior to a point that is beyond most people's capacity for understanding.

(Grandin 1995, 146, 102)

Autistic fixity of focus is a quality that enables another characteristic of autistic cognition, what Oliver Sacks refers to as a "gift for mimesis" (Sacks 1995, 241). People with autism, especially those with so-called "savant skills," often have prodigious rote memories.[34] The autistic cognitive and artistic style often involves doing one single thing with great intensity, again and again.

Private Meanings

Autistic thinking is based on locally coherent networks of private associations.[35]

Like poetry, especially modernist poetry, autistic language often involves unusual, idiosyncratic combinations of elements and images, with as much pleasure associated with the sounds of the words as with their meaning. In Kristina Chew's words, "Autistic language is a fractioned idiom, its vocabulary created from contextual and seemingly arbitrary associations of word and thing, and peculiar to its sole speaker alone . . . Autistic language users think metonymically, connecting and ordering concepts according to seemingly chance and arbitrary occurrences in an 'autistic idiolect'" (Chew 2008, 142, 133). More broadly, a search for privacy—a space safe and secure from the incessant demands of what Julia Rodas calls "compulsory sociality"—is a persistent theme in autism narratives (Rodas 2004 and 2008). Temple Grandin expresses the same notion in personal terms:

> One of my students remarked that horses don't think, they must make associations. If making associations is not considered thought, then I would have to conclude that I am unable to think. Thinking in visual pictures and making associations is simply a different form of thinking from verbal-based linear thought. There are advantages and disadvantages to both kinds of thinking. Ask any artist or accountant.[36]

Autistic expression is often introverted, directed inward rather than outward. Instead of a chain of logical inference, one often finds rich networks of associations, often private in nature. Often these networks consist of richly observed specific details: autistic thinking tends to be concrete rather than abstract.

In its search for private meaning, the autistic imagination often ends up not so much defying conventions as simply ignoring them. People with autism are generally not particularly eager to please, which frees them to ignore the social niceties. In speech and in writing, the autistic style is often direct to the point of rudeness, unconstrained by social conventions. As Gerland observes of her own behavior, "This apparent disregard for the conventions contributed to my appearing to be brave. In fact, I had absolutely no idea that there *were* such things as conventions" (Gerland 1997, 90). In autistic writing, music, and art, one often finds a striking originality with its roots in the drive toward private meaning with relatively little concern for normal social conventions and normal communication styles.

Autistic Writing

Recent years have witnessed an explosion of writing, both in print and on the Web, by people who identify themselves as autistic. While there has been a small amount of poetry and fiction, the dominant genre by far is that of autobiography or personal memoir.[37] For some critics, the authorship of these narratives is inherently problematic: if people are really autistic, with the difficulties in communication that entails, then they will be unable to write, and if they are able to write, that means they are not really autistic. Autism autobiographies, like those by people with other sorts of cognitive or developmental disabilities, have often required some degree of mediation (from co-authors or editors) and, at least in the early years, often came with forewords from certified autism experts to vouch for their authenticity.[38] It is true that autistic discourse has sometimes had to be mediated to some degree to make it comprehensible to a mainstream (neurotypical) audience, and it is possible that this might, in some sense, compromise a pure, authentically autistic vision. Nazeer (2006), writing as a person with autism, observes,

> There may be something distinctive about autistic minds, but at least some of that

autism has to be removed, or eased, before autistic people can communicate meaningfully, even with one another, and set their minds upon the world. While there's no autistic equivalent of sign language, some level of intervention is necessary (227).

Despite the necessity, in at least some cases, for "some level of intervention," the sheer number of autism memoirs now available, and the qualities they almost universally share, make it possible to treat them both as a coherent body of literature and as one that expresses a reliably authentic autistic world view.[39] In these memoirs, and allowing for considerable individual variation, the features of autistic consciousness discussed above—local coherence, fixity of focus, and private meanings—strongly shape the style of writing. Mark Osteen's comment about Williams 1992 applies to a broad range of autism memoirs: "Williams's voice and viewpoint—blunt, headlong, self-obsessed but curiously unreflective—bespeaks an *autistic* consciousness that rarely generalizes or condenses, shows little comprehension of or interest in how others think, and possesses a weak grasp of narrative connection" (Osteen 2008a, 27). These memoirs generally share a narrow emotional range, often with an appearance of distance between the observer and the events experienced and narrated. They often lack narrative cohesion, preferring to string together brief episodes. They often feel literal-minded and concrete, with little in the way of humor or irony. The fixed, repetitive interests that are described are mirrored in a repetitive, bland style of writing.

As for overall narrative shape, autistic memoirs occasionally appear to conform to the standard ways of narrating disability, namely as a story of overcoming (cure, or the triumph of the human spirit over adversity) or a story of conversion (lessons learned by the passage through a terrible experience).[40] Certainly these are the narratives adopted within the even larger genre of autism memoirs by parents. But the memoirs by autists themselves generally deviate from the standard script (see Waltz 2005). The title of Grandin 1986 (*Emergence*), is somewhat misleading: the emergence she describes is at best equivocal. Rather than celebrating a triumphant cure, she learns to get along in the normal world, but without changing herself in fundamental ways. Williams 1992 is something closer to a traditional "narrative of normalization" (Osteen 2008b, 28), but even here, the ending is hardly triumphant. More recent memoirs depart even farther from the usual narratives: these authors tell more of self-discovery, of finding and insisting on their essential autistic selves, than they do of overcoming or conversion. They are more like what Frank 1995 calls "chaos stories" in their defiance of traditional narrative order and their resistance to what Osteen 2008b calls "the tyranny of the comic plot" (16).

This difference in narrative shape is reflected also in the metaphors that the authors use to describe autism. In narratives of autism by parents and professionals, the most common images are those of a wall or the alien. The first of these suggests that the person with autism is concealed or imprisoned, inaccessible to the outside world, which is implicitly invited to tear the wall down. The best-known uses of this metaphor are those of Bettelheim (*The Empty Fortress*) and Park (*The Siege*), but there are many others as well. The second of these suggests that the person with autism is a foreigner, a visitor from a different land, or perhaps even a different planet. This metaphor engages the mythical, archetypal figures of the alien, the changeling, the child bewitched (Sacks 1995, 190), and is related to the Romantic notion that cognitive difference, like blindness, may both exemplify and confer a deeper, more spiritual vision. It is related also to the familiar idea of "compensatory faculties":

people with disabilities are often assumed to have gifts that compensate for and may result from their deficiencies—certainly that is the way that autistic "savant" skills are often described.

Clinicians seem particularly prone to these romanticizing notions: Asperger describes one of the children he studied as looking like he had "just fallen from the sky" (Asperger 1944/1991, 60) and Uta Frith refers to their "haunting and somehow otherworldly beauty" (Frith 2003, 1). In a similar but more prosaic vein, Grinker imagines autism as an exotic country whose inhabitants need to be better studied by anthropologists.[41] Grandin neatly turns this image around by imagining herself as an anthropologist trying to make sense of normate culture, which to her is exotic (Sacks 1995). Similarly, Miller 2003, a compilation of memoirs and conversations by autistic women, answers its title question, "Women from Another Planet?" with a resounding no:

> We are *not* from another planet. We tricked you. We made you look. We are from right here, Planet Earth. We are an integral part of this earth's ecosystems, its intricately inter-dependent network of niches and potentialities . . . We are the first wave of a new liberation movement. . . . We are part of the groundswell of what I want to call Neurological Liberation (xii).

The metaphors used in autistic memoirs rarely have to do with walls and aliens. Much more commonly, we find a metaphors of doors (Grandin 1995) and glass (Dawn Prince-Hughes 2004; Wendy Lawson 2000). Both involve an idea of separation—the autistic world and the normate world are distinct—but the boundary between them permits people on both sides to see through (it's not an impermeable wall), and possibly to move through as well. Autism culture is distinct, but it's still a human culture.

Autistic Art

Jessica Park and Stephen Wiltshire are autistic painters who have had some degree of public attention and commercial success. Jessica Park came to public attention at an early age through one of the first and most important personal narratives of autism by her mother, Clara Park. A later book by Clara Park brought the story up through 2001, and encompassed Jessica Park's burgeoning career as a painter.[42] At an earlier stage of her career, Jessica Park painted mostly heaters, radio dials or mileage gauges, while now she devotes herself almost exclusively to individual architectural structures, mostly houses, painted against an astronomically correct starry sky. Throughout, her work is characterized by vivid sharp lines, geometrical shapes, and bright colors, and imbued with private codes and associations.[43] Each element is separate and distinct—no smudging or blurring—and rendered in astonishing detail. Here is Clara Park's description of the paintings, together with her interpretation of them as expressive of autism:

> There is no vagueness in her painting, no clashing brushwork, no atmospheric washes. It's hard-edge stuff . . . Her art is autistic in other ways too. Autistic literalism has its visual equivalent; Jessy's eye acts like a camera . . . Cameras do not ponder, they record. And there is the lack of shading . . . Most of her colors remain flat. Indeed, that unsettling tension between the prevailing flatness and the few bits of round is part of what makes her realism surreal. No shading. No nuance. If Jessy's painting bespeaks her handicap, it is a handicap not surmounted but transmuted into something rich and strange. Here is autism in its core characteristics, literal, repetitive, obsessively exact—yet beautiful. In her paintings, reality has been transfigured.
>
> (Park 2001, 130–31)

Jessica Park's work, in all of its rich individuality, resonates with the three features of autistic imagination discussed above: local coherence, fixity of focus, and private meanings. I think it is a mistake, however, to overemphasize the camera-like, literal quality of these paintings. While they are meticulously observed and rendered, they are also richly imaginative and interpretive, vibrating with energy and life and, in their incongruous juxtapositions of brilliant colors, and of brightly sunlit houses against a nighttime sky, even humor.

Some of the same issues arise in the work of Stephen Wiltshire which has been extravagantly admired, some would say "enfreaked," for its astonishing, camera-like literalism. Wiltshire draws and paints cityscapes, and he is best known for panoramic views of major cities (including London, Rome, Tokyo, Frankfurt, Madrid, and Jerusalem), often produced after shockingly brief exposure to the sights he depicts in such naturalistic and accurate detail.[44] The ubiquitous Oliver Sacks, who has championed and written about both Wiltshire and Jessica Park, has questioned the extent to which Wiltshire's art can be considered truly creative, given its literal fidelity to his subjects: perhaps his art is too purely imitative to be taken seriously as creative art.[45] I think that underestimates the individual and interpretive aspects of Wiltshire's artistic vision: even a camera offers a particular view, not an unmediated glimpse of reality. Wiltshire's art unfolds within a distinctive culture of autistic perception and cognition, including local coherence (it would be hard to imagine an art richer in detail), fixity of focus (Sacks's "gift for mimesis"), and private meanings (the work vibrates with networks of visual associations), but betrays also a distinctively individual way of seeing the world.

Autistic Music

The autistic style can be felt both in the way autistic people perceive music and they way they make music, as composers and performers. In the domain of pitch perception, I note that Absolute Pitch (AP) is significantly more prevalent among people with autism than in the general population. As a non-relational strategy of pitch perception, one based on the internal qualities of a tone without respect to other tones, AP would seem to epitomize an autistic cognition of music, based on local rather than central coherence.[46] More generally, we might speculate that, if normal, non-autistic listening emphasizes contextualization and patterning, autistic listening emphasizes the integrity of the discrete event, an orientation toward the part rather then the whole.

Autistic listeners may be more attuned to private, idiosyncratic associations than larger shared meanings. Autistic hearing is both private and "fractionated." If normal hearing involves the creation of hierarchies, autistic hearing involves the creation of associative networks.[47] Individual events are not so much clumped together to create larger patterns as they are appreciated both for their own sake and for the associations they may suggest with other individual events. Autistic listeners may have a preference for repetition and the cognitive capacity for recalling extended musical passages in full detail. Like absolute pitch, prodigious rote memory epitomizes autistic hearing.

In the portrait I have painted here, an autistic listener is someone who attends to the discrete musical event in all of its concrete detail (local coherence); who prefers the part to the whole; who is adept at creating associative networks (often involving private or idiosyncratic meanings); and who may have absolute pitch and a prodigious rote memory. In each of these respects, autistic hearing challenges normal hearing, which is presumed to be oriented toward global coherence, the synthesis of wholes from parts, the creation of relationships among discrete events, the subsuming context, and the creation of conceptual hierarchies, particularly in the domain of pitch.

In many ways, the legendary Canadian pianist, Glenn Gould, epitomizes autistic perception of music in his extraordinary performances. In his lifetime, Gould was as famous for his personal eccentricities as for the shocking originality of his musical interpretations, and I would argue that both have a common source in his autism.[48] He disliked the spontaneous give and take, the socially interactive nature of live performance and, fairly early in his career, abandoned the concert stage for the privacy and isolation of the recording studio. His profound social disengagement isolated him not only from the live concert audience but also from the community of past and present pianists—this may thus have contributed to the astonishing originality of his musical interpretations.

Specific aspects of Gould's playing may also be related to his autism, including his preference for extreme isolation of individual tones through persistent staccato articulation. One of the distinctive hallmarks of Gould's playing is separation and detachment: he separates the lines within a polyphonic texture and within each line he separates the notes from each other.[49] The detachment of lines from other lines, and notes from other notes is a striking musical affirmation of an autistic preference for local coherence. In this sense, Gould's autism provides a way of understanding his life and his art in an integrated way. Instead of seeing his famous "eccentricities" as distracting, inessential personal mannerisms, we can see them as part of an autistic worldview.

Although I have emphasized autistic high culture—writing, art, and music— there is also a much broader autistic culture of everyday life, encompassing the sorts of things that autistic people do in their daily lives to express and represent themselves. I am thinking of activities like calendar calculation, puzzle solving, mathematical manipulation, and engagement with and possible memorization of favorite television shows or movies. These do not result in works of art, but they do express the same autistic values of local coherence, private meaning, and fixity of focus that also characterize autistic high art. Autism, like other disabilities, can be thought of, at least in part as a kind of performance: not something you are, but something you do.[50] By performing autistically, gifted writers, artists, and musicians, along with just-average autistics, participate in the construction of autism and in building a community of autistic people.

CLAIMING AUTISM

We are living in a period in which a culture of autism, constructed not by medical professionals but by people with autism, has begun to emerge. Like other cultures in our multicultural landscape, autism culture has involved a search for historical roots. Where were the people we now think of as autistic before the category was created in 1943? Are there historical figures who might be claimed as progenitors, who might be held up as a source of communal pride and identification? The identification of prehistoric (i.e. pre-1943) figures with autism has become a small cottage industry, and many names have been proposed, including the Wild Boy of Aveyron and other "wild boys," Kaspar Hauser, Hugh Blair, John Howard (Frith 2003); Isaac Newton, Albert Einstein, Andy Warhol (Collins 2004); Wolfgang Mozart, Ludwig van Beethoven, Herman Melville, Ludwig Wittgenstein, Lewis Carroll, Charles Darwin, Vincent van Gogh, Béla Bartók, W. B. Yeats (Fitzgerald 2004).[51]

Historical genealogies of this kind are extremely problematic. First, there is the lack of direct observation—for many of these figures it is hard to know reliably many significant personal details, much less if they met the elaborate and changing criteria for a condition that did not even have a name until 1943. Second, there is the problem of feedback—what Hacking 1999 calls "bioloooping." When people are identified with a particular condition, like autism, they may receive certain treatments (both in the sense of medical interventions and responsive behaviors from others), and these may in turn alter the condition. Whatever their underlying neurology, people who live with autism today are behaviorally and cognitively different from earlier generations precisely because of the consequences of being classified as autistic. Third, and most important, to the extent that autism is a social and cultural phenomenon rather than (or in addition to) a medical diagnosis—the central contention of this essay—it simply did not exist or, at best, existed in an entirely different form.[52] Until very recently, people born with the characteristic neurology of autism would have been abandoned or placed in institutions for the insane or feebleminded. In a few cases, if they had remarkable skills, they might have been tolerated as eccentrics, but their eccentricities would not have coalesced into anything very much like autism as it appears today. In my view, the search for ancestors must either be abandoned or pursued in an appropriately tentative way. We will have to content ourselves with the emergence of a community that is new, tracing its roots back only to 1943, but one that is now coalescing and burgeoning.

As autism culture takes shape, with its distinctive cognitive style and worldview, it is becoming a source of identity and pride within a rapidly growing community. More and more, just as self-aware people with disabilities have learned to claim disability (Linton 1998), autists are claiming autism:

I believe autism can be a beautiful way of seeing the world. I believe that within autism there is not only the group—the label—but the individual as well; there is strength in it, and there is terror in its power. When I speak of emerging from the darkness of autism, I do not mean that I offer a success story neatly wrapped and finished with a "cure." I and the others who are autistic do not want to be cured. What I mean when I say "emergence" is that my soul was lifted from the context of my earlier autism and became autistic in another context, one filled with wonder and discovery and full of the feelings that so poetically inform each human life. . . . Much like the deaf community, we autistics are building an emergent culture. We individuals, with our cultures of one, are building a culture of many.

(Prince-Hughes 2004, 2–3, 7)

I totally agree with the need for those with an Autism Spectrum Condition (ASC not ASD [i.e. condition, not disorder]) to be recognized as a minority whose rights and needs need to be acknowledged and respected by the majority. But on the basis that they have a shared information processing difference to the majority of the population. . . . who often fail to provide forms of education, communication, social activities/networks, occupation, and employment most appropriate to this form of information processing.

(Williams 2006, 206)

While it is important for people with autism to maintain our own identities as a culture and a way of being, it is also important to learn how to interface with the vast majority of people who are not on the autism spectrum.

(Shore 2006, 201)

If I could snap my fingers and be nonautistic, I would not—because then I wouldn't be me. Autism is part of who I am . . . As I have said, it has only been recently that I realized the magnitude of the difference between me and most other people. During the past three years I have become fully aware that my visualization skills exceed those of most other people. I would never want to become so normal that I would lose these skills.

(Grandin 1995 60, 180)

We are women, living our ordinary lives, with joys and sorrows as our circumstances dictate/allow, doing many of the things non-autistic women do, feeling many of the same feelings, yet we are, in all of this, profoundly, astonishingly, and perfectly different.

(Miller 2003, xxiii)

Previously, we discussed the social and cultural conditions that made it possible for autism to be conceived as a psychiatric diagnosis, and for that diagnosis to proliferate. Now we are a position to summarize the social and cultural conditions that have made it possible for autism to emerge and flourish as a distinctive human culture with a shared worldview and cognitive style. First, there are the sheer numbers of people who are now either classified as autistic or who self-identify as autistic. Second, there is the recent addition to the ranks of the autistic of large numbers of people with relatively good linguistic, communication, and intellectual skills. These are among the first generation of people with autism to be able to represent themselves effectively in all of the artistic and popular media. Third, there is the Internet with its vast capacity for the formation of social networks, crucial for a group that has, by its very nature, difficulties with conventional social relatedness and communication. Finally, there is the emergence of the disability rights movement, the field of Disability Studies, and the new movement for "neurodiversity" that draws so extensively on both. Autism may remain as a serious psychiatric condition, and it may continue to seem to require medical intervention directed toward normalization and possible cure. But for a new generation of people with autism, it is not about what they can do despite autism (not about overcoming), but about what autism enables them to do, what they do through and with autism (Grandin 1995 describes herself as "a person whose disability has provided me with certain abilities" (204)). In that spirit, they have begun to forge a thriving community of like-minded people, committed to celebrating their shared difference.

NOTES

1. Both Kanner and Asperger took the term "autism" from a Eugen Bleuler, a Swiss psychiatrist of an earlier generation, who had coined it in 1908 with reference to the tendency of his patients with schizophrenia to withdraw from the external world into fantasy. Bleuler also coined the term "schizophrenia."

2. As Kanner (1943) observes: "It is quite possible that some such children have been viewed as feebleminded or schizophrenic. In fact, several children of our group were introduced to us as idiots or imbeciles, one still resides in a state school for the feebleminded, and two had been previously considered as schizophrenic" (242). Of the eleven children in Kanner's original study, only two achieved any degree of independence or self-sufficiency (Kanner 1971). The rest spent their lives in large institutions, with the extremely poor outcomes typical for people with autism in this era: "One cannot help but gain the impression that State Hospital admission was tantamount to a life sentence, with evanescence of the astounding facts of rote memory, abandonment of the earlier pathological yet active struggle for the maintenance of sameness, and loss of the interest in objects added to the basically poor relation to people—in other words, a total retreat to near-nothingness. These children were entered in institutions in which they were herded together with severely retarded coevals or kept in places in which they were housed with psychotic adults; two were eventually transferred from the former to the latter because of their advancing age" (Kanner 1971, 144). For a cultural history of "feeblemindedness" and "mental retardation," see Trent 1994.

3. Similar problems and contingencies of classification affect the natural sciences, too. Biologists, for example, grapple with what they call "the species problem," their ongoing and contentious attempts to carve the world of biological organisms into meaningful groups. See Mayr 1988, Hull 1989, and Ghiselin 1992.

4. This history of autism diagnoses is traced in

Grinker 2007. For vigorous critique of the DSM as more a pragmatic, social document than a scientific one—it functions primarily to provide stable, consistently identifiable populations for researchers to study, drug companies to medicate, and insurance companies to reimburse—see Kutchins and Kirk 1997 and Lewis 2006.

5. The remarkable growth of the autism population—often described as an "epidemic"—can be explained entirely by the equally remarkable relaxation and expansion of diagnostic criteria, together with increased public awareness of autism through the popular media and more vigorous case finding by educational and mental health professionals (Gernsbacher 2005; Grinker 2007).

6. Garland-Thomson 2004, 779–80: "This logic has produced conflicting, yet complementary, sets of practices and ideologies that American culture directs at what we think of broadly as disability. Such thinking draws a sharp distinction between disabled bodies imagined as redeemable and others considered disposable. One approach would rehabilitate disabled bodies; the other would eliminate them. I am positing the cultural logic of euthanasia broadly, not simply as ending a life for reasons of "mercy" or eliminating a group targeted as inferior or flawed—such as people with spina bifida or "mental retardation"—but as an umbrella concept, a mode of thought manifest in particular notions of choice, control, happiness, and suffering that underpin a wide range of practices and perceptions. Our culture encodes the logic of euthanasia in its celebration of concepts such as curing, repairing, or improving disabled bodies through procedures as diverse as reconstructive and aesthetic surgery, medication, technology, gene therapy, and faith healing. At the same time, this logic supports eradicating disabled bodies through practices directed at individuals—such as assisted suicide, mercy killing, and withholding nourishment—and those directed at certain groups deemed inferior—such as selective abortion, sterilization, euthanasia, eugenics, and institutionalization."

7. In an assessment of the state of Disability Studies in 2005, Lennard Davis observes, "The area of cognitive and affective disabilities is only just beginning to see the light of day. . . . The fact that academics are high-functioning people without, for the most part, serious cognitive disabilities has presented a kind of barrier to the construction of an autonomous subjecthood for people with cognitive disabilities. Furthermore, there is a pecking order for affective disorders, so that obsessive-compulsive disorder, depression,

and anxiety disorders are more likely to be represented positively than schizophrenia (so-called), other psychoses, and mental retardation. (Davis 2005, 530–31). On cognitive disability and problem of narration, see Bérubé 2005. On narratives of autism generally, see Murray 2008.

8. Three important recent studies both epitomize and encourage a shift from thinking about autism as a psychiatric illness to thinking about it as a social and cultural phenomenon: Nadeson 2005, Osteen 2008a, and Murray 2008.

9. Bettleheim was an influential public intellectual of his time, speaking and writing widely on the subject of autism, on which he was the universally acknowledged expert. His best-known publication, Bettelheim 1967, describes his experiences with children he treated at his "Orthogenic School" at the University of Chicago. The falsehood of Bettelheim's claims about his life and his work has been widely documented—see Severson 2008 and Schreibman 2005. Bettelheim borrowed the term "refrigerator mother" from Kanner, who related autism to "emotional frigidity in the typical autistic family" and "almost total absence of emotional warmth in child rearing" (Eisenberg and Kanner 1958, 8, 9), attributed autism to a "genuine lack of maternal warmth" (Kanner 1949), and described the mothers of autistic children as "just happening to defrost enough to produce a child" (quoted in *Time Magazine* 25 July 1960). He later repudiated this notion in a speech in 1969 to the newly formed National Society for Autistic Children (now the Autism Society of America): "Herewith I especially acquit you people as parents" (quoted in Park 2001, 11).

10. For summary and critique of all three, see Nadeson 2005, 114–34.

11. See Frith and Happé 1999, Frith 2003, and Happé 2005. Like the "theory of mind" and "executive function" theories discussed below, the "weak central coherence" theory remains controversial due to its lack of demonstrable neurological or biological basis (see Schreibman 2005).

12. According to Uta Frith, the principal proponent of this theory, "We have now enough evidence to formulate a hypothesis about the nature of the intellectual dysfunction in autism. In the normal cognitive system there is a built-in property to form coherence over as wide a range of stimuli as possible, and to generalize over as wide a range of contexts as possible. It is this drive that results in grand systems of thought, and it is this capacity for coherence that is diminished in children with autism. As a result, their information-processing systems, like their very beings, are characterized

by detachment. Detachment, as a technical term, refers to a quality of thought. It could be due either to a lack of global coherence or to a resistance to such coherence" (Frith 2003, 160).

13. Frith 2003, Baron-Cohen 1993, 1997, 2001a, 2001b, 2004. The offensive term "mindblindness" is sometimes used to name this cognitive deficit. "Theory of mind" has encountered significant resistance in the literature. On its absence of biological basis, see Schreibman 2005. On its refutation by the presence of numerous first-person accounts by autistic authors, replete with representations of their own mental states and the mental states of others, see McGeer 2004. For a critique from within the autism community, see Nazeer 2006, esp. 68–75.

14. According to Simon Baron-Cohen, the principal proponent of this theory, "A theory of mind remains one of the quintessential abilities that makes us human. By theory of mind we mean being able to infer the full range of mental states (beliefs, desires, intentions, imagination, emotions, etc.) that cause action. In brief, having a theory of mind is to be able to reflect on the contents of one's own and other's minds. Difficulty in understanding other minds is a core cognitive feature of autism spectrum conditions. The theory of mind difficulties seem to be universal among such individuals" (Baron-Cohen 2001b, 3). Baron-Cohen's clear implication is that the lack of a theory of mind renders people with autism less than fully human.

15. According to Ozonoff 1991, "Executive function is defined as the ability to maintain an appropriate problem-solving set for attainment of a future goal; it includes behaviors such as planning, impulse control, inhibition of prepotent but irrelevant responses, set maintenance, organized search, and flexibility of thought and action. Some features of autism are reminiscent of executive function deficits. The behavior of autistic people often appears rigid and inflexible: many autistic children become extremely distressed over trivial changes in the environment and insist on following routines in precise detail. They are often perseverative, focusing on one narrow interest or repetitively engaging in one stereotyped behavior. Their cognition often seems to lack executive functions; autistic individuals do not appear future-oriented, do not anticipate long-term consequences of behavior well, and have great difficulty self-reflecting and self-monitoring. They frequently appear impulsive, as if unable to delay or inhibit responses (1083). . . . The universality of executive function deficits in the present sample [including subjects

with both "classic high-functioning autism" and Asperger syndrome] and suggests that it might be a primary deficit of autism" (1099). See also Ozonoff 2005 and the essays in Russell 1997.

16. "Asperger syndrome is a severe and chronic developmental disorder closely related to autistic disorder and pervasive developmental disorder not otherwise specified, and, together, these disorders comprise a continuum referred to as the *autism spectrum disorders*. Having autism as the paradigmatic and anchoring disorder in this diagnostic category, the ASDs more generally are characterized by marked and enduring impairments within the domains of social interaction, communication, play and imagination, and a restricted range of behaviors or interests" (Klin 2005, 88).

17. The metaphors around autism comprise what Roy Porter calls an "analogy-based explanatory system." He is speaking of the humors (blood, choler, phlegm, and melancholy), among the earliest medicalized attempts to understand madness, but his observation extends to current theories of autism as well: "Analogy-based explanatory systems of this kind were not just plausible but indispensable so long as science had little direct access to what went on beneath the skin or in the head" (Porter 2002, 40).

18. "The real potential value of genetic research in autism lies in the probability that it will provide invaluable leads for biological studies that will succeed eventually in identifying the neural basis of autism. Identification of the susceptibility genes will not, of course, do that on its own. Genes code for proteins and not for psychiatric disorders or behaviors. Many areas of science will be needed in delineating the indirect pathways leading from susceptibility genes through effects on proteins and protein products, through physiological and neurochemical processes, and ultimately to the proximal pathway that leads to the syndrome of autism" (Rutter 2005, 443).

19. Anderson 2005, 464: "On surveying the field of neurochemical research in autism, it is notable how few replicated differences have been found between autistic and normal subjects." Rutter 2005, 443–44: "At present, the clinical payoff from genetic research has been quite modest and it remains to be seen just what it will deliver."

20. Hacking 1998 identifies a group of what he calls "transient mental illnesses," by which he refers to "an illness that appears in a time, in a place, and later fades away" (1). He adduces hysteria as one such transient illness and devotes much of the book to "fugue" as another. See also Hacking 1999, which identifies transient mental illnesses,

including hysteria and anorexia, as ones that "show up only at some times and some places, for reasons which we can only suppose are connected with the culture of those times and places" (100). It's not that real people don't live, and possibly suffer, with real symptoms; rather, that these disease entities are provisional and contingent ways of grouping and labeling them.

21. Volkmar 2005, 6: "Today there is broad agreement that autism and associated disorders represent the behavioral manifestations of underlying disfunctions in the functioning of the central nervous system, and that sustained educational and behavioral interventions are useful and constitute the core of treatment." Schreibman 2005, 133: "Few people would argue with the statement that today the treatment of choice is that based on the behavioral model. In fact, behavioral treatment is the only treatment that has been empirically demonstrated to be effective for children with autism."

22. For a discussion of genetic testing from a Disability Studies point of view, see Wilson 2006, Hubbard 2006, Saxton 2006, and Garland-Thomson 2004.

23. Geneticists are already eying psychiatric diagnoses for the possibility of significant reconfiguration of the categories on a genetic basis. "One area that might benefit from genetic disease classification is psychiatry. Because of the difficulty of measuring the brain, psychiatric diagnoses are still mainly based on symptoms. The Diagnostic and Statistical Manual of Mental Disorders contains descriptions of conditions as diverse as acute stress disorder and voyeurism. Scientists have found that certain genes appear to be associated with both schizophrenia and bipolar disorder. Those links, and the fact that some drugs work for both diseases, have prompted a debate over whether they are truly distinct disorders. 'The way we categorize these into two separate entities is almost certainly not correct,' said Dr. Wade H. Berretini, a professor of psychiatry at the University of Pennsylvania" (Andrew Pollack, "Redefining Disease, Genes and All," *New York Times* May 6, 2008).

24. This conclusion—that autism may be productively thought of as a cultural phenomenon rather than a medical pathology—tracks that of Nadeson 2008, which is worth quoting at some length. "This genealogy questions whether autism is a homogeneous, pathological condition that can be exhaustively known—or transparently represented—by scientists and their representational technologies (e.g., MRIs). Although I deconstruct the idea of autism as a

uniform, biological essence shared by all people labeled as "autistic," I do *not* reject the idea that biological phenomena contribute to the expression of "autistic" symptoms. I believe we need to explore how various institutional relationships, expert authorities, and bodies of knowledge have sought to represent, divide, understand, and act on biologically based, but socially shaped and expressed, behavioral and cognitive differences such as autism. . . . In our everyday thinking and communication, most of us visualize disease as either caused by a scientifically discernable agent such as a virus or bacterium (e.g., AIDS or meningitis) or as emanating from a detectable, localized bodily dysfunction (e.g., heart disease or diabetes). The disease-causing agent or diseased bodily system is seen as objective, available to visual representation (through a microscope, electromagnetic scan, or scientific diagram), and ultimately treatable (even if a "cure" eludes current medical understanding). In effect, disease is represented in our everyday understanding as available to empirical identification, interpretation, and intervention. . . . But autism is probably a heterogeneous condition that is more properly called a syndrome than a disease. Moreover, the causal pathways engendering autistic symptoms are most likely multiple and contingent on level upon level of loosely coupled, synergistic, biological and social systems" (79–80).

25. Similarly, see Hacking 1998 and 1999.

26. "The long-dominant biomedical model provides [a] comprehensive and dubious grand narrative: a theory that reduces every illness to a biological mechanism of cause and effect. By contrast, my argument—that postmodern illness is defined by an awareness of the elaborate interconnections between biology and culture—does not aspire to the status of a grand narrative. It does not seek to explain every affliction on the planet, but rather to describe a new, transitional, and unfinished understanding of illness that typifies numerous industrial societies during the second half of the twentieth century" (Morris 1998, 11). Similarly, see Nadeson 2008: "In short, disease, disability, and bodily difference are at once material and symbolic, both socially constructed and materially inscribed. . . . The biological and the cultural [are] mutually constitutive, inseparable in their constitution of personhood" (81).

27. Linton 1998, 11–12: "The medicalization of disability casts human variation as deviance from the norm, as pathological condition, as deficit, and, significantly, as an individual burden and personal tragedy. Society, in agreeing to assign medical meaning to disability, colludes to keep

the issue within the purview of the medical establishment, to keep it a personal matter and 'treat' the condition and the person with the condition rather than 'treating' the social processes and policies that construct disabled people's lives. The disability studies' and disability rights movement's position is critical of the domination of the medical definition and views it as a major stumbling block to the reinterpretation of disability as a political category and to the social changes that could follow such a shift." Similarly, see Longmore and Umansky 2001.

28. Garland-Thomson 1997, 7. Similarly, see Longmore 2003.

29. Siebers 2008, 3–4: "While seen historically as a matter for medical intervention, disability has been described more recently in disability studies as a minority identity that must be addressed not as personal misfortune or individual defect but as the product of a disabling social and built environment. Tired of discrimination and claiming disability as a positive identity, people with disabilities insist on the pertinence of disability to the human condition, on the value of disability as a form of diversity, and on the power of disability as a critical concept for thinking about human identity in general."

30. Similarly, see Biklen 2005, 65: "I argue that autism is best understood as a social and cultural construction, that the particular aspects of autism's construction are complex and multilayered, and that people classified autistic as well as those around them, including the autism field, have choices to make concerning which constructions to privilege. Autism is not a given condition or set of realities—at least, it is not 'given' or 'real' *on its own*. Rather, autism is and will be, in part, what any of us make it."

31. In order to deflect any charge of essentialism, I want to make clear that I am not suggesting that all autistic people approach the world in the ways I describe, or that anyone who approaches the world in these ways must be autistic. People with autism comprise a diverse community—there are many ways to be autistic—and the qualities that I am describing as autistic are also present, in varying degrees, in the neurotypical population as well. The notion of an autistic cognitive style functions somewhat in the manner of a notion like "Jewish humor"—a provisional point of departure for inquiry and, possibly, a useful tool in establishing a group identity for strategic political purposes.

32. For more on the recasting of the deficit of "weak central coherence" as the difference of "local coherence," see Mills 2008 and Belmonte 2008.

33. This preference involves recasting Kanner's "sameness," deficiencies in "executive function," and the emphasis in the DSM-IV on "restricted, repetitive, and stereotyped patterns of behavior, interests, and activities."

34. There is an extensive literature on autistic savants, formerly known as "idiot savants." While the offensiveness of the first word in that earlier label is clear enough, even the term "savant" itself is problematic. First, it entails an invidious comparison between the narrow ability (the "splinter skill") and the larger disability—it might be better to see the variety of skills possessed by an individual person in the same way we see the variety of skills possessed by groups of people: aspects of naturally occurring and desirable diversity. Second, it carries an impulse toward "enfreakment": the special skill provokes amazement and wonder, and also a sense of irreducible otherness (the skill seems almost inhuman). Third, the "autistic savant" comes to play the same role with respect to the population of autistic people that the "supercrip" does with respect to disabled people: it minimizes the challenges that most people with disabilities face and implies an additional burden, possibly a moral burden, of failing to measure up to an unrealistic standard.

35. The idea of "private meaning" resonates with Kanner's "aloneness," with deficiencies in "theory of mind," and with the deficits in social interaction and communication described in the DSM.

36. Grandin 1995, 173.

37. A very partial list would include Grandin 1986 and Williams 1992 (these are the first two published autistic memoirs), as well as Gerland 1997, Willey 1999, Lawson 2000, Miller 2003, Shore 2003, Prince-Hughes 2004, Ariel 2006, Tammet 2006, Nazeer 2006, and Robison 2007. For a general discussion of autism memoirs, see Cumberland 2008.

38. Bérubé 2000. Grandin 1986 has a co-author (Margaret M. Scariano) and a foreword from Bernard Rimland, at the time a leading figure in autism research—he also wrote the authenticating foreword for Williams 1992. Grandin 1995 has a foreword from Oliver Sacks. Publishers of more recent autistic autobiographies have been more willing to allow their autistic authors to stand on their own.

39. Rose 2008, 47: "I contend, therefore, that the collection of texts that comprise the corpus of autistic life narratives is now such that it enacts a community response to the individuation

of impairment, as each text enacts Couser's antipathological impulse to write back against the more restrictive discursive limits of being diagnosed as autistic." The reference is to Couser 1997.

40. Couser 1997. See also Frank 1995 and Hawkins 1999. On conversion narratives and autism, see Fisher 2008. On autism narratives generally, see Murray 2008.

41. Grinker 2007, 13: "The process of understanding autism itself parallels the work that anthropologists do, since the minds of people with autism are sometimes as hard to understand as foreign cultures."

42. Park 1982 and Park 2001.

43. On the network of private meanings that permeate Jessica Park's life and artistic work, see Park 2001. See also Chew 2008.

44. Wiltshire's paintings can be seen on the Web and in four books: Wiltshire 1987, 1989, 1991, and 1993.

45. Sacks 1995. See discussion in Osteen 2008b, 12–14.

46. Absolute pitch is the ability to name a pitch or produce a pitch identified by name without using an external source. For a survey of work on absolute pitch (AP), including the autism connection, see Ward 1999. Mottron et al. 1999 suggests "a causal relationship between AP and autism," which they relate to an "atypical tendency to focus on the stimulus rather than its context" (486). See also Brown et al. 2003: "Reports of a relatively high prevalence of absolute pitch (AP) in autistic disorder suggest that AP is associated with some of the distinctive cognitive and social characteristics seen in autism spectrum disorders. . . . Piecemeal information processing, of which AP is an extreme and rare example, is characteristic of autism and may be associated as well with subclinical variants in language and behavior. We speculate that the gene or genes that underlie AP may be among the genes that contribute to autism. . . . Inasmuch as AP possessors can identify the individual pitches in a melody, AP is an extreme example of piecemeal information processing. . . . The link between autism and AP points to other neuropsychological processes that might underlie AP. A number of the special abilities found in autistic savants—prodigious memory and AP among them—can be characterized as high-fidelity information processing. . . ." (166).

47. Headlam 2006 makes a similar argument.

48. Maloney 2006 persuasively places Gould on the autism spectrum through careful study of the extensive written and video archive: "Autism is the solution to the perplexing riddle of [Glenn] Gould's existence and is therefore arguably the fundamental story of his life. It leads us to a coherent understanding of both the man and the musician. Not only does it gather all his strange behavioral and lifestyle eccentricities into a unified *gestalt*, it also furnishes intriguing insights into important aspects of his music-making" (134). Autism remains a controversial issue in Gould studies. Ostwald 1997 is a psychobiography that raises but does not pursue the issue of autism. Bazzana 2004 discounts autism, preferring instead a mixed account based on anxiety, depression, hypochondria, and "a variety of obsessional, schizoid, and narcissistic traits" (370).

49. According to Bazzana 1997, "As a general rule, Gould preferred articulation that can best be described as non-legato or detaché . . . His desire for clarity, so basic to his musical personality, extended to his rendering of phrases and even individual notes . . . Detaché was the norm for Gould regardless of tempo" (215–16).

50. Sandahl and Auslander 2005: "Part of sociology's legacy to performance studies is the idea that we do not just live our "real life" identities, we *perform* them . . . Goffman argues that who we are socially is bound up with who we are perceived to be by those around us (our audience) and that we behave as actors in order to control the impressions we make on others. This understanding of everyday behavior emphasizes that identity does not simply reside in individuals but is the product of social interactions among individuals. This perspective is congruent with the view of disability as something that is not an intrinsic characteristic of certain bodies but a construct produced through the interaction of those bodies with socially based norms that frame the way those bodies are generally perceived" (215).

51. A similar list of fictional characters from the pre-autism era who have been placed on the autism spectrum would include Bartelby (Garland-Thomson 2004 and Murray 2008); Jane Eyre (Rodas 2008); Sherlock Holmes (Fitzgerald 2004); and Barnaby Rudge (Grove 1987 and Murray 2008).

52. McDonagh 2008: "My resistance to reading historical figures or literary characters as autistic or aspergian is based on one of the fundamental precepts of this paper: that autism, should it turn out to be a single pathology with an organic cause and thus 'real,' is also perceived within a social dynamic, and our recognition and understanding of autism takes form within this

dynamic. If the social circumstances allowing us to perceive autism did not exist before some point relatively early in the twentieth century, and if the perception and articulation of autism is an important part of its being, then to what extent can we say the condition existed previously?. . . . The biological component of autism, the "indifferent" element [the reference is to Hacking 1999], may have a long history upon which biomedical and neurological research might one day shed some light, but autism as a diagnostic category has also, since its creation, been engaged in a dynamic social exchange that is as crucial as its indifferent element. Thus, although a pre-twentieth-century autism is possible in terms of simple pathology, it seems to be something of a conceptual anachronism" (100).

WORKS CITED

Anderson, George M. and Yoshihiko Hoshino. 2005. "Neurochemical Studies of Autism." In *Handbook of Autism and Pervasive Developmental Disorders*, third edition, ed. Fred R. Volkmar, Rhea Paul, Ami Klin, and Donald Cohen, 435–472. Hoboken, NJ: John Wiley & Sons.

Ariel, Cindy N. and Naseef, Robert A. eds. 2006. *Voices from the Spectrum: Parents, Grandparents, Siblings, People with Autism, and Professionals Share Their Wisdom*. London: Jessica Kingsley.

Asperger, Hans. 1944/1991. "'Autistic Psychopathy' in Childhood," trans. Uta Frith. In Uta Frith, *Autism and Asperger Syndrome*, 37–92. Cambridge: Cambridge University Press.

Baron-Cohen, Simon, ed. 1993. *Understanding Other Minds: Perspectives from Autism*. Oxford: Oxford University Press.

Baron-Cohen, Simon. 1997. *Mindblindness: An Essay on Autism and Theory of Mind*. Cambridge, MA: MIT Press.

Baron-Cohen, Simon. 2001a. "Theory of Mind and Autism: A Review." Special Issue of *The International Review of Mental Retardation* 23 (2001): 169–184.

Baron-Cohen, Simon. 2001b. "Theory of Mind in Normal Development and Autism." *Prisme 34*, 174–183.

Baron-Cohen, Simon. 2004. *The Essential Difference*. London: Penguin.

Bazzana, Kevin. 1997. *Glenn Gould, The Performer in the Work: A Study in Performance Practice*. Oxford: Clarendon Press.

Bazzana, Kevin. 2004. *Wondrous Strange: The Life and Art of Glenn Gould*. Oxford: Oxford University Press.

Belmonte, Matthew K. 2008. "Human, but More So: what the Autistic Brain Tells Us about the Process of Narrative." In Mark Osteen, ed. *Autism and Representation*, 166–180. New York: Routledge.

Bérubé, Michael. 2000. "Autobiography as Performative Utterance." *American Quarterly* 52: 339–343.

Bérubé, Michael. 2005. "Disability and Narrative." *PMLA* 120/2: 568–576.

Bettelheim, Bruno. 1967. *The Empty Fortress: Infantile Autism and the Birth of the Self*. New York: Free Press.

Biklen, Douglas. 2005. *Autism and the Myth of the Person Alone*. New York: New York University Press.

Brown, Walter A., Cammuso, Karen, Sachs, Henry, et al. 2003. "Autism-Related Language, Personality, and Cognition in People with Absolute Pitch: Results of a Preliminary Study." *Journal of Autism and Developmental Disorders* 33/2: 163–167.

Chew, Kristina. 2008. "Fractioned Idiom: Metonymy and the Language of Autism." In Mark Osteen, ed. *Autism and Representation*, 133–144. New York: Routledge.

Collins, Paul. 2004. *Not Even Wrong. Adventures in Autism*. New York and London: Bloomsbury.

Couser, G. Thomas. 1997. *Recovering Bodies: Illness, Disability and Life Writing*. Madison and London: University of Wisconsin Press.

Cumberland, Debra L. 2008. "Crossing Over: Writing the Autistic Memoir." In Mark Osteen, ed. *Autism and Representation*, 183–196. New York: Routledge.

Dawson, Geraldine, Sara Webb, Gerard D. Schellenberg, Stephen Dager, Seth Friedman, Elizabeth Aylward, and Todd Richards. 2002. "Defining the Broader Phenotype of Autism: Genetic, Brain, and Behavioral Perspectives." *Development and Psychopathology* 14: 581–611.

Davis, Lennard. 2005. "Disability: The Next Wave or Twilight of the Gods?" PMLA 120/2: 527–532.

Davis, Lennard. 2008. *Obsession: A History*. Chicago: University of Chicago Press.

Eisenberg, Leon and Leo Kanner. 1958. "Early Infantile Autism, 1933–1955." In *Psychopathology*, ed. Charles Reed, Irving Alexander, and Sylvan Tomkins, 3–14. Cambridge, MA: Harvard University Press.

Fisher, James T. 2008. "No Search, No Subject? Autism and the American Conversion Narrative." In Mark Osteen, ed. *Autism and Representation*, 51–64. New York: Routledge.

Fitzgerald, Michael 2004. *Autism and Creativity: Is there a Link between Autism in Men and Exceptional Creativity?* New York: Routledge.

Fombonne, Eric. 2005. "Epidemiological Studies of Pervasive Developmental Disorders." In *Handbook of Autism and Pervasive Developmental Disorders*, third edition, ed. Fred R. Volkmar, Rhea Paul, Ami Klin, and Donald Cohen, 42–69. Hoboken, NJ: John Wiley & Sons.

Frank, Arthur W. Frank. 1995. *The Wounded Storyteller: Body, Illness, and Ethics*. Chicago: University of Chicago Press.

Frith, Uta. 2003. *Autism: Explaining the Enigma*, 2nd ed. Oxford: Blackwell.

Frith, Uta and Happé, Francesca. 1999. "Theory of Mind and Self-Consciousness: What is it Like to be Autistic?" *Mind and Language* 14/1: 1–22.

Garland-Thomson, Rosemarie. 1997. *Extraordinary Bodies: Figuring Physical Disability in American Culture and Literature*. New York: Columbia University Press.

Garland-Thomson, Rosemarie. 2004. "The Cultural Logic of Euthanasia: 'Sad Fancyings' in Herman Melville's 'Bartelby.'" *American Literature* 76/4 (2004): 777–806.

Gerland, Gunilla. 1997. *A Real Person: Life on the Outside*, trans. Joan Tate. London: Souvenir Press.

Gernsbacher, Morton Ann, Michelle Dawson, and H. Hill Goldsmith. 2005 "Three Reasons Not to Believe in an Autism Epidemic." *Current Directions in Psychological Science* 14/2: 55–58.

Ghiselin, Michael. 1992. "A Radical Solution to the Species Problem." In Marc Ereshefsky (ed.), *The Units of Evolution: Essays on the Nature of Species*, 279–292. Cambridge, MA: The MIT Press.

Grandin, Temple. 1995. *Thinking in Pictures and Other Reports from My Life with Autism*. New York: Doubleday Books.

Grandin, Temple and Margaret M. Scariano. 1986. *Emergence: Labeled Autistic*. New York: Warner Books.

Grinker, Roy. 2007. *Unstrange Minds: Remapping the World of Autism*. New York: Basic Books.

Grove, Thelma. 1987. "Barnaby Rudge: A Case Study in Autism." *Dickensian* 83: 139–148.

Hacking, Ian. 1998. *Mad Travelers: Reflections on the Reality of Transient Mental Illnesses*. Cambridge, MA: Harvard University Press.

Hacking, Ian. 1999. *The Social Construction of What?* Cambridge, MA: Harvard University Press.

Happé, Francesca. 2005. "The Weak Central Coherence Account of Autism." In *Handbook of Autism and Pervasive Developmental Disorders*, third edition, ed. Fred R. Volkmar, Rhea Paul, Ami Klin, and Donald Cohen, 640–49. Hoboken, NJ: John Wiley & Sons.

Hawkins, Anne Hunsaker. 1999. *Reconstructing Illness: Studies in Pathography*, 2nd ed. West Lafayette, IN: Purdue University Press.

Headlam, Dave. 2006. "Learning to Hear Autistically." In *Sounding Off: Theorizing Disability in Music*, ed.

Neil Lerner and Joseph N. Straus, 109–120. New York: Routledge.

Hubbard, Ruth. 2006. "Abortion and Disability: Who Should and Who Should Not Inhabit the World?" In *The Disability Studies Reader*, 2nd ed., ed. Lennard Davis, 93–104. New York: Routledge.

Hull, David. 1989. *The Metaphysics of Evolution*. Albany, NY: State University of New York Press.

Kanner, Leo. 1943. "Autistic Disturbances of Affective Contact." *The Nervous Child* 2: 217–250.

Kanner, Leo. 1949. "Problems of Nosology and Psychodynamics in Early Childhood Autism." *American Journal of Orthopsychiatry* 19: 416–426.

Kanner, Leo. 1971. "Follow-up Study of Eleven Autistic Children Originally Reported in 1943." *Journal of Autism and Developmental Disorders* 1/2: 119–145.

Klin, Ami, James McPartland, and Fred Volkmar. 2005. "Asperger Syndrome." In *Handbook of Autism and Pervasive Developmental Disorders*, third edition, ed. Fred R. Volkmar, Rhea Paul, Ami Klin, and Donald Cohen, 88–125. Hoboken, NJ: John Wiley & Sons.

Kutchins, Herb and Stuart A. Kirk. 1997. *Making us Crazy: DSM: The Psychiatric Bible and the Creation of Mental Disorders*. New York: The Free Press.

Ladd-Taylor, Molly and Lauri Umanski. 1998. *"Bad" Mothers: The Politics of Blame in Twentieth-Century America*. New York: NYU Press.

Landsman, Gail. 1998. "Reconstructing Motherhood in the Age of 'Perfect' Babies: Mothers of Infants and Toddlers with Disabilities." *Signs: Journal of Women in Culture and Society* 24: 69–99.

Lawson, Wendy. 2000. *Life Behind Glass: A Personal Account of Autism Spectrum Disorder*. London: Jessica Kingsley.

Lewis, Bradley. 2006. *Moving Beyond Prozac, DSM, and the New Psychiatry: The Birth of Postpsychiatry*. Ann Arbor: University of Michigan Press.

Linton, Simi. 1998. *Claiming Disability: Knowledge and Identity*. New York: New York University Press.

Longmore, Paul. 2003. "Introduction." In *Why I Burned My Book and Other Essays on Disability*, 1–18. Philadelphia: Temple University Press, 2003.

Longmore, Paul and Lauri Umansky. 2001. "Introduction: Disability History: From the Margins to the Mainstream." In *The New Disability History: American Perspectives*, ed. Paul Longmore and Lauri Umansky, 1–32. New York: New York University Press.

Maloney, Timothy. 2006. "Glenn Gould, Autistic Savant." In *Sounding Off: Theorizing Disability in Music*, ed. Neil Lerner and Joseph N. Straus, 121–136. New York: Routledge.

Mayr, Ernst. 1988. *Toward a New Philosophy of Biology: Observations of an Evolutionist*. Cambridge, MA: Harvard University Press.

McDonagh, Patrick. 2008. "Autism and Modernism: A Genealogical Exploration." In Mark Osteen, ed. *Autism and Representation*, 99–116. New York: Routledge.

McGeer, Victoria. 2004. "Autistic Self-Awareness." *Philosophy, Psychiatry, & Psychology* 11/3: 235–251.

McRuer, Robert. 2006. *Crip Theory: Cultural Signs of Queerness and Disability*. New York: New York University Press.

Miller, Jean Kearns. 2003. *Women from Another Planet? Our Lives in the Universe of Autism*. Bloomington, IN: First Books.

Mills, Bruce. 2008. "Autism and the Imagination." In Mark Osteen, ed. *Autism and Representation*, 117–132. New York: Routledge.

Minshew, Nancy J, John A. Sweeney, Margaret L. Bauman, and Sara Jane Webb. 2005. "Neurologic Aspects of Autism." In *Handbook of Autism and Pervasive Developmental Disorders*, third edition, ed. Fred R. Volkmar, Rhea Paul, Ami Klin, and Donald Cohen, 473–514. Hoboken, NJ: John Wiley & Sons.

Morris, David. 1998. *Illness and Culture in the Postmodern Age*. Berkeley: University of California Press.

Mottron, L., Peretz, I., Belleville, S. and Rouleau, N. 1999. "Absolute Pitch in Autism: A Case-study." *Neurocase* 5: 485–501.

Murray, Stuart. 2008. *Representing Autism: Culture, Narrative, Fascination*. Liverpool: Liverpool University Press.

Nadeson, Majia Holmer. 2005. *Constructing Autism: Unraveling the "Truth" and Understanding the Social*. New York: Routledge.

Nadeson, Majia Holmer. 2008. "Constructing Autism: A Brief Genealogy." In Mark Osteen, ed. *Autism and Representation*, 78–96. New York: Routledge.

Nazeer, Kamran. 2006. *Send in the Idiots: Stories from the Other Side of Autism*. New York and London: Bloomsbury.

Osteen, Mark, ed. 2008a. *Autism and Representation*. New York: Routledge.

Osteen, Mark. 2008b. "Autism and Representation: A Comprehensive Introduction." In Mark Osteen, ed. *Autism and Representation*, 1–48. New York: Routledge.

Ostwald, Peter. 1997. *Glenn Gould: The Ecstasy and Tragedy of Genius*. New York: Norton.

Ozonoff, Sally, B. F. Pennington, and S. J. Rogers. 1991. "Executive Function Deficits in High-Functioning Autistic Individuals: Relationship to Theory of Mind." *Journal of Child Psychology and Psychiatry and Allied Disciplines* 32: 1081–1105.

Ozonoff, Sally, Mikle South, and Sherri Provencal. 2005. "Executive Functions." In *Handbook of Autism and Pervasive Developmental Disorders*, third edition, ed. Fred R. Volkmar, Rhea Paul, Ami Klin, and Donald Cohen, 606–627. Hoboken, NJ: John Wiley & Sons.

Park, Clara Claiborne. 1982. *The Siege: A Family's Journey Into the World of an Autistic Child*. Boston: Back Bay Books.

Park, Clara Claiborne. 2001. *Exiting Nirvana: A Daughter's Life with Autism*. Boston: Little, Brown and Company.

Pickles, A., E. Starr, S. Kazak, P. Bolton, K. Papanikolaou, A. Bailey, R. Goodman and M. Rutter. 2000. "Variable Expression of the Autism Broader Phenotype: Findings from Extended Pedigrees." *The Journal of Child Psychology and Psychiatry and Allied* Disciplines 41: 491–502.

Porter. Roy. 2002. *Madness: A Brief History*. Oxford: Oxford University Press.

Prince-Hughes, Dawn. 2004. *Songs of the Gorilla Nation: My Journey Through Autism*. New York: Harmony.

Robison, John Elder. 2007. *Look Me In The Eye: My Life with Asperger's*. New York: Crown Publishers.

Rodas, Julia Miele. 2004. "Tiny Tim, Blind Bertha, and the Resistance of Miss Mowcher: Charles Dickens and the Uses of Disability." *Dickens Studies Annual* 34: 51–97.

Rodas, Julia Miele. 2008. "'On the Spectrum': Rereading Contact and Affect in *Jane Eyre*." *Nineteenth-Century Gender Studie*s 4/2.

Rose, Irene. 2008. "Autistic Biography or Autistic Life Narrative?" *Journal of Literary Disability* 2/1: 44–54.

Russel, James, ed. 1997. *Autism as an Executive Disorder*. Oxford: Oxford University Press.

Rutter, Michael. 2005. "Genetic Influences and Autism." In *Handbook of Autism and Pervasive Developmental Disorders*, third edition, ed. Fred R. Volkmar, Rhea Paul, Ami Klin, and Donald Cohen, 425–452. Hoboken, NJ: John Wiley & Sons.

Sacks, Oliver. 1995. *An Anthropologist on Mars: Seven Paradoxical Tales*. New York: Knopf.

Sandahl, Carrie and Philip Auslander, ed. 2005. *Bodies in Commotion: Disability and Performance*. Ann Arbor: University of Michigan Press.

Saxton, Marsha. 2006. "Disability Rights and Selective Abortion." In *The Disability Studies Reader*, 2nd ed., ed. Lennard Davis, 105–116. New York: Routledge.

Schreibman, Laura. 2005. *The Science and Fiction of Autism*. Cambridge, MA: Harvard University Press.

Schultz, Robert T. and Diana L. Robins. 2005. "Functional Neuroimaging Studies of Autism Spectrum Disorders." In *Handbook of Autism and Pervasive Developmental Disorders*, third edition, ed. Fred R. Volkmar, Rhea Paul, Ami Klin, and Donald Cohen, 515–533. Hoboken, NJ: John Wiley & Sons.

Severson, Katherine DeMaria, James Arnt Aune, and Denise Jodlowski. 2008. "Bruno Bettelheim, Autism, and the Rhetoric of Scientific Authority." In Mark Osteen, ed. *Autism and Representation*, 65–77. New York: Routledge.

Shore, Stephen. 2003. *Beyond the Wall: Personal Experiences with Autism and Asperger Syndrome*. Shawnee Mission, KS: Autism Asperger Publishing Co.

Shore, Stephen. 2006. "The Importance of Parents in the Success of People with Autism." In *Voices from the Spectrum: Parents, Grandparents, Siblings, People with Autism, and Professionals Share Their Wisdom*, ed. Cindy N. Ariel and Robert A. Naseef, 199–203. London: Jessica Kingsley Publishers.

Siebers, Tobin. 2008. *Disability Theory*. Ann Arbor: University of Michigan Press.

Sontag, Susan. 1978. *Illness as Metaphor*. New York: Farrar, Straus, and Giroux.

Tammet, Daniel. 2006. *Born on a Blue Day*. New York: Free Press.

Trent, James W. *Inventing the Feeble Mind: A History of Mental Retardation in the United States*. Berkeley: University of California Press, 1994.

Volkmar, Fred R and Ami Klin. 2005. "Issues in the Classification of Autism and Related Conditions." In *Handbook of Autism and Pervasive Developmental Disorders*, third edition, ed. Fred R. Volkmar, Rhea Paul, Ami Klin, and Donald Cohen, 5–41. Hoboken, NJ: John Wiley & Sons.

Waltz, Mitzi. 2005. "Reading Case Studies of People with Autistic Spectrum Disorders: a cultural studies approach to issues of disability representation." *Disability & Society* 20/4: 421–435.

Ward, W. Dixon. 1999. "Absolute Pitch." In *The Psychology of Music*, 2nd ed., ed. Diana Deutsch, 265–298. San Diego: Academic Press.

Willey, Liane Holliday. 1999. *Pretending to be Normal: Living with Asperger's Syndrome*. London: Jessica Kingsley.

Williams, Donna. 1992. *Nobody, Nowhere: The Extraordinary Autobiography of an Autistic*. New York: Harper Collins.

Williams, Donna. 2006. "Culture, Conditions, and Personhood: A Response to the Cure Debate on Autism." In *Voices from the Spectrum: Parents, Grandparents, Siblings, People with Autism, and Professionals Share Their Wisdom*, ed. Cindy N. Ariel and Robert A. Naseef, 204–208. London: Jessica Kingsley Publishers.

Wilson, James C. 2006. "(Re)Writing the Genetic Body-Text: Disability, Textuality, and the Human Genome Project." In *The Disability Studies Reader*, 2nd ed., ed. Lennard Davis, 67–78. New York: Routledge.

Wiltshire, Stephen. 1987. *Drawings*. London: J.M. Dent & Sons.

Wiltshire, Stephen. 1989. *Cities*. London: J.M. Dent & Sons.

Wiltshire, Stephen. 1991. *Floating Cities: Venice, Amsterdam, Leningrad, and Moscow*. New York: Summit Books.

Wiltshire, Stephen. 1993. *American Dream*. London: Michael Joseph Ltd.

CHAPTER 35

Disability, Design, and Branding: Rethinking Disability within the 21st Century

Elizabeth DePoy and Stephen Gilson

SETTING THE CONTEXT

Reflecting on the 21st century reveals communities which are no longer defined by their geographic or even physical boundaries. Individuals can be in several places at one time (Bugeja, 2005), can increasingly participate in global events when they happen through viewing them in action on screens that can even be carried in a pocket. Work no longer needs to take place in a physical "workplace." We can create and revise our own virtual identities, appearances, functionality, and methods of interacting. We can shop internationally from our living rooms and enter virtual and actual theme parks that provide us with familiarity and comfort. We can communicate with great immediacy across the globe in languages that we may not even speak. We text message, e-mail, log on, blog, podcast, and become actors on virtual stages of our own films. We can access libraries, museums, across the globe from our homes and can meet face to face even if we are physically situated in different continents. Time is no longer simply a linear chronological measurement. We live among people who originated from distant geographic locations throughout the globe. And we can uncouple ourselves from our bodies as we interact, earn, play, and even engage in sex in virtual spaces.

Critical to thinking and theorizing about disability within these contemporary chronological times, we challenge the intellectual status quo of separate disciplines and discuss concepts such as intersectionality, symbols, theming (Bryman, 2004; Lukas, 2007), and constructed realities. The uncertainties and relativism of recent intellectual trends have been provocative of new thinking in which unlikely disciplines mingle and create new opportunities for context-relevant thinking and informed action. We now discuss these contemporary themes within disability studies.

POSTMODERNISM AND POST-POSTMODERNISM WITHIN DISABILITY STUDIES

Over the past few decades, postmodern theories that emerged in opposition to modernism caught the intellectual gaze of many disability studies theorists. Because postmodernism challenged the tyranny of normalcy (DePoy & Gilson, 2009) post-modernism provided both power and comfort in denuding grand narratives which disparage bodies and experiences that do not fit within + two standard deviations from the mean on measures based in traditional longitudinal and behavioral theories. While postmodernism opened a portal through which disability studies could oppose the medicalized 20th century notion of disability, its carnivalesque gaze and focus on the nonsense of language and symbol (Baudrillard, 1995) have left too many vacancies when looking to theory to inform human rights and equality of opportunity for groups which have historically been excluded, disenfranchised, or exploited for profit.

Despite its limitations, by dismantling narrative and theorizing its political ambiguity and even duplicity, post-modernism has left important intellectual rubble to be refitted into new theoretical configurations. What has appealed to us about postmodernism and its successors is simultaneous acceptance of diverse bodies of evidence beyond traditional positivist designs but including them as well, and its eschewal of prescribed world-views. These elements can support new theorizing that does contemporary-relevant intellectual and applied work. What we mean by work is the intellectual, analytical and knowledge base to inform understanding and equality of human rights.

Post-post modernist theorists are mining the disparate gems in the debris that the postmodernists left as they interrogated and unpacked enlightenment thinking. The post-postmodern contemporary genre for us integrates the "best of all explanatory worlds" by synthesizing the advantages of diverse fields. Post-postmodernism has gifted disability explorations and explanations with both intellectual and utilitarian richness. Consider for example the metaphoric propinquity of the designer disability items, orthopedic shoes, queerness, and evolutionary theory (Fries, 2007). Fries elucidates stunning relationships among his own travels and phylogenic theories of natural selection, legitimately reintegrating science into discussions of dis-

ability. Similarly the neurodiversity literature allows for the reintroduction of biology into explanations of disability while advancing progressive views in so doing. As example, using this postpostmodern view, diagnoses of brain disorder such as bipolar disorder, schizophrenia, autism, and so forth are reframed as diverse rather than as pathological (Antonetta, 2007; Seidel, 2004–2009).

Bolstered by post-postmodern scholarship, our recent work proposing two frameworks, "Disability as Disjuncture" and "Disability as Logo" have the potential to be theoretically robust in informing innovative contemporary responses aimed at equalizing human rights (DePoy & Gilson, 2006; Gilson & DePoy, 2007; 2008). We turn to these now.

DISABILITY AS DISJUNCTURE

Building on seminal works over the past decade, Disjuncture Theory indicts the interstices between environment and body as the locus for disability. As early as 1999, National Institute on Disability and Rehabilitation Research published the following explanation: "disability is a product of the interaction between characteristics of the individual (e.g., conditions or impairments, functional status, or personal and social qualities) and the characteristics of the natural, built, cultural, and social environments" (NIDRR, 2007). This synthetic explanation positions disability as mobile and context embedded but fails to identify the point or range at which the "interactive product" moves from ability to disability. Within NIDRR's viewpoint, the atypical body remains the habitat of disability as depicted in the parenthetical clarifier in the definition above.

Davis (2002) also was influential in looking at disability beyond the "body or environment" binary. Proceeding on his position that disability is an unstable category in need of reconceptualization, Davis posited the revision of the category to include every "body" regardless of its current status as disabled or not. This important viewpoint foregrounded the limitations of outdated models of identity politics that crafted policy responses for sub-populations even with the recognition that everyone can join the membership roster of disability. Similar to NIDRR's definition, Davis retained the body as the entry point into the disability club, referring to Christopher Reeve as exemplary of how quickly one can change embodied status.

This foundational work precedes and shapes disjuncture as one of many explanations that could form a solid axiological as well as praxis foundation for legitimate disability determination and response. Unlike NIDRR and Davis, however, we do not look to the body for the initial entrance into disability. Rather, Disjuncture Theory locates disability at the intersection of bodies and environments. Through this lens, disability is an ill-fit between embodied experience and diverse environments in which bodies act, emote, think, sense, communicate, and broadly experience. Disjuncture Theory therefore recognizes body and environment as equal vestibules leading into the category of disability. Disjuncture is a continuum rather than a binary, with ascending degrees of separation between environment and body denoting more severe disjuncture and visa versa.

Full juncture is the non-example of disability and thus is the desirable that drives our theorizing and application to praxis. In this state, embodied presence fits well within environmental features.

Curiously, our initial thinking about disjuncture emerged from a conversation in a disability studies class about design, beginning our foray into design as an important element of disability as well as a critical consideration in healing disjuncture.

DESIGN

Design is a complex construct which been increasingly used to describe abs____ and concrete human intention and activity, and to name a property of virtual, physical, and even abstract phenomena. The Appendix presents representative lexical definitions of design.

As reflected in the definitions and consistent with post-postmodern thought, design is purposive and may refer to decoration, plan, fashion, functionality, and influence. What is evident in the diverse definitions is the broad scope of phenomena to which design applies, including but not limited to the activities of conceptualizing, planning, creating, and claiming credit for ones ideas, products, and entities as well as the inherent intentional or patterned characteristics of bodies, spaces, and ideas (Margolin, 2002; Munari, Fames, Eamon, Guixe, & Dey, 2003).

Despite the ubiquitous and diverse use of the term, of particular note is the post-postmodern commonality in all definitions of design as purposive and intentional. That is to say, design is not frivolous but rather is cultural iconography which is powerful, political, and is both shaped by and explanatory of notions of standards, acceptability, membership, and desirability (Foster, 2003; Munari et al., 2003). Purposive design therefore has the potential to shape constraint, maintain the status quo, or effect profound change.

It is therefore curious that built and virtual environmental and product design standards are constructed around Enlightenment ideals of the human body, its balance, proportion, emphasis, rhythm, and unity (DePoy & Gilson, 2008; Margolin, 2002). This practice creates disjuncture and thus significant disability for numerous bodies, including many that fit within the typical ranges.

But the built environment is not the only target of design. Bodies themselves are "designed" through medical measurement and practice, fashion, fitness, education, counseling, and so forth. As example, consider the recent book by Little and McGuff (2008) entitled *Body by Science*. This title and the contents propose the role of empirically supported strategies to "design" the ideal body shape, tone, and even energy level for anyone who is willing. This trend is particularly relevant to the 21st century in which design has been enthroned not only as an aesthetic but also as cultural icon, logo, empirical method, and signifier of value. This point provides the segue to branding as simultaneously instigative of disability containment and liberation from stigma.

DISABILITY AS LOGO: BRANDING

In contemporary western economies, design is closely related to branding. Given the emergence of branding from the fields of marketing and advertising, brands within this constrained conceptual framework are defined as the purposive design and ascription of logos to a product for the intent of public recognition, addition of value, and consumption, Of particular importance to disability explanations within the scaffold of branding is the construct of value-added. Interpreted broadly, the addition of value does not necessarily imply an increase or elevation, but denotes the cultural inscription of value that can span the continuum from extremely pejorative to most desirable.

More recently, scholars have enlarged the definitional scope of branding as a critical culturally embedded symbolic set that commodifies and reciprocally represents and shapes value, ideas, and identities. Brands are design stories that unfurl and take on meaning as they are articulated and shared by multiple authors, so to speak.

Because symbolism and dynamism both inhere in branding, Holt (2004) has suggested the term cultural branding, which elevates brands to the status of icon, and marker of identity and idea. While Holt's term is relatively new, the notion of branding as explanatory of one's cultural, social, and individual identity and comparative social worth was originated in the early and mid 20th century by thinkers such as Horkheimer, Adorono, Noerr, and Jepgcott (2002) and McKluhan and Fiore (2005). Although divergent in ontology and domain of concern, these scholars were seminal in introducing branding as an identity-inscribing and projecting entity. That is to say, through the process of choosing and adopting cultural iconography in the form of products, fashions, food, music, and so forth one ostensibly defines the self and displays value to others (Holt, 2004).

While grand narrative suggests that brands can be chosen to depict and publically display a preferred identity (McLuhan & Fiore, 2005) we do not necessarily agree with this principle as universal. Rather through post-postmodern analysis, the purposive nature of design and branding can be revealed as manipulating individuals and groups into believing that they can and do autonomously choose their identities when they cannot. The conceptual portal of design and branding viewed through a teleological lens splays open the purposive, political, and profit-driven nature of embodied labeling, identity formation and recognition, stereotyping, and responses that explain disability and give meaning to it both as a category and as a fiscally productive market. The explanatory importance of this conceptual framework lies in the processes and purposes of design and branding as deliberate, complex, and potentially able to manipulate meaning of self, others, and categories (Licht & O'Rourke, 2007). The result of branding, which can span exploitation through liberation, is dependent on depth of understanding as well as skill in putting this market strategy to work.

In previous work, we have examined how design of visuals, such as objects, brand those who use disability specific products as disabled (DePoy & Gilson, in press). However, design and branding reach out more expansively and abstractly in explaining disability populations and affixing their value. Visual logos do not have to be present in order for disability to be recognized and valuated or "branded." Understanding disability through the powerful contemporary post-post modern lens is particularly timely and thought provocative within advanced global market environments (DePoy & Gilson, in press; Pasquinelli, 2005).

In a recent presentation that we gave at the Society for Disability Studies in 2009, a participant remarked that marketing theory did not do explanatory justice to understanding disability as a cultural group that experiences social discrimination and exclusion. In concert with Riley (2006) we respectfully disagreed, suggesting that in the 21st century and consistent with post-postmodern thinking, disability is no longer exempt from the market economy, business, and its design and branding processes (Adair, 2002; Pullin, 2009; Riley, 2006). Rather this synthetic lens is seminal to explaining disability as marked, circumscribed, and commodified by designated products, spaces, and abstracts that not only brand its members but position them as a target market segment ripe for commodification and economic exploitation. However, this complex analysis reveals new actionable pathways to social change as well.

As early as 1992, Gill and then Albrecht, in 2001, published scholarship that revealed the economic advantage derived from disability by providers, professionals, product manufacturers, and so forth. DePoy and Gilson (2004) referred to this phenomenon as the disability industry and more recently, building on the work of Lukas (2007) and Bryman (2004), the disability park (DePoy & Gilson, 2008) in which economic survival and profit drive design of themed or branded spaces which too frequently trump the goals of facilitating meaningful, full participation in community, work, recreation, and civic life for people who are considered or identify themselves as disabled.

Our more recent thinking asserts that in the current global context, disability, economic advantage, and value-added design not only can co-exist but must do so in order to reveal and dismantle the disability park and replace it with value added branding for diverse bodies. Policy has a significant role in this design and branding effort as we now discuss.

POLICY AS DESIGNED AND BRANDED DISABILITY

Aligned with disability products, spaces, and services which serve to brand those who use and inhabit disability geographies and parks, the very design of disability policy as a separate entity is an exemplar of abstract (non-visual) branding through segmentation. We refer to this policy segment as disability explicit, in that policies that exclusively target disability retain the abstract of the disability park as separate. However, disability policy is not located solely within the disability explicit world. Policy responses to disability can be located within identity politic policies that create "special" responses for population subcategories (referred to as disability-embedded policy), or in disability implicit policies which do not name disability but design it as devalued and undesirable through other political mechanisms such as measurement, prevention, and so forth. We are not suggesting that prevention of injury and illness at any stage of human existence is pejorative. Rather, we are urging a post-postmodern examination of policy such as public health strategies, particularly with regard to how they design and brand the value of designed bodies, populations, and behaviors and then hang valued outcomes on these policy doorposts.

Within disability-explicit and some embedded policy, two major lexical divisions exist: policies that guide the provisions of disability services and resources, such as the Social Security Disability Insurance Act (SSDI) (established by the Social Security Amendments of 1956), in the United States, and more recently those, such as the Americans with Disabilities Act (ADA, 1990), The ADA Amendments Act (2008), and the UN Convention on the Rights of Persons with Disabilities that purport to protect and advance the civil rights of populations that are considered or identity as legitimately disabled.

Building on this binary taxonomy, we suggest that that policy is much more complex than its explicit verbiage and articulated outcomes. As noted by Kymlicka (2007) in his recent analysis of multiculturalism, global human rights policy is plagued by two overarching problems. The first is the failure of current categorical frameworks to do viable work in carving up humanity into useful categories. Kymlicka's assertion provides one of the foundational pillars of our view, as we question the legitimacy of so many diverse and vague explanations for disability and thus the usefulness of the category for achieving the asserted purposes of full participation.

The second problem identified by Kymlicka (2007) is the time sequence of designing and implementing targeted and generic policy. Applied to disability, we suggest that targeted distributive and protective legislation in itself designates and designs legitimate disability. Those who qualify for benefits and protections of disability policy are not only defined as disabled if they meet the explanatory criteria, but their lives are designed in order to maintain benefits.

We assert that separate disability policies, which we referred to above as disability explicit policy, institutionalize disability explanations and the disability park by partitioning and "logofying" abstract principles and language and applying them differentially to disabled and non-disabled individuals (Tregakis, 2004). As an example, above we noted that people who are considered disabled are enabled by disability explicit policy to obtain often without cost, but within the disability park, products which are branded as "assistive technology" while non-disabled people who use identical products use technology, or as Seymour (2008) asserts, use items branded as fashionable technology. Consider the need for help that is designed as part of disability identity in the word "assistive" and the inscription of this branded concept in the Assistive Technology Act passed in the United States in late 20th century.

Another consideration regarding the sequencing of targeted and generic policy was illuminated by Badinter (2006) in her discussion of gender equality. She suggested that the maintenance of "specialized rights and policies" negates their articulated aims of equality. This insidious process occurs by surreptitious design in which recipients of resources and rights only granted by specialized policies are defined by their eligibility for protection and thus continue to be branded as victims. Those who are covered under disability policy therefore are designed and branded as vulnerable, in need of specialized assistance, and in the disability park that provides employment and economic opportunity and advantage to providers and disability designers. Analysis of disability explicit and embedded policy reveals it as a grand narrative, a brand of designed identity policy that on the surface speaks of resources and equity, but in essence serves up populations identified or identifying as disabled or otherwise vulnerable to the disability park and thus designs disability by location of service consumer within the park.

Similarly, The UN Convention on the Rights of Persons with Disabilities, a disability-embedded policy in that other vulnerable groups are named as well, while theoretically enacted to raise awareness and reduce discrimination and disadvantage experienced by populations identified or identifying as disabled, is often persuasive in the abstract but lacks substantive content. Thus it is explanatory as well. The presence of specialized and protected policy worldwide and the location of disability adjacent to other groups design all of these groups as needy of legal protection rather than as citizens with the rights and responsibilities afforded to typical citizens.

Both nationally and internationally, we recognize the temporary value of these policies for redressing discrimination and exclusion, particularly in a context in which population specific policies and resources are the predominant distributive model. However, through a post-postmodern lens, the explicit intent of disability explicit and embedded policy is open for interrogation and analysis as the basis to advance social change and equality of opportunity in the long-term, and to move from the oxymoron of population specific equality to population-wide equality and justice.

Theorizing and practice of design and branding, therefore, are not only central but critical in framing responses that we see as promoting full juncture. We therefore urge disability scholars and activists to capture and use design, branding and market theorizing and related praxis not simply to bemoan exclusion and exploitation from others who apply these strategies to design and maintain the disability park but rather to harness these contemporary-

relevant ideas and skills to promote positive social change. Referring to Kymlica's (2007) criticisms of categorization and the timing of expanding specialized policy citizen-wide, design and branding have significant potential to redesign and rebrand bodies and environments to produce goodness of-fit and full juncture.

APPENDIX: DEFINITIONS OF DESIGN

- To create, fashion, execute, or construct according to plan: DEVISE, CONTRIVE (Merriam Webster, 2006–7)
- Means any design, logo, drawing, specification, printed matter, instructions or information (as appropriate) provided by the Purchaser in relation to the Goods (http://simply-small.com/tandc.html)
- Design is a set of fields for problem-solving that uses user-centric approaches to understand user needs (as well as business, economic, environmental, social, and other requirements) to create successful solutions that solve real problems. Design is often used as a process to create real change within a system or market. Too often, Design is defined only as visual problem solving or communication because of the predominance of graphic designers. (http://www.nathan.com/ed/glossary/)
- The plan or arrangement of elements in a work of art. The ideal is one where the assembled elements result in a unity or harmony. (http://www.worldimages.com/art%5fglossary.php)
- Both the process and the result of structuring the elements of visual form; composition. (http://www.ackland.org/tours/classes/glossary.html)
- A clear specification for the structure, organization, appearance, etc. of a deliverable. (http://www.portfoliostep.com/390.1TerminologyDefinitions.htm)

- Intend or have as a purpose; "She designed to go far in the world of business" (http://wordnet.princeton.edu/perl/webwn)
- A plan for arranging elements in a certain way as to best accomplish a particular purpose (Eames, 1969 in Munari, Eames, Guixe & Bey, 2003).

REFERENCES

Adair, V. (2002). *Branded with infamy: Inscriptions of poverty and class in the United States.* Chicago, IL: The University of Chicago Press.

Albrecht, G., Seelman, K., & Bury, M. (2001). *Disability studies handbook.* Thousand Oaks, CA: Sage.

Antonetta, S. (2007). *A mind apart: Travels in a neurodiverse world.* New York: Tarcher.

Badinter, E. (2006). *Dead end feminism.* Cambridge, UK: Polity Press.

Baudrillard, J. (1995). *Simulacra and simulation: The body in theory: histories of cultural materialism* (S. F. Glaser, Trans.). Ann Arbor, MI: University of Michigan Press.

Bryman, A. (2004). *The Disneyization of society.* Thousand Oaks, CA: Sage.

Bujega, M. (2005). *Interpersonal divide: The search for community in a technological age.* New York, NY: Oxford University Press.

Davis, L. (2003). *Bending over backwards: Disability dismodernism and other difficult positions.* New York, NY: New York University Press.

DePoy, E., & Gilson, S.F. (in press). Disability by design. *Review of Disability Studies.*

DePoy, E., & Gilson, S.F. (2008–2009, Winter). Social work practice with disability: Moving from the perpetuation of a client category to human rights and social justice. *Journal of Social Work Values and Ethics,* 5(3). Access: http://www.socialworker.com.avoserv.library.fordham.edu/jswve/content/view/103/66/.

DePoy, E., & Gilson S. (2008). Healing the disjuncture: Social work disability practice. In K.M. Sowers & C.N. Dulmus (Series Editors) & B.W. White (Vol. Ed.), *Comprehensive Handbook of Social Work and Social Welfare: Vol. 1. The Profession of Social Work* (pp. 267–282). Hoboken, NJ: Wiley.

DePoy, E., & Gilson, S.F. (2008). Designer diversity: Moving beyond categorical branding. *The Journal of Comparative Social Welfare,* 25, 59–70.

DePoy, E., & Gilson, S.F. (2004). *Rethinking disability: Principles for professional and social change.* Pacific Grove, CA: Brooks-Cole.

Fitzgibbon, K. (2005). *Who owns the past?* New Brunswick, NJ: Rutgers University Press.

Foster, H. (2003). *Design and crime (and other diatribes).* New York: Verso.

Fries, K. (2007). *The History of my shoes and the evolution of Darwin's theory.* Cambridge, MA: Da Capo Press.

Fussell, P. (1992). *Class: A guide through the American status system.* New York, NY: Touchstone.

Galician, M.L. (2004). *Handbook of product placement in the mass media: New strategies in marketing theory, practice, trends, and ethics.* New York, NY: Routledge.

Gill, C. (1992, November). Who gets the profits? Workplace oppression devalues the disability experience. *Mainstream,* 12, 14–17.

Gilson, S.F., & DePoy, E. (2007). DaVinci's ill-fated design legacy: Homogenization and standardization. *International Journal of the Humanities,* 4, http://www.HumanitiesJournal.com

Gilson, S.F., & DePoy, E. (2008). Explanatory legitimacy: A model for disability policy development and analysis. In I. Colby (Ed.). *Social Work Practice and Social Policy and Policy Practice.* Hoboken, NJ: John Wiley & Sons.

Gilson, S.F., & DePoy, E. (2005/2006). Reinventing atypical bodies in art, literature and technology. *International Journal of Technology, Knowledge and Society,* 3, 7, http://www.Technology-Journal.com.

Holt, D. B. (2004). *How brands become icons: The principles of cultural branding.* Cambridge, MA: Harvard Business School Press.

Horkheimer, M., Adorono, T. Noerr, G.S., & Jepgcott, E. (2002). *Dialectic of enlightenment.* Palo Alto, CA: Stanford University Press.

Kymlicka, W (2007). *Multicultural odysseys.* Oxford, UK: Oxford University Press.

Lefebvre, H. (1991). *The production of space.* Oxford, UK: Blackwell.

Licht, A. & O'Rourke, J. (2007). *Sound art: Beyond*

music, between categories. New York, NY: Rizzoli.

Little, J., & McDuff, D. (2008). *Body by science.* New York, NY: McGraw Hill.

Lukas, S. (2007). *The themed space: Locating culture, nation, and self.* Lexington, MA: Lexington Books.

Margolin, V. (2002). *The politics of the artificial: Essays on design and design studies.* Chicago, IL: University of Chicago Press.

McLuhan, M. & Fiore, Q. (2005). *The medium is the massage.* New York, NY: Ginko Press.

Merriam Webster, Inc. (2009). *Merriam Webster Online.* Retrieved January 4, 2009, from http://www.merriam-webster.com/

Munari, B., Eames, C, Eames, R., Guixe, M., & Bey, J. (2003). *Bright minds, beautiful ideas.* Amsterdam, NE: Bis.

Nussbaum, M. (2007). *Frontiers of justice.* New York, NY: Belnap.

Pasquinelli, M, (2005). An Assault on neurospace. Accessed: http://info.interactivist.net/node/4531

Phillips, S. (2008). Out from under: Disability, history and things to remember {zigzag} Dropping. Accessed. http://www.rom.on.ca/media/podcasts/out%5ffrom%5funder%5faudlo.php?id=5

Pullin, G. (2009). *Design meets disability.* Boston, MA: MIT Press.

Riley, C. (2006). *Disability and business.* Lebanon, NH: University of New England Press.

Salvendy, G. (2006). *Handbook of human factors and ergonomics.* Hoboken, NJ: Wiley.

Scott , A.O. (2008). Metropolis now. *NY Times Magazine Section,* June 9.

Seidel, K. (2004–2009). Neurodiversity Weblog. Retrieved July 4, 2009, from Neurodiversity.com: http://www.neurodiversity.com/main.html

Seymour, S. (2008). *Fashionable technology: The intersection of design, fashion, science, and technology.* New York: Springer.

Tregaskis, C. (2004). *Constructions of disability: researching the interface between disabled and nondisabled people.* London, UK: Routledge.

U.S. Department of Education, Office of Special Education and Rehabilitative Services, National Institute on Disability and Rehabilitation Research. (2007). NIDRR Long Range Plan For Fiscal Years 2005–09. Executive Summary. Accessed May 25, 2010 from http://www2.ed.gov/rschstat/research/…/nidrr-lrp-05-09-exec-summ.pdf

PART VII

*F*iction, Memoir, and Poetry

CHAPTER 36

Stones in My Pockets, Stones in My Heart

Eli Clare

Gender reaches into disability; disability wraps around class; class strains against abuse; abuse snarls into sexuality; sexuality folds on top of race . . . everything finally piling into a single human body. To write about any aspect of identity, any aspect of the body, means writing about this entire maze. This I know, and yet the question remains: where to start? Maybe with my white skin, stubbly red hair, left ear pierced, shoulders set slightly off center, left riding higher than right, hands tremoring, traced with veins, legs well-muscled. Or with me in the mirror, dressing to go out, knotting my tie, slipping into my blazer, curve of hip and breast vanishing beneath my clothes. Or possibly with the memory of how my body felt swimming in the river, chinook fingerlings nibbling at my toes. There are a million ways to start, but how do I reach beneath the skin?

*   *   *

Age 13, hair curling down around my ears, glasses threatening to slide off my nose, I work with my father every weekend building a big wooden barn of a house. I wear overalls, my favorite flannel shirt, sleeves rolled up over a long-john top, and well-worn work boots. Over the years, my mother and I have fought about my hair. I want to cut the curls off; she thinks they're pretty. All morning I have sawed 2 × 12 girders to length, helped my father pound them into place. I come home from the building site to pick up a crowbar and eat lunch. A hammer hangs from my hammer loop; a utility knife rides in my bib pocket. I ask my mother, "Am I feminine?" My memory stops here. I do not remember what possessed me to ask that question, what I wanted to know, what my mother answered.

*   *   *

Feminine. Female. Girl. I watched my younger sister spend hours in the bathroom with a curling iron, my mother with her nail file and eyebrow tweezers. I watched and listened to the girls in my school talk about boys, go behind the equipment shed to kiss them, later whisper in algebra class about fucking them. I watched from the other side of a stone wall, a wall that was part self-preservation, part bones and blood of aloneness, part the impossible assumptions I could not shape my body around.

Dresses. Make-up. High heels. Perfume. I tried wearing the skirts my mother sewed for me. She urged me into Girl Scouts, slumber parties, the 4-H knitting and sewing clubs. I failed, not wanting any part of these activities. I loved my work boots and overalls long after all the other girls had discovered pantyhose and mini-skirts. But failing left a hole in my heart; I wanted to belong somewhere.

Am I feminine? Maybe I meant: "What am I, a girl, a boy, something else entirely?" Maybe I meant: "Can I be a girl *like this*?" Or maybe I was simply trying to say: "Mama, I don't understand." What did I want her to say? At 13, I didn't have a clue what it meant to be feminine or, for that matter, masculine. Those words were empty signifiers, important only because I knew I was supposed to have an attachment to femininity. At 13, my most sustaining relations were not in the human world. I collected stones—red, green, gray, rust, white speckled with black, black streaked with silver—and kept them in my pockets, their hard surfaces warming slowly to my body heat. Spent long days at the river learning what I could from the salmon, frogs, and salamanders. Roamed the beaches at high tide and low, starfish, mussels, barnacles clinging to the rocks. Wandered in the hills thick with moss, fern, liverwort, bramble, tree. Only here did I have a sense of body. Those stones warm in my pockets, I knew them to be the steadiest, only inviolate parts of myself. I wanted to be a hermit, to live alone with my stones and trees, neither a boy nor a girl. And now 20 years later, how do I reach beneath the skin to write, not about the stones, but the body that warmed them, the heat itself?

*   *   *

I could start with the ways my body has been stolen from me. Start slowly, reluctantly, with my parents. My father who raised me, his eldest daughter, as an almost son. My father who started raping me so young I can't remember when he first forced his penis into me. My mother who tells me she didn't know about his violence. I believe her because I know how her spirit vacated the premises, leaving only her body as a marker. My mother who closed her eyes and turned her back, who said to my father, "She's yours to raise as you see fit." My mother who was shaped entirely by absence and my father who taught me the hills and woods: they were the first thieves.

But tell me, if I start here by placing the issues of violence and neglect on the table alongside my queerness, what will happen next? Will my words be used against me, twisted to bolster the belief that sexual abuse causes homosexuality, contorted to provide evidence that transgressive gender identity is linked directly to neglect? Most feminist and queer activists reject these linkages and for good reason. Conservatives often use them to discredit lesbian, gay, bi, and trans identities and to argue for our conversion rather than our liberation. But this strategy of denial, rejecting any possibility of connection between abuse and gender identity, abuse and sexuality, slams a door on the messy reality of how our bodies are stolen.

*   *   *

I question my mother about that day when I asked, "Am I feminine?" I hope she will remember my question and her answer and offer me some clues about what I wanted to know. She has no memory of that day, but reminds me of something else. One year during the long rainy season we called winter, the Lions Club held a carnival in the old, falling-down junior high gymnasium. I wasted money on "the man-eating fish," only to see Tiny Lawrence eating tuna from a can, laughed at the boys throwing wet sponges at the volunteer firemen, then stood watching a woman draw quick cartoon-like portraits, each signed "Betsy Hammond" with a flourish. She was new to town, and I, curious, eventually paid my dollar to sit down in front of her easel. I recognized myself in the resulting drawing, liked the hard lines that defined my face, the angle of my jaw, the toughness in my mouth.

Weeks later in the grocery store, my mother introduced herself to Betsy. They started talking about husbands and children, and soon my mother mentioned me, her eldest daughter, and the portrait I had brought home from the carnival. Betsy didn't know what my mother was talking about. Finally after much confusion, she asked, "Didn't I draw your son?" I remember the complete joy I felt when my mother came home with this story. I looked again and again at the portrait, thinking, "Right here, right now, I am a boy." It made me smile secretly for weeks, reach down into my pockets to squeeze a stone tight in each fist. I felt as if I were looking in a mirror and finally seeing myself, rather than some distorted fun-house image.

* * *

How do I write not about the stones, but the heat itself? I could start by asking some hard, risky questions. Really, I'd rather hang out with my ten-year-old self and share in her moment of glee as she looked in the mirror. But truly, those questions feel inevitable, and my boyhood pleasure turns cold when I dip into the messy reality of how my body was stolen. So, whatever the risk, let me ask.

How did my father's violence, his brutal taking of me over and over again, help shape and damage my body, my sexuality, my gender identity? How did his gendered abuse—and in this culture vaginal rape is certainly gendered—reinforce my sense of not being a girl? How did his non-abusive treatment of me as an almost son interact with the ways in which his fists and penis and knives told me in no uncertain terms that I was a girl? How did watching him sexually abuse other children—both boys

and girls—complicate what I knew of being girl, being boy? How did my mother's willful ignorance of the hurt he inflicted on me influence what I absorbed about femininity and masculinity?

* * *

Little did I know back then as I carried that carnival caricature home with me that the experience of being called sir, assumed to be a young man, would become a regular occurrence. This gender ambiguity, being seen as a woman at one turn and a teenage boy at the next, marks to a large extent my queerness. When people stumble over their pronouns, stammer, blush, or apologize in embarrassment, I often think of Riki Anne Wilchins' description of her friend Holly Boswell:

> Holly is a delicate Southern belle of long acquaintance. . . . S/he has tender features, long, wavy blonde hair, a soft Carolina accent, a delicate feminine bosom, and no interest in surgery. Holly lives as an open transgendered mother of two in Ashville, North Carolina. Her comforting advice to confused citizens struggling with whether to use Sir or Madam is, "Don't give it a second thought. You don't have a pronoun yet for me."[1]

Sometimes when I'm read as a woman, I actively miss hearing "sir," "ma'am" sounding foreign, distant, unfamiliar, even wrong to me. Usually I feel safer, somewhat buffered from men's violence against women, walking the streets after dark, knowing my night-time outline and stride are frequently read as male. But mostly, I feel matter-of-fact: "Oh yeah, this is happening again."

Many dykes feel angered, irritated, dismayed, shamed by the experience of being read as male, feel the need to assert their womanhood. And in the same vein, I hear all the time about gay men who pump up their masculinity. To defend and strengthen one's authentic gender identity is important. But all too often I hear defensiveness in the argument that butch dykes don't mimic men but carve out new ways of being women; in the gay male personals that dismiss femmes and drag queens out of hand. Is this our one and only response to a heterosexist world that refuses to recognize feminine males and masculine females, that challenges our very queerness?

In the past decade, the burgeoning transgender/transsexual movement has questioned and started to wage a struggle against the binary gender system that automatically links female-bodied people to femininity to womanhood and male-bodied people to masculinity to manhood. Even the binary of female-bodied and male-bodied appears more and more to be a social construction as intersexed people—people who for any number of reasons are born with or develop ambiguous genitals, reproductive organs, and/or secondary sex characteristics—begin to speak publicly of their lives and the medical intrusion they've faced. How natural are the rigid, mutually exclusive definitions of male and female if they have to be defended by genital surgery performed on intersexed people? The trans movement suggests a world full of gender and sex variation, a world much more complex than one divided into female-bodied women and male-bodied men. Many trans activists argue for an end, not to the genders of woman and man, but to the socially constructed binary.

Within this context, to answer the homophobes becomes easy, those folks who want to dehumanize, erase, make invisible the lives of butch dykes and nellie fags. We shrug. We laugh. We tell them: your definitions of woman and man suck. We tell them: your binary stinks. We say: here we are in all our glory—male, female, intersexed, trans, butch, nellie, studly, femme, king, androgynous, queen, some of us carving out new ways of being women, others of us new ways of being men, and still others new ways of being something else entirely. *You don't have pronouns yet for us.*

* * *

How do I write not about the stones, but the heat itself? I could start with the brutal, intimate details of my father's thievery, of his hands clamping around my neck, tearing into me, claiming my body as his own. The brutal, intimate details, but listen: I get afraid that the homophobes are right, that maybe in truth I live as a transgendered butch because he raped me, my mother neglected me. I lose the bigger picture, forget that woven through and around the private and intimate is always the public and political.

We live in a time of epidemic child abuse, in a world where sexual and physical violence against children isn't only a personal tragedy and a symptom of power run amok, but also a form of social control. When a father rapes his daughter, a mother beats her son, a white schoolteacher sexually fondles a Black student, a middle-class man uses a working-class boy to make child pornography, a nondisabled caregiver leaves a disabled kid to sit in her/his urine for hours, these adults teach children bodily lessons about power and hierarchy, about being boys, being girls, being children, being Black, being working-class, being disabled.

What better way to maintain a power structure—white supremacy, male supremacy, capitalism, a binary and rigid gender system—than to drill the lessons of who is dominant and who is subordinate into the bodies of children. No, not every individual perpetrator thinks, "This kid has stepped too far outside. I need to beat/rape her back into line." But certainly the power imbalances out of which child abuse arises are larger than any individual perpetrator's conscious intentions. Social control happens exactly at the junctures where the existing power structure is—consciously or not—maintained and strengthened.

And here is the answer to my fear. Child abuse is not the cause of but rather a response to—among other things—transgressive gender identity and/or sexuality. The theory I'm trying to shape is not as simple as "My father abused me because I was a queer child who—by the time I had any awareness of gender—was not at all sure of my girlness," although some genderqueer kids do get raped specifically because of their queerness. Rather I want to say, "My father raped me for many reasons, and inside his acts of violence I learned about what it meant to be female, to be a child, to live in my particular body, and those lessons served the larger power structure and hierarchy well."

*   *   *

At the same time, our bodies are not merely blank slates upon which the powers-that-be write their lessons. We cannot ignore the body itself: the sensory, mostly non-verbal experience of our hearts and lungs, muscles and tendons, telling us and the world who we are. My childhood sense of being neither girl nor boy arose in part from the external lessons of abuse and neglect, from the confusing messages about masculinity and femininity that I could not comprehend; I would be a fool to claim otherwise. But just as certainly, there was a knowing that resided in my bones, in the stretch of my legs and arch of my back, in the stones lying against my skin, a knowing that whispered, "not girl, not boy."

Butch, nellie, studly, femme, king, androgynous, queen: how have we negotiated the lies and thievery, the ways gender is influenced by divisions of labor, by images of masculinity and femininity, by racism, sexism, classism, ableism, by the notions of "real" men and "real" women? And how, at the same time, have we listened to our own bodies? For me the answer is not simple.

I think about my disabled body. For too long, I hated my trembling hands, my precarious balance, my spastic muscles so repeatedly overtaken by tension and tremor, tried to hide them at all costs. More than once I wished to amputate my right arm so it wouldn't shake. Self-mutilation is shame of the baldest kind. All the lies contained in the words *retard, monkey, defect*; in the gawking, the pats on my head, and the tears cried on my shoulder; in the moments where I became someone's supercrip or tragedy: all those lies became my second skin.

I think about my disabled body, how as a teenager I escaped the endless pressure to have a boyfriend, to shave my legs, to wear make-up. The same lies that cast me as genderless, asexual, and undesirable also framed a space in which I was left alone to be my quiet, bookish, tomboy self, neither girl nor boy. Even then, I was grateful. But listen, if I had wanted to date boys, wear lipstick and mascara, play with feminine clothes—the silk skirt and pumps, the low-cut blouse, the outrageous prom dress—I would have had to struggle much longer and harder than my nondisabled counterparts. The sheer physical acts of shaving my legs and putting on make-up would have been hard enough. Harder still would have been the relentless arguing with my parents, resisting their image of me as asexual or vulnerable to assault, persuading them that I could in truth take care of myself at the movies with Brent Miller or Dave Wilson.[2] But in truth I didn't want to date Brent or wear the low-cut blouse. I shuddered at the thought. How would I have reacted to the gendered pressures my younger, nondisabled sister faced? For her the path of least resistance pointed in the direction of femininity; for me it led toward not-girl-not-boy. But to cast my abiding sense of gendered self simply as a reaction to ableism is to ignore my body and what it had to tell me. When I look around me in disability community, I see an amazing range of gender expression, running the gamut from feminine to androgynous to masculine, mixed and swirled in many patterns. Clearly we respond in a myriad of ways to the ableist construction of gender.

How do we negotiate the lies and listen to our bodies? I think about my disabled body, my queer butch body read as a teenage boy. The markers of masculinity—my shaved head and broad stance, direct gaze and muscled arms—are unmistakable. And so are the markers of disability—my heavy-heeled gait; my halting, uneven speech; the tremors in my hands, arms, and shoulders. They all twine together to shape me in the ableist world as either genderless or a teenage boy. The first is all too familiar to disabled people. The second arises from the gender binary, where if I am not recognized as a woman, then I am presumed to be a man or more likely, given my lack of height and facial hair, a teenage boy. These external perceptions match in large part my internal sense of gender, my bodily comfort with gender ambiguity. But if the external and internal didn't match, what then?

Once I sat in a writing workshop with straight, feminine, disabled women, and we talked for an entire afternoon about gender identity, precisely because of the damage inflicted when the external ableist perceptions don't match the internal sense of self. All too often, the thieves plant their lies, and our bodies absorb them as the only truth. Is it any surprise that sometimes my heart fills with small gray stones, which never warm to my body heat?

* * *

The work of thieves: certainly external perception, stereotypes, lies, false images, and oppression hold a tremendous amount of power. They define and create who we are, how we think of our bodies, our gendered selves. How do I write not about the stones, but the body that warms them, the heat itself? That question haunts me because I lived by splitting body from mind, body from consciousness, body from physical sensation, body from emotion as the bullies threw rocks and called *retard,* as my father and his buddies tied me down, pulled out their knives. My body became an empty house, one to which I seldom returned. I lived in exile; the stones rattling in my heart, resting in my pockets, were my one and only true body.

But just as the stolen body exists, so does the reclaimed body. I think of disabled people challenging the conception of a "perfect" body/mind. Ed Roberts sits out front of his house talking about crip liberation. Ellen Stohl shapes herself into a sex symbol for the disability community. I think of queer people pushing upon the dominant culture's containment of gender, pleasure, and sex. Drag queens and kings work the stage. Dykes take to the streets. Gay men defend public sex. Trans people of all varieties say, "This is how we can be men, women, how we can inhabit all the spaces in between." Radical faeries swirl in their pagan finery. Bisexual people resist a neat compartmentalizing of sexuality. I think of people of color, poor people, working-class people all thumbing their noses at the notion of assimilation. Over and over again, we take the lies and crumble them into dust.

But how do I write about *my* body reclaimed, full of pride and pleasure? It is easy to say that abuse and ableism and homophobia stole my body away, broke my desire, removed me from my pleasure in the stones warm against my skin, the damp sponginess of moss growing on a rotten log, the taste of spring water dripping out of rock. Harder to express how that break becomes healed, a bone once fractured, now whole, but different from the bone never broken. And harder still to follow the path between the two. How do I mark this place where my body is no longer an empty house, desire whistling lonely through the cracks, but not yet a house fully lived in? For me the path from stolen body to reclaimed body started with my coming out as a dyke.

* * *

I was 18 and had just moved to the city. I didn't want to be a girl, nor was I a boy. I hid my body, tried as much as possible to ignore it. During my first week of college, I started meeting dykes. In three weeks I began asking, "Am I a lesbian?" Once before, I had faced this question and known the answer. The summer I was 12, two women, friends of my parents, came visiting from Arkansas. I adored Suzanne and Susan, showed them my favorite spots, the best blackberry brambles, where the muskrat built her den. I wanted them to stay with me in my river valley. They came out to my parents, and later I overheard my father say that Suzanne was gay, his face growing tight and silent. Somehow I knew what that word meant, even though I barely understood *homosexual* and had only heard *lesbian* as a taunt. It made me smile. The image of Suzanne and Susan holding hands as we walked Battle Rock Beach stuck with me for weeks. I knew somewhere deep inside me, rising up to press against my sternum, that I was like them. This I knew, but by the time I turned 13, it had vanished.

Now at the age of 18, I picked the question up again. I had never kissed a boy, never had a boyfriend or girlfriend. I knew nothing about sexual desire. For me sex was bound together with abuse. I had learned the details from my father just as I had learned how to mix a wheelbarrow of concrete, frame a stud wall. Sex meant rape—that simple, that complicated. The only thing I knew about desire was the raw, split-openness that rampaged through me after he was done, how those feelings could overtake my body again late at night in my own bed, mounting up uncontainably. I was not in love with a woman; I didn't even have a crush. And yet the question "Am I a lesbian?" hung with me.

I went to dyke events, read dyke books, listened to dyke music, hung out at my first dyke bar, went to my first dyke dance. I adored watching those women talk, laugh, hold hands, dance, kiss. Those soft butch women who would never have claimed their butchness then, during the lesbian-feminist androgyny of the '70s and early '80s. Those women with buzzed hair and well-defined biceps, jeans faded and soft. Those women who looked me in the eye. Watching them was like polishing my favorite stone to its brightest glint. I knew I could be *this* kind of woman and so slowly over the course of that year came to know myself as a dyke. I waited another four years to kiss a woman.

My coming out wasn't as much about discovering sexual desire and knowledge as it was about dealing with gender identity. Simply put, the disabled, mixed-class tomboy who asked her mother, "Am I feminine?" didn't discover a sexuality among dykes, but rather a definition of woman large enough to be comfortable for many years. And if that definition hadn't been large enough, what then? Would I have sought out hormones and/or surgery? If I had been born a hundred years ago when a specifically lesbian definition didn't exist, would I have been a "passing woman"? If I live long enough to see the world break free of the gender binary, will I find home not as a butch dyke, a woman by default, but as some third, fourth, fifth gender? Some gender that seems more possible since trans people have started to organize, build community, speak out about our lives. Some gender that I have already started reaching toward.

* * *

In queer community, I found a place to belong and abandoned my desire to be a hermit. Among crips, I learned how to embrace my strong, spastic body. Through feminist work around sexual violence—political activism, theoretical analysis, emotional recovery—I came to terms with the sexual abuse and physical torture done to me. And somewhere along the line, I pulled desire to the surface, gave it room to breathe. Let me write not about the stones, but the heat itself.

I think of the first woman I dated. She and I spent many nights eating pizza, watching movies, and talking halfway until dawn. I fell in love but never even kissed her, too afraid to even say, "This is what I want," much less to lean over and put my lips to hers. It made sense only years later when my memories of rape came flooding back. I think of the butch woman, once my lover, now a good friend. One night as we lay in bed, she told me, "I like when your hands tremble over my body. It feels good, like extra touching." Her words pushed against the lies. But all too often, sex was a bodiless, mechanical act for me as I repeatedly fled my body. We decided we'd be happier as friends. I think of the woman who called me her dream butchy *shiksa* and made me smile. I took so long to realize what had flared between us she almost gave up waiting. With her, desire traced my body, vivid and unmistakable, returning me to the taste of spring water, the texture of tree bark as I climbed toward sky. With her, I understood finally what it meant to want my hand on a lover's skin, the weight of a lover's body against mine. A bone long fractured, now mending.

I turn my pockets and heart inside out, set the stones—quartz, obsidian, shale, agate, scoria, granite—along the scoured top of the wall I once lived behind, the wall I still use for refuge. They shine in the sun, some translucent to the light, others dense, solid, opaque. I lean my body into the big unbreakable expanse, tracing which stones need to melt, which will crack wide, geode to crystal, and which are content just as they are.

* * *

But before I make it too simple, let me tell another story about coming to queer community, queer identity. Five or six years after I came out, I lived in Oakland, California, still learning the habits and manners of urban dykes. I remember a weekend when 20 of us, mostly dykes, helped move a friend from north Oakland to west Berkeley. The apartment filled with laughter as we carried endless boxes to the moving van, flexed our muscles over the couch, teased the lovers who sneaked a kiss in the empty closet. That mix of friends, lovers, and ex-lovers, butch dykes, femme dykes, androgynous dykes: we elbowed and jostled and gossiped. Leslie and I hauled a table to the van. On our way back, she off-handedly said how she was glad to be wearing her steel-toed boots, but that her feet were beginning to hurt. I wanted to get to know Leslie better. She was butch and knew it. I liked watching her from across the room, feeling something less than attraction but more than curiosity. I hadn't yet named myself butch but knew I had much in common with Leslie's butchness. So when she mentioned her steel-toed boots, I asked where she worked, assuming she'd have a story about forklifts or hi-los, a warehouse, bailer, mill, factory, or mine. I thought about the summer I was 15 working in the woods. I was the only girl who started the summer with work boots already broken in. The other girls envied me for weeks as they nursed their blistered feet. Leslie said, "I just bought them as a fashion statement." I felt as if I'd been exposed as a hick yet again, caught assuming she was someone I might have grown up with. *A fashion statement.* What did I have in common with Leslie? I felt the stones in my heart grind deep.

Today, more than decade after watching Leslie from across the room, I have settled into a certain butch identity. Often I don't feel drawn to the urban markers of being butch—the leather jacket, the steel-toed boots, the black-on-black look, the arc of chain from wallet to belt loop—but I do understand how certain clothes make me feel inside my body. I learned to dress by watching the loggers and fishermen I grew up around, learned to love t-shirts and torn jeans, dusty work boots and faded flannel shirts from them. The girls with whom I went to school also wore their share of flannel and denim, but when it came time to learn how to dress like "women," they turned to *Vogue* and *Glamour.* To emulate the dress of their working-class mothers was somehow shameful. They wanted their lessons to come from the middle- and upper-class beauty mags. The boys on the other hand never thought to dress like anyone except the working-class men around them. For me, *Vogue* and *Glamour* held none of the appeal that Walt Maya did, dressed in his checked shirt, cowboy boots, and wide-brimmed hat. I joined the boys in their emulation.

I knew early on the feel of boots and denim, knew I would never learn to walk in a skirt. I loved how my body felt as I swung an ax, how my mind felt as I worked through the last and hardest algebra problem in Mr. Johnson's advanced math class, the most elusive metaphor in Mr. Beckman's poetry class. I knew I never wanted a child or a husband. I knew these things but could never have put words to them, knew them in spite of all that stole me away from my body.

How did I "know" I never wanted a husband, would never learn to walk in a skirt? What does it mean when I write that I "felt" like neither a girl nor a boy? The words *know* and *feel* are slippery in their vagueness. I pull out an old photo of myself from the night of my high school graduation. I stand outside on our front deck; behind me are the deep greens of western Oregon in May. I wear a white dress, flowers embroidered on the front panel, the plainest, simplest dress my mother would let me buy. I look painfully uncomfortable, as if I have no idea what to do with my body, hands clasped awkwardly behind me, shoulders caved inward, immobilized, almost fearful beneath my smile. I am in clumsy, unconsenting drag. This is one of the last times I wore a dress. This is my body's definition of *know* and *feel.*

And yet those things I knew and felt were also deeply shaped and colored by the rural, white, working class culture of Port Orford. They were cradled not so much by an unconscious baby butch sensibility, but in a working-class town where at weddings and funerals everyone looked as if they had been stuffed into their dress clothes. They were nurtured in the small town hardware store and lumber yard, where, even though George always asked if I could handle the 50-pound bags of cement, I was Bob's eccentric, "handicapped" kid and was never told to stop. They were underlined by my parents' desperate upward scramble toward the middle class and their corresponding passion for formal education. They were molded by the common knowledge that most of the girls in town would catch their lives on too many kids, most of the boys on alcohol and guns, and only a few of us would leave the county for good.

*   *   *

The stolen body, the reclaimed body, the body that knows itself and the world, the stone and the heat which warms it: my body has never been singular. Disability snarls into gender. Class wraps around race. Sexuality strains against abuse. *This* is how to reach beneath the skin.

Friday nights I go to the local queer bar, nurse a single Corona, hang out with my dyke friends. Mostly I go to watch one of the wait staff, a woman with long brown hair, sharp nose, and ready smile. She flirts with everyone, moving table to table, making eye contact, hunkering down to have a quiet word or laugh amidst the noise. She flirts with me too, catching me in her wide smile, appreciative gaze. I am under no illusion: this is simply how she works her job. But after a lifetime of numbness I adore her attention, adore tipping back my chair, spreading my legs wide, and watching her from across the room.

I want to take the stone between my tremoring hands—trembling with CP, with desire, with the last remnants of fear, trembling because this is how my body moves—and warm it gentle, but not, as I have always done before, ride roughshod over it. I want to enter as a not-girl-not-boy transgendered butch—gendered differently than when I first came out, thinking simply, "*This* is how I'll be a woman," never imagining there might be a day when the word *woman* was too small; differently from the tomboy who wanted to be a hermit; but still connected to both. Enter with my pockets and heart half-full of stone. Enter knowing that the muscled grip of desire is a wild, half-grown horse, ready to bolt but too curious to stay away.

* * *

In the end, I will sit on the wide, flat top of my wall, legs dangling over those big, uncrackable stones, weathered smooth and clean. Sit with butch women, femme dykes, nellie men, studly fags, radical faeries, drag queens and kings, transsexual people who want nothing more than to be women and men, intersexed people, hermaphrodites with attitudes, transgendered, pangendered, bigendered, polygendered, ungendered, androgynous people of many varieties and trade stories long into the night. Laugh and cry and tell stories. Sad stories about bodies stolen, bodies no longer here. Enraging stories about false images, devastating lies, untold violence. Bold, brash stories about reclaiming our bodies and changing the world.

NOTES

1. Wilchins, Riki Anne, *Read My Lips* (Ithaca, New York: Firebrand Books, 1997), p. 118.
2. I now recognize the disturbing irony of this, given the ways in which my father was sexually using me.

CHAPTER 37

Unspeakable Conversations

Harriet McBryde Johnson

He insists he doesn't want to kill me. He simply thinks it would have been better, all things considered, to have given my parents the option of killing the baby I once was, and to let other parents kill similar babies as they come along and thereby avoid the suffering that comes with lives like mine and satisfy the reasonable preferences of parents for a different kind of child. It has nothing to do with me. I should not feel threatened.

Whenever I try to wrap my head around his tight string of syllogisms, my brain gets so fried it's . . . almost fun. Mercy! It's like "Alice in Wonderland."

It is a chilly Monday in late March, just less than a year ago. I am at Princeton University. My host is Prof. Peter Singer, often called—and not just by his book publicist—the most influential philosopher of our time. He is the man who wants me dead. No, that's not at all fair. He wants to legalize the killing of certain babies who might come to be like me if allowed to live. He also says he believes that it should be lawful under some circumstances to kill, at any age, individuals with cognitive impairments so severe that he doesn't consider them "persons." What does it take to be a person? Awareness of your own existence in time. The capacity to harbor preferences as to the future, including the preference for continuing to live.

At this stage of my life, he says, I am a person. However, as an infant, I wasn't. I, like all humans, was born without self-awareness. And eventually, assuming my brain finally gets so fried that I fall into that wonderland where self and other and present and past and future blur into one boundless, formless all or nothing, then I'll lose my personhood and therefore my right to life. Then, he says, my family and doctors might put me out of my misery, or out of my bliss or oblivion, and no one count it murder.

I have agreed to two speaking engagements. In the morning, I talk to 150 undergraduates on selective infanticide. In the evening, it is a convivial discussion, over dinner, of assisted suicide. I am the token cripple with an opposing view.

I had several reasons for accepting Singer's invitation, some grounded in my involvement in the disability rights movement, others entirely personal. For the movement, it seemed an unusual opportunity to experiment with modes of discourse that might work with very tough audiences and bridge the divide between our perceptions and theirs. I didn't expect to straighten out Singer's head, but maybe I could reach a student or two. Among the personal reasons: I was sure it would make a great story, first for telling and then for writing down.

By now I've told it to family and friends and colleagues, over lunches and dinners, on long car trips, in scads of e-mail messages and a couple of formal speeches. But it seems to be a story that just won't settle down. After all these tellings, it still lacks a coherent structure; I'm miles away from a rational argument. I keep getting interrupted by questions—like these:

Q: Was he totally grossed out by your physical appearance?

A: He gave no sign of it. None whatsoever.

Q: How did he handle having to interact with someone like you?

A: He behaved in every way appropriately, treated me as a respected professional acquaintance and was a gracious and accommodating host.

Q: Was it emotionally difficult for you to take part in a public discussion of whether your life should have happened?

A: It was very difficult. And horribly easy.

Q: Did he get that job at Princeton because they like his ideas on killing disabled babies?

A: It apparently didn't hurt, but he's most famous for animal rights. He's the author of "Animal Liberation."

Q: How can he put so much value on animal life and so little value on human life?

That last question is the only one I avoid. I used to say I don't know; it doesn't make sense. But now I've read some of Singer's writing, and I admit it does make sense—within the conceptual world of Peter Singer. But I don't want to go there. Or at least not for long.

So I will start from those other questions and see where the story goes this time.

That first question, about my physical appearance, needs some explaining.

It's not that I'm ugly. It's more that most people don't know how to look at me. The sight of me is routinely discombobulating. The power wheelchair is enough to inspire gawking, but that's the least of it. Much more impressive is the impact on my body of more than four decades of a muscle-wasting disease. At this stage of my life, I'm Karen Carpenter thin, flesh mostly vanished, a jumble of bones in a floppy bag of skin. When, in childhood, my muscles got too weak to hold up my spine, I tried a brace for a while, but fortunately a skittish anesthesiologist said no to fusion, plates and pins—all the apparatus that might have kept me straight. At 15, I threw away the back brace and let my spine reshape itself into a deep twisty S-curve. Now my right side is two deep canyons. To keep myself upright, I lean forward, rest my rib cage on my lap, plant my elbows beside my knees. Since my backbone found its own natural shape, I've been entirely comfortable in my skin.

I am in the first generation to survive to such decrepitude. Because antibiotics were available, we didn't die from the childhood pneumonias that often come with weakened respiratory systems. I guess it is natural enough that most people don't know what to make of us.

Two or three times in my life—I recall particularly one largely crip, largely lesbian cookout halfway across the continent—I have been looked at as a rare kind of beauty. There is also the bizarre fact that where I live, Charleston, S.C., some people call me Good Luck Lady: they consider it propitious to cross my path when a hurricane is coming and to kiss my head just before voting day. But most often the reactions are decidedly negative. Strangers on the street are moved to comment:

I admire you for being out; most people would give up.

God bless you! I'll pray for you.

You don't let the pain hold you back, do you?

If I had to live like you, I think I'd kill myself.

I used to try to explain that In fact I enjoy my life, that it's a great sensual pleasure to zoom by power chair on these delicious muggy streets, that I have no more reason to kill myself than most people. But it gets tedious. God didn't put me on this street to provide disability awareness training to the likes of them. In fact, no god put anyone anywhere for any reason, if you want to know.

But they don't want to know. They think they know everything there is to know, just by looking at me. That's how stereotypes work. They don't know that they're confused, that they're really expressing the discombobulation that comes in my wake.

So. What stands out when I recall first meeting Peter Singer in the spring of 2001 is his apparent Immunity to my looks, his apparent lack of discombobulation, his immediate ability to deal with me as a person with a particular point of view.

Then, 2001. Singer has been invited to the College of Charleston, not two blocks from my house. He is to lecture on "Rethinking Life and Death." I have been dispatched by Not Dead Yet, the national organization leading the disability-rights opposition to legalized assisted suicide and disability-based killing. I am to put out a leaflet and do something during the Q. and A.

On arriving almost an hour early to reconnoiter, I find the scene almost entirely peaceful; even the boisterous display of South Carolina spring is muted by gray wisps of Spanish moss and mottled oak bark.

I roll around the corner of the building and am confronted with the unnerving sight of two people I know sitting on a park bench eating veggie pitas with Singer. Sharon is a veteran activist for human rights. Herb is South Carolina's most famous atheist. Good people, I've always thought—now sharing veggie pitas and conversation with a proponent of genocide. I try to beat a retreat, but Herb and Sharon have seen mo. Sharon tosses her trash and comes over. After we exchange the usual courtesies, she asks, "Would you like to meet Professor Singer?"

She doesn't have a clue. She probably likes his book on animal rights. "I'll just talk to him in the Q. and A."

But Herb, with Singer at his side, is fast approaching. They are looking at me, and Herb is talking, no doubt saying nice things about me. He'll be saying that I'm a disability rights lawyer and that I gave a talk against assisted suicide at his secular humanist group a while back. He didn't agree with everything I said, he'll say, but I was brilliant. Singer appears interested, engaged. I sit where I'm parked. Herb makes an introduction. Singer extends his hand.

I hesitate. I shouldn't shake hands with the Evil One. But he is Herb's guest, and I simply can't snub Herb's guest at the college where Herb teaches. Hereabouts, the rule is that if you're not prepared to shoot on sight, you have to be prepared to shake hands. I give Singer the three fingers on my right hand that still work. "Good afternoon, Mr. Singer. I'm here for Not Dead Yet." I want to think he flinches just a little. Not Dead Yet did everything possible to disrupt his first week at Princeton. I sent a check to the fund for the 14 arrestees, who included comrades in power chairs. But if Singer flinches, he instantly recovers. He answers my questions about the lecture format. When he says he looks forward to an interesting exchange, he seems entirely sincere.

It is an interesting exchange. In the lecture hall that afternoon, Singer lays it all out. The "illogic" of allowing abortion but not infanticide, of allowing withdrawal of life support but not active killing. Applying the basic assumptions of preference utilitarianism, he spins out his bone-chilling argument for letting parents kill disabled babies and replace them with nondisabled babies who have a greater chance at happiness. It is all about allowing as many individuals as possible to fulfill as many of their preferences as possible.

As soon as he's done, I get the microphone and say I'd like to discuss selective infanticide. As a lawyer, I disagree with his jurisprudential assumptions. Logical inconsistency is not a sufficient reason to change the law. As an atheist, I object to his using religious terms ("the doctrine of the sanctity of human life") to characterize his critics. Singer takes a note pad out of his pocket and jots down my points, apparently eager to take them on, and I proceed to the heart of my argument: that the presence or absence of a disability doesn't predict quality of life. I question his replacement-baby theory, with its assumption of "other things equal," arguing that people are not fungible. I draw out a comparison of myself and my nondisabled brother Mac (the next-born after me), each of us with a combination of gifts and flaws so peculiar that we can't be measured on the same scale.

He responds to each point with clear and lucid counterarguments. He proceeds with the assumption that I am one of the people who might rightly have been killed at birth. He sticks to his guns, conceding just enough to show himself open-minded and flexible. We go back and forth for 10 long minutes. Even as I am horrified by what he says, and by the fact that I have been sucked into a civil discussion of whether I ought to exist, I can't help being dazzled by his verbal facility. He is so respectful, so free of condescension, so focused on the argument, that by the time the show is over, I'm not exactly angry with him. Yes, I am shaking, furious, enraged—but it's for the big room, 200 of my fellow Charlestonians who have listened with polite interest, when in decency they should have run him out of town on a rail.

My encounter with Peter Singer merits a mention in my annual canned letter that December. I decide to send Singer a copy. In response, he sends me the nicest possible e-mail message. Dear Harriet (if he may) . . . Just back from Australia, where he's from. Agrees with my comments on the world situation. Supports my work against institutionalization. And then some pointed questions to clarify my views on selective infanticide.

I reply. Fine, call me Harriet, and I'll reciprocate in the interest of equality, though I'm accustomed to more formality. Skipping agreeable preambles, I answer his questions on disability-based infanticide and pose some of my own. Answers and more questions come back. Back and forth over several weeks it proceeds, an engaging discussion of baby killing, disability prejudice and related points of law and philosophy. Dear Harriet. Dear Peter.

Singer seems curious to learn how someone who is as good an atheist as he is could disagree with his entirely reasonable views. At the same time, I am trying to plumb his theories. What has him so convinced it would be best to allow parents to kill babies with severe disabilities, and not other kinds of babies, if no infant is a "person" with a right to life? I learn it is partly that both biological and adoptive parents prefer healthy babies. But I have trouble with basing life-and-death decisions on market considerations when the market is structured by prejudice. I offer a hypothetical comparison: "What about mixed-race babies, especially when the combination is entirely nonwhite, who I believe are just about as unadoptable as babies with disabilities?" Wouldn't a law allowing the killing of these undervalued babies validate race prejudice? Singer agrees there is a problem. "It would be horrible," he says, "to see mixed-race babies being killed because they can't be adopted, whereas white ones could be." What's the difference? Preferences based on race are unreasonable. Preferences based on ability are not. Why? To Singer, it's pretty simple: disability makes a person "worse off."

Are we "worse off"? I don't think so. Not in any meaningful sense. There are too many variables. For those of us with congenital conditions, disability shapes all we are. Those disabled later in life adapt. We take constraints that no one would choose and build rich and satisfying lives within them. We enjoy pleasures other people enjoy, and pleasures peculiarly our own. We have something the world needs.

Pressing me to admit a negative correlation between disability and happiness, Singer presents a situation: imagine a disabled child on the beach, watching the other children play.

It's right out of the telethon. I expected something more sophisticated from a professional thinker. I respond. "As a little girl playing on the beach, I was already aware that some people felt sorry for me, that I wasn't frolicking with the same level of frenzy as other children. This annoyed me, and still does." I take the time to write a detailed description of how I, in fact, had fun playing on the beach, without the need of standing, walking or running. But, really, I've had enough. I suggest to Singer that we have exhausted our topic, and I'll be back in touch when I get around to writing about him.

He responds by inviting me to Princeton. I fire off an immediate maybe.

Of course I'm flattered. Mama will be impressed.

But there are things to consider. Not Dead Yet says—and I completely agree—that we should not legitimate Singer's views by giving them a forum. We should not make disabled lives subject to debate. Moreover, any spokesman chosen by the opposition is by definition a token. But even if I'm a token, I won't have to act like one. And anyway, I'm kind of stuck. If I decline, Singer can make some hay: "I offered them a platform, but they refuse rational discussion." It's an old trick, and I've laid myself wide open.

My invitation is to have an exchange of views with Singer during his undergraduate course. He also proposes a second "exchange," open to the whole university, later in the day. This sounds a lot like debating my life—and on my opponent's turf, with my opponent moderating, to boot. I offer a counterproposal, to which Singer proves amenable. I will open the class with some comments on infanticide and related issues and then let Singer grill me as hard as he likes before we open it up for the students. Later in the day, I might take part in a discussion of some other disability issue in a neutral forum. Singer suggests a faculty-student discussion group sponsored by his department but with cross-departmental membership. The topic I select is "Assisted Suicide, Disability Discrimination and the Illusion of Choice: A Disability Rights Perspective." I inform a few movement colleagues of this turn of events, and advice starts rolling in. I decide to go with the advisers who counsel me to do the gig, lie low and get out of Dodge.

I ask Singer to refer me to the person who arranges travel at Princeton. I imagine some capable and unflappable woman like my sister, Beth, whose varied job description at a North Carolina university includes handling visiting artists. Singer refers me to his own assistant, who certainly seems capable and unflappable enough. However, almost immediately Singer jumps back in via e-mail. It seems the nearest hotel has only one wheelchair-accessible suite, available with two rooms for $600 per night. What to do? I know I shouldn't be so accommodating, but I say I can make do with an inaccessible room if it has certain features. Other logistical issues come up. We go back and forth. Questions and answers. Do I really need a lift-equipped vehicle at the airport? Can't my assistant assist me into a conventional car? How wide is my wheelchair?

By the time we're done, Singer knows that I am 28 inches wide. I have trouble controlling my wheelchair if my hand gets cold. I am accustomed to driving on rough, irregular surfaces, but I get nervous turning on steep slopes. Even one step is too many. I can swallow purées, soft bread and grapes. I use a bedpan, not a toilet. None of this is a secret; none of it cause for angst. But I do wonder whether Singer is jotting down my specs in his little note pad as evidence of how "bad off" people like me really are.

I realize I must put one more issue on the table: etiquette. I was criticized within the movement when I confessed to shaking Singer's hand in Charleston, and some are appalled that I have agreed to break bread with him in Princeton. I think they have a very good point, but, again, I'm stuck. I'm engaged for a day of discussion, not a picket line. It is not in my power to marginalize Singer at Princeton; nothing would be accomplished by displays of personal disrespect. However, chumminess is clearly inappropriate. I tell Singer that in the lecture hall it can't be Harriet and Peter; it must be Ms. Johnson and Mr. Singer.

He seems genuinely nettled. Shouldn't it be Ms. Johnson and Professor Singer, if I want to be formal? To counter, I invoke the ceremonial low-country usage, Attorney Johnson and Professor Singer, but point out that Mr./Ms. is the custom in American political debates and might seem more normal in New Jersey. All right, he says. Ms./Mr. it will be.

I describe this awkward social situation to the lawyer in my office who has served as my default lunch partner for the past 14 years. He gives forth a full-body shudder.

"That poor, sorry son of a bitch! He has no idea what he's in for."

Being a disability rights lawyer lecturing at Princeton does confer some cachet at the Newark airport. I need all the cachet I can get. Delta Airlines has torn up my power chair. It is a fairly frequent occurrence for any air traveler on wheels.

When they inform me of the damage in Atlanta, I throw a monumental fit and tell them to have a repair person meet me in Newark with new batteries to replace the ones inexplicably destroyed. Then I am told no new batteries can be had until the morning. It's Sunday night. On arrival in Newark, I'm told of a plan to put me up there for the night and get me repaired and driven to Princeton by 10 a.m.

"That won't work. I'm lecturing at 10. I need to get there tonight, go to sleep and be in my right mind tomorrow."

"What? You're lecturing? They told us it was a conference. We need to get you fixed tonight!"

Carla, the gate agent, relieves me of the need to throw any further fits by undertaking on my behalf the fit of all fits.

Carmen, the personal assistant with whom I'm traveling, pushes me in my disabled chair around the airport in search of a place to use the bedpan. However, instead of diaper-changing tables, which are functional though far from private, we find a flip-down plastic shelf that doesn't look like it would hold my 70 pounds of body weight. It's no big deal; I've restricted my fluids. But Carmen is a little freaked. It is her first adventure in power-chair air travel. I thought I prepared her for the trip, but I guess I neglected to warn her about the probability of wheelchair destruction. I keep forgetting that even people who know me well don't know much about my world.

We reach the hotel at 10:15 p.m., four hours late.

I wake up tired. I slept better than I would have slept in Newark with an unrepaired chair, but any hotel bed is a near guarantee of morning crankiness. I tell Carmen to leave the TV off. I don't want to hear the temperature.

I do the morning stretch. Medical people call it passive movement, but it's not really passive. Carmen's hands move my limbs, following my precise instructions, her strength giving effect to my will. Carmen knows the routine, so it is in near silence that we begin easing slowly into the day. I let myself be propped up to eat oatmeal and drink tea. Then there's the bedpan and then bathing and dressing, still in bed. As the caffeine kicks in, silence gives way to conversation about practical things. Carmen lifts me into my chair and straps a rolled towel under my ribs for comfort and stability. She tugs at my clothes to remove wrinkles that could cause pressure sores. She switches on my motors and gives me the means of moving without anyone's help. They don't call it a power chair for nothing.

I drive to the mirror. I do my hair in one long braid. Even this primal hairdo requires, at this stage of my life, joint effort. I undo yesterday's braid, fix the part and comb the hair in front. Carmen combs where I can't reach. I divide the mass into three long hanks and start the braid just behind my left ear. Section by section, I hand it over to her, and her unimpaired young fingers pull tight, crisscross, until the braid is fully formed.

A big polyester scarf completes my costume. Carmen lays it over my back. I tie it the way I want it, but Carmen starts fussing with it, trying to tuck it down in the back. I tell her that it's fine, and she stops.

On top of the scarf, she wraps the two big shawls that I hope will substitute for an overcoat. I don't own any real winter clothes. I just stay out of the cold, such cold as we get in Charleston.

We review her instructions for the day. Keep me in view and earshot. Be instantly available but not intrusive. Be polite, but don't answer any questions about me. I am glad that she has agreed to come. She's strong, smart, adaptable and very loyal. But now she is digging under the shawls, fussing with that scarf again.

"Carmen. What are you doing?"

"I thought I could hide this furry thing you sit on."

"Leave it. Singer knows lots of people eat meat. Now he'll know some crips sit on sheepskin."

The walk is cold but mercifully short. The hotel is just across the street from Princeton's wrought-iron gate and a few short blocks from the building where Singer's assistant shows us to the elevator. The elevator doubles as the janitor's closet—the cart with the big trash can and all the accouterments is rolled aside so I can get in. Evidently there aren't a lot of wheelchair people using this building.

We ride the broom closet down to the basement and are led down a long passageway to a big lecture hall. As the students drift in, I engage in light badinage with the sound technician. He is squeamish about touching me, but I insist that the cordless lavaliere is my mike of choice. I invite him to clip it to the big polyester scarf.

The students enter from the rear door, way up at ground level, and walk down stairs to their seats. I feel like an animal in the zoo. I hadn't reckoned on the architecture, those tiers of steps that separate me from a human wall of apparent physical and mental perfection, that keep me confined down here in my pit.

It is 5 before 10. Singer is loping down the stairs. I feel like signaling to Carmen to open the door, summon the broom closet and get me out of here. But Singer greets me pleasantly and hands me Princeton's check for $500, the fee he offered with apologies for its inadequacy.

So. On with the show.

My talk to the students is pretty Southern. I've decided to pound them with heart, hammer them with narrative and say "y'all" and "folks." I play with the emotional tone, giving them little peaks and valleys, modulating three times in one 45-second patch. I talk about justice. Even beauty and love. I figure they haven't been getting much of that from Singer.

Of course, I give them some argument too. I mean to honor my contractual obligations. I lead with the hypothetical about mixed-race, nonwhite babies and build the ending around the question of who should have the burden of proof as to the quality of disabled lives. And woven throughout the talk is the presentation of myself as a representative of a minority group that has been rendered invisible by prejudice and oppression, a participant in a discussion that would not occur in a just world.

I let it go a little longer than I should. Their faces show they're going where I'm leading, and I don't look forward to letting them go. But the clock on the wall reminds me of promises I mean to keep, and I stop talking and submit myself to examination and inquiry.

Singer's response is surprisingly soft. Maybe after hearing that this discussion is insulting and painful to me, he doesn't want to exacerbate my discomfort. His reframing of the issues is almost pro forma, abstract, entirely impersonal. Likewise, the students' inquiries are abstract and fairly predictable: anencephaly, permanent unconsciousness, eugenic abortion. I respond to some of them with stories, but mostly I give answers I could have e-mailed in.

I call on a young man near the top of the room.

"Do you eat meat?"

"Yes, I do."

"Then how do you justify—"

"I haven't made any study of animal rights, so anything I could say on the subject wouldn't be worth everyone's time."

The next student wants to work the comparison of disability and race, and Singer joins the discussion until he elicits a comment from me that he can characterize as racist. He scores a point, but that's all right. I've never claimed to be free of prejudice, just struggling with it.

Singer proposes taking me on a walk around campus, unless I think it would be too cold. What the hell? "It's probably warmed up some. Let's go out and see how I do."

He doesn't know how to get out of the building without using the stairs, so this time it is my assistant leading the way. Carmen has learned of another elevator, which arrives empty. When we get out of the building, she falls behind a couple of paces, like a respectful chaperone.

In the classroom there was a question about keeping alive the unconscious. In response, I told a story about a family I knew as a child, which took loving care of a nonresponsive teenage girl, acting out their unconditional commitment to each other, making all the other children, and me as their visitor, feel safe. This doesn't satisfy Singer. "Let's assume we can prove, absolutely, that the individual is totally unconscious and that we can know, absolutely, that the individual will never regain consciousness."

I see no need to state an objection, with no stenographer present to record it; I'll play the game and let him continue.

"Assuming all that," he says, "don't you think continuing to take care of that individual would be a bit—weird?"

"No. Done right, it could be profoundly beautiful."

"But what about the caregiver, a woman typically, who is forced to provide all this service to a family member, unable to work, unable to have a life of her own?"

"That's not the way it should be. Not the way it has to be. As a society, we should pay workers to provide that care, in the home. In some places, it's been done that way for years. That woman shouldn't be forced to do it, any more than my family should be forced to do my care."

Singer takes me around the architectural smorgasbord that is Princeton University by a route that includes not one step, unramped curb or turn on a slope. Within the strange limits of this strange assignment, it seems Singer is doing all he can to make me comfortable.

He asks what I thought of the students' questions.

"They were fine, about what I expected. I was a little surprised by the question about meat eating."

"I apologize for that. That was out of left field. But—I think what he wanted to know is how you can have such high respect for human life and so little respect for animal life."

"People have lately been asking me the converse, how you can have so much respect for animal life and so little respect for human life."

"And what do you answer?"

"I say I don't know. It doesn't make a lot of sense to me."

"Well, in my view—"

"Look. I have lived in blissful ignorance all these years, and I'm not prepared to give that up today."

"Fair enough," he says and proceeds to recount bits of Princeton history. He stops. "This will be of particular interest to you, I think. This is where your colleagues with Not Dead Yet set up their blockade." I'm grateful for the reminder. My brothers and sisters were here before me and behaved far more appropriately than I am doing.

A van delivers Carmen and me early for the evening forum. Singer says he hopes I had a pleasant afternoon.

Yes, indeed. I report a pleasant lunch and a very pleasant nap, and I tell him about the Christopher Reeve Suite in the hotel, which has been remodeled to accommodate Reeve, who has family in the area.

"Do you suppose that's the $600 accessible suite they told me about?"

"Without doubt. And if I'd known it was the Christopher Reeve Suite, I would have held out for it."

"Of course you would have!" Singer laughs. "And we'd have had no choice, would we?"

We talk about the disability rights critique of Reeve and various other topics. Singer is easy to talk to, good company. Too bad he sees lives like mine as avoidable mistakes.

I'm looking forward to the soft vegetarian meal that has been arranged; I'm hungry. Assisted suicide, as difficult as it is, doesn't cause the kind of agony I felt discussing disability-based infanticide. In this one, I understand, and to some degree can sympathize with, the opposing point of view—misguided though it is.

My opening sticks to the five-minute time limit. I introduce the issue as framed by academic articles Not Dead Yet recommended for my use. Andrew Batavia argues for assisted suicide based on autonomy, a principle generally held high in the disability rights movement. In general, he says, the movement fights for our right to control our own lives; when we need assistance to effect our choices, assistance should be available to us as a matter of right. If the choice is to end our lives, he says, we should have assistance then as well. But Carol Gill says that it is differential treatment—disability discrimination—to try to prevent most suicides while facilitating the suicides of ill and disabled people. The social-science literature suggests that the public in general, and physicians in particular, tend to underestimate the quality of life of disabled people, compared with our own assessments of our lives. The case for assisted suicide rests on stereotypes that our lives are inherently so bad that it is entirely rational if we want to die.

I side with Gill. What worries me most about the proposals for legalized assisted suicide is their veneer of beneficence—the medical determination that, for a given individual, suicide is reasonable or right. It is not about autonomy but about nondisabled people telling us what's good for us.

In the discussion that follows, I argue that choice is illusory in a context of pervasive inequality. Choices are structured by oppression. We shouldn't offer assistance with suicide until we all have the assistance we need to get out of bed in the morning and live a good life. Common causes of suicidality—dependence, institutional confinement, being a burden—are entirely curable. Singer, seated on my right, participates in the discussion but doesn't dominate it. During the meal, I occasionally ask him to put things within my reach, and he competently complies.

I feel as if I'm getting to a few of them, when a student asks me a question. The words are all familiar, but they're strung together in a way so meaningless that I can't even retain them—it's like a long sentence in Tagalog. I can only admit my limitations. "That question's too abstract for me to deal with. Can you rephrase it?"

He indicates that it is as clear as he can make it, so I move on.

A little while later, my right elbow slips out from under me. This is awkward. Normally I get whoever is on my right to do this sort of thing. Why not now? I gesture to Singer. He leans over, and I whisper, "Grasp this wrist and pull forward one inch, without lifting." He follows my instructions to the letter. He sees that now I can again reach my food with my fork. And he may now understand what I was saying a minute ago, that most of the assistance disabled people need does not demand medical training.

A philosophy professor says, "It appears that your objections to assisted suicide are essentially tactical."

"Excuse me?"

"By that I mean they are grounded in current conditions of political, social and economic inequality. What if we assume that such conditions do not exist?"

"Why would we want to do that?"

"I want to get to the real basis for the position you take."

I feel as if I'm losing caste. It is suddenly very clear that I'm not a philosopher. I'm like one of those old practitioners who used to visit my law school, full of bluster about life in the real world. Such a bore! A once-sharp mind gone muddy! And I'm only 44—not all that old.

The forum is ended, and I've been able to eat very little of my puréed food. I ask Carmen to find the caterer and get me a container. Singer jumps up to take care of it. He returns with a box and obligingly packs my food to go.

When I get home, people are clamoring for the story. The lawyers want the blow-by-blow of my forensic triumph over the formidable foe; when I tell them it wasn't like that, they insist that it was. Within the disability rights community, there is less confidence. It is generally assumed that I handled the substantive discussion well, but people worry that my civility may have given Singer a new kind of legitimacy. I hear from Laura, a beloved movement sister. She is appalled that I let Singer provide even minor physical assistance at the dinner. "Where was your assistant?" she wants to know. How could I put myself in a relationship with Singer that made him appear so human, even kind?

I struggle to explain. I didn't feel disempowered; quite the contrary, it seemed a good thing to make him do some useful work. And then, the hard part: I've come to believe that Singer actually is human, even kind in his way. There ensues a discussion of good and evil and personal assistance and power and philosophy and tactics for which I'm profoundly grateful.

I e-mail Laura again. This time I inform her that I've changed my will. She will inherit a book that Singer gave me, a collection of his writings with a weirdly appropriate inscription: "To Harriet Johnson, So that you will have a better answer to questions about animals. And thanks for coming to Princeton. Peter Singer. March 25, 2002." She responds that she is changing her will, too. I'll get the autographed photo of Jerry Lewis she received as an M.D.A. poster child. We joke that each of us has given the other a "reason to live."

I have had a nice e-mail message from Singer, hoping Carmen and I and the chair got home without injury, relaying positive feedback from my audiences—and taking me to task for a statement that isn't supported by a relevant legal authority, which he looked up. I report that we got home exhausted but unharmed and concede that he has caught me in a generalization that should have been qualified. It's clear that the conversation will continue.

I am soon sucked into the daily demands of law practice, family, community and politics. In the closing days of the state legislative session, I help get a bill passed that I hope will move us one small step toward a world in which killing won't be such an appealing solution to the "problem" of disability. It is good to focus on this kind of work. But the conversations with and about Singer continue. Unable to muster the appropriate moral judgments, I ask myself a tough question: am I in fact a silly little lady whose head is easily turned by a man who gives her a kind of attention she enjoys? I hope not, but I confess that I've never been able to sustain righteous anger for more than about 30 minutes at a time. My view of life tends more toward tragedy.

The tragic view comes closest to describing how I now look at Peter Singer. He is a man of unusual gifts, reaching for the heights. He writes that he is trying to create a system of ethics derived from fact and reason, that largely throws off the perspectives of religion, place, family, tribe, community and maybe even species—to "take the point of view of the universe," His is a grand, heroic undertaking.

But like the protagonist in a classical drama, Singer has his flaw. It is his unexamined assumption that disabled people are inherently "worse off," that we "suffer," that we have lesser "prospects of a happy life." Because of this all-too-common prejudice, and his rare courage in taking it to its logical conclusion, catastrophe looms. Here in the midpoint of the play, I can't look at him without fellow-feeling.

I am regularly confronted by people who tell me that Singer doesn't deserve my human sympathy. I should make him an object of implacable wrath, to be cut off, silenced, destroyed absolutely. And I find myself lacking a logical argument to the contrary.

I am talking to my sister Beth on the phone. "You kind of like the monster, don't you?" she says.

I find myself unable to evade, certainly unwilling to lie. "Yeah, in a way. And he's not exactly a monster."

"You know, Harriet, there were some very pleasant Nazis. They say the SS guards went home and played on the floor with their children every night."

She can tell that I'm chastened; she changes the topic, lets me off the hook. Her harshness has come as a surprise. She isn't inclined to moralizing; in our family, I'm the one who sets people straight.

When I put the phone down, my argumentative nature feels frustrated. In my mind, I replay the conversation, but this time defend my position.

"He's not exactly a monster. He just has some strange ways of looking at things."

"He's advocating genocide."

"That's the thing. In his mind, he isn't. He's only giving parents a choice. He thinks the humans he is talking about aren't people, aren't 'persons.'"

"But that's the way it always works, isn't it? They're always animals or vermin or chattel goods. Objects, not persons. He's repackaging some old ideas. Making them acceptable."

"I think his ideas are new, in a way. It's not old-fashioned hate. It's a twisted, mis-informed, warped kind of beneficence. His motive is to do good."

"What do you care about motives?" she asks. "Doesn't this beneficent killing make disabled brothers and sisters just as dead?"

"But he isn't killing anyone. It's just talk."

"Just talk? It's talk with an agenda, talk aimed at forming policy. Talk that's get-ting a receptive audience. You of all people know the power of that kind of talk."

"Well, sure, but—"

"If talk didn't matter, would you make it your life's work?"

"But," I say, "his talk won't matter in the end. He won't succeed in reinventing morality. He stirs the pot, brings things out into the open. But ultimately we'll make a world that's fit to live in, a society that has room for all its flawed creatures. History will remember Singer as a curious example of the bizarre things that can happen when paradigms collide."

"What if you're wrong? What if he con-vinces people that there's no morally sig-nificant difference between a fetus and a newborn, and just as disabled fetuses are routinely aborted now, so disabled babies are routinely killed? Might some future generation take it further than Singer wants to go? Might some say there's no morally significant line between a newborn and a 3-year-old?"

"Sure. Singer concedes that a bright line cannot be drawn. But he doesn't propose killing anyone who prefers to live."

"That overarching respect for the indi-vidual's preference for life—might some

say it's a fiction, a fetish, a quasi-religious belief?"

"Yes," I say. "That's pretty close to what I think. As an atheist, I think all preferences are moot once you kill someone. The injury is entirely to the surviving community."

"So what if that view wins out, but you can't break disability prejudice? What if you wind up in a world where the disabled person's 'irrational' preference to live must yield to society's 'rational' interest in reduc-ing the incidence of disability? Doesn't horror kick in somewhere? Maybe as you watch the door close behind whoever has wheeled you into the gas chamber?"

"That's not going to happen."

"Do you have empirical evidence?" she asks. "A logical argument?"

"Of course not. And I know it's hap-pened before, in what was considered the most progressive medical community in the world. But it won't happen. I have to believe that."

Belief. Is that what it comes down to? Am I a person of faith after all? Or am I clinging to foolish hope that the tragic protagonist, this one time, will shift course before it's too late?

I don't think so. It's less about belief, less about hope, than about a practical need for definitions I can live with.

If I define Singer's kind of disability prejudice as an ultimate evil, and him as a monster, then I must so define all who believe disabled lives are inherently worse off or that a life without a certain kind of consciousness lacks value. That definition would make monsters of many of the peo-ple with whom I move on the sidewalks, do business, break bread, swap stories and share the grunt work of local politics. It would reach some of my family and most of my nondisabled friends, people who show me personal kindness and who sometimes manage to love me through their ignorance. I can't live with a definition of ultimate evil that encompasses all of them. I can't refuse the monster-majority basic respect and human sympathy. It's not in my heart to deny every single one of them, categorically, my affection and my love.

The peculiar drama of my life has placed me in a world that by and large thinks it would be better if people like me did not exist. My fight has been for accommodation, the world to me and me to the world.

As a disability pariah, I must struggle for a place, for kinship, for community, for connection. Because I am still seeking acceptance of my humanity, Singer's call to get past species seems a luxury way beyond my reach. My goal isn't to shed the perspective that comes from my particular experience, but to give voice to it. I want to be engaged in the tribal fury that rages when opposing perspectives are let loose.

As a shield from the terrible purity of Singer's vision, I'll look to the corruption that comes from interconnectedness. To justify my hopes that Singer's theoretical world—and its entirely logical extensions—won't become real, I'll invoke the muck and mess and undeniable reality of disabled lives well lived. That's the best I can do.

CHAPTER 38

Helen and Frida

Anne Finger

I'm lying on the couch downstairs in the TV room in the house where I grew up, a farmhouse with sloping floors in upstate New York. I'm nine years old. I've had surgery, and I'm home, my leg in a plaster cast. Everyone else is off at work or school. My mother recovered this couch by hemming a piece of fabric that she bought from a bin at the Woolworth's in Utica ("Bargains! Bargains! Bargains! Remnants Priced as Marked") and laying it over the torn upholstery. Autumn leaves—carrot, jaundice, brick—drift sluggishly across a liver-brown background. I'm watching *The Million Dollar Movie* on our black-and-white television: today it's *Singing in the Rain*. These movies always make me think of the world that my mother lived in before I was born, a world where women wore hats and gloves and had cinched-waist suits with padded shoulders as if they were in the army. My mother told me that in *The Little Colonel*, Shirley Temple had pointed her finger and said, "As red as those roses over there," and then the roses had turned red and everything in the movie was in color after that. I thought that was how it had been when I was born, everything in the world becoming both more vivid and more ordinary, and the black-and-white world, the world of magic and shadows, disappearing forever in my wake.

Now it's the scene where the men in blue-jean coveralls are wheeling props and sweeping the stage, carpenters shouldering boards, moving behind Gene Kelly as Don Lockwood and Donald O'Connor as Cosmo. Cosmo is about to pull his hat down over his forehead and sing, "Make 'em laugh . . ." and hoof across the stage, pulling open doors that open onto brick walls, careening up what appears to be a lengthy marble-floored corridor but is in fact a painted backdrop.

Suddenly, all the color drains from the room: not just from the mottled sofa I'm lying on, but also from the orange wallpaper that looked so good on the shelf at Streeter's (and was only $1.29 a roll), the chipped blue-willow plate: everything's black and silver now. I'm on a movie set, sitting in the director's chair. I'm grown-up suddenly, eighteen or thirty-five.

Places, please!

Quiet on the set!

Speed, the soundman calls, and I point my index finger at the camera, the clapper claps the board and I see that the movie we are making is called "Helen and Frida." I slice my finger quickly through the air, and the camera rolls slowly forward towards Helen Keller and Frida Kahlo, standing on a veranda, with balustrades that appear to be made of carved stone, but are in fact made of plaster.

The part of Helen Keller isn't played by Patty Duke this time; there's no *Miracle Worker* wild child to spunky rebel in under 100 minutes, no grainy film stock, none of that Alabama sun that bleaches out every soft shadow, leaving only harshness, glare. This time Helen is played by Jean Harlow.

Don't laugh: set pictures of the two of them side by side and you'll see that it's all there, the fair hair lying in looping curls against both faces, the same broad-cheeked bone structure. Imagine that Helen's eyebrows are plucked into a thin arch and penciled, lashes mascared top and bottom, lips cloisonned vermillion. Put Helen in pale peach mousseline-de-soie, hand her a white gardenia, bleach her hair from its original honey blonde to platinum, like Harlow's was, recline her on a *Bombshell* chaise with a white swan gliding in front, a palm fan being waved overhead, while an ardent lover presses sweet nothings into her hand.

I play the part of Frida Kahlo.

It isn't so hard to imagine that the two of them might meet. They moved after all, in not so different circles, fashionable and radical: Helen Keller meeting Charlie Chaplin and Mary Pickford, joining the Wobblies, writing in the *New York Times*, "I love the red flag . . . and if I could I should gladly march it past the offices of the *Times* and let all the reporters and photographers make the most of the spectacle . . ."; Frida, friend of Henry Ford and Sergei Eisenstein, painting a hammer and sickle on her body cast, leaving her bed in 1954, a few weeks before her death, to march in her wheelchair with a babushka tied under her chin, protesting the overthrow of the Arbenz regime in Guatemala.

Of course, the years are all wrong. But that's the thing about *The Million Dollar Movie*. During Frank Sinatra Week, on Monday Frank would be young and

handsome in *It Happened in Brooklyn*, on Tuesday he'd have grey temples and crow's feet, be older than my father, on Wednesday, be even younger than he had been on Monday. You could pour the different decades in a bowl together and give them a single quick fold with the smooth edge of a spatula, the way my mother did when she made black and white marble cake from two Betty Crocker mixes. It would be 1912, and Big Bill Haywood would be waving the check Helen had sent over his head at a rally for the Little Falls strikers, and you, Frida, would be in the crowd, not as a five-year-old child, before the polio, before the bus accident, but as a grown woman, cheering along with the strikers. Half an inch away, it would be August 31, 1932, and both of you would be standing on the roof of the Detroit Institute of the Arts, along with Diego, Frida looking up through smoked glass at the eclipse of the sun, Helen's face turned upwards to feel the chill of night descending, to hear the birds greeting the midday dusk.

Let's get one thing straight right away. This isn't going to be one of those movies where they put their words into our mouths. This isn't *Magnificent Obsession*, blind Jane Wyman isn't going to blink back a tear when the doctors tell her they can't cure her after all, saying, "and I thought I was going to be able to get rid of these," gesturing with her ridiculous rhinestone-studded, catseye dark glasses (and we think, "*Really*, Jane,"); she's not going to tell Rock Hudson she can't marry him: "I won't have you pitied because of me. I love you too much," and "I could only be a burden," and then disappear until the last scene when, lingering on the border between death and cure (the only two acceptable states), Rock saves her life and her sight and they live happily ever after. It's not going to be *A Patch of Blue*: when the sterling young Negro hands us the dark glasses and, in answer to our question: "But what are they for?" says "Never mind, put them on," we're not going to grab them, hide our stone Medusa gaze, grateful for the magic that's made us a pretty girl. This isn't *Johnny Belinda*, we're not sweetly mute, surrounded by an aura of silence. No, in this movie the blind women have milky eyes that make the sighted uncomfortable. The deaf women drag metal against metal, oblivious to the jarring sound, make odd cries of delight at the sight of the ocean, squawk when we are angry.

So now the two female icons of disability have met: Helen, who is nothing but, who swells to fill up the category, sweet Helen with her drooping dresses covering drooping bosom, who is Blind and Deaf, her vocation; and Frida, who lifts her skirt to reveal the gaping, cunt-like wound on her leg, who rips her body open to reveal her back, a broken column, her back corset with its white canvas straps framing her beautiful breasts, her body stuck with nails: but she can't be Disabled, she's Sexual.

Here stands Frida, who this afternoon, in the midst of a row with Diego, cropped off her jet-black hair ("Now see what you've made me do!"), and has schlepped herself to the ball in one of his suits. Nothing Dietrichish and coy about this drag: Diego won't get to parade his beautiful wife. Now she's snatched up Helen and walked with her out here onto the veranda.

In the other room, drunken Diego lurches, his body rolling forward before his feet manage to shuffle themselves ahead on the marble floor, giving himself more than ever the appearance of being one of those children's toys, bottom-weighted with sand, that when punched, roll back and then forward, an eternal red grin painted on their rubber faces. His huge belly shakes with laughter, his laughter a gale that blows above the smoke curling up towards the distant, gilded ceiling, gusting above the knots of men in tuxedos and women with marcelled hair, the black of their satin dresses setting off the glitter of their diamonds.

But the noises of the party, Diego's drunken roar, will be added later by the Foley artists.

Helen's thirty-six. She's just come back from Montgomery. Her mother had dragged her down there after she and Peter Fagan took out a marriage license, and the Boston papers got hold of the story. For so many years, men had been telling her that she was beautiful, that they worshipped her, that when Peter declared himself in the parlor at Wrentham, she had at first thought this was just more palaver about his pure love for her soul. But no, this was the real thing: carnal and thrilling and forbidden. How could you, her mother said. How people will laugh at you! The shame, the shame. Her mother whisked her off to Montgomery, Peter trailing after the two of them. There her brother-in-law chased Peter off the porch with a good old Southern shotgun. Helen's written her poem:

> What earthly consolation is there for one like me
> Whom fate has denied a husband and the joy of motherhood?...
> I shall have confidence as always,
> That my unfilled longings will be gloriously satisfied
> In a world where eyes never grow dim, nor ears dull.
> Poor Helen, waiting, waiting to get fucked in heaven.

But not Frida. She's so narcissistic. What a relief to Helen! None of those interrogations passing for conversation she usually has to endure. (After the standard pile of praise is heaped upon her—I've read your book five, ten, twenty times, I've admired you ever since . . . come the questions: Do you mind if I ask you: Is everything black? Is Mrs. Macy always with you?): no, Frida launches right into the tale of Diego's betrayal ". . . of course, I have my fun, too, but one doesn't want to have one's nose rubbed in the shit . . ." she signs into Helen's hand.

Helen is delighted and shocked. In her circles, Free Love is believed in, spoken of solemnly, dutifully. Her ardent young circle of socialists want to do away with the sordid marketplace of prostitution, bourgeois marriage, where women barter their hymens and throw in their souls to sweeten the deal; Helen has read Emma, she has read Isadora; she believes in a holy, golden monogamy, an unfettered, eternal meeting of two souls-in-flesh. And here Frida speaks of the act so casually that Helen, like a timid schoolgirl, stutters,

"You really? I mean, the both of you, you . . .?"

Frida throws her magnificent head back and laughs.

"Yes, really," Frida strokes gently into her hand. "He fucks other women and I fuck other men—and other women."

"F–U–C–K?" Helen asks. "What is this word?"

Frida explains it to her. "Now I've shocked you," Frida says,

"Yes, you have . . . I suppose it's your Latin nature . . ."

I'm not in the director's chair anymore. I'm sitting in the audience of the Castro Theatre in San Francisco watching this unfold. I'm twenty-seven. When I was a kid, I thought being grown up would be like living in the movies, that I'd be Rosalind Russell in *Sister Kenny*, riding a horse through the Australian outback or that I'd dance every night in a sleek satin gown under paper palms at the Coconut Grove. Now I go out to the movies, two, three, four times a week.

The film cuts from the two figures on the balcony to the night sky. It's technicolor: the pale gold stars against midnight blue. We're close to the equator now: there's the Southern Cross, and the Clouds of Magellan, and you feel the press of the stars, the mocking closeness of the heavens as you can only feel it in the tropics. The veranda on which we are now standing is part of a colonial Spanish palace, built in a clearing in a jungle that daily spreads its roots and tendrils closer, closer. A macaw perches atop a broken Mayan statue and calls, "I am queen/I am queen/I am queen" A few yards into the jungle, a spider monkey shits on the face of a dead god.

Wait a minute. What's going on? Is that someone out in the lobby talking? But it's so loud—

Dolores del Rio strides into the film, shouting, "Latin nature! Who wrote this shit?" She's wearing black silk pants and a white linen blouse; she plants her fists on her hips and demands: "Huh? Who wrote this shit?"

I look to my left, my right, shrug, stand up in the audience and say, "I guess I did."

"Latin nature! And a white woman? Playing Frida? *I* should be playing Frida."

"You?"

"Listen, honey." She's striding down the aisle towards me now. "I know I filmed that Hollywood crap. Six movies in one year: crook reformation romance, romantic Klondike melodrama, California romance, costume bedroom farce, passion in a jungle camp among chicle workers, romantic drama of the Russian revolution. I know David Selznick said: 'I don't care what story you use so long as we call it *Bird of Paradise* and Del Rio jumps into a flaming volcano at the finish.' They couldn't tell a Hawaiian from a Mexican from a lesbian. But I loved Frida and she loved me. She painted 'What the Water Gave Me' for me. At the end of her life, we were fighting, and she threatened to send me her amputated leg on a silver tray. If that's not love, I don't know what is—"

I'm still twenty-seven, but now it's the year 2015. The Castro's still there, the organ still rises up out of the floor with the organist playing "San Francisco, open your Golden Gate. . . ." In the lobby now, alongside the photos of the original opening of the Castro in 1927, are photos in black and white of lounging hustlers and leather

queens, circa 1979, a photographic reproduction of the door of the women's room
a few years later ("If they can send men to
the moon, why don't they?") Underneath,
in Braille, Spanish, and English: "In the
1960s, the development of the felt-tip pen,
combined with a growing philosophy of
personal expression caused an explosion
of graffiti . . . sadly unappreciated in its day,
this portion of a bathroom stall, believed
by many experts to have originated in the
women's room right here at the Castro
Theater, sold recently at Sotheby's for $5
million. . . ."

Of course, the Castro's now totally accessible, not just integrated wheelchair seat-
ing, but every film captioned, a voice loop
that interprets the action for blind people,
over which now come the words: "As Dolores del Rio argues with the actress playing
Frida, Helen Keller waits patiently—"

A woman in the audience stands up and
shouts, "Patiently! What the fuck are you
talking about, patiently? You can't tell the
difference between patience and power-
lessness. She's being *ignored*." The stage
is stormed by angry women, one of whom
leaps into the screen and begins signing
to Helen, "Dolores del Rio's just come out
and—"

"Enough already!" someone in the audience shouts. "Can't we please just get on
with the story!"

Now that Frida is played by Dolores,
she's long-haired again, wearing one of her
white Tehuana skirts with a deep red shawl.
She takes Helen's hand in hers, that hand
that has been cradled by so many great
men and great women.

"Latin nature?" Frida says, and laughs. "I
think perhaps it is rather your cold Yankee
nature that causes your reaction. . . ." And
before Helen can object to being called a
Yankee, Frida says, "But enough about Diego. . . ."

It's the hand that fascinates Frida, in its
infinite, unpassive receptivity: she prattles

on. When she makes the letters "z" and "j"
in sign, she gets to stroke the shape of the
letter into Helen's palm. She so likes the
sensation that she keeps trying to work
words with those letters in them into the
conversation. The camera moves in close
to Helen's hand as Frida says, "Here on
the edge of the Yucatan jungle, one sometimes see jaguars, although never jackals. I
understand jackals are sometimes seen in
Zanzibar. I have never been there, nor have
I been to Zagreb nor Japan nor the Zermatt,
nor Java. I have seen the Oaxacan mountain Zempoaltepec. Once in a zoo in Zur-
ich I saw a zebu and a zebra. Afterwards, we
sat in a small cafe and ate cherries jubilee
and zabaglione, washed down with glasses
of zinfandel. Or perhaps my memory is
confused: perhaps that day we ate jam on
ziewback crusts and drank a juniper tea,
while an old Jew played a zither. . . ."

"Oh," says Helen.

Frida falls silent. Frida, you painted
those endless self-portraits, but you always
looked at yourself level, straight on, in full
light. This is different: this time your face is
tilted, played over by shadows. In all those
self-portraits, you are simultaneously artist
and subject, lover and beloved, the bride of
yourself. Now, here, in the movies, it's different: the camera stands in for the eye of
the lover. But you're caught in the unforgiv-
ing blank stare of a blind woman.

And now, we cut from that face to the face
of Helen. Here I don't put in any soothing
music, nothing low and sweet with violins,
to make the audience more comfortable
as the camera moves in for its close-up.
You understand why early audiences were
frightened by these looming heads. In all
the movies with blind women in them—or,
let's be real, sighted women playing the
role of blind woman—Jane Wyman and
Merle Oberon in the different versions of
Magnificent Obsession, Audrey Hepburn in
Wait Until Dark, Uma Thurman in *Jennifer
8*, we've never seen a blind woman shot this

way before: never seen the camera come in and linger lovingly on her face the way it does here. We gaze at their faces only when bracketed by others, or in moments of terror when beautiful young blind women are being stalked. We've never seen before this frightening blank inward turning of passion, a face that has never seen itself in the mirror, that does not arrange itself for consumption.

Lack = inferiority? Try it right now. Finish reading this paragraph and then close your eyes, push the flaps of your ears shut, and sit. Not just for a minute: give it five or ten. Not in that meditative state, designed to take you out of your mind, your body. Just the opposite. Feel the press of hand crossed over hand: without any distraction, you feel your body with the same distinctness as a lover's touch makes you feel yourself. You fold into yourself, you know the rhythm of your breathing, the beating of your heart, the odd independent twitch of a muscle: now in a shoulder, now in a thigh. Your cunt, in all its patient hunger.

We cut back to Frida in close up. But now Helen's fingers enter the frame, travel across that face, stroking the downy moustache above Frida's upper lip, the fleshy nose, the thick-lobed ears.

Now, it's Frida's turn to be shocked: shocked at the hunger of these hands, at the almost-feral sniff, at the freedom with which Helen blurs the line between knowing and needing.

"May I kiss you?" Helen asks.

"Yes," Frida says.

Helen's hands cup themselves around Frida's face.

I'm not at the Castro anymore. I'm back home on the fold-out sofa in the slapped-together TV room, watching grainy images flickering on the tiny screen set in the wooden console. I'm nine years old again, used to Hays-office kisses, two mouths with teeth clenched, lips held rigid, pressing stonily against each other. I'm not ready for the way that Helen's tongue probes into Frida's mouth, the tongue that seems to be not so much interested in giving pleasure as in finding an answer in the emptiness of her mouth.

I shout, "Cut," but the two of them keep right on. Now we see Helen's face, her wide-open eyes that stare at nothing revealing a passion blank and insatiable, a void into which you could plunge and never, never, never touch bottom. Now she begins to make noises, animal mewlings and cries.

I will the screen to turn to snow, the sound to static. I do not want to watch this, hear this. My leg is in a thick plaster cast, inside of which scars are growing like mushrooms, thick and white in the dark damp. I think that I must be a lesbian, a word I have read once in a book, because I know I am not like the women on television, with their high heels and shapely calves and their firm asses swaying inside of satin dresses waiting, waiting for a man, nor am I like the women I know, the mothers with milky breasts, and what else can there be?

I look at the screen and they are merging into each other, Frida and Helen, the dark-haired and the light, the one who will be disabled and nothing more, the other who will be everything but. I can't yet imagine a world where these two might meet: the face that does not live under the reign of its own reflection with the face that has spent its life looking in the mirror; the woman who turns her rapt face up towards others and the woman who exhibits her scars as talismans, the one who is only, only and the one who is everything but. I will the screen to turn to snow.

CHAPTER 39

"I Am Not One of The" and "Cripple Lullaby"

Cheryl Marie Wade

I AM NOT ONE OF THE

I am not one of the physically
    challenged—

I'm a sock in the eye with a gnarled fist
I'm a French kiss with cleft tongue
I'm orthopedic shoes sewn on a last of
    your fears

I am not one of the differently abled—

I'm an epitaph for a million imperfect
    babies left untreated
I'm an ikon carved from bones in a mass
    grave in Tiergarten, Germany—
I'm withered legs hidden with a blanket

I am not one of the able disabled—

I'm a black panther with green eyes and
    scars like a picket fence
I'm pink lace panties teasing a stub of milk
    white thigh
I'm the Evil Eye

I'm the first cell divided
I'm mud that talks
I'm Eve   I'm Kali
I'm The Mountain That Never Moves
I've been forever   I'll be here forever
I'm the Gimp
I'm the Cripple
I'm the Crazy Lady
I'm The Woman With Juice

CRIPPLE LULLABY

I'm trickster coyote in a gnarly-bone suit
I'm a fate worse than death in
    shit-kickin' boots

I'm the nightmare booga you flirt with in
    dreams
'Cause I emphatically demonstrate: It ain't
    what it seems

I'm a whisper, I'm a heartbeat, I'm "that
    accident," and goodbye
One thing I am not is a reason to die.

I'm homeless in the driveway of your
    manicured street
I'm Evening Magazine's SuperCrip of the
    Week

I'm the girl in the doorway with no
    illusions to spare
I'm a kid dosed on chemo, so who said life
    is fair

I'm a whisper, I'm a heartbeat, I'm "let's
    call it suicide," and a sigh
One thing I am not is a reason to die
I'm the poster child with doom-dipped
    eyes
I'm the ancient remnant set adrift on ice

I'm that Valley girl, you know, dying
    of thin
I'm all that is left of the Cheshire
    Cat's grin

I'm the Wheelchair Athlete, I'm every dead
    Baby Doe
I'm Earth's last volcano, and I am ready to
    blow

I'm a whisper, I'm a heartbeat, I'm a geno-
    cide survivor, and Why?
One thing I am not is a reason to die.

I am not a reason to die.

CHAPTER 40

"Beauty and Variations"

Kenny Fries

1.

What is it like to be so beautiful? I dip
my hands inside you, come up with—
    what?

Beauty, at birth applied, does not
    transfer
to my hands. But every night, your hands

touch my scars, raise my twisted limbs to
graze against your lips. Lips that never

form the words—*you are beautiful*—
    transform
my deformed bones into—*what?*—if not
    beauty.

Can only one of us be beautiful? Is this
    your
plan? Are your sculpted thighs more
    powerful

driving into mine? Your hands find their
    way
inside me, scrape against my heart. Look

at your hands. Pieces of my skin trail
    from
your fingers. What do you make of this?

Your hands that know my scars, that lift
    me to your
lips, now drip my blood. Can blood be
    beautiful?

2.

I want to break your bones. Make them so
they look like mine. Force you to walk on

twisted legs. Then, will your lips still
    beg
for mine? Or will that disturb the
    balance

of our desire? Even as it inspires, your
    body
terrifies. And once again I find your hands

inside me. Why do you touch my scars?
    You
can't make them beautiful any more than
    I can

tear your skin apart. Beneath my scars,
between my twisted bones, hides my
    heart.

Why don't you let me leave my mark? With
    no
flaws on your skin—how can I find your
    heart?

3.

How much beauty can a person bear? Your
    smooth
skin is no relief from the danger of your
    eyes.

My hands would leave you scarred. Knead the muscles
of your thighs. I want to tear your skin, reach

inside you—your secrets tightly held. Breathe
deep. Release them. Let them fall into my palms.

My secrets are on my skin. Could this be why
each night I let you deep inside? Is that

where my beauty lies? Your eyes, without secrets,
would be two scars. I want to seal your eyes,

they know my every flaw. Your smooth skin, love's
wounds ignore. My skin won't mend, is calloused, raw.

4.

Who can mend my bones? At night, your hands press
into my skin. My feet against your chest, you mold

my twisted bones. What attracts you to my legs? Not
sex. What brings your fingers to my scars is beyond

desire. Why do you persist? Why do you touch me
as if my skin were yours? Seal your lips. No kiss

can heal these wounds. No words unbend my bones.
Beauty is a two-faced god. As your fingers soothe

my scars, they scrape against my heart. Was this

birth's plan—to tie desire to my pain, to stain
love's touch with blood? If my skin won't heal, how
can I escape? My scars are in the shape of my love.

5.

How else can I quench this thirst? My lips
travel down your spine, drink the smooth-ness

of your skin. I am searching for the core:
What is beautiful? Who decides? Can the laws

of nature be defied? Your body tells me: come
close. But beauty distances even as it draws

me near. What does my body want from yourn?
My twisted legs around your neck. You bend

me back. Even though you can't give the bones
at birth I wasn't given, I let you deep inside.

You give me—*what?* Peeling back my skin, you
expose my missing bones. And my heart, long

before you came, just as broken. I don't know who
to blame. So each night, naked on the bed, my body

doesn't want repair, but longs for inno-cence. If
innocent, despite the flaws I wear, I am beautiful.

CHAPTER 41

Selections from *Planet of the Blind*

Steve Kuusisto

I believe that in every blind person's imagination there are landscapes. The world is gray and marine blue, then a clump of brown shingled houses stands revealed by rays of sun, appearing now as bison—shaggy and still. These are the places learned by rote, their multiple effects of color made stranger by fast-moving clouds. The unknown is worse, an epic terrain that, in the mind's eye, could prevent a blind person from leaving home.

Since I know the miniature world of Geneva, New York, I decide to attend college there. On campus, though, there are sudden skateboards. I wish for a magic necklace to ward them away. The quadrangle is a world of predatory watching, and so I begin affecting a scowl. I look serious, as if my corpuscles have turned into hot pearls. I'm the angriest-looking boy on earth.

The dean's office knows about my eyes. I have a first-floor room in the dorm in case of fire. The theory is that with a vision impairment, I might not make it down the fire escape. This is the extent of the campus's support service for disabled students in 1973. The unreadable print in books, the dark dormitory room, the inaccessible library books—all these are things left to my dissemblings.

In the classroom I gravitate toward literature. The prevailing pedagogy is still centered on the New Criticism, a method of reading and analysis born in the years after World War II. This is a lucky break for me: the stress here is on the close reading of texts.

One simply has to read a poem to death.

The professor chain-smokes and takes the class line by line through turgid Victorian prosody. We crawl in the nicotine haze through the comma splices of Thomas Hardy.

I listen, hunched in my chair as the machinery of poets is dissected. We are eighteenth-century clock makers: nothing is too small for our rational little universe.

In the dim library I move through the stacks, pressing my nose to the spines. In my pocket I carry a letter from the eye doctor addressed "To Whom It May Concern"—it avows that too much reading is dangerous for me. "The scanning motions inherent in reading make retinal tearing more likely. Therefore Mr. Kuusisto should read in moderation."

Like all true talismans, this letter is frightening. It's designed to protect me from professors who may demand too much from me. But in my pocket it feels like a letter bomb.

Reading is hazardous!

And to me the words of poetry are

onions, garlic, fennel, basil; the book itself an earthenware vessel.

Reading alone with a magnifying glass, nothing on earth makes more sense to me than Wallace Stevens's poem "The Pleasures of Merely Circulating": "The angel flew round in the garden/the garden flew round with the clouds,/and the clouds flew around, and the clouds flew around,/and the clouds flew around with the clouds."

My spastic eye takes in every word like a red star seen on a winter night. Every syllable is acquired with pain. But poetry furnishes me with a lyric anger, and suddenly poems are wholly necessary. Robert Bly's book *The Light Around the Body*, for example, expresses an almost mystical combination of wonder and rage about "the Great Society." He depicts a world gone so awry that the very pine stumps start speaking of Goethe and Jesus, the insects dance, there are murdered kings in the light bulbs outside movie theaters. All of it is glorious, and like my boyhood discovery of Caruso in the attic, Bly's voice, among others—Breton, Nerval, Lorca—follows me in the dark.

*   *   *

I move in a solitude fueled by secrecy. O Lord, let me never be seen with the white cane. Let me roll through the heavy oceans like the beluga whale, filled with dark seeds, always coursing forward. Let no one find me out! This is my lacerating tune. Leaning over my private page, I shake with effort.

Weakness and *lack of affect* are the synonyms for the word *blind*. In Roget's Thesaurus one finds also: *ignorant, oblivious, obtuse, unaware, blocked, concealed, obstructed, hidden, illiterate, backward, crude, uneducated,* and worst of all, *unversed.*

At twilight I walk in the botanical gardens, the night smells richly of lilac. I've read that Immanuel Kant could not bear to visit his friends in sickness; after they died,

he would repress all memories of them. There are limits to cognition and reason. What would he think in the mad purple twilight where I live. Would he visit himself?

I hear radios and TV sets from the open windows on campus.

Under the violet streetlights my glasses, thick as dishes, fill with aberrations at the edges of their thick curves.

College is brutally difficult for me. One poem must take the place of the bulky novel I cannot read, or at least not read in a week. I often go home from the library with the few words I've been able to see and absorb still vivid in my imagination. Alone, I take the words apart and rearrange them like Marcel Duchamp playing chess with his own private rules. Still, I need extra time for every assignment. But exploring what words can do when placed side by side, I'm starting to build the instrument that will turn my blindness into a manner of seeing.

Still, walking around, feigning sight, I step in the rain-washed gutter, brush the street sign, and make a hundred slapstick gestures. In a flash I'm Stan Laurel, the angel of nutty innocence. This can happen without warning. It might be the telephone that does it. A friend calls, saying she'll meet me downstairs in half an hour. She drives a red Chrysler.

I walk down to the street and approach the car. I reach for the door on the passenger's side and give it a tug, but it's locked. I rap on the window, but my friend doesn't seem to hear. I rap again, tug on the door, rap and tug. Then I walk around to her side of the car. Is she in some Wagnerian trance, Brünnhilde at the wheel? When I lean down to her window, I see at last the face of a genuinely terrified Chinese woman. I motion to her to roll down her window. She won't. I try to explain my mistake in sign language—pointing to my eyes, telling her loudly that I've mistaken her car for that of a friend. I begin backing away from her into the street like an ungainly kid on roller skates.

My embarrassments are legion. I know the white cane has become a necessity for the maintenance of my psychological health. I enter bathrooms marked "Ladies," and entering restaurants, I trip down short flights of steps. I appear misty eyed and drunk and walk about in circles looking for exits and entrances.

Without the cane, who will understand me? But it will be another eighteen years before I receive proper Orientation and Mobility training. Before I will accept it.

* * *

In one of my last trips without a cane I visit the great Prado museum in Madrid, where I find I cannot see the famous paintings of Velázquez and Goya because they are hanging behind ropes that prohibit the vandals from drawing too close. Since I can't draw near, I see oceans of mud in vast gilded frames instead of the ceremonial world of court or the sprawl of lusty peasants.

I've waited years to get to the Prado, and now I'm wandering through its broad hallways thwarted by guards and ropes. Of course I should be carrying a white cane. But of course I'm carrying nothing except my sense of not-quite-belonging, which I'm fighting like a man swatting hornets.

At a souvenir counter I buy a museum guide—I'll read about the paintings I can't see—but the print is microscopic. Instead of a book, I find I'm holding a little cup full of sand.

The light in the Prado is alternately prismatic, then dark as a jail. I stand in the sunbeams under the oval skylights and watch the world break up into rainbows, then turn a corner into a great vaulted darkness, where an important painting hangs behind a veil, black as an abandoned lighthouse.

But I've traveled so far to see the paintings, and I hate to be circumscribed by tricks of the light, so I fall in with a group of American tourists. They are dutifully following a Spanish woman tour-guide who is describing paintings in the gallery at which I've arrived. But she spots me as an impostor, a freeloading listener, and as I strain to see the fetlock of a painted horse, she points me out to the group.

"This man is not in our tour," she says. "Sir, you will have to leave."

And I walk from the museum, a flapping windmill of a man, and find myself doing a muddy umbrella-dance in the icy wet park. Two students approach and ask if I'll buy a comic book to help disabled schoolchildren. I give them some money and think that some kid will get a break.

* * *

Dusk is the hour when I'm most likely to misjudge the speed and flow of traffic. It's rush hour—people hurrying home in the autumn rush hour, some on foot, some in cars. In such moments I often feel prematurely aged: I want some help in crossing the street. I want to reach for someone's arm.

Ironically, though, as things visual are in doubt, they grow in unconventional beauty. Dear Jackson Pollock, I've entered your *Autumn Rhythm*. The irregular or sometimes certain flight of color and shape is a wild skein, a tassel of sudden blue here, a wash of red. The very air has turned to hand-blown glass with its imperfect bubbles of amethyst or hazel blue. I stand on the ordinary street corner as if I've awakened at the bottom of a stemware vase. The glassblower's molten rose has landed in my eyes.

I shift my glasses—a slow moon rises on my path, things appear and disappear, and the days are like Zen-autumn.

* * *

A benevolent shakespeare professor finds me a reader. Enter Ramona, a classics major who comes in the afternoons three days a week.

We sit in a sunbeam in a steep room somewhere toward the rear of the library. It's a storage space, old encyclopedias line the shelves. The librarian thinks no one will hear Ramona reading to me in this spot. He's given us two wooden chairs. We stack our books on them and sit on the floor. Soon we have a blanket, which we assiduously roll up and store each night in a closet.

Ramona is a tremendous reader, the shadowy forms of things, ideas, gestalt, whatever, they move as she talks. Together we cross the ancient hot plateaus where words are as mighty as numbers. She reads Gilgamesh, the poems of the Cid. And flat on my back in that tall room, I never fall asleep. What stranger miracles are there? Sometimes she stops, and I learn not to interrupt her silence: she's performing a calculation. It's a lesson for me in absorption. My own nervousness tends to exclude such moments.

Oddly enough, eros, syllables, and alchemy are facts, particularly in the lives of young people. Beside Ramona, listening, my habitual shyness around women begins to fall away. Outside the library, I find myself conversing with my female classmates with ease. For the first time, I discover how conversations between men and women can be like warm soap dissolving in a bath.

In the old student pub—a dark cellar, I meet a strange new girl named Bettina. We talk and drink German beer. Bettina is a polymath, angry, rebelling against her father, who is an executive at a television network.

"The bastard, he'd have been comfortable during the Crusades!" she says, and stubs her cigarette out in an ashtray on the bar.

With this altogether irreverent young woman, I experience puppy love. She's an Irish country girl with long, thrilling, unkempt red hair. Red leaning back toward gold.

Bettina cooks spaghetti over a gas ring in a basement. (She never has an apartment of her own, instead she occupies other people's places without self-consciousness. She knows everyone.) I accept a glass of wine, I'm wrapped in earth tones and sparks. My hands stink of Gauloises cigarettes, my fingers spasm from the nicotine.

She squeezes the juice of a lemon into the salad. Puts Tabasco in the pasta sauce. She throws raw carrot chunks in there too.

"Why are you putting carrots in the tomato sauce? That's disgusting!"

"Oh, shut up, if you'd eaten more carrots, your eyes would be better."

"I ate lots of carrots! My eyes went bad from masturbation!"

"Well, maybe you don't need to do that anymore."

I can't speak, because she's kissing me. It's a potent kiss, her tongue is wet and vital in my mouth.

She draws me to the floor, pulls down my pants, guides me inside her. I can't believe how quickly she does it, my brain is still stuck on the word *carrot*.

She's on top, loosening buttons down the front of her black dress. As her breasts touch my outstretched hands, I come with every ounce of my viscera. I come the way all virgin-boys should—with surrender and reverence. I'm trying to say something.

"It's okay," she whispers. "I'm wearing a diaphragm."

I start to rise on my elbows.

"I'm sorry, I—"

"Shhhhh!"

Her face closes in, her red hair falls over my eyes, tickles, smells faintly of shampoo. She guides my fingers gently to her clitoris. She's an open meadow! A birch tree at midsummer, the sunlight seeming to be above and inside her.

Like all virgins, I'm a narcissist: surely no one has ever experienced this abundant wet circle of girl before? Not like this!

I'm on a rug in a spot of lamplight. The sauce simmers behind us. There's a clatter of water pipes, there are apartments above. Dishes rattle somewhere. Bettina is astride me, and leaning, she kisses me forcefully, filling my mouth with her sip of cabernet.

For the first time the vast silence that follows sex expands in my chest.

"I love you!" I say it. "I love you!"

I begin to cry. I who cannot see a woman's face, who can't look someone in the eye, I, I, who, what, never thought this could happen. I'm crying in earnest, copious sparkles.

"Shhhhh!"

She arches her back, I slip from her, a little fish, laughing and weeping.

Bettina refastens her dress, retrieves a tortoiseshell hair clasp, arranges it, sings very softly some lines from Yeats: "'Ah penny, brown penny, I am looped in the loops of her hair.'"

* * *

Nights. november. books. Smoke. Pierre Reverdy. Emily Dickinson. The windows open, a sweet smell of fallen leaves. I stroke Bettina's neck as she reads from Rexroth's Chinese poems: "'The same clear glory extends for ten thousand miles. The twilit trees are full of crows.'"

I'm unimaginably blessed. The crystallography of sharpened syntax, image, her voice behind it, wash of water on stones.

"'My soul wandered, happy, sad, unending.'" (Neruda)

"'The branches are dying of love.'" (Lorca)

"'Show me, dear Christ, thy spouse, so bright and clear.'" (Donne)

"'Here is the shadow of truth, for only the shadow is true.'" (Warren)

* * *

In the library Bettina finds a box of discarded records. These are Caedmon recordings of Yeats, an actor reading Baudelaire, poems by Carl Sandburg, John Crowe Ransom. The recordings are in miserable condition. And there at the bottom of the pile is a recorded bird-watching disk. A British narrator talks the listener through encounters with dozens of different birds. The birds sing on command, precise, silver, optimistic.

"Listen to the plover!" says the voice. "He's stirring on a spring morning!"

The plover obeys, lets loose its porous notes.

"Now the nightingale. Bird of poetry!"

The nightingale sounds brighter and better rested than the plover. Clearly it is a happy bird.

"The blackbird."

"The oriole."

In some places the needle sticks. The oriole hiccups over and over.

Here come the wild swans.

I'm completely jazzed: all my life I've been a stranger in this neighborhood. I've never seen a bird. Now, hearing them has made a place in my imagination. The birds! The damned birds! I've been missing out on something huge. But where are they?

Someone tells me about the ornithology collection in the biology building. I go there alone on a Saturday, when I know that the building will be deserted. The birds are arranged in display cases on both sides of the first-floor corridor. I press my nose to the glass specimen case and try not to breathe, for breathing fogs the glass. I see cocoon shapes, brown as cordovan shoes. These are the taxidermied and long-fallen members of the parliament, as strange to me as Roman coins and nails.

The labs are empty, the lights off. There is a hum of large refrigerators, a percolating sound. I tap the glass case with my forefinger, and it swings open as if by magic! Perhaps some student assistant has forgotten to lock the case!

Imagine never having seen a bird. And now your hands are free to explore the vagaries of the bird-tomb. How weightless they are, light as dinner rolls! But the feathers are stiff, almost lacquered, like the tiny ribs of a corset I once held in an antique shop. This can't be what a live bird's plumage would feel like. These birds are stiff, Victorian, spent.

But what a miracle of pipe stems and ligatures, the legs and wings joined with such supple delicacy.

I lift a large thing from its perch, hold it to my face, just barely making out its predatory look. A hawk? It's large as a basketball, light as a throwaway newspaper.

Here I am, twentysomething, standing in a deserted corridor, fondling birds. I feel like a frotteurist: a person who has orgasms from casual touch with strangers. I'm some kind of pervert, alone with these dead birds, running my hands over their heads, tracing their beaks with my fingernails. What if a security guard were to appear and ask me what I'm doing?

"I'm blind, sir, and this is my first experience with birds!"

"My name is Kid Geronimo, and I live in the elevator!"

"Have you ever touched a plover, sir?"

"My name is Wigglesworth, I'm searching for insects."

This is a lifelong habit, imaginary conversations with authority figures, usually when I'm touching something, when I'm on the verge of an understanding.

All the birds smell like vintage hats. As I run my hands over their prickly backs, I put names to them, since I have no idea what they are.

"Leather-breasted barnacle chomper."

"Blue-throated Javanese son of Zero."

Outside I sit under a tree and listen to the living catbirds, a thrush, the chickadee. What I wish for is to see a live bird. So one afternoon shortly thereafter, I convince my friend and teacher Jim Crenner to go bird-watching with me. Jim is a poet, a student of anything that possesses color. He is a mosaic man with a Peterson's guide and at least two pairs of binoculars.

We walk into a meadow, talking of poets, Leopardi, Rumi, Eliot.

Jim knows I can't see well but figures he can point me to colors, fix me on a glittering stone from Ravenna, a goldfinch on a fencepost.

"Hold still, right there is a fat finch big as a Spanish gold piece!" he says, whispering through his mustache, as if he were reading aloud in one of his classes.

"There's a red-winged blackbird."

"A vireo."

"A scarlet tanager."

How toothsome they all sound! How thrilling it must be to spy them on their April branches, blond chaff from the skies, afterthoughts of a blue atmosphere.

When I look through binoculars, I see a coral blue/green bubble, perhaps my own eye, but nothing like a bird. I can't quite bring myself to tell this to Jim, who is in a rapture of color and evolutionary wonder.

"To think these things evolved from primal mud without a god!" he says, alert to the sheer improbability of our planet. But by now I realize I am looking at the blue dish of self. My field glasses are trained on my own optic nerves.

I have a major bird thirst, something untranslatable, I can't share it, can't cry aloud at my frustration. Instead I pretend.

"Can you see him? He's right on that post, fat and horny," says Jim, and I look into my own dish of thickened green and say, "Look at him jump!" At the moment I say it, I mean it. I can see that bird hopping up and down, that goldfinch jumping like a penny on a railroad track.

I agree with everything Jim sees, adding my own intensifier and adjectives. I don't want to tell him I can't see the damned things, fearing it will make him self-conscious, for then our outing will become an exercise in description. He'll have to tell me what they look like. And I will have to appreciate them all the more. By pretending to see, I'm sparing us an ordeal. Sure I'm faking it with the binoculars, gloating over imaginary bluejays, but I'm alone with my own imagination, listening casually to an enthusiastic friend, my blindness locked away for the time.

I think Jim imagines I've seen some birds, and maybe I have.

CHAPTER 42

Selected Poems

Jim Ferris

POEMS WITH DISABILITIES

I'm sorry—this space is reserved
for poems with disabilities. I know
it's one of the best spaces in the book,
but the Poems with Disabilities Act
requires us to make all reasonable
accommodations for poems that aren't
normal. There is a nice space just
a few pages over—in fact (don't
tell anyone) I think it's better
than this one, I myself prefer it.
Actually I don't see any of those
poems right now myself, but you never know
when one might show up, so we have to keep
this space open. You can't always tell
just from looking at them, either. Sometimes
they'll look just like a regular poem
when they roll in . . . you're reading along
and suddenly everything
changes, the world tilts
a little, angle of vision
jumps, your entrails aren't
where you left them. You
remember your aunt died
of cancer at just your age
and maybe yesterday's twinge means
something after all. Your sloppy,
fragile heart beats
a little faster
and then you know.
You just know:
the poem
is right
where it
belongs.

FROM THE SURGEONS: DRS. SOFIELD, LOUIS, HARK, ALFINI, MILLAR, BAEHR, BEVAN-THOMAS, TSATSOS, ERICSON, AND BENNAN

6–10–60. History. This child is the second of three

children— the other two are perfectly normal. He was the product

of a normal pregnancy and delivery. At birth it was noted

that the left lower extremity was shorter than the right. The child

had a fragmentation and rodding of the left femur

for stimulation of bone growth. Prior to that procedure a 2" discrepancy

existed. This procedure was repeated in 1957 and again in 1958. Prior

to the procedure in 1958 a 2" discrepancy was again noted. The child's

early development was normal. He has, of course, been periodically set back

in his physical progress because of the surgical procedures.

6–10–60. Physical Examination. Head: There is nothing

abnormal about the head. Left lower extremity: There appears

to be only a very moderate degree of atrophy in the left thigh, but

this is explainable on the basis of his surgical procedures.

Gait is moderately abnormal but caused only

by the leg length discrepancy.

7–28–61. History. He began sitting at six months of age, walked

at one year, and began talking at about one year of age. There have been

some periods of regression following the early surgical procedures. The boy

is attending school and is apparently well adjusted.

7–28–61. Physical Examination. Examination reveals a slight

compensatory scoliosis. This is corrected by equalization of leg lengths.

This boy walks with a left short leg limp. He is able to run without difficulty,

and can hop on his right foot, but he is unable to hop on his left foot.

When performing the duck waddle his left leg leads the right.

12–7–62. Neurological Examination. Deep tendon reflexes

are physiological. There is a slight diminution of the left knee jerk

as contrasted with that on the right. No sensory loss nor pathologic reflexes.

8–28–63. Progress Notes. The mother relates that the boy has been

stumbling more and more in recent weeks. His quadriceps are

quite weak, probably from the multiple surgical procedures

done on this thigh. Quadriceps are rather bound down at the knee.

The leg length discrepancy is 3" and it is very difficult

to have a satisfactory shoe lift on this dimension. A long leg brace

was ordered with knee locks and with a 2" pylon extension.

11–8–63. Progress Notes. This boy has received his long leg brace

with the caliper extension today. The brace is satisfactory,

except for the fact that the ankle joint is rigid and

he has a great deal of difficulty getting his trousers on and off

and needs to split the seams.

8–14–64. Progress Notes. This child who is almost 10 years of age

is wearing a long leg brace with a stilt on it, but the mother says

that he objects to this and apparently is undergoing considerable
emotional disturbance. The mother has noticed this since his return
from the hospital at which time he had a repeat fragmentation and rodding.

4–7–67. Physical Examination. Lower extremities: Circumference:
There is obvious atrophy of the left thigh: This cannot
be accurately compared with the right because of the shortness
of the extremity and the dislocation of the patella.

6–6–69. History. The child is in the ninth grade and does fair
and goes to a regular school.

10–30–70. Progress Notes. Final Discharge. The patient is essentially
unchanged since last visit. His leg lengths measured to the heel
on the right measures 101 and 86 on the left from the anterior superior
iliac spine. He has occasional episodes of pain. He is still
wearing the long leg brace with the high lift below
and there was no indication on the mother's part that she plans
on having anything done in the near future.

POET OF CRIPPLES

Let me be a poet of cripples,
of hollow men and boys groping
to be whole, of girls limping toward
womanhood and women reaching back,
all slipping and falling toward the cavern
we carry within, our hidden void,
a place for each to become full, whole,
room of our own, space to grow in ways
unimaginable to the straight
and the narrow, the small and similar,
the poor, normal ones who do not know
their poverty. Look with care, look deep.
Know that you are a cripple too.
I sing for cripples; I sing for you.

NORMAL

Across Oak Park Avenue
is a city park, lush
and busy, where men play softball all

evening, too far away
to watch, their dim voices
drifting across the green. Their cars line

the streets as far
as I can see. Sammy and I,
Robert and I, Hoffman and I call out

the makes and models
as the cars pass. *Dodge Dart.*
Chevy Nova. We are seldom wrong—*Corvair,*

Pontiac GTO—we who drive
wheelchairs and banana carts—
Mustang, VW, Rambler American—who have not yet

rounded second—
'57 Chevy! My dad had one of those—
who watch out windows a world so soft—*T-bird*—

so fair—*Corvette*—
so normal—*Ford Fairlane*—
a world going on, going by, going home.

HIGH CONCEPT

I was just planning to be in LA
for a couple days—make a few calls, see
an old friend, sit on the beach for an hour.
Nothing special. Calling up

the Screen Actors Guild was just a whim.
A joke. I never dreamed that anything
would come of it. You know how the guild has a rule
that no two actors can use the same name.

I just called to see if they had anyone
using mine. That's all. Just a moment,
I'll check, the person says. She's back in
two minutes. Did you say Jim Ferris? Yes.

Of course you're registered, Mister Ferris.
One moment, please. What does she mean of course,
I'm thinking, when suddenly this poodle voice
yaps: Where have you *been* I've been

trying to get hold of you for a month
OK a week but you gotta talk
to me, check in once in a while. Excuse
me, but who *is* this? Oh, this is just great—

a week in the country and it's amnesia.
Hello—I'm your agent. You'd be nothing
without me. I'm quoting you here. Where are
you? I'm not thinking, I tell him the name

of the hotel. Nobody stays there,
he says. Ten minutes. And hangs up before
I can say I'm nobody, really.
But I'm curious too, so I go down

to the lobby to see what this agent
looks like—if he shows. He does—and in five
minutes. He doesn't go up to the desk,
he comes right over to me and sits down.

Why don't you call me I've been worried sick.
I'm about to say Because I don't know
you, but he's already on this great deal
he's cooked up for me—for this other guy.

I'm not an actor, I tell him. That's why
they want you, he says. I'm not the right guy,
I say. I don't know this business, I don't
know you or anybody in this town.

Nobody really knows anybody clse, do they.
Before I know it we're having lunch
and all these people are acting like they know
me. A couple I'd seen in movies—that's it.

Nobody believes that I'm not
who they think I am. I show them my brace—
no movie star wears a brace like this,
or walks like I do, unless they're trying

to win an Oscar. Cut it out, Jim, my agent says. You can't
keep pulling this stunt. What the hell, maybe
it will be fun, until they figure it out. But
they never do. I take the part my agent lined up

for that other Jim. I stand where they tell me,
look where they tell me, say my lines. Beats working.
I take more parts, do some deals, before you know it
I'm a player, a commodity, Mister Green Light,

as full of shit as anybody. What's become
of the other Jim Ferris? Maybe
he's back home, stepping into the light,
saying my lines right on cue.

FACTS OF LIFE

Where's the glory in it? I am not
a survivor. Whatever the state
of my legs, whatever happened
there, know this: I walk down the street
whole, whether I limp or stumble,
cane or crutches, roll in a chair.
This is my body. Look if you like.
This is my meat, substance
but not essence, essence but not
fate, sum of all its particles
back to the big one but particular
to no single interpretation
in a cosmos of possible ontologies
that we all try to limit with all
our soft might but which accepts
only the most temporary
instructions: you, sir, explain
that birthmark, and you, how about
that nose? We are not signs,
we do not live in spite of
or because of our facts,
we live with them, around them, among,
like we live around rivers, my cane,
your warts, like we live among animals,
your heart, my brace, like we live with,
despite, because of each other.

NO SUGAR, NO MILK

I'm going to get up out of this chair and throw it away and walk.
Christopher Reeve, February 1996

They're dying now, the old ones.
My people die too young.
When I first saw him fly I had no
   idea
he would join my clan,
faster than sound
he would fall to ground
and learn to love the rich, bitter taste
   of all grounds
      (no sugar, no milk)
when ground is what you know.
I may be an old one soon,
and when I offer this body
   to the fire
and my coal is ground out
and my name floats off to be
   forgotten,
know that this is your clan too.
Our clan is grounded,
grace is anchored
   in the dirt.
Our people die too young,
and when we go, our people
   come behind.

APOLOGIA

This poem
                does not need
to march
                across
the page.
This poem
                is free
                        to lean
                                and limp
                                                        and lurch
and tap the
                ground.
                        This poem will just be
here,
        as it claims
                        a place
                                on this
                        page, in this
                space, in this rolling,
                        stumbling,

stuttering,
            blinking,
                    fresh and stinking
                                    world of great
                        pain
and promise:
            this poem
                        does not explain
                                    its shape,
its struggles,
            its joys.
                    Explain yourself,
if you like,
            and that
                is yours.
                    This poem
                            is home
with every poem
                and with all
sparks
                        seeking a place
                                to light.

ENOUGH

Instead of putting cotton in my ears
to pretend I was deaf,
instead of closing my eyes and wearing sunglasses
to pretend I was blind,
I'd pretend I could walk
like my brother,
my neighbors, kids at school.

I'd pretend for days, for years,
that I walked like everybody else.
Someone would always correct me —
can he hobble over here and try this on? —
but I was persistent, insisting on
seeing myself as a regular kid,
standing out for my wit, my charm,

my intelligence, not my walk.
I still pretend — I think of my walking
as *walking*, not something
beautiful or unique.
Like a poem, it is enough
like all the rest to be recognized,
but different enough to move me

through the world.

LUCKY NUMBER

1. Here be monsters.
    Wherever here is.

2. When I speak
    I speak with one voice
    When I cry
    I cry with all

3. Poetry makes nothing happen.
    Line breaks

4. If death be the mother
                                   of beauty,
    the flower is

5. All rules are arbitrary.
    There are no rules.
    Violate them and you
        will be
                    punished.

6. Without you
    there is no
    thing

7. At night I dream
    of picket fences
    and well-cut diamonds,
    rows of crosses at Normandy.

8. That's funnier than a crutch.
    I mean it.

9. If the world were flat we'd yearn for mountains
    if the world were dry we'd write the sea

10. Is there something wrong
    with his eyes?
    Why won't he look at me
    when he talks to me?

11. The map is not the terrain.

    All are made things
    in the eyes of God.

12. Oh St. Francis Galton, cousin to Darwin,
      father of normal, defender of the bell-shaped curve,
         pray for us.

   From the morons
   from the imbeciles
   from the idiots
         protect us.

   From the three generations – wait:
      we are the generations, judge, judge not –
        it's never enough.
   We take us along wherever we go.

13. Wherever
        here is.

14.

FOR THE BETTERMENT OF HUMANITY

In Boston, by the Mother Church,
The Mary Baker Eddy Library
For the Betterment of Humanity.
This is not fair — the bricks are clean,
Though they snag and jounce the wheelchairs.
The reflecting pool shimmers in the night.
This is not fair — clean lines, sweeping curves,
Grace and the golden mean. Charity, prudence,
Temperance, all heavenly virtues.
This is not fair — nothing is fair. The fit
Thrive, and winners require losers. A rising tide
Lifts all boats — sediment sinks, scum floats.
When the gene pool gets too messy, reflect and purify.
The war to end all wars killed millions
For the Betterment of Humanity.
Save us from the selfless – may they each earn a self.
Save us from those who would do good.
Efforts to Improve Humanity have killed
People like you. Our children waste away.

Something on the plaza catches the white cane's tip.
A carpenter sweeps up sawdust, picks up his tools
And limps home.

Blessed are the wayward, for they shall comfort the righteous.
Blessed are the righteous, for they know who they are.
Blessed are the suckers, for they shall be suckered.
Blessed are those who feed the fear, for they shall find nourishment.
Blessed are they who deny the past, for the future shall find them.
Save us from those who would fix our flaws,
You who have so much to answer for,
Save us from the righteous healers.
But we need the healers — who will stanch
Our blood? Who will ease our aches?
Who will tell us we are normal after all?

Save us from the tyranny of the norm.
Blessed are the unfit, the twisted, the shamed,
Blessed are the naked and the nude.
Blessed are they who will not get better.
Blessed are those who shock the pool.
Save us from the saviours, from your saints,
From those who know what's best. Save us from progress —
Some day we may Get Better. Till we do,
Let me learn to live as if living might matter,

As if we won't be punished for our hope, trust, love,
Save us from ourselves, be fast and true, while we
Save ourselves from what's above, while we
Save ourselves, at last, from you.

CLUBBING

My foot is a club
the sight of it batters
the ten fingers ten toes
as long as it's healthy
anything goes, praise for the normal
thank God we're normal
exceptionally normal club
that seems to start in the head—
keep the head of the club level, keep
your head down, the competition is all
in your head, remember that cute baby
   harp seal—
or does it start at the foot of the bed,
or is it a berth, in the club car,
my foot was clubbed at birth
but my training has progressed,
the lub-dub heart club requests
the pleasure of your bequests,
preserve your pious normate face,
your demure coquette heart tart

from which all else deviates,
make mine a club sandwich,
the universe is a club-
like thing, infinite memberships—
do you really want in a club
that accepts members like
you? Opt out now from this unkempt
circle with unlimited centers
(quit thinking in so few dimensions,
in this universe all have extension),
every man a king, the king of clubs,
the club will foot the bill,
every night there's a line to get in,
my club is a foot long exactly,
release your inner amputee,
send all your clannish limbs to me,
as long as they are healthy, they
can keep your phantom pain some
   company,
send me ten fingers, ten toes,
give or take a foot—our secret handshake,
normally, nobody knows.

Contributors

Clare Barker is Lecturer in English at the University of Leeds. She is the author of *Postcolonial Fiction and Disability: Exceptional Children, Metaphor and Materiality* (2011) and, with Stuart Murray, co-edited a special issue of the *Journal of Literary and Cultural Disability Studies* entitled "Disabling Postcolonialism."

Cynthia Barounis is a Postdoctoral Fellow in Women, Gender, and Sexuality Studies at Washington University in St. Louis. Her work has appeared or is forthcoming in the *Journal of Visual Culture*, the *Journal of Medical Humanities* and the *Journal of Literary and Cultural Disability Studies*.

H-Dirksen L. Bauman is Professor of Deaf Studies at Gallaudet University where he serves as Coordinator of the MA program in Deaf Studies. He is the editor of *Open Your Eyes: Deaf Studies Talking* (U of Minnesota P, 2008) and co-editor of *Signing the Body Poetic: Essays in American Sign Language Literature* (U of California P, 2006). Dr. Bauman is also an Executive Editor of the *Deaf Studies Digital Journal*.

Douglas C. Baynton, Associate Professor of History at the University of Iowa, is the author of *Forbidden Signs: American Culture and the Campaign Against Sign Language* (University of Chicago Press, 1996), and co-author with Jack Gannon and Jean Bergey of *Through Deaf Eyes: A Photographic History of an American Community* (Gallaudet University Press, 2007).

Liat Ben-Moshe is a Postdoctoral Fellow in the Department of Disability and Human Development at the University of Illinois at Chicago. Her PhD dissertation examined the connections between deinstitutionalization in the fields of intellectual disabilities and mental health and the prison abolition movement in the U.S. Liat has written on such topics as the International Symbol of Access; inclusive pedagogy; academic repression; disability, anti-capitalism and anarchism; queerness and disability; deinstitutionalization and incarceration and the politics of abolition.

Michael Bérubé is the Paterno Family Professor in Literature at Pennsylvania State University and the author of *Life As We Know It: A Father, A Family, and an Exceptional Child* (Pantheon, 1996).

Lerita Coleman Brown is Ayse I. Carden Distinguished Professor of Psychology and Director of the Science Center for Women at Agnes Scott College in Decatur, Georgia. Professor Brown's early work centered on nonverbal behavior (particularly communicated toward stigmatized individuals), and stigma, identity and self-concept. Her most recent articles include, "Advising a Diverse Student Body: Lessons I've Learned from Trading Places" published in *Liberal Education* and "An Ordinary Mystic: Contemplation, Inner Authority, and Spiritual Direction in the Life and Work of Howard Thurman," published in *Presence: An International Journal of Spiritual Direction.*

Eli Clare, writer and activist, lives in the Green Mountains of Vermont and is the author of a book of essays *Exile and Pride: Disability, Queerness, and Liberation* and a collection of poetry *The Marrow's Telling: Words in Motion.*

G. Thomas Couser retired in 2011 from Hofstra University, where he was a Professor of English and founding director of the Disability Studies Program. He is the author of *American Autobiography: The Prophetic Mode* (Massachusetts, 1979), *Altered Egos: Authority in American Autobiography* (Oxford, 1989), *Recovering Bodies: Illness, Disability, and Life Writing* (Wisconsin, 1997), *Vulnerable Subjects: Ethics and Life Writing* (Cornell, 2004), *Signifying Bodies: Disability in Contemporary Life Writing* (Michigan, 2009), and *Memoir: An Introduction* (Oxford, 2012). He has completed a memoir of his father and is writing a book about contemporary American patriography (memoirs of fathers).

Lennard J. Davis, the editor of this volume, is Distinguished Professor of Liberal Arts and Sciences at the University of Illinois at Chicago in the Departments of Disability and Human Development, English, and Medical Education. He is the author of *Enforcing Normalcy: Disability, Deafness and the Body; Bending Over Backwards: Disability, Dismodernism, and Other Difficult Positions; Obsession: A History,* for which he received

a Guggenheim Fellowship, and *The End of Normal: Identity in a Biocultural Era.*

Elizabeth DePoy, who currently holds academic appointments in disability studies, mechanical engineering and international policy, is a recognized scholar in research and evaluation methods, theory development focusing on disability as disjuncture and more recently disability as design and branded. Currently, she is conducting collaborative research on contemporary design and fabrication of robotic and Internet technology to improve usability of physical and virtual spaces and resources.

Elizabeth F. Emens is a Professor of Law at Columbia University. She earned her JD from Yale and her PhD in English from King's College, Cambridge. She teaches and writes in the areas of disability law, employment discrimination, and law and sexuality.

Nirmala Erevelles is Professor of Social and Cultural Studies in Education at the University of Alabama. Her book, *Disability and Difference in Global Contexts: Enabling a Transformative Body Politic,* was published by Palgrave Macmillan in 2011. She has published articles in journals such as *Educational Theory, Teachers College Record,* the *American Educational Research Journal, Disability & Society,* among others in the areas of sociology of education, disability studies, transnational feminist theory, and curriculum studies.

Jim Ferris is author of *The Hospital Poems* (2004), *Facts of Life*, (2005), and *Slouching Towards Guantanamo* (2011). Ferris has won awards for creative nonfiction and performance as well as for his poetry. He holds the Ability Center Endowed Chair in Disability Studies at the University of Toledo.

Anne Finger's most recent book is a short story collection, *Call Me Ahab*, which won the Prairie Schooner Award and was published by University of Nebraska Press. She has also written other short fiction, memoirs, and a novel.

Kenny Fries is the author of *The History of My Shoes and the Evolution of Darwin's Theory* and *Body, Remember: A Memoir*, as well as the editor of *Staring Back: The Disability Experience from the Inside Out*. His books of poems include *Anesthesia* and *Desert Walking*. He has been a Creative Arts Fellow of the Japan/US Friendship Commission and the National Endowment for the Arts and a Fulbright Scholar to Japan. He teaches in the MFA in Creative Writing Program at Goddard College.

Rosemarie Garland-Thomson is Professor of Women's Studies and English at Emory University. Her fields of study are feminist theory, American literature, and disability studies. Her work develops the field of disability studies in the humanities and women's and gender studies. Her most recent book is *Staring: How We Look*.

Stephen Gilson, Professor and Coordinator of Interdisciplinary Disability Studies and Faculty in International Policy and Administration, is internationally and nationally recognized for his creative, collaborative scholarship. Bringing an interdisciplinary background as an artist and neuroscientist to theory development and policy analysis, Gilson's current research interests and publications have focused on technology design, disability theory, disability as disjuncture, and most recently, disability as design and branding.

Faye Ginsburg is Kriser Professor of Anthropology at NYU where she is also Co-Director of the Council for the Study of Disability.

David Hevey is a British disabled photographer and writer. His book, *The Creatures that Time Forgot*, examines the representation of disabled people—in advertising, particularly that produced by disability charities, and in the work of photographers such as Diane Arbus and Gary Winogrand. He shows how such images construct disabled people as "creatures," the tragic-but-brave objects of the photographic gaze.

Ruth Hubbard is Professor Emerita of Biology at Harvard University, where she was the first woman to hold a tenured professorship position in biology. She is the author of *The Politics of Women's Biology* (1990*)* and *Profitable Promises: Essays on Women, Science & Health* (1995).

Georgina Kleege teaches creative writing and disability studies at the University of California, Berkeley. Her recent books include *Sight Unseen* (1999) and *Blind Rage: Letters to Helen Keller* (2006). Kleege's current work is concerned with blindness and visual art: how blindness is represented in art, how blindness affects the lives of visual artists, how museums can make visual art accessible to people who are blind and visually impaired. She has lectured and served as consultant to art institutions around the world including the Metropolitan Museum of Art in New York and the Tate Modern in London.

Steve Kuusisto teaches in the Center on Human Policy, Law, and Disability Studies at Syracuse University. He is the author of the memoirs *Planet of the Blind* and *Eavesdropping* as well as two collections of poems, " *Only Bread, Only Light* " and " *Letters to Borges* ".

Bradley Lewis MD, PhD is an Associate Professor at New York University's Gallatin School of Individualized Study. He has interdisciplinary training is in humanities and psychiatry and writes at the interface of psychiatry, cultural studies, and disability studies. His recent books are Narrative Psychiatry: How Stories Shape Clinical Practice and Depression: Integrating Science, Culture, and Humanities.

Paul Longmore (1946–2010) was Professor of History at San Francisco State University and winner of the Henry B. Betts Award from the American Association of People with Disabilities. An activist and a scholar, he published two key books in disability studies, *The New Disability History: American Perspectives* (ed. with Lauri Umansky, 2001) and *Why I Burned My Book and Other Essays on Disability* (2003). A team of disability historians who benefitted from the field he founded is completing his book on Telethons.

Josh Lukin teaches at Temple University. He is the editor of *Invisible Suburbs: Recovering Protest Fiction of the 1950s United States* (UP of Mississippi 2008) and *It Walks in Beauty: Selected Prose of Chandler Davis* (Aqueduct Press 2010).

Harriet McBryde Johnson (July 8, 1957–June 4, 2008) was a lawyer, writer, and disability activist. Her writing on disability has appeared in numerous publications including *New Mobility, South Carolina Lawyer, Review of Public Personnel Administration,* and the *New York Times.* She is the author of the memoir *Too Late to Die Young: Nearly True Tales from a Life* (2005) and the novel *Accidents of Nature* (2006).

Robert McRuer is Professor of English and Chair of the Department of English at The George Washington University. He is author of *Crip Theory: Cultural Signs of Queerness and Disability* (NYU, 2006) and *The Queer Renaissance: Contemporary American Literature and the Reinvention of Lesbian and Gay Identities* (NYU, 1997). With Anna Mol-

low, he co-edited *Sex and Disability* (Duke, 2012). His articles have appeared in PMLA, Radical History Review, GLQ: A Journal of Lesbian and Gay Studies, and numerous other locations.

Ann Millett-Gallant is an art historian and a lecturing fellow for the University of North Carolina at Greensboro. Her research focuses on representations of the disabled body in art and visual culture, and her book, *The Disabled Body in Contemporary Art* (2010) is the first to cross the disciplines of art history and disability studies. She has also published essays and reviews of art and film in disability studies journals and art magazines.

Andrea Minear is Assistant Professor of Elementary Education in the Department of Elementary Education at the University of West Alabama. Her areas of expertise are early childhood literacy, social justice and equity in education, and narrative research.

David Mitchell and Sharon Snyder are the authors of *Narrative Prosthesis: Disability and the Dependencies of Discourse* (Ann Arbor: U of Michigan P, 20000) and *Cultural Locations of Disability* (Chicago: U of Chicago P, 2006). They are also the creators of three award-winning films about disability arts, history, and culture. Together they helped found the Committee on Disability Issues in the Profession at the Modern Languages Association as well as researched, wrote, and curated a Chicago Disability History Exhibit for Bodies of Work: Disability Arts and Culture Festival. Currently, they are completing work on a new book titled, *The Geo-Politics of Disability,* and also a producing a new film on the social and surgical issues involved with esophageal atresia.

Anna Mollow is a PhD candidate at the University of California, Berkeley, where she is completing a dissertation entitled "The Disability Drive: Lesbian Feminist Disability Theory." She is co-editor, with Robert McRuer, of *Sex and Disability* (Duke UP 2012). Her articles have appeared or are forthcoming in the *Journal of Literary and Cultural Disability Studies, Women's Studies Quarterly, MELUS,* and *Michigan Quarterly Review.*

Joseph J. Murray is a historian whose work in Deaf Studies explores transnational interactions among deaf people and the intersections between deaf and hearing people in historical perspective.

Stuart Murray is Professor of Contemporary Literatures and Film in the School of English at the University of Leeds, where he is also the Director of the interdisciplinary Leeds Centre for Medical Humanities. He has written widely on issues connected to disability representation, and his last book was Autism (Routledge, 2012).

Catherine Prendergast is Professor of English at the University of Illinois at Urbana-Champaign. An editorial board member of the *Journal of Literary and Cultural Disability Studies*, she is co-editor with Elizabeth Donaldson of a special issue of that journal on "Representing Emotion and Disability" (2011).

Margaret Price is an associate professor of writing at Spelman College and co-editor of reviews for *Disability Studies Quarterly*. Her book *Mad at School: Rhetorics of Mental Disability and Academic Life* appeared in 2011 (University of Michigan Press). She is at work on a second book about the naming and un-naming of mental disability among faculty.

Jasbir K. Puar is Associate Professor of Women's & Gender Studies at Rutgers University. She is the author of *Terrorist Assemblages: Homonationalism in Queer Times* (Duke University Press 2007) winner of the Cultural Studies Book Award from the Association for Asian American Studies. Her articles appear in *Gender, Place, and Culture, Social Text, Radical History Review, Antipode: A Radical Journal of Geography, Signs: Journal of Women in Culture and Society,* and *Feminist Legal Studies.* Her edited volumes include a special issue of *GLQ* titled, "Queer Tourism: Geographies of Globalization" and co-edited volumes of *Society and Space* ("Sexuality and Space"), *Social Text* ("Interspecies"), and *Women's Studies Quarterly* ("Viral"). Professor Puar has been awarded the Edward Said Chair of American Studies at the American University of Beirut for 2012–13.

Ato Quayson did his BA at the University of Ghana and his PhD at the University of Cambridge. He is currently Professor of English and inaugural Director of the Centre for Diaspora and Transnational Studies at the University of Toronto. His publications include *Calibrations: Reading for the Social* (2003), *Aesthetic Nervousness: Disability and the Crisis of Representation* (2007) and he was also editor of the 2-volume *Cambridge History of Postcolonial Literature* (2012).

Rayna Rapp is Professor of Anthropology at NYU and Associate Chair of the Department of Anthropology. Faye Ginsburg and she are currently engaged in a study of cultural innovation and learning disabilities.

Ellen Samuels is Assistant Professor of Gender & Women's Studies and English at the University of Wisconsin at Madison. Her critical writing on disability has appeared in numerous journals and anthologies, and was awarded the Catherine Stimpson Prize for Outstanding Feminist Scholarship in 2011.

Marsha Saxton, Ph.D. teaches Disability Studies at the University of California, Berkeley. She is Director of Research and

Training at the World Institute on Disability, in Oakland, CA. She has published extensively about disability rights, women's health, health care disparities, abuse and violence prevention and genetic screening issues. She has been a board member of the Our Bodies, Ourselves Collective and the National Institutes of Health (NIH) Ethical, Legal Social Implications (ELSI) Working Group of the Human Genome Initiative. Her new book is *Sticks and Stones: Disabled People's Stories of Abuse, Defiance and Resilience*, www.wid.org/cape.

Tom Shakespeare is a sociologist and bioethicist. After researching and teaching at the Universities of Cambridge, Sunderland, Leeds and Newcastle, he moved to the World Health Organization in 2008. His books include *Disability Rights and Wrongs, The Sexual Politics of Disability* and *Genetic Politics: from eugenics to genome.*

Tobin Siebers is V. L. Parrington Collegiate Professor of English and Art and Design at the University of Michigan. He is the author of thirteen books, including *The Body Aesthetic: From Fine Art to Body Modification* (Michigan 2000), *Disability Theory (Michigan 2008), and Disability Aesthetics* (Michigan, 2010. Siebers is a past fellow of the Michigan Society of Fellows, the Mellon Foundation, the Columbia Society of Fellows, and the Guggenheim Foundation. In 2011 he was named the recipient of the Senior Scholar Award of the Society for Disability Studies.

Sharon Snyder, PhD, is co-writer along with David Mitchell of *Narrative Prosthesis* and *Cultural Locations of Disability.* She has directed and co-directed films on disability including *A World Without Bodies.*

Joseph N. Straus is Distinguished Professor of Music at the Graduate Center, City University of New York. He is a co-editor of *Sounding Off: Theorizing Disability in Music* (Routledge, 2006) and the author of *Extraordinary Measures: Disability in Music* (Oxford University Press, 2011). He is a former president of the Society for Music Theory.

Cheryl Marie Wade is a pioneer of disability arts and culture and one of the first physically disabled performance artists to gain critical acclaim. Wade used her "crippled" body onstage, along with raw, vibrant poetry, autobiographical storytelling and what has been described as "in your face" narrative, to carve out her particular style and niche as a performance artist.

Susan Wendell is the author of *The Rejected Body: Feminist Philosophical Reflections on Disability* (1996, Routledge). She is Professor Emerita at Simon Fraser University. She has lived with ME disease (CFIDS) since 1985.

Credit Lines

[11] Lerita Coleman Brown, "Stigma: An Enigma Demystified" from *The Dilemma of Difference: A Multidisciplinary View of Stigma* by Stephen C Ainlay, Gaylene Becker, and Lerita M Coleman. Reprinted by permission of Plenum.

[12] Susan Wendell, "Unhealthy Disabled: Treating Chronic Illnesses as Disabilities" from Hypatia 16.4 (Autumn 2001). Copyright © 2010 by Hypatia, Inc. Reprinted with the permission of John Wiley & Sons, Inc.

[13] Jasbir K. Puar, "The Cost of Getting Better: Suicide, Sensation, Switchpoints" from *GLQ: A Journal of Lesbian and Gay Studies* 18, no 1 (2011): 149–158. Copyright © 2011 by Duke University Press. Reprinted by permission of the publisher, www.dukepress.edu.

[14] Faye Ginsberg and Rayna Rapp, "Enabling Disability: Rewriting Kinship, Reimagining Citizenship" from *Public Culture* 13 (2001). Copyright © 2001 by Duke University. Reprinted by permission of the publisher, www.dukepress.edu.

[15] Ato Quayson, excerpt from *Aesthetic Nervousness: Disability and the Crisis of Representation.* Copyright © 2007 by Columbia University Press. Reprinted with the permission of the publisher.

[16] Tom Shakespeare "The Social Model of Disability." Reprinted by permission.

[17] David T. Mitchell and Sharon L. Snyder, excerpt from *Narrative Prosthesis: Disability and the Dependencies of Discourse.* Copyright © 2001 by The University of Michigan. Reprinted with permission.

[18] Catherine Prendergast, "The Unexpected Schizophrenic: A Post-Postmodern Introduction." Reprinted by permission.

[19] H-Dirksen L. Baumann and Joseph J. Murray, "Deaf Studies in the 21st Century: 'Deaf-gain' and the Future of Human Diversity" in *The Oxford Handbook of Deaf Studies, Language, and Education, Volume 2.* Copyright © 2010 by Oxford University Press. Reprinted with permission.

[20] Lennard Davis, "The End of Identity Politics: On Disability as an Unstable Category." Reprinted by permission.

[21] Tobin Siebers, "Disability and the Theory of Complex Embodiment(For Identity Politics in a New Register" from *Disability Theory.* Copyright © 2008. Reprinted with the permission of The University of Michigan Press.

[22] Margaret Price, "Naming and Definition" from (Introduction" from *Mad at School: Rhetorics of Mental Disability and Academic Life.* Copyright © 2011 University of Michigan. Reprinted with permission. This contains excerpts from Johnnie Lacy, "Director, Community Resources For Independent Living: An African-American Woman's Perspective on The Independent Living Movement in The Bay Area, 1960s–1980s" (interview conducted by David Landes, 1998) and (Minority vs. Disability Identity," both from *Disability Rights and Independent Living Movement Oral History Series* (UC Berkeley, 2000). Also excerpts from Donald Galloway, from (Blind Services and Advocacy and the Independent Living Movement in Berkeley" interviews conducted by Sharon Bonney and Fred Pelka (2000–2002) in *Disability Rights and Independent Living Movement Oral History Series* (UC Berkeley, 2004). All courtesy The Bancroft Library, University of California, Berkeley.

[23] Josh Lukin, "Black Disability Studies" from *Temple University) Faculty Herald* 36.4 (February 14, 2006). Reprinted with the permission of the author.

[24] Ellen Samuels, "My Body, My Closet: Invisible Disability and the Limits of Coming-Out Discourse" from *GLQ: A Journal of Lesbian and Gay Studies* 9, 1–2 (2003): 233–255. Copyright © 2003 by Duke University Press. Reprinted by permission of the publisher, www.dukepress.edu.

[25] Rosemarie Garland-Thomson, "Integrating Disability, Transforming Feminist Theory" from *National Women's Studies Association Journal* 14.3 (Fall 2002). Copyright © 2002. Reprinted with permission.

[26] Nirmala Erevelles and Andrea Minear, "Unspeakable Offenses: Untangling Race and Disability in Discourses of Intersectionality" from *Journal of Literary & Cultural Disability Studies* 4.2 (2010). Copyright © Liverpool University Press. Reprinted with permission.

[27] Robert McRuer, "Compulsory Able-Bodiedness and Queer/Disabled Exist ence" from *Disability Studies: Enabling the Humanities*, edited by Rosemarie Garland Thomson, Brenda Jo Brueggemann, and Sharon L. Snyder. Copyright © 2002. Reprinted with permission.

[28] Cynthia Barounis, "Crippling Heterosexuality, Queering Able-Bodiedness Murderball, Brokeback Mountain and the Contested Masculine Body." Reprinted by permission.

[29] Ann Millett-Gallant, "Sculpting Body Ideals: Alison Lapper Pregnant and the Public Display of Disability" from *Disability Studies Quarterly* 28:3 (Summer 2008). Reprinted with the permission of the author.

[30] Anna Mollow, "When Black Women Start Going on Prozac. . .': The Politics of Race, Gender, and Emotional Distress in Meri Nana-Ama Danquah's *Willow Weep for Me*." Reprinted by permission.

[31] David Hevey, "The Enfreakment of Photography." Reprinted by permission.

[32] Georgina Kleege, "Blindness and Visual Culture: An Eyewitness Account" from *Journal of Visual Culture* 4, no. 2 (August 2005). Copyright © 2005 by Sage Publications, Inc. Reprinted by with permission.

[33] G. Thomas Couser, "Disability, Life Narrative, and Representation" from *PMLA* 120, No. 2 (March 2005): 602606. Copyright © 2005. Reprinted with permission.

[34] Joseph N. Straus, "Autism as Culture." Reprinted by permission.

[35] Elizabeth DePoy and Stephen Gilson, "Disability, Design, and Branding: Rethinking Disability within the 21st Century" from *Disability Studies Quarterly* 30.2 (2010). Copyright © 2010. Reprinted with permission.

[36] Eli Clare, "Stones in My Pockets, Stones in My Heart" from *Sojourner: The Women's Forum* (November 1996). Copyright © 1996. Reprinted with the permission of South End Press.

[37] Harriet McBryde Johnson, "Unspeakable Conversations" from *The New York Times Magazine* (February 16, 2003). Copyright © 2003 by The New York Times Company. Reprinted with permission.

[38] Anne Finger, "Helen and Frida" from *The Kenyon Review* 16, no. 3 (Summer, 1994): 17. Copyright © 1994 Kenyon College. Reprinted with permission.

[39] Cheryl Marie Wade, "I Am Not One of The" and (Cripple Lullaby." Reprinted with the permission of Cheryl Marie Wade.

[40] Kenny Fries, "Beauty and Variations." Reprinted by permission.

Index